W9-AYE-292

# MOON HANDBOOKS®
# CONNECTICUT

© ANDREW COLLINS

Wake Robin Inn

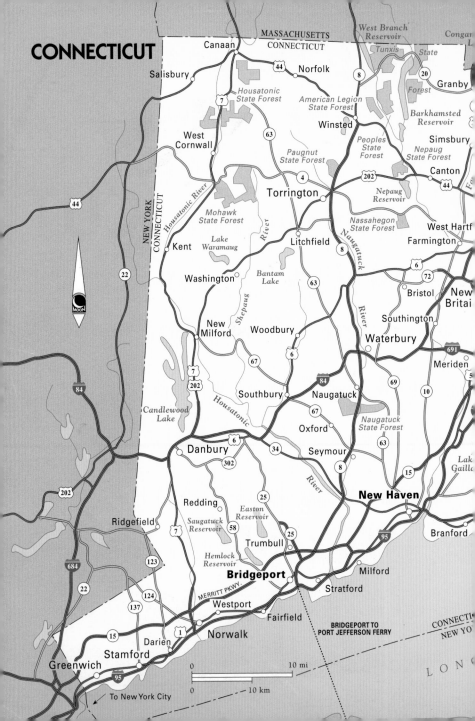

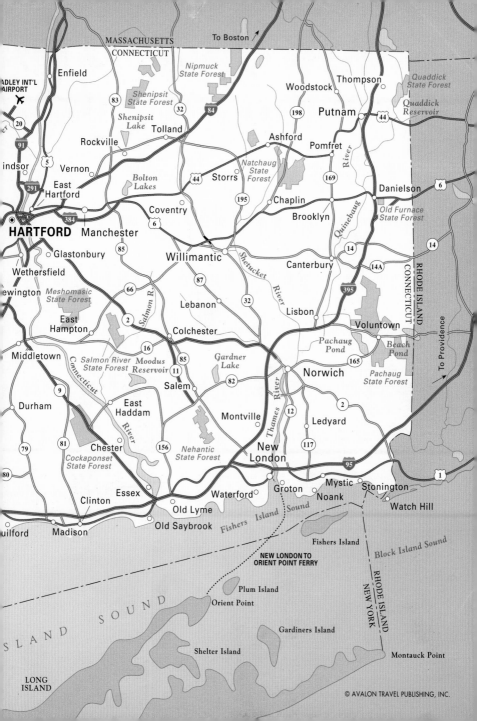

Queen of Tarts Bakery in Chester

© ANDREW COLLINS

# MOON HANDBOOKS®
# CONNECTICUT

SECOND EDITION

**ANDREW COLLINS**

AVALON
TRAVEL

# MAPS

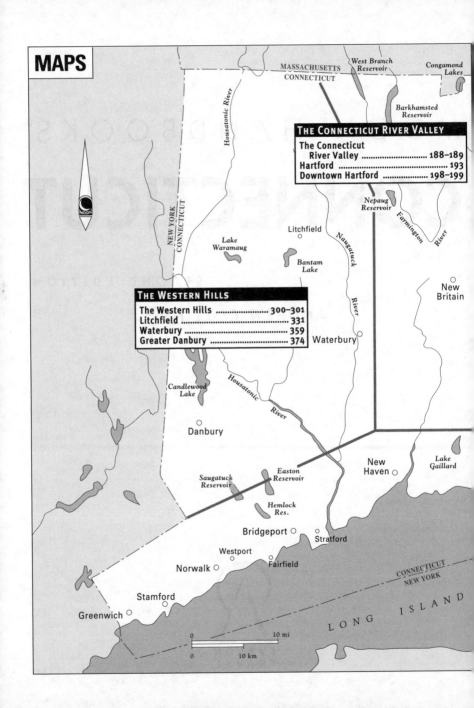

MASSACHUSETTS
CONNECTICUT

West Branch
Reservoir

Congamond
Lakes

Barkhamsted
Reservoir

Housatonic River

NEW YORK
CONNECTICUT

Nepaug
Reservoir

### THE CONNECTICUT RIVER VALLEY

**The Connecticut
   River Valley** ............................ 188–189
**Hartford** ................................................ 193
**Downtown Hartford** .................... 198–199

Farmington River

Litchfield

Lake
Waramaug

Bantam
Lake

Naugatuck River

New
Britain

### THE WESTERN HILLS

**The Western Hills** .................... 300–301
**Litchfield** ............................................ 331
**Waterbury** .......................................... 359
**Greater Danbury** ................................ 374

Waterbury

Candlewood
Lake

Housatonic River

Danbury

Saugatuck
Reservoir

Easton
Reservoir

New
Haven

Lake
Gaillard

Hemlock
Res.

Bridgeport

Stratford

Westport

Fairfield

CONNECTICUT
NEW YORK

Norwalk

Stamford

Greenwich

LONG ISLAND

0                 10 mi

0            10 km

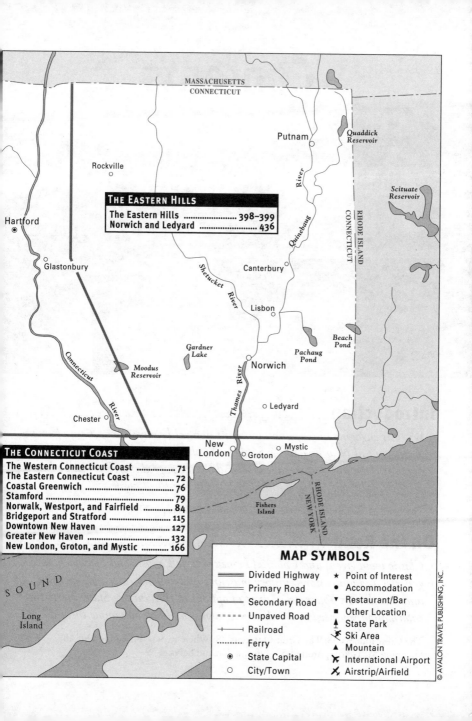

MASSACHUSETTS
CONNECTICUT

Putnam

Quaddick
Reservoir

Rockville

Scituate
Reservoir

Hartford

**THE EASTERN HILLS**

The Eastern Hills ........................ 398–399
Norwich and Ledyard ......................... 436

Glastonbury

Shetucket River

Canterbury

RHODE ISLAND
CONNECTICUT

Lisbon

Connecticut

River

Gardner
Lake

Moodus
Reservoir

Pachaug
Pond

Beach
Pond

Norwich

Thames River

Ledyard

Chester

New
London

Groton

Mystic

**THE CONNECTICUT COAST**

The Western Connecticut Coast ................. 71
The Eastern Connecticut Coast ................. 72
Coastal Greenwich ................................. 76
Stamford ............................................. 79
Norwalk, Westport, and Fairfield ............. 84
Bridgeport and Stratford ...................... 115
Downtown New Haven ........................... 127
Greater New Haven .............................. 132
New London, Groton, and Mystic ........... 166

RHODE ISLAND
NEW YORK

Fishers
Island

S O U N D

Long
Island

## MAP SYMBOLS

| | |
|---|---|
| ══════ Divided Highway | ★ Point of Interest |
| ────── Primary Road | ● Accommodation |
| ────── Secondary Road | ▼ Restaurant/Bar |
| ------ Unpaved Road | ■ Other Location |
| ┼──┼ Railroad | ▲ State Park |
| ········· Ferry | ⚡ Ski Area |
| ⊙ State Capital | ▲ Mountain |
| ○ City/Town | ✈ International Airport |
| | ✈ Airstrip/Airfield |

# Contents

© ANDREW COLLINS

## Introduction . . . . . . . . . . . . . . . . . . . . . . . . . . . . . . . . . . . . . . . . . . 1

*With its engaging history and abundant natural beauty, Connecticut offers the quintessential New England experience. Stroll along Main Street, taste maple sugar at the country store, take a hike along the rugged shoreline—all of these delights and more can be found within these tree-lined borders.*

The Land 2; History 12; Government, Economy, and People 24

## On the Road . . . . . . . . . . . . . . . . . . . . . . . . . . . . . . . . . . . . . . . . . . 33

*Classic town greens and Colonial homesteads, folk music and blackjack, art galleries and outlet stores, history museums and amphitheaters, leaf-peeping and fine dining: You're never short of options in the Nutmeg State. Here's the information you need to decide where, when, and how to sample them all.*

The Great Indoors 33; The Great Outdoors 38; Where to Stay 44; Eating Out 48; Shopping 51; Getting Around 53; Information and Services 59

# The Connecticut Coast ....................70

*Amid the buzzing cities and golden beaches along the Connecticut Coast, you'll always be just moments away from a peaceful wooded retreat or a bowl of steaming clam chowder. Whether you're an antiques junkie on a treasure hunt or a water baby in search of the perfect tan, you'll find plenty of inspiration here.*

**THE GOLD COAST** .......................................................73
Greenwich to Darien; Stamford; New Canaan; Norwalk; Westport and Environs; Fairfield

**BRIDGEPORT AND VICINITY** ...........................................114
Bridgeport; Stratford

**NEW HAVEN AND VICINITY** ............................................126
New Haven; Greater New Haven

**THE CENTRAL SHORELINE** ..............................................148
Branford to Madison; Clinton to Old Saybrook

**THE SOUTHEAST COASTLINE** ..........................................163
Old Lyme to New London; Groton to Stonington

# The Connecticut River Valley .........187

*Beyond this valley's tranquil expanse of water and clapboard Victorian villages lie two rapidly revitalizing urban playgrounds: the vibrant streetscape of New Haven and the capital city of Hartford, which is shaking off its tough reputation with a flurry of new restaurants, performing arts venues, and popular attractions.*

**HARTFORD** ............................................................192

**FARMINGTON RIVER VALLEY** ..........................................226
West Hartford to Farmington; Canton to Simsbury; New Hartford to Hartland

**TOBACCO COUNTRY** ...................................................244
Western Tobacco Country; East of the River

**THE HEART OF CONNECTICUT** .........................................260
Wethersfield to Berlin; Plainville and Bristol; Southington to Meriden; Middletown; Cromwell to East Hartford

**THE LOWER CONNECTICUT RIVER VALLEY** ............................285
Haddam to Chester; Chester to Essex

# The Western Hills ........................ 298

*Home to captivating landscapes and well-heeled captains of industry alike, the Western Hills offer quietly sophisticated living with easy access to New York City. In this rustic and even primitive setting, you may be surprised to find a multitude of exceptional eateries, elegant antiques shops, and fine country inns.*

**WESTERN LITCHFIELD COUNTY** ........................................ 302
New Milford to Washington; Kent to Cornwall; Sharon to Salisbury; Falls Village and Canaan
**THE EASTERN LITCHFIELD HILLS** ...................................... 324
Norfolk to Winsted; Torrington and Harwinton; Litchfield, Bantam, and Goshen; Morris to Southbury
**WATERBURY AND THE NAUGATUCK VALLEY** ........................... 357
Waterbury; North and West of Waterbury; South of Waterbury
**DANBURY AND THE LOWER HOUSATONIC VALLEY** ..................... 373
Danbury; South of Danbury; North of Danbury; Along the Lower Housatonic

# The Eastern Hills ............................. 397

*Less heralded than its livelier neighbors, this quiet and unhurried area comprises dense woodland, sparkling lakes, and Colonial hamlets. With uncluttered roads and sleepy agricultural and industrial communities, the Eastern Hills provide a gentler—and less expensive— foray into New England.*

**THE QUIET CORNER** ..................................................... 402
Woodstock to Pomfret; Brooklyn to Scotland; Willimantic and Lebanon; Coventry, Storrs, and Mansfield
**VERNON, MANCHESTER, AND ENVIRONS** .............................. 427
**NORWICH AND CASINO COUNTRY** .................................... 435
Mohegan Sun; Foxwoods

# Resources .......................................... 451

**SUGGESTED READING** ................................................... 452
**INTERNET RESOURCES** ................................................. 458
**INDEX** .................................................................. 460

# ABOUT THE AUTHOR
# Andrew Collins

Travel writer Andrew Collins spends most of his life on the road, driving back and forth across North America, logging about 40,000 miles annually. He has visited more than 1,700 of the nation's 3,145 counties, and has spent more than 2,000 nights residing in hotel rooms, slumming with friends, or crashing with various relatives—he is always most appreciative of his hosts' kind generosity. In recent years, he has lived in Manhattan, Brooklyn, and rural New Hampshire, and has spent extended periods in Atlanta, Boston, San Francisco, and Rhode Island, as well as overseas in London and Amsterdam. Although he currently lives in Santa Fe, New Mexico, he grew up in Connecticut, where he graduated from Wesleyan University in 1991. Andrew continues to spend several months a year in the quiet Litchfield County village of Roxbury.

Following college, he joined Fodor's Travel Publications, where he edited or co-edited more than a dozen travel guides. Since leaving Fodor's to pursue a freelance career in 1993, he has contributed to more than 120 travel books as both writer and editor, authoring *Fodor's Gay Guide to the USA, Moon Handbooks Rhode Island,* and this brand-new edition of *Moon Handbooks Connecticut.* He recently co-authored *Fodor's 1001 Travel Tips,* and his next book, *Moon Handbooks New Orleans,* is due out in 2004. Andrew's travel column, "Out of Town," appears in dozens of gay and lesbian newspapers throughout North America; his work has also appeared in numerous magazines, including *Travel + Leisure* and *Sunset.*

On those rare occasions when he's not on the road, Andrew can be found browsing the goods at farmers markets and gourmet food stores, or putting them to use in his kitchen. He also enjoys a variety of outdoors activities, including jogging, kayaking, and hiking, and follows professional baseball with a disturbing degree of fanaticism. A confessed pop-culture junkie, he scans online newspapers and newswires every day in search of odd trivia and amusing gossip about has-been celebrities. After finishing one of his guidebooks, he's been known to watch reruns of sitcoms and made-for-TV movies for hours on end, until fading blissfully into a trance-like stupor. Such is the life of the professional traveler . . . .

# Introduction

Whereas certain states in this country conjure up fairly distinct images when we think of them, Connecticut—despite being small and easily accessible—resists pigeonholing and instead presents a series of intriguing, and often pleasing, contradictions. It's one of the most densely populated states, and yet even its most bustling suburbs have a wooded, countrified air about them. Connecticut is little more than 100 miles wide at its broadest point—it's considerably smaller than Adirondacks State Park in New York—and yet it encompasses laid-back shoreline villages, a precipitous stretch of the Appalachian Trail, several scrappy cities, and among the wealthiest suburbs in the nation. It has a blue-blooded, WASPy reputation in parts, and thriving Polish, Lithuanian, Indian, Native American, African American, and Vietnamese communities in others. The close proximity of its disparate elements only underscores the state's considerable diversity.

Spend a whole lot of time searching for the "real Connecticut," and you'll probably come away empty-handed. The regional identity manifests itself in both unexpected and obvious places, and no one town or museum or neighborhood even vaguely represents the state as a whole. Collectively, however, the varied regions of Connecticut do reveal a true microcosm of greater New England. If you believe you have to penetrate the far reaches of the Northeast to experience "authentic" Yankee country, think again; whatever it is you're looking for—lobster shacks, art museums, country inns, outlet shops, rugged bike trails, or antiques stores—it's here within the borders of Connecticut.

© ANDREW COLLINS

Milford harbor

A study of the state's most recognized and easily defined regions helps to illuminate Connecticut's numerous offerings. The Mystic area is a smaller and more accessible slice of the same coastal joys found throughout the rest of New England, from Rhode Island to the eastern tip of Maine. There are maritime concerns, fishing villages, art galleries, seafood shanties, and outlet shops; and just a few minutes inland, two casinos have put the region on the national map.

The lower Connecticut River Valley is classic Victorian Americana: quiet clapboard villages overlooking a peaceful expanse of a wide river—countryside that outsiders might think exists only in Vermont and New Hampshire. Nearby New Haven is a rapidly revitalizing base to one of the world's leading bastions of knowledge, and a great theater center. Its downtown bustles with shops and restaurants and possesses easily the most lively streetscape of any city in the state.

The Litchfield Hills, meanwhile, offer a glimpse of a New England more accessible and more sophisticated than any other part of the Northeast, with a restaurant scene that rivals California's Wine Country (in quality if not quantity), as well as a bounty of sleepy, beautifully preserved town greens and Colonial homesteads.

It is quintessential New England, with the cultural panache and fine shopping of Manhattan.

And Fairfield County blends the classic town greens and clapboard Colonial architecture of the rest of New England with the trappings of New York City suburbia. Heavy traffic, building booms, and an almost frenetic pace characterize the county, especially along the coast, but the region's old-money dignity and wealth have managed to keep these towns neat as a pin and highly exclusive. Fine restaurants and shops prosper, while local zoning boards fight tooth-and-nail to limit unbecoming and garish development. Well-endowed historical societies and nature centers preserve Fairfield County's Colonial legacy. If parts of the area seem a bit uppity, never mind that. Come and enjoy the wealth—the wealth of beautiful surroundings and acclaimed cultural offerings.

The state has been described by some tourism officials as a "microcosm of America." Indeed, the vast state encompasses a great many identities and flavors. Just as nationally there is fierce loyalty and even rivalry among states, and a healthy distrust of federal government and centralization, Connecticut's towns function in very much the same manner.

## The Land

This relatively tiny state (at about 5,000 square miles) supports a tremendously varied landscape. With fine examples of rugged northern woodland (in the northwestern corner of the state), fertile river plains (most notably the Connecticut River Valley), and coastal habitats (along Long Island Sound), Connecticut is an environmental microcosm of New England as a whole. The climate is cool enough in northwestern Connecticut to sustain, albeit in limited numbers, animals and trees that you might expect to see only in Vermont and New Hampshire (e.g., black bears, coyotes, hooded mergansers, pileated woodpeckers, black spruce, mountain maple), yet warm enough along the southeastern coast to support marine and migratory birdlife year-round and all manner of coastal shrubs and berries.

The very northwestern tip of Connecticut supports dense broadleaf forest, the type that dominates northern New England. Beyond this swath, whose boundary falls roughly along the section of the Appalachian Trail that cuts through the state, is a band of transitional woodland—this terrain also characterizes the highest elevations of the eastern hills, around Woodstock and Union. But most of the rest of the state, east from Litchfield County and south from about I-84, is characterized by oak-hickory forest.

Unquestionably, the most developed part of the state is the coast, and also a swath of suburban and industrial sprawl running from New Haven north through Hartford and clear up the upper Connecticut River Valley. Cities such as Groton, New London, New Haven, Bridgeport, Norwalk,

© ANDREW COLLINS

Connecticut's gently rolling hills are on display on the grounds of the Hill-Stead Museum, Farmington.

INTRODUCTION

and Stamford are strung evenly along the shoreline, with relatively dense suburban towns squeezed between them. Even in picturesque seaside communities like Stonington village, Saybrook Point, and Rowayton, the neighborhoods nearest the water are jammed with clapboard and shingle vacation homes. For this reason, Connecticut's 100 miles of coastline (and 250 miles of overall shoreline, including rivers and estuaries) are something less of a nature lover's retreat than outer Cape Cod's or central Maine's. However, birdwatching is still a fascinating and increasingly popular pastime along the Connecticut shore, and established parks and preserves encourage these habitats.

One aspect of Connecticut that stands out today is its dense thickets of woodland, often producing a sense of seclusion in even the most developed communities. Were you able to wander the tree-studded hillsides during the 19th century, however, you'd have observed an almost entirely deforested state of rolling meadows and pastures, tilled to the hilt. You'd be quite able to see your neighbor's homestead a half mile down the country road, much the way the Irish and Scottish countrysides still appear, whereas today residential architects are quite careful to ensure that neighbors living a mere 200 feet apart are obscured from one another.

The coming of the industrial age, which arguably affected Connecticut's physical appearance, population composition, and economy as much as any other state's in the Union, largely put an end to this pastoral landscape. The percentage of open and bare land has diminished at a rapid rate every decade since the late 19th century. In low-lying river valleys abetted by strong transportation ties and easily developed land, the fields of crops gave way to magnificent mills and manufactories. In the rocky and craggy uplands, farming continued to be a force well into current times, but certainly no longer to the extent it was. Fields were given up or developed residentially, first for summer estates and eventually for year-round permanent housing. Trees were allowed to repopulate the region.

Mill sites and ironworks are strung throughout the state, often protected with historic status on the National Register, such as New Roxbury Ironworks Site in Woodstock and Hammonasset Paper Mill Site in Madison. There isn't a tremendous amount to see at most of these sites, usually foundations and clearings that once served as manufactories of varying sizes, but often good hikes lead to them, and they offer a glimpse into an era now long-forgotten and obsolete.

## GEOLOGY

Connecticut is divided into four key geological divisions: the western and eastern hills, which extend (and rise gradually in elevation) from just a few miles inland from the shore all the way north to the Massachusetts border; the fertile central valley, which divides the eastern and western hills and runs north–south through the center of the state (the upper span of it following the course of the Connecticut River); and a relatively narrow coastal plain that forms the state's southern border, and is fringed by the Long Island Sound.

The characteristics and topography of these four zones has greatly influenced how the state was settled. Early settlers gravitated toward the river valley, which was suitable for farming and was navigable via the Connecticut River. They then settled along the shore, which also lent itself fairly well to farming and was easily accessible. The state's oldest settlements are found in these regions, while the harsher, rockier, and hillier

# CONNECTICUT HIGH POINTS

If you've ever stayed in a high-rise hotel or at a mountainside inn, you know that the rooms on the highest floors and with the most stupendous views command the dearest rates. A great view is one of life's universal pleasures, as it informs our sense of place and literally elevates our perspective upon the world around us. You'll never look same way again at Paris after you've gazed down upon it from the Eiffel Tower, and you cannot fully appreciate nor comprehend the magnificence of the southwestern United States until you've stood at the rim of the Grand Canyon.

Connecticut, in the overall world scheme, is vertically challenged. Sure, it's hilly. In fact, it's one, long, more-or-less continuous slope from the Massachusetts border to Long Island Sound, slit by tortuous river valleys and punctuated by rugged ridge lines and rocky outcroppings. Anybody who's ever hiked or biked across the state knows there's nary a flat square mile to be found, even down close to the shoreline. Truly high points, whether natural or man-made, are few and far between—and it sometimes takes a little effort to find them. Here then are a few of the best bird's-eye views of the Nutmeg State, from Connecticut's highest mountain to its most distinctive skyscraper.

## Bear Mountain, Salisbury

Not surprisingly, most of Connecticut's high points are in the northern reaches of the state. The highest summit is Bear Mountain, just a couple miles short of the Massachusetts border in the extreme northwest hills of Litchfield County. A particularly arduous and dramatic stretch of the legendary Appalachian Trail cuts directly over the peak and rewards hikers with arresting views of the surrounding Berkshire foothills and a few taller peaks in the far-off distance.

Before tackling Bear Mountain, keep a few things in mind. This is no simple jaunt that can be attempted without planning, at the spur of the moment. The Appalachian Trail and the blue-blazed side trails leading to it are steep in many places, and the vertical rise from the main trailhead to the summit is 1,600 feet. You'll need to climb hand-over-foot along some stretches of this round-trip hike, which demands a four- or five-hour, seven-mile investment of sweat and stamina. If you thought gentle little Connecticut was without serious outdoors challenges, you're in for a surprise. A final caveat is that this peak is highly popular, and so you'll find little solitude along these nevertheless majestic trails.

Bear Mountain is in the northwestern corner of Connecticut, in the town of Salisbury. From Fairfield County, follow I-84 east to Rte. 8, and head north to U.S. 44 in Winsted. Drive west to Salisbury, making a right turn onto Rte. 41 and following it about 3.2 miles to the parking area for the blue-blazed Undermountain Trail. Shortly into the trail you'll find a bulletin board with trail maps and regulations. For further information, see the Appalachian Mountain Club website at www.ct-amc.org.

## Soapstone Mountain, Somers

If mountain biking is your passion, it's worth making a trip to the sparsely populated northeastern reaches of the Connecticut River Valley, where twisting dirt, gravel, and paved roads lead through 6,000 acres of densely wooded Shenipsit State Forest to 1,075-foot Soapstone Mountain. At the top of this relatively underutilized peak, you'll find picnic tables, a massive weather station, and an easily climbed wooden observation tower. From the top deck of the tower, you'll be treated to views of Springfield and the Pioneer Valley, plus miles of northern Connecticut farmland that once yielded the state's greatest cash crop, tobacco. The tobacco boom ended years ago as better and more abundant sources of it were discovered elsewhere, but this unspoiled landscape still retains a sleepy pace that recalls its agrarian past. Bring a pair of binoculars with you—on the clearest days, you can see the nation's most-climbed peak, Monadnock Mountain in New Hampshire.

Soapstone Mountain is in Somers, accessed from Parker Road, off Rte. 83. Take I-84 east past Hartford, turning north at exit 64 onto Rte. 83, and following it through Vernon and Ellington, into Somers. Parker Road is your first right turn after crossing the Somers town line; there's no designated parking here, but it's safe to park along the side of the road. From here, begin your bike ride 1.2 miles up Parker Road (the last third of this is rough and unpaved), turn left at the four-way intersection (onto Soapstone Mountain Road), and continue 1.3 miles to reach the short paved turnoff for the tower. For information on the hiking trails and other good biking roads in the park, phone the ranger's office at Shenipsit State Forest (860/684-3430) or contact the State Parks Department of the Bureau of Outdoor Recreation.

### Travelers Tower, Hartford

You may be wondering: Does every good view in the state necessitate an investment in hiking boots or a mountain bike? Not at all. Beginning with the earliest days of mild spring weather, usually the first or second week of May, that sovereign figure reigning regally over Hartford's skyline, Travelers Tower, opens its 27th-floor observation deck to the public.

This 527-foot-tall home of the first American insurance company to issue accident coverage was the tallest structure in New England (and the seventh-tallest in the nation) when it was completed in 1919. It's faced in pink granite and crowned with an 81-foot pyramidal copper cupola, the base of which is lined with a chest-high stone balustrade. From behind the balustrade, visitors can take in tremendous views in all directions, up and down the Connecticut River Valley and well into the state's eastern and western uplands. High above the deck, on the 34th floor, a 72,000-watt beacon emits an eerie beam of light that can be seen for miles.

Travelers Tower is in downtown Hartford. Take I-84 to exit 48, or I-91 to exit 29A. Travelers Tower is at 1 Tower Square, the intersection of Main Street and Athenaeum Square. The observation deck is open May –October, weekdays only; tours are free, but by reservation only (even for individuals); call 860/277-4208 or 860/277-0111.

---

uplands were settled later, as they were harder to penetrate, had colder winters (and therefore shorter growing seasons), and had rocky and less arable soil.

In the post-Colonial age, growth continued in the Connecticut River Valley, as it did in dozens of smaller river valleys in the state, where swift-flowing waterways were harnessed for industry. Several coastal communities continued to grow as centers of transportation and shipping. To this day, the most densely settled parts of the state are along the coast, the Connecticut River Valley, and a handful of less prominent river valleys. And every one of the state's present-day urban concentrations sits along a river except New Britain. The hilliest sections of the western and eastern uplands, although prized for their scenic beauty and thus popular with weekend visitors, remain amazingly remote and sparsely populated in many areas.

You'll find two basic kinds of matter beneath your feet as you venture around Connecticut (well, not counting pavement and other man-made materials, which are, alas, covering more of the state every year): bedrock, the stuff that

comprises the Earth's crust that lies the farthest down below us, and drift, a conglomerate of sand, silt, pebbles, and rocks that has been spread over the surface of the land like icing on a cake thanks to glaciation.

Connecticut offers a classic view of how glaciers form the land—virtually every square foot of the state owes its current appearance to the encroachment, and then recession, of a massive glacial formation that ended in about 8000 B.C., just a split-second ago in geological terms.

A block of ice perhaps a mile high drifted as far south as the present shoreline of Connecticut during the most recent Ice Age. This catastrophic action scarred the soil, lifting boulders, rocks, and sediment and carrying them hundreds of miles south from northern New England to the ocean, depositing a mound of debris at the glacier's leading edge. This mound is called terminal moraine, and it's the main ingredient of Long Island, which lies just across the Long Island Sound from the Connecticut coast. Geologically speaking, Long Island has almost nothing in common with Connecticut's shore, but it's rather like the other islands stuck out in the Atlantic, such as Block Island in Rhode Island, and Martha's Vineyard and Nantucket off Cape Cod.

As the Earth's temperature rose, the glaciers began to melt or retreat in a northerly direction, toward the part of North America with the coldest climate. Picture a large snowball filled with gravel, rocks, and debris that faces a slightly downhill heat source in one direction and a cold source slightly uphill in the other direction. The side of the mass facing the heat source will melt first, giving the appearance that it is receding or retreating toward the cold source. In its wake, the snowball will leave a large pool of water and will deposit the gravel, rocks, and debris where it melts—and because the warmer side is at a lower elevation than the colder side, gravity helps carry both the melted water and the debris in that direction. Long Island is terminal moraine, which marks the leading edge of the glacier.

Back along the Connecticut mainland, there's a narrow fringe of sandy coastal plain that lies along the shore, from Stonington west all the way to the New York border. This swath was formed in part, and in some places, when there was a pause in the glacial recession. Let's say the giant snowball had melted for a time, and then suddenly somebody turned off the heater—during this pause, the snowball might even gain a little mass once again, before continuing its recession once the heat was turned back on. In glacier terms, there was likely a change in the Earth's climate where the warming process of the last Ice Age stalled for a time, and so the glacial recession paused, perhaps it even moved forward again briefly, and then continued its recession once the Earth warmed again. This pause left another deposit of sand and debris, this time farther north than the original terminal moraine, called recessional moraine.

Incidentally, if you're curious why Connecticut, coastal southeastern Massachusetts, New York, and Rhode Island all share a similar topography—that of a downward slope of hilly and rocky earth ending with a coastline of recessional moraine, and then, farther out, islands formed by terminal moraine—it's because the major icecap that formed over what is now the Northeastern United States only advanced as far south as about Long Island. It stopped there at the ocean, and

across the lower Hudson River Valley in New York, the northern end of New Jersey, and then central Pennsylvania, but it never extended to the coastline of New Jersey, Delaware, Maryland, and points south, which are defined by a broad, low-elevation coastal plain. The formation of the Eastern Seaboard's shoreline from Long Island and Connecticut, north to Maine and into Canada, is glacial, while the formation of the shoreline south of that point is not.

Other than the extreme edge of coastline, most of the land of Connecticut was not deposited by glaciers, although every inch of it—as is the case all over New England—was shaped by glacial movement. Prior to the Ice Age, this land would have stood many, many yards higher in elevation and would have looked much different than it does today. To imagine the effects of the glacier on the land, remember the relative size and mass of the aforementioned snowball in relation to the ground it covered and then receded from. This powerful pile of ice scraped and scrubbed the landscape, eroding and grinding down the softest bedrock and scattering the landscape with debris and glacial drift as it retreated.

Throughout the state's interior, you'll see other evidence of glacial activity—boulders deposited from parts of northern New England and Canada, rock formations positioned as a result of glacial retreat. Some of the state's many freshwater ponds and natural reservoirs were formed when a chunk of glacier broke off and glacial debris settled around it and over it. Eventually, the piece of ice melted, and the thin layer of land over it then collapsed and sunk. What remained was a pond of water, called a kettle pond—these are all around Connecticut. In other cases, freshwater bodies formed where soil consisted of rather weak rock that was less able to resist glacial movement than adjacent areas consisting of crystalline rock.

The igneous and metamorphic rocks of interior Connecticut are mostly granite. Most of the rock was formed by molten lava that has, over many millions of millennia, pushed its way out from the Earth's core, but has never actually reached the surface, as in the case of a volcano. Instead, it

## AVERAGE CONNECTICUT TEMPERATURES

| Month | High/Low in °F |
|-------|----------------|
| January | 35/18 |
| February | 36/19 |
| March | 46/28 |
| April | 59/38 |
| May | 70/48 |
| June | 79/57 |
| July | 84/63 |
| August | 81/61 |
| September | 74/53 |
| October | 64/42 |
| November | 51/33 |
| December | 38/23 |

cooled and solidified into hard rock that's very resistant to erosion. Over time, the softer soil between it and the Earth's surface eroded from wind and rain, and then gave way even more dramatically during the last glacial recession. The jagged, sharp rocky ridges you sometimes see rising out of the soil in Connecticut formed this way. Many thousands of feet of soil once buried this layer of igneous rock.

The fascinating tale of how geological and meteorological conditions, and more recently people, have shaped the region is rendered with great skill and detail in Michael Bell's *The Face of Connecticut—People, Geology, and the Land,* which was published in 1985 by the Connecticut Geological and Natural History Survey. It's an invaluable resource if you have a serious interest in this subject, and it's a surprisingly captivating read no matter how much you know about geology. Another excellent source of information is the 1906 *Manual of the Geology of Connecticut,* by William N. Rice and Herbert E. Gregory.

For further information, visit the Bureau of Outdoor Recreation at the Connecticut Department of Environmental Protection, or DEP (79 Elm St., Hartford, CT 06106, 860/424-3200, www.dep.state.ct.us).

## CLIMATE

This is a small enough state that the climate is relatively consistent anywhere you go, although the very extreme northwestern hills typically register temperatures as many as 10°F cooler than in the rest of the state, and the coastal areas are typically 5–10°F warmer than elsewhere (except during the summer, when it's actually a bit cooler along the water). Precipitation is fairly constant year-round, ranging from about 49 inches (that's combined rain and snow) in northwestern Litchfield County to perhaps 40 down near the southeastern coastline. Again, the northwestern Litchfield Hills—which stay below freezing throughout most of winter—pick up significantly more snow than the rest of the state, and it's not uncommon in towns like Norfolk and Salisbury for there to be snow cover for 8–10 consecutive weeks. Otherwise, Connecticut—with Rhode Island—is the mildest of New England's states, with temperatures dropping below zero only six or seven times a year on average.

## FLORA AND FAUNA
### Trees and Shrubs

About 50 species of tree are common to New England and therefore present in at least limited numbers throughout parts of Connecticut, although varieties found mostly in northern and western New England are found only in the very northwestern tip of the state, close to the Massachusetts and New York borders.

Broadly speaking, trees are either conifers (the softwood "evergreens" with needlelike leaves that maintain their look and shape year-round) or broadleafs (hardwood flowering trees that are, at least in the four-season climate of Connecticut, deciduous). Common conifers throughout the state include the conical eastern red cedars, shrubby junipers that sport bluish berries, towering reddish-brown tamarack trees, prickly blue spruce, white and red pine, hemlocks, and redberried Canada yew trees. Along the shore, you may also see gnarled pitch pine.

Of broadleaf trees, note that the peak time for watching them burst with bright foliage is mid-October for most of the state, and late October along the coast and at least midway up the Connecticut River Valley. Oaks, of which there are 11 species in New England, abound and can be quite brilliant in the fall—locally you're most likely to see white, scarlet, swamp white, scrub, post, chestnut, and black oak trees. More dramatic, however, are the several species of maple trees, which are more popular in northern New England than in Connecticut. Still, you'll notice quite a few red, sugar, and silver maple trees putting on shows around the state.

Some of the other tall Connecticut broadleafs include beech, birch (the pretty white birch are more prevalent in the north), dogwoods (which flower beautifully all spring), elms (although many of these perished from disease during the middle of this century), holly, poplar, honey locust, cottonwood (especially in the Farmington, Connecticut, and Housatonic River Valleys), hickory, weeping willow, and aspen. If you wonder why so many roads in the state bear the name "Chestnut" but very few parts of state actually bear the trees themselves, it's because they were once nearly as common in the state as oaks and maples. Unfortunately, disease has wiped them out except in northern New England.

Smaller broadleaf trees and shrubs that dot the landscape, many of which bloom with a riot of colors, include speckled adler, dogwood, sumac, pink azalea, rhododendron, multiflora and beach rose, northern bayberry, and pussy willow. Connecticut also has a great many pick-your-own farms (covered under the heading "Agricultural Tourism" in the On the Road chapter).

Hundreds of varieties of wildflowers bloom across the state, beginning most vibrantly in June and remaining vital well into early fall. Some of the best spots for viewing them are Housatonic Meadows State Park in Cornwall, the White Memorial Foundation in Litchfield, and Pachaug State Forest in Voluntown.

## Invertebrates

Mammals, fish, and birds may get most of the attention when it comes to wildlife sighting, but the vast majority of critters crawling, flying, and swimming around Connecticut are—as is true

the world over—invertebrates, some of which are quite interesting to observe or, in the case of some mollusks or crustaceans, to eat.

Long Island Sound has long had a reputation for its abundance of shellfish—the oyster beds off Norwalk are among the largest and richest in the United States. But during much of the 20th century, pollution of the sound and overfishing have combined to deplete or spoil the region as a source of seafood. Thankfully, immensely ambitious efforts to clean up the waters off Connecticut, along with careful harvesting regulations, have restored the region's proliferation of these tasty creatures. Nevertheless, before collecting shellfish along the state shoreline, check first with the local town hall—in nearly all cases a license of some sort is required, and it's always a smart idea to ask about what's safe for consumption and what isn't.

A great range of marine invertebrates can be found off Connecticut's shoreline, including a number of jellyfish and sea anemones, most of which are harmless but for the large and extremely dangerous lion's mane jellyfish, which fortunately is more common in northern waters. Scour the beaches and rocks during low tide, and you'll find marine mollusks of every ilk, from Atlantic dogwinkles and edible common periwinkles to large (up to six inches long) knobbed whelks that live in those pretty yellow-gray shells that kids hold to their ears to hear the seashore. You'll also see tons of lively hermit crabs sidling about the beachline, living safely inside the mobile homes they've fashioned out of gastropod shells.

Tasty blue mussels cling to rocks and pilings. Bay scallops, eastern oysters, razor clams, hardshell northern quahogs (which include the prized cherrystone and littlenecks, the latter minced in clam chowder and atop pizzas), Atlantic surf clams, soft-shelled "steamer" clams, sea urchins (dangerous if stepped on), common green crabs, rock crabs, sand fiddlers, and the famously delicious blue crabs are found mostly in shallow, sometimes brackish waters usually burrowed in or scampering about sandy bottoms, rocks, and mudflats. Farther out, beginning in about 10 feet of water, sea scallops and lobsters make their homes, coming closest to the shore in summer.

Less endearing to most people are the many

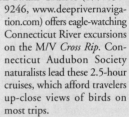

INTRODUCTION

# WAYS TO WATCH EAGLES

It was not long ago that the great soaring American icon, the bald eagle, stood on the brink of extinction. Remarkably, it's now rather easy to see these birds as far south as Connecticut. They soar down the Connecticut River from Canada as far as they must to search for fish and ducks in waters free of ice. In particular, they've become cool-weather habitués of the lower Connecticut River Valley, generally during the most frigid months of the year—from about January to early March, and occasionally a bit earlier or later. More than 100 eagles have been found scouring the region for food between Hartford and Long Island Sound—imagine that as recently as 1950 there were only about 400 breeding pairs of eagles known to inhabit the contiguous United States, down from an estimated 250,000 during the late 1700s. More than 6,000 breeding pairs have been tracked in the lower 48 states in recent years.

BOB RACE

There are several ways to see these creatures. You can simply drive to some of the better and less developed access points along the river—such as the ferry landings at Glastonbury, Rocky Hill, Hadlyme, and Chester—pull out a good pair of binoculars, and wait until you see something. Or you can embark on one of the cruises plying the Connecticut River in winter, some of which are mentioned in the Coastal Connecticut chapter.

On Saturday mornings in mid-January through mid-March, **Mark Twain Cruises** (877/658-9246, www.deeprivernaviga-tion.com) offers eagle-watching Connecticut River excursions on the M/V *Cross Rip*. Connecticut Audubon Society naturalists lead these 2.5-hour cruises, which afford travelers up-close views of birds on most trips.

Over the Presidents' Day weekend each year, the Connecticut Audubon Society sponsors the phenomenally popular **Connecticut River Eagle Festival** (860/767-9795 or 800/714-7201, www.ctaudubon.org/eagle.htm), a free event (the only activity with a cost was an optional boat ride along the river, where participants reported seeing dozens of bald eagles). Heated tents are set up in downtown Essex to house live entertainment, food, interpretive displays, and ice-carving demonstrations. With so few festivals staged in Connecticut in February, this unusual event is a terrific way to break up the sometimes gloomy midwinter weather.

---

land invertebrates that slither and crawl about the state, and indeed some of these—ticks, mosquitoes, horse and deer flies, carpenter ants, yellow jackets, cockroaches, Japanese beetles—are a genuine nuisance. But on summer nights it's a comfort for most of us to fall asleep to the distinct chatter, trill, and staccato of the zillions of katydids and tree crickets. Spiders munch on most pests and rarely bother humans, as is true of the many beautiful dragonflies that swarm about our flower beds, and also ladybugs. And we can thank honeybees for one of the state's tastiest commodities.

Connecticut swarms with butterflies, usually from about May through September or Octo-ber. Most species lie dormant in winter. An exception is the glorious monarch butterflies, which show up in the spring and lay their eggs; they develop first into yellow, black, and white-banded caterpillars before slowly metamorphosing into brilliant orange and black butterflies—two or three generations pass until colder weather inspires the monarchs to begin their migration south, where they'll ultimately winter in Mexico before returning again the following spring.

## Birds and Fish

Because birdwatching and fishing are among Connecticutters' favorite pastimes, a description of the state's most common species and the places where you'll most likely find them appears in the On the Road chapter, within the Birdwatching and Fishing subheadings of the section on the Outdoors.

## Reptiles and Amphibians

There are 14 species of snakes in Connecticut, of which two are venomous: the timber rattlesnake and northern copperhead. Rattlesnakes are endangered and should never be destroyed—they're not common, but hikers often report seeing these four-foot-long creatures on rocks in the sun in the northwestern hills, especially along the Appalachian Trail. They are people-shy and will leave you alone if you pause upon seeing them and calmly back away. Copperheads are far more prevalent and can be very aggressive; again, if you see one, give it plenty of space and move off in a different direction. Note that many nonvenomous snakes resemble their venomous cousins; eastern hognose snakes look like copperheads, for instance.

finback whale

BOB RACE

Turtles are the other class of commonly found Connecticut reptiles, especially painted turtles, which are known to sunbathe in groups around rivers and swamps. Respect the space of the snapping turtle, whose sturdy jaws can leave you with a nasty bite. You won't see these very often, but they do love to swim and cavort about in muddy-bottomed rivers and other bodies of water.

Among amphibians, newts and salamanders aren't easy to see, as they often blend in well with their surroundings, but the yellow-spotted and red varieties do stand out a bit. They tend toward creeks and living under rocks and logs, and are most visible from March through October during the day. Frogs we all know from the often loud choruses of ribbeting and peeping we hear on spring and summer nights, when these loquacious animals seek out mates. Spring peepers, bull frogs, and Woodhouse's toads frequent ponds

and swamps, while common American toads and wood frogs prefer yards, fields, and wooded areas. Unfortunately, in spring, thousands of frogs and toads are hit by automobiles in areas where large numbers of these amphibians are headed toward popular breeding grounds.

## Mammals

The mammals you're mostly likely to see around Connecticut are eastern chipmunks, eastern gray squirrels, opossum, raccoons, striped skunks, and white-tailed deer. All of these are common to both secluded woodlands and developed suburbs, and even some urban areas, and most of these mammals are not easily startled by the presence of human beings.

Skunks, opossum, and raccoons are primarily nocturnal, and if you see one during the day you should keep a good distance, especially if it's behaving erratically or aggressively, as there's a fair chance it's carrying rabies. This disease can actually make an otherwise harmless animal bite at will, and should you ever come into any physical contact with such a creature, you should immediately contact an emergency physician. Several cases of attacks on humans by rabid animals have been reported in Connecticut in recent years, and the lives of people were saved only because anti-rabies shots were administered promptly. There is no cure for this 100 percent fatal disease once symptoms appear.

Happily, the state's mammal population poses few serious threats otherwise. White-tailed deer may forage through gardens, and raccoons through trash cans, but such is the price one pays for living in countrified suburbs.

Less commonly sighted Connecticut animals, which you have the best chances of seeing in state parks and preserves, include beavers, black bears (mainly in northwestern Connecticut), coyotes (again, mostly in the northern part of the state), eastern cottontail rabbits, fishers, gray and red foxes, meadow volesmink, river otters, and woodchucks. Some of the mostly nocturnal and quite beautiful bobcats prevalent in northern and western New England have also been sighted in Connecticut in recent years, as have a handful of moose. (A particularly large one lumbered through a busy section of suburban Vernon in July 1999—helicopters swirled overhead, police and wildlife agents chased after the beleaguered animal, and parts of I-84 and Rte. 30 were shut down when the moose wandered near these roads).

Whale-watching cruises operate out of southeastern Connecticut, but these dramatic sea mammals—once hunted to near extinction—primarily inhabit the waters just beyond Long Island Sound, in the Atlantic. Finback, humpback, and minke whales are most often sighted, as are the occasional schools of bottle-nosed dolphins. Whales are most common spring through fall, with small numbers summering off the coast and the majority passing through in April and May on their way north and back down again in October, November, and December during their migration to warmer waters.

Both harbor and gray seals, which have always been fairly common from Maine to Cape Cod, have made a recent comeback along Connecticut's shoreline. While not easy to find, they are seen on an increasingly regular basis playing around the rocks and on a few beaches near the shallower waters of Long Island Sound.

## ENVIRONMENTAL ISSUES

Connecticut is a densely populated state, and local battles often pit those in favor of development with those keen on preserving the state's diminishing open spaces. A constant environmental concern throughout Connecticut is wildlife management. There's actually a misconception that the farther north you go in New England the more likely you are to see wildlife. In fact, in Vermont, Maine, and New Hampshire, so much of the land is undeveloped that many animals steer clear of roads, villages, and humans—they have the luxury of rarely having to leave their remote and pristine habitats in order to find food and shelter, and they maintain a healthy fear of mankind.

Connecticut, however densely populated it may be, is actually an easy place to spot many animals. The state is heavily wooded, and there are countless parks and preserves, and yet it is also heavily developed. Wildlife and humanlife coexist, for better or for worse, within close proximity, and mammals in Connecticut tend to be less afraid of people—and best able to feed themselves by scavenging through backyards, compost heaps, and garbage cans—than in the more remote parts of New England. This is nice, of course, for wildlife-watchers who get a kick out of seeing deer racing across their lawns.

It's also unfortunate because wild animals have become increasingly dependent upon people and dangerously abundant in areas with heavy traffic, and in an environment that barely supports them. Where they are overpopulated, they are a nuisance in the eyes of many humans—blamed for spreading Lyme disease, ravaging gardens and yards, and causing traffic accidents. Evenly settled by people, Connecticut has relatively few hunting grounds, and attempts to catch and relocate the most prolific species, such as deer, have met with only limited success. Anybody who drives on a daily basis in Connecticut is sure to have seen deer (sometimes several at a time) leaping across roads, usually at night—an astoundingly high number of drivers have struck deer. The statistics are especially bad in Fairfield County, one of the most heavily populated, yet verdantly wooded, sections of the state. Studies have shown that there are 26 deer per square mile living in the area; there were about 600 deer-related traffic accidents reported in Fairfield County in 1999, the highest in Connecticut—deer-related car accidents in the county represent about one of every three in the state.

On a more positive note, Connecticut has made a great deal of headway in reintroducing species that were virtually extinct at one time. With all the talk of encroaching suburban sprawl—although this trend is one of the greatest threats facing the state in the 21st century—it's easy to forget that three out of every four acres of Connecticut were already deforested by the early 1800s, when the state's economy was almost entirely agrarian.

Ironically, the region's woodlands were saved not so much by conservation efforts, which didn't develop in earnest until the 20th century, but by the coming of the industrial revolution, which transformed Connecticut's developed landscape from mostly cleared farmland into a few dense pockets of urbanity. In places where the hilly and rocky terrain made fast and simple transportation routes impossible, or where a lack of rivers made hydropower impractical, the land was left largely to heal itself. And some of it was reforested in order to increase the state's supply of lumber, which ultimately fueled many factories.

By 1900, 45 percent of Connecticut was developed land, and 55 percent had returned to its original forested state. Since that time an active interest in preservation and ecology has gripped the state, and in recent years great efforts and plans have been set forth to permanently protect as much of the landscape as possible. Species that had disappeared entirely during the 19th century have begun making a comeback—these include bald eagles, black bears, coyotes, and wild turkeys. According to wildlife biologists with the Department of Environmental Protection (DEP), about 100 black bears live in Connecticut, mostly in the northwestern and northeastern hills, although they often make their way farther south. Furthermore, efforts to clean up Connecticut's shoreline have restored the region's abundance of marinelife. Even harbor seals now lumber from time to time about the

rocks off Connecticut—something you'd never have seen 10 years ago.

It's taken a while, but Connecticut residents have become increasingly foresighted about the environment in recent years. In 1967, the state passed the Clean Water Act, which became a blueprint for federal water pollution legislation passed in 1972. It was the first state to open a materials recycling facility, and the public is encouraged to check out the educational exhibits on waste management and recycling at facilities in Hartford and Stratford. Connecticut has also restored more than 1,500 acres of wetlands across the state, with private groups like the Nature Conservancy, the Connecticut Audubon Society, and the White Memorial Foundation continuing to secure even larger tracts.

In 1999 Governor John Rowland unveiled a proposal calling for 21 percent of Connecticut to be eventually protected as open space—this would be above the thousands of acres owned by private nonprofit groups and individual municipalities. The state's first purchase was Portland State Forest (now Meshomasic) in 1901. Right now DEP owns 224,000 acres (about 7 percent of the state's acreage) and will need to acquire approximately 440,000 more acres to fulfill its goal of 21 percent. The plans for land acquisition are remarkably varied and comprehensive, and include all types of water access, natural areas to protect endangered habitats, scenic and historically significant areas, greenways, and large forest tracts.

# History

## Before 1614

Countless tribes of indigenous peoples lived in what is now Connecticut when European settlers first began charting the region. As you drive around the state it's worth noting that a vast number of geographical names come from the state's Indian legacy, from mountains and forests to lakes and streams. Two incorporated towns, Norwalk and Naugatuck, along with many villages and sections of towns, bear Native American names, including Higganum, Moodus, Moosup, Niantic, Noank, Oneco, Pawcatuck, Poque-

tanuck, Quinebaug, Saugatuck, Uncasville, and Willimantic. The very name "Connecticut" is a variation on Quonitockut (meaning Long Tidal River), which is how area tribes referred to what we now call the Connecticut River.

Connecticut's tribes were many, but they fell into five broadly defined groups. The Nipmuck, who lived primarily in northeastern Connecticut and southern Massachusetts, were loosely organized and followed no one primary leader. The Pequots and the Mohegans were rival tribes living in the southeastern part of the state; they shared a similar tongue and, in all probability, like origins—their contentious relations would ultimately pit them against each other as whites colonized Connecticut, with the Mohegans befriending the colonists and the Pequots warring with them.

The Sequins (or River Indians) formed a league of independent but interrelated groups living throughout the Connecticut River Valley; tribes included Hammonasset, Machimodus, Podunk, Poquonnuc, Quinnipiac, Saukiaug, Tunxis, and Wangunk. The fifth grouping was known by the names Wappinger and Matabesec; they shared a vast region of the Hudson River Valley with the Mohicans, and included among their tribes in Connecticut were the Pootatuck, Siwanoy, Uncowa, and Wepawaug. All of these Connecticut tribes were raided at various times by New England's most powerful league, the Mohawks.

### 1614–1633

Europeans began settling the state in the 1630s, and within a few decades had displaced, massacred, or wiped out the Indians with the introduction of various diseases. By the time of the American Revolution 150 years later, the population was nearly 100 percent of English origin. However, Dutch traders laid the earliest claims upon the region, and it's a matter of historical happenstance that the state was not colonized formally by them, as was neighboring New York.

Adriaen Block, the Dutch explorer for whom Block Island is named, is credited with first navigating the Connecticut River in 1614, nearly a decade before the Plymouth and Massachusetts Bay colonies were laid out by Puritans of mostly British citizenship. In 1633 Dutch traders set up a post at what is now Hartford (the old Colt Armory stands on about this site). A year earlier, scouts from the Massachusetts area had begun exploring the Connecticut River and reporting back to the more restless factions there that a great fertile river plain awaited expansion-minded Puritans.

By now the Massachusetts Bay Colony had established several communities around what is now Boston, and indeed groups from Watertown, Dorchester, and New Town (later renamed Cambridge) had begun to express a desire for more land and greater autonomy.

### 1633–1659

If religious and political differences in Europe drove the Puritans to settle in Massachusetts, a similar climate of dissension split these Puritans into a number of smaller sects. There's a misconception that the Puritans formed a unified front. In fact, although they shared a common distrust of the Church of England and a history of severe persecution, they harbored a proclivity for infighting and were not averse to persecuting each other—much as different factions within today's larger religious movements often disagree vehemently on specific, and sometimes minute, issues of doctrine and church law.

What the Puritans shared was a rejection of the high ritualistic tone of the Church of England and a rabid fear and hatred of the pope and the Roman Catholic Church. These Congregationalists espoused an austere and solemn understanding of God's will and embraced an ethic that not only allowed for a capitalist society, but actually encouraged its followers to prosper through hard work, self-sufficiency, and thrift. These three virtues would define the essence of what it means to be a resident of Connecticut for centuries to come.

During the New World's first half-century, three Puritan colonies were established in addition to the two in Massachusetts. Two of them, Rhode Island and Connecticut, were founded by comparatively liberal and tolerant leaders who had split from the Massachusetts Bay Colony, which, more than the Plymouth Colony, governed with a strong arm and permitted only "spiritually worthy" members to partake of the political process.

The radically pluralistic Roger Williams founded Rhode Island, which welcomed settlers of virtually all religions and early on established

*Tensions escalated the following spring into the Pequot War of 1637, during which about 130 settlers from the Connecticut River towns, along with 70 allied Mohegans, developed a plan to destroy their enemy.*

America's first synagogue. An enlightened minister named Thomas Hooker brought his congregation to the banks of the Connecticut River, where he drew up a governing doctrine for the colony that still required membership in the Congregational Church, but nevertheless included policies that were quite progressive for the day. The fifth and final colony, New Haven, was established by devout English Puritans a few years after Hooker. Eventually, awkwardly, these two colonies would merge.

In 1634, the first group of dissidents from the Massachusetts Colony established a settlement a few miles north of the Dutch trading post, in what is now Windsor. A brutal winter sent the majority back down to the brand-new military post at the mouth of the Connecticut River, on Long Island Sound, which was established by a group of British speculators whose ranks included a Lord Say and Sele and a Lord Brook—Saybrook remains the name of this community.

The following spring, Windsor was resettled, and Hooker led his band to a spot on the river immediately north of the Dutch post and christened it Hartford (after the British town from which his assistant hailed). A third group of Puritans encamped a few miles south to create Wethersfield. The first couple of years continued to test the wills of the new transplants, but the three towns quickly developed into a cohesive political and religious power led by the Reverend Hooker.

The Sequin River Indians of the region befriended these early settlers, as did the Mohegans, who lived not far to the east—in fact, the Mohegans had helped persuade the earliest British visitors to the region to colonize here. The rival Pequots, however, perhaps wisely intuited the presence of white settlers as a potential hazard, sensing correctly that these newcomers would—with the Mohegans—form a dangerous alliance.

The Pequots left their first calling card in the 1630s when they killed a pair of British merchants whom they encountered sailing up the Connecticut River on a trading mission. They further raised the ire of the settlers when they murdered the respected explorer John Oldham off the coast of Block Island in 1636, an act that led almost immediately to reprisals such as burn-

The headstones in Hartford's Ancient Burying Ground stand in the shadows of Main Street's office towers.

ings and raids by British troops. The Pequots continued to strike out, attacking and murdering several of the Wethersfield families during the winter of 1636–1637 and unsuccessfully attempting to establish a warring pact with their neighbors, the formidable Narragansett Indians of nearby Rhode Island.

These tensions escalated the following spring into the Pequot War of 1637, during which about 130 settlers from the Connecticut River towns, along with 70 allied Mohegans, developed a plan to destroy their enemy. Believing it wise to approach from the least likely side, the group attacked from the east, sailing to Narragansett Bay and marching in a westerly direction, with a force of about 400 Narragansetts looking on.

The Pequots were concentrated in a pair of encampments near what is now Norwich, each comprising a several-acre enclosure of a few dozen wigwams. The settlers, led by John Mason, struck the largest Pequot community at dawn and virtually obliterated its inhabitants, burning the wigwams and shooting any people who attempted to flee. The second Pequot encampment attempted to thwart the invasion but was easily driven to retreat. Over the next two months, the remaining severely crippled Pequot league edged its way west toward New York but was met in a massive swamp (in what would become Fairfield) by Mason and his battalion. Again a great slaughter was carried out, with the remaining 180 Pequots being taken hostage and brought to Hartford.

The Pequots could not have been subdued without the assistance of the Mohegans and the Narragansetts, with whom the English signed a treaty of friendship in 1637. But peace between the Native Americans and the English would last for only a few decades.

Feeling confident that the Connecticut Colony was there to stay, Thomas Hooker guided the settlement's most respected legal mind, Roger Ludlow, to draw up a governing doctrine of self-rule, which would be ratified by the General Court of Hartford in 1639 as the Fundamental Orders. The towns of Windsor, Hartford, and Wethersfield thereby formed "one publike State or Commonwealth," and thus was born what is often called the world's earliest working constitution (although historians have, over the centuries, weakened the thrust of this claim by pointing out a number of flaws and conditions that disqualify the document's status as a genuine constitution).

The Orders were based on principles that were, at the time, considered radical in their democratic spirit. They sought to limit the power of government and to break it down into three branches of elected officials: a single governor (whom today we would call the executive branch), a cabinet of magistrates (today's judicial branch), and a general court of assembly (today's legislative branch). A key tenet was popular sovereignty, meaning that the governor's powers were greatly limited by the voting of the general court and the rulings of the magistrates.

Hooker disapproved of the exclusive and right-eous terms of the Massachusetts Bay and designed a settlement in which each hardworking church-going man was granted membership in the church and political representation in the colony's government. Enlightened though the Fundamental Orders were, property was nevertheless a requirement for voter rights, church was most definitely not separate from state, only men were permitted to vote, and thus power fell entirely within the hands of male Christian landowners. In fact, it was not until the mid-19th century that non-Christians were allowed to build or secure a formal place of worship on any piece of Connecticut land.

New Haven Colony, meanwhile, was founded in 1638 by British merchants John Davenport and Theophilus Eaton. They established the very kind of governing body Hooker had sought to avoid, a theocracy whose orthodox laws were derived strictly and literally from the Bible's Mosaic Code. Over the next two decades, New Haven residents further settled in Guilford (which began first as its own independent colony), Milford, Stamford, Greenwich, Branford, and Southhold (which is across the sound from Connecticut, on the North Fork of eastern Long Island, now part of New York). Simultaneously, Connecticut Colony branched out along the Connecticut River and west into the Litchfield Hills.

These loose collections of communities governed by rival schools of Puritan doctrine legitimized their settlements by signing pacts with the Indians from whom they typically purchased the land, and sometimes by securing warrants and charters from Britain. But there were land disputes early on—the New Haven colonists were seen largely as squatters by their nemeses, and the whole issue of propriety, land rights, and independence became increasingly confusing and precarious. Neither colony possessed a document that truly validated its existence in the eyes of the king of England.

## 1659–1675

In 1658, the Puritan-sympathetic ruler of Great Britain—Oliver Cromwell—died, and in 1659 Catholic monarch Charles II was returned to England's throne. The mood in Connecticut suddenly turned from concern to near panic. Hartford's governor, John Winthrop, Jr., recognized the region's political vulnerability in the wake of this restoration of anti-Puritan rule—the mother country's laissez-faire attitude toward its colonies could no longer be expected.

Winthrop sailed to England, and, in a show of commendable diplomatic acumen, convinced the new king to grant Connecticut a royal charter, one that Winthrop himself largely drafted according to the basic principles of the Fundamental Orders. This document recognized the Connecticut Colony's geographical boundaries as Narragansett Bay (now part of Rhode Island) to the east, Long Island Sound to the south, Massachusetts to the north, and the Pacific Ocean to the west (yes, what we now know as the country's western border was at one time the very western reaches of the Litchfield Hills).

The residents of New Haven Colony considered neither Winthrop its ambassador nor Connecticut its greater identity, and so its leadership took angrily to their subsumption under the terms of the royal charter, relenting only in 1664 when it became painfully clear that any attempt to secede from Connecticut might result in being swallowed up within the colony of New York (a fate apparently even less palatable than joining with Hartford).

At this time, the charter-recognized Connecticut Colony consisted of 21 towns, 15 from the original Hartford Colony and 6 from New Haven. The rivalry between these two factions played itself out over the next three centuries and remains strong, in many circles, today. In fact, the state's legislative body met alternately in Hartford and New Haven until 1875, when a state referendum deemed that Hartford should be the state's sole capital.

By the 1670s, while the various towns of newly formed Connecticut struggled to see eye to eye politically, tensions between the region's indigenous and settling factions had increased dramatically, as whites snared acres of the best farming and hunting land for themselves and continued to infringe upon the traditions of the Native Americans by persistently seeking to convert them to Christianity.

In Rhode Island, the leader of the Wampanoag tribe, Philip, sought to unify New England's many Indian tribes in an ambitious and perhaps desperate conspiracy to overthrow the Puritan lock on the region. A Christian Indian loyal to the settlers betrayed King Philip's intentions and was quickly rubbed out by Philip's men in a move that could easily have been played out today in a Mario Puzo novel. As with the Pequot situation in 1637, the settlers upped the ante by capturing and executing the murderers of the Christian informant, and so began King Philip's War, an infamous campaign that would ultimately seal the fate of Native Americans in the northeastern United States.

The war took place principally near the Rhode Island and Massachusetts border, where Philip's tribe occupied a fort at Mount Hope. After several residents of the town of Swansea were murdered by the tribe, about 300 Connecticut troops and 150 Mohegan and (now-loyal) Pequot Indians joined the English army of about 1,000 and descended upon Mount Hope.

In the end, although a great many colonists were killed in the debacle, the raid was successful, and all of the region's Indian tribes were ultimately contained. Many of the defeated survivors of King Philip's War fled either north into Vermont and New Hampshire or south and west to New York State. A few bands remained behind, including a mix of western tribesmen who established the still-extant Schaghticokes Reservation in the Litchfield County town of Kent.

Best-known today are the groups that have sprung from the remaining Pequots and Mohegans, who were permitted to form reservations in Stonington, Ledyard, and Montville. The WPA's guide to Connecticut describes the Ledyard group as of 1930 as consisting of nine surviving members living on about "130 acres of rough land. Aside from these few State wards, 31 descendants of the Mohegan tribe are living as members of the community in the town of Montville." These few remaining Mohegans and Pequots may have been down by the middle of the 20th century, but they clearly weren't out. In 1993 the Pequots opened Foxwoods Casino, and in

1996, the Mohegans followed suit in nearby Uncasville. These two controversial gaming-and-entertainment complexes are today among the most lucrative businesses in New England.

## 1675–1700

In 1687, another shift in British rule again threatened Connecticut's independence. Charles II died and was succeeded by his brother, James II. Ever the autocrat and bureaucrat, the new king decided it was about time to consolidate the uneasily maintained British colonies under the aegis of one formal Dominion of New York and New England, with one royal governor, Sir Edmund Andros. All of the neighboring states gradually abandoned their patents and charters but for Connecticut, which stalled and held out until finally Governor Andros and 75 of his regents paid a personal visit to Hartford and its governor, Robert Treat.

The visit became forever known as the Charter Oak incident. Facing the threat of losing the charter to Andros, a stealthy witness to the negotiations (or perhaps a few them) stole away with the document and hid it in the trunk of an enormous old oak tree. This move, though romantic, ended rather unhappily—at least in the short run—as Andros nevertheless incorporated Connecticut within the Dominion of New York and New England.

Connecticut has enjoyed independent state rule for the entire duration of its political formation excepting the two years during which James II ruled the British Empire. England's Glorious Revolution of 1689 spelled the end of the king's controversial regime, and Parliament replaced him with his Protestant daughter, Mary, and her husband, William of Orange. The Dominion of New York and New England came to an abrupt end, and Andros was called back to England.

Connecticut's legislature voted immediately to return to the rule of the original charter, and the state was governed exactly according to it until a new constitution was deployed during the Constitutional Convention of 1818 (the revised version of that year remains the oldest extant state constitution in America).

## 1700–1770

Connecticut enjoyed a quietly prosperous century following its return to self-rule. The legislature maintained a low profile, doing little to raise eyebrows across the Atlantic. With few obvious assets and a position of no particular strategic value, England's rulers more or less left the little state to its own devices. The agrarian economy succeeded to the point of feeding the state's population but barely beyond that—it had no key crop that England sought to regulate.

Connecticut supplied troops for a variety of Colonial military campaigns throughout the late 1600s and early 1700s. The state also quibbled constantly with its neighbors over boundaries, at various times laying claim to eastern Long Island and Westchester County in New York, several prominent chunks of Pennsylvania, and smaller bits of Rhode Island and Massachusetts. These skirmishes even escalated into small battles on a few occasions, but by the time of the American Independence Connecticut had become, geographically, the state we know it to be today.

Little influenced by the crown and dealing to a minimal degree with neighboring colonies, Connecticut also developed a provincialism that remained well into the 19th century and a libertarian spirit of independence that lasts to this day. Even within the Colonial borders, individual communities kept largely to themselves, and the same tensions over autonomy, religious doctrine, and land hunger that inspired Thomas Hooker to forsake Massachusetts for Connecticut inspired countless communities to petition the legislature for incorporated town status or the right to settle new unchartered towns.

Residents identified themselves more as living in a particular village or grouping of towns than in the greater colony of Connecticut. The colony possessed no unifying identity or purpose but for its individual parts to operate free from a heavy-handed government, and to prosper as individual units within the greater realm.

Connecticutters cherished their ability to serve themselves and rely little on the outside world. There was no great source of income, except for a few port communities that benefited from the triangular trade route among New England, the

West Indies, and Africa. Other than the Connecticut River Valley, the land was rough and hard, studded with rocks and boulders that today crisscross the land in the form of beautiful stone walls. Connecticut Yankees fed their families and carried forward entirely through hard work and resourcefulness, invention and economy.

Despite having been founded by persons who were vilified on the basis of their religious beliefs, Connecticut remained amazingly intolerant of non-Puritans during its first couple hundred years. Until 1705, state law banned the practices of Quakers and any others who failed to agree to the tenets of Congregationalism. Catholicism was widely condemned, and the state's earliest Catholics, who arrived beginning in the 1700s, were forced to renounce their allegiance to the pope as a condition of citizenship. Where there was religious infighting in Europe and the New World during these times, intolerance was fought typically with intolerance, fear with fear, hostility with hostility. And so Connecticut's early leaders were often little more progressive and accepting than those from whom their ancestors fled.

The tight conservative grip of Congregationalism loosened ever so slightly through the 1700s, as Baptists, Episcopalians, Methodists, and Presbyterians slowly worked their platforms into the inclusion of state politics—although it would not be until 1818 that Congregationalism was formally done away with as the official church of the state. The hostility toward Catholics would not soften until the American Revolution, when allied Frenchmen served in Connecticut under Rochambeau and immediately earned the respect of locals.

By then of course, Tories had become the latest group worthy of ignominy. When talk of the American Revolution spread throughout the colonies, Connecticut's overwhelming distrust of the British Crown compelled its population to support full-scale revolt—comparatively few Connecticutters remained sympathetic to England.

## 1770–1800

Given its position, geographically, between Pennsylvania and Massachusetts, and considering its great ability to provide for its own people despite limited resources, Connecticut developed a reputation during the war as the Provisions State, supplying the Continental Army with food, munitions, and supplies. A handful of moderately important battles were staged in Connecticut during the Revolution, and the state gave us the war hero Ethan Allen and hero-turned-goat, Benedict Arnold. Throughout the campaign, the Colonial governor Jonathan Trumbull continued to serve the state, the only non-Tory governor in all of the colonies.

The state that emerged following independence had changed little during the past century, its population having increased little. Ask around today, and you'll find precious few Connecticutters who can trace their local roots to much earlier than the Revolutionary War.

It's entirely appropriate that the nation's greatest symbol of westward expansion, the Gateway Arch, stands over the city of St. Louis, but a case could be made that at least a miniature of this monument ought to go up somewhere along the Connecticut River. For it was this region's earliest inhabitants who planted the seeds for full-fledged expansion. Vast numbers of citizens left during the 1700s, migrating north to Vermont and west to western New York, Pennsylvania, Ohio, and eventually the Midwest.

By default, those who remained in Connecticut and became responsible for shaping its regional identity were an industrious, clever, and thrifty bunch, steady in their will and conservative in their method.

By the end of the 1700s, a thriving shipbuilding, trading, and whaling industry had grown to ease the state's economic dependence upon agriculture and increase its prominence as a mercantile entity. With three major rivers and about 100 miles of coastline, plus several very good harbors, Connecticut made the most of its geographical link to the sea.

From the 1750s to the Civil War, shipbuilding along the Connecticut River Valley towns from Essex to Windsor prospered greatly. Connecticut provided the first ships to the Revolutionary War effort, mostly from boatyards in Essex—there were more than a dozen shipyards along the river at this time. Masters and sea captains hailed from these Connecticut towns nearest the mouth of the river. River ports developed in Middletown, Derby, and Norwich, and the deep harbors of Stonington, New London, and New Haven provided for trade along the coast.

Whalers sailed out of New London, and in fewer numbers from Mystic and Stonington. These three towns were part of a highly profitable whaling industry centered around southeastern Connecticut, Nantucket Island, and New Bedford (the regional whaling capital) in Massachusetts, and Sag Harbor on Long Island. The efforts were profitable until the Civil War, when Confederate ships attacked Union boats. Natural oil fields were found in Pennsylvania shortly thereafter, spelling the end of this practice by lowering the demand for sperm oil.

## 1800–1818

The state continued to march to the beat of its own drummer during the years following the Revolution, and did not support Thomas Jefferson and his trade embargoes during the War of 1812, protesting to the point of refusing the United States War Department any assistance in the form of men and provisions. It, Rhode Island, and Massachusetts opposed the war, which was completely detrimental to the trade interests of these states, for by now Connecticut had developed into a significant port. In the most extreme circles there was, or at least was rumored to be, talk of secession or a dissolution of the Union, and at the very least there grew a greater call in New England for individual state rights.

With their history of self-sufficiency, Nutmeggers had long developed a drive to build the better mousetrap—indeed, mousetraps were manufactured with great success in the town of Sharon—and the economic crisis of these years further spurred native talents to come up with new ways to make money and improve commerce and methods of manufacture. If necessity is the mother of all invention, Connecticut's necessity to remain economically viable during the War of 1812 turned it into the mother state of inventors.

Factories and mills opened at a rapid rate, and mass industrialization began in earnest (although the economic leader in the state would remain

farming until around the Civil War). Meanwhile, the good trade years of the two decades prior to the War of 1812 had inspired Connecticut to open banks and come up with ways to protect its vastly growing assets. From this need was born America's insurance industry, of which Hartford has been the capital since it developed the first companies at the beginning of the 19th century.

The maritime trade was a risky business; entire ships and valuable cargoes could be lost in a single storm or mishap, and so investors realized that their long-term success could be greatly improved by developing ways to sharing both the risks and the profits. Following the formation of the new country, Congress established the U.S. Bank in 1791. The Connecticut National Bank was chartered in Hartford with funds of $100,000 the following year. Banks were organized shortly after in Norwich, New London, Middletown, and New Haven—in short, just about any place where sea commerce played a major role in the local economy. In 1794, in Norwich, the Mutual Assurance Company was formed to protect investors from losses in the case of warehouse fires and marine accidents. Others, including Hartford Fire and Aetna, formed soon after.

Congregationalist-Federalists, the blue-blooded old-boys' network of the day, controlled most of the state's business interests, from the newly emerging banking and insurance communities to most of the state's largest trade and manufacturing concerns. In 1814, an Episcopalian tired of being denied capital and backing from the Congregationalist-controlled financial institutions formed Hartford's second bank, Phoenix (today one of the state's most prominent companies). This bold affront to the traditional quasi-Brahmin mentality of the day foreshadowed soon-to-unfold events that would forever alter state's personality and politics.

With so many of the descendants of the state's early families having left the state for better opportunities out west, the demographics of Connecticut began to change in the early 1800s. Although the state was still almost entirely northern European and white, a greater number of non-Congregational Protestants, Catholics, and

# THE FREEDOM TRAIL

One aspect of Connecticut history that focuses on the contribution of African Americans to the social and cultural fabric of the state is the Connecticut Freedom Trail, a permanent record and self-guided tour of sites associated with the experiences and accomplishments of black men and women in the state.

The Freedom Trail documents some 18 structures that served as way stations on Connecticut's **Underground Railroad.** After lawmakers in 1793 established grounds to capture and return any slaves who escaped from slaveholding states into free states, a secret network of "safe havens" gradually developed throughout the northern United States. Many escaped slaves ultimately fled into Canada, while others settled in northern New England; vast numbers passed through Connecticut, many of whom landed at some point in Farmington, the center of such underground activity (five of the houses on the Freedom Trail map are here). Most of these homes are not open to the public, the exceptions being **Randall's Ordinary Landmark Inn and Restaurant** in North Stonington and the **Joshua Hempstead House** museum in New London.

The Freedom Trail also sheds light on the infamous *Amistad* case, the subject of the 1997 Steven Spielberg film *Amistad.* The case concerns a shipload of kidnapped African slaves, which, while en route in 1839 from Havana, Cuba, to another part of the island, was commandeered by the 53 captives on board. In the slaves' power, the crew was directed to sail the ship back to Africa, but surreptitiously the sailors steered in a northerly direction in hopes of eventually landing in a U.S. slave port. The ship ended up in Long Island Sound, where it was intercepted by the U.S. Navy. In New Haven, a trial was held to determine the fate of the Africans, all of whom were placed in captivity for the duration of the ordeal, which ended up lasting nearly two full years. With former president John Quincy Adams defending the Africans, the U.S. Supreme Court eventually declared them free in February 1841. The 37 survivors, after living in Farmington while funds were raised to return them home, finally sailed back to Africa in November 1841, along with five U.S. missionaries. Most of the sites relevant to the ordeal are in Farmington and New Haven.

A final section of the Freedom Trail covers more than 30 sites, several of which are open to the public, which detail a vast and fascinating variety of people and places that have figured prominently in the state's African American history. These include the former homes of such luminaries as **Marian Anderson,** a noted singer and U.N. delegate who made her home on a farm at 46 Joe's Hill Road in Danbury, and **Paul Robeson,** the college football star, singer, and actor who for 12 years lived in a mansion in Enfield at 1221 Enfield Street. There are also numerous churches and gravesites; **Wadsworth Atheneum** in Hartford, which is home to the 6,000-piece Amistad Foundation African-American Collection; **Prudence Crandall House** in Canterbury, where a private academy for young black women was attempted in 1831; **Harriet Beecher Stowe Center** in Hartford, homestead of the *Uncle Tom's Cabin* author; and historic districts in New Haven and New London.

To become acquainted with the Freedom Trail, you can contact the **Connecticut Historical Commission** (59 S. Prospect St., Hartford, CT 06106, 860/566-3005, www.ctfreedomtrail.com) for a brochure and map.

Another excellent resource on the state's African American heritage is the **Amistad Committee** (Box 2936, Westville Station, New Haven, CT 06515, 203/387-0370, www.yaleslavery.org), which produces a book, video, and a couple of pamphlets on the Amistad Rebellion and other facets of the state's African American and slave history. You can also download well-researched material directly from the Committee's website.

even Jews settled here, and the Federalist politicians who controlled the legislature and vehemently opposed President Jefferson's radical republicanism slowly lost their overwhelming popularity among the general public.

In 1816 a fallen Federalist named Oliver Wolcott Jr., the son and grandson of earlier Federalist governors (his father having also been a signer of the Declaration of Independence), ran successfully for governor as a member of the Tolerationist Party. His election marked a shocking defeat to the Congregational-Federalist lock on power and a system that favored only those of certain parentage while ignoring virtually every other citizen in the state.

If the state's traditional white Anglo-Saxon rule didn't exactly fall away immediately, it certainly lost its sway by the end of the 19th century. Governor Wolcott served 10 years and effectively revolutionized government in Connecticut by formally separating the state from the church. Wolcott presided over the constitutional convention of 1818, during which the state constitution was fully reformed so that greater powers were granted to the governor, voting rights were increased to a greater number of residents, and religious freedom was assured to all.

## 1818–1865

Soon after Wolcott assumed power, Episcopalians established Trinity College (then Washington College) in Hartford, and Methodists founded Wesleyan in Middletown, thus providing some competition to that bastion of Congregationalism, Yale.

John Fitch, of South Windsor, developed the steamboat long before Robert Fulton actually made it practical and became famous for it. Steamboats came into vogue in 1815 and were a popular means of transport until the advent of railroads 20 years later. They continued to operate throughout the 19th century, transporting people and goods among Boston, Providence, Hartford, New Haven, New York, and other water-accessible U.S. cities. Connecticut even used steamships to transport runaway slaves on the Underground Railroad. The last steamship ran up the Connecticut River in 1931, but not before East Haddam developed the Goodspeed Opera House and became a major resort community thanks to steamer transport.

Ask around locally and you'll learn that car dealers in Connecticut have developed an almost unrivaled reputation for high-pressure sales tactics, gamesmanship, and haggling. One need only consider the state's tradition for peddling goods to understand where this tradition began. The term Nutmegger actually derives from a sneaky practice attributed to Yankee peddlers, who were known to carve bits of wood to resemble the valuable spice nutmeg and pass them off as such to unsuspecting buyers.

Peddling was a common means of earning a living in the state and in many ways precipitated the rise of Connecticut's preeminence as one of America's great manufacturing states of the 19th and early to mid-20th centuries. The tradition was begun by the Pattison brothers of Berlin, a town in the Central Connecticut River Valley. They opened a tinshop in 1740 and determined that they could most effectively sell their wares by carting them around from town to town. Within a few years, other metalworkers in the area began setting up similar operations, and by the time the method of mass production was perfected in the early 1800s by a pair of Connecticut natives—Simeon North and Eli Whitney—the Connecticut River Valley was abuzz with metalworks. Meriden became the cradle of America's silver manufacture, New Britain became famous for hardware and tools, Waterbury for brass, and Berlin for tinware.

As for the Yankee peddler, he remained a force from about the American Revolution until the Civil War and continued in lesser numbers to the 1960s in one form or another, hauling his cart of gadgets and doodads around the countryside and utilizing a vast battery of tricks and diversions to help improve upon his sales. A peddler often traveled for months on end, selling his horse and wagon at the end of his trip before finally returning home.

The mood in America for intense manufacturing growth was ripe, owing to free trade among the newly formed United States and a patriotic fervor that supported products made on national soil. But what most pushed America forward was mass production, a notion spearheaded in Connecticut by two inventors, Eli Whitney and Simeon North. Interestingly, the two worked not together but several miles apart (Whitney in New Haven and North in Berlin), and they each developed interchangeable parts simultaneously and largely without the knowledge of the other.

Both inventors harnessed this new technology to mass-produce firearms, which prior to this time had to be created individually by skilled craftsmen. Whitney and North each developed tools and machines that could make identical and interchangeable parts, so that potentially—and indeed eventually—anything from a rifle to an airplane could be created quickly and with the least manual labor. Factory output increased not twofold or tenfold but exponentially, and this one Connecticut invention forever and dramatically altered the course of history.

Locally, Connecticut's economy received a great boost from a number of additional inventions that utilized, or in some cases improved upon, the principles of mass production. Most obviously, New Britain became one of the world's centers of machine-part production, for the nation's new wave of technological know-how depended upon machines that could actually produce machines themselves, such as lathes and milling machines. New Britain is still known as the Hardware City and the home of the international toolmakers, Stanley Works.

The proliferation of smaller metalworks, the shipping embargoes of the 1810s, and the development of mass production turned the state into a major manufacturing center. A major silk mill was opened in Manchester and pretty soon all kinds of textile mills began opening in the eastern hills, throughout Windham and Tolland Counties. Somers produced wool, Rockville cassimere, and Norwich cotton, and Willimantic became a leader in thread.

Textile manufacture developed in Connecticut after the Revolution, largely as a way for the state to boost its economy at a time when England had a lock on this technology and its sea trade. The idea of producing textiles at home caught on,

and by 1816, Congress had passed the first tariff on the importation of woolen goods in an effort to keep America's production profitable.

To compete with the Erie Canal, and so that New Haven's merchant ports could steal a little thunder from Hartford's, a group of investors financed the Farmington Canal in 1822. By 1825 it connected New Haven to Cheshire, and by 1829 it ran clear to Northampton. Unfortunately, landslides and generally high maintenance costs plagued the canal for years, and the stockholders lost bundles of money before finally abandoning the canal in 1847. By then railroad transportation had become a major force, further damaging the canal trade.

Railroads prospered from the 1840s through the 1850s, spreading rapidly around the state. Despite opposition from holders of the state's lucrative Turnpike stocks, the first railroad charter was granted by the General Assembly in 1832 for the New York and Stonington Railroad. Following were railroads connecting Norwich to Worcester and Boston, the Hartford to New Haven and Springfield, the Bridgeport through the Litchfield Hills to western Massachusetts and Albany via the Housatonic Line, and so on. However, by the 1930s, many of the little-used rail tracks (such as the one from Newtown to Litchfield) were decommissioned and abandoned. And today rail service in Connecticut is limited to primarily along the coast and the Connecticut River Valley.

Most of the state's largest cities would increase in population by 100 percent to 200 percent every decade from the 1820s through the end of the century, as laborers were drawn in to work in the wealth of new factories. A famine in Ireland and a work shortage would turn Connecticut, like most other Northeast states, into an emigration center for the Irish, who would populate the earliest factories. Entire factory towns and villages went up almost overnight, complete with factory-created housing, schools, churches, and such, as did similar mill towns. Collinsville, for example, was founded in 1826 and named for Samuel Collins, who operated what would become one of the world's leading ax manufactories. Seymour was an early example of a town built around textile mills, having been started by David Humphreys in the early 1800s.

Eli Terry, after whom Terryville is named, developed a way to mass-produce wooden clocks, and before long Connecticut was the nation's leading teller of time, with most of the production set in the upper Naugatuck River Valley, around Bristol, Thomaston (named for clockmaker Seth Thomas), Plymouth, and Waterbury. A student of Terry, Chauncey Jerome, came up with a way to build cheaper and more efficient brass clocks, which further facilitated nearby Waterbury's rise in brass production. Eventually, the famed Timex watch-making corporation would be established just outside Waterbury.

Hitchcock chairs were mass-produced to great acclaim in the northern end of this region, and the original Lambert Hitchcock chair factory still operates alongside the Farmington River in Riverton. In Bridgeport, Elias Howe developed sewing machines, and Isaac Singer developed the leading sewing machine company in the world.

In the Ivoryton section of Essex, everything from ivory combs and toothpicks to pianos were made with great success. A small boom in copper mining in Simsbury led to the development of the Ensign-Bickford safety-fuse company, and in the Hazardville section of Enfield gunpowder was produced.

## 1865–1910

Eli Whitney and Simeon North had developed mass production largely as a way to increase the output of firearms. Appropriately, Connecticut would continue to excel in the munitions field and also in providing the U.S. military with warplanes and helicopters during the military campaigns of the 20th century. Christian Sharps gave us the breech-loading rifle, his plant becoming a leading employer in Hartford. Samuel Colt would amass one of the greatest fortunes of his day by inventing the revolver, with his Colt Armory in Hartford employing thousands. Another machine tool concern in Hartford, named for founders Francis Pratt and Amos Whitney, would develop eventually into the leader of airplane engines and into New England's largest employer. They, along with several other impor-

tant manufacturing pioneers of the day, learned their trade while working at the Colt factory. Another from Colt was Christopher Spencer, who gave us the Spencer repeating rifle.

Around the time of the Civil War, more than half of the nation's firearms came from Hartford and New Haven, brass buttons and hardware from Waterbury and New Britain, carriage axles from New Haven, and hats from Danbury. Rubber goods came from the Naugatuck area, owing to the invention by Charles Goodyear of vulcanized rubber, which could resist the effects of extreme heat, cold, and chemicals. The state was second in per capita manufacturing only to Massachusetts.

This led to great waves of immigration by French Canadians, Germans, Italians, Poles, Russians, and Slavs, as well as a high number of African Americans who began moving into the state to fill the many job openings.

Farming had greatly diminished in popularity as manufacturing replaced it as Connecticut's leading industry, but one crop remained highly viable. Tobacco production peaked in the 1880s and was the state's most valuable cash crop by 1920.

## 1910–1950

Out of the tradition of Yankee peddling, around World War I Al Fuller developed the phenomenally successful Fuller Brush company, whose sales rose from $87,000 during its first year to $15 million annually by 1923, less than a decade later—the company stood near the banks of the Connecticut River, in Hartford by the Windsor line. The ubiquitous Fuller Brush salesmen were a fixture in America until the 1950s, when the notion of peddling door-to-door finally lost its cachet.

A fairly primitive submarine was invented during the Revolutionary War by David Bushnell in the shipbuilding stronghold of Essex, but it was not too far away and about a century later that full-scale submarine manufacture took root in Groton, where the Electric Boat company become the largest submarine base in the country in 1904. The company produced 75 subs for the U.S. Navy during World War II and developed the first nuclear-powered submarine in 1955. Groton remains the world's leading sub manufacturer.

The Weed Sewing Machine became a strong producer in Hartford before turning its attention to the production of Columbia bicycles and some of America's earliest automobiles. In fact, the race to become auto-manufacturing capital of America fell entirely between Hartford and Detroit, but Henry Ford ended the rivalry with his great ideas about assembly-line production. The auto industry died in Hartford, but in 1925 the airplane engine business took hold at Pratt & Whitney, which prior to this time was best known for creating the standard inch and other high-precision measuring machines that further facilitated the mass production of goods.

Pratt & Whitney enjoyed limited success during the economically challenged 1930s but, like so many other Connecticut companies over the years, was given an amazing boost when America entered World War II and suddenly needed tens of thousands of new planes. The company produced more than 350,000 airplane engines for the World War II effort. The same Provisions State that helped fuel the American Revolution played a vital role as well during both World Wars, and perhaps spared the state the very worst of the Depression era (at least in some areas). Connecticut became a munitions center, and its factories greatly supplied the war efforts.

Igor Sikorsky took airplane engine–building a step further by inventing the helicopter at his plant in Stratford. The Russian émigré perfected the helicopters during the World War II years, and they became a major factor in the Korean War. Sikorsky was somewhat pained by the war uses of his invention, and took greater pride instead in its great application in emergency rescues and humanitarian deeds.

## 1950–Present

The manufacturing boom lasted through World War II and began to fizzle after that, falling rapidly in the 1960s. Companies closed and certain products gave way to new technologies elsewhere in the nation. Timex is still headquartered near the original clock center in Middlebury, and United Technologies, General Electric, and others continue to be major employers, but the percentage of residents employed in manufacturing has dropped from well over half to under a quarter.

Today, Connecticut ranks number two in the nation in industrial research facilities, with the Pfizer Pharmaceutical company being one of the major ones and United Technologies the leader. Connecticut continues to receive more U.S. military contracts per capita than any other state.

# Government, Economy, and People

From its inception, Connecticut allowed all of its "residents" to take part in the political process, although residents were defined as church-going, male landowners. Still, this limited definition of full suffrage exceeded the participation in government permitted in most other colonies. The political decisions of the day were decided at town meetings, usually monthly, which were typically presided over by a panel of three selectmen. Still today, more than half of Connecticut's 169 towns are governed this way, and local issues are still voted on by the citizens (now meaning all persons of the legal voting age, of course). Another 75 municipalities operate under a mayor-council form of government, and a few others function with representative town meetings where matters are voted on by regionally elected officers.

Additionally, Connecticut is one of only a few states that sanctions the formation of boroughs, which are basically communities within incorporated towns that provide for their own forms of taxation, zoning, and various local ordinances such as shop hours, liquor regulations, and the like. Boroughs were chartered typically when a village within the town felt that the existing laws no longer represented and spoke for its residents' best interests. Bridgeport, which was the first borough chartered out of a total of 27, and Groton, now an incorporated city, actually began as boroughs. Stonington Village, at the southern coastal tip of Stonington proper, was the second and remains one of the 11 of the state's independent boroughs, operating quite separately from the rest of the town.

The governing document of Connecticut during its earliest political incarnation, as the three colonies of Wethersfield, Hartford, and Windsor, was the Fundamental Orders, which placed the authority of the legislature above all branches of government. Until the constitution was strongly revised in 1818, Connecticut's governor was merely a figurehead and not the chief executive lawmaker of today.

In 1818, the state's legislature instituted the following conditions for the election of its electoral body: Each town was permitted one state representative, but no town more than two. The U.S. Supreme Court, with its "one man, one vote" decision, eventually ruled against this form of government because it allowed for a legislature that failed to accurately represent the will of the state population as a whole. For instance, a tiny town's sole representative might represent 600 residents, while a larger city's two representatives might represent 60,000 residents each.

Sometimes this meant that while 75 percent of the state was registered Democrat, 75 percent of the state legislature was Republican. Large cities found themselves without the political clout to serve themselves adequately. This setup dated to the state's earliest history, when a Yankee desire to maintain political autonomy among individual towns made sense, especially given the degree to which different Connecticut settlements had been founded upon differing religious and political ideals. Connecticutters didn't then and still do not today embrace any all-encompassing state identity and platform and rather cherish their rights to govern locally in their best interests.

The issue didn't really begin to show itself as unfair until the industrial revolution saw immense population swings in certain cities and the 20th century continued to see a huge swell in the state's immigrant population. This political system accounts in large part for the disparity that now exists, economically and socially, between the state's wealthier suburbs and rural communities and its faltering cities, which have staggered economi-

cally since the loss of Connecticut's manufacturing base in the 1950s and 1960s.

This early desire for an autonomous representative democracy also formed the basis for the state's traditionally pragmatic and centrist views and its healthy encouragement of independent bipartisan politicians. Locally, the Democratic and Republican political machines are as strident as ever, but rarely are there major differences voiced on most social issues. Abortion, homosexuality, gun control, environmentalism, and other buzz words are not commonly played up by the state's successful politicians.

Voters show a willingness to vote against party lines and also to support independent candidates, and the majority harbor a suspicion of extremists and overly negative campaigners. There is plenty of infighting and at times emotionally charged campaigning and politicking—after all, this is true throughout the nation—but in this state politicians have shown an uncanny ability to stay out of the national spotlight and stick to serving their local constituents.

Today, Connecticut has five U.S. representatives (having lost one of its seats in Congress in the redistricting that followed the 2000 census) in addition to its two U.S. senators. The state legislature consists of 151 state representatives and 36 state senators.

## THE ECONOMY

It's often believed that because the state's per capita income of $42,435 (as of 2001) is the highest in America, Connecticut is a land of millionaires. Further adding to this perception are the number of high-profile celebrities living in the state. In fact, although Fairfield County is one of the wealthiest few in the country, Connecticut as a whole is extremely varied economically and has some of the poorest cities in the nation, a number of small lower- to middle-class mill towns, and mostly middle class suburbs surrounding its largest cities—Bridgeport, Hartford, New Haven, and Waterbury.

Where average salaries are indeed higher even in the state's middle-income towns than in most of America, remember that the consistently high cost of living limits the buying power of the state's residents. In the most expensive towns, real-estate costs are staggering. The average house price in Greenwich is well over $1.2 million, and nearby New Canaan, Weston, Darien, Westport, and Wilton all post averages of more than $650,000. Average per capita income in these towns is above $80,000.

Amazingly, Bridgeport is just 15 miles from some of these towns yet has a per capita average income of $20,000—the average house there costs just $85,000, but a relatively high crime rate, substandard public schools, and a gritty downtown that was subjected to some awful urban planning during the 1950s and 1960s have tarnished the city's reputation. An ambitious mayor and a number of positive new plans to revitalize the city have helped boost the city's cachet in recent years, but Bridgeport, like every other major Connecticut city, has a long way to go toward full revitalization. Stamford, a trove of important corporate headquarters, enjoys a fairly positive—if dull—perception among the state's larger cities. Additionally, fast-gentrifying downtown New Haven, with its abundance of great restaurants, theaters, nightclubs, shops, and museums, has become one of New England's best urban success stories.

In general, the western half of the state is wealthier, but also more expensive, than the eastern half. As of 2002, according to *Connecticut Magazine,* there were nine towns in the state where the median housing price was greater than $300,000, and all of these were in Fairfield County. A total of 33 towns had median housing prices greater than $200,000, and all but one of these was west of the Connecticut River (the exception, Lyme, is on the eastern border of the river). Most were in Fairfield County, several others in lower Litchfield County (Bridgewater, Roxbury, Woodbury, Washington, and Warren), and still others just outside Hartford (Avon and Simsbury) and near the shore outside New Haven (Orange, Woodbridge, Guilford, Madison, and Killingworth). There were also 33 towns with median housing prices below $110,000; 14 of these were in the northeast corner of the state, and nearly all the rest were Connecticut's key

urban hubs: Bridgeport, Bristol, East Hartford, Hartford, Meriden, Middletown, New Britain, New Haven, New London, Torrington, Waterbury, Windsor Locks, and a handful of others.

Dozens of major companies are based in Connecticut, including General Electric, International Paper, Timex, United Technologies, Pratt & Whitney, the Stanley Works, Xerox, Pitney Bowes, Aetna, Champion, Playtex, Swiss Army Brands, and Praxair—to name a few.

Overall, the state began the 21st century with cautious economic optimism. After a recession that flattened the tires of the state's workforce and real-estate values ended in 1992, things picked up steadily throughout the 1990s. Unemployment slowed to around 2 percent by spring 2001, the lowest in the United States. That figure more than doubled, however, following the more recent economic recession and the effects of the September 11 terrorist attacks on the tri-state area—by mid-2003, the rate stood at about 5.2 percent.

Furthermore, Connecticut faces a major labor shortage, especially in skilled labor and middle-level office type jobs, and in teaching, medicine, and other sectors of the service industry. While this has helped raise wages, the sharp economic extremes that define the state remain a problem for this kind of worker, who is likely to earn an income that is too low to afford real estate in many suburbs. Many other parts of the country, in contrast, have tremendous job growth in similar areas and a much lower cost of living.

Where Connecticut's cost of living is fairly low—its cities—few workers with middle-class salaries wish to live, and the school systems are poor enough off that families are unwilling to raise kids there. And the areas with plentiful land, decent schools, and relatively affordable housing—the northwestern and northeastern hills—are usually too long a commute for most workers.

Experts and economists love to debate the bind that Connecticut has found itself in economically, but there's little question that the failure of the state's wealthiest regions to help subsidize its poorest ones, especially during the tough second half of the century, have cost the state as a whole. Cities were left to rot, and the disparity between desirable and undesirable communities, in terms of crime and economy, has widened sharply in Connecticut, so that the notion of a solid and desirable middle-class suburbia is an elusive dream in much of the state.

The record economic growth felt in much of the state during the late 1990s was tied largely to the windfall from the stock market, the overall comeback of Northeast cities like New York and Boston, and to a growth in technologies and industries that can replace the defunct factories of years gone by. But a more recent decline in industry has begun to hamper the state's economic growth.

Economics aside, cities like Hartford, New Haven, and Bridgeport contain the state's most-visited attractions and are all hotbeds of culture, dining, and nightlife. While the urban manufacturing base has fallen off a bit, tourism continues to become a major player in the economy—both in cities and elsewhere.

Still, since the September 11 attacks, some of which occurred less than 40 miles from Connecticut's southwestern border, and the economic recession that began around 2000, tourism has experienced ups and downs similar to the rest of the country. There's been a renewed interest in short weekend destinations where people can drive, rather than having to fly, which has helped parts of the state popular with New Yorkers and others in the Northeast. Additionally, Connecticut's more rural areas have attracted those seeking a vacation someplace perceived as safe and relaxed. However, some cities have experienced a downfall for the exact opposite reason. Connecticut underwent a hotel-building boom in the late 1990s, at the height of the nation's economic boom, and with so many midrange business-oriented hotels having opened all around the state, occupancy rates have suffered in certain markets. This, of course, sometimes translates to favorable deals on hotel rooms.

## THE PEOPLE

At the end of 2002, the state population stood at 460,563; it has grown slightly, by 3.6 percent, since 1990, when the population stood at 3,287,116. Only three states (Pennsylvania, West Virginia, and North Dakota) experienced a lower population growth during the same decade. The most populous cities include Bridgeport, 139,000; New Haven, 122,000; Hartford, 120,000; Stamford 118,000; Waterbury, 107,000; Norwalk, 83,000; Danbury 76,000; and New Britain 71,000.

Connecticut has attained a somewhat undeserved reputation for blue-blood homogeneity. Within the Northeast, it's often thought that the residents of this state are a mostly WASPy uniform blend of descendants from the *Mayflower,* and the state holds a national reputation as a haven for famous actors and writers. It's where Lucy and Ricky (of *I Love Lucy* fame) move to when they leave New York City for life in the "country." The town of Westport, even in the 1950s, hardly qualified as this, having already become a commuter suburb.

Because it's a wealthy place, and because it's near enough to New York City to be seen within the spotlight that shines constantly upon Gotham, Fairfield County—the very southwestern corner of the state—has become the lens through which outsiders sometimes view Connecticut as a whole. To be completely fair, even Fairfield County is varied culturally and economically. Regardless, the state is remarkable in its diversity of ethnic backgrounds.

The Connecticut Yankee of legend still roams a few remote villages, like Woodstock in the northeast, Chester in the Connecticut River Valley, or Goshen in the Litchfield Hills. Here, living uneasily beside transplanted and weekending New Yorkers, there are still a few old-timers—folks who can recall a time when much of the state was agrarian and when these secluded areas were effectively cut off from the rest of the state. Customs were preserved, and the post office and Congregational church were the primary social forums. People lived off the land, farmed in the warmer months, and produced maple sugar in late winter.

Many of these small towns still look incredibly quaint, like throwbacks to an earlier era. A great example is Roxbury, just 20 minutes north of I-84, in the lower end of Litchfield County. Drive

# CONNECTICUT CELEBRITIES

Ever buy one of those star maps on a trip to Los Angeles? A big part of tourism for visitors to La La Land is the possibility of running into a famous face—but with many millions of people living in that part of the world, your odds of having a brush with fame are tiny. Maybe what you really need to do is forget Hollywood and plan a trip to the Nutmeg State. That's right: Connecticut may be the home of more celebrities per square mile than just about any state in the country.

Stars often end up here because of Connecticut's proximity to New York City, combined with its relative insularity and rustic landscape. The western half of the state, from coastal Fairfield County clear up to the Litchfield Hills, is crawling with glitterati. Most locals in these towns are well aware that luminaries live within their midst, and most won't admit to caring one way or the other whether they ever see one of these famous figures.

You won't find anybody hawking maps to the stars' homes in Connecticut, but what follows is a somewhat random list of well-known figures and the general regions in which they presently reside or have once lived (quite a few on this list are no longer living, period). Of course, people come and go, and there's no definitive source on this kind of information, although *Connecticut Magazine* columnist Pat Grandjean frequently discusses celebrities in her writings.

### Greater Greenwich, Norwalk, Stamford, and New Canaan

Arthur Ashe, Henri Bendel, Victor Borge, Jesse Bradford, William F. Buckley, Jr., former president George H. W. Bush (raised here), Harry Connick, Jr. and Jill Goodacre, Alice Cooper, Glenn Close (raised here), Norman Cousins, Morton Dean, Tommy Dorsey, Howard Fast, George Foster, Jim Fowler, Frank and Kathie Lee Gifford, Tony Goldwyn, Benny Goodman, Topher Grace, Eileen Hackert and Jack Yankee, June Havoc, Tommy Hilfiger, Mick Jagger, Carolyn Bessette Kennedy, Philip Johnson, Victor Kiam, Ralph Kiner, Angela Lansbury, Ring Lardner, David Letterman, Vince McMahon, Robert Motherwell and Renata Ponsold, Gerry Mulligan, Reuben Nakian, Jack Paar, Maxwell Perkins, Regis Philbin, Orville Prescott, Pat Riley, Andy Rooney, Diana Ross, Louis Rukeyser, Rick Schroder (raised here), George C. Scott, Tom Seaver, John Cameron Swayze, Leon Trotsky, Donald Trump, Ivana Trump, Bobby Valentine, Mort Walker, Mats Wilander, Gene Wilder (and formerly Gilda Radner).

### Greater Fairfield, Westport, Weston, and Wilton

Mason Adams, Ashford and Simpson, Elizabeth Ashley, Leonard Bernstein, Theodore Bikel, Judy Blume, Michael Bolton, Dave Brubeck, Paul Cadmus, David Canary, Spencer Christian, Frank Converse and Maureen Anderman, Hume Cronyn (and formerly Jessica Tandy), Rodney Dangerfield, Bette Davis, Jim Davis, Frank Deford, Sandy Dennis, Phil Donahue and Marlo Thomas, Jose Feliciano, Linda Fiorentino, F. Scott and Zelda Fitzgerald, Keir Dullea and Susie Fuller, Chris Frantz and Tina Weymouth, Ace Frehley, Peter Golenbock, Frank Gorshin, Robert and Francis Sheridan Goulet, David Marshall Grant, Charles Grodin, William S. Hart, Sterling Hayden, A.E. Hotchner, Hulk Hogan, Linda Hunt, Don Imus, Erica Jong, Madeline Kahn, Lincoln Kirstein, Shirley Knight, Alfred Knopf, Jr., Arthur Kopit, Danny Kortchmar, Hilton Kramer, Ira Levin, Raymond Massey, Meadowlark Lemon, Christopher Lloyd, Justin Long, Lucille Lortel, John Malkovich, Jim McKay, Meatloaf, Dickie Moore and Jane Powell, Brent Musberger, Jim Nantz, James Naughton, Paul Newman and Joanne Woodward, Joe Pantoliano, Christopher Plummer, Robert Redford, Keith Richards and Patti Hansen, Lee Richardson, Jason Robards, Jr., Eric Roberts, Richard Rodgers, Meg Ryan (born here), Neil Sedaka, Patricia Hearst Shaw, Sergeant Slaughter, Brett Somers, Southside Johnny, Martha Stewart, Donna Summer, Elizabeth Taylor, Christopher Walken, Harvey Weinstein, Edgar Winter, Robert Wright.

**Ridgefield, Redding, and Greater Danbury**
Jonathan Brandis (born here), Roz Chast, Judy
Collins, Harvey Fierstein, Ira Joe Fisher, Waylon
Jennings, Elia Kazan, Dick Morris, Maxim
Shostakovich, Ronnie Spector, Maurice Sendak,
Jane and Michael Stern, Mary Travers, Mark Twain,
Robert Vaughn.

**Bridgeport, New Haven, and Environs**
Captain Lou Albano, Ernest Borgnine (born
here), P.T. Barnum, Richard Belzer, Nancy Marc-
hand and Paul Sparer, Glenn Miller, Kevin Nealon
(born here), John Ratzenberger, Tom Thumb,
Thornton Wilder. Additionally, Yale faculty and
alumni have included: William Bailey, Angela
Bassett, Jennifer Beals, Harold Bloom, Sorrell
Booke, William F. Buckley, Jr., Claire Danes, David Duchovny,
George W. Bush, Claire Danes, David Duchovny,
Gerald Ford, Jodie Foster, Harry Hamlin, Bill
and Hillary Clinton, James Earl Jones, Henry
Luce, Gabriel Mann, David Hyde Pierce, Donald
Margulies, Paul Newman, Cesar Pelli, Vincent
Price, Richard Selzer, Robert Stone, Meryl Streep,
James Tobin, Gary Trudeau, Rudy Vallee, Sam
Waterston, Henry Winkler, Bob Woodward,
Efrem Zimbalist, Jr.

**Greater Hartford and Waterbury**
Chris Berman, Bob Crane (born here), Will
Friedle, Greg Gumbel, Katharine Hepburn (born
here), Gordie Howe, Gayle King, Ted Knight
(born here), Eriq La Salle, Dylan McDermott
(born here), Gene Pitney, Rosalind Russell (born
here), Wallace Stevens, Mark Twain, Katrina
Witt, and James Van Der Beek (born and raised
here). Additionally, various Wesleyan University
faculty and alumni have included Jeanine and
John Basinger, Bill Belichick, William Christopher, Annie Dillard, Laurent de Brunhoff and
Phyllis Rose, Dana Delany, Akiva Goldsman,
the Highwaymen (folk band), Paul Horgan,
Robert Ludlum, William Manchester, Kit Reed,
Paul Theroux, Joss Whedon, Dar Williams,
Bradley Whitford.

**Central and Eastern Coastal Connecticut**
Art Carney, Brian Dennehy, Dominick Dunne,
Harrison Ford, Katharine Hepburn, Charles Kuralt,
Eugene O'Neill, Jane Pauley and Gary Trudeau,
chef Jacques Pépin, Morley Safer, Max Showalter.

**New Milford, Roxbury, Washington, and Environs**
Robert Anderson and Teresa Wright, Christine
Baranski and Matt Cowles, Carl Bernstein, Bill
Blass, Alexander Calder, Graydon Carter, Linda
Dano and Frank Attardi, Jim Dine, Peter Duchin
and Brooke Hayward, Mia Farrow, Peter Gallagher,
Lois Gold, George Grizzard, A.R. Gurney, Ruth
and Skitch Henderson, Barbara Hershey, Dustin
Hoffman, Alfred Kazin, Susan and William Kin-
solving, Larry Kramer, Dennis Leary, Walter
Matthau, Frank McCourt, Arthur Miller (and for-
merly Marilyn Monroe) and Inge Morath, Wendell
Minor and Karen Valentine, Mike Nichols and
Diane Sawyer, Conan O'Brien, Moses Pendleton,
Peter Poskas, Gene Rayburn, Rex Reed, Philip
Roth (and formerly Claire Bloom), Stephen Sond-
heim, Joan and Fred Mustard Stewart, William
and Rose Styron, James Taylor, Sada Thompson,
Diane Von Furstenberg, Richard Widmark, Stuart
Woods, Michael Zaslow, Susan Hufford.

**Kent, Cornwall, Salisbury, Sharon, and Environs**
Kevin Bacon and Kyra Sedgwick, Sandra Boyn-
ton, Barbara Taylor Bradford, Tom Brokaw,
William F. Buckley, Jr., Joyce Chopra, Jane Curtain,
Oscar de la Renta, Milos Forman, Michael J. Fox
and Tracy Pollan, Whoopi Goldberg, Jane Kacz-
marek and Bradley Whitford, Henry Kissinger,
Patti Lupone, Seth MacFarlane (born here), M.
Scott Peck, Campbell Scott, George Segal, Isaac
Stern, Meryl Streep, Rip Torn, Michael Walsh,
Sam Waterston, Ezra Winter, Jerry Zaks.

**Northern and Eastern Litchfield County**
Gary Burghoff, Brendan Gill, Ivan Lendl, Susan St.
James and Dick Ebersol, Arthur Schwartz, Paul
Winter, Alfred Uhry, Efrem Zimbalist, Jr.

through town and you'll find no businesses but for a Colonial building in the center of the village, which includes a country store, a realtor, a post office, a small bank, and a gas station. One small sandwich place sits farther on down the road.

It is here that you might expect to find honest Connecticutters. Roxbury is no backwater in fact, but through aggressive preservation and zoning it has resisted the growth that has marred many neighboring towns. Arthur Miller, Dustin Hoffman, William Styron, Richard Widmark, and Mia Farrow are among the town's residents, along with countless business executives and successful artists. Most of the farms here are of the gentleman's variety, and most of these creaky old white houses cost several hundred thousand dollars. It's a beautiful town, and it's difficult to imagine a more inviting place to call home. It wouldn't be fair to say that Roxbury doesn't accurately reflect a real and valid side of Connecticut's people—but it's important to point out that while it looks the way Connecticut towns did 150 years ago, its population reflects the demographic trends of today.

Roxbury is emblematic of Litchfield County. The county is less suburban than any other part of the state, and so the people here tend to be either middle-class and employed locally at shops, small businesses, schools, and other such jobs, or quite well off and in many cases living here part-time. This latter grouping may include some antiques dealers and restaurateurs, but more likely entertainers, artists, and an increasing number of self-employed consultants and executives with positions that allow them to work at home all or most of the time.

In Litchfield County, it's rather common that locals will call anybody foreign to them a New Yorker, whether he or she hails from New York or not. It's a label that is not necessarily derisive, but does nevertheless imply that the said person is apt to be a bit pushier and more demanding than the local population, and to be perhaps a bit green in the ways of such local pastimes as forestry, hunting, fly-fishing, and hiking. Monied outsiders are also the reason Litchfield County has one of the best restaurant scenes of any rural area in America, not to mention an abundance of restored historic

homes and beautifully kept properties. The influx of tourists and weekenders has poured a great deal of money into a part of Connecticut that would otherwise have had few things going for it economically since the Industrial Revolution, when the state's growth and income jumped in the river valleys and along the coast, largely bypassing the rugged northwestern hills.

What has long been and remains a defining aspect of the peoplescape in Litchfield County is the large degree of socializing among many walks of life at local taverns and hangouts. Restaurants and bars in these parts very often favor one kind of Litchfielder or another, but there are a decent number of spots that serve both high-end nouvelle cooking and affordable and simple pub grub, and at these you're apt to see a mix of Mercedeses and Range Rovers, beat-up pickup trucks and old jeeps.

The northeastern hills are less the domain of weekending New Yorkers than the northwestern hills, and they are considerably less gentrified and lower-heeled as a result. Many of the towns up here—Putnam, Grovsnerdale, and such—were old mill communities where Eastern Europeans, Germans, Italians, and Scandinavians migrated around the turn of the 20th century, and they retain this legacy. If you drive through the eastern side of the state, from the northeastern hills down through the blue-collar communities of Dayville and Norwich and on toward the coastal cities of New London and Groton, you'll note a preponderance of social clubs created for one specific nationality or another: Italian, Latvian, Polish, Swedish, Ukrainian.

There are, in the northeastern hills, often called the "Quiet Corner," a good many B&Bs and, particularly in Putnam, a growing number of antiques dealers. The beauty and history of this region has begun earning it great tourism cachet, but the typical town profile still favors a solidly middle-class, Catholic base of persons descended from the factory and mill workers who settled here a century ago. The population has leveled off quite a bit—there is not a huge number of jobs available, and young people who grow up here tend to move on to more populated areas once they finish high school or college.

The area that was the most urbanized and industrialized beginning in the mid-19th century is the Connecticut River Valley. Hartford and New Haven both grew dramatically, first drawing Irish immigrants during the potato famine of the 1840s and 1850s and then large numbers of Germans, Italians, Poles, and Russians. Into the early 20th century, many blacks relocated here from the southern states, taking advantage of better job opportunities. And into the middle of this century, a significant number of Puerto Ricans and Central Americans have come for work.

By 1790, 96 percent of the state was of English ancestry and 99.7 percent was English, Scotch, or Irish. By the beginning of the Civil War, the Irish led the numbers of foreign-born residents (with twice as many entering the state in the 1860s than all other immigrants combined). They remained the dominant group until the turn of the 20th century, but by then Eastern and Central Europeans were catching up. During the 1920s and 1930s, Italians led the pack, with 167,000 immigrants, followed by Polish (97,000), Irish (86,000), Russian (64,000), Canadian (mostly French-Canadian—63,000), German (45,000), English (44,000), Swedish (35,000), Lithuanian (25,000), Hungarian (21,000), Austrian (20,000), Czechoslovakian (18,000), and Scottish (17,000).

By the 1880s, a third of the state was foreign-born, and countless Connecticut natives had settled elsewhere in the nation. Between 1789 and 1889, there were 34 U.S. senators and 187 U.S. representatives born in Connecticut but serving from other states. By the 1930s, more than half of the state's residents were foreign born, and only 34 percent were of native Connecticut parentage.

If you wonder why there is a large contingent of Jamaicans living in northern Hartford and Bloomfield and on up through the northern Connecticut River Valley, it's explained by the fact that the tobacco industry that once thrived in this region essentially got too big to be sustained along by the local population. Both Jamaicans and Puerto Ricans were among those immigrants who were recruited to move here and work the tobacco crops, and even after this form of farming had been sharply scaled back, many of the descendants of the original workers remain.

In New Britain, you'll find as visible a Polish community as anywhere in the state, with a couple of neighborhoods that are especially pronounced in this regard and have preserved their heritage. A more recent change has been the influx of Asians, especially Indian and Pakistani, throughout the state. A huge number of small businesses, from restaurants to convenience stores and gas stations to motels, are now operated by Asian immigrants.

Back in Fairfield County, indeed the reputation for being largely upper class and white holds true in many towns. Outside of the cities of Bridgeport, Stamford, Norwalk, and Danbury, the county is 90–95 percent white. And the income levels in some of the largest towns, along with the cost or real estate, are among the highest in the world.

In the most general sense, the face of Connecticut has changed at a much slower rate over the past few decades than it did between the 1850s and the 1950s, when booming immigration altered the racial, religious, and ethnic background dramatically. A combination of factors has actually led to a drop in population in Connecticut, albeit slight. It's a small state, so when job growth was stunted by the movement of most industrial concerns to more affordable Southern and Midwestern states, workers left in larger numbers than they came in.

Furthermore, there's simply a limited amount of land left for people to build new homes on. Even in Fairfield County, whose economy improved rapidly throughout the 1990s and even held up pretty well during the recession of the past few years, the population has not increased to any great degree. And there's not much land left for building homes, which is why the trend of renovating older homes or buying houses and tearing them down to make way for new ones has been a major (and controversial) one in towns, especially ones along the so-called Gold Coast, extending from Greenwich to Fairfield.

There's been the greatest growth in the towns on the outskirts of Fairfield County, such as New

Milford, Newtown, Southbury, and Brookfield—regions that were once as agrarian as the Litchfield Hills but because of the creation in 1960s of I-84 and the growth of the white-collar job base in both Stamford and Danbury have effectively developed into bedroom communities.

Another hot spot has been the northern Connecticut River Valley, where much of the farmland that once contained tobacco crops has been sold and replanted with condos and housing developments, as well as a number of industrial parks and corporate campuses. The economy has shifted so that leading companies in this area tend toward service industries, technologies, research, and the like.

While New England's population rose slightly over the past few years, it's still a slow growth. Nevertheless, people moved from New England at record numbers in the early 1990s, when the economy was at its weakest, and this bleed of out-migration has largely ceased as job growth in the state is back on track.

In keeping with the rest of New England, ethnic immigration to Connecticut has slowed to a trickle in recent years, again because there are better economic opportunities elsewhere in America. Also, the immigrants who moved here in a huge boom in the early part of the century are now aged, and so there is a fairly high death rate. In many parts of Connecticut, there are either too few jobs or too high a cost of living to attract young couples and families, and so the birthrate in the state is also quite low. Even with a rejuvenated economy, most forecasters predict that population growth in Connecticut will remain very slow.

# On the Road

## The Great Indoors

Connecticut has 20–30 must-see indoor attractions, ranging from aquariums to art museums to amusement parks to historic homes—the sorts of places that qualify as destinations unto themselves. Many visitors build their entire vacations around just one or two of these major sites, especially if a special exhibit is showing or a festival is scheduled. These attractions—Mystic Seaport, the Maritime Aquarium at Norwalk, the Wadsworth Atheneum, the Mark Twain House, and the Peabody Museum of Natural History, to name but a handful—are typically open year-round and often charge a relatively substantial admission ($5 per person or more), not because they're greedy, but because these kinds of attractions tend to have high operating expenses.

At the opposite end of the spectrum are perhaps 150–200 smaller and often underrated attractions, including local historical societies and house-museums and museums focusing on fairly

Main Street in Essex

specific topics, such as locks or cartoon memorabilia. Remember that many of these museums are among the most fascinating in Connecticut, as their existence tends to rely more on the devotion and enthusiasm of their staff than on their commercial potential. You're also more likely to receive personal attention at smaller attractions and less likely to have your enthusiasm dampened by overcrowding, long lines, or a sense that you need to rush around and see every last exhibit to feel that you've gotten your money's worth.

In addition to the headliners and the sleepers, dozens of attractions fall somewhere between; hours, admission, and visitor appeal vary greatly depending on any number of factors, from location to subject matter. Some of the most visited attractions in the state are parks, concert halls, theaters, and casinos, all of which are covered separately in this chapter.

## Hours and Admission

Hours at many of these smaller attractions can be very complicated and change frequently throughout the year. For this reason, *Moon Handbooks Connecticut* lists an attraction's hours only when they're fairly straightforward and reliable; in all other cases the hours are listed as either "limited" or "seasonal," which means you should phone ahead to ensure that the place will be open on the day that interests you.

As a general rule, the smallest house-museums and historic attractions are open only on weekends (usually afternoons) from about Memorial Day to Columbus Day—you're especially likely to find this in the colder and more rural inland communities, where the low off-season visitation and high cost of heating the buildings make regular hours impractical. Along the coast, where there are more visitors and warmer temperatures, many smaller museums stay open Apr.–Nov. or Christmas and may open two to five days a week, late morning to late afternoon.

Don't be put off by the limited hours—in most cases, if you phone a week or two ahead and ask to see one of these smaller attractions by appointment, you'll be encouraged to set up a private visit. Most establishments are operated by volunteers and curated through bequeaths

Established in 1842, Hartford's Wadsworth Atheneum is one of the oldest art museums in America.

and gifts; they typically charge a nominal entrance fee or perhaps request a donation.

Those attractions with a fairly steady flow of visitors offer the same hours you might expect of most local businesses and shops: 9 A.M.–5 P.M., five to seven days a week (Mondays or Tuesdays are the most common days for attractions to close). In many cases, hours are reduced on Sundays. In summer you'll notice that some of these attractions increase their hours to 6 or 7 P.M., and in winter some of them close at 4 P.M. or don't open until 10 or 11 A.M.

The admission given for each attraction in this book is for adults. At the vast majority of attractions, very young children are admitted free; grade-school kids, college students, and senior citizens very often receive discounts of 25–50 percent.

Whatever these general rules of thumb, and whatever hours and admission charges are listed in this book, remember that hours (and other policies) may change with no notice. It's highly advisable to phone ahead before visiting any attraction in Connecticut.

For additional information on attractions across the state, it's a good idea to get a free copy of the *Connecticut Planner* from the state tourist board, 800/CT-BOUND. You can find web links to many museums and attractions at the state Internet address, www.tourism.state.ct.us.

For information on local historic sites and

related attractions, contact the **Connecticut Historical Commission** (59 S. Prospect St., Hartford, CT 06131, 860/566-3005, www.chc .state.ct.us). The commission is behind many projects relevant to local history and architecture, including thematic architectural surveys, the Save Outdoor Sculpture Project, town architecture surveys, a full inventory of the state's 170 town greens, and an inventory of some 90,000 Connecticut properties of historic or architectural importance (complete with detailed notes, photographs, and maps). This latter project, called the Statewide Historic Resource Inventory, can be viewed on paper in Storrs at the University of Connecticut's **Homer D. Babbidge Library** (860/486-2524) and on microfiche at several locations; contact the commission for further details. The library also has a tremendous collection of historic maps, photos, and related exhibits at its Map and Geographic Information Center (MAGIC), which is open to the public or can be viewed through its website, http://magic.lib.uconn.edu.

If you've a strong interest in the area's architectural history and in helping to preserve the state's many historic sites, consider joining the **Connecticut Trust for Historic Preservation** (940 Whitney Ave., Hamden, 203/562-6312, www.cttrust.org), which publishes a useful and informative bimonthly journal, *Connecticut Preservation News*.

## THE PERFORMING ARTS

Connecticut's cities are deservedly the high points when it comes to theater, live music (both popular and classical), and dance, but highly esteemed performance spaces also hide in secluded and often beautiful settings. Unquestionably, having so many outstanding musicians and actors living in the state has helped endow Connecticut with an unusually strong arts scene.

Best known among the state's more isolated venues are excellent theaters in Berlin, Chester, East Haddam, Ivoryton, Putnam, Sharon, and Westport, and acclaimed music festivals or performance halls in Clinton, Falls Village, Litchfield, Norfolk, Thomaston, and Waterford.

New Haven has easily the greatest reputation for theater of any Connecticut city, as it has long been a proving ground for productions with aspirations toward Broadway. Hartford's Bushnell Hall is one of the Northeast's premier performance facilities (which recently underwent a major expansion); the city is also home to the acclaimed Hartford Stage. Bridgeport, Danbury, New Haven, New London, Torrington, and Waterbury are also home to regionally, and in some cases nationally, acclaimed performance facilities. Mohegan Sun Casino in Norwich and Foxwoods Casino in Ledyard also merit mention.

Several universities present a varied and impressive array of musical and dramatic productions to which the public is welcome, including Connecticut College (New London), Fairfield University (Fairfield), Trinity (Hartford), UConn (Storrs), University of Hartford, Wesleyan (Middletown), WestConn (Danbury), and Yale (New Haven).

For general information, listings, and calendars pertaining to the arts, contact the **Connecticut Commission on the Arts** (755 Main St., Hartford, CT 06103, 860/566-4770, www.ctarts.org).

## ARTS AND CRAFTS GALLERIES

While there are no artistic or crafts forms specific to just Connecticut, the state has a long and prolific history of nautical and maritime art, from oil paintings and watercolors of ships and sea scenes to different kinds of sculpture, woodworking, and metalworking relevant to the ocean and seafarers. You'll especially find these kinds of works in Mystic, which has a number galleries, and in many other towns along the coast. The state's other acclaimed arts-and-crafts gallery hub is Litchfield County.

The state office of tourism has also developed a **Trail of Connecticut Craft Centers,** 888/CT-CRAFT, which provides information on major crafts centers in Avon, www.fvac.net; Brookfield, www.brookfieldcraftcenter.org; Guilford, www.handcraftcenter.org; Middletown, www.wesleyanpotters.com; and New Haven, www.creativeartsworkshop.org.

## FESTIVALS

Connecticut's most enduring festivals seem to involve one or more of the following four things: music, seafood, agriculture, and the fine arts. As you might expect of a state whose tourism booms in summer and slacks off during the colder months, the most popular festivals occur from late spring through early fall. Some of the state's most famous events and festivals are mentioned below, but you'll find a wealth of additional listings, along with phone numbers and sometimes websites, listed in the "Festivals and Events" sections of this book's individual chapters.

### Winter

Hartford is one of a number of U.S. cities that ushers in the New Year with a rollicking **First Night** celebration, which occurs at several locations around the city and consists of music, food, and other activities. The 10 towns of the upper Connecticut River Valley, north of Hartford, put on a rousing **Holidayfest,** which includes activities, concerts, and parties at a variety of shops, farms, and museums. Also leading up to Christmas, Mystic Seaport offers nightly **Lantern Light Tours,** which allow visitors to ride a horse-drawn omnibus through the seaport, which is festooned with holiday decorations.

In Middletown, the **Wesleyan Potters Exhibit and Sale,** runs for two weeks beginning just after Thanksgiving—this is one of the largest juried crafts shows in New England. Similarly, the **Brookfield Craft Exhibition & Sale,** shows the wares of more than 300 of the nation's top craft artists—it's a great opportunity to search for holiday gifts. Lastly, just as winter begins to wear out its welcome in Connecticut, the **Connecticut Flower & Garden Show** rolls into Hartford's Connecticut Expo Center the last weekend in February; more than 200 exhibitors show off their flowers, plants, herbs, and gardening and landscaping products.

### Spring

In mid-April, Hamden's **Goldenbells Festivals** is a sure sign that spring has sprung; gather in the center of town for concerts, nature walks, crafts shows, and other wholesome fun. Meriden's **Daffodil Festival** is another lively April event. May sees the **Sound Winds Kite Festival** at Hammonassett Beach State Park in Madison, and the ever delicious **Lobsterfest** at Mystic Seaport. Up in Lakeville, the **Lime Rock Park Grand Prix** draws sports car–racing enthusiasts from all over the country.

Bargain hunters and furniture junkies shouldn't miss the **Farmington Antiques Weekend** in June, which pulls in some 600 antiques dealers from all over the country. What's fast becoming one of the most exciting and dynamic events in the Northeast, New Haven's **International Festival of Arts & Ideas** presents two June weeks of cutting-edge theater, dance, opera, music, film, puppetry, and visual arts to venues all over the city; most of these events are free.

### Summer

As the warmest days of the year heat up in Connecticut, the festival season really starts to boom. Some of the best **Fourth of July celebrations** are held in Norwich, Enfield, and in Groton at the Naval Submarine Base athletic field complex. **Riverfest,** which takes place along the banks of the Connecticut River in Hartford and East Hartford, also takes place around the Fourth of July and includes concerts by big-name performers and a stunning fireworks display. One of the largest fireworks displays is the **Mashantucket Pequot Thames River** event overlooking Groton and New London, which takes place the weekend after the Fourth of July. That same weekend, New London is home to **Sailfest,** a harborside party with amusement rides, tall ships, a car show and parade, crafts exhibits, and varied food offerings.

Music lovers should head to Guilford for the **Great Connecticut Jazz Festival,** in late July, and to Goshen for the fast-growing **Litchfield Jazz Festival,** in early August; the latter has become one of the top such events in nation. Check out the acclaimed **Pilot Pen Tennis Women's Championship** in New Haven in mid-August; this nine-day tournament draws some of the world's top-seeded female tennis players. One of the first big "aggie" fairs in the state kicks off in late August: the **Woodstock Fair** is the state's second-oldest. Other popular events include the **Connecticut Agricultural Fair** and **Litchfield County 4-H Fair** in Goshen in July; the **Windham County 4-H Fair** in Brooklyn in July; the **Bridgewater Country Fair** in Bridgewater in August; the **Bethlehem Fair** in Bethlehem in early September; and the largest of them all, the **Durham Fair** in Durham, held in late September.

## Fall

Festival-wise, activities don't much slack off until mid-October. One of the top early Fall events is the **Norwalk Oyster Festival,** which has been going strong at Veteran's Memorial Park on Long Island Sound for decades. Come to observe the arts and crafts, historic boats, and fireworks, and sample tasty seafood and other fine foods while catching a host of excellent concerts. Foodies also flock to the **Chowderfest** at Mystic Seaport in mid-October. **Boats, Books, and Brushes** is a maritime-themed literary festival held at Waterfront Park in New London in mid-September.

Come October, Southington's **Apple Harvest Festival** is great fun for fans of the forbidden fruit—apple products of every imaginable type are offered, along with a road race, a parade, and arts and crafts stalls. Start getting yourself into shape if you want to participate in the **Greater Hartford Marathon,** in mid-October. Strollers, on the other hand, might want to check out the **Walking Weekend,** which takes places among some 35 towns in the state's Quiet Corner over Columbus Day Weekend; featured are about 60 guided walks through historic districts, parks, preserves, and other scenic areas within the Quinebaug and Shetucket Rivers Valley National Heritage Corridor.

## NIGHTLIFE

When Nutmeggers get serious about partying, they tend to head for New York City and Boston—there's no denying that these two cities possess the lion's share of the Northeast's hottest warehouse discos and highest-profile live-music clubs. Happily, Connecticut's proximity to these cities makes it a popular testing ground for quite a few aspiring rock and alternative acts, as well as comedians, balladeers, folk singers, and the like. Important national acts also appear regularly at the major performance venues in Hartford, New Haven, Norwich (Mohegan Sun Casino), and Ledyard (Foxwoods Casino), and occasionally in New Haven and Stamford.

For the latest scoop on live music at local clubs and discos, check out the *Hartford Advocate, New Haven Advocate,* and *Fairfield County Weekly,* all of which are free and have helpful websites. These papers also list the state's best dance clubs, from tribal to swing, and also note poetry readings, open mike sessions, and every other conceivable sort of nightlife option.

There is a smattering of gay and lesbian nightclubs around the state, with a few such venues in both Hartford and New Haven, two in New London, and one each in Danbury, Waterbury, and Westport.

As you might expect, nightlife options exist in direct proportion to population density, meaning that there's far more to do at night in towns along the shoreline and in the Connecticut River Valley than in the northeastern and northwestern hills. In places like Litchfield and Woodstock, the dance scene might consist of jitterbugging to old Glenn Miller records in your bed-and-breakfast's rec room, and the singles scene might center around the local luncheonette or, if you're lucky enough to be near one, coffeehouse. Note that many java joints around Connecticut are reviewed in the Food sections of this book, and socializing over coffee or tea has definitely evolved into a wildly popular activity in recent years.

# The Great Outdoors

Among the 8,000 miles of rivers and streams and the 6,000 lakes and ponds, you'll discover 108 boat launches, 93 state parks, and 32 state forests covering some 200,000 acres. Not to mention hundreds of municipal parks and dozens of privately administered nonprofit nature preserves and sanctuaries. Hiking and birdwatching are encouraged at the vast majority of these facilities, and many also welcome mountain biking, cross-country skiing, boating, fishing, and camping.

Parks are typically open sunrise to sundown, and very often fees are assessed during the busiest part of the day or on weekends (and, especially at state parks, from late spring through early autumn).

## GENERAL RESOURCES

There are several excellent resources for learning more about the state's wealth of outdoors diversions. A good way to begin is by contacting the Bureau of Outdoor Recreation at the **Connecticut Department of Environmental Protection,** or DEP (79 Elm St., Hartford, CT 06106, 860/424-3200). You can write or phone to request brochures on the state parks and on any of the aforementioned activities, or visit DEP's website (it's one of the best out there) at http://dep.state.ct.us.

You can also drop by the **DEP Bookstore** and the **Maps and Publications Office of the Natural Resources Center,** both at DEP's Elm Street headquarters. The bookstore sells excellent books and maps covering every facet of outdoors recreation, and the resources center dispenses plenty of advice and can also provide many brochures and free booklets. DEP store and center visitor hours are Mon.–Thurs. 9 A.M.–3:30 P.M. (or by appointment). You can also call with orders and questions, 860/424-3555, or visit http://dep.state.ct .us/store/index.htm.

The DEP can also give you the lowdown on each of the state parks and forests—individuals park profiles, complete with history, acreage, ac-

tivities, directions, and fees, are found on the Web at http://dep.state.ct.us/stateparks. Connecticut's state parks and forests are open year-round 8 A.M.–sunset. Parking and entry fees vary from park to park (many are free) and are typically in effect May–October; seasonal passes are available to state residents for $40 and to non-residents for $60, and free passes are available to Connecticut residents over the age of 65.

A wonderful way to learn about Connecticut's outdoors and become involved with keeping it clean and desirable is to join the Connecticut chapter of the **Nature Conservancy** (55 High St., Middletown, CT 06457, 860/344-0716, http://nature.org). This highly respected and influential organization was founded in 1951, and Dr. Richard Goodwin, a botany professor at New London's Connecticut College, was instrumental in organizing the Connecticut chapter the following year. One of the first acquisitions was Beckly Bog in Norfolk, a very rare black spruce bog that anchors a 600-acre preserve. The chapter maintains 55 nature preserves covering more than 27,000 acres, the most visited of which is the 1,700-acre Devil's Den, in Weston and Redding, which offers some of the most rugged and exciting hiking in the state.

An equally important conservation advocate and resource is the **Connecticut Audubon Society,** (2325 Burr St., Fairfield, CT 06430, 203/259-6305, http://ctaudubon.org), which manages 19 sanctuaries (some 2,200 acres) across the state, including extensive facilities—museums, classrooms, educational programs—at the centers in Fairfield, Milford Point, Glastonbury, Pomfret, Brooklyn, and Hampton.

Helpful, too, are the **Connecticut Forest and Park Association,** or CFPA (860/346-2372, www.ctwoodlands.org), and the **Appalachian Mountain Club** (www.ct-amc.org), as well as the conservation museum and 4,100 acres of trails and protected preserve at the **White Memorial Foundation** (860/567-0857, www.white-memorialcc.org).

## HOT AIR BALLOONS

Several Connecticut companies provide aerial tours via this increasingly popular means of touring the state. In Southington, **Berkshire Balloons** (203/250-8441, www.berkshireballoons.com) runs daily flights early each morning, spanning more than an hour and covering 5–15 miles depending on wind conditions. Of course, once you ascend to some 4,000 feet, you'll enjoy views of the entire Farmington River Valley, most of central Connecticut, and even Massachusetts and Long Island Sound in the distance. Following the flight, guests (the balloons accommodate from four to six passengers) enjoy complimentary snacks and a champagne toast on the ground; a van, which follows the balloon from the ground, whisks everyone back to the destination point.

This is an entirely safe and quite fascinating way to earn a new perspective on a state you may think you already know quite well. Even if you've crossed Connecticut in a commercial jet, you've most likely been too high off the ground to fully grasp the scenery. Most flights leave early, just after sunrise, although Berkshire offers some late-afternoon flights. The cost is $250 per person and $475 per couple, but you may also want to opt for a Bed, Breakfast, and Ballooning package at $650 per couple. This includes accommodation for one night at the nearby Chimney Crest Manor, the early morning balloon ride, and full breakfast back at the inn upon your return.

There are several other balloon companies in the state, many listed individually in other chapters—they are most popular and commonplace in the Farmington River Valley and Litchfield County. With so many balloons frequently flying over Connecticut, you may wonder why you don't see them overhead on a regular basis. Most likely, this is because you're sound asleep when the majority of these rainbow-hued vehicles make their journeys. At sunrise or just prior to sunset, the air is calmest and pilots have the easiest time navigating their crafts.

ON THE ROAD

## AGRICULTURAL TOURISM

This once agrarian stronghold has relatively little private farmland today—there are more than 3,000 farms statewide (nearly 250 open to the public), and this number drops every year as profits continue to falter and real-estate developers continue to swoop in and pounce on these desirable tracts of mostly cleared land. The farms that remain in business do so largely through the hard work and dedication of a small number of proud owners, some of whom are 10th or 12th generation descendants of the settlers who first tilled the land. Many have increased revenues and the public's interest in their survival by welcoming visitors to partake of many activities.

You might pick your own produce or buy milk and homemade ice cream, cut your own Christmas tree or pick up a quart of fresh maple syrup. Pick-your-own farms make for an especially fun outing, whether alone or with a group of friends or family—from early spring through late fall, you'll find fresh fruits and vegetables for your kitchen table. Regional specialties include apples, fresh and dried herbs, peaches, pears, pumpkins, raspberries, squash, strawberries, sweet corn, and tomatoes. For a list of farms (listed by county with directions, hours, and descriptions of what you can pick at each farm and when), send a SASE to the **Connecticut Department of Agriculture,** or DOAG (765 Asylum Ave., Hartford, CT 06105, 860/713-2503), or download this document from the Internet at www.state.ct.us/doag.

Another way to support local farming while also obtaining wonderful produce, fish and game, jams and jellies, cheeses and yogurts, flowers and shrubs, syrups and honeys, and other specialty-food products is to visit any of the 65 farmers markets held year-round across the state, usually once a week. This activity has grown enormously in popularity in recent years, and you can obtain a free brochure listing each market (by county, with days, hours, and addresses) by contacting the DOAG.

You can also send away for or download brochures (at www.state.ct.us/doag) on the following Connecticut agricultural topics: agricultural fairs, apple growers and retailers, certified organic farms, cordwood farms, cut-your-own Christmas trees, dairy farms, hay and honey producers, maple sugarhouses, regional food products, turkey farms, and wineries.

## BIKING

Most of Connecticut is excellent biking terrain, hilly but not overly so, and extremely scenic. The only real drawbacks are the relatively high amount of auto traffic, even in the most scenic areas, and the many narrow and winding roads. Connecticut drivers are also rather infamous for their love of speeding.

Fortunately, there are designated bike routes all over the place, and you can phone or send away to receive the excellent and detailed bike map produced by the Connecticut Department of Transportation. Two excellent books cover biking in Connecticut: one, the *Connecticut Bicycle Book,* is produced by the DEP and sold at its bookstore, and the other, the *Connecticut Bike Book,* is produced by the **Connecticut Bicycle Coalition** (1 Union Place, Hartford, CT 06103, 860/527-5200, www.ctbike.org). This organization also produces a useful brochure, *Connecticut by Bike.* Another good resource is *Short Bike Rides in Connecticut,* published by Globe Pequot Press, 888/249-7586, www.globe-pequot.com.

Mountain biking trails are found at the Winding Trails Recreation Area in Farmington and at the Woodbury Ski and Racquet Area.

## BIRD-WATCHING

From yuppies to senior citizens, families to singles, every kind of Nutmegger seems to be taking up bird-watching these days, especially those folks who live around the coastal regions. The popularity makes a lot of sense, for as hobbies go, this is one of the least expensive and most educational. Best of all, birds are abundant in the state year-round, though of course the individual species you're likely to see depend on the sea-

son. You may see more than 200 species throughout Connecticut.

In addition to the several excellent parks and preserves mentioned below (and detailed in the regional chapters of the book), the state has an excellent birding resource, the **Connecticut Ornithological Association,** www.ctbirding.org, which publishes both a quarterly bulletin and a journal called *The Connecticut Warbler.* The association, which provides lists of the best birding spots and sponsors conferences and field trips around the state, is headquartered at the Connecticut Audubon Society's **Birdcraft Museum,** (314 Unquowa Rd., Fairfield, 203/259-0416). The nearby **Connecticut Audubon Center** at Fairfield houses a fascinating raptor rehabilitation facility, which is a terrific place to observe these proud and stern-looking creatures.

A wealth of additional information, as well as many excellent links to related sites, can be accessed through the **Connecticut Birding Website,** http://pages.cthome.net/jbair/ctbirds.htm. Here you'll find descriptions of many excellent local birding areas, from airports to parks.

Much of the best birding is along the coast, where you'll see myriad waterfowl year-round and magnificent blue heron October through April. Peregrine falcons and hawks regularly fly about marshes and estuaries, and in August and September you'll see warblers and thrushes. A huge population of sparrows descends upon the coastal points during the fall. Owls are not easy to find, but they do live around the state—it's reported that at least five species of this mysterious bird live in the cedar groves along the road at Hammonasset Beach State Park, between the park gate and the rotary.

An extraordinary spot for bird-watching, year-round, is the **Connecticut Audubon Coastal Center Bird Sanctuary** at Milford Point. Ducks and heron live among the marshes, and least terns, piping plovers, and American oystercatchers are a few of the most distinctive creatures that forage about the mudflats and are especially abundant at low tide. Orioles, finches, and sparrows live among the bushes and thickets of beach shrubs. Nearby **Lighthouse Point Park,** at New Haven, also hums with birding activity and has become rather famous Sept.–Nov. for the annual procession of some 20,000–30,000 hawks, ospreys, northern harriers, American kestrels, and peregrine falcons that pass through the area en route to warmer climes. Another excellent spot for coastal birding is the **Stuart B. McKinney National Wildlife Refuge** in Westbrook, which includes nearly three miles of trails through woods, fields, and salt marshes.

In the state's interior, good nature exploration and wildlife sighting is had at some of the state parks in the northwestern and northeastern hills. The **Sharon Audubon Center,** which has an exhibit commemorating the works of New England naturalist and author Hal Borland, has 754 acres of trails on which you might glimpse the distinctive pileated woodpecker (or at least hear it) or a ruffed grouse. Woodchucks, beavers, river otters, red foxes, and white-tailed deer traverse the region, as they do around the magnificent 4,100-acre **White Memorial Foundation** in Litchfield, which has 35 miles of maintained trails. The park's Caitlin Woods section is one of the state's greatest stands of old-growth eastern hemlocks and eastern white pines—barred and great horned owls live among them. Also, wild turkeys, for which Ben Franklin once lobbied for designation as the national bird and which were hunted to near-extinction a century ago, now live throughout Connecticut, especially in the Litchfield Hills.

## CAMPING

There are two basic forms of camping in Connecticut: the more primitive tent-and-backpack activity offered at both commercial grounds and many state parks and forests, and the downright cushy RV camping available exclusively at commercial sites.

The Connecticut DEP administers the roughly 1,400 sites at state parks and forests. Officially, the season kicks off in mid-April and runs until the end of September, but several parks offer camping only from Memorial Day to Labor Day. Check-in at sites is from 1 P.M. on, and check-out is by noon; you may camp for a maximum of 14 straight nights at inland parks and for up to 21

consecutive days at the Hammonasset Beach and Rocky Neck State Parks along the coast.

If you'll be camping for more than two nights, you can reserve your site ahead of time through the DEP; this can only be done by mail, and applications for the coming year must be received after January 15 (those postmarked earlier will be returned to you) and at least 10 days before your expected date of arrival. It's prudent to reserve ahead, as many sites fill up quickly on weekends.

For details on how to submit a reservation and on the various camping rules, costs, and facilities at each park, contact the State Parks Division of the Bureau of Outdoor Recreation at the Connecticut DEP (79 Elm St., Hartford, CT 06106, 860/424-3200). All of this information can also be found at the DEP camping website, http://dep.state.ct.us/stateparks.

There are private commercial campgrounds throughout the state, most of them in the northeastern or northwestern hills, or along the coast. You can obtain a directory of these facilities by contacting the **Connecticut Campground Owners Association, Inc.** (14 Rumford St., West Hartford, CT 06107, 860/521-4704, www.camp conn.com).

## FISHING AND HUNTING

Among the state's hundreds of great fishing holes and swift rivers, the upper Housatonic in Litchfield County and the lake at Bigelow Hollow State Park are among the best sources of trout fishing. In fact, you'll find several fly-fishing outfitters along the Housatonic, and even an excellent fly-fishing school. Other common freshwater catches (some tasty and some usually thrown back) include banded sunfish, black crappie, bluegills, smallmouth and largemouth bass, and yellow perch.

Largemouth bass and certain varieties of trout may be found also in brackish waters, and some species of anadromous fish (those that spawn in fresh water but live most of their lives in salt water) regularly make their way inland from Long Island Sound up Connecticut's rivers: these include shad, sturgeon, and Atlantic salmon. The early spring shad run up the Connecticut

River is an especially celebrated event among fishermen and connoisseurs of this plank-cooked member of the herring family, whose gamey-tasting roe is a delicacy.

Along Connecticut's shoreline, bluefish, cod, striped bass, and sturgeon are popular game fish, as are a variety of shellfish, including mussels, oysters, lobsters, and crabs. For a chance to fish for these and New England's many deep-sea species—such as black sea bass, bluefin tuna, bonito, haddock, mackerel, and swordfish—consider booking a trip on any of the state's 40 private fishing charter boats, many of which are listed in the Connecticut Coast chapter of this book, and all of which are listed in the *Connecticut Vacation Guide,* available free from the state office of tourism, 800/CT-BOUND.

Saltwater fishing does not require a license except for lobstering; additionally, most forms of shellfishing are regulated locally, so you should check with the area town hall before setting out. Freshwater fishing requires a seasonal license, which costs $20 for residents ($40 nonresidents). Or, for just $16, out-of-state visitors can buy a three-day fishing license. These may be obtained at town halls and many bait and tackle shops, as can the DEP-produced *Angler's Guide,* which lists rules and regulations, lakes and public boat ramps, site access for the handicapped, and the best of the state's fishing areas.

If you're serious about fishing, you should phone the DEP, 860/424-FISH, and request the *Angler's Guide* and any other information or advice pertaining to your specific interests, or check out the DEP website, dep.state.ct.us. From this site you can download the entire Angler's Guide in PDF format, plus applications for fishing licenses, as well as permits and detailed guides on every kind of hunting (trapping, waterfowl, deer, turkey, firearms, archery, etc.).

## GOLFING

Hartford's own Mark Twain is often quoted as having described golf as "a good walk spoiled," and indeed the state had a handful of very nice courses even back in Twain's day. The number and variety of courses—from winding, relatively flat, and rather tight links courses to lush, narrow, and hilly woodland layouts—have mushroomed over the years. Many of the best public golf facilities are described in this book's individual regional chapters.

If you live and play regularly in Connecticut, it makes sense to join the 54,000-member **Connecticut State Golf Association,** Golf House (35 Cold Spring Rd., Suite 212, Rocky Hill, CT 06067, 860/257-4171, www.csgalinks.org). The website lists some 165 member clubs, upcoming local tournaments, and many additional resources.

For visitors just wanting to learn a bit about the ins and outs of the state's 100 public courses, the **Connecticut Golfer** website (www.ct-golfer.com) is an outstanding resource containing detailed information on course and driving-range fees, hours, statistics, difficulty, terrain, and layout. Each public course has its own page, from which you can read the comments made by other golfers or leave comments of your own. So, the next time a bumpy green costs you a crucial putt, get even by leaving a scathing review of the greenskeeping on this website—of course, all duffers know deep down that we have only ourselves to blame for poor scores, but it's nice to be able to vent.

## HIKING

Connecticut has more than 400 miles of trails for hiking and biking, and contrary to what you might expect, you don't have to travel to the most remote northwestern and northeastern reaches to find the most rugged and pristine scenery. Wonderful parks and trails are within a 10-minute drive of every city and town in Connecticut.

Many of the resources, parks, and preserves detailed elsewhere in this section are of great use to hikers, especially those under the General Resources, Biking, Bird-watching, and Skiing subheadings. However, anybody with more than a passing interest in trailblazing should contact, and consider joining, the **Connecticut Forest and Park Association (CFPA),** Middlefield (16 Meriden Rd., Rockfall 06481, 860/346-2372, www.ctwoodlands.org). It costs just $35 to join. For $21, you can also buy the invaluable *Con-*

necticut *Walk Book,* a complete guide to the organization's 700-mile Blue-Blazed Hiking Trail System. You'll also get *Connecticut Woodlands* magazine and the *CFPA News* and be invited to recreational, conservation, and forestry events and seminars throughout the year.

A terrific introduction to the CFPA is attending **Connecticut Trail Day,** when volunteers spend the day helping to maintain and improve the Blue-Blazed Hiking Trail System. Tasks include pruning and clearing, installing waterbars, adding steps and brides to help prevent erosion, and other general upkeep. It's a great way to learn about the state's many excellent trails, as this event takes place on more than 50 different spans of the system. Contact CFPA for details and a brochure.

The state's most serious and revered hiking is along the 52 miles of the Appalachian Trail traversing the very northwestern corner of the state. Detailed information on this highly challenging but rewarding trail is found in the Western Hills chapter, but you can also contact the state branch of the **Appalachian Mountain Club,** www.ct-amc.org, which includes a trail map and details of what you'll encounter along the 52 miles.

## SKIING

Connecticut's ski season has long lacked the respect it deserves—certainly New England's top ski resorts are spread across Vermont, New Hampshire, and Maine. But Connecticut's five downhill facilities are perfect for day outings, brushing up on your skills, and families.

The largest, with 23 trails, is Mohawk Mountain in Cornwall, but others (each with 14 or 18 trails) include Mount Southington in Southington, Powder Ridge in Middlefield, Ski Sundown in New Hartford, and Woodbury Ski and Racquet in Woodbury. All have at least four surface or chair lifts, night skiing, snowmaking, and food concessions.

Woodbury Ski and Racquet and Mohawk Mountain also have excellent cross-country ski trails, in addition to Cedar Brook Cross Country Ski Area in West Suffield, the White Memorial Foundation in Litchfield, and the Winding Trails Cross Country Ski Center in Farmington.

For the latest conditions and information on ski resorts in Connecticut, check out www.goski.com.

## TAKING TO THE WATER

There are aquatic outfitters and tour providers throughout the state, with the most popular river sports (such as canoeing and kayaking) along the Farmington, Connecticut, and the upper Housatonic. Other opportunities include kayak tours of the Norwalk Islands or, in New Milford, Lake Lillinonah. Individual canoeing, kayaking, rafting, and tubing outfitters are listed in their appropriate regional chapters.

About 20 tour operators offer cruises in Long Island Sound. Some in Branford go out to the Thimble Islands, several in the southeastern part of the state offer sunset cruises and wildlife (whales, seals, migratory birds) cruises, and others explore the coast of New Haven and Fairfield County. Several additional companies offer cruises that ply the state's inland waterways, including the lake at Quassy Amusement Park in Middlebury and the Branford, Connecticut, Mystic, Quinnipiak, Thames, and West Rivers.

**Riverboat Rides,** 860/526-4954, www.deep-rivernavigation.com, offers three different tours in vintage riverboats along the Connecticut River and Long Island Sound. Tours from Hartford's Charter Oak Landing run up- and downriver and to Rocky Hill, and they also offer cocktail excursions. Tours from Middletown's Harborpark run quite a way down the river to Gillette Castle in East Haddam, and they're offered in fall

## WATER QUALITY AND CONDITIONS

The New England office of the U.S. Environmental Protection Agency sponsors a program at the University of Connecticut that monitors the water quality and conditions on Long Island Sound via a network of radio transmitters and buoys. If you're trying to find out the most current conditions before swimming or fishing, you can now visit the program's website (www.mysound.uconn.edu).

ON THE ROAD

only (to take advantage of the foliage). Old Saybrook's Saybrook Point runs take visitors to Essex Harbor, Duck Island, and along the Saybrook waterfront to Outer Lighthouse. Many additional types of special-interest cruises are offered seasonally, including winter eagle watches and Hartford-to-the-Sound excursions. Most regularly scheduled runs are one–two hours and cost $8–12 per person.

The *Connecticut Vacation Guide,* available free by calling the state tourism office (800/CT-BOUND), supplies a full list of aquatic outfitters, cruise-tour operators, and charters. Many of the state's lakes and ponds allow boating, and marinas and launches are strung along Long Island Sound from Greenwich to Stonington. For rules and regulations and a complete list of public boat launches, get the free booklet *Connecticut Boater's Guide* by contacting the DEP Boating Division, 860/434-8638; the guide is also available at most marinas and boat shows and can be downloaded from the DEP at www.dep.state.ct.us/rec.

# Where to Stay

No part of the state is without a healthy variety of lodging options, although some regions tend more toward smaller inns and bed-and-breakfasts, while others favor the presence of chain motels and hotels. As you might expect, the most densely populated areas—along the Interstates, in cities, and near industrial and corporate campuses—tend to favor the larger properties.

Many of the smaller inns and B&Bs in Connecticut close either seasonally or at will, according to the needs and in some cases the whims of their owners. It's always a good idea to book your accommodations as far ahead as possible, and it's imperative that you do so when planning a stay at an inn or B&B.

## PRICE CATEGORIES

Accommodations in this book are grouped according to the following price categories: Under $50, $50–100, $100–150, $150–250, and over $250. These ranges are based on the cost of an establishment's standard room, double-occupancy, during high season. Expect to pay more during holidays or during a few exceptionally popular weekends (i.e., weekends in October during peak foliage), for suites or rooms that sleep more than two, and for rooms with special amenities, such as fireplaces, hot tubs, and decks. Expect to pay less (often as much as 50 percent less) off-season (i.e., winter along the shore), during the week with leisure-oriented country inns and B&Bs, during weekends for urban hotels and motels, and for rooms with fewer amenities (shared baths, twin beds, brick-wall views, no TV, etc.).

## WHAT IT WILL COST

There are two basic factors on which accommodations base their highest and lowest rates, both tied in closely to supply and demand. Price ranges indicated this book reflect the highest rates, double-occupancy, during the most expensive times. Don't be put off if you see a hotel listed in the $150–250 range when you're seeking something under $100 nightly. There are hotels in Connecticut whose highest rates hover around $200 nightly but drop to as low as $70 during slow times—it's always a good idea to phone ahead or visit a property's website and ask about special packages and seasonal, weekday, or weekend discounts.

At properties that rely principally on leisure travelers, rates are nearly always seasonal and always lower on weekdays than on weekends. This category includes bed-and-breakfasts, country inns, and a small number of larger hotels and motels in the more tourism-dependent sections of the state, such as Litchfield County, the lower Connecticut River Valley, the Quiet Corner, and the Mystic/Stonington area. In most of the state, rates tend to be highest from late spring (anywhere from Easter to Memorial Day) until late October (just after the peak foliage periods). The rest of the year, you can anticipate price breaks anywhere from 30–50 percent, although the most popular establishments (particularly in Litchfield County and around the casinos in southeastern Connecticut) often stay busy year-round, and so don't reduce their rates by as much. Also, some hotels keep their rates up until January, as tourism (at least on weekends) can remain fairly strong through the Christmas holidays.

In the most desirable regions during peak season, it's next to impossible to get a weekend room at the last minute—book as early as possible (at least two weeks ahead) and expect to find two-night minimums in shore locations in summer and inland locations during fall foliage (three-day minimums are the norm on holiday weekends). Typically, once you make a reservation, whether through a reservations service or directly through an inn, you'll be required to leave as much as a 50 percent deposit. The refund of this deposit is contingent upon the property's being able to rebook your room—at the very least, you'll be charged a significant "processing" fee. Note the rules of deposit and payment carefully (not all places accept credit cards, either) when making your reservation, and don't expect anybody to bend on these policies once you've booked your room. Remember, the laws of accommodations depend entirely upon supply and demand.

At properties that rely principally on business travelers, rates are the least affected by the season and the most influenced by day of the week. In this regard, their prices are usually the inverse of what you'd pay at a B&B in the country: On weekdays, when corporate travelers descend on the place, rates are at their highest, but on weekends, they can drop 30–70 percent. This rule holds most true in greater Hartford, greater New Haven, Danbury, and coastal Fairfield County from Greenwich to Bridgeport. You are also more likely to see dramatic rate swings at upscale properties than you will at low-end or moderate ones. For example, the top hotels in Hartford (the Goodwin, the Hilton, and the Crowne Plaza) all reduce their rates significantly on weekends, yet the bare-bones Ramada maintains the same rate seven nights a week. What does this mean for the economy-minded traveler visiting Hartford Wednesday through Saturday? Stay at the

Ramada the first two nights, and switch to one of the upscale properties over the weekend.

There are a few notable exceptions to the above. Fairfield County, including the lower Housatonic River Valley, is the one part of the state with a high number of small inns and B&Bs that draw an even mix of leisure and business travelers. For this reason, you'll find that rates at these establishments don't vary much according to the day of the week or the season. Whatever the time of year, accommodations in Fairfield County are generally more expensive than elsewhere in the state—it's the closest region to New York City and it registers the highest cost of living in New England.

Another set of rules applies to the dozens of chain properties lining the major Interstates (I-95 along the coast, I-84 from Danbury to the Massachusetts border, and I-91 from New Haven to Enfield). The vast majority of the guests at these properties are passing through en route to another part of the Northeast. Rates tend to be constant throughout the year, although if you call these kinds of properties on a slow night, you'll find that the manager on duty is often willing to cut you a nice deal, lower than you'll be quoted by phoning the chain's toll-free central-reservations number.

## CHOOSING AN ACCOMMODATION

No matter what it says in a property's brochure, remember that nothing at your hotel—breakfast, a pool, an exercise room, turndown service, local phone calls—is free. These extras may be included in the rate, but this means that rates at properties with oodles of perks, amenities, and facilities are going to be higher than rates at properties without them. These extras are all well and good, provided you're really going to take advantage of them, but think seriously about booking a room at a country inn that's renowned for its lavish full breakfasts or an upscale hotel whose business and conference facilities are renowned. Do you eat breakfast? Are you in town on business?

As the old real estate cliché goes, location is everything when it comes to finding the right place to encamp—even if just for the night. Once you've established what you're willing to spend and what level of accommodation will suit you, make a very careful study about where you plan to spend most of your visit. Are you looking to hide away with your mate in a romantic suite, rarely emerging until checkout? Or will you be spending as little time as possible in your room or even in the town where you're staying? Does a view matter? How about being within walking distance of shops and restaurants? Chances are strong that to satisfy one of these needs, you may have to sacrifice another—the vast majority of Connecticut's accommodations are either scenic and charming but remote, or basic and lacking a picturesque setting, but convenient to local attractions.

For the record, 10 accommodations that satisfy all of the above criteria are the Avon Old Farms Inn (Avon), the Elms Inn (Ridgefield), the Farmington Inn (Farmington), the Goodwin Hotel (Hartford), Homestead Inn (New Milford), the Inn at National Hall (Westport), Steamboat Inn (Mystic), the Stonington Inn (Stonington), the Three Chimneys (New Haven), and the Westin Hotel (Stamford). There are many others, but these are among the best.

One major caveat before relying heavily on the state-produced *Connecticut Vacation Guide* and the brochures produced by the local tourist boards: The organizations that produce these publications are funded by a hotel tax (12 percent) that is added on to your room rate. As long as a lodging pays this tax, it is entitled to be included in any literature published by the state and local tourist boards. This means that these brochures and publications cannot refuse a listing to even the seediest, dreariest, and most horrible establishment.

What does this mean in practice? Having anonymously inspected most of the properties listed in the *Connecticut Vacation Guide,* I can say that 10–20 percent of them are highly suspect, and several make the hotel in *The Shining* look like a Ritz-Carlton. You would think that some sort of ratings system would be in place to keep properties that are truly unsanitary, substandard, or unsafe from being recommended unconditionally by organizations aiming to promote tourism, but such are the mysterious ways of governmental bureaucracies.

This is not to suggest that establishments omitted from this book are substandard—there are simply too many hotels to review in this guide, and thus you'll only find the most characterful and appealing properties in the state in each price category. In cities with an unusually high number of similar chain motels, I've selected those representing the greatest value, which is figured roughly by considering the rates, the location, the facilities, and the level of cleanliness and staff professionalism I encountered. A change in management can raise or lower the quality of a property almost overnight, but it's safe to say that at press time, I'd have recommended every single property in this book to my mother (and that's saying a lot).

## Country Inns and Bed-and-Breakfasts

To get a real feel for the area you're visiting, consider choosing a B&B or country inn over the typical cookie-cutter chain property. Some may believe that chains offer better rates, more consistent standards, better amenities for business travelers, and greater anonymity, but this is far from always—or even often—the case. Many of the smaller B&Bs, especially those that offer shared baths, have among the least-expensive rooms in Connecticut (if fewer than four rooms they're also exempt from the state's hotel tax), and most of them have higher-quality furnishings and amenities than similarly priced chains.

Furthermore, staying at a small historic property need not involve socializing with either your hosts or the fellow guests, or placing phone calls and sending faxes from a common area. An increasing number of higher-end inns (this is less true of B&Bs) have recognized the needs of business travelers and begun installing in-room direct-dial phones, data ports, and cable TV. If privacy is important to you, ask if any of the rooms have separate outdoor entrances. You'll be surprised how many places do, often in carriage houses or outbuildings set away from the main house.

All of this is not to suggest that warm and welcoming country inns and B&Bs are not plentiful—the kinds of places where guests compare notes on their finest antiquing conquests before a roaring evening fire, or conspire together to attack the area's most challenging hiking trails over a four-course breakfast. The most successful innkeepers have learned to leave alone the independent travelers, but gently direct the ones seeking local advice and connections, like hard-to-score dinner reservations and directions to secret fishing holes that you'll never find in brochures or even in this book. If it's your wish, a B&B can offer both camaraderie and a personal concierge—and these perks come with no extra charges.

In the broadest sense, B&Bs are smaller than country inns. B&Bs tend to have fewer than 10 rooms (sometimes only one or two), and the owners often live on the premises. Breakfasts tend to be intimate and social, common areas small and homey, and facilities and amenities minimal (rarely are there phones or TVs in guest rooms, nor is there a restaurant or exercise room). At inns, you may find anywhere from several to 100 rooms, a full staff of employees (the owners often live off-property), breakfasts served in dining rooms and often at your own private table, spacious and more formal common areas, and an array of facilities and amenities.

More often than not, breakfast at a country inn is continental, and breakfast at a B&B is full (i.e., includes a hot entrée and often three or four courses). It's less of a rule, but country inns typically charge more than B&Bs, and, although they're often less personable and quirky, they maintain a higher standard of luxury and offer a greater degree of privacy. These are general differences, and in many cases the lines between country inns and B&Bs blur considerably. Regardless of these distinctions, inns and B&Bs share many traits: usually they are historic or designed in a historic style, rooms typically vary in layout and are decorated individually in period style, and settings are often rural or scenic.

The smallest variety of B&B is generally not covered individually in this book, because these places are very often operated discreetly or part-time (many are not licensed and do not seek the publicity of a guidebook) and are best booked by contacting one of the several reservations services below. The smallest B&Bs are more like one- or two-room private homestays, where you may find yourself interacting closely with your hosts. It's important that you explain your privacy preferences when speaking with reservations services. These booking services cover a variety of properties, and some even represent larger hotels.

## Hotels and Motels

The majority of the state's hotels and motels are perfectly nice, and a few are downright homey and charming. However, most of the unacceptable accommodations in Connecticut are lower-end chain motels, many of them located off the Interstates. There are exceptions, of course, as there are some truly awful B&Bs out there, and some surprisingly unkempt and poorly run moderate-to-upscale hotels. You can increase your odds of picking a good property by keeping a few things in mind:

Look for *recent* stickers in lobby windows that indicate the hotel has been approved by AAA or the Mobil guides, and avoid motels on busy roads within earshot of a major highway (they're not only apt to be noisy, but they're more likely to be rendezvous points for any number of illicit activities). Motels that rent rooms by the hour are usually not very savory, and there are plenty of them—especially along I-95.

However, if you've a penchant for campy decorating and kitschy love nests, by all means give some of the more tawdry motels a whirl. The funnier (but still clean and safe) of these are reviewed in this book and may include such memorable amenities as heart-shaped (often water-filled) beds, heart-shaped double whirlpool tubs, and other heart-shaped accoutrements of romance. The most glamorous "suites" at these sorts of establishments—they still usually rent for under $75—are typically offered in one of the following themes: safari, jungle, Camelot/medieval, tropical, or the unpredictable "honeymoon."

At any property with which you're unfamiliar, ask to see the room before you check in, and if the front desk refuses—or even hesitates—you can safely assume they're harboring secrets that shall be revealed to you only after you have left a credit-card imprint (like the postage-stamp size guest towels are frayed and threadbare, and the air conditioner is broken). If you see plants or personal effects on the sills of guest-room windows, or rusty cars in the parking lot, you have no doubt stumbled upon a residential hotel with facilities that are probably not up to the expectations of most travelers. (This may sound like a joke, but quite a few of these places are listed in the brochures produced by tourist boards.)

A few chains are consistently reputable or have especially good products in Connecticut, including most of the high-end ones. Of economical and moderately priced chains, best bets include Comfort Inn, Courtyard by Marriott, Four Points, Hampton Inn, Holiday Inn Express, Motel 6 (the best bare-bones chain in the state), and Quality Inn. Independently operated budget motels are inherently no better or worse than chain properties—don't rule them out just because you've never heard of them. But do check them out carefully ahead of time.

# Eating Out

Like so much of America, Connecticut's culinary scene has been blessed with an unparalleled wave of inventiveness and sophistication since the 1990s. Dining out, from affordable diners and pizza parlors to upscale bistros and trattorias, yields pleasurable results across the state, with the greatest concentration of high-caliber eateries found in western Fairfield County and much of Litchfield County. Greater Hartford, greater New Haven, Mystic and Stonington, the lower Connecticut River Valley, the central shoreline, and eastern Fairfield County are also rife with memorable dining options.

The variety and high standards that characterize the state's dining scene can be traced to several factors. First, Connecticut has a number of wealthy areas where both ordinary diners and business types are willing on a regular basis to spend a good bit of money on food. The venerable Zagat survey reports that Connecticut residents dine out about 3.5 times per week, more than in such restaurant meccas as New York City and San Francisco. This sort of interest in, and respect for, good cooking make it both economically rewarding and professionally satisfying for outstanding chefs to open restaurants in the state.

This is also an area where it's quite possible for chefs to become known among the rich and famous. It no doubt pleases the kitchen wizards of such notable Litchfield County eateries as the Good News Cafe and the West Street Grill to know that local glitterati, like Rose and William Styron, Diane Sawyer and Mike Nichols, and Dustin Hoffman, are among their contented patrons. No doubt the chefs at Rebecca's in Greenwich and Miramar in Westport are happy knowing they may be preparing dinner on any given night for Paul Newman and Joanne Woodward, Phil Donahue and Marlo Thomas, Diana Ross, or Mel Gibson.

Numerous celebrated food writers also call Connecticut home, including cookbook gurus Jacques Pépin and Mark Bittman; the authors of the quirky dining bible *Road Food,* Jane and Michael Stern; *New York Times* food critic Patricia Brooks; Arthur Schwartz of WOR radio's "Food Talk"; NPR's "Food Schmooze" host, Faith Middleton; the controversial doyenne of entertaining, Martha Stewart; and an array of travel and food writers from national publications large and small.

Another reason for the wealth of reputable cutting-edge chefs is the proximity of the renowned Culinary Institute of America, in nearby Westchester County, New York, plus a fair share of cooking academies in New York City. Ruth Henderson, the wife of the well-known bandleader Skitch Henderson (think early *Tonight Show*), runs her own cooking school in New Milford, along with an emporium of gourmet foods and cookery called the Silo. In short, Nutmeggers are knowledgeable, demanding, and savvy when it comes to eating out.

Connecticut is close enough to New York City and Boston to feel the influences of both of these world-class cooking capitals, and yet it's refreshingly out of the hustle and bustle of either place. Fairfield County is the most like Manhattan in terms of having several dozen loud, high-profile,

And what if you've got kids in tow, or you've been out hiking or fishing all day and are neither dressed for, nor especially inclined toward, dinner at a big-name restaurant? First, remember that all but a handful of even the best restaurants in the state welcome casual attire, put up with (if not wholly accept) children, and eschew fanfare and formality. Next, consider the plethora of outstanding cheap and casual eateries set around the state.

Connecticut has a bevy of diners, many open 24 hours. The largest ones—with streaks of neon tubing and shimmering stainless-steel facades—are very often Greek-owned, and so feature a few Hellenic specialties, plus just about every variety of sandwich, breaded fish, omelette, and blue-plate special (e.g., liver and onions, chicken parmigiana, pork chops with applesauce) known to humanity. They also offer the requisite Greek salad, side plates piled high with french fries or hash browns, "dieter's delights" consisting of cottage cheese and canned peaches or pears, and glimmering, shimmering glass bowls of Jell-O in both expected and disturbing Day-Glo colors.

Connecticut is not unlike other parts of New England when it comes to inexpensive local staples: the Americanized order-by-number Chinese restaurant, the sports bar or English-style pub with TGIF-style munchies and bar snacks, the family-run red-sauce Italian restaurant with predictable but ultimately satisfying pasta and veal dishes, and the venerable Colonial tavern complete with creaky wide-plank floors, dark-wood tables and bentwood chairs, Revolutionary War kitsch, and a long list of Old Yankee favorites, such as pot roast, broiled haddock, clam chowder, filet mignon, and peach cobbler á la mode. These sorts of midpriced independent restaurants are widespread, if not necessarily of a higher quality than the better chain eateries lining the state's busiest roads.

Here in Connecticut, the everyman contribution to dining that stands out above any other is pizza—no other state in the Union matches up. Considering its sheer size and reputation for creative cooking and fresh ingredients, California might be able to give Connecticut a run for its money. But those elaborate, almost decadent,

urbane, and pricey eateries of great regional acclaim—cynics may argue that for what you'll pay at the best restaurants in Fairfield County you may as well make the trip to New York. But there's no denying the bounty of good restaurants in this part of the state.

Litchfield County proves the better value, as you'll find a significant number of restaurants offering dining experiences as good as any in New England for $18–25 per entrée, and that's at the best of the bunch. This area depends heavily on the deep pockets of both tourists and New Yorkers who weekend or summer here, and so in order to keep the restaurants busy during weekdays and slow months, menu prices remain agreeable year-round.

The news is similarly good at the top dining haunts elsewhere in Connecticut, where even in cities like Hartford and New Haven two people can enjoy a world-class, three-course dinner with a decent bottle of wine for $125 and a very good meal at a lower-profile eatery for under $75. Cut out the bottle of wine, or try sharing an appetizer or dessert, and good dining becomes an affordable reality for many budgets.

Wolfgang Puck–style pies known all over the West Coast and in most major U.S. cities are not pizzas at all, but rather complicated dinner entrées slopped over a slab of bread and baked in an oven.

Genuine pizza, the kind introduced at America's first and still-going-strong pizza parlor—Frank Pepe's of New Haven—is prepared using thin crusts, a brick oven, and but a handful of basic but fresh ingredients that complement one another. Connecticut is especially known for white sauce-less pies baked with a simple but satisfying base of oregano, garlic, olive oil, a few choice Italian herbs, and maybe some Parmesan cheese. Among white pizzas, the variety heaped with fresh minced quahog clams and shreds of cured bacon is a specialty with no rival. But don't get too fancy and start asking for sundried tomatoes or walnuts—at traditional Connecticut pizza parlors, ask for more than a couple ordinary toppings and you'll get a cold stare from the person who takes your order.

*Here in Connecticut, the everyman contribution to dining that stands out above any other is pizza—no other state in the Union matches up.*

Seafood is another regional strength—outsiders sometimes forget that while Connecticut lies on the Long Island Sound rather than the open Atlantic Ocean, fish don't seem to know the difference—especially with far-reaching and highly successful efforts over the past decade to clean up the sound. Fresh, locally caught clams, mussels, oysters, and many varieties of fish are again common. Dozens of fish eateries dot the coast, many with "in-the-rough" seating either on or near the water, and a surprising plethora of fine seafood restaurants lie inland.

The state of ethnic cooking in Connecticut is something of an enigma. For the most part, restaurants offering Asian cuisine are quite good, if a bit tepid, when it comes to seasoning and a bit impatient when it comes to preparation. For a while, you couldn't get Yankees to sample exotic or spicy food unless you toned down the more biting ingredients and cooked food as quickly and efficiently as possible. This sensibility encouraged chefs to pan-fry and deep-fry many dishes that would never have been drowned in hot oil if prepared in their native lands.

Finally, the tongues of Nutmeggers have caught up and begun to demand Indian and Japanese restaurants to the point where these sorts of places have opened in nearly every city or large town in the state. A smaller number of Afghan, Korean, Malaysian, Thai, and Vietnamese eateries have followed. Unfortunately, the chefs at Asian restaurants still tend to Americanize their dishes for fear that New Englanders won't give authentic and spicy seasoning a chance. If, however, you request that your meal be prepared as though you were native to the cuisine, many chefs will comply.

The quality of Japanese restaurants is the highest of any ethnic type in the state, with outstanding purveyors of both sushi and hot Japanese dishes opening at a breakneck speed. Chinese restaurants remain consistently bland throughout the state, although a handful has begun serving more vibrant cuisine. Also, an increasing number of contemporary American and Continental restaurants have begun experimenting with Asian ingredients and techniques, yielding a fusion cuisine that is quite good in these parts, if not as consistently exemplary as the best cutting-edge fusion cooking in San Francisco or Seattle.

Many contemporary menus now also offer dishes with a Latin-American or Mexican bent, but it's virtually impossible to find authentic regional Mexican or Southwestern fare in Connecticut. Even the greasy, mushy, so-called Tex-Mex offered at most of the state's Mexican restaurants lacks anything near the punchy zest of authentic Tex-Mex as prepared in Houston or Austin.

In the end, while many of the ethnic eateries in the state fall short in terms of authenticity and subtly of seasoning, they nevertheless offer food that is reasonably tasty and ingredients that are fairly fresh. If you can forget that the food you're eating at the vast majority of the state's "cantinas" is supposed to be Mexican, you may actually overlook the kitchen's gross breaches of culinary integrity and enjoy your meal. If this kind of cooking is no better than your average all-Amer-

ican cheeseburger or fried chicken, it's really no
worse either.

## Restaurant Hours and Prices
Most restaurants in either urban or suburban
parts of the state serve lunch from 11 A.M. or
noon until 2 or 3 P.M., and dinner from 5 or
6 P.M. until 10 P.M. In some of the more rural
parts of the state, especially the Litchfield Hills
and the Quiet Corner, expect lunch to end by
2 P.M. and dinner by 9 P.M.

Following the phone numbers of most restaurants included in this book, the average range of
the cost of dinner entrées has been provided
(e.g., $5–15). This is a general range that does
not take into account the occasional high-priced
special or unusual dish on a menu. For coffeehouses, gourmet markets, and some of the fast
food–oriented eateries in the book, no range
has been given. And for restaurants where dinner is not served, the cost range of lunch entrées has been given.

# Shopping

In Connecticut, shopping is about as serious a
pastime as surfing is in Hawaii or skiing in
Vermont—it could easily be called the state
sport. Specifically, Connecticut is at the forefront of the nation's antiques scene, and both
bargain-hunters and serious collectors will find
a visit here immensely rewarding. But all other
forms of shopping proliferate around the state,
with the exception of especially cutting-edge
and out-there clothiers—New York, and to a
lesser degree Boston still maintain a stronghold where European boutiques and runway
wear are concerned. Same goes for home furnishings and art (although a fair number of
daring contemporary galleries exist across the
state); the emphasis is on traditional stuff: maritime painting, New England landscapes, historic portraiture, etc. This is a fairly conservative
state where style is concerned, as the goods
sold here reflect.

## Major Shopping Regions
Hulking shopping malls abound in Connecticut, but only a few are large and exciting enough
to truly cause excitement among tourists—the
rest, while containing the usual chain shops, are
no different than you'll find elsewhere in the nation. The four with the greatest cachet are Stamford Town Center (which doubled as a ritzy
Beverly Hills mall in the *Scenes from a Mall*),
the Danbury Fair Mall, the Buckland Hills Mall
(in Manchester), and the Westfarms Mall (on
the Farmington–West Hartford border).

As far as urban shopping is concerned, only
New Haven could truly qualify as having an engaging retail streetscape, with many of its stores
set around the green and close to the campus of
Yale University. This is a great city for books
(both new and antiquarian), records, and cheap
funky clothing—owing largely to the significant
student population.

Hartford is sadly without an appealing retail
base, and it's not yet clear how much of a retail
component there will be at the much-anticipated
Adriaen's Landing riverfront development when it
opens. Downtowns with especially engaging and
walkable streets for browsing and window shopping include Branford, Greenwich, Guilford,
Kent, Litchfield, Mystic, New Canaan, Norwalk
(in the SoNo area), Old Saybrook, Putnam,
Ridgefield, Stonington, West Hartford, and Westport, to name a few. Westport is probably the
most controversial of these, at least among nostalgic locals who lament that that the town's
charming Main Street has been transformed from
a friendly row of independent dry-goods and
workaday retailers into a slew of impersonal high-
end chain boutiques.

Outlet shopping has grown in popularity over
the years, especially in the southeastern part of the
state. Clinton, Mystic, and Westbrook have extremely popular outlet centers.

## Antiques
**Organizations and Publications:** Whether a
novice or an expert, your antiquing success will be

enhanced greatly if you consult a few publications before setting out. The country's leading resource is *Antiques And The Arts Weekly* (The Bee Publishing Co., P.O. Box 5503, Newtown, CT 06470, 203/426-3141, www.antiquesand thearts.com), a mammoth 200-page feast of detailed auctions (with photos), museum and gallery exhibits, book reviews, antiques show calendars, shopping tips, and engaging features. Subscriptions are $67 annually. The paper has a fine website, whose most helpful and unusual resource is an exhaustive list of antiquarian books and their authors.

Although based in Massachusetts, the monthly **New England Antiques Journal** (P.O. Box 120, Ware, MA 01082, 800/432-3505, www.antiquesjournal.com) has some coverage on Connecticut (subscriptions are $17.95 annually). On the Internet, **New England Antiquing** (www.antiquing.com) has links to shows and events, dealers, towns that are good for antiquing, and other useful stuff.

Connecticut also has numerous crafts centers, where groups of today's best artisans work in a variety of media: glassblowing, woodworking, pottery, ceramics, jewelry-making, printmaking, and so on. For a free guide to the state's major crafts centers, call 888/CT-CRAFT (888/282-7238).

**A Regional Overview:** You'll find a smattering of antiques shops in nearly every community, but a few regions stand out in particular. Litchfield County, in the northwestern hills, is best known for its plethora of shops, the greatest number of them in Woodbury (the state's an-

tiquing capital), New Preston (part of Washington), Salisbury, and Litchfield itself (especially in the Bantam section of town). Kent has a few antiques dealers, but is perhaps better known for possessing a couple of the Northeast's most esteemed art galleries. The state's northeastern hills are similarly rife with old clapboard houses brimming with antiques, and the entire downtown of the old mill community, Putnam, has given way to multi-dealer antique shops in recent years.

The upper half of the Connecticut River Valley, around Hartford, is perhaps the most underrated part of the state with regard to antiquing—there are plenty of great deals to be had in these parts. Places like Plainville, South Windsor, and—more expectedly—Farmington (especially the Unionville section) have a good many shops, and another old mill community, Collinsville, has been virtually transformed into a year-round antiques fair.

Coastal Connecticut has several communities strong on antiquing, especially in Fairfield County, where you may not find many bargains but you will see museum-quality wares. There aren't as many concentrations of shops in these parts—they tend to be spread all around, although there are major multi-dealer antiques centers in Stratford and Stamford. The central shoreline and the little towns around the mouth of the Connecticut River foster a great many antiques dealers, particularly Essex, Old Saybrook, and Guilford, and farther east you'll find excellent shops—many specializing in maritime pieces—around Stonington and Mystic.

# Getting Around

Connecticut is small, crossed by major Interstates and railway tracks, served by New England's second-largest airport and within 90 minutes of five other major ones, and easily reached from every major city in the Northeast. Perhaps no other state in America is more easily accessed, from corner to corner, than Connecticut.

For general information on commuting, getting to and from Connecticut, and getting around the state, contact the **Connecticut Department of Transportation,** or DOT (2800 Berlin Tpke., Newington, CT 06131, 860/594-2000, www.dot.state.ct.us). The DOT website offers extensive information on numerous publications, traveler resources and road conditions, licenses and permits, upcoming roadwork and projects, legal notices, and construction bid notices.

An excellent resource for online transportation information in the state is www.apta.com/sites/transus/ct.htm, which has links to countless related sites.

## DRIVING

This is a great state for scenic drives, whether on major highways or local two-lane surface roads. Alas, there are also plenty of major routes that make for lousy sightseeing and suffer from heavy congestion. Following is a list of highlights and lowlights.

### Road Names and Labels

Connecticutters invariably refer to all numbered roads, whether Interstate or local, as "routes." It would be typical, for instance, for a local describing the best way from Ridgefield to New Fairfield to suggest taking "Route 7 north to Route 84 east to Route 39 north." Look on a map, and you'll find that you actually need to take U.S. Highway 7 north to I-84 east to State Road 39 north. Because you the reader may or may not be from around the northeast, this book follows a clearer format in referring to numbered roads. All Interstate highways are indicated with an "I" before the number (I-95,

I-84, I-91, etc.), all national highways are referred to with a "U.S." before the number (U.S. 7, U.S. 202, U.S. 1, etc.), and all other numbered state and local roads are referred to with a "Rte." before the number (Rte. 8, Rte. 63, Rte. 302, etc.).

### Scenic Versus Dreary Drives

Of major limited-access highways, try to drive along the Merritt Parkway (from Greenwich to Stratford), Rte. 8 (from Bridgeport to Colebrook), Rte. 9 (from Old Saybrook to Middletown), Rte. 2 (from Glastonbury to Norwich), and I-395 (from New London to Thompson). Avoid I-95 (from Greenwich to North Stonington). The other two biggies, I-84 (from Danbury to Union) and I-91 (from New Haven to Enfield), will get you where you need to go, but are both prone to traffic jams (especially near Hartford) and aren't especially attractive.

Of other highways (U.S. and state routes), top picks for scenery include U.S. 7 (from New Milford to Canaan), Rtes. 39 and 37 (from Danbury to Sherman), Rte. 58 (from Trumbull to Bethel), Rte. 67 (from Seymour to New Milford), Rte. 109 (from New Milford to Thomaston), Rte. 4 (from Sharon to Farmington), U.S. 44 (from Lakeville to Canton and from Bolton to East Putnam), Rte. 20 (from Winsted to Granby), Rte. 69 (from Prospect to New Haven), Rte. 63 (from Canaan to New Haven), Rtes. 142 and 146 (from Branford to Guilford), Rte. 77 (from Guilford to Durham), Rte. 154 (from Higganum to Essex), Rte. 190 (from Suffield to Union), Rte. 140 (from East Windsor to Stafford Springs), Rte. 164 (from Ledyard to Jewett City), Rte. 169 (from Norwich to Woodstock), Rte. 156 (from Moodus to New London), Rte. 215 (from Groton to Mystic), and Rte. 49 (from North Stonington to Plainfield).

Other highways (U.S. and state routes) that should be avoided because they tend to be congested and heavily developed include U.S. 1 (from Greenwich to Pawcatuck), U.S. 202/U.S. 7 (from Norwalk to New Milford), U.S. 6 (from

Plymouth to Manchester), U.S. 5 (from Enfield to New Haven), Rte. 69 (from Waterbury to Bristol), Rte. 75 (in Windsor Locks), Rte. 12 (from Plainfield to Groton), and Rte. 71 (from Meriden to New Britain).

### Speed Limits

In 1998, Connecticut became the 49th state in the nation to raise the maximum speed limit on certain limited-access highways from 55 to 65 mph (Delaware is the only state that hasn't followed suit). Except where highways pass through urban areas, and along I-95 from Greenwich to New Haven (a notoriously congested and dangerous stretch of roadway), you can drive 65 mph. This policy does not alter the fact that speeding fines statewide are among the highest in the nation (strictly speaking, driving 66 mph could lead to a hefty fine, whether in a 65 or 55 mph zone). As in most states, however, officers typically don't pull over offenders who keep within 5–8 mph of the posted limit. Roads have never been heavily patrolled in Connecticut, partly because the number of highways with narrow or dangerous shoulders makes it difficult for troopers to pull over drivers. Popular wisdom suggests that the police most heavily target drivers who fail to slow down when passing from the 65 mph zones into slower ones.

Connecticut has, by far, the highest gas tax in the nation; expect stations here to charge 10–30 cents per gallon more than in most of the border states. And if you happen to be approaching from New Jersey, fill up there—that state has one of the lowest gas taxes in the nation.

## MASS TRANSIT

Connecticut has tried very hard in recent years to make the most of its rail and bus systems, both intercity and municipal, but for touring the area a car is still the best way to go. However, parts of the state can be visited quite easily by train, namely New Haven and Hartford. Most of the rail service, however, is geared toward commuters.

Still, it is quite possible and economically fea-

## DRIVING DISTANCES FROM HARTFORD

| Albany, New York | 109 miles |
|---|---|
| Anchorage, Alaska | 4,519 miles |
| Atlanta, Georgia | 1,000 miles |
| Boston, Massachusetts | 103 miles |
| Burlington, Vermont | 236 miles |
| Chicago, Illinois | 892 miles |
| Cleveland, Ohio | 557 miles |
| Concord, New Hampshire | 154 miles |
| Hartford, Washington | 2,977 miles |
| Hyannis, Massachusetts | 161 miles |
| Mexico City, Mexico | 2,909 miles |
| Miami, Florida | 1,398 miles |
| Montréal, Québec | 332 miles |
| Nashville, Tennessee | 1,000 miles |
| New Connecticut, New York | 255 miles |
| New Haven, Connecticut | 39 miles |
| New London, Connecticut | 48 miles |
| New York, New York | 116 miles |
| Northampton, Massachusetts | 46 miles |
| Philadelphia, Pennsylvania | 212 miles |
| Portland, Maine | 199 miles |
| Providence, Rhode Island | 73 miles |
| Stamford, Connecticut | 78 miles |
| Toronto, Ontario | 493 miles |
| Washington, D.C. | 348 miles |

• Interestingly, few state capitals are closer together than Hartford and Providence, but they are not directly connected by an Interstate highway. You have to either drive down I-91 to the coast and then continue up I-95, or take surface roads.
• Five cities that share Connecticut's approximate latitude: Ankara, Turkey; Baku, Azerbaijan; Beijing, China; Madrid, Spain; Salt Lake City, Utah.
• Five cities that share Connecticut's approximate longitude: Bogota, Colombia; Lima, Peru; Port-Au-Prince, Haiti; Santiago, Chile; Trois-Rivières, Québec.

sible to visit Connecticut without using a car. If, for example, you're visiting Westport from New York City, you could get into town by train on Metro-North and then use a bus to travel to and from the beaches, downtown, the train station, and some of the shopping areas. A cab would work for any areas you can't otherwise cover by bus. Much of Coastal Connecticut is similarly doable with a combination of trains, buses, and taxis—and even with the seemingly high cost of a cab, think how much renting a car (plus gas and possibly additional insurance) in New York City costs.

It's also fairly easy to explore the Connecticut River Valley using this combination of mass-transit options. To make the most of the eastern and western hills (excepting perhaps Waterbury and Danbury), you really are better off with a car. You could, in a pinch, take a Bonanza bus to Cornwall or Canaan in Litchfield County or Danielson in the northeastern hills, then use local bus service to get around area towns; but your flexibility will be severely restricted. On the other hand, if all you're doing is hiding away inside a country inn for the weekend, this option might work fine.

Another strategy is to use rail service to reach the state and then rent a car to get around locally once you arrive. This saves having to rent a car from an expensive city (rentals are far cheaper in Connecticut than in Manhattan, for instance) or using your own car for a very long drive (from, say, Washington, D.C. or Boston).

Given the sheer volume of auto traffic in Connecticut, it's helpful to try to choose an alternative means of transport. If you're moving to the state and are interested in opportunities for carpooling, vanpooling, and public transportation information, contact any of the state's three ridesharing organizations. For Southwestern Connecticut and New York's Lower Hudson Valley Region, call **MetroPool** (800/FIND-RIDE, www.metropool.com); for greater New Haven and Waterbury, call **Rideworks** (800/ALL-RIDE, www.rideworks.com); and in greater Hartford, north-central, and southeast Connecticut, call **Rideshare** (800/842-2150, www.rideshare.com).

## Amtrak

Numerous Amtrak trains (800/872-7245, www.amtrak.com) run through the state daily. This is a fairly hassle-free way to get to the state from Boston, Montreal, New York City, Philadelphia, and other major metro regions. There are four basic Amtrak routes in Connecticut, two of them beginning in Washington, D.C., and terminating in Boston. Of these two, the inland route makes stops in Stamford, Bridgeport, New Haven, Wallingford, Meriden, Berlin/New Britain, Hartford, and Windsor Locks; the shore route stops in Stamford, Bridgeport, New Haven, Old Saybrook, New London, and Mystic. The third route is the New Haven to Springfield run, which makes the same stops as the inland D.C.–Boston route described above, from New Haven to Windsor Locks. Finally, a fourth route runs from New York City to St. Albans, Vermont, with Connecticut stops in Stamford, Bridgeport, New Haven, and Hartford.

High-speed Amtrak rail service, the first in America, was developed between Washington, DC and Boston in 2000 and can greatly reduce travel times between Connecticut and other cities. Sample train times to New Haven are as follows (shorter times are for high-speed express trains): 4.5–5 hours from Washington, D.C.; 3–3.5 hours from Philadelphia; 2–2.5 hours from Boston; 1.5–2 hours from Providence; and about 90 minutes from New York City.

## Commuter Rail

Making far more stops, and costing a bit less than Amtrak between New Haven and New York City's Grand Central Station (in Midtown, at 42nd St. between Lexington and Park Aves.), is the New Haven Line of **Metro-North** (800/638-7646, www.mta.nyc.ny.us). Metro-North also has spurs to Waterbury, Danbury, and New Canaan (where it was featured in the movie *The Ice Storm*). Virtually every town between New Haven and Greenwich—and each town on the Waterbury, Danbury, and New Canaan spurs—has at least one Metro-North stop. Sample travel times from Grand Central Station are about 45–60 minutes to Greenwich or Stamford, 75 minutes to Bridgeport, 100 minutes to New

Haven, 110 minutes to Danbury (requires a change at South Norwalk), and 140 minutes to Waterbury (requires a change at Bridgeport).

If you're planning to use a car where you're headed, consider taking the train to Stamford, which is served by Avis, Alamo, and Thrifty; or to Norwalk, which is served by Avis and Budget. New Haven and Bridgeport are additional options, although you might as well take the train to the nearest station to New York City. In general, car-rental rates are much lower in Connecticut than in New York City—and, you don't have to worry about driving a car in Manhattan, which can be nerve-wracking if you're not used to it.

A last option for using Metro-North is to use the Harlem Line, rather than the New Haven Line. This makes sense if you're going to rent a car and explore northern Fairfield County or the Litchfield Hills, as you can take the train to White Plains, which takes just 50 minutes from New York City. The White Plains station is served by Hertz, Budget, Avis, and National rental-car agencies, and then it's a relatively easy drive up I-684 to I-84 to reach Connecticut. (This route generally has less traffic and better scenery than the highways serving Stamford and other parts of Fairfield County, but it will put you farther from Coastal Connecticut). Or, if friends with a car can meet you at the train station, take the Harlem Line all the way up to its last stop, Brewster, New York (105 minutes), which puts you just 15 miles west of Danbury and quite close to Litchfield County. This station is served more frequently than Danbury's station, it does not require a change of trains (which Danbury does), and it's a very scenic train ride, at least north of White Plains.

Between New Haven and the towns east as far as New London (but with more frequent service as far east as Old Saybrook), you can train it via **Shore Line East** (800/255-7433, www.shorelineeast.com). This is strictly a commuter line: Trains run only in the morning and in the evening—there is no service on weekends or holidays.

## Excursion Trains

Connecticut has a few scenic rail and trolley tour companies, which are detailed in the regional

chapters. These are in Danbury, East Haven, East Windsor, Essex, and Waterbury.

## Interstate Bus Providers

If it has been a while since you traveled by bus, be prepared for a shock: Many improvements have been made, as there are movies shown and the rides are quite comfortable (and less expensive than Amtrak). Two interstate bus lines make stops in Connecticut. **Bonanza** (800/556-3815, www.bonanzabus.com) is a New England regional line with service to Bridgeport, Canaan, Cornwall Bridge, Danbury, Danielson, Falls Village, Farmington, Gaylordsville, Hartford, Kent, Manchester, New Milford, Southbury, Storrs, Waterbury, and Willimantic.

**Greyhound** (800/231-2222, www.greyhound.com) serves Bradley Airport, Bridgeport, Enfield, Farmington, Foxwoods Casino, Hartford, Meriden, Middletown, New Britain, New Haven, New London, Middletown, Stamford, and Suffield and makes connections nationwide.

## Intercity Bus Providers

Both fixed route and commuter express buses run throughout Connecticut. There are local bus districts all over the state (the more useful of which are detailed in individual chapters): Torrington/Northwest Connecticut, Greater Hartford (www.cttransit.com), Windham Region, Greater Waterbury (www.gwtd.org), Meriden (www.cityofmeriden.com/services/transit), Middletown, Danbury/Bethel/New Milford (www.hartct.org), Greater Stamford (www.cttransit.com), Norwalk (www.norwalktransit.com), Westport, Greater Bridgeport (www.gbtabus.com), Ansonia/Debry/Seymour/Shelton (http://electronicvalley.org/vtd), Milford, Greater New Haven (www.cttransit.com), Southeast Connecticut, and New Britain/Bristol (www.nbtrans.com).

Most of these bus services are practical solely for locals and commuters, but if you're resourceful and adventuresome, it is possible to see a good bit of the state by bus.

## Ferries

A number of ferry services connect Connecticut to Long Island, including one high-speed provider. These services reduce the time it takes to travel from New London to eastern Long Island from about five or six hours by car to as little as 90 minutes. It is always highly advisable to phone as far ahead as possible when considering ferry plans, as the summer weekend runs often fill up quickly, especially the automobile reservations.

Most Connecticut ferries leave from New London's ferry terminal, handily located by the city's Amtrak station, and run year-round to Orient Point (860/443-5281 or 631/323-2525, www.longislandferry.com); there are two kinds of ferries, the traditional car ferries that hold 22–120 cars and 130–1,000 passengers and take about 80 minutes, and the high-speed express passenger-only boats that carry up to 400 passengers (and no cars) and take just 40 minutes.

Other ferries from New London run to Fishers Island (a small resort island that is part of New York state but is just off the coast of New London), 860/443-6851 or 860/442-0165 or 631/788-7463, www.benkard.com/ferry. These auto ferries accommodate up to 250 passengers and operate year-round. In summer, from early June to early September, there is also ferry service from New London to Rhode Island's Block Island (401/783-4613, www.blockislandferry.com). Sailing time is two hours, and both pedestrians and motor vehicles are accommodated.

If traveling between central or western Connecticut and Long Island, considering crossing via the Bridgeport–Port Jefferson ferry (203/335-2040 or 631/473-0286 or 888/44-FERRY, www.bpjferry.com). This ferry, which tranports 90–100 automobiles year-round, carries 1,000 passengers in summer and 500 in winter. The ride takes 90 minutes, and the Connecticut terminal is in Bridgeport, a block from the municipal bus terminal and an easy walk from the city's Amtrak station.

Foxwoods Casino runs a high-speed, luxury ferry, **Fox Navigation,** 888/SAILFOX, www.fox-navigation.com, between the ferry terminal in New London and Glen Cove Ferry Terminal in Long Island, just east of New York City. The trip takes just two hours and 15 minutes. Service is mostly on weekends, but is more frequent during the summer season.

A new company, **SeaConn** (www.sea-conn.com), was as at press time planning to unveil high-speed passenger service that would run from New Haven to Manhattan. It's expected that this service will become available sometime in 2004.

There are also short passenger ferry crossings across the Connecticut River, one from **Chester to Hadlyme** and the other from **Glastonbury to Rocky Hill,** www.dot.state.ct.us.

## Airports

Connecticut is served by **Bradley International Airport** (888/624-1533, www.bradleyairport.com). New England's second-largest such facility, it's 12 miles north of downtown Hartford via I-91, exit 40. Bradley is served by 15 passenger airlines (including Air Canada Jazz, American, American Eagle, America West, Continental, Continental Express, Delta, Midwest Express, Northwest, Southwest, United, United Express, US Airways, and US Airways Express) with flights to virtually every major city in United States, as well as some service to Canada and the Caribbean. Popular cities served nonstop from Bradley include Atlanta, Cancun, Chicago, Dallas, Miami, Minneapolis, Montreal, Orlando, Phoenix, St. Louis, San Juan, Tampa, Toronto, and a number of additional cities in the Northeast and Mid-Atlantic regions. Unfortunately, you'll need to connect in a different city to reach the West Coast and a number of other major cities, including Denver, Houston, New Orleans, and Salt Lake.

Bradley is in the process of receiving a comprehensive $135 million expansion, which is ultimately expected to increase passenger capacity by 60 percent by 2010. These renovations are expected to attract even more major airlines to this airport, which is seen as an increasingly desirable alternative to the congested facilities in Boston and New York City. The first phase of construction saw the addition of more gates, new restaurants and shops, a huge new on-site parking garage, and better overall facilities. More than 6.8 million passengers walked through Bradley's gates in 2001, just under the record of more than 7 million in 2000. Even with all the changes,

Bradley remains a relatively small, hassle-free facility when compared with the congested, bigger airports in New York City and Boston.

Nevertheless, remember that parts of Connecticut are also within a 90-minute drive of the similarly pleasant and recently expanded Providence's T. F. Green Airport, as well as Boston's Logan Airport, New Jersey's Newark Airport, New York's Westchester and Stewart airports, and New York City's JFK and LaGuardia airports. It's easy enough to fly in via Hartford, but you may find that certain airlines offer better fares to some of the airports in neighboring states, which also sometimes offer the only nonstop flights to certain destinations.

Two smaller regional airports are also served by major airlines: **Groton/New London Airport** (860/445-8549, www.grotonnewlondonairport.com) on the state's southeastern coast, is served by US Airways Express (with daily service to Philadelphia). And **Tweed-New Haven Airport** (203/946-8285, www.tweednewhavenairport.com) is served by US Airways Express (with daily service to Philadelphia). For information on many smaller regional airports in the state, visit the DOT's airport website, www.dot.state.ct.us.

## Car-Rental Agencies

Major car rental agencies at Bradley International Airport include **Alamo** (860/292-5380 or 800/GO-ALAMO); **Avis** (860/627-3500 or 800/331-1212); **Budget** (860/627-3660 or 800/527-0700); **Dollar** (860/627-9048 or 800/800-4000); **Enterprise** (860/292-7061 or 800/325-8007); **Hertz** (860/627-3850 or 800/654-3131); **National** (860/627-3470 or 800/227-7368); and **Thrifty** (860/623-8214 or 800/367-2277).

## Transportation to and from the Airports

There are several ways to get from the airport to major towns. **Connecticut Limousine Service** (800/472-5466, www.ctlimo.com) offers many daily bus and van trips between Bridgeport, Danbury, Hartford, New Haven, and several other major Connecticut towns and cities to New York City's La Guardia and JFK airports, New Jersey's Newark Airport, and Bradley Airport. Tickets can be purchased at the terminals in each town or on the bus. You can either call Connecticut Limo directly or book by going to the ground transportation counter at the airport where you arrive. **Greyhound** (800/231-2222, www.greyhound.com) has direct service from Bradley to a number of cities in Connecticut. There are also several regional airport shuttles and limo services, which provide door-to-door service from Bradley to points throughout the state and many neighboring states. You can learn about these services by visiting the ground transportation desk at Bradley, or by visiting Bradley's online ground transportation link from www.bradleyairport.com.

The least expensive option is **Connecticut Transit** (860/522-8101, www.cttransit.com, which provides frequent service from Bradley to downtown Hartford.

# Information and Services

## PERSONAL SAFETY

### Crime

As with any part of the country that is densely populated, concerns about crime and traffic are germane to planning a trip to Connecticut.

Without generalizing, Nutmeggers have a reputation for being fairly aggressive on the roads and in a hurry to get from place to place—if you're driving in parts of the state that are unfamiliar to you and slowing down to read street numbers or admire the scenery, you will no doubt incur the wrath of the drivers behind you. It is a very good idea to pull off the road from time to time to allow others to pass you, whether you feel their rush is justified or not. There are few roads with passing lanes in this state of hilly and winding terrain, and you stand to gain nothing by inciting road rage in either yourself or other drivers. Whenever possible, back down and let the speed demons around you get by.

Crime is not a major concern in Connecticut, although random acts of both serious violent crime and petty theft are about as common in the state's urban areas as they are in New York City or Boston. In other words, most crime occurs in the rougher parts of town, well away from tourist attractions and the heart of downtown. It's a good idea when walking in Bridgeport, Hartford, New Haven, and Waterbury to keep your eyes forward and carry yourself discreetly, without shows of jewelry or cash. But the crime rate has dropped sharply in every major city in the state, just as it has elsewhere in the Northeast; virtually no community in Connecticut is so dicey that you shouldn't feel safe driving around and walking major thoroughfares.

If you have a cell phone, bring it along in the car with you, as it's always a comfort to know you can phone for help should you end up lost or with a disabled vehicle. In an emergency, you can reach the appropriate dispatcher by dialing 911. There are hospitals in every city and quite a few smaller regional hospitals in some of the more remote parts of the state—locations of these are given in the regional sections of the book.

### Hospitals and Health Care

Because of Connecticut's high population density, you're never terribly far from a hospital when you're in the Nutmeg State.

Some major hospitals and their contact information include: **Bridgeport Hospital** (267 Grant St., 203/384-3000, www.bridgeporthospital.org); **Charlotte Hungerford Hospital** (540 Litchfield St., Torrington, 860/496-6666, www.charlottesweb.hungerford.org); **Danbury Hospital** (24 Hospital Ave., 203/797-7000, www.danhosp.org); **Day Kimball Hospital** (320 Pomfret St., Putnam, 860/928-6541, www.hnne.org); **Greenwich Hospital** (5 Perryridge Rd., 203/863-3000, www.greenhosp.org); **Hartford Hospital** (80 Seymour St., 860/545-555, www.harthosp .org); **Lawrence & Memorial Hospital** (365 Montauk Ave., New London, 860/442-0711, www.lmhospital.org); **Manchester Memorial** (71 Haynes St., 860/646-1222, www.echn.org); **Middlesex Hospital** (28 Crescent St., Middletown, 860/344-6000, www.middlesexhealth.org); **Natchaug Hospital** (189 Storrs Rd., Mansfield Center, 860/426-7792, www.natchaug.org); **New Britain General Hospital** (100 Grand St., 860/224-5011, www.nbgh.org); **New Milford Hospital** (21 Elm St., 860/355-2611, www.new milfordhospital.org); **Norwalk Hospital** (24 Stevens St., 203/852-2000, www.norwalkhosp .org); **Sharon Hospital** (50 Hospital Rd., 860/364-4141, www.sharonhospital.org); **Stamford Hospital** (Shelburne Rd. and W. Broad St., 203/325-7000, www.stamhealth.org); **Waterbury Hospital** (64 Robbins St., 203/573-6000, www.waterburyhospital.org); **William W. Backus Hospital** (326 Washington St., Norwich, 860/889-8331, www.backushospital.org); **Windham Community Memorial Hospital** (112 Mansfield Ave., Willimantic, 860/456-9116, www.windhamhospital.org); **Yale-New Haven Hospital** (20 York St., 203/688-2000, www.ynhh.org).

## Pharmacies

You'll find pharmacies, many of them open until 9 or 10 P.M., throughout Connecticut, the only exceptions being the more remote towns in the Northwest and Northeast parts of the state, as well as in the Lower Connecticut River Valley. The leading chain in Connecticut is **CVS** (888/607-4287, www.cvs.com). CVS Pharmacies open 24 hours are found in Ansonia, Bridgeport, Bristol, Fairfield, Groton, New Britain, Norwalk, Riverside (Greenwich), Southington, Stamford, Vernon, Waterbury, West Hartford, Westport, and Wethersfield.

## Travel Insurance

Purchasing travel insurance makes sense if you've invested a great deal in a trip with prepaid accommodations, airfare, and other services, especially if you have any reason to be concerned about your ability to make the trip—perhaps impending medical concerns (check, however, the fine print regarding pre-existing conditions). It's a good idea to purchase insurance from a major provider, such as **Access America** (800/346-9265, www.etravelprotection.com), or **Travel Guard International** (800/826-1300, www.travelguard.com). Typically, these policies can cover unexpected occurrences, such as trip cancellations, interruptions, and delays, as well as medical expenses incurred during your travels.

## Water Safety

As Connecticut is a likely spot for activities on the water, it's a good idea to supervise children and exercise caution when boating, swimming, or even fishing. Common sense applies here—use life vests and or other floating devices whenever possible, avoid swimming in areas that don't have lifeguards (the case at many of the state's smaller beaches), and observe local regulations concerning boating, sailing, and fishing (see also Fishing and Hunting, and Taking to the Water, above). Shark attacks have never occurred in Connecticut waters, which are also mostly free from other dangerous creatures, including jellyfish

Motion sickness can be a serious, and sometimes unexpected, problem for passengers on boats. If you're at all concerned about this, or you've had bouts with seasickness in the past, consider taking Dramamine, Bonine, or another over-the-counter drug before setting sail. You may even want to consult with a physician before your trip, especially if you're interested in the Transderm Scop patch, which slowly releases medication into your system to prevent seasickness, but is not without potential side effects. In general, try to avoid sailing on an empty stomach or on too little sleep, keep your eyes on the horizon, and avoid reading or focusing intently on anything that's small or moving with the rock of the boat. Stick as close as possible to the center of a ship, and consider staying above deck (if weather permits), as breathing fresh air often helps.

## Wildlife Encounters

Connecticut, because it has relatively few truly wild areas, presents few threats in terms of encounters you might have with dangerous or menacing animals. However, the northern reaches of Litchfield County, parts of the Northeast corner, and even some areas of Fairfield County and the Lower Connecticut River Valley are remote enough to attract bears, coyotes, rattlesnakes and copperheads, and even bobcats and moose. Do keep in mind that rabies is a relatively rare but persistent problem statewide, occurring most often in skunks, opossums, raccoons, and other mostly nocturnal animals. This is a disease that can actually make an otherwise harmless animal bite at will, and should you ever come into any physical contact with such a creature, you should immediately contact an emergency physician.

Insects can be a problem in summer, but fortunately the state is without the nasty black flies that so commonly ruin the days of late spring in colder northern New England climes. Do watch out for ticks, however, and also be alert to the recent spread of West Nile Virus throughout the United States, carried by mosquitoes and birds; Connecticut has reported some cases of West Nile Virus in birds, mosquitos, and in a handful of cases, human beings. If you feel at all feverish or sick after having been nibbled on by mosquitoes, and this condition persists, it's a good idea to consult with a physician.

# LYME DISEASE

It's well-documented that southeastern New England has one of the highest per-square-mile deer populations of any human-settled area in the country, and it is the close proximity of deer with human beings that has contributed to the painfully debilitating disease named for the small Connecticut town in which it was first diagnosed: Lyme disease. It was around 1975 that Yale–New Haven Hospital's Section of Rheumatology first diagnosed this strange bacterial disease that was causing severe arthritic pain in people of all ages.

Evidence finally linked the victims to bites from infinitesimal deer ticks carrying spiral-shaped bacterium called spirochete—although identified in New England, Lyme disease was actually carried to the United States from Europe some time during the early part of the 20th century, according to speculation. Symptoms vary considerably from victim to victim, and one common problem is delayed diagnosis—the longer you go without treating this problem, the more severe its effects.

In most cases, a victim of Lyme disease will exhibit a red-ring–shaped rash around the bite from the deer tick. The rash somewhat resembles a little bull's eye, and will appear anywhere from a week to many weeks after the incident. Flu-like symptoms often follow—fever, achy joints, and swelling—and if the disease is left untreated for more than a couple of months, chronic arthritis may set in. Lyme disease may also attack the nervous system, causing a loss or reduction of motor skills, severe headaches, paralysis of some facial muscles, and general fatigue—and in somewhat rare cases, patients have also developed heart problems. This is in no way a disease to be taken lightly.

Unfortunately, testing for Lyme disease is a sketchy business at best, as no definitive method has yet been developed. Doctors typically rely on a series of blood tests, and more often than that rely simply on observation of various symptoms. Research is currently underway to come up with new and more reliable tests. In the meantime, you should consult with your healthcare provider the second you develop any of the symptoms outlined above—especially if you've been spending time in areas where ticks, and deer, are commonplace, such as wooded terrain, meadows, and coastal scrub.

**deer tick**

When spending time in areas where tick infestation is a problem, wear long-sleeved clothing and slacks, tuck your pant-legs into your boots and/or socks, apply tick and insect repellent generously, and check yourself carefully for signs of ticks or bites. It's a good idea to don light-colored clothing, as you'll have an easier time sighting ticks, which are dark. Remember that the more commonly found wood ticks do not carry the disease, and that deer ticks are extremely small—about the size of a pinhead.

Should you be found to carry the disease, you'll most likely be treated with a fairly standard round of antibiotics, such as doxycycline, and amoxicillin. And if you're diagnosed early enough, these treatments will, in most cases, do the job. Research over the past few years has also led to some vaccines, both for human beings and for certain animals (dogs, horses, etc.). These vaccines vary in their availability and their suitability for different types of patients, and it's best to speak with your doctor if you're curious about whether you'd make a good candidate. In any case, the vaccines are purely preventative, and they will not help you once you're infected with the disease.

BOB RACE

ON THE ROAD

# SPECIAL INTERESTS

## Gay and Lesbian Travelers

The Hartford-based biweekly, **Metro Line** (860/233-8334, www.metroline-online.com), is the region's main gay and lesbian newspaper, with nightlife listings and local news and listings. Serving all of New England, but with specific coverage of Rhode Island, is Boston-based *In Newsweekly* (617/426-8246, www.innewsweekly.com). This publication is free and distributed at most of the state's several gay bars, certain bookstores, and a few restaurants.

Close to such gay-popular vacation spots as Fire Island (New York), Northampton (Massachusetts), Ogunquit (Maine), and Provincetown (Massachusetts), and several major cities with visible and vibrant gay neighborhoods, Connecticut is a relatively progressive and accepting state when it comes to gay issues. Discrimination on the basis of sexual orientation is illegal (as it is on the basis of race, religion, gender, or age), and the vast majority of the restaurants, hotels, inns, and businesses in the state are quite accustomed to, and comfortable with, the presence of same-sex couples.

In addition to bars and clubs with a specifically and predominantly gay following, there are several restaurants covered in this book with an especially pronounced gay following, including the Bistro (New Milford), Bloodroot Caf– (Bridgeport), Claire's (New Haven), Emerald City Café (Bethel), and G. W. Tavern (Washington). Bloodroot is also a bookstore.

## Senior Citizens

Connecticut is less famous as a destination among senior travelers than Cape Cod or certain parts of coastal Maine, which draw many visitors in their senior years, but it's definitely a place where all travelers, no matter their age, will not feel out of place. Connecticut is a highly family-friendly state, and as multigenerational travel has become an increasingly popular trend—grandparents traveling with grandkids, or several generations of families vacationing together—the state's most family-oriented areas, such as coastal Connecticut, have become popular for such groups of travelers.

Depending on the attraction or hotel, you may qualify for certain age-related discounts—the thresholds can range from 50 to 65. It can also help if you're a member of the **American Association of Retired Persons**, or AARP (800/424-3410, www.aarp.org). For a nominal annual membership fee, you'll receive all sorts of travel discounts as well as a newsletter that often touches on travel issues. **Elderhostel** (877/426-8056, www.elderhostel.org) organizes a wide variety of educationally oriented tours and vacations geared toward 55-and-over individuals or couples of whom one member is that age.

## Students

New Haven is one of the most student-friendly big cities in New England, whether you're actually studying there or visiting from another place. Especially along Chapel Street and around the New Haven Green, you'll find cafés, shops, and other businesses catering toward, and sometimes run by, area students. You'll also find all kinds of resources and like-minded and like-aged company at the libraries and student unions of Yale, Connecticut College, UConn (and the other University of Connecticut branches in Danbury, Groton, New Haven, Stamford, Torrington, and Waterbury), Trinity, Wesleyan, University of Hartford, Quinnipiac, Fairfield University, and other schools across the state.

**STA Travel** (9 Whitney Ave., New Haven, 800/836-4115, www.statravel.com) caters to student travelers and is a great resource when you're looking for good deals. Connecticut has one youth hostel, operated by **American Youth Hostel Inc., Yankee Council** (181 Broad St., Windsor, CT 06095, 860/683-2847, www.hiayh.org). The hostel is in Hartford's West End at 131 Tremont St., 860/523-7255.

Many Connecticut museums and attractions offer student discounts; always bring your university or school I.D. card with you, and ask even if such reduced prices or admissions aren't posted.

## Travelers with Children

Connecticut is an excellent, if not quite stellar, state for families and travelers with children. Amusement parks, children's museums, science centers, and other attractions geared toward kids and families are set evenly along the shoreline and in the Connecticut River Valley. Less appropriate are the northwest and northeast corners of the state, where romantic adult-oriented inns and restaurants predominate, although you'll still find plenty of kid-friendly things to do and places to stay even in these areas.

The state's cities have some of the best family attractions, especially places like Bridgeport (with a zoo, the P.T. Barnum Museum, and the Museum, plus minor league sports stadiums), Danbury (Military Museum of Southern New England and the Danbury Railway Museum) and Norwalk, with the Maritime Aquarium and a new children's museums. Other towns with children's museums include Manchester, Middletown, New Haven, New Britain, and Niantic. Other attractions around the state include Mystic Seaport, the Bruce Museum in Greenwich, the Stamford Museum and Nature Center, the Shore Line Trolley Museum in East Haven, the Mashantucket Pequot Museum by Foxwoods, the New England Air Museum in Bradley Airport, the Connecticut Trolley Museum in East Windsor, the Mark Twain Museum in Hartford, and the Science Museum of Connecticut in West Hartford.

*The hands-down capital of family travel in Connecticut . . . is the shoreline, especially east of New Haven.*

The hands-down capital of family travel in Connecticut, however, is the shoreline, especially east of New Haven. From here to the Rhode Island border you'll find great beaches, miniature golf and amusement parks, events tailored toward kids, and family-friendly accommodations (such as midpriced motels and hotels with efficiency and other kitchen units, and also a vast selection of cottage rentals).

Many chain hotels and other accommodations throughout Connecticut allow kids to stay in their parents' rooms free or at a discount, and many restaurants in the state have kids' menus. You'll also find a number of clam shacks and ice-cream stands, especially in the state's coastal regions. Also fear not if you're headed to a seafood house with finicky kids who aren't wild about fish or clams—it's the very rare restaurant that

doesn't offer a few chicken, burger, or grilled cheese options. Many museums and other attractions offer greatly reduced admission.

## Travelers with Disabilities

Connecticut is on par with other Northeastern states in the degree to which establishments conform to the guidelines set by the American's with Disabilities Act's (ADA). With new hotels, larger and recently built restaurants, and most major attractions, you can expect to find wheelchair-accessible restrooms, entrance ramps, and other necessary specifications. But Connecticut has many hole-in-the-wall cafés, historic house-museums with narrow staircases or uneven thresholds, tiny B&Bs, and other buildings that are not easily accessible to persons using wheelchairs. If you're traveling with a guide animal, always call ahead and even consider getting written or faxed permission to bring one with you to a particular hotel or even restaurant; it's the rare instance in Connecticut when you won't be permitted to arrive with a guide dog.

A useful resource is the **Society for the Advancement of Travel for the Handicapped** (212/447-7284, www.sath.org).

# MONEY
## Banks, ATMs, and Credit Cards

Banks are plentiful throughout Connecticut, although fewer and farther between in the handful of rural areas. Finding a bank that's open in a rural area may require looking around a bit. Most banks are open weekdays from 9 A.M. until anywhere between 3 and 5 P.M., and on Saturdays 9 A.M.–noon.

ATMs (Automated Teller Machines) are abundant in Connecticut; most of those found at banks are open 24 hours and accept a wide range of bank cards (typically Cirrus and/or Plus, for example) and credit cards. You'll also find ATMs in airports and at many bus and train stations, in many convenience stores and gas stations (especially larger ones that keep late hours), hotel lobbies, and increasingly in some bars and taverns. ATMs typically charge a fee ranging from about $1 to $2, unless you use a bank card issued by the bank whose ATM you're using. While crime is not a huge problem in Connecticut, you should exercise discretion—especially if you're alone—when using ATM machines late at night, especially in urban areas. Walk away and choose a different machine if you see anybody suspicious lurking nearby or actually loitering inside the vestibule in which the machine is located, and never leave your car unlocked and running while you step out to use the machine.

Credit cards and—increasingly—bank cards are acceptable forms of payment at virtually all gas stations and hotels, many inns and B&Bs (but definitely not some of the very small ones, which will take traveler's checks and sometimes personal checks), most restaurants (the exceptions tend to be inexpensive places, small cafés, diners, and the like), and most shops (again, the exception tends to be small, independent stores). Never assume that any shop accepts credit cards.

## Currency

Connecticut receives very few international visitors traveling directly from their countries of origin—in Hartford, flights are handled only from Canada and a couple of Caribbean nations. Therefore, currency exchange booths and services are limited in the state. It's best to make these changes in whatever city you fly into from your country of origin. Connecticut is far enough south of Canada that Canadian currency is not generally accepted in the state.

Currency exchange rates may change during the lifetime of this book, but here are a few very approximate samples from some major English-speaking nations: one British pound equals about US$1.60; $1 Canadian equals about US$.65; $1 Australian equals about US$.55; $1 New Zealand equals about US$.52; and one Euro equals about US$1.15.

## Costs

Depending on where in the state you visit, travel costs in Connecticut can be as expensive as some of the most costly U.S. cities, such as Boston or New York City, or as inexpensive as many average-priced destinations. Compared with other parts of the United States, no area of Connecticut could be called inexpensive.

Fairfield County has some of the highest hotel rates in New England, with rooms at top properties easily exceeding $250 nightly. However, if you search a bit, or consider some of the chain properties out in neighboring counties, you can find rooms as low as $50 per night. Restaurants are pricey in Fairfield County, and increasingly so in New Haven and some of the trendier parts of Litchfield County—but you can also find a number of independent and chain eateries with rates similar to those in the Northeast (in general, perhaps 10–20 percent more costly than the average U.S. region). In wealthy towns, like Greenwich, Westport, and New Canaan, you can expect restaurant prices to mirror those in New York City.

In general, much of Connecticut is priced similarly to the rest of southern New England, with low-end chains charging as little (but rarely less than) $50 or $60 nightly, and better-class properties charging as much as $200 per night.

Shopping in Connecticut is not markedly more or less than in other parts of New England, although you'll find some very pricey, upscale boutiques and galleries Fairfield County, some of the other fancy towns along the shore, and some parts of Litchfield. Connecticut has the highest gas tax in the nation, so gas stations tend to be very expensive here.

Connecticut's sales tax is 6 percent.

## Tipping

Tipping practices are fairly constant and widely observed in the tipping-oriented United States, but in larger cities and especially in the more urbanized Northeast, people customarily tip slightly higher than the national average, especially at restaurants and hotels. This means that you might want to edge toward the higher end of the usual 15 to 20 percent range that Americans use to tip waiters at restaurants, obviously factoring in the level of service you receive. You might round up your change or leave as much as $1 when ordering a drink at a bar or a cup of espresso at a coffeehouse (some coffeehouses and cafés have "tip jars" on their counters and appreciate, but don't necessarily expect, you to drop in a little change). If you're ordering multiple drinks, tip more along the lines of 15 percent for the total bill. At nightclubs, the theater, or other places with this service, tip the coat-check staff $1 per coat or bag.

Tip taxi drivers and hairstylists 15 to 20 percent. At hotels, tip parking valets $1 or $2 each time they retrieve your car; tip bellhops 50 cents to $1 per bag; and leave $1 or $2 for hotel housecleaning staff in your room. If the concierge performs any special tasks for you, tip $5 to $10. Room-service gratuities are typically built into the total bill, so leaving an additional tip is unnecessary and should only be done at your discretion; tip the local pizza or other food delivery person who brings dinner to your hotel room $2 or $5 depending on the total bill. At small inns and B&Bs, it's customary to leave somewhat more than this for cleaning and other staff. You may find an envelope left in your room especially for the purpose of tipping the staff. There's no real consensus about what to leave at small properties, but aim for a minimum of $2–3 per day, $5–10 per day if you received a great deal of personal service (such as help with sightseeing and restaurant reservations) or stayed in an especially luxurious suite that required lots of cleaning. At small B&Bs that are cleaned and serviced by the owners themselves, it is not necessary or even appropriate to leave a tip.

If you use the services of an individual tour guide, consider tipping 10 to 15 percent of the total cost. The practice varies greatly on package tours, but drivers and guides generally expect to receive anywhere from several to $10 per person per day, unless gratuities have already been included in the total price of the tour.

## MEDIA

Connecticut has nearly 150 newspapers, a dozen TV stations, and roughly 80 radio stations. Additionally, you'll find a number of local magazines and periodicals covering individual regions within the state.

*Connecticut Magazine* (203/380-6600, www.connecticutmag.com) is a fine monthly; especially fun are Elise Maclay's dining commentary and Julie Wilson's travel pieces. A journalist named Pat Grandjean regularly writes about local personalities and seems always to have the latest scoop on who lives where.

*Fairfield Weekly* (203/406-2406, www.fairfieldweekly.com) is a free arts and entertainment alternative newsweekly, with highly iconoclastic and often very funny news coverage; the scoop on clubs, music, the gay scene, and eating out; loads of personals and useful classifieds; fiery letters to the editor, and other good clean fun. It's published by New Mass Media, which also publishes the *Hartford Advocate* (860/548-9300, www.hartfordadvocate.com) and the *New Haven Advocate* (203/789-0010, www.newhavenadvocate.com). All of these papers use similar formats and are quite excellent.

*Litchfield County Times Monthly* (860/355-4141) is filled with features about antiquing, local celebs and important people, restaurant news, and other information as helpful for locals as it is for tourists. If you have even an ancillary interest in this region, it's worth subscribing.

The website **www.ctnow.com** contains content from most of the above publications, as well as from the *Hartford Courant*; it's an indispensable resource packed with local and state news, dining reviews, events listings, and other useful information.

## COMMUNICATION
### Phones and Area Codes

Connecticut has two main area codes: most of Fairfield and New Haven Counties retain the original 203 code, while the majority of the rest of the state uses 860. A few towns along the border counties are exceptions to this rule. Two new area overlay codes were added in 2000—475 works within the area served by 203, and 959 works within the area served by 860. However, thus far, relatively few numbers have been issued with these new codes. When dialing within your local calling region, it's unnecessary to use the area code (except when calling from one area code to another, in which case—if it's a local call—you must dial the area code but you do not dial "1" first). Outside your local calling region, you need to first dial 1 and the area code, even if you're calling within the same area code. For directory assistance, dial 411 (there's a charge for this call, typically 50 to 75 cents).

In this book, the local telephone number, where there is one, always precedes any possible toll-free number. Note too that toll-free numbers may have area codes of 800, 866, 877, or 888.

Pay phones generally charge $.50 for local calls, and they also add a $.25 surcharge for calls placed collect or using a calling card. Most hotels charge a $.50–1.50 surcharge for local calls, toll-free calls, or just about any other kind of call placed from their phones. Long-distance rates are outrageous at many hotels, and it's generally a good idea—if you don't already have a cell phone with an economical calling plan—to use your own calling card or buy a prepaid one. The latter are available at many convenience stores and gas stations, and at a wide range of prices. If you're a member of Costco, Sam's Club, or another wholesale discount store, consider buying one of the prepaid Sprint, MCI, or AT&T phone cards sold at these stores—often you can find cards that end up costing just two or three cents per minute.

## Cellular Phones

Cell phones increasingly have become a way of life in the United States, and relatively few frequent travelers go anywhere without them. If you're a subscriber to one of the nation's major networks, such as Sprint PCS, T-Mobile, Verizon, or AT&T, you'll find full coverage throughout most of Connecticut. Patches of the state where coverage is limited or unavailable tend to be the least populated parts of Litchfield and Putnam counties, a few northern reaches of Fairfield County, and some rural areas in the eastern half of the state. Virtually every city, the entire coastline and Connecticut River Valley, and most of the region around Southeastern Connecticut (near Mystic and the Casinos) are covered. Even in rural areas, you should have no trouble receiving the more expensive "roaming" service.

For now, it's legal to jabber away on your cell phone while driving, but it's not a good idea, especially if you're unfamiliar with where you're

going. When possible, try to pull off to the side of the road; if traveling on a multilane highway, try to stay in the right and center lane and drive defensively if you must talk on your cell phone. And even if you're not speaking on your phone, be aware of drivers around you who are. Some states and cities in the United States have banned cell phone use while driving, and the trend seems to be in this direction. You can, legally, circumvent this trend by purchasing a hands-free attachment, which allows you to talk on your cell phone while driving without having actually to hold the phone.

You can avoid the ire of those around you by either turning off your phone, or setting its volume to "off" or "vibrate," when in restaurants, hotel lobbies, shops, and other confined spaces. Do not talk on your cell phone in libraries or fancy restaurants, and avoid doing so in general when you're in shops or even fast-food or seemingly casual venues. If you must do so, try to keep the call short and speak quietly.

## Internet Services and Computers

There are an increasing number of places throughout the United States, especially in fairly urbanized states like Connecticut, where you can check the Internet—even some airport pay phones are now providing this service. The best, and most convenient, place to check email and surf the Web is the public library; there's one in virtually every Connecticut town, although only those in larger communities tend to have public computers. Libraries at Connecticut's several universities and colleges are also open to the public, but their policies vary regarding computer use; some only allow computer access to students, faculty, and staff. Libraries generally allow you to use their computers for short periods, ranging from 15–60 minutes.

A handful of cafés around the state have pay Internet stations, as does **Kinko's**, which has branches in Fairfield (1427 Post Rd., 203/319-0500), Farmington (1599 Southeast Rd., 860/561-3900), Glastonbury (175 Glastonbury Blvd., Suite 3, 860/657-9797), Greenwich (48 W. Putnam Ave., 203/863-0099), Hartford (544 Farmington Ave., 860/233-8245; and 196 Trumbull St., 860/246-0202), New Haven (55 Church St., 203/777-5725), Norwalk (596

Westport Ave., 203/847-7004; 464 Main Ave., 203/847-8143; and 777 Connecticut Ave., 203/299-1616), Orange (400 Boston Post Rd., 203/799-2679), Shelton (707 Bridgeport Ave., 203/944-9600), and Stamford (980 Highridge Rd., 203/968-8100; and 81 Summer St., 203/357-1100); it's open 24 hours. Kinko's is an excellent traveler's business and work resource, as it's also a place to make copies, buy some office supplies, use Federal Express and other shipping services, and rent time on computers.

If you're traveling with your laptop and looking to go online from your hotel, keep a few things in mind. First, check with your Internet Service Provider (ISP) about how to access them from outside your local area; if it's a local provider, you'll most likely have to call long-distance from another part of the world. Some ISPs issue toll-free numbers or have local access numbers in other regions. Major U.S. ISPs (such as Earthlink and America Online) have several local access numbers in Connecticut. If you subscribe to one of these providers, you'll probably be able to access them making a local call in Bridgeport, Cornwall, Danbury, Deep River, Fairfield, Greenwich, Groton, Hartford, Harwinton, Ledyard, Middletown, Moodus, New Britain, New Haven, New London, Norwalk, Norwich, Old Saybrook, Putnam, Southington, Stamford, Torrington, Waterbury, Westport, and Wolcott. This covers virtually all of the state's local calling areas, but you may have trouble making a local connection in a few remote parts of Litchfield and Putnam counties.

These days, it's easy to plug your laptop computer into the phone jack at virtually any motel or hotel, whether they have phones with dedicated data ports or not. It's a good idea to bring your own phone cord and cord "coupler," which enables you to extend an existing hotel-room phone cord on the chance that it's very short or inconveniently located. Additionally, some of the major midrange and upscale hotel chains now offer high-speed Internet service—for a daily noon–noon fee (often $8–10), you'll enjoy unlimited high-speed access. This service generally works on any recent-model laptop with either a USB port or an Ethernet port (cables are typically provided in the hotel rooms, but to be perfectly safe, you might want to bring your own).

If logging on using your laptop is important to you, ask about phone policies before booking a room at a B&B or small inn. It's usually not an issue if you have a phone in your room, but in smaller places, more than one guest room may be sharing a line, which means that you won't be able to log on for long periods without inconveniencing fellow guests. Some inns have only a common phone, and innkeepers are often very accommodating of guests who wish to log onto the Internet using their laptops if it's just a brief call—but if you're planning to be online a great deal, it's best to avoid staying at properties that don't offer in-room phones.

## VISITOR INFORMATION

In fall 2003, Connecticut consolidated its 11 tourist districts into 5, each of which has its own offices, brochures, and staff. It's wise to work directly with these offices when planning a trip to a specific area within the state—contact information for these offices is given in the appropriate chapters throughout the book. In many cases, the towns that make up a particular section of this book fall into more than one of the aforementioned tourism regions, meaning you may want to call two or three local offices to best plan out your itinerary and cull advice on upcoming events, attractions, and such.

The statewide information bureau is the **Office of Tourism, Connecticut Department of Economic and Community Development** (505 Hudson St., Hartford, CT 06106, 800/CT-BOUND, www.tourism.state.ct.us), which will send you a free 175-page travel planner on the state and can also book hotel rooms. A backup resource if you have further general questions that can't be answered by the regional tourist boards is the **Connecticut Lodging Association** (731 Hebron Ave., Glastonbury, CT 06033, 860/657-2259, www.ctlodgingassoc.com).

A number of visitor centers are located throughout the state; some are unstaffed, and others are open only seasonally (Memorial Day

ON THE ROAD

through Columbus Day). These all contain an array of brochures and range from quite helpful to not very—they're nice in a pinch or for basic questions, but you're always better off phoning ahead and obtaining local brochures and advice from the extremely useful regional boards.

## Business Hours

Most restaurants in either urban or suburban parts of the state serve lunch from 11 A.M. or noon–2 or 3 P.M. and dinner from 5 or 6 P.M.–10 P.M. In some of the more rural parts of the state, especially the northeast and northwest sections, expect lunch to end by 2 P.M. and dinner by 9 P.M. The post office is usually open 8 A.M.–5 P.M. on weekdays and also on Saturday mornings.

There's no reliable rule for typical shop hours, except that they seem to be getting gradually longer over time, to the point that major chain shops and stores in big shopping malls often stay open from 9 or 10 A.M.–9 or 10 P.M., typically with shorter hours on Sundays. Local, independently operated boutiques and shops often don't open until late morning (especially in resort areas), and they often close by 5 or 6 P.M.; these same shops may not open at all on Sundays, or even on Mondays or Tuesdays. In some densely populated areas you'll be able to find 24-hour full-service grocery stores, and 24-hour gas stations and convenience stores are found in several parts of the state, especially near highway exits off major Interstates. Because shop hours vary so greatly, it's important to phone ahead if you're concerned about a particular business being open when you arrive.

Also see Museums and Attractions, near the front of this chapter, for advice on their general hours and admission policies.

## Electricity

The standard in Connecticut and the rest of the United States and Canada is AC, 110 volts/60 cycles. Plugs have two flat, parallel prongs.

## Time Zone

Like the rest of New England, Connecticut falls entirely within the Eastern Standard Time (EST) zone, as is true all along the U.S. Eastern Seaboard. Chicago is an hour behind, Los Angeles three hours behind. The Canadian Maritimes are an hour ahead; London, England is five hours ahead; and Israel is seven hours ahead.

Remember that hours behind and ahead are affected by the fact that Connecticut, like most American states and Canadian Provinces, observes Eastern Daylight Time (EDT): on the last Sunday in October, clocks are set back one hour through the first Sunday in April, when they are set ahead an hour.

## When to Go

Keeping in mind special events and festivals that may influence your travel plans, Connecticut is generally a year-round destination. If you're planning to take advantage of the state's vast access to the water, whether it be in the form of boating or beachcombing, you may want to focus your visit around the warmest months, generally from mid-May through mid-October, but especially from mid-June through Labor Day. Keep in mind, however, that in seaside vacations towns like Mystic, Stonington, and Madison, you'll be competing with throngs of other sea-lovers for space and parking at the beach, a table at restaurants, and hotel rooms. These can be very crowded and very expensive times to visit the state's coastal regions. In recent years, coastal areas have made more of an effort to attract off-season visitors. Some museums have begun keeping longer winter hours, and many hotels and other organizations now offer special rates and deals in the off-season. This can be a pleasant time to tour coastal Connecticut, as the crowds are at a minimum.

Summer is also popular for inland Connecticut, especially in the Quiet Corner and Litchfield Hills, whose higher elevations and pastoral scenery can feel very appealing during the hottest months, especially to urban dwellers. But fall, especially the six weeks from Labor Day through mid-October, is the most visited time in the hilly, scenic interior, as droves of leaf-peepers attack the countryside, cameras in hand. Country Inns and even highway-side chain motels fill up quickly during these times.

Connecticut's cities can be appealing any time of year, and where colleges affect the social vibe, such as in New Haven and even in Middletown, fall through spring is ideal, as the influx of students livens up the restaurant, nightlife, and arts scenes. Winters are not brutally cold in coastal Connecticut, but can get quite chilly—and snowy—in the upper elevations of Litchfield County and the Quiet Corner. Then, of course, a different breed of traveler comes to Connecticut—the type who loves snuggling up before a roaring fire in the den of a bed-and-breakfast, and snowshoeing or cross-country skiing across the rolling terrain.

For others, the most bewitching and scenic season in Connecticut is spring, when the entire state is abloom with greenery and flowers. Many museums, parks, and public gardens flourish during these months, or offer special garden-themed tours.

## What to Pack

Packing for a trip to Connecticut is not unlike planning for any other trip in Southern New England, or to any city or town with a four-season climate—just remember that certain rules apply to visitors heading to the sea. This is a small, somewhat industrialized state with relatively few opportunities for true wilderness hiking and camping, so unless you're planning a very specific adventure of this kind, it's not necessary to think much in terms of advanced camping gear. Also, virtually nowhere in the state are you very far from almost any kind of household, clothing, food, or travel supply—distances in Connecticut between gas stations, grocery stores, and department stores are very short. The only exceptions would be the northwest and northeast corners of the state, where it's a good idea to stock up on necessities, as you may find yourself a half-hour's drive from the nearest big grocery or department store.

Winters are not as brutally cold here as they are in northern New England, but it can snow as early as late October and as late as April (or even in early May, though rarely). So, especially when visiting during the spring or fall, prepare for a wide range of weather conditions. You may need shorts and short-sleeve shirts in October or April, or you might want to bundle up at these times, too.

If you're headed toward the shore, as so many vacationers to Connecticut are, consider toting along the kinds of clothing and shoes that are ideal for beachcombing and boating, such as sandals, swimwear, and windbreakers (even in summer, as it can be very cool if you're out on the water sailing). Also, while it's easy to find sunscreen and other conveniences at shops all throughout the shore towns, it's more economical to bring these supplies yourself. Sunscreen, film, and other supplies cost much more at small, beachside convenience stores than they might in big grocery or discount department stores back home.

# The Connecticut Coast

The roughly 100 miles of shoreline between Greenwich and Stonington contain the vast majority of the state's most-visited attractions, restaurants, and hotels—for many visitors, this jagged band of beaches and small cities is reason alone to visit. Like the Connecticut River Valley, the coastal points were settled by Europeans starting in the late 1630s, and already comprised a number of significant-sized communities by the time of the Revolutionary War. It's no surprise that today, few areas along the shore have been left undeveloped, and traffic on the region's main thoroughfares is correspondingly thick and congested much of the time.

Fortunately, permanently protected preserves span parts of the shore, helping to make up for the relative lack of beaches that welcome nonresidents (at least during the summer months). You're also never far from wooded state parks and quieter inland villages, even when you're standing in the heart of the region's most densely populated cities.

But crowds clearly define this part of the state, and many visitors enjoy the buzz of lobster shacks, the body-saturated beaches, and lively shopping districts that dot the coastline. Several sizable cities, including Stamford, Bridgeport, New Haven, and Groton/New London, interrupt the long stretches of suburbia—wealthy and exclusive from Greenwich to Fairfield, unpretentious and modest from Stratford to West Haven, dense with vacation homes and seafood restaurants from Branford to Waterford, and rich with maritime history from Mystic to Stonington.

If tranquility is more your scene, don't rule out a tour of the shoreline during the off-season—a time that can be rewarding

New London beachfront

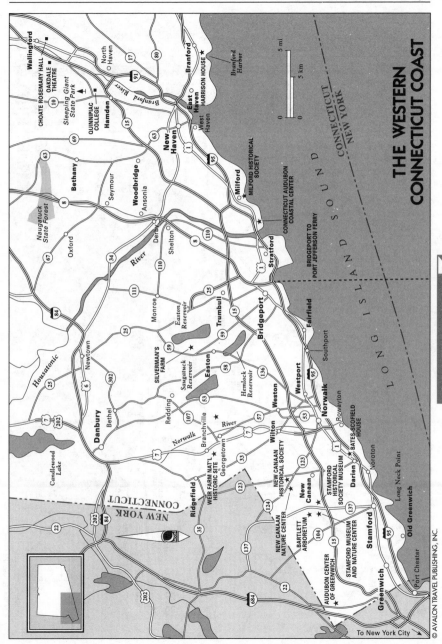

THE WESTERN CONNECTICUT COAST

N THE CONNECTICUT COAST

© AVALON TRAVEL PUBLISHING, INC.

THE CONNECTICUT COAST

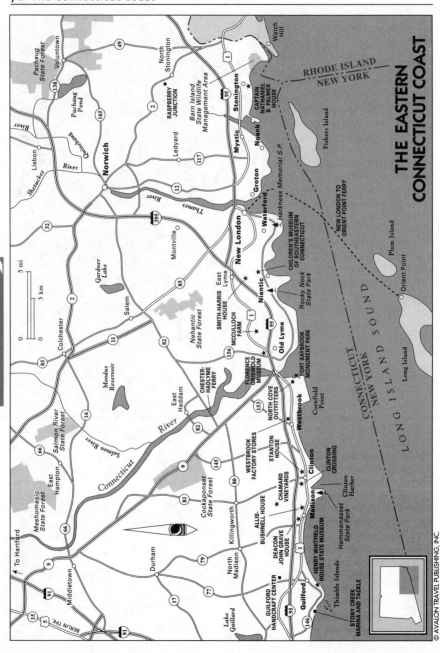

THE EASTERN CONNECTICUT COAST

© AVALON TRAVEL PUBLISHING, INC.

not only because you're apt to encounter fewer fellow travelers, but also because prices come down at restaurants and hotels, and the blustery weather makes it a fine time to curl up before a fire in an old captain's mansion-turned-B&B, or to sup on a steaming bowl of bouillabaisse at a convivial French bistro. The cities, as well as the commuter towns in Fairfield County, are less seasonal than areas like Mystic, Old Lyme, and Madison, and you'll find a number of important year-round museums, performing arts venues, and shopping districts in those areas.

## A FEW PRACTICALITIES
### Media
The **New Haven Advocate** (203/789-0010, www.newhavenadvocate.com), like its siblings in Hartford and Fairfield County, offers the 411 on local dining, the club scene, and all kinds of cultural events—plus plenty of flip commentary.

### Tours
**Downtown New Haven** walking tours leave from outside the Yale Visitor Information Center (149 Elm St., 203/432-2302, www.yale.edu/visitor/core.html), and focus squarely on the his-

toric green and the many important buildings near and on campus. Tours depart weekdays at 10:30 A.M. and 2 P.M., and on weekends at 1:30 P.M..

### Getting There
Traffic-jammed East–West I-95 (where it's marked "I-95 North," it runs in an easterly direction across the shore, and where it's marked "I-95 South," it really runs west) is the region's major limited access highway. Busy U.S. 1 also runs along the coast, but has few stretches where the speed limit exceeds 35 miles per hour (and is, for the most part, heinous-looking). State roads connect the region with other parts of the state, as well as with western Rhode Island and New York's Westchester County.

An extensive network of interstate train, bus, and ferry providers serves the Connecticut coastline. The region is also served by Bradley International Airport, an hour inland from New Haven. The western coastal towns are convenient to New York City's JFK and La Guardia airports, and upstate New York's Westchester and Stewart airports. The eastern coastal towns are extremely close to T.F. Green Airport, in Providence, Rhode Island.

## The Gold Coast

The stretch of coastal Fairfield County comprising Fairfield, Greenwich, Norwalk, Stamford, Westport, and a smattering of smaller communities feels in many ways more like a suburb of Manhattan than a slice of New England—indeed, these towns share many traits of both regions. Greenwich, in fact, like New York, was settled by the Dutch rather than the British in the 1600s—it's the only town in New England for which this is true. And as its upscale downtown is just 35 miles from Manhattan, it maintains close ties there.

Throughout much of this region, residents have commuted regularly to New York, although the emergence of Stamford since the 1980s into a corporate stronghold has changed this to some

extent. Now most area residents work elsewhere in Fairfield County, if not in Stamford then in the many office buildings that have popped up in Fairfield, Norwalk, Westport, and Wilton.

To be sure, these are densely settled suburbs—they're not quaint the way Litchfield County and the Quiet Corner are, and they lack the rustic maritime air of points farther east along the coast. But this chunk of Connecticut nevertheless possesses a rich and varied cultural base, including some of the best—and well-endowed—historical societies in the state, some outstanding nature preserves, and a few first-rate museums.

Another major draw is shopping, particularly at antiques shops. To the chagrin of some residents, an invasion of mid- to upscale chain stores (e.g.,

## THE MERRITT PARKWAY: HIGHWAY AS ART

The Merritt Parkway is one of the state's great treasures, and one that residents hold dear. Completed on June 29, 1938, this narrow four-lane highway runs from Greenwich—where it meets with New York state's Hutchinson River Parkway and feeds down toward New York City—to Stratford, where a bridge leads the road across the Housatonic River. From there, it continues as the later-constructed Wilbur Cross Parkway. The road cuts through Fairfield County's most scenic wooded countryside—billboards, commercial development of any kind, and concrete walls appear nowhere and are expressly forbidden. Preservationists revere this road, which is actually a designated National Historic Site.

The Merritt was the very first limited-access highway to cut through Connecticut, and it immediately turned the towns in southwestern-most Fairfield County into commuter suburbs of New York City. What had essentially been a rural, and somewhat remote, patch of countryside was transformed almost overnight—nowadays most Fairfield County commuters work elsewhere in the county, and those who do work in Gotham more often than not use the Metro-North railroad.

For the most part, the Merritt has been only slightly and respectfully altered in recent years—some of the exit ramps have been lengthened for safety, and various other improvements have been made. Also, the tollbooths that stood at frequent intervals along the road were forever dismantled in the 1980s.

What people love most about the Merritt are its 68 bridges, each with a unique design by George Dunkleberger, which carry parkway traffic over surface roads and vice versa. Many of these structures are crowned with elaborate sculptures, or their abutments are carved with artful images. Three of them wear a stone veneer, including a particularly handsome arched bridge that carries Guinea Road over the Merritt in Stamford. Still three others are clad entirely in intricately wrought steel. Art deco ornamentation graces the abutments of the Long Ridge Road overpass in Stamford and the sleek New Canaan Avenue bridge in New Canaan. Frilly iron railings line many of the bridges. Collectively, they make for a fascinating architectural and design tour of the styles so popular in America during the 1930s.

Unfortunately, the Merritt is in constant danger of being widened or "improved" in such a way as to destroy its beauty. It has been pointed out by the *Connecticut Preservation News* that traveling this 37.5-mile historic road at a speed of 65 miles per hour, rather than the posted 55, reduces the length of the trip by just six minutes to a total of 35. The point is made because rising traffic speeds on the road have led to increased concerns about safety, and therefore the Department of Transportation (DOT) plans to make the road wider, at least around certain curves.

Unfortunately, one major reason it's so tempting to speed on the Merritt has little to do with saving time, and more to do with pretending you're a race-car driver. In today's handling-happy autos—and Fairfield County is home to a disproportionately high number of expensive ones—drivers crave a swift drive along this sleek, beautiful highway, even when they're in no particular hurry to get wherever it is they're going.

But if the accident rates continue, almost certainly the thus-far highly cooperative DOT will be forced to damage the grace of this dashing track. So, if you want to do your utmost to keep the Merritt looking the way it does, keep exactly to the speed limit. At worst, if you creep above the limit, try to do so along the straightaways and when traffic is light. Tailgating is an atrocious problem on the parkway, partly because well-meaning but stubborn proponents of speed reduction sometimes insist on driving 55 in the left lane, thereby enraging equally stubborn and often aggressive speeders behind them. It's much wiser to yield to dangerous drivers, perhaps copying down a license plate number if it comes to that.

Finally, the vast majority of accidents, especially injurious ones, occur during wet conditions. The Merritt is highly prone to hydroplaning. Quite simply, if you drive at high speeds during wet conditions, especially during a heavy rainfall, you're greatly increasing the danger for yourself, your passengers, the drivers around you, and, ultimately, the historic integrity of this beautiful road.

Gap, Talbot's) has swept through Fairfield County with alarming force, substantially altering the character of many downtowns—and putting independently-owned shops out of business. Parts of Westport, New Canaan, and Greenwich, for example, now feel like fancy outdoor shopping centers. Nevertheless, if retail consumption is your game, you'll find plenty to keep you busy.

On a similar note, Fairfield County's restaurant scene is among the highest-profile of any nonurban area in America—it seems like every couple of weeks another well-known chef from New York City, Boston, or even California swoops down into one of the area's trendy downtowns and opens a hot new eatery. It used to be that eating out in communities like Westport and New Canaan represented substantial savings compared with midtown Manhattan, but times have changed. Expect to eat well in these parts, and to pay dearly for your meal.

Despite the pricey state of things, and the fact that Fairfield County is bursting at the seams in terms of population, much of the region retains a semi-rural feel. As you drive along the winding back roads of these towns—even the city of Stamford—you'll encounter wooded vistas and sweeping lawns traced by ancient stone walls. Much of the county is divvied up into picture-perfect two-acre lots of suburban paradise, quite of few of them with disproportionately palatial homes plopped down in the center.

## GREENWICH TO DARIEN

### Greenwich

Greenwich is an enormous old-money town consisting of several villages. There are a few worthwhile attractions, and it's also a popular town for country driving. The one downtown attraction is the **Bruce Museum** (1 Museum Dr., off Arch St. at exit 3 of I-95, 203/869-0376, www.brucemuseum.org), which is quite well known for the uniformly high quality of its changing art and historical exhibits and its outstanding lecture series and special programs (open Tues.–Sat. 10 A.M.–5 P.M. and Sun. 1–5 P.M.; $5). The art collection is astounding for so small a facility—paintings date back to 14th-century

Italy, and include Renaissance and Baroque. A bronze Degas statue of a young dancer is a highlight, as is one of only two self-portraits ever painted by Manet. Other works worth noting include *Paysage l'Ile de la Grande Jatte,* one of George Seurat's famous pointillist landscapes; famous portraits by Rembrandt Peale of George Washington; and New England landscapes by several members of the Cos Cob art colony (and their Connecticut peers), including Willard Metcalf, Elmer Livington MacRae, John Twachtman, and Childe Hassam. Accompanying the paintings are extensive interpretations and notes about the artists, far better material than you often find in much larger art museums.

Across the corridor from the art collection is the children's natural history wing, filled with mounted wildlife and other exhibits on flora and fauna specific to the region, especially of common Long Island Sound birdlife. One excellent exhibit illustrates how man's use of land has altered the ecology and landscape of the region, and another details Connecticut's geology and minerals.

West of the Bruce Museum, much of the exclusive neighborhood of **Belle Haven** is private (i.e., no trespassing), and you may be turned away at the gatehouse—but if you look at all like you know where you're going, no one will bother you. It's worth poking your head around just to see the collection of mature estates, with a diverse range of architecture dating principally from the 1870s to 1930s. As is true in so much of Greenwich, nothing here is done on a small scale. You can reach Belle Haven by heading west of downtown along Railroad Avenue (from Greenwich Ave.) and turning left onto Field Point Road; follow this road beneath the rail tracks.

Head back downtown, park the car, and wander up Greenwich Avenue for some great storefront browsing. Greenwich's primary commercial thoroughfare, Greenwich Avenue, slopes up and under a rail bridge and then ascends to U.S. 1, where you'll find still more shops. It's a picturesque retail center that looks quintessentially all-American in many respects. A traffic cop directs cars midway down the street. At one junction there's a flag pole and a narrow obelisk war memorial. Quite a few locally owned businesses still thrive,

THE CONNECTICUT COAST

despite the very high rents and the intrusion of a few chain businesses. Overlooking the center of action is the former town hall, with its copper greenish-blue cupola; it now houses a senior center and the town's acclaimed arts center. Curiously, the statue of a yak stands guard outside the building—perhaps a lion was too expensive.

At the top of Greenwich Avenue, you'll come to U.S. 1, the ubiquitous and busy highway that spans Connecticut's coast from Greenwich clear to Stonington on the Rhode Island border—it is, of course, but a link of the entire highway extending from Maine to Key West, Florida. In these parts it's lined with more fine shops, ritzy car dealers west of

downtown toward the New York border, and quite a few fine restaurants east of downtown, in the Cos Cob and Old Greenwich sections.

Before heading east, consider a country drive along some of the town's back roads. A somewhat common custom, especially on Sunday afternoons, is for visitors to drive around the town peering past high hedges and brick walls to gain a peek at some of the town's dramatic buildings. There are quite a few neighborhoods of great historic and architectural significance, including the Round Hill Historic District (along Round Hill Rd. and John St., a bit north of the Merritt Parkway).

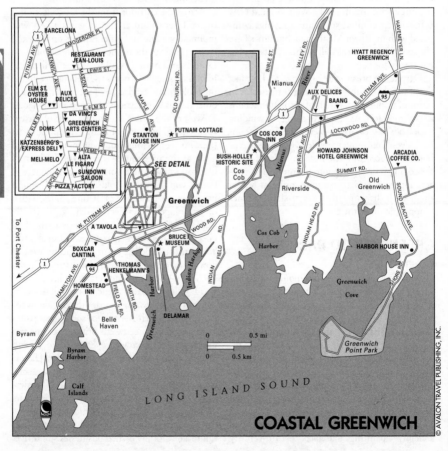

COASTAL GREENWICH

© AVALON TRAVEL PUBLISHING, INC.

© ANDREW COLLINS

**THE CONNECTICUT COAST**

Miller Motorcars, Greenwich

Up in these northern reaches of town, near massive $15-million estates, is the **Audubon Center of Greenwich** (613 Riversville Rd., 203/869-5272, www.audubon.org, open 9 A.M.–5 P.M. daily, $3). From downtown, follow Putnam Avenue (U.S. 1) west a short way from Greenwich Avenue, turn right onto Deerfield Drive, continue through the rotary onto Lake Avenue, and follow this north a little more than a mile and make a left onto Round Hill Road. Continue for nearly five miles, crossing the Merritt Parkway and making a left onto John Street, which leads right to the entrance of the park on Riversville Road.

Back in the center of town on U.S. 1, head east to reach **Putnam Cottage** (243 E. Putnam Ave., or U.S. 1, 203/869-9697, open Wed., Fri., and Sun. afternoons, best to phone ahead, free), a center-chimney 1734 Colonial house with carefully restored red-scalloped siding, wide wooden floors, and original post-and-beam details. Built and opened as Knapp Tavern, the building served as General Israel Putnam's military headquarters during the American Revolution; it was here that Putnam—General Washington's second in command—met with Rochambeau.

## Cos Cob

Continue east into the Cos Cob section of town and make a right onto Strickland Road (a bit before you reach the Mianus River) to reach the **Bush-Holley Historic Site and Visitor Center** (39 Strickland Rd., 203/869-6899, www.hstg.org, open noon–4 P.M. Tues.–Sun., call for exact tour hours, $6). The striking yellow house dates from 1730, but was a major center of American impressionist painting in the late 19th and early 20th centuries, when hundreds of artists lived here at what was then called Holley's Boarding House. Childe Hassam, John Henry Twachtman, and J. Alden Weir are among the distinguished painters to have spent time here. The house now contains a fine collection of early Connecticut furnishings and also impressionist art. You can also tour the re-created studio of artist Elmer MacRae.

## Old Greenwich

Hop back on U.S. 1 and continue east, and just after passing the entrance to I-95, make a right turn onto Sound Beach Avenue, and follow the signs into Old Greenwich (this is a circuitous but interesting way to reach Stamford; for a more direct route, stick with U.S. 1 or I-95). Like

Greenwich proper, Old Greenwich has lots and lots of grand Victorians, Colonials, and other enormous homes with neatly manicured lawns, quite a few of which are down "private drives." The folks around here do not appreciate attention, and don't even think for a minute about scurrying onto the local beach at the end of Shore Road—a posse of officious sand troopers will testily rebuff any invasions from nonresidents. Greenwich, especially near the water, is essentially one big Keep Out sign.

Follow Sound Beach Avenue all the way through the village until you dead-end at Shore Road, and take a left turn, which will lead you into Stamford.

## Stamford

Stamford is Connecticut's most prosperous city, a refuge of corporate headquarters and a thoroughly modern-looking downtown dominated by contemporary office buildings—companies including Xerox, GTE, Pitney Bowes, and International Paper are based here. You don't get the sense, driving or walking through Stamford, that it's the same kind of Connecticut city found elsewhere in the state, as little evidence exists today of its early industrial legacy. Only in the somewhat dodgy neighborhood south of the rail tracks and I-95 will you see hulking old factory buildings and a few blocks of older urban architecture; in this part of town, a hot new antiques scene has rapidly emerged in recent years.

Also, unlike most cities, Stamford really isn't a place to park the car and walk around. The main downtown retail draw is the massive indoor Stamford Town Center shopping mall, which anchors the very center of town but is more accessible by car than on foot. Likewise, most of the more interesting attractions are in the northern section of town, where a car is definitely needed. Main drags like Summer Street, Atlantic Street, and Bedford Street, which all run north–south, are lined with some very good restaurants, popular nightclubs, and a smattering of interesting shops, but downtown is mostly the domain of busy suit-clad nine-to-fivers. There's also a fertile performing arts scene in Stamford, with its two most prominent

venues—the Palace Theatre and the Rich Forum—right downtown on Atlantic Street.

As you happen by the Palace Theatre, make note of the three elegant 19th-century brick townhouses to the immediate north; they house offices and the public can't wander inside, but they're worth admiring, just to get a quick sense of what this city must have looked like several decades ago.

Once you've finished checking out downtown, hop in your car and proceed north up Atlantic Street, which becomes Bedford Street once you cross Broad. Note the funny-looking church on your right a few blocks farther; from the outside, the contemporary **First Presbyterian Church** (1101 Bedford St., 203/324-9522, www.fishchurch.org, open weekdays and for services on Sundays, free) looks something like a large grounded ship. Wander inside, however, and you'll realize that this long, curving, Wallace K. Harrison–designed icon actually resembles a fish, with stunning stained-glass panels created by French artist Gabriel Loire, plus the largest mechanical pipe organ in all of Connecticut.

## North Stamford

Continue north on Bedford for just under a mile, until you reach the large four-way intersection of Rtes. 104 and 137. Make a right turn onto Rte. 137 (High Ridge Rd.), and follow it through central Stamford. You'll pass by several shopping centers and go under the Merritt Parkway (Rte. 15) for nearly four miles before bearing left on Scofieldtown Road, to reach one of Fairfield County's favorite attractions (especially for kids)—the **Stamford Museum and Nature Center** (39 Scofieldtown Rd., 203/322-1646, www.stamford museum.org, open 9 A.M.–5 P.M. Mon.–Sat., 11 A.M.–5 P.M. Sun.). The museum's general admission is $6, but there are additional fees for the planetarium and observatory shows. It's sometimes forgotten that Stamford is more than a fast-paced blur of glitzy corporate offices and fancy shopping centers. Especially north of the Merritt Parkway, the city look gives way to some of the county's prettiest woodlands. This sprawling 118-acre complex, which occupies

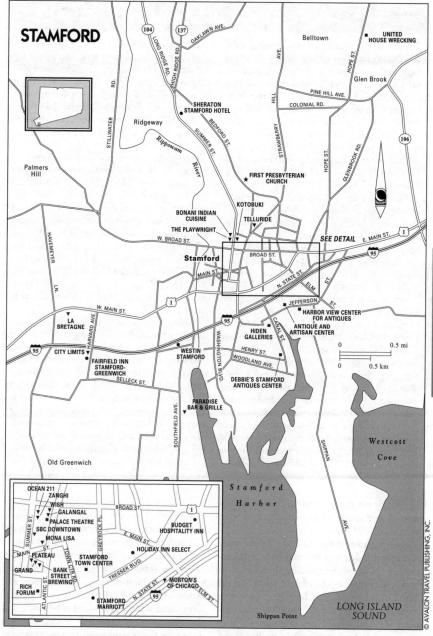

# STAMFORD

Belltown

UNITED HOUSE WRECKING

Glen Brook

OAKLAWN AVE.

104  137

LONG RIDGE RD.

HIGH RIDGE RD.

PINE HILL AVE.

COLONIAL RD.

AVE.

HILL

Ridgeway

STILLWATER RD.

SHERATON STAMFORD HOTEL

Rippowam River

SUMMER ST.

BEDFORD ST.

HOPE ST.

STRAWBERRY

HOPE ST.

GLENBROOK RD.

106

Palmers Hill

FIRST PRESBYTERIAN CHURCH

KOTOBUKI

BONANI INDIAN CUISINE

TELLURIDE

THE PLAYWRIGHT

HAVEMEYER LN.

W. BROAD ST.

SEE DETAIL

E. MAIN ST.

1

**Stamford**

BROAD ST.

95

MAIN ST.

N. STATE ST.

ELM ST.

JEFFERSON

W. MAIN ST.

HARVARD AVE.

1

95

HARBOR VIEW CENTER FOR ANTIQUES

LA BRETAGNE

CANAL ST.

ANTIQUE AND ARTISAN CENTER

CITY LIMITS

WASHINGTON BLVD.

HIDEN GALLERIES

0          0.5 mi

FAIRFIELD INN STAMFORD-GREENWICH

WESTIN STAMFORD

HENRY ST.

0       0.5 km

SELLECK ST.

WOODLAND AVE.

DEBBIE'S STAMFORD ANTIQUES CENTER

SHIPPAN

PARADISE BAR & GRILLE

SOUTHFIELD AVE.

*Westcott Cove*

Old Greenwich

*Stamford Harbor*

AVE.

OCEAN 211

ZANGHI

WISH

GALANGAL

BROAD ST.

1

PALACE THEATRE

SBC DOWNTOWN

SUMMER ST.

GREYROCK PL.

BUDGET HOSPITALITY INN

MONA LISA

E. MAIN ST.

PLATEAU

ST.

HOLIDAY INN SELECT

MAIN ST.

STAMFORD TOWN CENTER

GRAND

BANK STREET BREWING

ATLANTIC ST.

TRESSER BLVD.

*LONG ISLAND SOUND*

RICH FORUM

MORTON'S OF CHICAGO

N. STATE ST.

ELM ST.

STAMFORD MARRIOTT

95

Shippan Point

THE CONNECTICUT COAST

© AVALON TRAVEL PUBLISHING, INC.

## ANTIQUING IN STAMFORD

In the 17th–19th centuries, coastal Connecticut's shopkeepers and traders did a brisk business. Hard work and thrift defined the early Connecticut ethic, and these traits encouraged local Yankees to trade with merchants from around the world, to save even the most trivial belongings for generations, and to keep their furnishings in the best possible condition. Prosperity reigned, and the influx of wealthy industrialists throughout the late 19th and early 20th centuries further fattened Fairfield County's booty.

The result is an abundance of riches for modern-day antiques lovers in a region now considered one of America's great repositories of fine collectibles. While Greenwich, New Canaan, Ridgefield, Southport, Westport, and Wilton and have always boasted a bevy of smaller antiques stores, Stamford has become a hub of multi-dealer shops.

Several such facilities are within walking distance of each other in an industrial neighborhood south of the rail tracks downtown. A favorite here is **Debbie's Stamford Antiques Center** (735–737 Canal St., 888/329-3546), a 150-dealer showroom inside an old factory building. Offerings range from crystal stemware and Tiffany glass to the kitschy 1950s household goods that dominate the stalls in the center aisle. Two outer aisles showcase furnishings and paintings—mostly American and European—of some 80 specialists. Debbie's approach is friendly and downright fun: Treasures range from elegant tiger-maple chests to a plaster "Elvis on Hawaii Tour" bust.

**E.J. Kassery & Co.** (735 Canal St., 203/975-0545) specializes in silver-plating, metal polishing and repairs, and chandeliers. The **Warehouse** (425 Fairfield Ave., 203/975-7177) claims to have the largest selection of vintage dining and bedroom sets in the area. **Braswell Galleries** (733 Canal St., 203/357-0753) is another of the fine options in the neighborhood, specializing in art, bronzes, porcelain, and crystal.

One of the newest spots in this burgeoning mecca is the **Harbor View Center for Antiques** (101 Jefferson St., 203/325-8070), an 80-dealer store that specializes in very fine 18th- and 19th-century furniture and decorative arts. Others in the neighborhood include the venerable **Antique and Artisan Center** (62 Jefferson St., 203/327-6022), where the emphasis is on period and decorative furnishings, books, garden pieces, and art and bronzes; and **Hiden Galleries** (481 Canal St., 203/323-9090), where you're apt to find ornamental and decorative arts and a few architectural pieces, paintings, textiles, and furniture.

No journey to Stamford is complete without visiting the granddaddy of furnishings and other treasures salvaged from estates: **United House Wrecking** (535 Hope St., 203/348-5371, www.unitedhousewrecking.com). This 35,000-square-foot compound was established in the 1950s, when many of the area's finest homes were razed to make way for I-95. Here you'll discover an unparalleled collection of marvelous architectural remnants, from stained-glass transoms, ornately carved mahogany mantels, and cast-iron urns to terra-cotta pots, birdbaths, and copper weather vanes.

the courtly estate and mansion of the former Henri Bendel estate, offers an engaging glimpse into this side of town.

The main house is a grand Tudor Revival stone château with a slate roof. Its main floor houses exhibition space, where rotating shows tend to focus on difference aspects of Americana—model railroads and teddy bears have been shown in recent years. There's also an art gallery whose installations tend toward contemporary—and in many cases rather provocative. On the second

level, dioramas illustrate the region's Native American history. The solar system can be explored both in the museum's observatory, which contains a 22-inch telescope, and also in a planetarium.

The Overbrook Nature Center merits a visit. In this small building a few small, modest exhibits reveal the habitats of turtles, frogs, and snakes. Outside the center, there's a wonderful playground with slides, wooden benches, and play equipment. A 300-foot boardwalk runs alongside a serene creek; you can press buttons at various stations along the walk and hear a narrative on local flora and fauna. The boardwalk easily facilitates parents using strollers or visitors using wheelchairs. Nearby picnic tables and benches overlook a duck-filled pond, over which a footbridge leads to Heckscher Farm.

Kids love wandering through the farm, admiring goats, pigs, and sheep behind Colonial-style fences, a 1750 restored barn, which contains authentic implements, and a fine herb garden. Best of all is a pair of inquisitive river otters who happily cavort through mud puddles and splash about pools, racing back and forth in their large pen to the delight of human observers. In March there are maple-sugaring demonstrations at the farm.

The museum also offers workshops for young people and adults, on topics ranging from astronomy to children's books to creative dance to child-and-parent seminars.

Just around the corner from the Stamford Museum is **Stamford Historical Society Museum** (1508 High Ridge Rd., or Rte. 137, 203/329-1183, www.stamfordhistory.org, open noon–4 P.M. Tues.–Sat.) an imposing fieldstone mansion that has permanent exhibits on mostly local history, plus a research and genealogy library. Collections on early textiles and tools are a highlight. The museum also operates the 1699 **Hoyt Barnum House** (713 Bedford St., 203/329-1183); it's downtown, across from the Stamford Suites Hotel, and has frequent exhibitions.

Continue north on Rte. 137 about three-quarters of a mile, making a left turn onto Brookdale Road. Shortly after on your right, you'll come to an old yellow farmhouse that marks the entrance to the **Bartlett Arboretum** (151 Brookdale Rd., 203/322-6971, http://bartlett.arboretum.uconn.edu, grounds open daily 8:30 A.M.–sunset, visitor center open 8:30 A.M.–4:30 P.M. weekdays, free). A 63-acre spread of natural woodlands, hiking trails, and beautifully laid out gardens, including a pond and a large greenhouse. In addition to guided tours, workshops and classes are offered.

## New Canaan

From Stamford, it's a quick hop along the Merritt Parkway and east to exit 36; head north a short way on Rte. 106 to reach downtown New Canaan, a quintessential Fairfield County town of low-key blue bloods and a yachting mentality—even though it doesn't actually front Long Island Sound. Many locals resented the town's depiction in the depressing but breathtakingly beautiful Ang Lee film The Ice Storm, with Kevin Kline, Sigourney Weaver, Christina Ricci, Elijah Wood, Tobey Maguire, and Joan Allen. Many shots in the movie show New Canaan's picture-perfect downtown of white-clapboard and redbrick shopfronts—several of which house upscale clothiers, antiques stores, and flashy high-caliber restaurants.

Head north from downtown just up Oenoke Ridge (Rte. 124) toward the New York border; just up the hill, you'll find the **New Canaan Historical Society** (13 Oenoke Ridge, 203/966-1776, http://nchistory.org, open 10 A.M.–4:30 P.M. Tues.–Sat., donation suggested), one of the finest in Fairfield County. It includes a 1799 one-room schoolhouse, a 19th-century printing press, and historic shoe-making equipment (the town was a major shoe manufacturer back in the middle of the 19th century). Hanford-Silliman House dates from the 1760s and is the key to the historical center, with fine furniture and a great doll collection. Also, the 1870s studio of sculptor John Rogers is here.

A bit farther up the street, you'll see the entrance to the **New Canaan Nature Center** (144 Oenoke Ridge, 203/966-9577, www.newcanaannature.org, open 9 A.M.–4 P.M., Mon.–Sat., grounds open dawn–dusk daily, free), where some 40 acres of hiking trails crisscross contrasting habitats. Bird, butterfly, perennial, herb, and wildflower gardens bloom spring through fall, and various educational programs reveal techniques in cider-making and maple-sugaring. Visitors also have the opportunity to interact with live animals of many kinds. As with the historical society, this is one of the best around, with a wonderful visitor center built in 1999, a 4,000-square-foot greenhouse, and a first-rate nature gift shop. In fall 2002, the Nature Center underwent a partnership with the Nature Conservancy to manage Devil's Den Preserve, in Weston.

# NEW CANAAN'S ARCHITECTURAL LANDMARKS

In 1997, architect Philip Johnson's simple but stunning **Glass House,** in a heavily wooded section of New Canaan, was named a National Historic Landmark. When Johnson dies, his estate—which consists of the 1949 house, a 1962 pavilion, a 1965 painting gallery, a 1970 sculpture gallery, a 1980 study, the 1985 Lincoln Kirstein Tower, and a 1995 visitors center—will be opened to the public, and will no

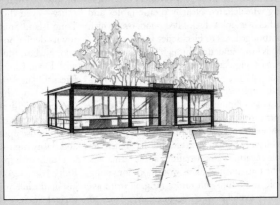

BOB RACE

doubt become one of America's germinal architectural sites. It's one of about 40 landmark houses that were built in New Canaan during the 1930s, 1940s, and 1950s on through the present day, including one designed by Frank Lloyd Wright. None is open to the public, and most are well hidden with shrubbery and large plots of woodland.

In eastern New Canaan, near the Norwalk and Wilton lines, rotating art installations are mounted at the **Silvermine Guild Arts Center** (1037 Silvermine Rd., off Rte. 106, 203/966-9700, www.silvermineart.org, open 11 A.M.–5 P.M. Tues.–Sat., 1–5 P.M. Sun.) founded by sculptor Solon Borglum, whose brother Gutzon created South Dakota's Mt. Rushmore; the guild shop sells jewelry, art, and crafts. Right around the corner is the historic Silvermine Tavern.

## Darien

Retrace your steps from downtown New Canaan south along Rte. 123, passing over the Merritt Parkway and continuing into Darien, a wealthy coastal community with the same kinds of beautiful estates and country clubs typical of New Canaan and Greenwich. This town, too, also fared rather badly, if less inconspicuously, in the movies. In the classic musical *Auntie Mame,* the lead character is heard to exclaim that she shall never let her precious nephew become "an aryan from Darien."

There's little, formally, to see or do in Darien that's not on the dreary Post Road, so visitors sometimes fail to get a true sense of just how pretty the town is—this seems fine with most residents of this insular and affluent place. But to really see the fine homes and pretty roads, be sure to venture off U.S. 1.

Where Rte. 124 intersects with U.S. 1, make a left turn toward Norwalk to reach the historic **Bates-Scofield House** (45 Old Kings Hwy. N, 203/655-9233, http://historical.darien.org, open Tues.–Fri., best to phone ahead, $3), a lovely old 1736 saltbox house-museum filled with 18th- and 19th-century regional antiques. The Colonial history of Middlesex Parish, the name of this town before it became Darien in 1820, is traced through many exhibits. Actual guided tours of the house are given Wednesdays and Thursdays, 2–4 P.M. Also notable are the immense central chimney and fireplace, original beehive oven, and garden containing some 30 herbs used commonly in 18th-century Connecticut.

# NORWALK

## Rowayton

From downtown Darien, drive south on Rte. 136 through the quiet boating community of Noroton and into the similar Rowayton section of Norwalk. Marinas and beach houses line the Five Mile River, and the jagged points poking into Long Island Sound. It's no surprise that the name Norwalk is an ancient Indian word, Norruck, meaning "Point of Land." In Rowayton, the **Rowayton Arts Center** (145 Rowayton Ave., 203/866-2744, www.rowaytonartscenter.org), shows changing exhibits by local artists and also offers art classes.

## South Norwalk

Much of this small city with an impressive maritime history fronts the sound and the dramatically revitalized South Norwalk (SoNo) neighborhood, which you'll reach if you continue along Rte. 136 through some inner-city sections. SoNo straddles the Norwalk River and contains the highly acclaimed **Maritime Aquarium at Norwalk** (10 N. Water St., 203/852-0700, www.maritimeaquarium.org, 10 A.M.–5 P.M. daily, open an hour later in summer, museum $9.25, IMAX $7, combined $14), a top-notch museum that has been the cornerstone of South Norwalk's redevelopment.

The aquarium, which faces Norwalk Harbor, occupies a dramatic 19th-century foundry, with exposed brick, arched windows, and other original industrial-architectural elements. The facility captivates children of all ages with an aquarium of 20 habitats containing more than 1,000 animals indigenous to Long Island Sound. The youngest visitors gather eagerly to watch agile and spirited harbor seals bark for raw fish during three scheduled daily feedings (11:45 A.M., 1:45 P.M., and 3:45 P.M.) and to stroke the shells of horseshoe crabs and razor clams in a shallow touch-tank manned by chatty volunteers. (Seals, incidentally, have started to make a comeback in Long Island Sound, because hunting them off the coast is now illegal, the waters have been greatly cleaned up, and the northern Atlantic has had much of its fishing stock depleted.)

Slightly older kids flock wide-eyed to the 110,000-gallon shark tank (the regular Sunday feedings are a great time to watch these magnificent creatures in action).

The museum's two-story Maritime Hall contains an interactive boat shop, where kids and their parents can not only watch staff and volunteers construct handsome wooden vessels, they can work together to create their very own dinghy (call to learn about upcoming programs). If you've a teen or two among your brood, be sure to treat them to a show on the 8-story-by-6-story IMAX screen, where a 24,000-watt sound system rumbles and roars through such presentations as *Mysteries of Egypt* and *Whales.* In warmer weather, tours of the harbor are given aboard the museum's RV, *Oceanic,* which scoops up samples from the sound for environmental analysis. In 2001, a café and a hands-on Environmental Education Center were added.

Extending from one to three miles off of the Norwalk shoreline are a number of small islands. From Memorial Day through September a daily ferry operated by the U.S. Coast Guard shuttles passengers from just outside Hope Dock, by the Maritime Aquarium, to the **Sheffield Island Lighthouse** (www.soundnavigation.com), a four-level 10-room beacon dating to 1868 that's great fun to explore. You can wander about this secluded three-acre island, picnicking if you'd like (a clambake is held on Thursday evenings). Adjoining the lighthouse property is the Stuart B. McKinney U.S. Fish and Wildlife Sanctuary. Keep in mind that ferry service is not always offered, notably when the Coast Guard is called into active duty; in 2002, for example, the shuttle did not operate. It's always best to check with the **Norwalk Seaport Association** (203/838-9444, www.seaport.org) for details.

This neighborhood is also home to the **Norwalk Museum** (41 N. Main St., 203/866-0202, www.culinarymenus.com/norwalkmuseum.htm, open afternoons Tues.–Sun., free), which opened in 1999 inside the 1913 former city hall in South Norwalk, near the Regent Cinema. The museum contains a variety of exhibits, maps, a museum shop, and a gallery that shows changing exhibitions.

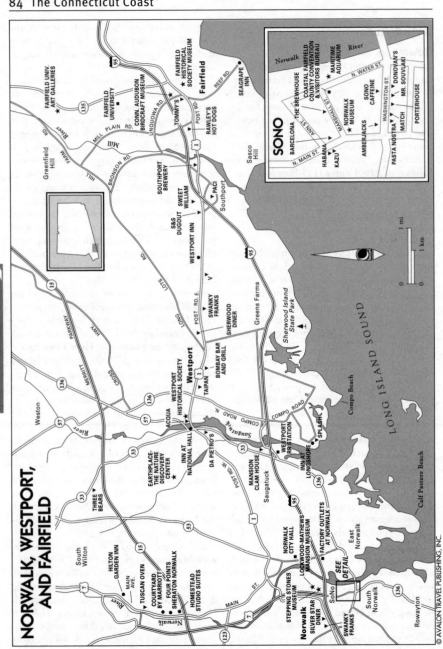

# NORWALK, WESTPORT, AND FAIRFIELD

FAIRFIELD UNIV. ART GALLERIES

FAIRFIELD UNIVERSITY

CONN. AUDUBON BIRDCRAFT MUSEUM

FAIRFIELD HISTORICAL SOCIETY MUSEUM

Fairfield

SEAGRAPE INN

TOMMY'S

RAWLEY'S HOT DOGS

MILL PLAIN RD.

UNQUOWA RD.

POST RD.

REEF RD.

Greenfield Hill

Sasco Hill

Southport

SOUTHPORT BREWERY

SWEET WILLIAM

PACI

S&S DUGOUT

WESTPORT INN

Greens Farms

SWANKY FRANKS

SHERWOOD DINER

Sherwood Island State Park

BOMBAY BAR AND GRILL

Westport

TAIPAN

WESTPORT HISTORICAL SOCIETY

ACQUA

INN AT NATIONAL HALL

DA PIETRO'S

EARTHPLACE-THE NATURE DISCOVERY CENTER

MANSION CLAM HOUSE

Saugatuck

WESTPORT RR STATION

SPLASH

INN AT LONGSHORE

Compo Beach

LONG ISLAND SOUND

Calf Pasture Beach

Weston

THREE BEARS

South Wilton

HILTON GARDEN INN

TUSCAN OVEN

COURTYARD BY MARRIOTT

FOUR POINTS SHERATON NORWALK

HOMESTEAD STUDIO SUITES

MAIN AVE.

Norwalk

NORWALK CITY HALL

LOCKWOOD-MATHEWS MANSION MUSEUM

FACTORY OUTLETS AT NORWALK

East Norwalk

STEPPING STONES MUSEUM

SILVER STAR DINER

SWANKY FRANKS

SoNo

South Norwalk

Rowayton

SEE DETAIL

## SONO

Norwalk River

BARCELONA

THE BREWHOUSE

COASTAL FAIRFIELD COUNTY CONVENTION & VISITORS BUREAU

MARITIME AQUARIUM

N. WATER ST.

N. MAIN ST.

ANN ST.

MARSHALL ST.

WASHINGTON ST.

NORWALK MUSEUM

SONO CAFFEINE

DONOVAN'S

MR. SOUVLAKI

HABANA

KAZU

AMBERJACKS

PASTA NOSTRA

MATCH

PORTERHOUSE

1 mi

1 km

From South Norwalk, work your way north along West Ave. to see the rest of the city. Just after crossing the I-95 overpass, you'll find the **Lockwood-Mathews Mansion Museum** (295 West Ave., 203/838-9799, www.lockwoodmathews.org, open noon–5 P.M. Wed.–Sun. mid-Mar.–Dec., by appointment off-season, $8), which has been called America's earliest château. It's one of the earliest and best-preserved examples of a Second Empire home, with a decadent mansard roofline marked by crockets, finials, and turrets. This 52-room Victorian palace, built by banker and railroad mogul LeGrand Lockwood in 1864, took four years to build. Lockwood died a few years later, and the house was sold to a wealthy Staten Island merchant named Charles D. Mathews, who lived here with his wife until 1938. The city of Norwalk bought the place in 1941 and converted it into a city park.

Like so many grand estates, Lockwood-Mathews was threatened with demolition during the 1950s, but a group of local preservations fought successfully to keep it going. Today, it retains its original stenciled walls, inlaid exotic woodworking, and a magnificent skylighted rotunda. Rooms are filled with some 4,000 decorative objects, textiles, paintings, and research materials on area history—an intentionally varied and quite fascinating collection that places this museum among the most curious in southwestern Connecticut.

On the Lockwood-Mathews grounds is the **Connecticut GraphicArts Center and Museum** (203/899-7999, open 9 A.M.–5 P.M. Mon.–Sat, free), which focuses exclusively on print works, photography, and artists; exhibits change throughout the year.

Opened in 2000, the popular **Stepping Stones Museum for Children** (Mathews Park, 303 West Ave., 203/899-0606, www.steppingstonesmuseum.org, open 10 A.M.–5 P.M. Tues.–Sun., also Mondays in summer, $7), comprises several key learning areas. A 27-foot-tall kinetic sculpture called the ColorCoaster whirls in a colorful play of light and color; Toddler Terrain is an ages-three-and-under area with puppets, books, and other playthings; a giant waterscape re-creates the movements of pools and rivers, and even has a fog machine; and Express Yourself is an arts and music area where kids can experiment with sound effects, video instruments, and play musical instruments. There's also a café that can be rented for parties.

## Downtown Norwalk

Continue up the road to the true center of the city, which doesn't quite yet look as good and trendy as SoNo. This area lacks much in the way of personality, but there are some pretty buildings and a large town green at the intersection of Wall Street and East Avenue, on the other side of the Norwalk River. Pop inside the **Norwalk City Hall** (125 East Ave., 203/866-0202, www.norwalkct.org), which houses impressive WPA (Works Progress Administration) murals from the 1930s and 1940s. If you phone ahead, you can arrange for a guided tour; but at any time during regular weekday office hours, you can examine these for yourself.

# WESTPORT AND ENVIRONS
## Saugatuck

Drive south down East Avenue and back over I-95 into East Norwalk, where a left turn back onto Rte. 136 will lead you into the coastal Saugatuck section of Westport.

"Tucks" are rather common in the names of Connecticut villages and rivers; *tuk* is an Indian word meaning "tidal river," and indeed Westport's Saugatuck River is just such a body of water. As you enter the small village of Saugatuck via Rte. 136, you'll find a small and appealing community of shops and houses set in the shadows of the giant overhead I-95 and railroad bridges.

While Westport fits in with Fairfield County's well-heeled, urbane personality, in spirit the town is more like the fashionable Hamptons of Long Island than it is its Connecticut neighbor. It's a major commuter stop on the Metro-North New Haven rail line, perhaps the easternmost Fairfield County town taken seriously as a suburb of New York City, as few workers are willing to live any farther from their offices. Westport's an hour from Manhattan by train, but factor in the drive to the train station and a possible subway ride from Grand

Central to the office and many commutes take as long as two hours each way.

Hang around the train station on a weekday evening to witness a scene fresh out of a John Cheever novel: On each side of the track stands a rickety old turn-of-the-20th-century station, and on the southbound side, across the street, is a row of engaging little shops—from a bustling newsstand to a stylish frame shop to a chichi trattoria to a florist—the whole collection anchored by one of the town's longest running institutions, Mario's Italian Restaurant.

Beginning around 6 P.M. on weekday evenings, watch the suits and dresses debark from the first trains, many of them dashing through the track's underpass to meet friends or spouses for a drink at Mario's, or to pick up a dozen roses before heading home to their families. Other commuters rush off the train into waiting cars filled with moon-eyed sons and daughters and family dogs. Within 15 minutes of the train having dropped off its cargo, a stillness descends again upon the station and platforms—only to be interrupted a half-hour later by the next train, when this routine renews itself.

The station is not in Westport's true commercial center, but a few miles downriver in Saugatuck, land that was once (and still is, to a certain extent) dominated by the sight of haggard fishing boats and the Italian and Portuguese immigrants who manned them. Saugatuck retains a slightly less rarefied air than the rest of town. Just up Riverside Street from the train station, trendy restaurants have opened near the Rte. 136 bridge, giving the area a shot of gentrification. But one of the best dining experiences is still at the ancient Mansion Clam House, a rickety, red, clapboard tavern that looks as though the next strong wind may send it tumbling off its foundation. Real locals slurp down plate after plate of raw oysters and hot steamers.

## Westport

Considering its many charms, Westport is notably not, in fact, a Colonial Connecticut town. In the early days, the village of Westport was ignored in favor of Fairfield and Norwalk, whose ports were far larger than and superior to the lit-

tle inlet of Saugatuck. But in 1835 some feisty locals petitioned the state legislature for the right to start a new town, one that took in the eastern fringes of Norwalk, the southern fringes of Weston, and the western fringes of Fairfield.

Westport made very few waves until the upper classes began buying property near the shore, converting sleepy farms into magnificent summer estates. F. Scott Fitzgerald lived in a charming cottage along Compo Road in 1920, during the first summer of his marriage to Zelda. This first brush with immense wealth and high society was partly Fitzgerald's inspiration for West Egg, Long Island, the fictitious setting of *The Great Gatsby*.

With the birth during the early 20th century of commuting, Westport developed into a bedroom suburb of New York City, while retaining its reputation as a quiet country town. Fans of *I Love Lucy* will remember that it's to Westport where Lucy and Ricky eventually move from Manhattan to build their farmhouse in the country. *Bewitched* was also set here, and the television station Nick at Nite has had great fun with this while running old reruns of the series. Of course it wasn't filmed here, and so during a scene with Larry and Darren driving in a convertible, the late-night station sarcastically points out the famous "palm trees of Westport, Connecticut." Bits of Westport and the Merritt Parkway are also visible in the opening credits of *Who's the Boss?*, the 1980s Tony Danza, Alisa Milano, Judith Light, and Katherine Helmond vehicle also set here. Even the *Dick Van Dyke Show* made use of Westport's reputation as an early commuter town, with Rob Petrie's boss said to hail from here (Carl Reiner's character, Alan Brady). The Petries themselves lived not far from the Connecticut border, in New Rochelle, New York.

In real life, dozens of celebrities have made the trek out here, either to perform for a summer at the esteemed Westport Playhouse (Elizabeth Taylor and Bette Davis are among the alums) or to move here permanently. Paul Newman and Joanne Woodward are two of the town's most famous residents, and the iron-fisted, embattled, yet resolutely upbeat doyenne of contemporary entertaining, Martha Stewart, films her popular television show from both her compound on Turkey Hill Road and a newer studio downtown.

Plenty of people live in Westport, but not everybody's a local. This is a town of transplants. Many residents have arrived via Manhattan and other such harried metropolises. Westport is desirable because it offers the verdant greenery of other Connecticut towns, while providing the level of services, shopping, culture, and dining of many Manhattan neighborhoods.

In that regard, the town has changed drastically over the past decade. Downtown centers on a bridge that carries the Boston Post Road (U.S. 1) over the Saugatuck River. Ten years ago, on the west side of the river, you used to see a poorly planned, mixed-use stretch of office buildings and junky shops. Rather suddenly, this neighborhood, whose crux is at the intersection of U.S. 1 and Rte. 33, has been transformed into a tony settlement of restored redbrick beauties—including one of New England's most luxurious small hotels, the Inn at National Hall—plus a few good restaurants and several crafts boutiques and specialty shops. The bridge has been widened to include a handsome promenade—and on clear summer nights, it's hard to walk across it without imagining you've suddenly been transported to Sag Harbor or the Hamptons.

The commercial spine of downtown, on the east side of the Saugatuck River, is Main Street, which is interesting from U.S. 1 north for two blocks. Lined a decade ago with mundane dry-goods shops, Main Street is now the redbrick-sidewalk outdoor equivalent of an upscale shopping mall. To the dismay of independent-business owners and some of the town's old-timers, the storefronts have been invaded by a who's who of high-end chain shopping, including J.Crew, Eddie Bauer, Ann Taylor, Brooks Brothers, Coach, and William Sonoma. Several of the little side streets in the vicinity are also rife with opportunities to shop and explore, and along U.S. 1 all the way to the Fairfield border, ritzy shopping centers and trendy restaurants continue to spring up at a dizzying pace.

If you've an interest in history, make a right onto Avery Place at the top of the shopping drag along Main Street. Having been fully restored in 1996, the octagonal (well, actually seven-sided, but with an octagonal roof) **Bradley-Wheeler Cobblestone Barn** became the **Museum of Westport,** which along with the adjoining 1795 **Wheeler House,** comprises the **Westport Historical Society** (25 Avery Place, 203/222-1424, www.westporthistory.org, open 10 A.M.–4 p.m. weekdays, 11 A.M.–3 P.M. weekends, donation suggested). The Wheeler House, though it dates from Colonial times, was vastly remodeled in the 1860s, and now there's an ornate Italianate exterior—it was purchased by the society in 1981 following a fund-raising drive spearheaded by Westport residents and community activists Paul Newman and Joanne Woodward. In these buildings you'll see changing exhibitions on the town's local history, collections of local photographs and maps, restored period rooms, a collection of vintage costumes, and genealogical archives.

When you tire of window-shopping and indoor diversions, especially if you've got kids with you, drive south of downtown on U.S. 1, almost to the Norwalk border, and make a right onto Woodside Lane to reach **Earthplace—The Nature Discovery Center** (10 Woodside Ln., 203/227-7253), a 62-acre wildlife sanctuary with an extensive network of five nature trails and a small natural history and ecology museum (grounds open 7 A.M.–dusk daily, museum open 9 A.M.–5 P.M. Mon.–Sat., 1–4 P.M. Sun., $3). Exhibits in the museum include dioramas of natural history; a kid-oriented Discovery Room with nature games, puzzles, puppets, and books; and an ecology resource lab where visitors can observe and sometimes touch minerals and both live and mounted animals. A bird-and-butterfly garden makes for a pleasant stroll in warm weather.

## Compo Beach and Greens Farms

Westport is a wonderful town for leisurely driving, and perhaps nowhere is the sightseeing more spectacular than along the waterfront, east of Saugatuck and below U.S. 1. It's best to begin at the intersection of Compo Road and Bridge Street (Rte. 136). Turn onto Compo Road and follow it south beneath the railroad trestle; it soon curves along the shore, past beautiful Compo Beach (which is officially open to all, year-round, but from Memorial Day to Labor Day it has parking only for Westport and Weston residents). At the end of Compo Beach, veer right onto Hills Point Road; follow it until it passes over I-95, then turn right onto Greens Farms Road. This posh trail leads into the wealthy residential enclave of Greens Farms, where eventually you bear right onto Beachside Avenue, whose mansions are the biggest and most ostentatious in town. The drive ends at the compact but inviting town beach of Southport, which is just over the Westport–Fairfield town line.

As you follow Greens Farms Road east, before you enter Fairfield you'll first pass Sherwood Island Road, where a right turn leads you to a major exit from I-95 and then to the entrance of **Sherwood Island State Park** (203/226-6983), one of the largest and prettiest public beaches in Connecticut. Unfortunately, the dearth of public access points to Long Island Sound results in huge summertime crowds at this 1.5-mile-long beach. Nevertheless, it's a well-maintained facility with picnic groves, sports fields, fishing, swimming, concessions in summer, and changing facilities. Presently, construction is underway at the park on Connecticut's official memorial to the victims of the September 11 terrorist attacks. This sculpture garden will include a memorial stone and bench and landscaping, all laid out to face across Long Island Sound toward the New York City skyline, which can sometimes be seen on clear days. Admission ranges $7–14 per vehicle depending on the time of year and whether you have in- or out-of-state license plates; off-season admission is free.

## Wilton

Before continuing east along the shoreline into the town of Fairfield, consider making a detour up into three more countrified suburbs: Wilton, Weston, and Easton. These towns all have relatively few attractions, except for a fascinating National Historic site in Wilton and a huge Nature Conservancy sanctuary in Weston, but if you explore the back roads, you'll encounter some beautiful vistas and pass alongside some grand Colonial and Victorian estates. These towns are all rather hilly, but nevertheless make for good bicycling terrain.

Wilton's historic 1852 rail depot, at Cannondale Crossing antiques village

From downtown Westport, follow Rte. 33 until the road joins with U.S. 7 and leads directly into Wilton center. On your left, as you approach the center of town, is the **Wilton Heritage Museum** (224 Danbury Rd., or U.S. 7/Rte. 33, 203/762-7257, open 9 A.M.–4 P.M. Mon.–Thurs., 1–4 P.M. Sun, $2). Inside this 1750s classic center-chimney house, the rooms are furnished with period furnishings and costumes. Highlights include a large exhibit of toys, dolls, and dollhouses and an exhibit of Norwalk-made redware and stoneware. A parlor contains lovely Queen Anne pieces and a fine collection of ceramics. The museum also operates two additional house-museums in town, the 1735 **Blackmar House** and the 1724 **Lambert House**, which both contain additional period pieces and host various rotating exhibits. On the grounds of Lambert House, at the junction of Rte. 33 and U.S. 7, are the town's first railroad station (ca. 1852), an 1880s general store and post office, a Greek Revival one-room schoolhouse, and a few more outbuildings.

Turn left where Rte. 33 branches off from U.S. 7, and follow it through the center of town and north toward Ridgefield. After about two miles make a right turn onto Nod Hill Road, a narrow country lane that twists northward through some of the area's prettiest countryside. After about two miles you have the option to bear left onto Whipstick Road. Continue another three-quarters of a mile and make a left onto Antler Road to reach the **Woodcock Nature**

© ANDREW COLLINS

Center (56 Deer Run Rd., 203/762-7280, www.woodcocknaturecenter.org), a 146-acre sanctuary that extends into Ridgefield and has self-guided boardwalk trails, a nature store, and interpretive exhibits.

Or, continue along Nod Hill Road for another mile or so to reach the 153-acre **Weir Farm National Historic Site** (735 Nod Hill Rd., 203/834-1896, www.nps.gov/wefa, grounds open dawn–dusk daily, visitor center open 8:30 A.M.–5 P.M. Wed.–Sun., free), the state's only national park. Landscape painter J. Alden Weir (1852–1919) purchased a farm in Wilton, straddling the Ridgefield border, in 1882—he paid $10 and one painting for this piece of land. Weir soon built a studio, laid out a garden, and enlisted the talented aid of the McKim, Mead, & White architectural firm in expanding the main house. Weir created countless portraits here, and he also invited fellow painters Childe Hassam, John Twachtman, and John Singer Sargent to spend time here—it became a mini artists' colony of considerable repute. The legacy of the artist is preserved in an appropriately informal manner as the Weir Farm National Historic Site. You can pick up the $2 brochure *Weir Farm Historic Painting Sites Trail* to visit the actual vantage points on the property from which works were painted—more than 250 were completed here. Most of the historic buildings are concentrated by the entrance, just off Nod Hill Road by the Wilton–Ridgefield border. The actual Weir House and surrounding outbuildings are privately owned and occupied, and guests should not visit them.

## Weston

From the park, double back south a short distance, turning left onto Indian Hill Road and then left again at the T intersection onto Mountain Road, which will bring you down to U.S. 7 in the Georgetown section of Wilton. At the intersection, bear right and cross U.S. 7, taking Rte. 107 two-tenths of a mile and making a right turn (south) onto Georgetown Road (Rte. 57), which will lead you into Weston. About three miles later, make a left turn onto Godfrey Road, and then shortly after a left onto Pent Road,

where signs lead to **Devil's Den** (33 Pent Rd., 203/966-9577, www.newcanaannature.org/devils_den). At 1,756 acres, this is the largest sanctuary of the Connecticut chapter of the Nature Conservancy. The New Canaan Nature Center became the manager of Devil's Den in fall 2002.

Back on Rte. 57, continue south and you'll eventually dip into the tiny center of town. This is the exemplary sleepy New England village, yet smack in the middle of Fairfield County's posh suburbs. Though ritzy, it's quiet and without so much as a single commercial district. Most residents shop or dine in Westport to the south or Wilton to the west. At the core of the town, where Rtes. 53 and 57 are one road, there's a cute redbrick complex of Colonial-style shops, a market, a pharmacy, and a deli. Across the street, hedges and bushes obscure a large school complex, which takes in all of the town's schools. Here, too, are the town hall and some churches.

From here, the quickest way into neighboring Easton is to drive south into the northern end of Westport and make a left turn onto Rte. 136 north, which leads directly into town. However, a far more scenic and engaging way is to turn back north from downtown Weston and continue for about five miles until you reach the sterling evergreen-shaded shoreline of the placid Saugatuck Reservoir, a popular spot for fishing. You're actually in the eastern fringes of the aforementioned Devil's Den Preserve. If you follow Rte. 53 north around the entire reservoir you'll enter Redding. However, turn east from Rte. 53 onto Valley Forge Road to continue along this tour. You'll fringe the beautiful southwestern shore of the reservoir; after several twists and turns on this tortuous country road, make a left turn onto Old Redding Road and follow it south until it dead-ends with Westport Road (Rte. 136).

## Easton

A left turn onto Rte. 136 brings you the remaining couple of miles to Rte. 59—this junction marks the center of Easton, which is similar to Weston and offers an even more picturesque view of the town center. An ancient Congregational church sits high overlooking the intersection, and there's also a general store, antiques shop, and service station. **Greiser's Store and Deli** (203/459-1678), across from the church, is a good spot for provisions, an ice-cold drink, a sandwich, and some browsing. Attached in the same old yellow-brown clapboard building is the post office. The little spot is a true community hub, the kind you'd expect to see in northern Vermont. Interestingly, this scene is almost more authentic than what you might see in northwestern Connecticut.

Turn south on Rte. 59 (Sport Hill Road), which leads past **Silverman's Farm** (Sport Hill Rd., 203/261-3306, www.silvermansfarm.com), a great place to finish up a tour of the area. There's a farmers market, an animal farm with a petting zoo, a working cider mill, and seasonal pick-your-own crops (open daily; $2). At this point, you can continue down Rte. 59 into Bridgeport or hop onto the Merritt Parkway heading west, getting back off at either the Fairfield or Westport exit to return to the coast.

## FAIRFIELD

With more residents (58,000) than some of Connecticut's smaller cities, Fairfield is nonetheless a quintessential bedroom community. Other than General Electric's headquarters, the town is without much in the way of major industry. It's along the shore and the Metro-North railroad line to New Haven, and it's the last bastion of semi-serenity before reaching the state's largest city, Bridgeport.

Explored first by Roger Ludlow, Fairfield is one of the state's earliest settlements, a town whose initial prowess was in agriculture and then, concurrently, in shipping. Fairfield was begun as a strict Puritan settlement, but by the 1770s had become a true Yankee town, where wealth and merchant success was the measure of all virtue. It was called Fairfield because of its rich salt marshes, which made excellent grazing spots for cattle.

During the American Revolution, British general William Tryon and his troops landed in Fairfield three times, intending to march northward to Danbury—a major repository of munitions. During the first landing, the troops quickly moved through and headed to Danbury. The

second time, Fairfield was not so lucky. Few civilians had stayed behind at this point, but those who had were treated quite badly by the invading Brits. Ultimately, the redcoats burned about 100 homes and 100 additional structures.

The cost of rebuilding hit Fairfield hard. Agricultural yields, which had up to that point been a great source of prosperity, now had to be bartered for lumber to build homes. The city's shipping industry also died following the British raid, as many crafts were burned. Compared with New Haven and Norwalk, the other two towns greatly destroyed by raids, Fairfield saw the greatest forfeit of wealth. Despite its Colonial misfortune, however, Fairfield still has a bounty of 18th- and 19th-century homes.

As Newfield, later Bridgeport, began to grow next door because of its river access and sheltered harbor, Fairfield slumped, as it had little in the way of strategic importance. Still an important town by 1800, things really took a turn for the worse during the 19th century. Little of the industrial revolution's boom made its way to Fairfield, and shipping and agriculture boomed elsewhere in the state, quickly eclipsing that which had been established in Fairfield. The War of 1812, during which the British implemented a blockade of the Long Island Sound, resulted in docking what remained of the town's mercantile shipping fleet.

Untouched by the industrial revolution, farming (particularly of onions) continued to serve as Fairfield's primary source of income. Trade with the West Indies and foreign powers died following the war. Fairfield's fleet turned toward domestic trade, but generated little revenue. Many residents, unable to survive on the reduced wages, moved elsewhere, often to Vermont and New Hampshire. With zero population growth for the first half of the 19th century, because so many sons and daughters had moved elsewhere, those who remained seemed content with agrarian ways, and subsistence became the only real goal of residents. This mentality would prevent the economy from going anywhere for the next 50 years.

A further blow was struck when a new town, Westport, was incorporated from existing sections of Fairfield and Norwalk. Bridgeport, Danbury, and Norwalk thrived industrially; Fairfield spun its wheels. Bridgeport eventually stole Fairfield's status as county seat by building a county courthouse, and because Fairfield lacked proper facilities to house visiting lawyers and court persons, while Bridgeport had a nice big hotel.

The town found itself in immense debt by the 20th century. Several times manufacturers considered moving plants to Fairfield, but this rarely took hold. Fairfield's only remaining hope lay in reinventing itself as a resort community—most of this transformation occurred in Southport, on desirable Sasco Hill, which overlooks Long Island Sound. Two (now long-gone) grand hotels began to thrive in Fairfield, as New Yorkers discovered the area's summertime virtues. Bridgeport's new industrialists also began moving into large mansions in nearby Fairfield.

The small, coastal division of the town, **Southport**—a former shipbuilding community—turned during the early 20th century into a dignified yachting enclave, today one of the most prestigious in the Northeast. Southport's main drag, Pequot Avenue (accessed just off U.S. 1 at the Westport border), is lined with little redbrick and white clapboard buildings, some containing antiques shops and boutiques. It's a picture-perfect neighborhood with many great homes and mansions.

As opposed to other Fairfield County towns, but like the area's cities, Fairfield's waterfront neighborhoods, outside of posh Southport, are modest and simple, consisting of rows of neat bungalows and 1950s ranch-style homes. Not surprisingly, the working-class neighborhoods nearest Bridgeport have a grittier feel about them.

In points north, the verdant and grand **Greenfield Hill** neighborhood has many of the town's prettiest homesteads—scads of dogwood trees, too. About 50,000 of these trees were planted in Fairfield during the early 1800s, and every May since 1936, a **dogwood festival** (203/259-5596, www.greenfieldhillvis.org/dogwood.htm) has been staged on the grounds of the Greenfield Hills Congregational Church (the site of the estate once owned by Dr. Isaac Bronson, who is said to have begun the dogwood craze). Various homes and properties are

open for touring, and festivities include art shows, tag sales, and food stalls.

Architectural buffs might stop by the **Fairfield Historical Society** to obtain a driving tour of houses built in the 1920s to 1940s by Cameron Clark, Colonial Revival homes whose seem right out of *Mr. Blandings Builds His Dream House*. The tour extends through Fairfield proper, Greenfield Hill, and Southport. None of these homes is open to the public, but all can easily be admired from the roadside.

The Jesuit **Fairfield University,** a preppy, small liberal arts college in the mold of a suburban Boston College, is popular with kids from the Boston suburbs looking to go to school as far from Boston as possible (by Boston's somewhat provincial standards, Fairfield University may as well be in Tahiti). Fairfield University has been something of a best-kept secret among Jesuit colleges, but it's risen to prominence in recent years, prompting some to declare it ranks right up there with Boston College as New England's leading such institution. Visitors don't tend to flock here in droves, but the campus is not without its charms, including the **Fairfield University Art Galleries** (N. Benson Rd., Fairfield, 203/254-4000, ext. 2969, www.fairfield.edu). Here the **Thomas J. Walsh Art Gallery** offers engaging rotating exhibits and student works. Also on campus, the unbecomingly named **Gallery of the Center for Financial Studies** (open 11 A.M.–5 P.M. Tues.–Sat., noon–4 P.M. Sun., free) has exhibits.

The **Connecticut Audubon Birdcraft Museum** (314 Unquowa Rd., 203/259-0416, www.ctaudubon.org, open 10 A.M.–5 P.M., Tues.–Fri., noon–4 P.M. weekends, $2) opened in 1914 as the first nature center in America. Set on a six-acre wildlife sanctuary, the odd little museum is a National Historic Landmark; inside are dioramas, wildlife exhibits, dinosaur footprints, and other fun things to look at and play with. More than 120 species of bird have been documented on the property. A related site that's also very popular with outdoors enthusiasts is the **Connecticut Audubon Center at Fairfield** (2325 Burr St., 203/259-6305, www.ctaudubon.org, sanctuary open dawn–dusk daily, center open

## FAIRFIELD COUNTY BABYLON

*Only the little people pay taxes.*

—*Leona Helmsley*

W ho doesn't love a good scandal? Of course, bad things happen to bad people all the time. Connecticut has probably endured no greater number of wrongdoings than any other place—and they've happened all over the state, no more often in one region than any other.

But somehow, the salacious headlines surrounding misdeeds in Fairfield County generate more buzz than those in say, Waterbury, where former mayor and failed 2000 Republican U.S. Senate contender Philip A. Giordano was involved in a rank scandal concerning allegations of felony and sex with children. Fairfield County is famously rich and famously famous. Had the Giordano case occurred there, it would have received far more attention than it has, especially from the national media. There seems to be a fascination, traceable right back to Greek mythology, with powerful people who start living according to their own laws—and then get nabbed.

Few observers, for example, could resist watching real-estate and hotel tycoon and reputed megalomaniac Leona Helmsley go down on tax evasion charges a few years back. It played especially well that the so-called "Queen of Mean" was forced to abandon her palatial Greenwich digs in exchange for 18 months of not-so-hard time at a minimum security prison in Danbury.

Greenwich is the hometown of Kathie Lee Gifford, who's spent more time on the covers of tabloid scandal rags than most; her former co-host Regis Philbin lives in Greenwich, too. It's also the hometown of the late Carolyn Bissette Kennedy, who perished in the infamous 1999 plane crash off the coast of Martha's Vineyard with her husband, John F. Kennedy, Jr., and her sister, Lauren.

But the Kennedy connection goes much deeper.

The unsolved 1975 murder of Greenwich teen Martha Moxley, immortalized in two 1998 nonfiction bestsellers (the most famous, *Murder in Greenwich,* was penned by Dominick Dunne and O.J. Simpson detective Mark Fuhrman), has helped solidify the region's status as a Babylon of sorts. The most often-named suspect in the case had long been Thomas Skakel, nephew of Ethel and the late Robert Kennedy. The Skakel family lived next door to the Moxleys in the exclusive Belle Haven neighborhood, and Martha was bludgeoned to death with a golf club that belonged to this famous-by-association family, who stopped cooperating with police soon after the murder.

For years, nobody was formally charged, and accusations were tossed around that various persons had paid off various other persons to keep the case from ever being solved. That all changed in January 2000. In a surprising move, Thomas Skakel's older brother, Michael, was charged with the murder; he surrendered to police the following day, and a long trial ensued. In summer 2002, a Connecticut jury convicted Michael Skakel of the murder of Martha Moxley. At press time, Skakel (who's serving a prison sentence of 20 years to life) is appealing his conviction.

Upscale Darien popped up in the headlines in recent years with regard to the courtroom drama of accused rapist Alex Kelly. (The story later made it to the small screen, in the form of a tabloid-style made-for-television movie and a dime-store true crime book). Kelly has been depicted as having lived a life of privilege and ease in the face of great evil. After he was charged with the rape of a schoolmate, he fled the country and bounced around posh ski resorts in Switzerland and France for the better part of a decade—supposedly supported through secret payments from his parents. This episode, like those illuminated in Rick Moody's novel (and Ang Lee film) *The Ice Storm* and Ira

Levin's famous novel-turned-movie *The Stepford Wives*, shows a sinister underside of Fairfield County.

One of the most tragic and bizarre county scandals was the plight of Margaret Ray, a mentally ill woman who repeatedly broke into the New Canaan home of television talk-show host David Letterman. She was once caught at a tollbooth at the Lincoln Tunnel, driving Letterman's Porsche and claiming to be his wife and the mother of his child. At other times, the star arrived home to find Ray in his house. Letterman handled the situation with considerable compassion, trying to minimize publicity, never condemning the woman for her actions, and declining to press charges in hopes that she would eventually get the help she needed. He added in a 1994 interview with *Playboy*, "this woman has, in my assessment, been failed by the judicial system, failed by the state psychiatric system—if in fact there is one—failed by her family, and failed by her friends."

Eventually, Ray stopped stalking Letterman and moved on to astronaut Story Musgrave. She committed suicide in Colorado in October 1998. In 2002, Letterman sold his New Canaan house and moved to a lavish estate across the border in New York's Westchester County.

And then there's Martha. Entire books have been written on the scandalous life of Westport's love-her-or-hate-her arbiter of interior decorating, event-planning, cooking, and crafts. In the minds of many, Martha Stewart epitomizes the good and the bad of Fairfield County. Ironically, she herself chided Westport in 2000 for becoming "more elitist"—she still owns an estate there on Turkey Hill Road, where some of her television programs are filmed, but her official residence is now a 153-acre estate in Bedford, New York. More than a few bemused and amused locals have noted that to whatever extent Westport has become elitist, Martha herself is partly responsible.

It's a financial scandal that beset Stewart and her empire. In June 2003, Stewart was indicted on nine charges related to insider trading and obstruction of justice, resulting from her decision to sell off 4,000 shares of ImClone stock the day before the company was to receive terrible news concerning a new anticancer drug. This led many to conclude that she has at least done something highly unethical, if not necessarily illegal. It has been alleged that Stewart received inside information from her friend, ImClone founder Sam Waksal, who dumped an enormous amount of his own stock prior to the government's announcement that it would reject the anti-cancer drug. Waksal eventually pleaded guilty to fraud and insider trading, and began serving a seven-year sentence in summer 2003.

Of course, tales of financial scandal are nothing new here. Back in 1932, a Darien businessman made headlines for skimming a huge amount of money from the state of Connecticut. Former Republican state representative G. Leroy Kemp, a local realtor, was hired to purchase private lands on which the newly proposed Merritt Parkway would eventually be built. Kemp was charged with purchasing about 2,600 acres of prime Fairfield County real estate, and he found a great way to make a little money for himself on the side.

Kemp became cozy with a few area realtors, whom he tipped off about parcels of land the state would soon be seeking. The realtors then approached the prospective landowners and negotiated the sale of the land to Kemp. In return for these tips, the realtors agreed to split their realtor fees with Kemp fifty-fifty.

The residents of Fairfield County's wealthiest towns are, of course, no more inherently likely to commit acts of avarice and hubris than the citizens of any other place in America. It's just that when they do, you can safely bet that nobody feels too sorry for them.

9 A.M.–4:30 P.M. Tues.–Sat., also open noon–4:30 P.M. Sun. spring and fall, sanctuary $2, center free), which comprises 152 acres of woodland and pond-side trails. The center has a walk designed specifically for the elderly, the blind, and the physically impaired, and runs a very interesting operation for wounded birds.

One can walk around Fairfield center, admiring large homes, including the Burr Homestead, in which John Hancock wed Dorothy Quincy in 1775. One can sit on the town green, admiring a large gazebo. Down near the center of town, the **Fairfield Historical Society Museum** (636 Old Post Rd., 203/259-1598, www.fairfieldhistoricalsociety.org, open 10 A.M.–4:30 P.M. Tues.–Sat., 1 P.M.–4:30 P.M. Sun., $3) documents Fairfield's 350-year history with a library of genealogy and both changing and permanent exhibits. The museum is contained within the Ogden House Museum and Gardens, an exceptionally well-preserved Colonial saltbox typical of 18th-century Fairfield; unlike most houses of that time it survived the British burning of the town during the War of Independence.

## SHOPPING

Spending money is serious sport in Fairfield County, and evidence of the fervor with which residents pursue this activity lies in just about every downtown in the region. A limited sampling of the area's retail highlights appears below.

### Greenwich

On Putnam Avenue (U.S. 1), there's a procession of fine shops. You'll pass by Sotheby's Realty, where you can seek out just the right furnishings for that mansion you're building. The home-furnishings stores stock everything from Oriental rugs to handcrafted cabinets from New Hampshire to Provençal fabrics. Chain stores like Baccarat, Simon Pearce, Gap, and Banana Republic line nearby Greenwich Ave., and Prada, Gucci, and Donna Karan window displays at Saks make a feast for fashionable eyes.

### Norwalk

The SoNo section of town is your best bet for shopping, as you'll find unusual shops along Washington and Main Streets as well as the blocks near them. **Oddz** (136 Washington St., 203/866-8818) has the latest alternative duds, plus a reasonable selection of more sensible ones. **SAGA** (119 Washington St., 203/855-1900) carries a fascinating array of artifacts, skulls, Day of the Dead curios, and other handcrafts from Latin American and the U.S. Southwest. **M&M Cigar and Gifts** (83 Washington St., 203/853-9748) has the largest selection of stogies in the area.

The **Giving Tree** (181 Main St., Norwalk, 203/840-1515) is an enormous consignment store famous not only for its children's clothing and accessories, Christian and Jewish books, study and teaching aids, and designer women's clothing, but also for raising money for the Children's Special Needs charity (the store goal is to raise $2,000 monthly, and it donates the first $800). The Norwalk branch is fairly new, and the Stamford one has been around for a while.

It's not as impressive a shopping center as those farther east along the coast, but the **Factory Outlets at Norwalk** (East Ave. at exit 16 of I-95, 203/838-1349) does have a handful of useful shops with cut-rate prices: Bed Bath & Beyond, Famous Footwear, Royal Doulton, and Van Heusen among them.

### Stamford

In addition to the burgeoning antiques district downtown, shoppers in this city love to browse to their heart's content at **Stamford Town Center** (Tresser Blvd. between Atlantic and Elm Sts., 203/324-0935, www.shopstamfordtowncenter.com), an upscale nine-level indoor mall anchored by Saks 5th Avenue, Macy's, and Filene's—it also stood in for the Beverly Hills Mall in the Woody Allen and Bette Midler flick *Scenes from a Mall*.

**Shanti Bithi Nursery** (3047 High Ridge Rd., Stamford, 203/329-0768) is one of the nation's leading growers and importers of bonsai, with more than 3,000 for sale. The nursery also offers classes on bonsai and sells Japanese stone lanterns.

## DEVIL'S DEN PRESERVE: FAIRFIELD COUNTY'S NATURAL TREASURE

Straddling the Weston-Redding border, the 1,756-acre **Devil's Den Preserve** has long been one of Fairfield County's most treasured sanctuaries; it's the jewel of the Connecticut chapter of the Nature Conservancy (the preserve is managed by the New Canaan Nature Center). This maze of rock ledges and dense woodlands remains appealing to hikers, birdwatchers, and other outdoors enthusiasts year-round.

A favorite way to visit the park, especially if you've got children with you, is to partake in one of the sanctuary's monthly family nature walks. Walk participants can identify century-old oak and maple trees and lichen-clad geological outcroppings and discuss the history of this immense tract of land by examining the remains of an 1850s sawmill and a re-created charcoal-making site. (Bushels of this messy gray substance, which fueled Colonial Connecticut's pig-iron forges and blacksmith shops, were distilled from this forest's seemingly endless supply of non-resinous hardwoods throughout the 18th and early 19th centuries.)

Of course, you can also come and wander the park on your own; 21 miles of hiking and cross-country ski trails traverse it. About 145 species of birds pass through the park, including wood duck, ruffed grouse, and pileated woodpeckers, plus mammals including bobcats, coyotes, and red foxes. The Nature Conservancy also operates the smaller **Katharine Ordway Preserve,** 165 Goodhill Rd., which has fields of wildflowers and stands of mountain laurel, as well as an arboretum of trees from around the world. Devil's Den Preserve is in Weston at 33 Pent Rd., 203/226-4991.

### Elsewhere

**Gilbertie's Herb Farm** (7 Sylvan Ln.,off Rte. 33, Westport, 203/227-4175) is a must-see for gardening enthusiasts. Owner Sal Gilbertie has written books about herbs, and his staff is highly knowledgeable and holds workshops and demonstrations throughout the year. In Darien, **Morgans** (21 Tokeneke Rd., 203/655-9476) is a 17-dealer antiques center in a converted 19th-century schoolhouse.

## RECREATION

### Bicycling

The terrain in coastal Fairfield County is relatively flat and in many places exceptionally picturesque. The tours described above through Greenwich and Westport are particularly appealing, as are the country roads inland a bit in New Canaan, Wilton, Weston, and Easton. Just remember that as auto traffic has increased many-fold in recent decades, the roads remain treacherously narrow and winding in places. If you're planning to conquer Fairfield County by bike, wear the appropriate gear and be very careful.

Rental shops include **Dave's Cycle** (78 Valley Rd., the Cos Cob section of Greenwich, 203/661-7736) and the **Stamford Cycle Center** (1492 High Ridge Rd., Stamford, 203/968-1100).

### Day Spas

Day spas are a booming trend in tony Fairfield County, with several prominent facilities throughout the region. Favorites include **Born of Earth Spa** (375-2 Post Rd. W, Westport, 203/226-BORN, www.bornofearth.com); **Hands on Massage** (282 Railroad Ave., Greenwich, 203/531-7929); **Judith Jackson Spa** (Inn at National Hall, 20 Wilton Rd., Westport, 203/226-7626); and **Noelle Spa for Beauty and Wellness** (1100 High Ridge Rd., Stamford, 203/322-3445). All offer a full range of facial, skin, foot, and nail treatments, plus mud wraps, massage, and sugar glows.

### Golf

Golfing is a hugely popular pastime in Fairfield County, but the vast majority of the area's dozens of courses are not only private, but they have long (as in a few years or more) waiting lists and both entry and annual fees that run well into five figures. Still, if you call ahead and reserve a tee

THE CONNECTICUT COAST

time as early as possible, you should be able to enjoy yourself at the following 18-hole public facilities: **Fairchild Wheeler Golf Course** (2390 Easton Tpke., Fairfield, 203/373-5911); **Oak Hills** (165 Fillow Ave., Norwalk, 203/838-0303); **Smith-Richardson** (2425 Morehouse Hwy., Fairfield, 203/255-7300); and arguably the most acclaimed and popular (but short, at 6,400 yards) of the bunch, **Sterling Farms** (1349 Newfield Ave., Stamford, 203/461-9090).

## Hiking

In addition to many acres of rugged woodland worth exploring in Devil's Den, keep in mind some of the nature centers and attractions described above if you're interested in hiking. These especially include the Audubon Center of Greenwich, the Bartlett Arboretum and the Stamford Museum and Nature Center in Stamford, the Connecticut Audubon Center in Fairfield, Weir Farm in Wilton, and the New Canaan Nature Center.

## ENTERTAINMENT AND NIGHTLIFE

### Theater and Performing Arts

Fairfield County, like much of the coast, is dense with arts venues, including some excellent year-round and summer-stock theaters, some of them nationally acclaimed.

The **Connecticut Grand Opera & Orchestra** (15 Bank St., Stamford, 203/359-0009, www.ctgrandopera.org) performs at the Palace Theatre in Stamford, 61 Atlantic St., 203/325-4466. The **Palace Theatre,** part of the **Stamford Center for the Arts** (www.onlyatsca.com), was designed as a vaudeville venue in the late 1920s by renowned theater architect Thomas Lamb; it offers theatrical and musical shows year-round. The building is presently undergoing a dramatic restoration that will rehabilitate the terra cotta facade, create a new outer lobby and other public areas, and develop a smaller 194-seat theater for experimental and newer works—this renovation is expected to be completed in 2003. Just down the street is the center's other venue, the larger **Rich Forum** (307 Atlantic St., 203/325-4466), which

is one of the most impressive performing arts facilities in the state, regularly showing Broadway-bound shows, national touring productions, and concerts by popular bands and musicians. The Palace and Forum also host the **Stamford Symphony Orchestra** (203/325-4466, www.stamfordsymphony.org).

On a smaller scale, **Curtain Call** (1349 Newfield Ave., Stamford, 203/329-8207, www.curtaincallinc.com) stages local plays, concerts, and workshops; **Stamford Theatre Works** (200 Strawberry Hill Ave., 203/359-4414) presents professional theater fall through spring.

Southwestern Connecticut is extremely fortunate to have so many high-caliber performance groups, including the **Fairfield Orchestra** (203/972-7400), which has concert series from fall through spring at both the Norwalk Concert Hall and the stately 1801 Federal-style Old Fairfield. The orchestra has performed in New York City at Carnegie Hall and hosted internationally renowned musicians, such as violinist Joshua Bell. Another interesting music group is the **Greenwich Symphony** (203/869-2664, www.greenwichsym.org), a well-respected orchestra that has been going strong since the early 1950s.

For 50 nights throughout the summer, performances of many kinds—from comedy to music—are held at Westport's **Levitt Pavilion for the Performing Arts,** (203/226-7600, www.levittpavilion.com) behind the Westport Public Library on Jesup Road. These shows are often outstanding and, in most cases, completely free. One of the best professional summer-stock theaters in the country, the **Westport Country Playhouse** (25 Powers Ct., off U.S. 1, 203/227-4177, www.westportplayhouse.org), is inside a characterful converted barn and regularly draws famous Hollywood and Broadway actors and actresses to its intimate stage. Summer-stock community theaters in the area include the **White Barn Theatre** (Newtown Tpke., Westport, 203/227-3768, www.whitebarntheatre.org), and the **Wilton Playshop** (Lovers Ln., Rtes. 33 and 106, 203/762-7629, www.wiltonplayshop.org).

Fairfield University's **Quick Center for the Arts** (Fairfield University, N. Benson Rd., Fairfield, 203/254-4010, www.fairfield.edu) has both the 750-seat Kelley Theatre and the 150-seat Wien Experimental Theatre; throughout the school year drama, poetry, music, family programming, and dance are presented on both stages. These include some student performances but also visits from major artists and groups, from the Chamber Music Society of Lincoln Center to the Trisha Brown dance company.

## Nightclubs and Hangouts

The renowned restaurant and inn, **Silvermine Tavern** (194 Perry Ave., 203/847-4558) is also worth noting for the Inn Late Jazz program; the tavern becomes a highly respected jazz club on Friday and Saturday nights beginning at 9 P.M., and also on some Thursday evenings. The program doesn't run in the summer. Norwalk's hip SoNo district is loaded with trendy New York–style cocktail lounges, cigar bars, and nightclubs, including **The Loft** (97 Washington St., 203/838-6555), a spirited martini bar and cigar lounge that's a study in posing. The high, pressed-tin ceiling and velvet drapes set the tone. Another hipster-infested dancing-and-drinking place is **Liquid** (112 Washington St., 203/866-0800). There are several other cool hangouts in the same neighborhood, which is the epicenter of Fairfield County's nightlife. The nearby **Deep Pockets Billiards** (50 Washington St., 203/831-0743) is the place to shoot pool.

In Stamford, for drinks stop by **Kennedy's** (600 Summer St., 203/325-1131), an authentic Irish pub with Guinness on tap and a true pub feel. Or consider the **Temple Bar and Druid Restaurant** (120 Bedford St., 203/708-9000), an immense pub and restaurant owned by a couple of Ireland's transplants. It's a hugely popular scene on weekends, when there's live music. It has beautiful artwork inside; note the architectural details. Stamford's favorite place for dancing is the **Art Bar** (84 W. Park Place, 203/973-0300). **Premiere** (129 Atlantic St., 203/323-1120) is another hot dance club in downtown Stamford.

Dozens of the restaurants in this chapter are major nightlife haunts, with bars and sometimes patios packed with Fairfield County's well-heeled martini-sippers, micro-beer guzzlers, and wine connoisseurs. Notables include the **Black Goose**

**Grille** in Darien; **Tommy's** in Fairfield; **Elm Street Oyster House** and **Sundown Saloon** in Greenwich; **Amberjack's, Donovan's, Habana, River Cat Grill,** and **The Brewhouse** (which is noted for its live music many nights) in Norwalk; **Bank Street Brewing Company,** the **Long Ridge Tavern, Ocean 211, Paradise Bar and Grille,** and **The Playwright** in Stamford; and **Mario's,** and **Splash** in Westport.

Westport's **Cedar Brook Cafe** (918 Post Rd. E, or U.S. 1, 203/221-7429) has been serving the gay and lesbian community since the 1950s, making it one of the oldest such clubs in the nation. There's a small dance floor, an outdoor patio, and a couple other rooms for mingling and watching the occasional drag show.

# FESTIVALS AND EVENTS

## Spring and Summer

In early May the **Fairfield Dogwood Festival** (Old Academy and Bronson Rds., Greenfield section of Fairfield, 203/259-5596) is a great way to usher in spring, with art shows, tag sales, food stalls. Homes and properties are also open for touring. An astounding assortment of bric-a-brac and bargain-priced collectibles is sold at the **Minks to Sinks Sale** (U.S. 7 and School Rd., Wilton, 203/834-1793), which lures droves of die-hard shoppers to town in May (and then again in early October). At the end of the month, drop by Staples High School to visit the **Westport Handcraft Show** (70 North Ave., 203/227-7844).

Summertime festivities in late June include the **Fairfield County Irish Festival** (Roger Ludlowe Field, Fairfield, 203/259-4025) and the **Norfield Church's Country Fair** (Norfield Congregational Church, Weston, 203/227-7886). Historic SoNo comes alive in July for the **Norwalk Harbor Splash!** (downtown SoNo, 203/838-9444). And there's a **Village Fair and Sidewalk Sale** (203/966-2004) in downtown New Canaan.

## Fall

In September, 20 food booths, 240 juried crafts artisans, a slew of historic ships and boats, sky diving, fireworks, and live music draw thousands to one of coastal Connecticut's most celebrated events, the **Norwalk Oyster Festival** (203/838-9444). Later in the month, the **Outdoor Arts Festival** (Bruce Museum, 203/869-0376) draws folks to Greenwich to check out the works of more than 80 artisans; a second festival is held at the Bruce in May.

In early October, Greenwich also hosts a popular **Apple Festival** (North Greenwich Congregational Church, 606 Riversville Rd., 203/869-7763), with rides, crafts vendors, baked apple goods, and children's books.

## ACCOMMODATIONS

You'll pay dearly for a hotel room in coastal Fairfield County, no matter the time of year. There are plenty of country inns and also fine upscale chain business hotels, but few offer regular rates below $100 nightly, and in downtown Stamford, the rule is closer to $200. However, virtually all of the high-end business properties dip their rates by as much as 50 percent on weekends. Conversely, you'll often pay more to stay at one of the inns on weekends, but Monday through Wednesday or Thursday, you may encounter a limited discount. Other than downtown Stamford and a relatively new stretch of chain properties just off the Merritt Parkway and U.S. 7 in Norwalk, hotels tend to be spread fairly evenly throughout the county.

### Hotels and Motels

**Over $250:** One of the most talked-about new hotels in New England, the 83-room **Delamar Greenwich Harbor** (500 Steamboat Rd., 203/661-9800), opened in 2003 in what had been a fading property with a stunning location overlooking Greenwich Harbor. The spacious rooms—with Frette linens, down pillows and duvets, flat-screen TVs, CD players, coral-marble bathrooms, and deep cast-iron soaking tubs—start at around $300 for a town view. Expect to pay around $700 for one of the enormous suites, with a wet bar, fireplace, whirlpool tub, and high-tech entertainment system. You can tie up your boat at the 600-foot dock, work out in the fitness center, and enjoy a meal at the fabulous L'Escale

Restaurant and Bar. Predictably, this hotel (which feels as though it was airlifted from a secluded Mediterranean island) has fast become a favorite hideaway for celebs and executives.

**$150–250:** One of Connecticut's few luxury full-service hotels, the **Hyatt Regency Greenwich** (1800 Putnam Ave., 203/637-1234) occupies the regal turreted former headquarters of the Condé Nast publishing empire. Its design, grounds, and setting are beautiful—the lobby feels like a Mediterranean cloister. Rooms received a much-needed overhaul in 2001 and now have lavish European bedding and soft gold-and-tan color schemes. The four-story, conservatory-style atrium, filled with tall trees and a babbling brook, hosts a memorable weekend brunch. Amenities include a heated indoor pool and sundeck, a full health club, and the Enza Riccobene Salon and Day Spa; the 375 guest rooms have dual-line phones, bathrobes and slippers, refrigerators, and CD players.

No hotel in the area has spiffier rooms and a more Manhattan-influenced aesthetic than the sumptuous **Westin Stamford** (1 First Stamford Place, 203/967-2222 or 800/WESTIN-1) where soft-wood finishes, muted tan and gray tones, fluffy warm duvets, and a full slate of in-room amenities await you. Westin also offers a comprehensive slate of children's programs, making it an ideal getaway for families. There's also a great health club, a large indoor pool, a tennis court, and a Jacuzzi. The Asian-American Area Restaurant and Tea Garden Lounge are quite trendy for dining or cocktails; room service is 24 hours. Rates are in line with other business hotels in Stamford, but the overall quality of this property is higher than most. Stamford's train station is within walking distance.

Another highly traditional option among corporate roosts is the **Stamford Marriott** (2 Stamford Forum, Tresser Blvd. and Canal St., 203/357-9555 or 800/732-9689), an immense 506-room property that's slightly less stylish than the Westin, but is just opposite the Stamford Town Center shopping mall and close to the train station and highway (and is also a stop for the New York City airport shuttle service, Connecticut Limousine). An asset is the revolving top-floor restaurant, Vuli, a fine Northern Italian eatery that shows just how far hotel dining has come in Connecticut over the years; live piano and jazz are performed nightly. A health club, indoor and outdoor pools, an American restaurant, a wine bar, a rooftop jogging track, a racquetball court, and a game room round out the amenities.

Across the street, the **Holiday Inn Select** (700 Main St., Stamford, 203/358-8400 or 800/408-7640) is a perfectly pleasant deluxe business hotel, but with the usual conservative chain-hotel furnishings that give the place a slightly less characterful feel than some of its competitors. But its rates also tend to be a bit lower. There are 383 rooms, a health club, an indoor pool, and a restaurant.

The **Sheraton Stamford Hotel** (2701 Summer St., 203/359-1300 or 800/325-3535) is a well-maintained, luxurious property that's a top pick among visiting business executives—it's also slightly removed from downtown and a bit closer to northern Stamford attractions. Many of the 450 rooms look into a soaring central atrium, where there's a restaurant. Off the atrium, you'll find the largest hotel health club in town and an indoor pool.

The **Westport Inn** (1595 Post Rd. E, 203/259-5236 or 800/446-8997, www.westportinn.com) is home to a new steakhouse, plus a health club with saunas, an atrium and an indoor pool, and very good business services. The brochures and advertising go to great lengths to give people the impression it's something along the lines of a country inn with hotel amenities, which, aesthetically anyway, it is not—it's a very nice motor lodge. Nevertheless, rooms are graciously furnished, and the exterior has been sheathed in a Colonial-style clapboard-and-glass facade that is an improvement on most motor lodges. A newer building in back contains larger suites with big sitting areas.

**$100–150:** Recently renovated, the **Fairfield Inn Stamford–Greenwich** (135 Harvard Ave., 203/357-7100 or 800/228-2800) has a dreary but handy location off I-95 in a semi-industrial neighborhood convenient to downtown Stamford and Greenwich. Rooms are large and attractive; the hotel is eight stories, so top floors have a view of downtown or Long Island Sound in the

distance. The attached retro-cool City Limits Diner is a terrific place for a meal (see below, under Food).

Near the Wilton border, **Courtyard By Marriott** (474 Main Ave., 203/849-9111 or 800/321-2211) is a very nice midrange business property, predictably popular with business travelers. The neighboring **Four Points Sheraton Norwalk** (426 Main Ave., 203/849-9828) is just slightly more upscale and expensive; it also has a decent Italian restaurant.

Another option along here is the **Hilton Garden Inn** (560 Main Ave., 203/523-4000 or 800/HILTONS), a recently opened 170-room property with a full-service restaurant, indoor pool and whirlpool, fitness center, 24-hour guest snack and gift shop, and self-serve laundry. **Homestead Studio Suites** (400 Main Ave., 203/847-6888) is a 135-room extended-stay property along the same stretch. All of these have a dull "Edge City" location off U.S. 7, right by the Merritt Parkway.

The **Seagrape Inn** (1160 Reef Rd., Fairfield, 203/255-6808, www.seagrapeinn.com) provides tasteful and large all-suite accommodations a short walk from Jennings Beach and Long Island Sound. Each unit of this contemporary building has a dining area, equipped kitchen, and in most cases a balcony. Rooms are themed for different places and style: the Arizona Room, the Nautical Room, and so on.

**$50–100:** With the cheapest rooms in Greenwich (and that's not saying much), the **Howard Johnson Hotel Greenwich** (1114 Boston Post Rd., or U.S. 1, 203/637-3691) doesn't look like a typical HoJo from the outside, with its red-brick motor-court exterior and frilly, black, wrought-iron grillwork. Rooms have somewhat dated dark-wood furnishings and could use some brightening and refurbishing, and some are permeated by the noise of neighboring I-95.

**Budget Hospitality Inn** (19 Clark's Hill Ave., Stamford, 203/327-4300 or 800/362-7666) is one of the cheapest in town, and it's the one with the best location; however, rates do not drop here on weekends, meaning you're probably better off spending the extra bucks at one of the luxury hotels that sometimes come down to under $100 on weekends. Weekdays, you'll save a ton of money here. Rooms have small desks, clean bathrooms, and basic furnishings, and there's a pleasant lobby with sofa and end chairs. Some units have limited kitchen facilities.

## Country Inns and Bed-and-Breakfasts

**Over $250:** The **Homestead Inn** (420 Field Point Rd., Greenwich, 203/869-7500), a stately mansion in the prestigious Belle Haven neighborhood, was built in 1799 and converted into an inn—with Italianate and Gothic touches—in 1859. Rooms are also in a pair of outbuildings, but those in the main house have the most character. On the other hand, rooms in the outer buildings are somewhat larger and newer, perhaps better suited for business travelers or those seeking privacy. The place needed a bit of TLC when Thomas Henkelmann and his wife Theresa Carroll bought it in 1997; they've done an amazing revamp of both the guest rooms and public spaces, where you'll find priceless artworks, top-quality antiques, rich fabrics, and elegant color schemes. An interesting literary note: Playwright William Inge was living in room 26 when he penned his most celebrated work, *Picnic*. The restaurant, which bears Henkelmann's name, is among the finest in the state.

One of the most exclusive accommodations in New England, the **Inn at National Hall** (2 Post Rd., or W. U.S. 1, 203/221-1351 or 800/NAT-HALL, www.innatnationalhall.com) was created from the shell of a three-story Italianate Victorian building overlooking the Saugatuck River and tony Westport. The 15 guest rooms and the public areas were decorated by exceptionally talented (and whimsically minded) local artisans who have filled the spaces with trompe l'oeil murals, carved cherry woodwork, and memorable antiques. A few loft suites have two-story ceilings and staircases leading into romantic second-level sleeping areas. Bathrooms are of limestone and marble and come with Turkish cotton robes and heated towel racks. You'll have a hard time imagining amenities that the innkeepers haven't thought of.

For over-the-top opulence, book a stay in the inn's own harem's den of sorts, the Turkistan Suite, which features an ottoman chest, gold-stenciled sage and rose walls, a curved balcony sleeping loft, and a two-story floor-to-ceiling staircase. Of course, on the flip side, this inn drips with pretension—but for many guests, that's part of the fun. Arthur Tauck, of the famed Tauck Tours, opened this property in 1993. A few rooms are priced around $300, but suites range $500–750. The restaurant, Miramar, is one of the hottest tickets in Connecticut. The luxe Judith Jackson Spa is on the same block.

**$150–250:** It's within walking distance of Long Island Sound and the town's exclusive beaches, but the **Harbor House Inn** (165 Shore Rd., Old Greenwich, 203/637-0145, www.hhinn.com) falls a little short of its potential considering the gaudy rates. This many-gabled, old white mansion exudes character and has a big homey lobby with plenty of comfy chairs to curl up in. Rooms have a comfortable hodgepodge of furnishings, wall-to-wall carpeting, and wood-paneled walls, but are otherwise undistinguished. Location is key. A few rooms have shared baths

The **Stanton House Inn** (76 Maple Ave., 203/869-2110, www.bbonline.com/ct/stanton) is within walking distance of downtown Greenwich and has beautiful furnishings in both the common and guest rooms, including hardwood floors and attractive Colonial reproduction furnishings. The grounds, which include a large pool, are also arresting, as is the surrounding residential neighborhood. Although the main structure dates from 1840, architect Stanford White redesigned and enlarged the house in 1899.

At one time a boarding house, and before that part of a large estate, the spiffy **Cos Cob Inn** (50 River Rd., Cos Cob Greenwich, 203/661-5845, www.coscobinn.com) has been beautifully restored. It's a subtly charming place, not overdone with frill, and popular with both business and leisure travelers. Common areas are limited to a small breakfast/sitting area, but rooms are gracious and sunny, many with fireplaces, refrigerators, and Jacuzzi tubs, and some with private entrances. A few smaller units have starting rates around $125. Across the street, the same owners operate Beacon Point Marine, on the

Mianus River—this full-service marina has nearly 300 boat slips.

The **Inn at Longshore** (260 Compo Rd. S, Westport, 203/226-3316, www.innatlongshore.com) was built at the turn of the 20th century as a private home and later functioned as a country club frequented by Rockefellers and Roosevelts. Nowadays, it's a swanky seaside hotel on 52 acres of woodlands, with a golf course and rolling lawns, a short stroll from town beaches and the town tennis courts. Rooms are pleasantly furnished, not necessarily fancy, with floral bedspreads and a mix of newer and older pieces, but they're clean and comfortable, and the rates aren't bad considering this wonderful setting, golf and tennis access, two swimming pools, stellar on-site restaurant, and see-and-be-seen hotel bar.

Tremendous attention to detail, lovely furnishings, and relatively (by New Canaan standards) reasonable rates, with some rooms going for less than $150 nightly, propel the 18th-century white-clapboard **Roger Sherman Inn** (195 Oenoke Ridge, 203/966-4541, www.rogershermaninn.com) into the upper echelons of Fairfield County's lodging scene. Rooms contain a full slate of modern amenities (TVs, phones, private baths) and a restrained tasteful selection of both older and newer country-style pieces. An adjoining carriage house, which was completely renovated in the late 1990s, contains an additional nine rooms. The attached restaurant is one of the best in town. Next door is another fine old country inn, the **Maples Inn** (179 Oenoke Ridge, 203/966-2927, www.maplesinnct.com), which is a dependable and slightly less pricey alternative to the Roger Sherman, though slightly worn in places. (It would also be fun to see this great old house with its original hardwood floors and minus a few modern interior updates). Nevertheless, pluses here include manor-like grounds, an easy and picturesque walk to downtown, and a thoughtful and congenial staff. Rooms on the top floor have the most light (some bathrooms have skylights). One final, and also relatively affordable, New Canaan lodging option is the **Village Inn** (122 Park St., 203/966-8413 or 800/370-2224, www.vil-

lageinnnc.com), a less fancy but still very nice property in the heart of town, just a block from train station featured in *The Ice Storm*. Proximity to so many shops and eateries can be a plus, as are the updated amenities (state-of-the-art voicemail, data ports, cable TV); some connecting rooms with kitchenettes can be booked together to form an apartment.

Visitors to Norwalk are often surprised to find the quaint and historic **Silvermine Tavern** (194 Perry Ave., 203/847-4558, www.silverminetavern.com) within city limits—albeit nestled near the New Canaan and Wilton borders. You may recognize the lobby and front door of this rambling 18th-century inn from the Jennifer Aniston–Paul Rudd film *The Object of My Affection*. Rooms vary in size, but most contain simple but inviting American antiques, canopy beds, hooked or braided rugs, and charmingly low sloped ceilings; a few have only showers and no baths, so ask if this is important to you. Some additional rooms are inside the neighboring coach house, which sits over an old general store that sells penny candy and assorted Early Americana.

## FOOD

Coastal Fairfield County has far more commendable restaurants than could possibly be squeezed into a general-interest guidebook covering the entire state, so bear in mind that a great many equally deserving restaurants have been left off the list below. Outstanding bastions of contemporary American and international cuisine dominate many of the area downtowns.

A flip side of the restaurant boom is that just about every eatery in the area has felt justified in upping its prices over the past few years by as much as 25–40 percent. In many cases, the very high-end establishments charging $25–40 per entrée truly do provide a dining experience that lives up to the prices, complete with gracious and knowing service, exotic ingredients, and high-quality furnishings. The problem lies more often with the second tier of restaurants—places that in many cases employ loosely trained staffs and serve freezer-paroled food, yet still charge $15–25 per plate. Finding a relatively comfortable sit-down restaurant where two people can enjoy a three-course meal for under $50 has become a near impossibility in Fairfield County.

With these caveats in mind, foodies should have no trouble eating themselves silly in this part of the state. On weekends, you may require reservations—sometimes a few days ahead—at some of the area's more exclusive eateries. But on slower nights, try simply parking your car near one of the county's many concentrations of restaurants, and stroll about looking at menus until you find something to your liking.

In Greenwich, a culinary row of sorts exists along Greenwich Ave. (and the side streets just off it). Note that for the most part, the fancier places are at the top of the hill, nearest U.S. 1—the rent on this road seems to decrease in proportion to the elevation, so you'll find more affordable options toward the bottom of the hill. In Stamford, Bedford and Summer Streets have quite a few eateries. Ditto for downtown Westport, Washington and Main Streets in South Norwalk, and downtown New Canaan.

## Greenwich to Darien

**Upscale:** One of the area's most remarkable and romantic restaurants, **Thomas Henkelmann's** (the Homestead Inn, 420 Field Point Rd., Greenwich, 203/869-7500, $29–40) presents an oft-changing menu of classic and contemporary French fare, including loin of lamb wrapped in spinach and watercress, a grilled lamb chop, fingerling potato-and-leek puree, crisp potato tart, and a lamb-thyme jus. This is one of the dressier spots in the county.

At the dramatic new Delamar Greenwich Harbor hotel, **L'Escale** (500 Steamboat Rd., 203/661-9800, $17–32) delights French-cooking connoisseurs with magnificently rendered Gallic cuisine and sterling views of the yachts and sailboats plying Greenwich Harbor. Consider the foie gras appetizer, resting in a broth of sweet peas dotted with bacon lardons. The grilled salmon with preserved lemon, oven-dried tomatoes, and baby fennel makes for a memorable entrée. Dine on the patio when weather permits. **Restaurant Jean-Louis** (61 Lewis St., Greenwich, 203/622-8450, $37–42) offers an old-

world experience in traditional French cooking, the kind that's been in vogue for decades and has avoided the come-and-go culinary trends of late. Chef Jean-Louis Gerin is a kitchenhold name in these parts, and his Scottish wood pigeon in cognac flambé is a masterpiece, as is the double oxtail consommé with foie gras (yup, that's a $29 bowl of soup). Housed in a simple pink-brick building off Greenwich Avenue, the interior is lush and somewhat formal.

The grand **Roger Sherman Inn** (195 Oenoke Ridge, New Canaan, 203/966-4541, $18–36), once a cliché-d and overpriced dining experience, has improved to become one of the best restaurants in the state. Memorable fare includes a Swiss-inspired poached rainbow trout with sorrel white wine sauce, or *les trois filets du chef* (medallion of veal, noisette of lamb, and tourne do of beef, each with its own sauce). Even the vegetarian options are presented with a flourish—note the spinach soufflé with a champignon soubise. Forget the usual after-dinner mints at this place; instead, dip into a dish of mini-Toblerone chocolates (which is not to say the silky rich desserts won't satisfy any cravings you have for sweets).

Set inauspiciously beside an Ethan Allen furniture showroom on the west side of Stamford, **La Bretagne** (2010 W. Main St., 203/324-9539, $22–32) offers a great old-fashioned French dining experience, complete with a doting and congenial waitstaff, formal but not overly dressy decor, and wonderfully inspired country French fare. Try the excellent sautéed frogs' legs in garlic butter, seafood crêpes with lobster sauce, and sweetbreads with tarragon sauce. **Zanghi** (201 Summer St., 203/327-3663, $24–$36), having moved from its former digs in the Inn at National Hall in Westport, occupies a similarly snazzy space in downtown Stamford that feels more urbane and sexy than its old locale. Osetra caviar on shallot toast, mustard-seed-crusted calves' liver with horseradish-whipped potatoes, and rack and saddle of lamb with fricassée of vegetables and fingerling potatoes are menu highlights. Wear something stylish for this place.

**Creative but Casual:** One of Greenwich's hottest restaurants, **Rebecca's Restaurant and Bar** (265 Glenville Rd., 203/532-9270, $27–42), is a spare space with molded blond-wood chairs and simple white linen-topped tables. All is spare and the crowd super chic, somewhat belying the modest location, across from the Glenville Firehouse. This is sit-up-and-take-notice fare—consider angel hair pasta with smoked salmon, Bibb lettuce, and sevruga caviar, or a sublime starter of duck foie gras with caramelized mango and ginger. **Alta** (363 Greenwich Ave., 203/622-5138, $24–35) offers some of the finest Scandinavian food you'll find in the United States, but a meal here doesn't come cheaply—the $24 prix fixe lunch is a good way to sample some of the better victuals, such as grilled salmon with curried vegetables and a mint-lingonberry chutney. Also try pan-seared duckling with armagnac-cherries, potato herb tart, and sugar snap peas. A great starter at dinner is the Scandinavian seafood plate of gravlax, smoked salmon, shrimp, beet salad, herring, and spinach potatoes. Panna cotta with sour cherries in a port wine sauce makes a memorable finale.

A counterpoint to the formal ambience and richly elaborate fare of Restaurant Jean-Louis is **Le Figaro Bistro de Paris** (372 Greenwich Ave., 203/622-0018, $19–29), an old-world bistro with lace curtain valances, old-fashioned lamps, mosaic floors, and mouthwatering fare like monkfish medallions with shrimp risotto and bisque sauce, or roasted free-range chicken with thyme pan drippings and French fries.

Bertrand, once the most well-regarded restaurant in all of Connecticut, closed its doors a few years back, only to be replaced by **Dome** (253 Greenwich Ave., 203/661-3443, $12–27), a colorful and whimsical two-tiered eatery on Greenwich Avenue. Entrées on the international menu mostly keep around $20 and include everything from a peppercorn-crusted Jack Daniel's burger with cheddar and caramelized onions, to ginger soy spare ribs with toasted coconut–crusted onion rings and a Polynesian dipping sauce. This is also a frenetically popular lunch spot.

**Telluride** (245 Bedford St., 203/357-7679, $11–20), with its rough-hewn wooden tables, hanging Navajo rugs, and lodge-like Western decor, is one of the most inviting restaurants in downtown Stamford. The great food is afford-able—if there's any drawback here, it's the staggering popularity of the place. The menu borrows ingredients from just about everywhere, including Asia, but concentrates on the Western and Southwestern United States. The sundance salad has arugula, grilled pears, oranges, grapefruit, Gorgonzola, spicy pecans, and a lemon-herb butter; hearty buffalo burgers come with grilled portobello mushrooms and red pepper marmalade; and lobster sushi roll tempura comes with miso sauce and wasabi. **Wish** (21 Atlantic St., 203/961-0690, $18–28) is a contemporary space with handsome decor and good-looking patrons to go with it. The menu emphasizes creative seafood, such as the starter of calamari-and-watercress salad with radicchio, bean sprouts, and a roasted-tomato chipotle vinaigrette, and a main course of pan-roasted monkfish with black barley, sautéed Swiss chard, and a tomato-butter sauce.

**Grand** (15 Bank St., Stamford, 203/323-3232, $13–25) is a dark and sexy see-and-be-seen sort of place that draws plenty of young execs. The menu is divided into "little," "big," and "bar" plates; mussels and frites, and mac and gruyère cheese with truffles, are tempting examples of the first. Pan-seared halibut with edamame, mushrooms, and preserved lemon makes an excellent large plate, while a bar favorite is the plate of cured meats with crusty bread.

Helmed by Waldy Malouf, the famous New York City chef who once ran the Rainbow Room at the World Trade Center, **Beacon** (183 Harbor Dr., Stamford, 203/327-4600, $19–32) overlooks the harbor at Stamford's gracious Shippan Point. It's a serious place for fine wine and exceptional contemporary American fare, but patrons feel just fine dressed casually as they nosh on wood-smoked baby-back ribs or grilled swordfish steak with capers and mustard. Predictably, Beacon fills up fast on warm-weather evenings, so book early for a chance to sample this stellar cooking.

Festive and friendly, with the real clatter and ambience of a Parisian bistro—not to mention exquisitely prepared food—New Canaan's **Bistro Bonne Nuit** (14 Forest St., 203/966-5303, $18–28) is a suave spot where dishes like warm calamari salad with olives, capers, sun-dried tomatoes, and roasted lemon, and pan-roasted sea scallops with black-truffle vinaigrette, chive-mashed potatoes, and haricots verts are specialties. The warmly lighted storefront locale, with rich lemon-yellow walls, makes for a romantic evening on the town.

New Canaan's tiny and refreshingly unstuffy **Bluewater Café** (15 Elm St., 203/972-1799, $17–23) presents a dependable and fairly short menu of mostly Italian and Continental dishes, such as fettuccine pescatore with mussels, squid, and shrimp, and coconut-crusted monkfish. The arugula and goat cheese salad here is a local favorite. Bonus points for having the friendliest staff in town.

The only quasi-serious dining venue in Darien, the **Black Goose Grille** (972 Boston Post Rd. or U.S. 1, 203/655-7107, $13–28) still qualifies chiefly as a neighborhood eatery, popular with commuters fresh from Metro-North trains that deposit at the rail station down the block. Inside is a clubby rear bar and a larger front dining room—wooden goose decoys, wood-paneled ceilings, and nautical prints impart a cozy and convivial ambience. The food, which is quite pricey, gets mixed reviews and ranges from hefty barbecued grilled salmon fillet with roasted corn and red onion couscous and corn bread to cheddar burgers with fried tobacco onions.

If it's atmosphere you seek, away from the crowds and urban feel of downtown Stamford, drive north nearly to the New York border for the **Long Ridge Tavern** (2635 Long Ridge Rd., 203/329-7818, $17–24), inside a dutifully restored three-story country barn that dates from the mid-19th century. This place is warm and filled with loud happy patrons most nights, and even live jazz and blues quite often. The food tends toward the hearty side—consider oven-roasted rock Cornish game hen stuffed with sun-cured cranberries, sweet sausage, toasted pecans, and wild rice. Maple pumpkin crème brûlée is a signature dessert. There's also a less pricey tavern menu.

**Ocean 211** (211 Summer St., 203/973-0494, $17–32) is an exceptional seafood in downtown Stamford, earning high kudos for such freshly and innovatively prepared dishes as crab cakes with mustard-caper remoulade and sweet corn–ji-came salad; and mahimahi with spring onions, wild mushrooms, truffle oil, haricots verts, and potatoes. This smart, hip space occupies two floors of a narrow town house; the upstairs space, with a bar, is the louder and livelier of the two.

A trendy Asian-fusion restaurant that has garnered outstanding reviews since it opened in the late 1990s, **Baang** (1191 E. Putnam Ave., Riverside, 203/637-2114, $23–34), consists of a futuristic-looking dining room with an open kitchen; it's usually swarming with beautiful people. Thai-spiced pork tenderloin with lemongrass-green curry broth and roasted sweet potatoes, and charred rare tuna with an avocado and tomato wasabi vinaigrette are representative of this very interesting menu. Some critics knock the high prices, but this is not your ordinary Asian fare. An always-crowded spot in the heart of downtown New Canaan, **Ching's Table** (64 Main St., New Canaan, 203/972-2830, $8–23) presents a varied and reasonably priced menu of pan-Asian cuisine, including a mix of Indonesian, Vietnamese, Malaysian, and Thai dishes. The hearty noodle plates; wok–ginger-glazed calamari with string beans; and pan-seared lobster tail with scallion and young ginger are memorable.

**Steak, Pizza, Pub Grub, and Seafood:** A grand place to while away a summer weekend afternoon, **Paradise Bar and Grille** (5 Stamford Landing, off Southfield Ave., Stamford, 203/323-1116, $15–32) attracts a lively crowd of yuppies to its airy dockside confines. There's plenty of outdoor and indoor seating, all with views of sailboats along the West Branch of Stamford Harbor. Big portions of decent but unexceptional American fare are served, including broiled grouper with sweet potatoes and a sauce of capers, basil, diced tomatoes, and lemon butter; spinach tortilla sandwiches; nachos; and buffalo wings. It's the setting that keeps this place going strong.

**SBC Downtown** (131 Summer St., Stamford, 203/327-2337, $9–22) occupies a grand new building with very high ceilings and tall windows. It's filled nightly with a loud and fun bunch. Hearty comfort food prepared with nouvelle twists can be expected, including tasty Maryland crab cake sandwiches, baby back ribs, brick-oven pizzas, and porterhouse steaks. It's a popular spot for drinks, especially after work.

A cozy Irish pub downtown, the **The Playwright** (488 Summer St., Stamford, 203/353-1120, $9–19) is a celebration of all things Irish, filled with Tiffany-style lamps, beautiful varnished wood paneling, and photos of Beckett and Wilde. It serves a mix of traditional and more inventive dishes—the Irish mixed grill with lamb chops, black pudding, white pudding, sirloin steak, Irish bacon Irish sausage, egg, and mashed potatoes is a favorite. There are additional branches of this handsome pub in New Haven and Hamden.

**Morton's of Chicago** (377 N. State St., 203/324-3939, $18–38) has hit the corporate world of Stamford, landing in the Swiss Bank Center Tower. Leather booths and dark-wood paneling give the place a country-club air, and seafood and prime beef are consistently good.

The **Bank Street Brewing Company** (65 Bank St., Stamford, 203/325-BREW, $9–24) occupies a remarkable neoclassical building with a soaring domed ceiling—there's bird's-eye seating on a mezzanine that allows a full sense of the decor. As is often the case, the food doesn't live up to the setting—nor does the often humorless service. You can generally count on decent bar victuals, like Cobb salad, cornmeal-crusted calamari, and blackened-chicken sandwiches, but beware any of the more ambitious entrées.

If inexpensive pub fare is all you're seeking, slip into **Sundown Saloon** (403 Greenwich Ave., 203/629-8212, $6–18), an old-fashioned saloon where barbecue shrimp, burgers, chili, and other hearty dishes prove that Greenwich is not without regular Joes in search of regular chow. There's live acoustic music here some nights. **Pizza Factory** (380 Greenwich Ave., 203/661-5188, $13–17 for large pies) has a Chicago tavern atmosphere, with fun old vintage advertising posters on the walls. Pizzas are available deep dish or thin crust, and several additional California-style individual pies are also offered. The Chicago Stinger, with fresh sausage, sliced onions, and sliced hot peppers, is a winner.

Befitting smart and upscale Greenwich, the **Elm Street Oyster House** (11 W. Elm St.,

203/629-5795, $18–24), is smart and upscale—not the usual fish shanties purists might insist upon. Still, there's no denying the high quality of preparation here, from the shrimp, mussels, and spinach over lobster-and-roasted-red-pepper ravioli to the Cuban-rubbed swordfish and roasted vegetables on a bed of mixed greens with citrus vinaigrette. Friendly and unpretentious service is an added plus.

An Italian restaurant with a fairly predictable menu, but plenty of panache in the dining room, **Da Vinci's** (235 Greenwich Ave., 203/661-5831, $13–27) evokes the spirit of a real Italian trattoria, with sponge-painted chairs, Raphael-like murals, and a gurgling fountain in the center of the room. The waitstaff is unpretentious and sweet, the food dependable. Try the fusilli padovana with a light pink cream sauce, peas, and prosciutto, or hearty spaghetti with meatballs. **A Tavola** (99 Railroad Ave., Greenwich, 203/422-0563, $10–17) occupies a sleek industrial space but serves surprisingly affordable Italian fare: brick-oven pizzas (the bomba has sweet and spicy sausages, pancetta, pepperoni, smoked bacon, garlic, and tomato sauce), penne Bolognese, and grilled calamari.

A hit with the local corporate crowd, as well as patrons of the nearby Atlantic Theatre, the endearingly decorated **Mona Lisa** (133 Atlantic St., Stamford, 203/348-1070, $14–22) is a cute storefront Italian with hanging brass pots and pans, exposed brick walls, Cinzano posters, and a thoroughly European milieu. The food here is as good or better than a number of pricier Italian restaurants in downtown Stamford; try salmon with mustard sauce, seafood risotto, homemade gnocchi, and a tasty zabaglione with fresh strawberries for dessert.

**City Limits** (135 Harvard Ave., 203/348-7000, $8–25) is Stamford's anti-diner, a delightful find despite being in a drab industrial area off I-95—it's a short drive from downtown. This is a sleeker, more sophisticated interpretation of diner deco than is common in much of Connecticut: turquoise-and-charcoal booths, dark woods, and a mosaic-tile floor along with some glass brick. But what really sets this place apart is the menu, including many draft beers, a good wine list, and a designer-martini roster. Tasty dishes include the sesame-crusted tuna with ginger-soy vinaigrette, grilled hanger steak with pepper-and-onion home fries, and double mustard-glazed pork chops with Swiss chard. There's a vast dessert selection.

**Ethnic Fare: Kotobuki** (457 Summer St., Stamford, 203/359-4747, $12–20) is an intimate little Japanese restaurant with excellent sushi; the many varieties of rolls include the Gene-San (asparagus and tuna), named for regular customer Gene Wilder. **Li's Brothers** (25–48 Old King's Hwy. N, Good Wives Shopping Center, Darien, 203/656-3550, $6–15) serves commendable Hunan- and Sichuan-style Chinese fare, including spicy lobster with garlic sauce, crispy lemon chicken, and Mandarin noodle soups. There's another location in Norwalk.

On Summer Street's busy restaurant row, **Bonani Indian Cuisine** (490 Summer St., Stamford, 203/348-8138, $10–21) has a great staff, well-seasoned food, and an exotic-looking dining room. It's a lot pricier than qualitatively similar Indian cooking just 35 minutes away in the East Village of Manhattan, but it's still awfully good. Shrimp biryani; whole roasted eggplant cooked in brown onion, garlic, and light spices; and chicken tikka masala are favorites. **Plateau** (25 Bank St., 203/961-9875, $8–22) is a sumptuous space with high ceilings and dark lighting. Exceptional Pan-Asian food is offered, from panfried egg noodles wok-seared with seafood, beef, or chicken, to crispy red snapper served with cucumber, tomatoes, and tamarind sauce.

**Thali** (87 Main St., New Canaan, 203/972-8332, $9–20) occupies a vintage, almost formal-looking bank building, but the decor inside is anything but staid—a waterfall trickles through the dining room, and the decor is bright and offbeat. Specialties from the kitchen include shrimp Malabar (with a coconut-mustard curry), tandoori-baked cubed leg of lamb with hand-rubbed spices, and eggplant marinated in spices and cooked in yogurt sauce. The sweet farmers cheese dumpling seasoned with cardamom and pistachio make a nice dessert.

**Galangal** (35 Atlantic St., 203/348-4888, $11–19) specializes in the varied cuisine of Southeast Asia, offering a range of treats from several culinary traditions. The Thai spring rolls are sublime, as are entrées like stir-fried spicy eggplant with a basil-sweet-chili sauce, and duck panang with coconut milk, chili, fresh string beans, and curry spices. Save room for the decadent fried bananas. The restaurant has an upscale feel with tropical decor, a breezy space with a popular bar.

With so many Mexican restaurants—most of them of varying repute—in Connecticut, it's nice to sample the subtly contrasting cuisine of New Mexico at **Boxcar Cantina** (44 Old Field Point Rd., Greenwich, 203/661-4774, www.boxcarcantina.com, $12–18). Indian posole soup reveals a recipe popular in the Four Corners region of the Southwest, while sweet potato tamales and carne adovada make excellent entrées, as do the salmon burritos that combine a favorite New England ingredient with Southwestern preparation. The dining room is decorated with Southwestern artwork and colors.

Mexican lasagna, empanadas, and delicious filling burritos (plus many veggie options) make little **Ole Mole** (1030 High Ridge Rd., Stamford, 203/461-9962, $4–9) a delicious choice for un-Americanized Mexican food. The mostly Oaxacan-influenced **Tequila Mockingbird** (6 Forest St., 203/966-2222, $9–18) offers the snappiest Mexican fare in Fairfield County. The goat cheese and oliveta appetizer actually seems more Mediterranean in origin, but south of the border specialties such as chicken with smoked pasilla-pepper enchiladas are among the great entrées. Chips come with fresh tomatillo and chipotle salsa. This bright dining room fills up fast on weekends and can be incredibly noisy.

**Quick Bites: Katzenberg's Express Deli** (342 Greenwich Ave., 203/625-0103, average meal $4–8) is a colorful, modern space for this regionally famous deli, known for awesome white-bean-and-chicken chili, Philly-style steak hoagies that taste amazingly like they were made in the City of Brotherly Love, and hearty salads and wraps. It's also a nice choice for a light breakfast. Another great nearby is **Meli-Melo** (362 Greenwich Ave., 203/629-6153, average meal $6–13), a cozy and classy crêperie and juice bar that's also a great spot for a dish of ice cream. The Sardagna buckwheat crêpe, with fontina cheese, spinach, sundried tomatoes, artichokes, fresh asparagus, olive oil, and pine nuts is a winner. Save room for the one of the dessert crêpes, such as green-apple sorbet flambéed with Calvados. Several excellent salads and sandwiches are offered, too.

**Java Joints:** There are some espresso bars along Greenwich Avenue in Greenwich, including ubiquitous Starbucks, but the most characterful hangout in town is the **Arcadia Coffee Co.** (20 Arcadia Rd., 203/637-8766), a homey (well, manorly is probably a better word in these parts) spot in the heart of Old Greenwich, inside a former bank building. Great gelato.

**Gourmet Goods and Picnic Supplies: Aux Delices** (1075 E. Putnam Ave., Old Greenwich, 203/698-1066, also 3 W. Elm St., Greenwich, 203/622-6644) is a one-stop shop for gourmet goodies and fabulous prepared foods—the owner, Debra Ponzek, used to head up the kitchen at the famed Montrachet in New York City. You can also stay and eat within the sunny Provence-inspired confines.

## Norwalk

**Upscale:** It's hard to find a prettier setting than that of the family-run **Silvermine Tavern** (194 Perry Ave., 203/847-4558, $18–30), a venerable country inn near the New Canaan and Wilton border. The menu presents a lively mix of traditional New England and contemporary recipes, from crab-stuffed fillet of sole with a basil-citrus beurre blanc to honey-glazed roast duck breast with caramelized peaches, braised baby turnips, toasted orzo, and a wild rice pilaf and duck-stock reduction. The antiques-filled dining rooms, with their Oriental rugs and old wooden tables, peer out over the swan- and duck-friendly Silvermine River and charming waterfall; in warm weather, book ahead to secure a table on the riverside deck. Thursday nights feature an all-you-can-eat buffet and live Dixieland music; Sunday brunch ($21 per person) is another fine tradition.

At unassuming **Pasta Nostra** (116 Washington St., South Norwalk, 203/854-9700, $17–30) the menu changes weekly. In the fall you might sample *cappellaci con zucca* (squash ravioli with butter sauce, hazelnuts, and prosciutto). A traditional Sicilian favorite, *pasta con sarde* (spaghetti

with a tomato sauce of olives, celery, onions, saffron, olive oil, and fresh sardines) is featured rather often. There's a tremendous array of antipasti available, too. On cold nights, the windows are fogged from the steam of simmering sauces. If there's any complaintm it's that prices are rather steep for even stellar pastas, but few Italian restaurants in Connecticut can rival Pastra Nostra in quality.

Sophisticated and sassy, with a frenetic bar on one side and a somewhat quieter and more romantic dining area on the left, **Barcelona** (63 N. Main St., Norwalk, 203/899-0088; also 18 W. Putnam Ave., Greenwich, tapas $4–9, entrées $15–24) rates as both a wild gathering spot and a first-rate restaurant. Among the more addictive tapas is roasted portobello mushrooms with fontina and aged sherry. As a main course, try chicken breast scarpiello with hot cherry peppers and roast potatoes or the traditional paella (for two or more), weighing in at a reasonable $17 per person.

A hip restaurant with the same owners as The Loft, **Match** (98 Washington St., 203/852-1088, $18–27) is a chic two-story post-industrial space that's yet another sexy SoNo spot for drinks, and also a good bet for designer brick-oven pizzas. Other good bets from the menu include port-poached pear and gorgonzola salad, and a surf and turf with tenderloin of beef, tempura lobster, and whipped potatoes, truffled pumpkin, and brandy gravy. This latter dish reaches new heights of decadence. Exposed brick, yellow floors and drapes, and orange walls create a colorful, sexy ambience.

Once just a casual dockside seafood place in an understatedly elegant yachting community, the **Restaurant at Rowayton Seafood** (89 Rowayton Ave., 203/866-4488, $18–32) took on a hot new chef a few years back, and suddenly this place began nearing the top of everybody's short list of favorite eateries. Dishes like salmon with tabouli, tzatziki, and black olives, and crispy soft-shell crab with black bean salad, pineapple teriyaki glaze, daikon radish sprouts, and sesame aioli reveal the kitchen's culinary mastery, as well as this restaurant's consistent use of the freshest seafood around. Standbys like oysters on the half shell and fried whole-belly clams prove excellent, too.

A crowd clad in Izod shorts, khakis, and boat shoes descends upon this place nightly, sitting in the happily simple dining room overlooking the Five Mile River. A more recent entry to the Rowayton scene is the **River Cat Grill** (148 Rowayton Ave., 203/854-0860, $6–16), where the premise is small tapas-style portions of big flavors: fresh mussels in a curry broth, clam chowder, Sichuan-style beef carpaccio—the idea is that a couple could easily order five or six selections to round out a meal. It's a busy scene, with a dining room typically abuzz with chatter, and there's live music many nights.

Not your ordinary steak place, **Porterhouse,** (124 Washington St., South Norwalk, 203/855-0441, $20–38) has garnered rave reviews for its contemporary suave ambience and innovative fare. Ochre walls, high ceilings, amber lighting, and soft music make this a top spot for a romantic evening, and dishes such as marinated venison pan-roasted in a berry and peppercorn sauce with a chestnut puree delight hungry patrons. But it's the steaks, including the restaurant's dry-aged namesake, that star at this show. There's also a "raw and claw" bar (two of you might opt for the tasting plate of lobster, shrimp, oysters, and clams) and a substantial list of wines, ports, draft beer, fine brandies and scotches, and other special spirits.

SoNo's **Habana** (70 N. Main St., 203/852-9790, $18–24) has successfully introduced a mouthwatering fusion of Cuban, Latin American, and Caribbean flavors to stodgy old New England: in addition to such showstoppers as ginger-crusted salmon with pomegranate sauce, black calamari rice, and haricot vert, and baby back ribs roasted with sweet and spicy guava sauce and boniato fries, the menu offers an array of fine imported rums and spirits (including the head-spinning Brazilian cachaca), plus fine cigars. Caipirnhas and mojitos are among the tasty drinks served. The intriguing dining room captures the laid-back yet elegant ambience of Key West and Havana, with lazily whirring ceiling fans, French doors, and several tables on a front patio. This is one of the best restaurants in this part of the state, with only the high noise level a slight detraction.

**Pizza, Pub Grub, and Seafood:** With lusty delicious burgers, hearty chili, and hefty sandwiches, the century-old **Donovan's,** (138 Washington St., 203/838-3430, $5–13) has survived some terrible times along Washington Street in SoNo, and remains popular even during the height of the neighborhood's gentrification. Vintage boxing photos, wooden booths, and ornate pressed-tin ceilings impart a festive big-city spirit to this old-fashioned tavern. Another spot in SoNo, as popular for its happy hour bar scene as it is for its extremely good food, is the the dark and sophisticated **Amberjacks** (99 Washington St., Norwalk, 203/853-4332, $13–25), which specializes in regional American seafood, such as wild mushroom-and-seafood risotto, Pacific Northwest seafood skewers, and grilled oysters. The list of nightly specials is also formidable, as is the balanced wine list.

Reasonably priced portions of hearty Northern Italian fare are served at **Tuscan Oven** (544 Main Ave., U.S. 7, 203/846-4600, Norwalk, $15–28), an attractive restaurant near the Wilton line, with lemon yellow and rose-colored walls, tile floors, and smooth helpful service. Thin-crust pizzas; veal- and pistachio-filled ravioli in a parmigiana rosemary sauce; and grilled skewers of Gulf shrimp and calamari served with field greens and fennel salad are among the tasty dishes offered.

The **Brewhouse** (13 Marshall St., 203/853-9110, $8–22) is one of the state's most atmospheric brewpubs, a wonderful place to tank up before or after a meal in one of the area's many good restaurants. The food here, incidentally, has never been as good as the ales and is priced awfully high to boot. But if you are eating here, stick with the sandwiches and pub fare, including great fish and chips, barbecued baby back ribs, and tasty burgers, and approach the more ambitious entrées with caution. The staff seems to have a good time, and the service is appropriately easygoing. The building, with its distinctive five-story Seth Thomas (as in Thomaston, Connecticut) clock tower, dates from the 1920s and contains a colorful and extensive collection of brewing memorabilia chronicling the nation's and the state's ale history.

**Ethnic Fare:** One of the many fine eateries

to enliven SoNo during the late 1990s, **Kazu** (64 N. Main St., 203/866-7492, $13–23) is a stellar Japanese restaurant with a sedate but very sleek, postmodern decor of small wooden chairs of many colors, distinctive hanging lanterns, broad windows, and flat-black floors. The menu is extensive and varied, with specialties such as *nabeyaki udon* (with soy-fish broth, shrimp tempura, spinach, bamboo shoots, mushrooms, and fish cakes), *negimaki* (sautéed sliced beef rolled over scallions), and chicken katsu with curry rice. The sushi isn't cheap, but items like the soft-shell-crab roll or tempura-style Hiru roll with eel, salmon, shrimp, asparagus will knock your socks off.

**Quick Bites:** The utter charmlessness of **Swanky Frank's** (Connecticut Ave., 182 Connecticut Ave., U.S. 1, just off exit 14 of I-95, 203/838-8969; 1050 Post Rd. E, Westport, 203/226-5355, average meal under $6) accounts, of course, for its incredible charm—this cruddy little Formica fanstasyland on a nondescript stretch of the Post Road speaks the romantic language of hot dogs (and fried clams, roast beef sandwiches, and fries—but it knows its dogs better than anything else). Folks drive considerable distances for Swanky's wieners—even actor Dennis Franz supposedly eats here. As it happens, a lot of the regulars here *look* like the gruff and portly thespian, so who knows. Whatever the truth, this place deserves its celebrity status.

In SoNo, where trendy and increasingly expensive restaurants proliferate, it's nice to know that **Mr. Souvlaki** (122 Washington St., 203/853-4546, $4–14) is around for cheap and reasonably tasty Greek and Middle Eastern fast food, including souvlaki, pizzas, and chicken kabob platters. The **Silver Star Diner** (210 Connecticut Ave., 203/866-5302, $5–18) has a mammoth menu, even by Connecticut diner standards, and that's saying a lot: chicken with a mango-habanero sauce, wraps, salads, wasabi-beef sandwiches, Cordon bleu burgers, buffalo chicken wings, calzones, seafood with penne in vodka sauce—you'll find a little of everything here. And decor-wise, this is no shrinking violet: It's a glitzy place with mauve booths, lots of chrome and glittery, and super-fast service.

**Java Joints: SoNo Caffeine Co.** (133 Washington St., 203/857-4224) is the definitive coffee and chocolate lounge. The interior is warm and a bit more sophisticated than the usual coffeehouses, with Edwardian furnishings and Middle Eastern accents. You'll find Belgian chocolates, gourmet foods, antiques for sale, live music some evenings—it's a mixed bag of epicurean delights.

## Westport and Environs

**Upscale:** You'll find few restaurants in Connecticut with more historic and romantic settings than the **Cobb's Mill Inn** (12 Old Mill Rd., Weston, 203/227-7221, www.cobbs millinn.com, $21–29), a rambling 18th-century former mill with creaky floors and views over a waterfall and duck-filled river—next door is a country store that once served as Weston's post office. It's the sort of place you might keep in mind for a special occasion, and the quality of food here has improved markedly in recent years. Grilled wild Irish salmon with a fennel confit and pinot noir reduction graced a recent menu—great stuff. And the storybook location completes the experience.

Tiffany-style lamps, old wooden floors, and kitschy bear sculptures in the foyer give the **Three Bears** (Rte. 33 and Newtown Rd., Westport, 203/227-7219, $18–27) the sensibility of a faded Colonial inn, and that seems to be exactly how devotees of this old-timer like it. It's a rambling old place that's not as finessed as some. Nevertheless, the food has improved greatly in recent years, and now features Continental and American fare like double-cut lamb chops with rosemary, a pine nut gremolata, three onion au jus, white bean salad, curried Israeli couscous, and garlic seared spinach, or pan-roasted rabbit with pappardelle pasta, cabbage greens, beefsteak tomatoes and caramelized pearl onions, and a marsala wine-green peppercorn sauce. The portions are impressive, too.

**Creative but Casual: Miramar** (Inn at National Hall, 2 Post Rd. W, 203/222-2267, $22–32) opened in the fanciest hotel in Fairfield County in 1998, showcasing the cuisine of Boston celebrity chef Todd English (author

THE CONNECTICUT COAST

of cookbooks and host of *Cooking In,* the PBS show). The much-hyped food lives up to its billing: Note the crab cakes with spicy mango salsa and shaved fennel salad among the starters, and grilled sirloin topped with Vidalia onions, Roquefort cream, and ham served over Tuscan bruschetta as a favorite entrée. The decor is understated but hip, the service good (though perhaps a notch below what you might expect).

**V** (1460 Post Rd. E, Westport, 203/259-1160, $12–19) combines the best attributes of a breezy wine bar and a moderately priced American bistro, all within an attractive high-ceilinged space with shelves of wine bottles and lovely dried floral arrangements lining the walls. Culinary offerings delight rather than dazzle—try the grilled Oriental chicken marinated with soy, honey, ginger, and hoisin with garlic-mashed potatoes, or the bay scallop risotto.

On ultra-trendy Main Street, **Acqua** (43 Main St., Westport, 203/222-8899, $17–30) is presided over by Christian Bertrand, who has helmed the kitchens of such celebrated temples as Stonehenge, Lutece, and his now-defunct eponymous restaurant in Greenwich. Bertrand appears right at home in this considerably less formal setting, where he conjures up such Mediterranean-inspired delights as T-bone lamb chops with niçoise ragout and French and white beans, and grilled striped bass with basmati rice, black fig–mango relish, and a pomegranate vinaigrette.

**Da Pietro's** (36 Riverside Ave., Westport, 203/454-1213, $21–30) has garnered rave reviews over the years, something that may surprise you if you simply drive or stroll by the modest storefront and poke your face up against the glass. It's comfy inside but hardly formal or elaborate. Southern French and Northern Italian fare are featured, often with subtle but inventive international and regional American influences: grilled Norwegian salmon finished with balsamic vinegar, olive oil, and fresh mint, or grilled polenta topped with sautéed shiitake, champignon, and oyster mushrooms, with white wine, shallots, and scallions. Chef-owner Pietro Scotti is a stickler for details, and every

ingredient is carefully thought out, every dish constructed like an intricate mosaic. Weekend reservations are nearly impossible to score, and Paul Newman and Joanne Woodward are said to be regulars.

People drive from all around the area for the singularly exceptional cooking at **Mediterranean Grill** (Stop & Shop Plaza, 5 River Rd., Wilton, 203/762-8484, $15–21), a first-rate restaurant from the airy white-washed dining room to the informal yet refined service. Selections include poached pear and endive salad topped with Cabrales blue cheese in a roasted beet vinaigrette; seafood risotto; roasted pork tenderloin with Catalan spinach served in a fig sauce; and Tunisian-style veal stew with almonds, yogurt, and Mediterranean spices.

**Splash** (Inn at Longshore, 260 S. Compo Rd., Westport, 203/454-7798, $20–38) serves meals in a loud but enjoyable dining room or on an expansive deck (first-come, first-served) with knockout views of Long Island Sound. A stellar but pricey, ultra-stylish restaurant in the otherwise sedate Inn at Longshore, Splash serves decadent pan-Asian fare, including macadamia-crusted swordfish with crispy spinach, ginger, and a lime sauce; a two-pound roast lobster with baby vegetables and a green chile vinaigrette; tuna tartare with caviar and crème fraîche.

One of the more inventive menus in the area—and that's saying a lot—is found at Westport's **Bridge Café** (5 Riverside Ave., 203/226-4800, $16–28), where a bright airy dining room has colorful murals and a Mediterranean feel, plus several seats on a terrace overlooking the Saugatuck River. This is one of several outstanding eateries around the intersection of Rte. 33 and U.S. 1. Typical entrées from the ever-changing menu include pan-roasted duck breast with fresh plum juice, wild rice risotto, and braised endive, or pan-seared Chilean sea bass with Japanese seven-spice, citrus vanilla sauce, basmati rice, and carrot-fennel slaw.

**Pizza, Pub Grub, and Seafood: Tom E Toes** (5 River Rd., 203/834-0733, large pies, $10–14) serves the best pizza in Wilton and among the best in the county (its pies have received both local and national awards). A long but fairly traditional list of toppings is offered, plus specialty pies like clams casino and barbecue chicken. A side specialty here is the Tom E Dog, brushed with barbecue sauce, smothered with provolone and mozzarella, and wrapped in pizza dough.

For excellent pizza, pay a visit to **DeRosa's at The Firehouse** (577 Riverside Ave., 203/221-1769, large pies $12–15). The restaurant is inside a restored redbrick firehouse, behind the Inn at National Hall. Red-checked tablecloths, tile floors, counter seating, and tables facing the enormous old garage doors of the firehouse lend a casual air to this place—it fills up very fast on weekends. Favorite creations include the pizza with sliced filet mignon and fresh gorgonzola, and also the cioppino pie with mussels, calamari, clams fra diavolo, and Romano and Parmesan cheeses.

Drop by **Mario's** (36 Railroad Place, Westport, 203/226-0308, $7–22) at 3 P.M. on a Tuesday and you'll find a ragtag crew congregated around the smoky bar—this place is the antithesis of pretentious, a hangout for commuters to unwind with a few cocktails and cheap red-sauce Italian fare. Dingy old carpet and dated furnishings paint a relaxed picture, to say the least—locals would never have it any other way. Steaks, baked haddock, lasagna, and ziti with clam sauce are offered.

The lovably low-keyed **Mansion Clam House** (541 Riverside Ave., 203/454-7979, $14–30) is a red clapboard tavern that looks as though the next strong wind may send it tumbling off its foundation. You're apt to find real locals slurping down plate after plate of raw oysters and hot steamers. The quality of food and preparation is uniformly excellent.

**Ethnic Fare:** You don't see **Tomiko** (15 River Rd., 203/761-6770, $13–20) in readers' and critics' polls cited as one of the best sources of sushi in Fairfield County, but it is—in fact, the creative rolls here place this elegant Japanese restaurant among the best in the state. It's a little hard to find, as it occupies the former commissary of a business park in Wilton Center. The service ranges from perfunctory to a bit weak, but once you've tasted smoked sea scallop, salmon and sundried tomato, and lobster tempura rolls, you'll

start singing the laurels of this place, too. The rolls aren't cheap, but they are unusually large (most of them eight pieces). Good noodle dishes and grills, too.

The trendy **Taipan** (376 Post Rd. E, Westport, 203/227-7400, $10–16) offers a full range of Asian dishes, borrowing from such cultures as Indonesia, China, and Thailand. Memorable dishes include the spicy Indonesian Rendang beef or chicken cooked with lemongrass, shallots, spices, and coconut sauce; the Mandarin duck pancakes; and a crispy tangerine sea bass fried whole with fresh chilies and scallions. Waterfalls, light fixtures inside bird cages, and exotic and eye-catching decor complement the great food. **The Little Kitchen of Westport** (423 Boston Post Rd., 203/454-5540, $12–20) is a very urbane and slick space despite its shopping center locale. It has red walls, bright and cheerful colors, and same owners as Taipan, nearly across the street. The food here is a little more upscale and urbane, but you won't go wrong at either restaurant. The lobster rolls are mesmerizing.

Your best bet among the many Indian restaurants that have cropped up over the years in southwestern Connecticut is **Bombay Bar and Grill** (616 Post Rd. E, Westport, 203/226-0211, $10–18). See for yourself whether "Martha Stewart's favorite malasa dosai" (a rice and lentil crêpe filled with spiced potatoes) lives up to its billing. Entrées include lamb in a mild cashew and cream sauce, shrimp in a hot coconut and tamarind sauce, and hot lobster vindaloo. There's a popular daily lunch and weekend brunch buffet, too, all served in an elegant narrow dining room with white napery, and distinctive chandeliers.

**Quick Bites:** The 24-hour **Sherwood Diner** (901 Post Rd. E, U.S. 1, Westport, 203/226-5535, $4–9) located in a redbrick building near the road to Sherwood Island State Park, draws everybody from suits to truck drivers during the day to blue-haired kids, post-clubbers, and, yes, truckers at night. The tuna and Swiss melt on rye is simply unrivaled elsewhere in the state, and the pancakes, Greek entrées, and pies are great.

**Java Joints:** The **Coffee an' Donut Shop** (343 Main St., Westport, 203/227-3808) makes the tastiest doughnuts in Fairfield County, and the coffee's not bad either. Downtown Westport may have lost its heart and soul to chain retail, but this unpretentious little spot continues to thrive.

The **Moonstruck Chocolatier** (22 Main St., 203/221-1321) occupies a cozy storefront amid the retail mania of downtown Westport—this handsome space, with faux-tile floors, gold walls, and murals of Italy, sells decadent truffles, a few light sandwiches and snack foods, and a large array of hot drinks from coffees to gourmet hot cocoas to frozen treats. It's a lovely spot for people-watching.

**Gourmet Goods and Picnic Supplies:** On your way to some picnicking at Weir Farm or Devil's Den, you might drop by Wilton's **Epicure** (991 Danbury Rd., 203/544-6000) for delectable pastries and fine foods to go. People think of **Abbondanza** (30 Charles St., 203/454-0840, average price $3–9), an elegant gourmet food store near the train station in Saugatuck, as mainly a "to go" spot—but there are also several tables here, where you can enjoy any of the delectable prepared foods, fresh sandwiches, and such. An old-school Italian market named for the main thoroughfare of Little Italy in the Bronx, **Arthur Avenue** (539 Riverside Ave., 203/221-1551) has smooth-as-silk gelato, fresh pasta, and other Italian groceries, and a few tables where you can sit around and savor your purchases. It's right beside the Mansion Clam House.

## Fairfield

**Creative but Casual:** Backed by a few high-profile chefs in the area, **Voila!** (70 Reef Rd., 203/254-2070 or, for the patisserie, 203/254-6036, $15–22) is set in a small red house with lace curtains and a stone fireplace; it overlooks the Fairfield green. Escargot with a Roquefort sauce makes for a memorable appetizer, after which you might move on to butter-filled Cornish hen grilled with garlic and herbs. The rich desserts are created in the restaurant's cleverly named patisserie, Marie Antoinette.

**Paci** (96 Station St., 203/259-9600, $19–29) is a bit off the main track, down a side street in the dainty village of Southport; in fact, it's right

inside the old rail station—a spare dining room with soaring vaulted ceiling, high brick walls, and indirect lighting. Very fine Italian fare is served, including a delicious house specialty of ravioli stuffed with fennel-sausage, radicchio, onions, parmigiano, and ricotta cheese. **Centro** (1435 Post Rd., Fairfield., 203/255-1210, $8–17) has one of the longest menus of any Italian restaurant in Fairfield County, with both traditional and contemporary offerings, including an always-delicious BLT with grilled chicken, bacon, fresh mozzarella, tomatoes, and fresh basil aioli, plus three-cheese rigatoni with grilled chicken, prosciutto, spinach, and Parmesan-herb bread crumbs, and a hearty balsamic-mustard glazed baked salmon over spinach risotto. You get to enjoy all these tasty things in a wonderful, airy contemporary space adjacent to the town green, with pastel-painted walls and courteous, smartly dressed staff. Additional branches are in Darien and Greenwich.

**Sarabande** (12 Unquowa Pl., Fairfield, 203/259-8084, $19–28) offers an exciting menu of creative contemporary American fare—it's one of the best restaurants in town. Consider an appetizer of anise-and-sesame-crusted seared raw tuna.

**Pizza, Pub Grub, and Seafood:** With several rambling informal dining rooms and a great stretch of sidewalk seating beside the Community Theater cinema, **Tommy's** (1418 Post Rd., 203/254-1478, $10–18) is a terrific place to socialize with a group of friends or even partake of Fairfield's yuppified social scene. The mostly Italian food has improved a great deal in recent years and has included gnocchi with sweet sausage and broccoli rabe, a wonderful seafood bisque, and chicken with spicy pomodoro sauce. The staff is fun and friendly but sometimes a little flighty.

Steel and brass brewing vats line the walls of the **Southport Brewery** (2600 Post Rd., 203/256-BEER, $5–20), a colorful spot near the Westport border with blond-wood floors, amber sponge-painted walls, and a nice, extensive selection of handcrafted beers on tap. The menu offers a range of familiar comfort foods: brick-oven pizzas, 20-ounce porterhouse fire-grilled steaks, Cobb salads, Maryland crab cakes, and some nice pasta dishes.

**Europa** (1342 Kings Hwy., Fairfield, 203/259-1960, $6–17) is a friendly and casual Greek and Italian restaurant in eastern Fairfield, with moderate prices and reliable fare. Chicken souvlaki, Greek salads, grinder, pan-pizzas, and moussaka are among the specialties.

**Ethnic Fare:** The family-run **Pearl of Budapest** (57 Unquowa Rd., Fairfield, 203/259-4777, $13–16) presents excellent and authentic Hungarian fare, like strips of steak sautéed with white asparagus, green beans, mushrooms, and chicken livers; Hungarian ratatouille with onions, peppers, smoked sausage, and spaetzle; herring salad; and potato latkes. The charming, old-world environment is accented by staff dressed in colorful vests. The Fairfield train station is steps away.

Like the Stamford branch, **Ole Mole** (2074 Black Rock Tpke., Rte. 58, Fairfield, 203/333-0400, entrées $4–9) is a cute hole-in-the-wall with a few tables and chairs and a colorful tile counter; it's tops in the area for excellent, authentic regional Mexican food.

**Quick Bites:** Grab a cheese dog at **Rawley's Hot Dogs** (1886 Post Rd., U.S. 1, Fairfield, 203/259-9023, under $6), yet another alleged favorite of Martha Stewart (it's difficult, but immensely enjoyable, to picture her slurping down a big dog with relish running down her forearm). This divey, short-order joint has been a local favorite since 1946.

Fairfield's **Firehouse Deli** (22 Reef Rd., 203/255-5527, under $8) might just make the best sandwich in Fairfield County. Unfortunately, everybody seems well aware of the great food available inside this quirky old red house facing the town green, so lines can be intense at lunchtime. The clam chowder is stellar, and in the morning there's a full range of muffins and coffee cakes. **S&S Dugout** (3449 Post Rd., Southport, 203/255-2579) is a casual hole-in-the-wall with incredibly tasty sausage and pepper sandwiches, among other delicacies.

**Java Joints:** Once a cushy antiques store, **Sweet William** (91 Southport Woods Dr., Fairfield, 203/256-9709) now specializes in breakfast, lunch, afternoon tea, and gourmet dinners to go.

# INFORMATION AND SERVICES

## Visitor Information

The region is served by the **Coastal Fairfield County Convention & Visitor Bureau** (20 Marshall St., Suite 102, Norwalk, CT 06854, 203/840-0770 or 800/866-7925, www.coastalct.com).

## Getting Around

Traffic in coastal Fairfield County has become a huge nuisance in recent years, as not only the area's population has increased dramatically but also its affluence (meaning more cars per family) and the aggressiveness of its drivers. There are times when getting through Stamford and Norwalk can feel not unlike negotiating midtown Manhattan—well, minus the cabs, anyway. Furthermore, U.S. 1—a busy surface road lined with strip malls—fills with traffic most days and has relatively few designated turn lanes, making for backups and all kinds of dangerous situations. Add to this situation the Mario Andrettis dominating the main limited-access roads, I-95 and the curvy Merritt Parkway, and you can see that getting around Fairfield County should be approached with a healthy dose of patience, lucidity, and maybe a dash of fatalism. You'll get where you're going, but it may take a bit longer than in other parts of Connecticut. On the plus side, major roads do connect the region with New York City, New Haven, and Danbury.

As for alternatives to driving, coastal Fairfield County is served by Metro-North, and this is a viable way to get around—although there's no denying that a car is generally more convenient. Still, the downtown dining and entertainment hubs of Greenwich, Stamford, Darien, New Canaan, Norwalk, and Fairfield are all within walking distance of the region's train stations. And even in Westport you can at least walk to a few fun restaurants in the Saugatuck area. If you're visiting Fairfield County from New York, Boston, or any point in between, you might consider doing so by train. It is possible to catch cabs at all of the major train stations to any points that require more than a walk.

THE CONNECTICUT COAST

# Bridgeport and Vicinity

It wouldn't be inaccurate, at least geographically, to say that greater Bridgeport extends as far west as Fairfield or even Westport, east to Milford, and north up to Shelton or even Monroe. But for the purposes of characterizing a particular region's demographics and personality, the city stands largely on its own. And these other nearby towns fit in more closely with other parts of the state. This is probably due in part to the fact that Bridgeport has endured an unflattering reputation during the latter half of the century, and residents of even its neighboring towns have tended to distance themselves.

By a few thousand residents, Bridgeport is Connecticut's largest city, one that has shown signs of progress and even an all-out turnaround since the mid-1990s. If momentum continues in its favor, perhaps it's just a matter of time before the southwestern end of the state actually embraces the downtrodden metropolis. In the meantime, keep an open mind about Bridgeport, and remember that it possesses some of southern New England's most popular attractions. Neighboring Stratford and Trumbull are also covered in this section, and each has some pretty back roads that make for a pleasing afternoon's drive.

## BRIDGEPORT

For many years, the less anybody wrote about Bridgeport, the better. For six decades, following its early 19th-century inception, the city experienced a rapid industrial rise. For the next six decades, it hovered between high and low periods—but the city always survived. But from the 1950s through at least the mid-1990s, Bridgeport's fortunes plummeted. It's ironic that the largest city in the nation's wealthiest state is one of the nation's poorest cities.

But over the past few years, Connecticut's residents and civic leaders have begun paying more attention to the state's faltering cities. Bridgeport lacks the corporate base of Stamford and the educational base of New Haven, and so it faces a continuous challenge in attempting to

lure young professionals—the lifeblood these days of any major urban renaissance. Given this, a serious comeback may take some time.

It's harder to fix things here than in many other cities. If only the local economy had bottomed out completely following World War II—if only Bridgeport had been rendered completely dead—today's planners might ride into town and set out to convert its dilapidated but charming mansions into condos or museums or offices, turn faded redbrick factories into atrium-anchored shopping malls, or turn an eroded riverfront into a cobbled pedestrian way with park benches and espresso stands.

Unfortunately—and ironically—it is because Bridgeport remained a somewhat viable force following World War II that so little of its early architecture and original layout have been preserved. True, there was a white flight to the suburbs, and many of the city's major employers either folded or moved south, where the labor was cheaper and the taxes lower. But many residents stayed behind, hoping to keep the city prosperous. Well-intentioned but ill-advised city leaders decided that Bridgeport's success in the face of a changing economy lay in full-on urban renewal.

The core of this dynamic metropolis was razed, right down to the last Gothic archway or Colonial church spire, and replaced with an endless series of concrete office blocks, monolithic parking garages, and almost shamefully impersonal housing projects. There were many cries from preservationists, but, for the most part, these drastic designs were executed as planned.

Flip ahead to 1993, perhaps the nadir in the city's history. That year Bridgeport filed unsuccessfully for bankruptcy. Then residents endured discussions that a massive casino-resort development might save the city (look around the country and you'll see that this strategy has mixed results, at best). Meanwhile, descendants of the area's original inhabitants, the Golden Hill Indians, put forth a lawsuit to fight for the land rights to much of downtown—prompting many observers to retort, "Let them have it!"

## History

Bridgeport—then with 3,400 residents—was incorporated as a town in 1821. It is younger, by more than 170 years, than its coastal neighbors Stratford and Fairfield, which shared rights to what would become Bridgeport throughout the 17th and 18th centuries. Part of the area, Golden Hill, had been established in 1660 as a reservation for the region's Paugusset Indians. And elsewhere, by the time of the Revolutionary War, perhaps 100 settlers lived here, raising sheep amid the marshy plains around what is now Bridgeport Harbor.

A few years after its incorporation, the birth of America's railroad industry spurred civic leaders into recognizing Bridgeport as a potentially important transportation center—it being on Long Island Sound and also at the foot of both the Housatonic and Naugatuck River Valleys. A city charter was established in 1836 so that municipal bonds could be issued to fund a massive railroad project, and industrial Bridgeport was born.

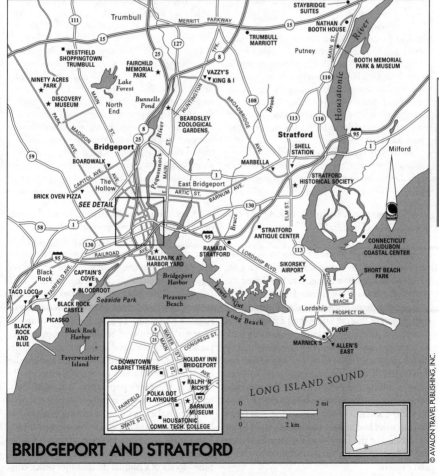

THE CONNECTICUT COAST

© AVALON TRAVEL PUBLISHING, INC.

**BRIDGEPORT AND STRATFORD**

## THE GOLDEN HILL INDIANS

Paugusset Indians first occupied the land on which the city of Bridgeport has developed. In the earliest days of the colonies, the neighboring settlements of Fairfield and Stratford held the Indians in terribly low regard. It was illegal for whites to sell them liquor, munitions, horses, or boats, and colonists were permitted to shoot dead any Indians caught roaming close to their homes at night. At one point, a rather dire attempt was made to Christianize these "poore lost, naked sonnes of Adam," but for the most part, the Paugussets were deemed incorrigible.

It's sometimes thought that the area was inhabited by Pequot Indians, but in fact, that tribe, which had been aggressively opposed to the English settlers, had merely sought refuge here among the other tribes. In 1637, a band of Brits surrounded the Pequots around Sasco Swamp and essentially massacred them; for many years, this event was listed as a "battle," as though both sides had entered into a even-handed war. In fact, the event was barbaric and bloody.

In 1659, 80 acres of Golden Hill (the sloping mound just west of the center of Bridgeport's current downtown, where the Pequonnock River emp-ties into Bridgeport Harbor) were granted to the Indians in exchange for their right to all other claims on Fairfield and Stratford. Around 1700, Indians sold half of their reservation to a local landowner, and by 1760, the Indian population had largely either died off or been driven away.

A few settlers had now begun encamping across the river in what is now the Newfield section of town, and still others began encroaching upon the reservation, with designs on the tribe's increasingly desirable land. After the Indians petitioned for restitution, a compromise was handed down by the state legislature, whereby the tribe ceded its rights to Golden Hill in exchange for about 20 acres of land in other, considerably less prominent, areas, plus some corn and blankets. In 1802, the Indians were deemed unable to put their remaining acres to productive use, and the land was auctioned off—the funds were used to support remaining tribe members. For the next two centuries, the few descendants from the original Golden Hill tribe continued to live in the area. Today, several tribe members are embroiled with the state in a tense legal battle over the land.

The Housatonic Railroad, linking the city north with Stockbridge, Massachusetts, was completed in 1841; the Naugatuck Railroad, which extended through Waterbury up to Winsted, was finished in 1849; and the New Haven line, which passed through Bridgeport and linked the city to Manhattan, was finished in 1850.

Logically then, the decade that followed the completion of this rail line—the 1850s—spelled prosperity. The city's already burgeoning saddle- and carriage-making factories were joined by major producers of sewing machines, cutlery, brass, steel, bronze, furniture, carpets, and numerous additional products. The Irish potato famine brought Irish settlers here in the 1840s—by 1850 a seventh of the population was Irish, and factories had an enormous labor pool to select from. For the next 50 years, these burgeoning industrial enterprises continued to thrive and expand.

Other immigrant groups soon joined the Irish in significant numbers. Bridgeport has long had a visible African American population. They were the city's first non-indigenous residents of non-British origin, and although their numbers grew most dramatically following World War II (when southern blacks came here to assume factory jobs), by as early as 1835 there was a pair of African Methodist Episcopal (AME) churches in town. Eastern and Southern Europeans, especially Hungarians and Italians, made up much of the immigration into Bridgeport during the late 19th century and early 20th century. By 1900, Bridgeport's population was more than half foreign-born and mostly blue collar.

Though the city's manufacturing base was robust, factory working conditions verged on inhuman, and strike activity began to rear its volatile head. Where the tradition of electing Protestant blue bloods of Colonial descent into office continued unabated in much of the state, increasing tension between the owning and working classes in Bridgeport led to a shift of political power into mostly immigrant, blue-collar hands.

The wealth of Bridgeport early factory owners translated to a grand downtown of elegant town houses and wedding cake mansions. But the rapid growth also led to unmanageable population surges and the potential for urban social ills. Chief among these, civic leaders worried about the 4,000 unmarried working women living in Bridgeport at this time, most likely aware of the potential distractions this posed to the many more thousands of unmarried working men. Concerns of this nature led planners to construct the first of Bridgeport's massive housing projects around 1915.

The outbreak of World War I may have spelled detestation throughout much of the modern world, but it thrust Bridgeport into a state of untold prosperity. Factories excelled in the manufacture of war materials, producing two-thirds of all the small arms and ammunition made in the United States during this period. In a matter of a couple years, the population exploded from 100,000 to 150,000. Following the war, the city experienced a mild depression in the early 1920s.

Corruption and debt plagued Bridgeport to such an extent that the state actually assumed control of the city's finances for a couple of years during the mid-1920s. Fortunes rose just as quickly as big players like General Electric and Dictaphone Corporation moved in, then fell to a certain degree during the Depression. But Bridgeport continued to excel in the manufacture of everything from submarines to gas meters to toasters to corsets. Local engineer Igor Sikorsky developed the helicopter, and the city became an aeronautical center as World War II began. The Second World War represented perhaps the pinnacle of Bridgeport's financial successes.

Following World War II, however, the city's bottom dropped out. Several companies moved to larger and newer locations outside of the city, many residents began settling into the greener suburbs, and a sizable chunk of Bridgeport's commercial and residential base bolted south. As the city's spirit sagged, Bridgeport

## THE PIE BAKERY THAT INVENTED THE FRISBEE

We have the employees of William R. Frisbee's Bridgeport pie-baking operation to thank for the invention of one of the great toys of America's beaches and parks: the Frisbee. In the mid-1930s, Frisbee's ovens produced upwards of 50,000 pies daily, but it's his pie *pan* for which the baker is now remembered. During lunch breaks, employees would toss the shallow disks back and forth, thereby inspiring Wham-O to mass-produce the pans in more user-friendly plastic.

set forth its ambitious but ultimately catastrophic plan to reinvent the city.

Plenty of things went wrong: The decision to build housing projects away from the city center had the unintended effect of draining downtown of its vibrancy, putting people miles away from everyday services and shops. Further destroying the city's character, in 1957 the 52-acre State Street Redevelopment Project resulted in the razing of hundreds of old churches, homes, and commercial buildings to make way for concrete boxes and super-highways. Church congregations and community organizations rebuilt in the suburbs, giving people even fewer reasons to come into town. P. T. Barnum's old Recreation Hall gave way to the city's first modern high-rise.

The final and most insulting blow was the senseless destruction of the city's greatest mansion, the sprawling, Gothic Harral-Wheeler House. It was bequeathed to the city in 1958, upon the death of the Wheeler family's last heir, for "educational and park purposes." Zealous mayor Joseph Tedesco interpreted such purposes to include the construction of a massive civic center. The mansion was bulldozed, and the civic center never built. Instead, a span of Rte. 8 now passes over most of the property.

The city continued to decline over the next few decades, but now some good things have begun to happen. A sports complex comprising a minor-league baseball stadium and sports arena has brought more life into the city, as have some new restaurants and performing arts spaces. There

# THE GREATEST SHOWMAN ON EARTH

The most famous man in Bridgeport's history, Phineas Taylor Barnum, was actually born up near Danbury in the village of Bethel, Connecticut, in 1810. The oldest of five children, P. T. was only 15 when his father died, leaving the family penniless. Barnum displayed keen entrepreneurial skills early on, developing several businesses that could be charitably described as sketchy.

Instant notoriety came with the founding of a newspaper, the *Herald of Freedom,* in 1831—one in which the young firebrand felt the freedom to libel people from time to time (he was successfully sued three times in the first three years, and was even jailed for 60 days at one point). He continued hustling a variety of odd jobs through the mid-1830s, when, while in Philadelphia, he purchased the freedom of a black woman named Joice Heth. Heth claimed to be 161 years old and the former nurse of George Washington, so Barnum began exhibiting her across America, claiming she was the nation's oldest living woman. In fact, Heth was only about 70 years old, and Barnum was eventually found out and then heavily criticized in a number of newspaper articles.

But Barnum had clearly found his talent: entertaining the masses, and using whatever tricks, half-truths, and hyperbole necessary to draw crowds. Among his successes, Barnum established the American Museum of New York in the 1840s, filling it with every imaginable kind of curiosity. The museum eventually burned, and Barnum rebuilt it, only for the second structure to go up in flames. All the while, the promoter was earning worldwide fame with the discovery of a personable 35-inch-tall young man he dubbed General Tom Thumb, and for presenting concerts given by the opportunistic Scandinavian

are still too many vacant storefronts downtown to say that Bridgeport has completely turned the page, but its future does look brighter.

## Northern Bridgeport

Long before Bridgeport began its recent and ambitious comeback, the city stood out for possessing three of the state's top family attractions, any two of which could easily be combined to make for a full-day outing. Two of these venues are north of downtown, in the northern reaches of Bridgeport.

Unquestionably, the **Discovery Museum** (4450 Park Ave., exit 47 from the Merritt Pkwy., 203/372-3521, www.discoverymuseum.org, open 10 A.M.–5 P.M. Tues.–Sat., noon–5 P.M. Sun., $7) gears itself for kids of all ages, although a spokesperson was quick to point out, rightfully, that adults, too, will find plenty here to jump-start their imaginations. This is a touch-friendly facility, where your children can press buttons and turn knobs to learn about electricity, machinery, and colors. You can arrange colored plastic on a light board, for example, to simulate stained glass. A few learning stations are either too primitive or too complicated to keep the attention of today's computer- and technology-savvy kids—the hands-on science exhibits

on the lower level are arguably the most fun and interactive. And Discovery's fascinating new Virtual Basketball exhibit will dazzle even jaded youngsters, as does a well-equipped Challenger Space Learning Center, a facility geared toward team-based activities that revolve around a Space Shuttle simulation and a Mission Control Unit. It's open to the general public on some Saturdays; call ahead for hours and to make reservations.

On the main floor, an art gallery is more than a nod to the cultural arts, with ever-changing exhibits presented in clever ways. There are frequently special programs, such as Sunday Celebrations (which draw musical performances, storytelling, and other lively events). Events often take place in the auditorium, which has a satellite down-link making it possible to host NASA video conferences. The Henry B. duPont, III Planetarium offers at least two programs daily, with a variety of themes. A contemporary light-filled building whose large windows face a densely wooded forest, the museum also has a small food court (with vending machines) and a gift shop on the second floor. Lots of places to sit.

Another important attraction in the northern end of the city is the **Beardsley Zoological Gar-**

opera singer, Jenny Lind (nicknamed the "Swedish Nightingale").

The eccentric promoter suffered from an inferiority complex in many respects, always striving to attain great wealth and to fit in with the upper classes that for the most part, especially early in his career, ridiculed him. He spent enormous sums of money building lavish mansions for himself and his family. The most famous of these was Iranistan, a truly one-of-a-kind palace built in 1848, incorporating Moorish, Byzantine, and Oriental design elements—it was, by all accounts, hideously ugly and garish. Iranistan stood for just nine years (it burned in 1857), but the Persian Palace made quite a statement long before any other U.S. mansion had anywhere near the same impact.

Barnum was a bit of a drinker early in life, but corrected his ways in the late 1840s and ultimately took a vow of abstention. He lectured on temperance throughout the remainder of his years.

It was actually rather late in his life, 1871, that Barnum founded the spectacle for which he is famous the world over, now called the Ringling Brothers Barnum & Bailey Circus. In Bridgeport, Barnum established a reputation as a great civic hero, serving as the city's mayor at one time and eventually as the local state representative in the Connecticut Assembly. He's widely credited with improving the growing industrial city's water supply, securing rights from Washington, D.C., for the dredging and construction of Bridgeport Harbor, and for building a number of city parks. Barnum passed away on April 7, 1891.

There's been renewed interest in Barnum in recent years, owing in part to some TV documentaries about his life and a 1999 miniseries on cable television's A&E channel starring Beau Bridges.

dens (1875 Noble Ave., exit 5 from the Rte. 8/25 connector, 203/394-6565, www.beardsleyzoo.org, open 9 A.M.–4 P.M. daily, $7). Frederick Law Olmsted designed adjoining Beardsley Park (open dawn–dusk, free), and the zoo was inspired by the fact that P.T. Barnum used to walk his circus animals in the park; indeed, the Barnum and Bailey Circus was the first to donate animals to the zoo in the 1920s. There are some 300 animals (125 species, mostly from North and South America) at the zoo, including free-roaming peacocks. The zoo occupies a wonderful setting in northern Bridgeport along Bunnells Pond, and a walking loop through the 32-acre zoo grounds reveals animals of many kinds: endangered species as red wolf, Siberian tiger, and spectacle bear. In a re-created indoor rainforest, you might see a scarlet ibis, broad-snouted caiman, or pygmy marmoset (the smallest primate in the world). The monkeys are a favorite for kids, and just about every toddler who passes through here manages to climb aboard one of the park's imposing stone lions (think photo op)—carved elephant fountains are also quite a splash in warmer weather.

In 1996, a carousel exhibit was added; the actual working carousel is a fiberglass reproduction, but surrounding it on the perimeter of the shed are authentic restored horses from the old carousel that once operated at Seaside Park. The shed offers nice views back toward the city, too; it's the highest point in Bridgeport. A master plan calls for construction of Victorian gardens and an Animal Conservation Center; work on the gardens commenced in 1999 and is ongoing. There's a nice gift shop at the carousel, and a more general shop, too, and the zoo also has a small café. In the summer, folk concerts are held at the picnic pavilion, right beside the carousel shed.

The zoo is sometimes assumed, incorrectly, to be closed in winter; in fact, it's open year-round, and advantages include more time to talk with and interact with zookeepers and volunteers. Certain heavy-coated animals, such as bison and tigers, are more active in colder weather, too. And if the weather is simply not cooperating, consider touring the warm and sultry rainforest exhibit.

## Downtown Bridgeport

Head south on the Rte. 8/25 connector to reach the jewel of downtown Bridgeport, the **Barnum Museum** (820 Main St., 203/331-1104, open 10 A.M.–4:30 P.M. Tues.–Sat., noon–4:30 P.M.

THE CONNECTICUT COAST

Sun., \$5). P. T. Barnum is perhaps best known for having founded in 1871 the circus that still bears his name, and many exhibits at this fascinating facility focus on his legacy as the "Greatest Showman on Earth."

On each floor, a few rooms show restored period pieces, some of which actually existed in Barnum's home, and many exhibits appeal to kids, especially those on the third floor. In the lobby, you'll pass beside six-foot, eight-inch, 700-pound Baby Bridgeport, the taxidermied baby elephant born in 1882, once a participant in Barnum's circus. Like the city after which it is named, Baby is a patchwork of old and new, having been repaired so many times that it's hard to say how much of the original animal truly exists today. Like many of the exhibits here, there's a slightly creepy but fascinating aura surrounding Baby Bridgeport. Exhibits on the first floor re-create rooms from Barnum's fantastic—some would say bombastic—mansion, Iranistan, as well as numerous biographical details on his life.

The second floor mixes exhibits on his life with others about the city's history, including one that displays many products manufactured here, including Underwood typewriters, Howe sewing machines, Sprague gas meters, Columbia records (the original plant was at 1473 Barnum Ave.), General Electric (whose headquarters were once at 1285 Boston Ave.), and Remington Fire Arms.

The top level focuses on Barnum and the museums of curiosity he operated in New York City prior to starting the circus—these facilities contained immense collections of the fantastic and the obscure. Oddities on this floor include a rather gory-looking Egyptian mummy that's said to date from 500 B.C., Siamese calves, a portrait of the Albino family (described as having "pure white skin, silken white hair, and pink eyes, though born of perfectly black parents"), letters and memorabilia concerning Jenny Lind, and the extraordinarily small carriages that transported Tom Thumb. Kids can stand beside life-size wall paintings of Bridgeport-born Tom Thumb and his newlywed bride, Lavinia Warren, on their wedding day, and in many cases tower over him. A handcarved mini circus shows amazing detail, right down to the twirling trapeze artist. The model is hand-carved and is a 1,000-square-foot replica of the actual circus, encircled by an elevated viewing ramp.

Note the elaborate exterior of the museum, a beautiful Romanesque red-sandstone-and-brick structure with terra-cotta friezes, which dates from 1893. The museum was established with funds Barnum bequeathed upon his death two years earlier. A comparatively new and quite snazzy-looking 7,000-square-foot special-exhibitions wing can prove to be a great additional draw depending on the particular show; these change a few times a year. Renowned architect Richard Meier designed this exhibit space, which opened in 1989, as well as the neighboring People's Bank Building, which with its white, gray, and brownstone panels and glass bricks will be readily recognized by anyone who has been to the new Meier-designed Getty Center in Los Angeles.

It's not well known, but the **Housatonic Community-Technical College** (900 Lafayette Blvd., 203/332-5000, www.hctc.commnet.edu) has a fine 5,000-piece collection of art, works of which hang in many of its public spaces as well as in the Burt Chernow Gallery (open weekdays; free). The donated works come from all walks of the art world and has originals by Warhol, Matisse, Rodin, and Picasso. Brochures allow a self-guided tour of the collection. The new campus of Housatonic Community-Tech College downtown has helped greatly to rejuvenate the area, and nearby, the Bluefish stadium is a highly impressive ballpark, as is new Arena at Harbor Yard, which hosts minor-league hockey and college basketball.

## Seaside Park and Black Rock

From downtown, follow either Main Street or Iranistan Avenue south to reach Seaside Park, the 325-acre jewel of Bridgeport's coastline, laid out shortly following the Civil War by renowned landscape experts Frederick Law Olmsted and Calvert Vaux. You can walk across grassy lawns and by several historic monuments and sculptures, and try to get a sense of this broad expanse of greenery as its greatest champion, P.T. Barnum, envisioned it. At the western tip of the park, a breakwater leads out to Fayerweather Island's natural wildlife preserve, on which stands a lighthouse that stood guard over Black Rock Harbor from the 1820s through 1932.

At **Captain's Cove** (1 Bostwick Ave., 203/335-1433, www.captainscoveseaport.com) in Black Rock Harbor, charter fishing boats and harbor cruises sail from the full-service 400-slip marina, and there's a small boardwalk with crafts shops, an ice-cream stand, a fish market, a casual 400-seat restaurant, and concerts and special events—basically, an array of attractions and diversions (open daily Mar.–Oct.; call about special events).

Dundon House, a Queen Anne Victorian moved to Captain's Cove in 1991, houses photos, models, and artifacts pertaining to the Black Rock section of coastal Bridgeport. One of the more intriguing curiosities here is the Whitehead Hangar, which sits at one end of the main dock and contains a half-scale model of an aircraft said to have been the first ever flown in the world—not by the Wright Brothers, but by one Gustave Whitehead, a German immigrant who moved to Bridgeport in 1900. Witnesses have verified having watched the aviation expert take a half-mile flight over Long Island Sound on August 14, 1901—more than two years before the Wright Brothers accomplished the feat in Kitty Hawk, North Carolina. Unfortunately, Whitehead lacked public relations savvy and either the means or the good sense to document his advances in aviation, and so the big prize—recognition—went to Orville and Wilbur Wright.

Black Rock is the one Bridgeport neighborhood that possesses a certain funky cachet; the main drag, Fairfield Avenue—south of I-95 to the Fairfield line—contains eateries and a few interesting shops.

# STRATFORD

Bridgeport's neighbor to the east, Stratford, is a bustling coastal suburb with a handful of interesting attractions; in many ways this tightly settled working-class community is an extension of Bridgeport. From Bridgeport, head east on either Stratford Avenue or I-95 to exit 30, and then follow Rte. 113 south a couple miles around the southern tip of Sikorsky Airport to the Lordship section of town, where beach cottages line Long Island Sound. It's a nice spot to get a glimpse of the water. Washington Parkway off Rte. 113 leads to Seascape and Allen's East, which both front the water and serve great seafood.

From here, continue along Rte. 113 north into the center of Stratford. Virtually any place in the world named Stratford seems to have a connection to England's Stratford-upon-Avon, the home of William Shakespeare. Indeed, Stratford in Connecticut has maintained ties for quite a while, although the **Stratford Shakespeare Festival Theater** (1850 Elm St.), which was begun in 1955, was all but a memory by the 1990s. Attempts have been made to bring back the theater, and in 2002 a committee was formed to determine the future plans for this facility.

Within walking distance of the theater to the north is the **Stratford Historical Society** (967 Academy Hill, 203/378-0630, www.stratford-historicalsociety.com), which is inside a restored red 1750 Captain David Judson house overlooking the historic town green, around which are several appealing old homes (open June–Oct., limited hours, $2). Inside the house are artifacts pertaining to the region's Indian and African American histories, documents describing the town's involvement in the French and Indian Wars, a piano that once belonged to framer of the U.S. Constitution William Samuel Johnson, an open-hearth kitchen, and regularly changing exhibits. It's the centerpiece of the Academy Hill Historic District, which includes a number of 18th- and 19th-century homes.

A small but interesting museum set inside the vintage rail station downtown, the **National Helicopter Museum** (2480 Main St., 203/375-5766, open afternoons Wed.–Sun., mid-May–mid-Oct., donations suggested), has exhibits and historic photos that trace the history of the helicopter, which was developed by Igor Sikorsky right here in Stratford.

A drive north on Rte. 113 to Rte. 110 into the more rural Putney section of town reveals a different side of Stratford. Here you'll find one of the quirkiest attractions in the county, the **Booth Memorial Park & Museum** (Main St., Putney, 203/381-2046, museum has limited

© ANDREW COLLINS

**old tollbooth from Merritt Parkway, Booth Memorial Park & Museum in Stratford**

hours, open June–Sept., free) on shaded sloping grounds with views of the Housatonic. It's in northern Stratford, just off the Merritt Parkway. Here is a grab bag of historic structures, a vintage toll booth plaza from the Merritt, a rose garden, picnic tables, and a children's playground. Kind of fun on a warm day, as you never can be sure what you'll stumble upon. Technocratic Cathedral was made in 1932 of redwood and glass-block windows, sort of like an art deco pagoda. Other buildings include a Victorian clock tower, a greenhouse, and a 1935 blacksmith shop notable for having 44 sides and 44 corners. The Booths were clearly eccentric. Roosters cluck away in a barnyard.

## SHOPPING

Stratford contains one of the best-known emporiums of antiques dealers in the state, containing some 200 dealers: the **Stratford Antique Center** (400 Honeyspot Rd., 203/378-7754, www.stratfordantique.com). The area's other big retail draw is the huge, 165-store **Westfield Shoppingtown Trumbull Mall** (Main St. at exit 48 of the Merritt Pkwy., 203/372-4500), which is anchored by Macy's, Lord & Taylor, Filene's, JCPenney, and Circuit City.

## RECREATION
### Baseball

The minor-league pro baseball team the **Bridgeport Bluefish** (Ballpark at Harbor Yard, 500 Main St., 203/345-4800 or 877/GO-BLUES, www.bridgeportbluefish.com) plays from April through September, drawing the best crowds of any team in its league. The sleek new stadium is a masterpiece, and you can picnic on the grounds while catching a game. The ballpark also hosts **Bridgeport Barrage Major League Lacrosse.**

### Hockey

The **Bridegport Tigers** (203/368-1000 or 203/334-GOAL, www.soundtigers.com) were Eastern Conference champs for 2001–2002; the season runs from October through early April. Games are held at the new **Arena at Harbor Yard** (600 Main St., 203/345-2400), which also hosts Fairfield University Stags basketball games. The arena is part of the new Harbor Yard development, just I-95 downtown.

## ENTERTAINMENT AND NIGHTLIFE

**J.C. Hillary's** (Shoppingtown Trumbull, 203/371-5700) has live acoustic music some nights and other specials and discounts depending on the timing. There's also an outpost of the popular **Ruby Tuesday** chain at the same mall, and popular lounges at the nearby Trumbull Marriott. Bridgeport itself has little in the way of nightlife, although some of the restaurants in Black Rock reviewed below (Arizona Flats, Black Rock Castle, and Black Rock and Blue) are popular with area college students and yuppies for cocktails. **Acoustic Cafe** (2926 Fairfield Ave., 203/335-3655) is a top venue for live music, including jazz, folk, and pop—a number of national acts perform here, along with local ones; there are also poetry readings and amateur nights. **Bear & Grill** (2000 Black Rock Tpke., Fairfield, 203/333-1522) is another fun spot for live music.

One of several great new things to happen in Bridgeport during the past couple years, the 220-seat **Polka Dot Playhouse** (177 State St., 203/333-3666, www.polkadotplayhouse.org) reopened in 1999 inside a classic late–19th-century building in the heart of downtown (it had lived for many years in the Pleasure Beach section of town). It's a beautiful space, and it's exciting to see this theater thriving in the heart of this city that's trying so hard to rebound. The season of this professional theater sees a mix of five Broadway-style musicals and more serious dramas. **Downtown Cabaret Theatre** (263 Golden Hill St., 203/576-1636, www.dtcab.com) is an extremely successful and popular facility with wonderful musical comedy, typically with upbeat lively themes. You can bring your own food if you'd like to picnic while watching the show, and a children's series is offered Oct.–May. The **Klein Memorial Auditorium** (910 Fairfield Ave., 203/576-8115) regularly hosts classical, jazz, choral, and operatic music performances—it's home to the **Greater Bridgeport Symphony Orchestra** (203/576-0263).

## FESTIVALS AND EVENTS

In late June, watch the fireworks, street parades, and other festivities surrounding the **Barnum Festival** at various locations in downtown Bridgeport, 203/367-8495. This is also the time for the **Russian Festival & Crafts Fair** (St. Nicholas Russian Orthodox Church, Stratford, 203/377-1515). The city also hosts the well-attended **Puerto Rican Parade of Fairfield County** (203/333-5193), held in July. A **Hungarian Bazaar** (Holy Trinity Byzantine Catholic Church Social Hall, 225 Scofield Ave., 203/334-7089) has been drawing crowds to Bridgeport each September since the late 1970s. Hungarian and American foods, games, and crafts highlight the occasion.

## ACCOMMODATIONS

You won't find a huge variety of lodging options in this area, despite the fact that Bridgeport is the largest city in the state. In fact, there's only one hotel in this entire municipality. However, bear in mind that Fairfield and Westport to the west, New Haven and Milford to the east, and Shelton to the north all have a wealth of accommodations. You certainly don't need to stay in Bridgeport to take advantage of its attractions, which are all easily accessed from major highways.

### Hotels and Motels
### $100–150

A great option if you'd like to be near Bridgeport's major attractions, but in a peaceful non-urban setting, the **Trumbull Marriott** (180 Hawley Ln., Trumbull, 203/378-1400 or 800/228-9290) is an upscale business-oriented facility with a very nice restaurant and a less formal café, two pools, full business center, exercise room, and 323 fully updated rooms.

Rooms at the nine-floor **Holiday Inn Bridgeport** (1070 Main St., 203/334-1234 or 800 /HOLIDAY) have been completely revamped, making what had been a so-so property quite respectable—and a reasonably priced one, considering that it's the only option in downtown Bridgeport. You'd have never imagined a leisure traveler actually choosing to stay in Bridgeport a few years back, but with continuing redevelopment and better attractions, these days the Holiday Inn is a great option no matter what your reasons for coming. There's a restaurant, indoor pool, room service, and free parking.

Opened in 2002, **Staybridge Suites** (6905 Main St., 203/377-3322 or 800/238-8000) has a wonderfully convenient yet quiet location on a wooded hilltop off the Housatonic River, overlooking the Merritt Parkway bridge and the Sikorsky helicopter facility nearby. This attractive complex of colonial-style buildings has large smartly decorated suites with full kitchens and ample living areas—they're especially popular with corporate travelers. But on weekends, a number of leisure travelers choose this property, since it's an easy drive from Bridgeport, Shelton, Waterbury, and New Haven. The staff is highly professional, the public areas warm and inviting, and the facilities top-notch—including a snack/grocery shop (open 24 hours), a business center, indoor pool, evening socials, a guest laundry, free local calls, and a complimentary breakfast buffet.

## $50–100

The 145-room **Ramada Stratford** (225 Lordship Blvd., exit 30 from I-95, 203/375-8866 or 888/298-2054) is a perfectly decent chain property in a dull, but convenient location. It's well-managed and the rooms are very clean, but the hotel could use a little updating. There's a nice lobby, a comfortable bar and restaurant, and an indoor pool. **Marnick's** (10 Washington Pkwy., Stratford, 203/377-6288) is a rather old-fashioned, family-run motel in the heart of Lordship's waterfront neighborhood—basic accommodations that show the wear of families and beach vacationers but are nevertheless bright, clean, and pleasant, with huge TVs, refrigerators, water views, and rates you won't beat. It's a real throwback to the kind of beach motels that once proliferated along the shore, and a somewhat hidden secret around these parts. A restaurant on the premises has traditional Italian and American favorites, and Seascape and Allen's East are a short stroll away.

## Country Inns and Bed-and-Breakfasts

**$100–150:** The **Nathan Booth House** (6080 Main St., 203/378-6489, www.bbonline.com /ct/nathanbooth) is a distinctive 1843 Greek Revival in the countrified village of Putney, right by a simple white 1844 chapel and a short walk from the Booth Museum. It's on a hill close to the Housatonic, and an expanse of lawn and shade trees—plus a big red barn—runs behind the house. You won't find a quieter and more secluded setting in greater Bridgeport. The four guest rooms have period furnishings, wide-plank chestnut floors, and original hardware and woodworking throughout.

## FOOD

Bridgeport has a disproportionately low number of marquee restaurants, considering the bounty of great dining options elsewhere in coastal Fairfield County and also in New Haven. Nevertheless, the city has a handful of very good options, and nearby Stratford has a few more.

### Creative but Casual

An intimate and dapper eatery on U.S. 1 near the Bridgeport border, **Marbella Restaurant and Tapas Bar** (1479 Barnum Ave., 203/378-6702, $15–18) is one of the better eateries in town, serving authentic Spanish and Mediterranean fare. You might sample grilled baby squid, with lemon, olive oil, and sherry vinegar; or paella Valenciana, with chicken, chorizo, shrimp, clams, mussels, and saffron rice. The service couldn't be friendlier, and a handsome bar in back is well-suited for single diners. Of the three seaside eateries in Stratford's Lordship neighborhood, **Plouf** (14 Beach Dr., Stratford, 203/386-1477, $14–20) serves unquestionably the best food. The unprepossessing dining room has closely spaced tables with festive, colorful napery and rows of windows overlooking Long Island Sound. Fine Parisian-inspired cooking is featured: Start with the delicious seafood crêpe before graduating to fillet of salmon in a puff pastry with dill sauce, or classic sautéed frogs' legs, butter, garlic, herbs, tomato, and white wine.

**Bloodroot** (85 Ferris St., Bridgeport, 203/576-9168, www.bloodroot.com, $6–12), in an unassuming brown building—a former machine shop—in a sleepy residential cul-de-sac overlooking Cedar Creek and Long Island Sound, is more than a vegetarian restaurant—it's also one of southern New England's foremost feminist collectives, and a well-respected bookstore, too. Of course, all are welcome to sample the healthful and creative vegetarian fare, including oyster-mushroom quiche, tempeh pot pie, and a salad of smoked eggplant with a lima-leek purée and sweet-and-sour pickles. Black-and-white pictures, plants, and various bric-a-brac give the place a happily cluttered and homey look; you order as you come in, pick up your food at the counter when it's ready, and clear your own table.

**Ralph 'n' Rich's** (121 Wall St., Bridgeport, 203/366-3597, $12–22), a clubby restaurant on a side street by the Holiday Inn, serves first-rate Italian fare—live piano is presented most evenings, and at lunchtime, you're sure to find a sea of area power-brokers and deal-makers schmoozing over freshly prepared pastas, seafood grills, and chicken and steak specialties. The outgoing staff works hard to please and even remembers the names of customers. A snazzy spot serving creative, contemporary American fare, **Picasso** (3074 Fairfield Ave., Bridgeport, 203/335-2500, $12–22) has an attractive mustard-cobalt-burgundy color scheme and a hip lounge that's often the site of live music.

## Pizza, Pub Grub, and Seafood

In a funky, medieval-inspired building, **Black Rock Castle** (2895 Fairfield Ave., 203/336-3990, $10–23) is a brewpub with a moderately interesting menu of Irish, English, and American dishes—best bets include Irish whisky steak, bangers and mash, and fish and chips. There's live music many nights. **Vazzy's** (Beardsley Plaza, 513 Broadbridge Ave., 203/371-8046, $9–17, 10-inch pies $7–11) serves not only the best brick-oven pizzas in

the area, but also superb and filling pastas. You can have the pasta served either traditionally or still sizzling in the pan in which it was cooked (the latter, of course, is a real crowd-pleaser; try spaghetti in white clam sauce this way). The mixed seafood sauté is another favorite. Just bear in mind the staggering popularity of this place—it can be tough to score a table, and service sometimes falters when the going gets tough.

A good place to bring the kids after a visit to the nearby Discovery Museum, **Brick Oven Pizza** (1581 Capitol Ave., 203/367-9958, $6–17, large pies $9–19) anchors a fairly quiet residential neighborhood near the Fairfield border. Specialty pies range from white broccoli to four seasons (sausage, pepperoni, mushrooms, and bacon).

A typically loud and vibrant college joint near the Fairfield border, **Black Rock and Blue** (3488 Fairfield Ave., 203/384-1167, $8–17) brings in a variety of music acts and specializes in hearty regional American fare, including Philly cheese steaks, sausage-pepper-and-eggs sandwiches, Cajun-seared chicken with Dijon sauce and pan-fried catfish. Not a quiet date place, but plenty of fun. Stratford's playfully named **Shell Station, Main St. Railroad Station W** (203/377-1648, $10–18) occupies the former rail station in the center of town but now traffics in fresh seafood, including a very nice selection of sushi and sashimi. Lace curtains and high ceilings, as well as a large fish tank built into one wall, make for an engaging setting. The food at **Allen's East** (60 Beach Dr., 203/378-0556, $8–15) doesn't measure up to aforementioned Seascape by a long shot, but it is the less expensive of the two, and you still get to enjoy great views of Long Island Sound from the large covered patio.

## Mexican

**Taco Loco** (3170 Fairfield Ave., 203/335-8228, $4–8), set in a stucco house with generous outdoor and indoor seating, is a pleasant choice for inexpensive and not-too-greasy Mexican food, such as chiles rellenos and steak and rice. The staff is friendly, and there's lively music playing in the background.

## Asian

Thai restaurants remain a rarity in Connecticut, despite the influx of Indian eateries. Bridgeport's **King & I** (545 Broadbridge Rd., 203/374-2081, $8–15) has been a stalwart since opening in 1987—one wonders if the management ever intends to move into a larger space, as the present two-tiered dining room in a shopping mall near Beardsley Park fills up fast on weekends. The cooking is generally excellent, with specialties like deep-fried quail in garlic, Thai herbs, and a sharp lemon sauce, or pan-fried squid with a ginger, onion, and a scallion brown sauce. Service can be brusque, but is fairly efficient nonetheless.

## Quick Bites

In case you're thinking fast-food burgers and fries would hit the spot right about now, consider forgoing the chain restaurants and pulling up alongside the **Boardwalk** (982 Madison Ave., 203/338-0649, most dishes under $5) where an annoying—but easy to recognize—strobe light beckons famished travelers. The Philly cheese steaks, hot dogs, thick shakes, and cheap breakfasts are worth braving this hole-in-the-wall's uninspired north-of-downtown neighborhood.

## INFORMATION AND SERVICES

### Visitor Information

The region is served by the **Coastal Fairfield County Convention & Visitor Bureau** (20 Marshall St., Suite 102, Norwalk, CT 06854, 203/840-0770 or 800/866-7925, www.coastalct.com).

### Getting Around

Bridgeport is easily reached from the rest of the state from both I-95 and, in the northern reaches, the Merritt Parkway. Also, Rte. 8 (a limited-access four-lane highway) runs north from downtown to Waterbury, Rte. 25 to Danbury. Both Bridgeport and Stratford are served by Metro-North from New York City to New Haven. Crime is a problem in Bridgeport, and you should be careful about walking around certain neighborhoods and parking your car on streets with which you're unfamiliar. All of the attractions described above have safe parking or are close to secure parking garages.

# New Haven and Vicinity

Even when times have been tough for New Haven, this midsize city facing Long Island Sound has remained a beacon of higher learning and culture. The city is synonymous with Yale University, which has infused downtown with several fine museums, an eclectic restaurant scene, and an intriguing blend of high-brow and offbeat shops. After Boston, New Haven also possesses the second most important theater scene in New England. The city suffers from the same urban ills that plague the rest of urban Connecticut, but New Haven has a tremendous amount going for it and definitely should be a part of any trip through the state.

Circling the city on the west, north, and east is a fringe of rather quiet bedroom communities, but you will find a smattering of attractions in these outlying towns, especially in the two largest of the region's municipalities, Milford and Hamden.

## NEW HAVEN

New Haven's history, architecture, and academic prestige make it potentially one of the best small urban destinations in the Northeast. Unfortunately, under the leadership of the same federally subsidized urban renewal that laid much of Hartford and Bridgeport to ruin, New Haven capsized during the middle of the century. Awkward, unseemly highways cut through the heart of the city, dividing neighborhoods and creating insular pockets of blight and neglect. Historic buildings were knocked down, and the suburban sprawl of neighboring towns sucked away the core of local shoppers. For the next few

THE CONNECTICUT COAST

# DOWNTOWN NEW HAVEN

**Streets and areas:**
CLARK ST.
PEARL ST.
BRADLEY ST.
LINCOLN ST.
ORANGE ST.
TRUMBULL ST.
STATE ST.
WILLIAM ST.
LYON ST.
GRAND AVE.
JEFFERSON ST.
CHESTNUT ST.
WOOSTER PL.
HUGHES PL.
JOHN ST.
SAINT ST.
GREENE ST.
COURT ST.
UNION ST.
OLIVE ST.
ACADEMY ST.
CHAPEL ST.
WOOSTER ST.
BREWERY ST.
AUDUBON ST.
ARTIZAN ST.
ORANGE ST.
CENTER ST.
CHURCH ST.
GEORGE ST.
STATE ST.
FAIR ST.
TEMPLE ST.
COLLEGE ST.
HIGH ST.
YORK ST.
PARK ST.
CROWN ST.
HOWE ST.
NORTH FRONTAGE RD.
SOUTH FRONTAGE RD.
CEDAR ST.
HOWARD AVE.
DWIGHT ST.
EDGEWOOD AVE.
LYNWOOD PL.
BROADWAY
TOWER PKWY.
ASHMUN ST.
GROVE ST.
PROSPECT ST.
HILLHOUSE AVE.
WHITNEY AVE.
TRUMBULL ST.
WALL ST.
ELM ST.
CHAPEL ST.
OAK ST. CONNECTOR (34)

**Labeled locations:**
- CHRISTOPHER MARTIN'S
- TRE SCALINI RISTORANTE
- FRANK PEPE'S
- LIBBY'S ITALIAN PASTRY SHOP
- THE MANSION INN
- SALLY'S APIZZA
- PEABODY MUSEUM OF NATURAL HISTORY
- NEW HAVEN COLONY HISTORICAL SOCIETY
- CREATIVE ARTS WORKSHOP
- ANNA LIFFEY'S
- JUDIE'S EUROPEAN BAKED GOODS
- CONNECTICUT CHILDREN'S MUSEUM
- YALE COLLECTION OF MUSICAL INSTRUMENTS
- WILLOUGHBY'S COFFEE & TEA
- YALE UNIVERSITY VISITOR INFORMATION
- GREATER NEW HAVEN CONVENTION AND VISITORS BUREAU
- AMISTAD MEMORIAL
- MISO
- ROYAL PALACE
- BENTARA
- BEINECKE RARE BOOK LIBRARY
- YALE UNIVERSITY
- New Haven Green
- WILLOUGHBY'S COFFEE & TEA
- UNION LEAGUE CAFE
- CLAIRE'S
- ANCHOR
- ZINC
- BOTTEGA
- THE PLAYWRIGHT
- OMNI NEW HAVEN HOTEL AT YALE
- NEW HAVEN HOTEL
- SHUBERT THEATER
- CAFFE ADULIS
- LOUIS' LUNCH
- CAFE ISTANBUL
- BAR
- IBIZA
- ROOMBA
- YALE UNIVERSITY ART GALLERY
- SEOUL
- ATTICUS CAFE
- YALE CENTER FOR BRITISH ART
- BANGKOK
- YALE REPERTORY THEATRE
- DUNCAN HOTEL
- COSI
- IVY NOODLE
- HOLIDAY INN AT YALE
- THE COLONY
- THREE CHIMNEYS
- MAMOUN'S
- INDOCHINE
- TANDOOR
- YALE NEW HAVEN HOSPITAL
- Yale Medical School
- Grove Street Cemetery

**Scale:**
0 — 300 yds
0 — 300 m

91

N

© AVALON TRAVEL PUBLISHING, INC.

decades, only the presence of Yale University sustained downtown New Haven.

In keeping with the slow but sure renaissance of Connecticut's cities, New Haven began to blossom again in the 1990s, however. An upscale Omni hotel now fringes the campus and stands tall over the still-lovely town green. Older buildings, most of them west and southwest of the green, have been refitted and reworked, and new construction has been planned out carefully with the aim of working intelligently with the existing streetscape. The Wooster Street neighborhood, a compact "Little Italy" whose character and culinary prowess nevertheless rivals any such enclave in America, has also made tremendous strides.

The Town Green Special Services District, a joint public-private coalition to oversee the renaissance of central New Haven, was formed in 1997. This organization is funded by a tax levied upon property owners within the district (plus a significant city government contribution), and the organization, whose annual budget is about a half million dollars, employs maintenance officers to keep the streets clean and security officers to watch for broken streetlights and assist pedestrians in getting around safely. They've installed planters throughout central downtown, which residents have helped to care for. And they've offered to consult for free with locals on how more attractively to landscape their properties. It's exciting to see groups such as these help put a new face on New Haven.

The city is also a trove of notable modern urban architecture, with Yale's presence having helped to draw some of the world's most prestigious architects to New Haven. The **Alliance for Architecture** produces a wonderful pamphlet and walking tour on the city's architecture during the second half of the 20th century; it's available free from the Greater New Haven Convention and Visitors Bureau. Works by Marcel Breuer, Gordon Bunshaft (of Skidmore, Owings, and Merrill), Frank Gehry, Philip Johnson, Louis I. Kahn, Cesar Pelli,

*The city is also a trove of notable modern urban architecture, with Yale's presence having helped to draw some of the world's most prestigious architects to New Haven.*

Kevin Roche, Eero Saarinen, and Robert Venturi are included on the tour.

Some talk of bringing about change in New Haven hinges on the high-speed train service between here and Manhattan. In late fall 1999, such service began running—reducing the time to New York City's Grand Central Station from about 90 minutes to just 45. This development could make it easier for residents of New Haven to commute into Manhattan, something that folks in Stamford do quite easily. More importantly, it may draw greater numbers of New Yorkers out to New Haven.

## Downtown New Haven

The best place to begin your explorations is at the **New Haven Green,** a large, stately plot of civic greenery that encompasses what was one of the original nine town squares laid out upon the village's inception in 1638. Three beautiful churches line the green: the Gothic Revival **Trinity Episcopal Church** (ca. 1814, designed by Ithiel Town), the Federal-style **Center Church Congregational** (ca. 1812, also by Town), and the Georgian **United Church** (ca. 1815, by David Hoadley), which served as the city's primary meetinghouse.

The campus of Yale University dominates most of the area immediately west of the green and also some of the blocks to the south and north of it. Drop by the **Yale University Visitor Information Center** (149 Elm St., 203/432-2300) from which one-hour free guided walking tours of the campus depart at 10:30 A.M. and 2 P.M. on weekdays and at 1:30 P.M. on weekends.

Walk west from the southern end of the green to appreciate the one area that has really begun to thrive over the past decade, the **College-Chapel District,** bounded roughly by College, Crown, York, and Chapel streets—near the west edge of Yale's campus and the New Haven Green. Great restaurants, fun shops, and a positive pedestrian buzz permeate the blocks in this neighborhood. Chapel Avenue is one of the few streets in Con-

# YALE UNIVERSITY AND THE HISTORY OF NEW HAVEN

Yale University enjoys a considerably more liberal-minded reputation today than its archrival, Harvard, yet New Haven was founded upon an amazingly strict and exclusionary set of laws—the so-called Blue Laws—which were based directly on the teachings of the Old Testament. During those early years, any child of 16 or older who cursed or struck a natural parent could be put to death. Another called for the branding, whipping, and expulsion from the colony of any person found to be a practicing Quaker.

It's interesting to note today that the WPA guide to Connecticut, published in 1938, also notes among these exceptionally harsh rules that "a law made smoking illegal except in a room in a private house; another law declared smoking illegal except on a journey of five miles away from home, which made it impossible for most servants to smoke." Obviously, the WPA writers would have been shocked to know that regarding one of these issues, society just a half-century later would return to its barbaric ways.

Yale University was founded in 1702 (originally in the town of Killingworth, and then Old Saybrook—it moved to New Haven in 1716), only about six decades after the city's founding. But it is this prestigious university for which Connecticut's third-largest city is best known, and indeed Yale has imbued New Haven with international clout and a rich cultural scene.

The Reverend John Davenport of London first settled the city in 1640, purchasing it from the region's Quinnipiac Native Americans for a sum that compared favorably to Peter Minuit's considerably more infamous New York City land transaction: 23 coats, 12 spoons and hatchets, 24 knives, and an assortment of scissors and hoes.

The rigidity with which Davenport ruled the colony, basing every move on the biblical laws of Moses, greatly influenced the handsome layout attributed to New Haven today. The first planned community in the New World was set around nine 16-acre squares, the central one being a town green that would contain a public market and cattle pasture. That green, whose character has been altered relatively little since its inception, remains the centerpiece of modern New Haven.

Davenport sought to develop a school of higher education in his new colony, but during his life no such enterprise happened. Harvard proved sufficient to handle the education of New England's young men until in 1701 a group of Harvard-graduated clergymen gathered inside a house in Branford and planned the creation of a second university.

A wealthy merchant named Elihu Yale, at the urging of friends, was convinced to part with a bounty of merchandise so that funds raised by its sale could help finance the nascent institution, which had by then just moved into New Haven. Yale's gift fetched the then-impressive sum of 562 pounds, and in exchange for his generosity, the heads of the school named it for him. Yale, like many wealthy men of the day, was no doubt inspired by the potential for recognition, and in that regard his gesture has certainly paid off. He died in 1721, never knowing just how important the little school that bore his name would become.

Early on, Yale University graduated a number of illustrious men, including theologian Jonathan Edwards, patriot-martyr Nathan Hale, lexicographer Noah Webster, and inventor Eli Whitney. And the school has continued to churn out distinguished statesmen, among them presidents Bill Clinton and George W. Bush. The school's abundance of Oxford- and Cambridge-inspired collegiate Gothic architecture permeates downtown New Haven—perhaps most famous is the 221-foot Harkness Tower, which rises high above the school's Memorial Quadrangle.

THE CONNECTICUT COAST

necticut where the streetlife compares with Boston or Manhattan. Just off Chapel, along Temple Street, **Temple Plaza** is a new landscaped courtyard with a few restaurants off of it, in a spot that was quite barren until recently. It's further evidence of how downtown New Haven has become increasingly walkable and attractive.

Art lovers should make a special point of visiting the **Yale University Art Gallery** (1111 Chapel St., 203/432-0600, www.yale.edu/artgallery, open 10 A.M.–5 P.M. Tues.–Sat., until 8 P.M. on Thurs., 1–6 P.M. Sun., free) whose specialties include remarkable troves of Egyptian, Etruscan, and Greek art; early Italian painted panels; impressionist and modernist works from both European and American masters, including Monet, van Gogh, Manet, and Picasso; and many works from Asia and Africa. Special exhibitions change often and have included works by Yale artists, retrospectives of major artists (Degas, for example, was featured in 2003), and relevant themes (such as "Justice on Trial: Ben Shahn's Case for Sacco and Vanzetti" in 2002). The building, designed in 1951 by Louis I. Kahn, is itself a marvel.

Across the street, the **Yale Center for British Art** (1080 Chapel St., 203/432-2800, www.yale.edu/ycba, open 10 A.M.–5 P.M. Tues.–Sat., noon–5 P.M.. Sun., free) is arguably the best gallery of English art outside of the United Kingdom, with many important originals by Turner, Reynolds, Gainesborough, Constable, Millay, Hogarth, Rosetti, and many others. The building's design is highly innovative and provocative, and the collection showcases works from Tudor times to the present. The museum store is particularly good. Through much of summer and fall, you'll be able to see the "Art of Bloomsbury" exhibition, one of the several excellent temporary events presented each year. Paul Mellon founded the center in 1966 by financing the cost of the building (designed by architect Louis I. Kahn) and donating the gallery's core art collection; he also bequeathed $90 million plus an art collection of undetermined value on his death in 1999.

Head to the north side of the green to see a different, less commercial side of downtown.

The ***Amistad*** **Memorial** (165 Church St., 203/387-0370) is directly in front of the New Haven City Hall. Designed in 1992 by renowned sculptor Ed Hamilton, the sculpture was created to commemorate the Amistad rebellion, which occurred in 1839 and was followed by two years of trials and hearings in New Haven courtrooms before the 53 kidnapped Africans were freed.

Note the 1938 Southern New England Telephone Building, one of the state's finest examples of art deco and one of only a handful of such skyscrapers. It's a 17-story structure whose lobby has nickel doors, fixtures, and fluted columns, as well as black marble walls with fountains.

Continue north along Church; it soon becomes Whitney Avenue, site of the **New Haven Colony Historical Society** (114 Whitney Ave., 203/562-4183, open 10 A.M.–5 p.m. Tues.–Fri., 2–5 P.M. weekends, $2) which contains historical and cultural exhibits tracing the city's growth from the 1630s to the present. There's also a remarkably complete survey of New Haven tableware, most of it dating from the 17th through 19th centuries, and a fine research library and photo archives.

Another of Yale's excellent attractions, the **Peabody Museum of Natural History** (170 Whitney Ave., 203/432-5099 or 203/432-3740, www.peabody.yale.edu, open 10 A.M.–5 P.M. Mon.–Sat., noon–5 P.M. Sun., $5) was developed in 1866 by a wealthy industrialist named George Peabody—at the behest of his nephew and Yale paleontology professor, Othniel Charles Marsh. The museum today contains more than 11 million specimens, from triceratops fossils, ceremonial crafts of Pacific Northwest indigenous inhabitants, artifacts from ancient Egypt, and the Hall of Connecticut Birds, whose ornithological collection encompasses three-quarters of all of the world's bird species.

At the intersection of Whitney and Trumbull, right by the Peabody, turn west (left if you're walking from the green, right if coming from the museum) and continue past Temple Street, then make your next left to reach the **Yale Collection of Musical Instruments** (15 Hillhouse Ave., 203/432-0822, www.yale.edu/musicalinstruments, open afternoons Tues.–Thurs. during the school year, $2) where some thousand rare and important instruments from the 1500s to the present reside. This is a fascinating place that's often overlooked because it keeps irregular hours and is somewhat off the beaten path. It's worth phoning ahead and making an appointment to view this collection, even if you have only an ancillary interest in music.

Back on Whitney, return toward the green, making a brief detour east on Audubon Street to see the **Creative Arts Workshop** (80 Audubon St., 203/562-4927, www.creativeartsworkshop.org), a small regional art school whose Hilles Gallery mounts rotating exhibits of student works. From Whitney, back near the green, make a right turn onto Wall Street to survey more of Yale's campus and to reach the **Beinecke Rare Book Library** (121 Wall St., 203/432-2977, www.library.yale.edu/beinecke), a distinctive 1963 building known for its translucent marble windows and sunken sculpture garden. Among the rarities contained in this collection are an original Gutenberg Bible and a fine set of original Audubon bird prints. The facility also contains the largest archive of late playwright and New London resident Eugene O'Neill (open 8:30 A.M.–5 P.M. weekdays, 10 A.M.–5 P.M. Sat. during the school year).

Two final New Haven attractions, in the northwestern end of town, are best reached by car. From the green, drive west on Chapel Street away from downtown, turn right onto Sherman Avenue, and then left onto Rte. 10 (Whalley Avenue); follow Rte. 10 until it becomes Fitch Street and leads up to the campus of Southern Connecticut State University. The college is home to the **Ethnic Heritage Center** (117 Wintergreen Building, 501 Crescent St., 203/392-6126, open Tues.–Fri., somewhat limited hours, free) where five ethnic groups trace their roles in the growth of New Haven. Here you'll find the Jewish Historical Society of Greater New Haven, the Connecticut Irish-American Historical Society, the Ukrainian-American Historical Society, the Italian-American Historical Society, and the Connecticut African-American Historical Society. Each archive contains a vast cache of information pertaining to the efforts of these groups to establish roots in the region.

Near campus are **West Rock Park** (203/789-7498) and the **West Rock Nature Center** (1020 Wintergreen Ave., 203/946-8016), a 40-acre center with native birds, reptiles, and other animals, plus wildlife displays.

One of the newest attractions in Connecticut is the **Knights of Columbus Museum** (1 State St., 203/865-0400, www.kofc.org), a short walk south east of the New Haven Green and the rapidly gentrifying Nine Square neighborhood—it's right off the Rte. 34 connector from I-95, near the train station. This spacious facility traces the history of this Catholic-family fraternal-service organization. But even if you don't have a strong interest in this organization, be sure to find out what temporary exhibits are featured—the museum presents some outstanding religious art and artifacts (open 10 A.M.–5 P.M. Wed.–Sat. Sept.–Apr., 10 A.M.–5 P.M. daily May–Aug.).

A few blocks north, the **Connecticut Children's Museum** (22 Wall St., 203/562-5437, www.childrensbuilding.org, open noon–5P.M. Fri.–Sat., $5) is a weekends-only interactive space for kids. Exhibits allow kids to sample and learn about music, mathematics, language, and nature.

## GREATER NEW HAVEN

Mostly quiet suburban towns fringe New Haven; Milford and Hamden offer very good dining options, and several main roads in this area prove quite engaging for bicycling or Sunday driving. There's also some good hiking in a few areas, but overall this mostly residential region has little to draw in the tourist.

### Milford

One of the best area attractions is the **Connecticut Audubon Coastal Center** (1 Milford Point Rd., 203/878-7440, www.ctaudubon.org, open 10 A.M.–4 P.M. Tues.–Sat., noon–4 P.M. Sun., $2), which occupies what has been for centuries a prolific source of wild marinelife—about 840 acres of pristine salt marsh. Any time you come here, the sound of birds calling punctuates the tranquil air of this dramatically situated beach park. In summer, along the tidal marsh, you'll spy zillions of fiddler crabs, which wiggle about in such abundance that some people mistake them at first for a plague of locusts. You'll also see many kinds of ducks, plus terns and great herons—many live along Nell's Island, a marshy tract behind the visitor center. A small museum houses exhibits on coastal wildlife in Connecticut, and a four-story observation deck offers great views of the marsh, the Housatonic, and Long Island Sound. Bring binoculars so you can clearly see all of the wildlife.

The fastest way here from New Haven is to follow I-95 west to exit 34, head back east a half mile on U.S. 1, make a right onto Meadows End Road, and then another right onto Milford Point Road, which leads a few miles down to the coast and the Audubon Center. An interesting way back to New Haven from the center is to follow the shoreline east along Sea View Avenue and then Broadway, passing through several popular summer communities and Silver Beach.

Make a left when you come to the end of this stretch, onto Seaside Avenue, and follow this into Milford's charming downtown. It's anchored by one of the longest, prettiest village greens in the area, with flower gardens, war monuments, and a gazebo—it all has the feel of a great old all-American town center. An increasingly trendy array of shops and eateries has opened along or just off Broad Street (runs the length of the green). Milford is very much a town whose star is rising, filling up with folks who want to live close to hip New Haven and avoid the rocket-high real-estate costs of Fairfield County. Appropriately, there's a

Subway Sandwich store anchoring one end of the green—the now-immense fast-food franchise was developed in Milford, and the town is still the home of Subway's headquarters.

This is a walkable downtown, and from the green you can stroll down High Street a couple of blocks to get a look at the pretty little harbor. There's free parking in a lot just across the street from Archie Moore's restaurants, near the town marina. Here, too, is the **Milford Historical Society** (34 High St., 203/874-2664, open 1–4 P.M. Sun. and by appointment, gardens

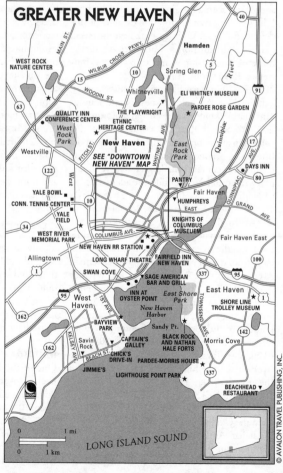

© AVALON TRAVEL PUBLISHING, INC.

© ANDREW COLLINS

**waterfall in Milford**

open daily May–Oct., free), which occupies three historic houses, presents special exhibits and a collection of Indian artifacts, and offers special programs from tours out to Faulkner Island Lighthouse to Christmas Candlelight house tours.

### West Haven

From the center of town, hop in your car and continue east on New Haven Avenue (Rte. 162), which leads eventually over the Oyster River and into West Haven. Just after crossing the border, make a right turn onto Ocean Avenue and follow it along Long Island Sound. The area around Jimmie's restaurant is now lined with rather characterless modern buildings, but years ago Savin Rock was famous for its long boardwalk and Coney Island-like seaside amusements. Alas, all was torn down many moons ago, but the beach itself is still intact and runs uninterrupted for a few miles back to New Haven—it's the longest stretch of public beach in Connecticut. Just stay along the various roads bordering the beachfront—great for jogging, strolling, or blading—to get back; you'll pass popular possibilities for fried seafood along the way.

### Bethany and Woodbridge

The towns due north of New Haven are quite peaceful and largely underdeveloped, surprisingly so considering their proximity not just to New Haven, but to Bridgeport, Waterbury, Meriden, and Hartford. One way to admire this terrain and some of the old Colonial homes in the area is to head north on Rte. 63 through the towns of Woodbridge and Bethany and return back down Rte. 69.

### Sleeping Giant State Park

There's more to see and do in the towns just east of here (and still north of New Haven); Hamden (a large semi-urban town with excellent hiking at its north end) and Wallingford (a middle-class community with a history of silver manufacturing).

From New Haven, drive north on Rte. 10, passing through the center of town and continuing several miles until you reach Mt. Carmel Road. Soon after turning right onto this street you'll see the attractive campus of **Quinnipiac College** (275 Mt. Carmel Ave., 203/582-8200, www.quinnipiac.edu), whose traditional redbrick buildings date mostly from the 1920s and 1930s. This small liberal arts school has grown steadily in prestige over the years, as it's well-known for both an excellent law school and its tradition of polling—you'll especially hear newscasters and political analysts discussing the latest Quinnipiac polls around the time of national elections.

Students here are fortunate to be just steps from one of the best state parks in Connecticut. **Sleeping Giant State Park** (200 Mt. Carmel Ave., just east of Rte. 10, Hamden, 203/789-7498), has been one of the state's favorite outdoors venues since it was granted park status in 1924. It consists of about 1,500 acres presently, but the Sleeping Giant Park Association continues to work with the state to acquire more land—this association is worth joining, incidentally, if you come to this area often. Membership entitles you to participate in the 14 group hikes held throughout the spring and fall.

The usual array of tables, restrooms, and pavilions is available near the main parking area, and several excellent trails then lead into the steep ridges contained within the park. The most popular (and typically quite crowded), the 1.6-mile Tower Trail, leads to a four-story stone tower built by the Works Progress Administration in the late 1930s. About 30 more miles of trails traverse the park. The name "Sleeping Giant" comes from the geological formation that can be seen from New Haven harbor and other points south—looking north, the ridge looks like a silhouette of a lying body, its feet pointed east and its head lying to the west. The tower sits atop the giant's left hip. There's also fishing (on the Mill River) and a self-guided nature trail. Of the 13 trails, most follow a steady ascent and run from one to three miles; there are also a couple of easy, nearly level trails, including the Tower Path, which is wide and easy. The most challenging hike is along the Blue Trail, a 5.1-mile trek that crosses by the Stone Tower and eventually joins with the Quinnipiac Trail, at the eastern end of the park. Rather quickly into this hike you'll climb the "chin" of the sleeping giant's head, at the western end of the park, which is rather rugged and involves a

bit of hand-over-foot climbing. The elevation ranges from about 100 to 750 feet depending on where you go.

## Wallingford

From the main park entrance, continue east on Mt. Carmel Road, turning left when you come to the Hartford Turnpike (which parallels the Wilbur Cross Parkway), and then turn right onto Rte. 150—after passing the Oakdale Theater—to reach downtown Wallingford. This isn't the most exciting town in Connecticut, but there are some neat historic buildings downtown, especially around the campus of the prestigious Choate-Rosemary Hall prep school. The Wallingford Historic Trust holds offices in a dramatic 1672 saltbox donated to the organization by Choate-Rosemary Hall, which had owned it for some 30 years. It's filled with antiques and was saved from demolition back in 1924 by Helen and Lucy Royce; it's called the Nehemiah Royce House.

## Hamden

From the center of Wallingford, return to Hamden by hopping onto the Wilbur Cross Parkway and heading west a few miles, leaving via exit 60 and heading south again along Rte. 10. Turn left a half mile later onto Mather Street and follow it until it runs into Whitney Avenue; make a right. You'll soon come to the entrance for East Rock Park and the **Eli Whitney Museum** (915 Whitney Ave., 203/777-1833, www.eliwhitney.org, open noon–5 P.M. Wed.–Fri. and Sun., 10 A.M.–3 P.M. Sat., call for schedule of performances at the barn, $3), a very kid-friendly tribute to the man often credited for singlehandedly propelling America into the throes of the industrial revolution. Displays trace Whitney's long and distinguished career as the inventor of the cotton gin and the one who perfected the notion of interchangeable parts. The museum also has an interactive learning lab and a summer barn where dances, concerts, and theater are sometimes presented in the summer.

Continue south a short distance, and right at the New Haven border make a left turn onto

East Rock Park Road to access the expansive and hilly **East Rock Park** (203/946-6086), which has a bird sanctuary, playgrounds and playing fields, nature trails, and excellent views in the distance toward Long Island Sound and New Haven Harbor. On the east side of the park is the **Pardee Rose Garden** (180 Park Rd., Hamden, 203/946-8021, open sunrise–sunset daily, free) where you can see (and smell) some 50 varieties of rose April–October. The flowers peak in June and July.

Whitney Ave. leads from East Rock Park back into the center of New Haven, depositing you right at New Haven Green.

## Eastern New Haven and East Haven

A final worthwhile excursion from downtown New Haven takes you along the shore east of the city, into the working-class and heavily industrialized town of East Haven—it's not much to look at from a car speeding along I-95, but if you investigate a bit you'll find some interesting parks and attractions. This trip greatly lends itself to children, and several of these attractions are still within New Haven's city limits—the border cuts down the center of the peninsula just east of New Haven Harbor.

Take either U.S. 1 or I-95 (to exit 50) east from New Haven, heading south on Woodward Avenue, until you come to the entrance of **Black Rock Fort and Fort Nathan Hale** (203/946-8790), the sites of a pair of old military garrisons. The foundation of Black Rock Fort dates from the Revolutionary War, and adjoining Nathan Hale Fort was used during the Civil War. Great views are had of New Haven Harbor and back toward the city itself.

Continue south on Woodward, turn right onto Townsend Avenue, and follow it a little less than a mile to Lighthouse Road, onto which you'll make a right turn. This historic neighborhood, now the site of many small beach cottages, contains the **Pardee-Morris House** (325 Lighthouse Rd., 203/562-4183, limited hours, free) a restored 1780 Colonial with period furnishings dating from the 1600s to the Victorian age. Continue south to **Lighthouse Point**

**Park** (2 Lighthouse Rd., 203/946-8005), an 82-acre sound-view park with nature trails, a good beach for swimming, picnic tables, and a vintage carousel. There's a seasonal fee of $3.50 for parking.

Back on Townsend, follow the road south around the grounds of Tweed-New Haven Airport until you've looped back around and are heading north on Hemingway Avenue (Rte. 142). Turn right onto River Street to reach the **Shore Line Trolley Museum** (17 River St., 203/467-6927, www.bera.org), which offers three-mile rides along a historic Central Shore route, through Branford. It's open May–Dec., primarily on weekends spring and fall (daily in summer). Admission is $6, which includes unlimited rides for the day. There's also a picnic area and displays of model trolleys.

It's a short drive back to New Haven. Or, you could return the other way on Rte. 142 and follow it along the shore into Branford.

## SHOPPING

In addition to the fact that New Haven is something of a book-buyer's mecca, you'll find many more one-of-a-kind shops and boutiques in the neighborhoods around the city green. Music aficionados should not miss **Cutler's** (33 Broadway, 203/777-6271) which predates the music superstore and yet offers a similarly exhaustive selection of CDs, tapes, and vinyl, with an especially notable selection of imports, used titles, and a separate classical store. The service is highly personalized, and the proximity to Yale's campus makes it a fun spot while touring the neighborhood.

New Haven and the neighboring area comprise a hotbed of arts studios, most private, although they are open to the public during an October weekend each year called **City-Wide Open Studios** (203/772-0850, www.cwos.org). Many artists open their private studios at this time, and still others exhibit their work in various public spaces around town.

Milford has a smattering of antiques shops near the town green, including **Antiquities on the Green** (125 Broad St., 203/783-0546).

## A NEW HAVEN BOOK BROWSE

Downtown New Haven offers a browsing experience that's refreshingly free of jostling crowds and brash "sale" signs—it's one of the great bookstore capitals of the Northeast. Most people know about the comprehensive **Yale Bookstore** (which is really a Barnes & Noble); (77 Broadway, 203/777-8440). But a number of smaller off-the-beaten-path shops in New Haven will bring a smile to the face of any serious bibliophile.

Head up along bustling Chapel Street, which buzzes with cafés and boutiques, and you'll find the student-popular **Book Trader Café** (1140 Chapel St., 203/787-6147), which is packed with used titles of all kinds (and has sunny seating and great sandwiches), and the cerebral **Yale Co-op** (924 Chapel St., 203/772-2200), where children's books, publisher's remainders, art books, and a fine selection of scholarly works keep the bookish happy for hours. Perhaps most engaging along this stretch is the funky and appealing **Atticus Bookstore** (1082 Chapel St., 203/776-4040), an expansive shop with a terrific adjoining café. A couple of blocks northeast of the town green, the Audubon neighborhood offers two small general-interest stores, **Bryn Mawr Book Shop** (56 Whitney Ave., 203/562-4217), and **Foundry Bookstore** (33 Whitney Ave., 203/624-8282). **Arethusa Bookstore** (87 Audubon St., 203/624-1848) has an outstanding collection of rare first editions and out-of-print art-and-architecture books.

Another part of town big with bookish-minded Yale students is the intersection of Broadway and York Streets, just down from Yale Bookstore. Here, **Book Haven** (290 York St., 203/787-2848), specializes in women's and gender studies and other left-of-center disciplines, and **Elm City Books** (282 York St., 203/772-1762) stocks a provocative selection of rare used early editions and hard-to-find newer ones—American studies, philosophy, and theology are particular strengths. If so much leafing through valuable manuscripts piques your curiosity, make a point of visiting New Haven's **Beinecke Rare Book Library** (121 Wall St., 203/432-2977), which contains, among other important tomes, a Gutenberg Bible.

If you've got the time, drive north on Rte. 69 about 10 miles to the town of Bethany, turning left on Morris Road when you see the sign pointing you toward **Whitlock Book Barn** (20 Sperry Rd., 203/393-1240), where two vintage barns are packed with used titles. In addition to the large selection of books, the second floor of the smaller barn contains an exhaustive selection of old maps of Connecticut towns and also of cities across the United States and the world. These remarkable and colorful documents are quite suitable for framing.

## RECREATION

### Amusement Parks

The **Smiles Amusement Center** (1607 Boston Post Rd., on U.S. 1, 203/877-3229) is a place to take the kids. You'll find the usual slew of outdoor and indoor amusements, arcade games, and similar such diversions.

### Golf

Popular public 18-hole courses in the area are **Alling Memorial** (35 Eastern St., New Haven, 203/946-8014); **Grassy Hill Country Club** (441 Clark Ln., Orange, 203/795-3100); **Laurel View Country Club** (310 W. Shepard Ave., Hamden, 203/288-1819); and **Orange Hills Country Club** (389 Racebrook Rd., 203/795-

4161). With greens fees starting at $100, the relatively new **Great River Golf Club** (130 Coram Ln., Milford, 203/876-8051), which fringes the Housatonic River, ranks among the pricier public courses in Connecticut. But devotees of this challenging course insist that playing the beautifully kept facility is worth every penny.

### Hiking

For a city, New Haven is blessed with one of the area's best venues for hiking, **West Rock Park,** near Southern Connecticut State University, where you'll have access to the **Regicides** and **Quinnipiac Trails.** Head north a short ways to Hamden to reach what may be the most popular spot for hiking in the region, **Sleeping Giant**

State Park, just east of Rte. 10, which is also traversed by the well-marked Quinnipiac Trail. Additionally, a span of the **Naugatuck Trail** cuts through a secluded and attractive section of Bethany, beginning off Rte. 42.

## Horseback Riding

**B&R Riding Stables** (120 Roaring Brook Rd., Prospect, 203/758-5031) is a 200-acre facility in the quiet northern New Haven suburbs. It gives guided trail rides for $25 per hour.

## Tennis

The **Pilot Pen Women's International Tennis Tournament** (Connecticut Tennis Center, 45 Yale Ave., 203/776-7331 or 888/99-PILOT, www.pilotpentennis.com) hosts many of the world's best female tennis stars; it's held every August.

## ENTERTAINMENT AND NIGHTLIFE

As you might guess, given the presence of many undergraduate and graduate students, New Haven has a number of great night spots, including the bars at several of the restaurants listed below (Anna Liffey's, Bar, Christopher Martin's, Humphrey's, Cosi, and Zinc—to name a few). **Cafe 9** (Crown and State Sts., 860/789-8281) bills itself the "musician's living room" and is one of the top live music venues in the city. **Back Room @ Bottega** (956 Chapel St. rear, enter off Temple Street Courtyard, 203/562-5566) is a hip lounge at the popular restaurant; the veranda and courtyard are popular in warm weather. In Milford, you can play pool and catch live tunes at **Sidepockets** (354 Woodmont Rd., 203/301-0764). In New Haven, **Toad's Place** (300 York St., 203/624-TOAD) has long been one of New England's leading venues for cutting-edge alternative music—many a then-unknown booking has gone on to attain worldwide fame. Equally esteemed for big-name music talents is the **Palace** (246 College St., 203/789-2120). Other terrific

*As you might guess, given the presence of many undergraduate and graduate students, New Haven has a number of great night spots.*

live-music venues include **Off the Hook** (216 Crown St., 203/789-9921), where soul and jazz are the specialties, to **Rudy's** (372 Elm St., no phone) where independent rock and jazz bands, both local and nationally known, perform. Depending on the night, you'll find anything from a predominantly gay and lesbian to a totally mixed crowd dancing at the hip **Gotham Citi** (130 Crown St., 203/498-CITI); **168 York St. Cafe** (168 York St., 203/789-1915), and **Partners** (365 Crown St., 203/776-1014) are also popular hangouts within the gay community. 168 York also serves excellent and reasonably priced food and is quite popular in this regard among both gay and straight patrons. **Yale Cabaret** (217 Park St., 203/432-1566) is a 95-seat basement theater that shows 20 lively musical and comic performances from October through April; Yale School of Drama students write and perform many of these shows. Dinner is also available.

The **Yale School of Music** (Sprague Memorial Hall, 470 College St., 203/432-4158, www.yale.edu/schmus) performs regularly during the school year and off-season you can catch performances by the **Yale Summer Cabaret** (217 Park St., 203/432-1567). Another impressive concert venue is **Woolsey Hall** (corner of College and Grove Sts, 203/432-2310), which books musical works throughout the year.

A jewel of New Haven has long been the **Shubert Theater** (247 College St., 203/562-5666 or 800/228-6622, www.shubert.com), an estimable house that dates from 1914 and had become outmoded before new management helped to restore the theater and bring in new talents. New Haven was for many years the pre-Broadway testing ground of choice, a reputation that waned for some years, but has enjoyed a revival since the late 1990s. The 1,600-seat Shubert presents top musicals as well as fairly traditional plays throughout the year. Offering similarly high quality drama (with fewer musical-oriented shows), the internationally acclaimed **Long Wharf Theatre** (222 Sargent Dr.,

203/787-4282, www.longwharf.org) runs September–June. The Long Wharf is both a testing ground for new potential Broadway shows and a great venue for classic dramatic works from both American and European playwrights, from Miller and O'Neill to Ibsen and Shaw. Nearly as famous as the Shubert and Long Wharf is the **Yale Repertory Theatre** (corner of York and Chapel Sts., 203/432-1234, www.yale.edu/yalerep), where both current stars and acting notables of tomorrow perform several plays throughout the school year.

Up in the northern section of town, at Southern Connecticut State University, dramatic and musical pieces are presented at the **Lyman Center for the Performing Arts** (501 Crescent St., 203/392-6154, www.southernct.edu/aboutscsu/lyman). The **Palace Performing Arts Center** (246–248 College St., 203/789-2120) shows a broad range of entertainment year-round. In East Haven, musicals are presented with a meal at the **Amarante Dinner Theatre** (62 Cove St., East Haven, 203/467-2531).

The region's impressive arts scene extends well outside of New Haven proper. In Wallingford, close to the Hamden line, the **Oakdale Theatre** (95 S. Turnpike Rd., 203/265-1501, www.oakdale.com) is the largest theater in New England and offers Broadway-style musicals, comedy acts, and shows October–May and a popular music series in summer that draws big-name performers. You can also dine before the show in the Oakdale Bistro, just off the lobby—it opens two hours before shows and serves reasonably good Continental and American fare ($12–25). At Quinnipiac College in Hamden, the **Clarice L. Buckman Theater & Alumni Hall** hosts popular jazz and chamber concert series, as well as student-produced theatrical productions during the school year.

## FESTIVALS AND EVENTS
### Fall and Winter
Early September's **North Haven Fair** (203/239-3700) features live music, foods and crafts, a petting zoo, a midway with rides and amusements, a pie-baking contest, and quilting demonstrations. An event that's really picked up in enthusiasm in recent years is September's **Film Fest New Haven** (York Square Cinema, Little Theatre & Whitney Humanities Center, New Haven, 203/776-6789, www.filmfest.org) during which dozens of independent features and shorts from around the world are screened. There are parties and symposiums with the filmmakers and screenwriters, as well as children's programs. The end of November culminates with the **Season of Celebration** (N. Main, S. Main, and Center Sts., town green at the railroad station, Wallingford, 203/284-1807) where you can watch ice-carving contests, carriage rides, a Frosty the Snowman parade, the arrival of Santa, and a Christmas tree lighting.

### Spring and Summer
In September, New Haven's historic Little Italy hosts the **Cherry Blossom Festival** (Wooster Square, 203/865-5842) with an orchestra, flower sale, and great foods from those famous Wooster Street restaurants. In mid-May, come to the **Annual Meet the Artists and Artisans** (Milford Green, 203/874-5672) where 200 artisans and craftsmakers compete in a juried festival. Milford Green is also the site of an early summer **fair** (203/874-1982).

Early July the Milford Green keys up for an **Annual New England Arts & Crafts Festival** (203/878-6647). For two weeks in early July, various venues in downtown New Haven partake of the renowned **International Festival of Arts and Ideas** (888/ART-IDEA, www.artidea.org), which includes international theater productions by the England's Royal Shakespeare Company; jazz, classical, and pop concerts; arts and poetry events; a street festival; and tours of historic buildings. A bit less cerebral and thus, in the minds of many, even more fun is West Haven's late-July **Savin Rock Festival** (Old Grove Park, 203/937-3511) where there's a crafts fair, shopping stalls, seafood, and carnival rides and amusements. In late August it's time for the long-running **Milford Oyster Festival** (downtown Milford, 203/878-5363), where there's also a classic car show, plus a canoe and kayak race, harbor activities, and a food court.

# ACCOMMODATIONS

New Haven has a broad and inviting range of accommodations, and the selection has improved greatly over the past decade with the opening of some new properties and refurbishment of some others. Additionally, you'll find several chain hotels in nearby Milford and also in some of the towns north of New Haven. New Haven doesn't have quite the corporate base that Hartford and Fairfield County do, and so it's not a given that weekday and weekend rates at area hostelries vary a great deal. This is especially true because New Haven draws quite a few parents and friends of Yale students on both weekends and weekdays.

## Hotels and Motels

**$150–250:** The **Omni New Haven Hotel at Yale** (155 Temple St., 203/772-6664 or 800/THE OMNI) has the cushiest rooms of any large hotel in town—in fact, they're the nicest in the state outside of Hartford and Stamford. The 306-room hotel only opened in 1998, and has quickly become the top luxury hotel in town. It has top-notch amenities, including a very nice health club and a popular rooftop restaurant, Galileo's, that offers stunning views of the New Haven Green and, in the distance, Long Island Sound. It's in the heart of the city's arts and entertainment district, just steps from Yale.

**$100–150:** A European-style property that opened in the early 1990s as a medical hotel affiliated with Yale–New Haven Hospital, the **New Haven Hotel** (229 George St., 203/498-3100 or 800/644-6835, www.newhavenhotel.com) is now a fine upscale business accommodation that's somewhat less known than others in town, and so offers a relatively good value. Because of its past incarnation, some of the amenities here are rather unusual: all bathrooms are wheelchair-accessible (but this means there are no tubs), every floor has a spacious common lounge, and guests have use of a heated therapeutic lap pool (plus health club privileges). The 92 rooms have eye-pleasing conservative color schemes and furnishings, high-speed Internet, and the hotel is a short walk from area theaters and restaurants (there's

also a full-service restaurant on-site). A plus is the highly personable and professional staff.

Having undergone a recent renovation, the **Holiday Inn at Yale** (30 Whalley Ave., New Haven, 203/777-6221, www.holiday-inn.com/newhavenct) now qualifies as one of the better chain properties in the city. It's right by York Square, steps from Yale's campus and a number of good shops and eateries. The 160 rooms have a sophisticated brown-and-gold color scheme, bathrooms with marble and granite accents, and a full slate of in-room amenities. There's also a full-service restaurant, exercise room, lounge, outdoor pool, and self-service laundry.

**The Colony** (1157 Chapel St., New Haven, 203/776-1234 or 800/458-8810, www.colony-atyale.com) sits on bustling Chapel Street in the heart of the city. The furnishings in this 86-room hotel have a retro feel about them, but everything is in surprisingly nice condition—the beds are covered with tasteful floral spreads, and the bathrooms have clean tile floors and walls. A popular (and also retro) steak house, T.J. Tucker's, occupies the ground floor and serves pretty good, inexpensive burgers, chops, and the like. The staff here is helpful and friendly, and the hotel offers some great weekend deals.

**$50–100:** The lovingly unrestored **Duncan Hotel** (1151 Chapel St., 203/787-1273) has the oldest hand-operated elevator in Connecticut—a ride in this sputtering, clanking contraption is a highlight of staying in this 100-room property with vintage shag carpeting, old TVs, clean but tired baths, and furnishings so dated they almost qualify as quaint. Hey, it ain't the Waldorf-Astoria, but then the rates are low, the location on Chapel Street is ideal, and the charming old-world lobby filled with vintage photos is great fun to hang out in (if only you could sleep in it). It's a favorite of students and artsy types.

With a peaceful location convenient to Hamden, Woodbridge, Meriden, and other greater New Haven towns, the **Quality Inn Conference Center** (100 Pond Lily Ave., exit 59 from the Wilbur Cross Pkwy., New Haven, 203/387-6651 or 800/228-5151) is a Colonial-style brick motor court whose warmly furnished rooms have floral bedspreads and tartan curtains; there's an indoor pool, a sundeck, and a well-outfitted gym. Several suites have Jacuzzis.

Just off I-95 a short drive from the city center, **Fairfield Inn New Haven** (400 Sargent Dr., 203/562-1111 or 800/228-2800) is a recently renovated and extremely nice property—it's close to Long Wharf Theater and looks directly over New Haven Harbor.

In Milford, a reliable option is the **Hampton Inn** (129 Plains Rd., exit 36 from I-95, 203/874-4400 or 800/HAMPTON); rooms are furnished tastefully, and the staff is first-rate. Another excellent Milford option is the new **Fairfield Inn Milford** (111 Schoolhouse Ln., 203/877-8588 or 800/228-2800), a handsome four-story property just off I-95 and a short drive from Silver Sands beach and the Milford Green. Rooms are nicely outfitted, and there's an outdoor pool and fully equipped exercise room.

One of the better in its chain, Milford's family-operated **Howard Johnson Lodge** (1052 U.S. 1, exit 39 from I-95, 203/878-4611 or 800/406-1411) sits on 12 acres and has a full slate of facilities, including an exercise room, indoor and outdoor pools, and satellite TV in the 160 guest rooms, some of which are apartment-style units with two or three bedrooms, kitchenettes, and living rooms with pullout sofas. Rates in standard rooms sometimes dip below $50, especially weekends. Others priced typically just over $50 include the **Red Roof Inn** (10 Rowe Ave., Milford, 203/877-6060 or 800/THEROOF), which is just off I-95 in the western end of town (near Stratford), and the **Days Inn** (270 Foxon Blvd., 203/469-0343 or 800/329-7466), which is in New Haven off I-91, convenient to East Haven and Wallingford.

## Country Inns and Bed-and-Breakfasts

**$150–250:** A sign in front of the **Three Chimneys** (1201 Chapel St., 203/789-1201 or 800/443-1554, www.threechimneysinn.com) admonishes "street girls brought in by sailors must be paid for in advance." This is obviously a joke—New Haven hasn't had sailors in years. Kidding aside, this glorious 1870s painted lady,

aglow in pinks, greens, and whites, might be the loveliest urban inn in Connecticut and one of the finest anywhere in the state. The guest and public rooms are decorated with rich colors and fabrics, high-quality antiques, Oriental rugs, four-poster beds, and yet many of the business amenities you might expect of an upscale chain hotel: large (but elegant) work desks, modern phones with data ports and voicemail, and cable TV. In the evening, you can relax in the sitting room before a gas fireplace; afternoon tea is presented in the library, and Continental breakfast is included. For an upscale inn with luxurious furnishings, the staff is refreshingly down-to-earth and the ambience low-key and fun.

The **Historic Mansion Inn** (600 Chapel St., 203/865-8324 or 888/512-6278, www.thehistoricmansioninn.com) anchors the heart of the historic Wooster Square neighborhood, where Italian restaurants abound. This 1842 Greek Revival home was transformed into an urbane bed-and-breakfast. Private baths have marble fixtures, and guest rooms have fireplaces. Lovely varnished mahogany woodwork fills the high-ceilinged public spaces, which include a library.

**$100–150:** Another wonderful small hostelry in New Haven, **Swan Cove** (115 Sea St., 203/776-3240, www.swancove.com) is a towering Queen Anne house in historic Oyster Point, right near the harbor, offering three large and homey suites filled with gracious antiques. Particularly notable is the Solarium Suite, with a library bedroom, a kitchenette, Mexican tiled floors, and a glass roof. Tree Tops has a living area looking out over Long Island Sound, and Safari Suite has a full kitchen and fireplace.

Around the corner, the delightful **Inn at Oyster Point** (104 Howard Ave., New Haven, 866/978—3778, www.oysterpointinn.com) occupies a striking 1902 mansion, with most of its original woodwork intact. There are five guest rooms occupying two upper floors, each with its own fully equipped communal kitchen—a huge convenience if you're planning a longer stay. This feature has helped make the inn popular with actors in New Haven shows; Lynn Redgrave rented the top floor for a few weeks while in town for a play in 2002. Each room has a different decorative theme, from urbane Italian to New England nautical; one room has a luxurious double whirlpool tub. Breakfast specialties include Grand Marnier–stuffed French toast; it's a full meal on weekends and Continental on weekdays. Host Vincent Cusenza is extremely knowledgeable about the area.

**Rainbow Gardens** (117 N. Broad St., 203/878-2500, www.bbonline.com/ct/rainbow) is a great find in Milford, facing the lovely town green, within walking distance of the train station, and a short drive from area beaches. There are three air-conditioned, antiques-filled rooms, which share one bath, in this elegantly restored 1855 house. A distinctive mansard-roof French Colonial on the Wepawaug River, very close to the shore and downtown, the **Lily Pond B&B** (44 Prospect St., Milford, 203/876-9996, www.bedandbreakfast.com) offers three charming rooms sharing a pair of baths. It's a relaxed, informal place whose rooms contain a mix of antiques and newer furnishings, mostly with a Victorian look. One guest room is "scent-free," set up specifically for guests who may have allergies. An English garden fronts the house.

# FOOD

You'd be hard-pressed to find a great wealth and variety of dining options in such a small city anywhere else in the Northeast, for New Haven abounds with great Asian eateries—many of them are near the campus of Yale, which also puts them within easy walking distance of area theaters and museums. A second culinary strength here is Italian food; America's version of the pizza was invented at Frank Pepe's on Wooster Street, which is in the heart of Little Italy, alongside several other great restaurants. Such diverse foods as hamburgers and lollipops were also invented in New Haven, and the city also has a notable history as a beer-brewing center.

You can walk along Chapel and Crown, southwest of the green, and College, High, and York streets, which intersect with them, to find many of New Haven's best culinary offerings. Another strip of good restaurants falls along State Street, northeast of downtown. Outlying towns with a strong dining presence include Milford and Hamden.

## Upscale

To experience true, big city elegance without ever leaving Connecticut, visit the **Union League Café** (1032 Chapel St., 203/562-4299, $15–24), a beautiful formal restaurant with detailed moldings, recessed lighting, a sedate dining room of whites and yellows, and a waitstaff clad in natty vests and bow ties. A meal is less pricey than you might expect, especially considering the high caliber of the refreshingly uncomplicated pheasant pie with fresh foie gras, endive, and juniper berry jus; and seared marinated duck breast with red wine and blackcurrants, poached pears, braised chestnuts, and celeriac. The wine list is among the best in town.

Inside an impeccably restored 1819 house at an otherwise dreadfully overbuilt intersection in Hamden, **Colonial Tymes** (2389 Dixwell Ave., 203/230-2301, $14–26) presents a consistently fine menu of mostly Italian and Continental favorites, such as sautéed broccoli rabe with chicken apple sausage, and tournedos of beef over portobello mushrooms with spinach, fried leeks, and a brandy sauce. It's a big place with a few dapper dining areas, plus an upstairs cigar loft. There's live piano entertainment many nights.

**Sage American Bar and Grill** (100 Water St., New Haven, 203/787-3466, $9–32) enjoys a dramatic setting by Oyster Point Marina, jutting into Long Island Sound. The two-story restaurant is staffed by gracious employees and has a lively upstairs lounge with pitched ceilings; great water views are available from all rooms. Sage offers a range of contemporary American entrées (chops, filet mignon, herb-crusted salmon), plus lighter fare such as burgers and lobster rolls.

## Creative but Casual

**Zinc** (964 Chapel St., 203/624-0507, $19–28) has taken downtown New Haven by storm with a short menu of reasonably priced, healthful, and daring, globally influenced American dishes including seared diver sea scallops, with fresh-basil pesto and lobster risotto. You could also make a nice meal of four or five appetizers—the

© ANDREW COLLINS

**Amberjack's restaurant, Milford**

smoked-duck nachos with fried wonton skins, spicy aioli, and lime crema are a knockout. This sexy restaurant filled with black-clad hipsters opened in a vintage building facing the New Haven Green a few years ago.

Head to increasingly trendy Temple Street to find **Diva** (152 Temple St., 203/777-3482, $14–26), which occupies an appropriately lavish space with high ceilings, long draperies, and rich reddish-brown walls. Depending on your mood, it's a martini bar, a place for nibbling on small plates, or a legitimate big-dinner venue. The food borrows from Asia, the Mediterranean, and Latin America—seared-rare tuna steaks, filet mignon, and complex pasta dishes vie for attention on the colorful menu. Get your hair done for this one.

**Roomba** (1044 Chapel St., 203/562-7666, $18–25) is one of the hottest tables in New Haven. Chef Arturo Franco Camacho, formerly of the outstanding Habana in South Norwalk, continues to work wonders with pan-Latin American ingredients here. Watch for dishes such as a duck confit–filled empanada with foie gras, mushrooms, and tropical fruit chutney; and pumpkin seed–crusted mahimahi with malanga root purée, eggplant caviar, and coconut-curry lemongrass

sauce. There's also a raw bar, and everything is served in a lively setting. Of course, getting a reservation—especially on weekends—isn't easy. Owner Camacho was planning to open a brand-new restaurant, Dish, on College Street in late 2003; big things are expected from this eatery, too.

With arguably the best service in town, **Ibiza** (39 High St., 203/865-1933, $17–23) makes for a wonderful dining experience if only to be treated like royalty by a staff that prides itself on anticipating patrons' every need, from refilling glasses to briskly replacing used plates with fresh ones. But it happens that the food scores high marks, too—authentic regional Spanish fare is served. Ibiza is in a high-ceilinged space a block off Chapel Street, with exposed brick walls and strings of garlic, onions, and peppers hanging from the ceiling.

**Amberjack's** (35 New Haven Ave., Milford, 203/882-9387, $11–24) enjoys an enviable setting overlooking the river in downtown Milford. Huge floor-to-ceiling windows afford spectacular views of the river and waterfall. It's a contemporary, minimalist space with curved varnished wood details. Outstanding locale. Moroccan-spiced chicken, grilled pork tenderloin with an apricot reduction, and penne rigate are favorite entrées, while a variety of salads, grilled pizzas, and tapas are available if you're seeking a light bite.

**Christopher Martin's** (860 State St., 203/776-8835, $12–22) has long been one of those dependable New Haven eateries with a warm cozy atmosphere where students, local suits, yuppies, and pub-crawlers can count on upscale food that nevertheless won't break the bank. Duck confit served warm with port wine, poached pears, walnuts, and blue cheese is a perfect starter, while more substantial dishes include sautéed veal and artichokes with a lemon butter sauce, and shrimp and roasted fennel over spinach fettuccine. The feel of an old-fashioned tavern characterizes the main dining room, while constant chatter and a large TV screen impart a more casual space with an Irish-pub milieu.

The sexy and fun **Back Room at Bottega** (956 Chapel St. rear, enter from Temple Street Courtyard, 203/562-5566, $10–22) is a stylish spot for a meal, drawing a youthful, hip crowd. Try porcini risotto, Bottega beans (white beans and sundried tomatoes with a light balsamic-herb dressing), or *pollo di peppe* (chicken breast topped with tomatoes, capers, olives, garlic, and olive oil). There's nothing fancy about the food here—it's just good, honest Italian fare in a memorable setting.

**Rainbow Gardens** (117 N. Broad St., on the Milford Green, 203/878-2500, $11–18), the dining component of a lovely yellow Victorian B&B in the center of Milford, offers a worldly dining experience that's something of a surprise given the almost frilly tearoom ambience. Varied dishes like curried coconut shrimp and Brazilian black bean cakes show the range of the kitchen, and save a little room for the fabulously rich desserts (the walnut bread pudding is a knockout dish). The dining room abounds with hanging and potted plants and stained-glass windows, and colorful dinner plates form a whimsical border for the gardens out front.

In the center of downtown Milford, **Citrus** (56 S. Broad St., 203/877-1138, $17–23) has pumpkin-shaded walls with a black ceiling of exposed airducts and beams—the design makes for great acoustics. At this restaurant, run by the former chef of another top Milford eatery, Jeffrey's, you might start with Maryland crab cakes topped with avocado, lime, and a native corn salsa, before moving on to house-made ravioli filled with fresh lobster, chives, goat cheese, and spinach over a sauce of yellow plum-tomato coulis drizzled with a black-tomato crème fraîche.

## Pizza, Pub Grub, and Seafood

It's hard to say which restaurant along Wooster Street is best, but Alto Basso has many fans, as does **Tre Scalini Ristorante** (100 Wooster St., 203/777-3373, $13–19), where you can dine inside a beautifully appointed dining room on reasonably priced and first-rate Italian fare. The menu goes on and on, with about 20 substantial appetizers, from escarole and beans over peasant bread to Gorgonzola polenta with wild mushrooms. The list of entrées is no less formidable, including a wonderfully tender monkfish baked with olives, raisins, pine nuts, and fresh tomatoes; and medallions of veal pan-sautéed with portobello, shiitake, and porcini mushrooms and a feathery tarragon-cognac reduction. Enter and park in back, around the corner from Wooster on Franklin Street.

For pizza, the original is **Frank Pepe's** (157 Wooster St., 203/865-5762, large pies $12–18), which is especially known for its heavenly white pies—the one with fresh-chopped clams is a favorite (order it with bacon for a little extra kick). There's nothing fancy about this place: you'll be seated, potentially after a long wait, at a wooden booth and order from a short list of pizzas posted on various walls throughout the restaurant. There are no grinders, pastas, or other dishes—nothing to take away from what this kitchen has been doing so well for much of this century. Equally popular and only slightly newer is **Sally's Apizza** (237 Wooster St., 203/624-5271, large pies $12–18), which also serves stellar pies in a somewhat similar format.

**Stonebridge** (50 Daniel St., Milford, 203/874-7947, $13–22) sits on the banks of the Wepawaug River, just as it flows beneath the stone Founder's Bridge and empties into Milford Harbor. In nice weather, you can dine overlooking the river (but you'll have to deal with the traffic over the bridge). Somewhat traditional seafood is the big draw, from char-grilled salmon with Caribbean herbs to baked stuffed jumbo shrimp; expect plenty of steak options, too. There are several large dining rooms—this place holds a lot of people. Maybe the only great culinary reason to trek up into North Haven is **D'Errico's** (343 Washington St., U.S. 5, 203/239-8051, $14–27). It's a serious Italian-fusion restaurant run by folks who truly care about both the presentation and the ingredients of what they're serving—dishes like pan-blackened sashimi tuna steak served over a pesto coulis, topped with seared blue point oysters; and black Angus steak with onion "straws" and fettuccine Alfredo score high marks. Desserts here are lavish.

**Archie Moore's** (15 Factory Ln., 203/876-5088; also 188 Willow St., New Haven, 203/773-9870, and 39 N. Main St., Wallingford, 203/265-7100, $3–8) has cheap pub food—the buffalo wings are especially good—and an attractive deck with seating looking down the street toward Milford Harbor. It's a good bet if you're hanging out with friends and expecting relatively little in the way of culinary creativity; bear in mind, too, the waitstaff seems almost willfully indolent.

Because East Haven is not a town with a great culinary presence, it's remarkable that **Beachhead Restaurant** (3 Cosey Beach Ave., 203/469-5450, $12–22) has stood firm all these years, since around World War II, pleasing both locals and summering tourists with fresh seafood year after year.

**Anna Liffey's** (17 Whitney Ave., 203/773-1776, $5–11) is a hip spot for drinks and dinner. This Irish pub is tucked down inside a cozy stone-walled and wood-paneled cellar, with a bar on one side and booth seating on the other. Meals are fairly simple, but quite good: fish and chips; haddock with scallions, tomatoes, mayo, and cheddar cheese; and so on. There's Irish music to get everybody in a festive mood.

Probably the best of the seafood restaurants along the beachfront in West Haven, **Captain's Galley** (19 Beach St., 203/932-1811, $11–22) specializes in stuffed and steamed lobsters, steamers, and also more substantial dishes like salmon with tomatoes, olives, anchovies, artichokes with

pasta, or zuppa de pesce with mussels, clams, shrimp, scallops, calamari, and crablegs.

One of the more famous seafood places in the area is **Chick's Drive-In** (183 Beach St., West Haven, 203/934-4510, $9–17), a honky-tonk counter-service restaurant that's overrated, but incredibly popular nonetheless. Portions are average-sized and quite pricey, the seafood is over-fried, service is almost nonexistent, and the bathrooms consist of portable toilets out back behind the outdoor dining area. A bit farther west, nearly at the Milford line, the casual **Oyster River Tavern** (38 Ocean Ave., 203/932-0440, $8–16) serves great buffalo wings, steamed mussels, and other casual American and seafood cooking.

A cheap and dependable Middle Eastern restaurant near Yale's campus, **Mamoun's** (85 Howe St., 203/562-8444, $3–8) serves hearty platters of kibbeh (cracked wheat shell stuffed with potatoes, onions, and walnuts), shish kebabs, baba ghanouj, and delicious Turkish Delight for dessert.

The simply named **Bar** (254 Crown St., New Haven, 203/495-1111, $8–14) is many more things than a watering hole. First, there's a student-popular brewpub with live music many nights. And should hunger pangs kick in, drop by for the wealth of brick-oven pizzas with both conventional and interesting (littleneck clams, mashed potatoes) toppings. A house favorite is the salad of seasonal greens, sliced pears, caramelized pecans, crumbled blue cheese, and light vinaigrette dressing.

Facing Long Island Sound in West Haven, **Jimmie's** (5 Rock St., 203/934-3212, $7–16) is practically an institution among seafood lovers. Unfortunately, this massive cafeteria-style space feels and operates a bit like an institution—it's less than ideal if intimacy, quiet, and romance are high on your list of priorities. Nevertheless, it's a dependable option for fried-fish platters, softshell crab, and the like.

The **Playwright** (144 Temple St., New Haven, 203/752-0450; also 1232 Whitney Ave., Hamden, 203/287-2401, $10–19), well-known since it opened in the 1990s in Stamford, also has two locations in greater New Haven. The one in Hamden opened first and is quite festive and homey, but the more recent downtown New Haven branch is the real show-stopper. This stunning space just off the newly developed Temple Square contains actual furnishings and architectural remnants of 19th-century churches and other buildings in Ireland—note the 1885 pulpit, the grand pipe organ, and even the double doors from the owners' great-grandparents' house. Apart from being an engaging space, the Playwright serves all the expected Irish ales and elixirs, along with commendable nouvelle Irish and American cooking, ranging from clams in white wine to traditional Irish lamb stew. **Humphreys** (175 Humphrey St., New Haven, 203/782-1506, $5–12) is an old-fashioned loud and local tavern on the ground floor of a four-story Victorian building on the east side of town near I-91. Despite being slightly off the beaten path, it's always packed with regulars who appreciate the hefty juicy hamburgers and other filling pub fare, and the selection of three-zillion-or-so beers on tap.

## Asian

**Bentara** (76 Orange St., New Haven, 203/562-2511, $8–18) is in an up-and-coming neighborhood of wonderful old redbrick buildings—a short walk south and east of the green. It serves traditional Malaysian fare along with a smattering of recipes culled from elsewhere in Southeast Asia. Overall, it's probably the best and most sophisticated of New Haven's many fine ethnic eateries. The food is fresh and subtly seasoned, often packing some serious punch—try the hot and spicy calamari, curried Prince Edward Island mussels, or egg noodles cooked with beef and vegetables in a peanut-base beef broth. Be sure to sample the one authentic Malaysian dessert on the menu: ABC, short for Air Batu Campur, a truly memorable concoction of grass jelly, palm seed, sweetened red beans, and cream of corn topped with red syrup, evaporated milk, and shaved ice. The staff is genuinely friendly and always on top of things, and the dining room is beautifully furnished with elegant wooden tables, benches imported from Asia, exposed brick, and a smattering of Malaysian artifacts.

**Royal Palace** (32 Orange St., 203/776-6663, $7–17) is one of the best Chinese restaurants in

the city, set in the heart of the Nine Squares neighborhood. Specialties in this simple dining room packed with regulars include lobster Cantonese-style with a fragrant white sauce, lemon chicken, scallion pancakes, and beef with oyster sauce. When you're hungry and low on funds, head to the **Ivy Noodle** (316 Elm St., 203/562-8800, $4–8), a cheap-and-cheerful noodle house typically packed with Yale students. Dozens of soups are offered, prepared your choice of eight noodles: spinach, lo mein (spaghetti), Cantonese, rice, flat white, udon, vermicelli, and egg. Curry shrimp is a top seller. It's a small, busy place.

Of the Thai restaurants in New Haven, and there are a few good ones, **Bangkok** (172 York St., 203/789-8684, $7–14) stands out for its kicky seasoning, affordable but also high-quality lunch deals, and its warm inviting dining room—the best seats are in a solarium-style space overlooking the street. Specialties include Chaiya noodles (shrimp and scallops cooked with yellow Chaiya noodles, bean sprouts, scallions, and a red curry sauce); in general, seafood is a major player on this menu, with several fine dishes. When the menu states that a dish is spicy, believe it (a rarity in Connecticut).

With a bright, open dining room and a menu that mixes Korean and Japanese (including sushi) standards, **Seoul** (345 Crown St., 203/497-9634, $10–17) is a refined but casual spot where there's apt to be classical music playing. Popular dishes include sea trout baked whole; flame-broiled pork marinated with chili sauce; beef in a scallion sauce; and any of the traditional Korean hot-pot cook dinners, such as clam stew and glazed monkfish.

**Miso** (15 Orange St., 203/848-6472, $14–24) is a postmodern space with high ceilings, blond-wood furniture, unfinished cement floors—the look is cool and crisp. Soothing music is piped in, putting patrons at the handsome sushi bar totally at ease, and ready to sample the traditional, superbly prepared selection of nigiri sushi, sashimi, and maki rolls. From the main menu, consider broiled-tuna teriyaki and *yosen nabi* (fish, clams, chicken, scallops, shrimp, fish cake, bean curd, and vegetables in a hot broth). It's elegant and chic, a great addition to the burgeoning Nine Squares neighborhood.

The menu at **Indochine** (1180 Chapel St., 203/865-5033, $6–15) spans several Asian cultures, including Vietnamese, Thai, and Laotian. Dishes like salmon mango curry, ginger soft-shell crab, spicy tofu with curried-coconut milk, rice vermicelli with sweet and sour sauce, and squid with ginger and bean sauce show off the kitchen's considerable skills. The dining room with pale green and raspberry decor, faux hanging plants, and vintage photos is warmly furnished. At $4.95, the lunch buffet is one of New Haven's top bargains.

Walk west on Chapel Street and you'll eventually come to a classic, stainless-steel, boxcar-style diner with stools at the counter, neon beer signage in the window, and a ubiquitous carved-enamel ceiling, but this place doesn't serve meatloaf and fries. Rather, **Tandoor** (1226 Chapel St., 203/776-6620, $8–13) presents a fairly traditional menu of very good Indian fare, such as homemade cheese paneer cooked in spinach and cream; shrimp in a hot vindaloo curry; and lamb biryani.

## Ethiopian

Soft lighting and high ceilings accent **Caffe Adulis** (228 College St., New Haven, 203/777-5081, $9–16), a comfy yet chic Ethiopian restaurant known for its traditional stews, such as red lentil with cilantro, as well as pan-seared jumbo shrimp with tomato basil sauce, unsweetened coconut, dates, basmati rice, Parmesan cheese, and a light cream sauce. Several Continental options are also available, including smoked bluefish on mesclun salad with capers, chopped tomatoes, onions, and a mustard vinaigrette.

## Turkish

On busy Crown Street, **Cafe Istanbul** (245 Crown St., New Haven, 203/787-3881, $11–17) is the state's first serious foray into Turkish cuisine, and so far it seems to be a hit. The exotically furnished space—complete with tall windows, ceiling fans, colorful decorative arts, and hostesses in authentic costumes—complements the intricately seasoned fare, like lemony Turkish hummus; grape leaves filled with rice, onions, pine nuts, herbs, and raisins; and succulent kebabs.

## Quick Bites

Frantically crowded with students and granola types most days and nights, **Claire's** (1000 Chapel St., 203/562-3888, $4–13) has pioneered creative vegetarian eating in New Haven. The space, with green-and-white linoleum floors and a few nominal decorative elements, is nothing to write home about, but the location opposite the New Haven Green is handy, and the food is uniformly fresh and tasty, often with Middle Eastern, Asian, and other international influences. Try the challah French toast, pizza bagels, veggie burgers, or Mexican lasagna. Claire's opened decades ago—long before actress Claire Danes attended Yale University. Nevertheless, appropriately, she is said to be a regular.

A tiny redbrick box by a parking lot on busy Crown Street, **Louis' Lunch** (263 Crown St., New Haven, 203/562-5507, $3–7) looks rather secretive with its red batten doors and arched windows, like some secret society of Yale. In fact, its legacy means more to many people than just some old Ivy League university—for in this tiny building began America's still-passionate love affair with hamburgers. The very first burger was served here some time around 1895. Burgers here have always been steamed and served on toast, a preparation that's new to many, but surprisingly easy to develop a taste for. Open until 2 A.M. on weekends.

Just off the Wilbur Cross Parkway at the Hamden-Wallingford line, the **Redwood Grille** (180 S. Turnpike Rd., Wallingford, 203/284-9651, meals $4–11) has a wonderful variety of both traditional (chili dogs, clam strips, grilled sweet Italian sausage sandwiches) and somewhat more refined (chicken focaccia sandwiches, grilled Cajun tuna steak rolls) fare, all at extremely reasonable prices. It's sort of a cross between a burger stand and a diner, with the best food from both. And it may just have the friendliest staff in greater New Haven. The popular Oakdale Theater is just up the road, but bear in mind that lines can be long here before popular shows.

In downtown Wallingford, **Half Moon Coffee and Grille** (50 N. Main St., 203/265-4571 $7–16) serves three meals daily, from scones and breakfast wraps to more substantial fare at dinner, including creatively topped pizzas and bountiful salads. In a town with few noteworthy restaurants, this delightful gourmet shop, coffeehouse, and restaurant is a great find.

The **Anchor** (272 College St., New Haven, 203/865-1512, dishes under $8), with its vintage neon sign, pressed-tin ceilings, deep leatherette booths, and old-fashioned lamps, looks like the kind of joint Mickey Spillane might feel comfortable in. It's certainly resisted the temptation to go trendy, like just about every other restaurant in the Chapel St. area. Expect cheap, filling fare like chops, corned beef hash, and baked ham with cole slaw.

An adjunct of the popular bookstore of the same name, **Atticus Café** (1082 Chapel St., 203/776-4040, dishes under $7) serves a full menu until midnight—a welcome rarity in downtown New Haven. Any time of day, the fresh sticky buns are wildly addictive; other goodies include delicious marzipan cakes dipped in chocolate with caramelized almonds; chai teas; hot cocoa; guacamole and cheddar cheese lavash; and velvety black bean soup. A locals' hangout just off busy State Street in the northeast corner of downtown, the **Pantry** (2 Mechanic St., 203/787-0392, under $5) might just serve the best breakfasts in metro New Haven, plus very good sandwiches through the afternoon (the place is closed at dinner time). Scrambled eggs and omelettes come in several permutations, none of which are especially fancy or daring—just good. Philly cheesesteak, cheese French toast, and club sandwiches are other specialties.

Ice-cream addicts should consider two great places for a rich yet refreshing treat. In Hamden, **Wentworth's Homemade Ice Cream** (3697 Whitney Ave., 203/281-7429) scores high marks, while in Milford, **Scoopy Doo's** (Milford Public Marina, off Helwig St., no phone) is a cute seasonal ice-cream stand that's ideal if you happen to be strolling by the marina or need a break from downtown shopping.

Dapper **Café Atlantique** (33 River St., 203/882-1602, $5–8) is a wonderful little find in downtown Milford, the perfect place for an iced coffee in summer or a warm white mocha latte in winter, but also for creative but light fare any time of day. Consider a baguette filled with spinach, apples, goat cheese, and honeyed almonds, or the chicken, broccoli, and cheddar crêpe. There's also an impressive range of desserts and pastries.

## Java Joints

**Cosi** (338 Elm St., 203/495-9869) is a lively urbane spot near Yale, with a mosaic facade and an especially good selection of pizzas on the menu.

Maybe it's the high number of students, but New Haven abounds with great coffeehouses, including the locally popular chain **Willoughby's Coffee & Tea** (1007 Chapel St., New Haven, 203/789-8400; 258 Church St., New Haven, 203/777-7400; 273 York St., New Haven, 203/773-1700; Temple Medical Center, 60 Temple St., New Haven, 203/498-0600). North of the city, **Jave Jive** (3000 Whitney Ave., Hamden, 203/248-3262) is a cozy hangout with tables and sofas—there's live music some nights.

## Gourmet Goods and Picnic Supplies

**Libby's Italian Pastry Shop** (139 Wooster St., New Haven, 203/772-0380) has earned an enormous following (literally—nobody's getting thin eating this stuff) for yummy pastries, gelato, and countless other fattening and devilishly delicious desserts.

A cozy bakery that used to be in Branford but now occupies a handsome space in downtown New Haven, **Judie's European Baked Goods** (63 Grove St., New Haven, 203/777-6300) has a near-cult following for its French-style peasant breads, chocolate croissants, baguettes, sandwiches, and some great soups, too (try the chicken and andouille gumbo when available).

**Gastronomique** (25 High St., New Haven, 203/776-7007), a teeny-tiny takeout spot near Yale's campus, doles out sublime French fare, from steak-and-cheese sandwiches and escargots to ginger-sage-pumpkin risotto. It's all wonderful, and the place doubles as a juice bar. Just keep in mind that you can barely move in this cute and confined takeaway café.

THE CONNECTICUT COAST

## INFORMATION AND SERVICES

### Visitor Information

Most of the region is served by the **Greater New Haven Convention and Visitors Bureau** (59 Elm St., New Haven, 203/777-8550 or 800/332-STAY, www.newhavencvb.org). Wallingford is served by the **Connecticut River Valley & Shoreline Visitors Council** (393 Main St., Middletown, CT 06457, 860/347-0028 or 800/486-3346, www.ctrivershore.com).

Another exceptionally helpful resource is www.newhavenweb.com, which provides links to a full slate of local websites, plus the lowdown on all events, dining, lodging, and attractions.

### Getting Around

New Haven lies at the intersection of two of the Northeast's most important highways, North–South I-91—which runs clear to the Canadian border—and the great monster of Interstates, I-95. New Haven, then, is easily reached from Boston, Hartford, New London, New York City, Stamford, and other major Northeastern cities. There's also a train station served by Amtrak and Metro-North right on the edge of downtown, and visiting New Haven by train is definitely a practical option. Several hotels are within walking distance or a short cab ride of the train station.

# The Central Shoreline

Connecticut's central shoreline, a jagged-tooth stretch of beach 'burbs stretching from New Haven Harbor for about 30 miles to the mouth of the Connecticut River in Old Saybrook, could be called a hybrid between the wealthy commuter towns of Fairfield County and the salt-aired maritime villages of Mystic and Stonington. Few attractions here merit more than a quick look—mostly creaky old house-museums with seasonal hours.

The draws are beaches; twisting country roads that trace the coves, points, and inlets of the coast; and stately captains' mansions that now contain elegant bed-and-breakfasts. Numerous seafood restaurants dot the landscape, from open-air, bare-bones lobster shacks to some extremely sophisticated eateries. Shopping is another major draw, from the enormous upscale outlet centers of Clinton and Westbrook to the dozens of galleries and antiques shops of Madison, Branford, and Old Saybrook.

I-95 divides the heavily developed coastal sections of these towns from their more rural and slower-paced northern reaches, where you'll find a handful of pick-your-own farms and some good hiking opportunities. Near the coast, I-95 and U.S. 1 can be flooded with traffic, especially on weekends and at rush hour on weekdays. This tour mostly follows less-trafficked, very scenic, but at times circuitous local roads, except from Madison through Westbrook, where U.S. 1 is your only viable option.

## BRANFORD TO MADISON

### Branford

Begin this trip by driving east from New Haven along I-95, taking exit 52 in East Haven, and following Rte. 142 through town to where it becomes Short Beach Road and leads east into Branford, through the Short Beach and Double Beach sections of town. Continue up into downtown, turning right onto Rte. 146, which leads through Branford's pretty village center. Branford possesses a broad town green, with a picture-perfect white Gothic church with big red front doors and authentic Tiffany windows. Engaging shops line the tree-shaded streets near the green, gussied up with redbrick sidewalks, old-fashioned wrought-iron and wooden benches, and street lamps. A bit west of the green stands **Harrison House** (124 Main St., 203/488-4828, open afternoons Fri.–Sat., June–Sept., free), a 1720s Colonial saltbox filled with antiques.

From downtown, Rte. 146 leads back down across the Branford River and into the scenic Indian Neck section of town—from this point on this state route could arguably be called the most enchanting coastal drive in the state. The highly irregular jagged run of Branford's and Guilford's shoreline has thwarted the development that has damaged other coastal Connecticut towns, so that actual shore access is intermittent. From many stretches of this road, however, you'll have gorgeous views of the sound and the many majestic Colonial and Victorian homes in this area.

## Stony Creek and the Thimble Islands

Route 146 jogs back inland slightly before again dipping down toward the sound as it passes the turnoff for Stony Creek, an alluring village with a few shops and eateries and, more notably, Stony Creek Marina and Tackle, from which scenic cruises of the Thimble Islands depart. A deli faces the harbor, with good lobster rolls, sandwiches, and chowder; a rustic mood prevails.

Legends of lost treasures surround the history of the hundreds of islands that make up the Thimbles. Some of these are little more than craggy rock piles visible only at low tide, while 23 of the more substantial ones are inhabited. Scrub pine and coastal hardwood provide a little bit of contrast against the mostly rocky terrain of these islands, a few of which were used as shipbuilding hubs during the American Revolution. The most-often told tale, however, concerns the treasures infamous pirate Captain William Kidd is said to have stashed somewhere in and around the Thimbles. Divers, researchers, and explorers have searched for the spoils to no avail—skeptics declare it's just an old myth with little basis in fact. Still, it's nice to dream.

Wealthy vacationers began building elaborate summer homes on the islands beginning in the late 19th century, and today more than 100 houses—many of them beautifully restored and preserved—guard the shores of the islands. In the 1930s, the Thimbles's heyday, a few small resort hotels even operated out here, but all are private residences today. A small fleet of ferry boats transports residents, goods, and mail to and from the islands and Stony Creek. Both the *Sea Mist II* (203/488-8905) and the *Volsunga*

*IV* (203/481-3345, http://thimbleislands.com) offer narrated tours of the islands, several times daily in summer and weekends and some weekdays in May, September, and early October (the fare is $8 for adults, $5 children). You'll get a very close look at some of the islands, and the crews of both boats give lively anecdotal narrations. Off-season, these boats often give charter seal and bird-watching cruises; call for details.

## Guilford

Back on Rte. 146, continue east into Guilford. For another coastal detour, make a right turn onto Sachems Head Road, which loops down around the scenic point of the same name. Route 146 then leads into the picturesque center of Guilford, which is anchored by one of the largest town greens in New England—it's shaded by towering leafy trees and crossed by walking paths. Shops and cafés line the west and south sides of this inviting expanse, and hardly a summer afternoon passes when this grassy oasis isn't the scene of sunbathers and picnickers.

> *Legends of lost treasures surround the history of the hundreds of islands that make up the Thimbles.*

The town's far-reaching history makes it a center of very old house-museums, including what is believed to be the very oldest masonry structure in Connecticut, and one of two in New England dating from before 1650. From the southwestern corner of the town green, drive south on Whitfield Street, about a half mile to reach the **Henry Whitfield House State Museum** (248 Old Whitfield St., 203/453-2457 or 860/566-3005, open 10 A.M.–4:30 P.M., other times by appointment, Wed.–Sun., Apr.–mid-Dec., $3.50). Parts of the museum's foundation date to 1639—although the house underwent major structural changes during restorations in both 1897 and the 1930s. During the latter, architect J. Frederick Kelly restored the house to its original plan of two floors with a dramatically steep roof, design elements heavily influenced by the English medieval period. The house was opened to the public in 1899 as the first state-owned museum in New England, and today it's filled with early weaving and textile equipment, as well

## SEARCHING FOR THE PERFECT BEACH

It may seem simple to find a great beach in Connecticut, with its 254 miles of shore fronting Long Island Sound. But any state resident who's keen on beaches knows there are certain obstacles in your quest for the perfect day at the shore. Although every inch of the coast is accessible to the public below the high-tide mark, getting to that elusive line in the sand can be challenging. Much of the shore abuts private property, and many beaches are restricted to the use of town residents.

Also consider what exactly you're seeking in a perfect beach experience. You may dislike pebbles—in which case much of Connecticut's shoreline may prove about as satisfying as sunbathing on a gravel driveway. Or, you may feel that a seaside sojourn lacks authenticity unless it involves clam strips, banana splits, and saltwater taffy.

Factoring in these criteria, a case could be made that **Madison,** between New Haven and Old Saybrook, is the state's best all-around beach getaway. Shore-goers began building shingled cottages here in the late 1800s, when rail and steamship travel were in vogue and the town's wharves welcomed throngs of resort visitors. It remains very popular today.

The community's sheltered shoreline overlooks Long Island Sound at one of its widest points, a full 19 miles from Riverhead, New York. A handful of picturesque municipal beaches are open only to residents and area hotel guests, Memorial Day–Labor Day. However, Madison's **Hammonasset State Park** welcomes everybody to its two-plus miles of golden sand—the longest stretch of public beach in the state. This peninsula became a member of the state park system in 1919 and is now Connecticut's most-visited attraction.

The facilities are top-notch, with a central pavilion and a few other picnic areas, spacious bathhouses, biking trails, and a boardwalk. The sand along the beach is coarse but not overly rocky. You can fish for bluefish and striped bass from a long jetty, or swim and sailboard right off the beach, under the watchful eye of lifeguards; there's also a boat launch and a 550-site campground.

An unusual feature of Hammonasset is the park's **Meigs Point Nature Center,** with fresh- and saltwater dioramas, a touch tank, and engaging exhibits on local sea and bird life. Nature programs are offered all summer, from canoe trips through the salt marshes to bird-watching strolls. In fact, this is one of the premier bird-watching habitats in southern New England, as acres of pristine marshland and bayberry thickets extend behind the beaches and provide a desirable habitat for sanderlings, thrushes, and warblers. Peregrine falcons, osprey, and sharp-shinned hawks patrol from above much of the year, and five species of owls have been known to nest here.

Because the park juts well into Long Island Sound, extending southeast from the coastline at about a 45-degree angle, with the beach running along this western flank, it's one of the few spots in Connecticut where you can sit on the beach and watch the sun set over the water. At the southern tip of the park, a small trail leads over a burly outcropping of rocks. Enjoy great views of the sound and the beach from the observation platform atop this hillock.

Hammonasset State Park (203/245-2785, open year-round 8 A.M.–sunset) is off I-95 at exit 62, just east of downtown Madison on the Boston Post Road (U.S. 1); Meigs Point Nature Center (203/245-1817) is open late Apr.–late Sept. Memorial Day–Labor Day, there's a per-vehicle fee of $5 (CT plates)/$8 (nonresident) on weekdays, $7 (CT plates)/$12 (nonresident) on weekends. Mid-Apr.–Memorial Day and Labor Day–mid-Oct., admission is free on weekdays and $5 (CT plates)/$7 (nonresidents) on weekends.

### Rocky Neck State Park
Contrary to its name, Rocky Neck State Park (off exit 72 of I-95, East Lyme, 860/739-5471) is arguably the least rocky beach in the state, a narrow but long crescent of soft sand just minutes off I-95, near the Niantic section of East Lyme. The typically light surf makes this an ideal swimming spot, and the large snack bar and picnic pavilion are a plus for groups and families. Oddly, rail tracks divide the parking area, changing facilities, and concessions from the beach—you walk under a rail bridge to get from one to the other. Hours and fees are the same as at Hammonasset State Park, above.

## Bluff Point State Park

It's small enough that including it in a guidebook seems slightly unfair—so please approach any visit to Groton's Bluff Point (off U.S. 1 via Depot Road, just east of Groton/New London Airport, 860/424-3200 or 860/445-1729) with the utmost respect for this pristine swath of tidal marsh, light forest, and undisturbed coastline. A visit here is less about sunning your buns (though this is one of the few spots along the coast where bathers have been known to bare all) and more about hiking and bird-watching. The park occupies the former farm of early Colonial governor John Winthrop—778 acres that became a part of the state park system in 1975. This sliver of paradise is minimally staffed and has no lifeguards, so be careful about swimming along its rocky shore. There's no charge for admission; park open daily dawn–dusk.

## DuBois Beach

Tiny DuBois Beach (end of Water St., 860/535-2476) is a little-known gem in the Colonial borough of Stonington, at the very eastern end of the state. It's at the southern tip of Water Street, facing Stonington Harbor and tucked between a pair of stone jetties. There are no facilities, just a tiny covered deck for unpacking your picnic basket and changing into flip-flops (lifeguard on duty daily in summer and weekends in late spring and early fall). Bereft of amenities, DuBois is nonetheless a gorgeous spot, offering 270-degree views that take in Fishers Island, New York, and the Victorian homes and hotels to the east in Watch Hill, Rhode Island.

The best thing about this beach may be that it requires an excursion through Stonington, one of Connecticut's prettiest Colonial villages, densely settled with clapboard and shingle homes dating to the 18th and 19th centuries. Some buildings contain galleries, boutiques, and eateries—so consider finishing your day at the beach with some shopping and noshing. The beach is open dawn to dusk, and the fee (including parking) is $2 weekdays and $3 weekends.

## Sherwood Island State Park

Fairfield County's own Sherwood Island State Park (exit 18 off I-95, Westport, 203/226-6983) fills up fast on summer weekends, as residents of the Bronx, Westchester County, and inland western Connecticut head here to enjoy the well-maintained facilities and 1.5 miles of sandy beach. The western beach looks out toward several islands off Norwalk and Westport and offers the calmest stretch for swimming, while the eastern beach looks 15 miles across the sound toward Stony Brook, Long Island. In addition to beaches, picnic areas, changing facilities, and food concessions, Sherwood has grassy meadows ideal for kites or Frisbee. It's also a fine spot for bird-watching, and in summer (Wed.–Sun.), you can visit the park's small nature center or take a self-guided nature stroll. As of this book's writing, a memorial to the Connecticut victims of the September 11, 2001 terrorist attacks was being built at the park—it looks out across Long Island Sound toward the Manhattan skyline. Hours and fees are the same as at Hammonasset State Park, above.

## Harkness Memorial State Park

Where's the best park in Connecticut to make believe you're a Vanderbilt? It's Harkness Memorial State Park (275 Great Neck Rd., Rte. 213, 860/443-5725) in the bucolic town of Waterford, just west of the New London border. Here the recently restored, turn-of-the-20th-century, 42-room mansion Eolia anchors the former estate of oil magnate Edward S. Harkness. There's a pristine beach for walking, sunning, and picnicking—but unsafe for swimming, which is prohibited (no lifeguards). A path from the parking lot leads through 250 acres of mature shade trees and well-manicured lawns to the water. You'll pass the colonnaded terrace and gardens of Eolia on the left (house open 10 A.M.–3 P.M. daily for touring in summer, weekends spring and fall). There is a per-vehicle fee of $4 (CT plates) or $5 (nonresidents) weekdays, $5 (CT plates) or $8 (nonresidents) weekends, Memorial Day–Labor Day. There's no additional charge for touring Eolia. The park is open 8 A.M.–sunset.

as the first clock tower made in the colonies (1726), and exhibits of local and state history. There's also an herb garden and museum shop on the premises.

Turn left out of Whitfield Street to reach Len Hubbard Marina, which has a small park that's popular with fishing enthusiasts and offers great views of the Sound and Faulkners Island Lighthouse in the distance. Drive back to the town green and turn right to continue along Rte. 146. Just east of the green you'll encounter two more historic houses open to the public. The 1660 **Hyland House** (84 Boston St., 203/453-9477, open seasonally, limited hours, $2) is an ancient hulking saltbox Colonial with three walk-in fireplaces and many rare furnishings and unusual decorative elements. The 1774 **Thomas Griswold House** (171 Boston St., 203/453-3176, www.thomasgriswoldhouse.com, open 11 A.M.–4 P.M. Tues.–Sun., June–Sept., $2) contains a restored blacksmith shop, early–19th-century antiques, and a small shop.

## Madison

Continue east on Rte. 146 a short distance before turning right onto U.S. 1, which leads into Madison, a town originally settled as part of Guilford. Today, this suburban community swells with visitors all summer long, as the beaches here are among the smoothest and prettiest in the state. Vacation homes dot the Madison shoreline—not the imposing monsters found in Fairfield County but typically simple and inviting shingle structures, many dating to the early half of this century.

Madison, which was incorporated in 1826 and named for our fourth president, was a shipbuilding and fishing center during the 19th century. As you motor through town, slow down as you pass through the Madison Green Historic District, where a number of preserved homes are situated around the dignified town common, where festivals and concerts are held throughout the summer.

Here you'll see perhaps the best-preserved of Connecticut's 17th-century homes, the **Deacon John Grave House** at Tuxis Farm (581 Boston Post Rd., U.S. 1, 203/245-4798, mid-June–Columbus Day, $2), which was built in

municipal Middle Beach, Madison

© ANDREW COLLINS

1675 and is notable for its hulking central chimney. The building, which has grown from a two-room cabin to a large Colonial saltbox, has served many functions during its existence, including school, war hospital and munitions depot, inn, tavern, and courthouse. You can also visit the 1785 **Allis-Bushnell House** (853 Boston Post Rd., on U.S. 1, 203/245-4567, home of the Madison Historical Society, June–late Sept., free). Highlights include exhibits of china, dolls, costumes, and spinning wheels.

Madison has an eminently walkable downtown, a wide Main Street brimming with shops, mostly white clapboard or redbrick facades, and trees looming over the sidewalk. There are some coffeehouses and cafés. A quiet, peaceful town, Madison has shore roads ideal for biking or jogging, level terrain that rewards with fine views. The town looks today largely as it did 20 years ago, save for a more sophisticated retail base downtown. The traditional no-frills Madison Coffee Shop, a place where blue-plate specials like meatloaf on toast keep the crowds coming back for more, now sits nearly across the street from a hip little java joint called Madison Gourmet Beanery. Antiques shops and galleries line this stretch of the Post Road, the town's main commercial thoroughfare, which in downtown Madison is edged by trees, sidewalks, and brick and clapboard storefronts. There are few chain stores, but rather a colorful swatch of independently owned one-of-a-kind businesses.

Access to Madison's wonderful town beaches is limited to residents (or guests of the town's hotels) from Memorial Day through October, but Madison's shoreline looks the way you'd expect an established family summer resort town to look—it's been carefully zoned and is free of commercial development and the honky-tonk ambience that can sometimes mar a seascape when done to an extreme. West Wharf Beach is one of the nicest little stretches of sand in the state, fronted by vintage beach houses and a couple hotels, with a protected cove that's good for swimming. You can't hang out here in summer unless you're a guest of the hotel, but off-season it's open to everybody and is a very nice place to stroll or watch the surf pound the shore during stormy weather.

**Hammonasset State Park** (off I-95 at exit 62, just east of downtown Madison on the Boston Post Rd., U.S. 1, 203/245-2785, admission $7–14 depending on time of year and whether you have in- or out-of-state plates, off-season free) is the state's premier beach, an enormous point that juts out into the sound so that visitors can actually watch the sunset over the water—a feat mostly unheard of in Connecticut. There are several beach parking areas, a large picnic pavilion, changing facilities, and a nature center. And from anywhere at this beach, the views are quite nice. Note that it can be chilly; it could be 80°F in protected Madison, at the town beaches, and 60°F here at the same time.

## CLINTON TO OLD SAYBROOK
### Clinton and Westbrook

US 1 leads east through two more suburbs with plenty of marinas, beaches, and B&Bs—Clinton and Westbrook. There isn't much to see or do in these communities, which are best known for the outlet shopping. But if you've some free time, pay a visit to the **Stanton House** (63 E. Main St., Clinton, 860/669-2132, limited hours, open June–Sept., free) a 1790s house-museum notable for its 18th- and 19th-century antiques, including a fine collection of Staffordshire dinnerware. In Westbrook, history buffs should stop by the **Military Historians Headquarters Museum** (N. Main St., 860/399-9460, open 8 A.M.–3:30 P.M. Tues.–Fri., free), which houses

the most comprehensive collection of American military uniforms in the country. A research and video library contains reams of archives, and other exhibits display artifacts and vehicles from various military campaigns.

Treat yourself to a bit of wine-tasting at **Chamard Vineyards** (115 Cow Hill Rd., Clinton, 860/664-0299, www.chamard.com, open Wed.–Sat. year-round). The modern vineyard, established in 1983, is set across 40 gently sloping acres just a couple of miles inland from Long Island Sound. Chamard produces chardonnay, cabernet sauvignon, pinot noir, merlot, and cabernet franc vintages.

### Old Saybrook

From Westbrook, continue along U.S. 1 into the town of Old Saybrook—the very first coastal community settled in the state of Connecticut. It's a town rich with history, although you'd hardly know it from busy U.S. 1, which eventually merges with I-95 in the eastern end of town before crossing over the Connecticut River and heading into Old Lyme.

For a look at the many lovely homes that show 350 years' worth of architectural change in Connecticut, turn right off of U.S. 1 onto Rte. 154 and follow it as it loops through several communities of both summer and year-round homes. This route passes alongside Long Island Sound, and then runs over a long causeway to Saybrook Point, which looks directly out at the mouth of the Connecticut River. You'll see the fancy Saybrook Point Inn on your right, the Dock and Dine seafood restaurant, and a parking lot beside a miniature-golf course. Here, also, is the entrance to **Fort Saybrook Monument Park** (Rte. 154, 860/395-3123, free) an 18-acre park where storyboards depict the founding of the original Saybrook Colony in 1635. This is a great spot for birdwatching, and a long boardwalk runs along the river.

## SHOPPING

The central shoreline towns are excellent sources of shopping, with a number of boutiques and stores within walking distance of one another in the downtowns of Branford, Guilford, Madison, and Old Saybrook, and major outlet malls in Clinton and Westbrook.

In the northern part of Branford, don't miss **Hilltop Orchards** (616 E. Main St., 203/488-0779) where U.S. 1 passes through. It's a great spot for pies, fresh berries and fruits in season, and other goodies. Apple pie is the big draw. The **Guilford Handcraft Center** (411 Church St., Rte. 77, 203/453-5947, www.handcraftcenter.org) is a school devoted to fine arts and handicrafts; it hosts some seven exhibitions annually; it also has an outstanding gift shop of handmade items, and it's open year-round.

Madison has an engaging downtown—there's something fun about any village whose main pharmacy is called Jolly's Drug Incorporated. One must-visit here is the independent bookstore **R. J. Julia** (768 Boston Post Rd., U.S. 1, 203/245-3959, www.rjjulia.com), one of the best sources for books in the state. It's famous statewide for its exceptional selection and knowledgeable staff, and it also has a nice little café. If you're the type whose toes tingle whenever somebody mentions trailblazing, fly-fishing, rock-climbing, and other such activities, you simply must check out **North Cove Outfitters** (75 Main St., Old Saybrook, 860/388-6585, www.northcove.com), a phenomenally well-stocked font of outdoors stuff, from books to boots to shiny fishing lures. The staff is extremely helpful, and demonstrations are sometimes held here on a range of outdoor topics.

Outlet shopping is a serious pastime along Connecticut's central and eastern shorelines, with two of the most popular venues a short drive from each other off I-95. The **Westbrook Factory Stores** (314 Flat Rock Place, exit 65 from I-95, Westbrook, 860/399-8656, www.shopwestbrook.com) has about 65 stores including Eddie Bauer, J.Crew, Jockey, Timberland, Reebok, Oneida, Pfaltzgraff, and Black & Decker. Higher end, by far, is **Clinton Crossing** (exit 63 from I-95, 860/664-0700, www.premiumoutlets.com), where 70 upscale shops like Barneys New York, Calvin Klein, Coach, Crate & Barrell, Donna Karan, Gap, Jones New York, Kenneth Cole, Coach, Perry Ellis, Mikasa, KB Toys, Ralph Lauren, Waterford Wedgwood, and Royal Doulton

await you and your credit cards. Of course, any retail diva will tell you that "outlet" stores don't always offer a significant discount off the prices you'll find in real stores, but loyal fans of these shopping centers insist that bargains abound.

## RECREATION

Boating, whether in sailboats, on fishing expeditions, or in big party boats, is the recreation of choice along the central shore, and there are dozens of outfitters sailing out of the hundreds of marinas found in the towns along this stretch.

## ENTERTAINMENT AND NIGHTLIFE

This region is an easy drive from the many performing arts venues of New Haven and also the lower Connecticut River Valley, but the central shoreline does possess one first-rate attraction of its own, the **Opera Theater of Connecticut** (Main St., Clinton, 860/669-8999, www.operatheater-ct.org), which offers fully produced operas all summer long. One of the quirkier performance spaces in Connecticut is the **Puppet House Theatre** (128 Thimble Island Rd., 203/488-5752, www.puppethouse.org), where puppet-themed plays and concerts are presented year-round.

## FESTIVALS AND EVENTS
### Spring and Summer

A major **Antiques Show** takes place at Adams Middle School (Rte. 77, Guilford, 203/458-9087) in early March. Military-history buffs congregate at Madison's Hammonasset Beach the first weekend in May for the **Annual Civil War Living History & Battles Encampment** (860/526-5086); a different battle is reenacted each year. Thinking about finally giving in and buying that little (or big) yacht you've always wanted? There's no better place to browse than at the **Old Saybrook Boat Show** (Old Saybrook Shopping Center, U.S. 1, 860/388-3266) a two-day event held mid-June.

In the same month, gather for food, games,

and local entertainment at the **Branford Festival** (Branford Town Green, Main St., 203/488-1255, ext. 135.). Craftsmakers and those who admire their wares head to the Guilford Green every July for the **Guilford Handcraft Exposition** (Whitfield St., 203/453-5947). Soon after, there's also an **Arts and Crafts Show** (860/388-3266) on the town green in Old Saybrook.

## Fall and Winter

Retail fanatics won't want to miss September's **World's Largest Sidewalk Sale** (Westbrook Factory Outlets, 314 Flat Rock Place, 860/399-8656); basically, it's a giant clearance sale at a 65-shop outlet center, complete with a Dixieland band and other live entertainment. Later that month, it's time for the **Guilford Fair** (Guilford Fairgrounds, Lovers Ln., 203/453-3543), with oldies and country-western music and a family circus that's a hit with the kids. Just as the leaves begin to turn, it's time to motor over to the **Old Saybrook Apple Festival** on the town green (Main St., 860/388-9362), for horse-drawn carriage rides, square dancing, quilt and bake sales, and arts and crafts displays. Madison ushers in Halloween with a **Pumpkin Festival,** downtown along the Boston Post Road (on U.S. 1, 203/245-7394 or 888/342-7394).

In November, check out the **Harvest Fair** (First Congregational Church, 122 Broad St., Guilford, 203/453-4227), where 18 stalls have been set up with holiday decorations, dried floral arrangements, jewelry and tools, and homemade baked goods. December's **Old Saybrook Torchlight Parade** (Main St., 860/399-9460) features holiday-themed floats and about 50 fife and drum corps.

# ACCOMMODATIONS

There's absolutely no shortage of accommodations, of every style and in every price range, along the Connecticut shoreline. The bulk are motels and chain hotels strung along I-95, many of which are sleazy and strange, and some of which are perfectly adequate but pricey for what they offer (the Super 8 in Old Saybrook and the Days Inn in Branford, for instance). Those reviewed below

are the best and most updated in each category, but if you go in summer—when the popularity of this area can surge to the point that rooms are scarce—you might consider simply driving along and popping into some of those not listed. However, bear in mind that any place that has not been rated by AAA or another reputable organization may feel strangely like the Bates Motel.

B&Bs are another option in these parts, as there are several handsome of properties—some of them restored captains' mansions—in this area.

## Hotels and Motels

**Over $250:** The luxurious **Saybrook Point Inn** (2 Bridge St., Old Saybrook, 860/395-2000 or 800/243-0212, www.saybrook.com) stands on the site of the once ever-so-fabulous Terra Mar Resort, which hosted everyone from Frank Sinatra to Tom Jones in its heyday and also played a role in the movie the *Parrish,* which was released in 1960 and starred Troy Donahue, Connie Stevens, Claudette Colbert, and Karl Malden. The Terra Mar fell on hard times eventually, was raided by the police, and underwent a series of indignities before facing the wrecking ball. The current Saybrook Point Inn opened in 1989, offering the very same enticing water and marina views. The exterior is pretty, but not especially dramatic—sort of like an upscale condo complex. But the 80 rooms and suites are elegant through and through, with gas fireplaces, sumptuous armchairs, baths of imported Italian tile, high-speed Internet, and in many cases balconies. Guests include yachters and sailors who pull right up to the dock. Visit the full-service spa for facials, massages, depilation, and the body works, or buff those bods in the health club or swim in the indoor and outdoor pools.

**$150–250:** The fancy **Water's Edge Resort and Country Club** (1525 Boston Post Rd., Westbrook, 860/399-5901 or 800/222-5901, www.watersedge-resort.com) is one of the state's only full-scale resort getaways, and a very nicely maintained one at that. The compound of gray-shingle villas with airy contemporary interiors and a main lodge sits on several acres of direct waterfront on Long Island Sound; many of the airy high-ceilinged rooms have unobstructed water views. Some of the two-bedroom units are resided in seasonally, but most are booked as standard hotel units. There's an extensive health spa and fitness center, an indoor pool, and a very nice Continental restaurant that's especially well-regarded for brunch and offers lovely water views from both the dining room and the terrace.

**$100–150:** Don't let its location on a busy road turn you off; the **Sandpiper** (1750 Boston Post Rd., on U.S. 1, Old Saybrook, 860/399-7973 or 800/323-7973, www.sandpipermotorinn.com) has a peaceful 4.5-acre setting on a pond, back from the road. Rooms at this 45-room motor lodge are clean and pleasant if with ordinary furnishings, but a few top-end rooms do have wet bars, work areas, and additional sofa beds; all units have refrigerators and micowaves. This is a well-run property in every respect, with a small but quaint common area, an outdoor pool, town-beach privileges, and Continental breakfast included.

Somewhat of a sleeper along a surprisingly peaceful and pleasant stretch of U.S. 1, the Colonial-style **Guilford Suites Hotel** (2300 Boston Post Rd., on U.S. 1, 203/453-0123 or 800/626-8604), is popular with families and relocating executives, as all of its units have separate living rooms with kitchens and sofas that convert into queen beds. It's a well-maintained facility, one of the best values in coastal Connecticut.

The attractive timber-sheathed **Days Inn Old Saybrook** (1430 Boston Post Rd., on U.S. 1, 860/388-3453 or 800/DAYS-INN) is a well-kept chain property with clean but unremarkable rooms and a nice location on a relatively quiet stretch of U.S. 1 near several good restaurants. The indoor rooftop pool is a definite plus, and the staff is courteous. Guests get free beach passes, and some suites have whirlpool baths or saunas.

The **Madison Beach Hotel** (94 W. Wharf Rd., Madison, 203/245-1404, www.madisonbeachhotel.com) is a great old seaside property, with a vintage mood, varnished wooden sink counters in the bathrooms, simple beachy decor, a friendly staff, and considerable character—it's a nice place to come for a week and relax by the beach. The 32 rooms all face the sound, and all have small balconies with partition walls for privacy; the two-room suites are perfect for families. In the early 1800s this place was a boarding house for area shipbuilders, but it's been a hotel since the 1920s. There's a decent seafood and pasta restaurant attached, from which room service is available.

**$50–100:** The **Ramada Limited** (3 Business Park Rd., off Leetes Island Rd., Branford, exit 56 off I-95, 203/488-4991 or 888/298-2054) is a top-notch chain hotel with 85 attractive, contemporary rooms, an indoor pool, a fitness room, a self-service laundry, and a few suites with kitchenettes or full kitchens. While it's pricier by $20–30 per night than other motels in Branford, it's far superior to all of them.

It's not a good choice for families, but adventuresome singles on a budget with an appreciation for roadside kitsch may just want to try out the **Branford Motel** (470 E. Main St., exit 55 off I-95, 203/488-5442), a strange little place of questionable repute whose rooms have color TVs, giant mirrors (some on the ceiling), and such special features as round beds, water beds, or heart-shaped tubs. Who can resist the special suite called the Jungle Room, with a safari suite? Or the glittery Disco Room? Some rooms are advertised as having "jell beds." It's not clear what these are, but one can't help but imagine they're plenty of fun. There are plenty of motels like this off I-95 throughout Connecticut, but this one is at least clean and courteously staffed. There's a Subway sandwich restaurant on the premises, and lovely gurgling fountains dot the grounds, which are strung with holiday lights. And yes, special "day rates" are available.

Another inexpensive option is the **Advanced Motel** (81 Leetes Island Rd., exit 56 from I-95, Branford, 203/481-4528), which is described in its brochure as being less than five minutes from the "roaring Atlantic Ocean." Well, sort of—it's about 10 minutes from gurgling Long Island Sound. No matter—rooms are clean and relatively tasteful, and many have refrigerators. And Stony Creek is a short drive away.

## Country Inns and Bed-and-Breakfasts

**$150–250:** The 1740 **Deacon Timothy Pratt House Bed and Breakfast** (325 Main St.,

860/395-1229, www.connecticut-bed-and-break-fast.com) is a remarkably well-preserved, pale-gray, 1746 Colonial with a steep wooden-shingle roof and a prime location on a main street. It's a short drive or bike ride away from the water, and you can hear the church bells chiming from a nearby historic church. The interior is decorated with very fine period pieces—four-poster beds, Chippendale highboys, and such—but without the clutter that typifies many old B&Bs; creaky wide-plank floors, hand-hewn beams, beehive ovens, Oriental rugs, and working fireplaces contribute to the historic ambience. Nearly every room has a fireplace and whirlpool tub. Original occupant Timothy Pratt was a deacon in the meetinghouse directly across the street. The inn also has a couple of rooms in the historic building next door, the 1790 James Gallery and Soda Fountain, a former apothecary where it's said that "Lafayette made a purchase in 1824." One of the rooms here is a studio that can sleep four and has a large kitchen. There's also a working soda fountain, open to the public, on the ground floor (it's closed from late fall to early spring). Innkeeper Shelley Nobile is a knowledgeable host with a great flair for decorating and restoration.

**$100–$150: By the Sea Inn and Spa** (107 Montowese St., Branford, 203/483-3333, www.bytheseainnspa.com) is a gracious 19th-century mansion with both a day spa and overnight accommodations. Beds are big and fluffy, with high-quality linens, lace-window treatments, polished hardwood floors, and up-scale furnishings. There are four rooms, among them a two-bedroom an apartment-style suite with its own private entrance, a den that can also be used as a second bedroom, and a kitchenette. All have private baths, and a Continental breakfast is included. Of course, the big draw here is the on-site day spa, where myriad treatments are available, from aromatherapy to seaweed body wraps. The inn is on the edge of downtown, within walking distance of many shops and eateries—it's not directly "by the sea," but the beach is just a short drive away.

The **Tidewater Inn** (949 Boston Post Rd., on U.S. 1, 203/245-8457, www.thetidewater.com) is a large Colonial-style property on a busy road,

within walking distance of the shops downtown, and not too long a stroll from Madison's East Wharf Beach. The nine rooms are furnished elaborately with antiques and canopy and four-poster beds with lacy linens; all have private bath. Two rooms have working fireplaces.

Facing Long Island Sound in Westbrook, the **Talcott House** (161 Seaside Ave., 860/399-5020) has the feel and look of a classic shingle-style New England beach house, complete with a twin-chimneyed hipped roofline. The house dates from 1890 and sits along the beach, just a half mile from Pilots Point Marina. There are four suites, all facing the ocean and all with crisp, tasteful furnishings and private baths.

The **Captain Stannard House** (138 S. Main St., 860/399-4634, www.stannardhouse.com) commands a regal presence over U.S. 1, with its distinctive cupola, steep roof, tall 12-over-12 windows, and Palladian front door. It's quite a mansion, evidence of the original owner's successes as a merchant sea captain. The public areas and eight guest rooms contain period antiques, there's a common TV in the library, and sweeping gardens extend behind the house. Westbrook's beaches are within easy walking distance.

## FOOD

For the better part of this century, there have been wonderful lobster shacks serving up shore dinners all along the central shoreline's busy U.S. 1. The authenticity of a seaside community is measured as much by the availability of its seafood as by the quality of its beaches. And in this department, Madison scores very high marks. Make a right turn onto the Boston Post Road, as you leave Hammonasset Park, and you'll come upon a slew of lobster and crab shacks, plus ice-cream parlors and pizza joints. Another strength of the region is its many fine Asian restaurants, especially in Old Saybrook and Branford. In fact, Branford has emerged in recent years as one of Connecticut's culinary hotbeds—perhaps restaurateurs are moving here to follow in the footsteps of celebrity chef Jacques Pépin, who lives in Branford. (An odd side note: the "wine" that Pépin's great friend Julia Child used to drink on her cooking show was actually a mixture of water and Gravy Master, a cooking sauce that's produced in Branford.)

## Creative but Casual

Steve and Eva Wilkinson, who ran the now-defunct Steve's Centerbrook Café near Essex, have opened **Esteva** (25 Whitfield St., 203/458-1300, $17–24), on the ground-floor of a dashing Second Empire Victorian mansion facing the Guilford Green. The snazzy dining room with blue-striped banquettes and warm lighting is staffed by a friendly, professional bunch. And, as at Steve's other acclaimed restaurants, the food here is outstanding—consider a starter of chorizo-and-crawfish beignets with a roasted–red pepper remoulade; and a main course of seared scallops with ginger rice, fried carrots, and a red soy and cashew sauce. Desserts are a real treat here—consider the Guinness cake with caramelized apples and green-apple sorbet.

You'll have no trouble understanding why the kitchen at **Terra Mar** (2 Bridge St., Old Saybrook, 860/388-1111, $23–34) has garnered important culinary achievement awards from the James Beard Foundation. The New American cooking here, infused with Continental influences, is uniformly excellent. You might start with a braised-rabbit spring roll with savoy cabbage, goat cheese, and roasted garlic, before moving on to entrées such as herb-seared haddock with roasted pepper–and–caper tapenade, lemon beurre blanc, and basmati rice. Wild game specials are offered frequently, and Sunday brunch is a weekly tradition. This snazzy space at the Saybrook Point Inn overlooks the hotel's marina—it's perfect in warm weather, when you can actually sup on the terrace.

Popular for his PBS cooking shows and columns in *Food & Wine,* Jacques Pépin eats frequently at **Le Petit Café** (225 Montowese St., Branford, 203/483-9791, $35 for four-course prix fixe), a charming little French restaurant where the menu changes on a near-daily basis—it's run by Pépin's niece. Tripe is frequently offered, and roasted rack of lamb Provençal with double-baked Granny Smith apple-and-turnip gratinée, roast Brussels sprouts, and rosemary

sauce. Also consider sautéed Icelandic char with five-spice sesame-seed crust, baby artichokes, grape tomatoes, chorizo, and lemongrass-port wine reduction. The intimate sunny dining room is unpretentious, with a black-and-white floor and small wooden tables.

With an absolutely tiny dining room with containing marble tables, a blackboard menu, and views into the similarly diminutive kitchen, **Pasta Cosi** (202 S. Montowese St., Branford, 203/483-9397, $8–16) may not look like much, but offers exceptionally fresh and tasty pasta platters. Order by mixing and matching your noodle of choice with any number of interesting sauces, including a divine blue crab sauce. Gorgonzola and walnut ravioli is often featured.

**Cafe Routier** (1353 Boston Post Rd., on U.S. 1, Westbrook, 860/399-8700, $14–19) serves food that could be called simple and straightforward in France (which means it's superb on this side of the pond). Consider the traditional salad of endive and arugula with toasted walnuts, apples, gorgonzola, and a sherry vinaigrette; or chicken fricassee with pearl onions, mushrooms, bacon lardons, tarragon, and basmati rice. There's even Mom's Meatloaf, in case you're homesick. This inviting restaurant moved into an attractive colonial house in 2001—it consists of an elegant cocktail bar to one side and a lovely dining room main dining room that's quite a bit larger than Routier's compact former quarters.

**Noodles** (508 Old Toll Rd., Madison, 203/421-5606, $9–20) is an inviting dining room with a relaxed and outgoing staff. The cuisine could best be described as upmarket comfort food, much of it with an Italian slant—crab cakes with a roasted red pepper and caper sauce; fish and chips; flank steak teriyaki. A plus is that most things are available in either full- or semi-sized portions.

**Wine and Roses** (150 Main St., 860/388-9646, $13–20), another small and casual eatery in downtown Old Saybrook, specializes in eclectic contemporary fare that thoughtfully blends classical preparations with both traditional and unexpected ingredients. The menu emphasizes Italian fare and might include crabmeat-filled ravioli with fresh corn, green onions, cream, and potato corncakes followed by roast leg of lamb seasoned with rosemary and garlic and served with sundried tomato couscous and a wild mushroom sauce. Expect to savor a meal you'll remember for some time, yet at extremely fair prices.

**Café Allegre** (725 Boston Post Rd., on U.S. 1, Madison, 203/245-8954, $9–22) sits inside an imposing downtown Madison Greek Revival building with narrow white columns and green trim. Inside the dining room, rush-seated ladderback chairs, polished wood floors, and red-and-white checkered curtains impart a bright, clean, Colonial ambience. Very good contemporary Italian fare is served, including Black Angus steak with scallions, shitake mushrooms, and a cognac demiglace, and fresh Maine lobster sautéed with shallots in a tomato cream sauce and served over angel-hair pasta. The focaccia here is addictive—try it topped with prosciutto and crumbled fontina cheese. A chief competitor of Café Allegre is **Aleia's** (1687 Boston Post Rd., Old Saybrook, 860/399-5050, $14–22), housed in a Colonial-style building near the Westbrook border. Here, in an expansive and elegant but unstuffy dining room, you might try Chilean sea bass with tapanade-flavored gnocchi and root vegetables, several great pasta entrées, or an exceptional appetizer of sesame-crusted seared tuna. Prices are reasonable for this level of cuisine.

## Pizza, Pub Grub, and Seafood

Exactly what the name of this restaurant suggests, the genuinely thoughtful staff at **Friends & Company** (11 Boston Post Rd., Madison, 203/245-0462, $10–20) welcomes all patrons as though they're members of the family—and many who eat here have become regulars. The casually furnished restaurant has a convivial bar on one side and a fireplace-warmed dining room on the other. Most of the American entrées are available in appetizer portions; these might include farm-raised salmon baked in parchment paper with fresh dill and seasonal veggies, or traditional chicken teriyaki. Try the fresh-baked cookies and breads, too.

**Pat's Kountry Kitchen** (70 Mill Rock Rd. E, Old Saybrook, 860/388-4784, $5–15) is right across from a red Greek Revival house containing Pat's Kountry Kollectibles. Apparently, Pat likes the letter "K." As you might guess, this restaurant is filled with homey knickknacks and Colonial memorabilia; in fact, the waitstaff dresses in neo-Puritan garb. From waffles with strawberries and cream to delicious clam hash, breakfast comes in heroic proportions. Dinner might be Delmonico steak, chicken potpie, jumbo stuffed shrimp, or any of several large sandwiches.

A pubby spot with wood-paneling and comfy booth seating, **Webster's** (1114 Main St., Branford, 203/488-8161, $7–18) pays homage to the Connecticut-born dictionary maker Noah Webster, as dishes and their ingredients appear on the menu as words with their definitions. About six kinds of burgers are offered, plus several seafood entrées, shrimp Française, honey-garlic chicken, and herbed salmon.

Another entry in the "best pizza in the state" pageant is **Alforno Ristorante** (1654 Boston Post Rd., on U.S. 1, 860/399-4166, $10–15, large pies $12–18), which has attained a near-celebrity status. A bright dining room with neon, high ceilings, and impressionistic splashes of color painted across the walls, Alforno serves similarly dynamic pizzas, including a mouthwatering scampi pie with garlic, oregano, thyme, Romano cheese, and olive oil. A few dependable pasta dishes are served, too.

Still another superb pizza restaurant in coastal Connecticut, **Born in America** (4 Brushy Plain Rd., Branford, 203/483-0211, $8–13, large pies $11–17) has chefs who clearly delight in inventive and unlikely pizza toppings, such as the Passion Pie of sliced tomatoes, chopped dill, salmon, Swiss and mozzarella cheese, and lumpfish caviar. Calzones, hefty sandwiches, and a few pasta dishes are also offered, but most folks come for these wild pies.

The football field–sized parking lot at **Lenny and Joe's Fish Tale** (1301 Boston Post Rd., on U.S. 1, Clinton-Madison line, 203/245-7289; also 86 Boston Post Rd., on U.S. 1, Westbrook, 860/669-0767, $4–15) attests to this fish house's enormous popularity—there are people who will drive from hours away to sample the mammoth whole belly clams and succulent oysters doled out here. Nobody's gonna accuse Lenny and Joe's of serving health food, but the frying here is done with cholesterol-free vegetable oil. And the coleslaw is fresh and flavorful. Just step in, order at the counter, wait for your number to come up, and haul your catch back to one of the simple wooden booths in the back.

After admiring the smiling-clam logo at **Clam Castle** (1324 Boston Post Rd., on U.S. 1, Madison, 203/245-4911, $4–12), it almost seems like a crime to eat the cute little critters. Alas (for the clams—and the soft-shell crabs and lobsters), people can't seem to eat enough of the fresh food at this informal fast-food-style eatery near the Clinton town line. Arguably, the Saybrook Fish House might have better food than **Dock and Dine** (Saybrook Pt., Old Saybrook, 860/388-4665, $14–25), but this seaside restaurant has one of the prettiest settings around—the spacious three-sided dining room has enormous windows that look out over the water. It's a relaxing, traditional place, a bit touristy but quite fun—steaks, bouillabaisse, and broiled fish are among the offerings. In summer, there's seating on the terrace. The **USS Chowder Pot III** (560 E. Main St., on U.S. 1, exit 56 from I-95, 203/481-2356, $9–28), with its own monthly newspaper and constant events and special theme nights, is not just a restaurant but an experience. The restaurant began in 1977 as a hot dog and chowder stand and has grown several times since then, often commanding waits of two hours for the fresh seafood. There's karaoke some nights, nautical furnishings, and on lobster night (Monday) you can sample any of 20 preparations of New England's favorite crustacean. Additionally, about 15 dinner platters, many fried-food platters, and several appetizers are available, plus chicken and ribs.

The **Saybrook Fish House** (99 Essex Rd., Old Saybrook, 860/388-4836, $12–26), which began here but now has three branches elsewhere in the state, is inside an unassuming house in northern Old Saybrook, near the shores of the Connecticut River. The dining room has a few old maritime paintings, butcher paper on the tables, and the odd flotsam and jetsam, but is far classier than many of the over-the-top fish

restaurants in coastal Connecticut. The best seafood dishes here have a distinctly Italian flavor—the Poseidon Adventure, for instance, comes with a selection of shrimp, scallops, lobster, crab, clams, mussels, squid, and whitefish simmered in a rich wine and garlic broth and served over linguine. Sole Dijon is another specialty.

The dining adjunct of the Madison Beach Hotel, the **Wharf** (94 West Wharf Rd., Madison, 203/245-0005, $8–23) offers great views of Long Island Sound from its second-floor dining room, which is decked in lobster traps and buoys and has the feel of a rustic boathouse. It's a terrific place for dinner or drinks when the sun is setting. Expect hefty portions in the way of filet mignon, lobster, fried oyster platters, horseradish-crusted salmon, sandwiches, and lobster rolls.

Among the three billion seafood restaurants along Post Road in Westbrook, **Frankie's** (359 Boston Post Rd., 860/399-5524) has been entertaining seafood lovers since 1959—the retro, castle-like building with a spacious rooftop deck looks as though it hasn't changed since the day it opened. The draws here, apart from the kitsch factor, are a wild happy hour that includes free bar food at cocktail hour, and the house-specialty prime rib.

Adjoining the Cedar Island Marina in Clinton, **Aqua** (34 Riverside Dr., 860/664-3788, $12–20) serves straightforward American and Italian fare with an emphasis on seafood. Fillet of sole Florentine, lobster and shrimp baked with breadcrumbs, and Gorgonzola-crusted fillet of beef are favorites. The decor is a bit tired and the overall dining experience something short of inspiring, but it's your best bet for a meal in Clinton. The restaurant closes Jan.–March.

It may have an ordinary name, but **The Place** (901 Boston Post Rd., on U.S. 1, Guilford, across from Bradlees shopping center, 203/453-9276, $5–11) is a highly unusual dining establishment. Behind a quirky little red house is the outdoor dining area (there are no seats inside), consisting of basic wooden tables and seats carved out of tree stumps. All the food is cooked over an open fire, giving dinner here the feel of a big family barbecue. Roast clams, lobster, bluefish, and roasted corn are about all you'll find on the menu, plus excellent cheesecake. And everything tastes great, perhaps in part because of the infectiously fun in-the-rough setting. The **Westbrook Lobster Market & Restaurant** (346 E. Main St., on U.S. 1, Clinton–Westbrook line, 860/664-9464) is an all-in-one market and dine-in eatery; grab a beer and fried seafood platter and enjoy the day.

## Asian

Near the Westbrook border, **Little Siam** (1745 Boston Post Rd., Old Saybrook, 860/399-8848, $8–16) has a strong following locally and serves quite good Thai seafood dishes—fried shrimp with garlic sauce, squid and shrimp curries—and some good fried appetizers. It's not overly spicy fare, but you can request it as such. The staff is gracious, and the dining rooms are attractive, with seascape murals, a fireplace, and pink napery.

Many of the state's best Asian restaurants are marred only by dull strip mall settings; clearly the owners of the delightful Vietnamese restaurant **Saigon City** (1315 Boston Post Rd., on U.S. 1, Old Saybrook, 860/388-6888, $10–16) looked hard to avoid this fate, opening their popular restaurant inside a rambling 1710 Colonial house. The dining rooms exude charm and character—it's a romantic yet unstuffy setting, a place to show off dazzling plates of food like spicy ginger pork, catfish baked in a clay pot with fragrant spices, and lemongrass tofu. Another great source of Asian fare along the shoreline is **Zhang's** (455 Boston Post Rd., on U.S. 1, Old Saybrook, 860/388-3999, $8–14), which sits beside an old rail depot off U.S. 1 and offers a wide selection of both Chinese and Japanese specialties is offered, including good sushi. Try the spicy tofu Szechuan-style or the "happy family" (with lobster, shrimp, chicken, and beef in a tangy brown sauce).

**Darbar India** (1070 Main St., Branford, 203/481-8994, $8–15) is one of the better Indian restaurants in the state, offering an extensive menu that includes coconut soup with pistachios, several Tandoori dishes, shrimp vindaloo in a fiery curry sauce with potato and tomato, and complete dinners (veggie or non-veggie) that are priced quite reasonably—a good way to go if you're unfamiliar with Indian menus. The lavishly decorated and always aromatic dining room has ornate wooden booths and is overseen by an attentive staff.

## Mexican

You'll find fairly standard fare, but better-than-average preparation at **Su Casa** (400 E. Main St., Branford, 203/481-5001, $8–17), a low-key Mexican eatery festooned with imported crafts and artwork. Good bets include tamales smothered with chile con carne and *pescado con salsa de tomate verde* (red snapper broiled with tomatillo and white wine sauce). **Cuckoo's Nest** (1712 Boston Post Rd., on U.S. 1, Old Saybrook, 860/399-9060, $7–17) is another longtime favorite, whose irresistibly engaging interior features a rustic-beamed ceiling and has the feel of an old hacienda. The Mexican food is given fresh Creole twists: catfish and red beans and rice are specialties, but also check out the grande chimichangas and the jalepeños stuffed with black beans and cheese and deep-fried with a remoulade sauce.

## Quick Bites

The **Front Parlour** at the British Shoppe (45 Wall St., Madison, 203/245-4521, $6–10; full afternoon teas $9–18), combines the best of a gourmet tea and food shop and a dainty tearoom. The most sumptuous of tea options, the Duchess of Bedford, encompasses a large selection of finger sandwiches, a slice of cake, scones, English preserves, and Devonshire cream. Traditional lunch entrées include the ploughman's platter and the farmer's lunch of pork pie. The setting, a 1690 red center-chimney house with an uneven wooden shingle roof, seems perfect for an anglophile experience —it almost looks as though a wealthy Tory family could have lived here 300 years ago.

It may look like a typical Greek-style greasy spoon, but the **Shoreline Diner & Vegetarian Enclave** (345 Boston Post Rd., on U.S. 1, Guilford, 203/458-7380, $4–12) serves—as the name suggests—plenty of veggie options, too.

Through flower-filled front windows, you'll see one of Madison's favorite little luncheries, the homey **Madison Coffee Shop** (765 Boston Post Rd., on U.S. 1, 203/245-4474, $4–10), where home-style favorites like meatloaf on toast, scrambled eggs, fried clam strips, ham sandwiches, and tasty pies are served amid unpretentious trappings. Come here if you've forgotten the difference between coffee shops and coffeehouses.

## Java Joints

There are two branches in the area of **Willoughby's Coffee & Tea,** Branford Business Center (550 E. Main St., Branford, 203/481-1700) and 752 Boston Post Rd. (U.S. 1, Madison, 203/245-1600). **Madison Gourmet Beanery** (712 Boston Post Rd., on U.S. 1, 203/245-1323) is a standard-issue coffeehouse in the center of Madison, with a couple of tables and a nice selection of light foods and specialty drinks (including Fresh Samantha juices).

Facing the green are several shops and eateries, including a small, lovely coffeehouse, **Common Grounds** (1096 Main St., Branford, 203/488-2326), which sells about 30 blends of coffees to go. But it's also a nice stop for bagels, tea and coffee, and great desserts if you're out exploring the area. The marble tables face a front window that overlooks the town green. On Main Street in Old Saybrook, **Caffe Toscana** (25 Main St., 860/388-1270) is a tiny ivy-colored cottage that looks like it was airlifted from the Italian countryside and plopped down here in coastal Connecticut. Inside you'll find a nice selection of espressos and coffee drinks, as well as light breakfasts and lunches.

## Gourmet Goods and Picnic Supplies

The **Indian Neck Store and Market** (2 Sybil Ave., Branford, 203/483-8220) and the adjoining **Bud's** (203/488-1019 or 800/348-1019), which share the same owners, offer a full range of gourmet items. Bud's is one of the finest seafood markets along the coast, specializing in sushi products, crab butter, "fruit-

of-the-sea" salad, and incredibly fresh and good fish—they'll ship lobsters and other delicious foods anywhere in the country. The Indian Neck Store and Market has an ice-cream stand, deli, prepared foods, and outdoor seating on a deck looking toward the water.

The diminutive **Sifting Bowl Pastry Shop** (168 Main St., Old Saybrook, 860/388-0022) is a great place to pick up fresh-baked cookies, various country gifts, and other culinary odds and ends. On the way to Hammonasset Beach, drop by **Perfect Parties** (885 Post Rd., 203/245-0250) for a memorable sandwich. It has many tempting kinds, from basic to quite special (the crab cake with cucumber dill comes to mind).

A comely gourmet market and coffeehouse overlooking the green in downtown Guilford, **Cilantro** (85 Whitfield St., 203/458-2555) is a great resource for specialty foods, sandwiches, and drinks—there are a few indoor seats.

# INFORMATION AND SERVICES
## Visitor Information

Most of the region is represented by the **Greater New Haven Convention and Visitors Bureau** (59 Elm St., New Haven, 203/777-8550 or 800/332-STAY, www.newhavencvb.org). Old Seabrook and Westbrook are served by the **Greater Hartford Tourism District** (31 Pratt St., 4th Fl., Hartford, CT 01063, 860/244-8181 or 800/793-4480, www.enjoyhartford.com).

## Getting Around

As with other shore points, U.S. 1 and I-95 are your main routes for navigating the region, although for the best scenery stick to the coastal state roads described throughout the chapter. There's limited commuter rail service between these towns and Groton and New Haven, but a car is your only real practical option.

# The Southeast Coastline

The southeastern corner, blessed with a whaling and shipbuilding heritage and several beautiful coastal communities, is a slice of Connecticut that many visitors are surprised to encounter. Perhaps they imagine that pier-side lobster shacks and handsome sea captains' mansions exist primarily in Cape Cod and coastal Maine, but this bustling little slice of Connecticut has such diversions in spades. Mystic, Noank, Groton Long Point, and Stonington make up a certifiably quaint and wonderful maritime region, complete with salt-aired villages and galleries proffering marine art and nautical memorabilia.

You'll find dozens of motels, hotels, and inns throughout these parts, as well as in the twin cities of Groton and New London. The former is best known as one of the world's leading manufacturing centers of submarines, while New London is the home of the U.S. Coast Guard Academy and a number of fine historic house-museums (including Eugene O'Neill's childhood home). Mystic Seaport, which anchors the chipper village of the same name, is among southern New England's most visited attractions and takes at least a couple days to explore all the way through.

Issues revolving around livability, pedestrian and auto traffic, urban planning (especially in Groton and New London), and development in general are hot topics around these parts—the opening of two major casinos just a few miles inland has only further challenged the regional infrastructure and the viability of the local economy. In particular, a number of the coastal communities in these parts are debating exactly how historic districts can retain their integrity without preventing development that might be beneficial to the economy.

Visitors should keep in mind that while there's plenty to see and do here, late spring through early fall see substantial crowding throughout the southeastern shoreline, and a bit of planning is ad-

*Mystic, Noank, Groton Long Point, and Stonington make up a certifiably quaint and wonderful maritime region, complete with salt-aired villages and galleries proffering marine art and nautical memorabilia.*

visable. Book rooms as far in advance as possible. Don't rule out a visit during the off-season, either. Mystic Seaport and most of the other regional attractions are open year-round, and there's something romantic about walking along the beach or slurping oysters on the half-shell during the moody, but evocative, winter months.

## OLD LYME TO NEW LONDON

### Old Lyme

As you cross the Connecticut River on I-95, take exit 70, which will deposit you onto Lyme Street in the heart of historic Old Lyme—it's here that America's impressionist art scene blossomed in the late 1800s. You can learn about the legacy, which included Barbizon-trained painter Henry Ward Ranger, as well as Willard Metcalfe and Childe Hassam, at the **Florence Griswold Museum** (96 Lyme St., 860/434-5542, www.flogris.org), which occupies 11 of the 12 original acres of the estate on which patroness of the arts Ms. Griswold hosted various painters (open 10 A.M.– 5 P.M. Tues.–Sat., 1–5 P.M. Sun., Apr.–Sept.; 1–5 P.M. Wed.–Sun. Jan.–Mar.; $7). The 1817 house is a marvel to begin with, sitting on the tranquil Lieutenant River and filled with fine period furnishings, including panels on the dining room wall that were painted by some of the house's famous guests. Historic gardens surround the house, and changing exhibits are mounted at the museum. In 2002, behind the original house and overlooking the Lieutenant River, the museum opened the Robert and Nancy Krieble Gallery, a new center celebrating American art in all its forms. Here in this dramatic, light-filled modern facility you'll find outstanding rotating exhibits; this is also the site of the excellent museum store.

In the same neighborhood, which is also anchored by a pair of historic inns—the Bee and

THE CONNECTICUT COAST

Florence Griswold Museum, Old Lyme

Thistle and the Old Lyme Inn—rotating art shows are presented at the **Lyme Academy of Fine Arts** (84 Lyme St., 860/434-5232, www.lymeacademy.edu, open Tues.–Sun., donation suggested), the 1817 John Still House that now serves as a fine arts college. The third component of the art colony is the **Lyme Art Association** (90 Lyme St., 860/434-7802, www.lymeart.com/oldlyme/laa), the oldest art gallery in the United States, which stages seven exhibitions throughout the year, showing both contemporary and traditional works.

Walk or drive just south of these buildings, and you'll find yourself in the heart of the Old Lyme Historic District, which has several small art galleries and antiques shops, and a great range of interesting buildings spanning from Colonial times to the early 20th century.

If you love horses or you've got kids with you, plan a detour to **McCulloch Farm** (100 Whippoorwill Rd., off U.S. 1, a little more than a mile north of the historic district, Old Lyme, 860/434-7355), which has been breeding prize Morgan horses longer than any other farm in Connecticut. Foals are generally born in April and May, but any time of year visitors may come to ad-

mire and pet the horses (call ahead to confirm it's a good time for visitors).

## East Lyme and Niantic

Back on Rte. 156, continue down through Old Lyme for several miles into East Lyme, which most people know by the name of its largest and most prominent village, Niantic. In fact, if you ask around, you'll learn that many Connecticut residents don't even know there is such a place as East Lyme. Niantic is a popular summer-vacation community, with cottages and weekend homes. It's also the site of one of the area's best public beaches, **Rocky Neck State Park** (Rte. 156 at exit 72 off I-95, 860/739-5471, admission $7–14 depending on time of year and whether you have in- or out-of-state plates, off-season free). A long, shaded road leads from the park entrance down to an immense parking area, which also has space for RVs. A path leads under a rail trestle to the broad expansive beach. Black Point is the stretch of land to the east of the park; jutting out and lined with vacation houses, it's opposite the park limits on the other side of the mouth of the Pattagansett River.

From Rocky Neck, drive another couple miles to reach the bustling village center of Niantic, which has quite a few small shops, a handful of accommodations, and some restaurants—all within walking distance of the sound. Among the many attractions for great fun with kids, the **Children's Museum of Southeastern Connecticut** (409 Main St., 860/691-1111, www.childrensmuseumsect.org) is geared mostly toward the 1–12 age group. The museum consists of numerous touch-friendly and interactive displays, from a scaled trail model of the entire Connecticut shoreline to an actual two-man submarine and a computer where kids can access appropriate websites; there's also a rock-climbing wall (open 9:30 A.M.–4:30 P.M. Tues.–Sat., noon–4 P.M. Sun., until 8 P.M. Fri. and on Mon. in summer and during school breaks, $5).

Nearby, and also appropriate for young ones, the **Millstone Information and Science Center** (278 Main St., 860/444-4207, open weekdays, daily in summer, free) has interactive exhibits on the Millstone Nuclear Power Station discussing nuclear and other forms of energy, from bicycle generators to nuclear reactors. There's also a marine aquarium with touch tanks.

Before continuing along Rte. 156 into the town of Waterford, history and architecture buffs might make a brief detour north on Rte. 161 about two miles and make a left onto Society Road, site of the **Smith-Harris House** (33 Society Rd., 860/739-0761, seasonal hours, free), a Greek Revival-style house filled with exhibits on local history. Also along Rte. 156 in Niantic is the **Thomas Lee House and Little Boston School** (860/739-6070 or 860/739-5079, open 1–4 P.M. Tues.–Sun., $2), a small complex comprising the state's oldest wood-frame schoolhouse (ca. 1660) and the first district school constructed between New York and Boston (ca. 1734). There's also an English herb garden.

## Waterford

In Waterford, continue the scenic tour of the shoreline by making a right turn from Rte. 156 onto Rte. 213, which winds down by the gracious lawns of **Harkness Memorial State Park** (275 Great Neck Rd., Rte. 213, 860/443-5725, open 10 A.M.–3 P.M. Tues.–Sun. Memorial Day–Labor Day), one of the state's most dra-

matic parks and oceanfront estates. The magnificent 42-room Italian villa is open to the public for free guided tours. The grounds sit on a point offering 270-degree views of Long Island Sound. From May to October, admission to the park grounds is $6–10 per car, depending on the day of the week and whether you have in-state license plates; off-season admission is free.

Just west of the park on Rte. 213, you'll pass the grounds of the **Eugene O'Neill Theater Center** (305 Great Neck Rd., 860/443-5378, www.oneilltheatercenter.org), where new theater works are developed and actors and other stage workers trained. Festivals and performances are held here periodically; call for details.

## New London

From Waterford, Rte. 213 passes into the southwestern end of New London, a small semi-industrial city at the mouth of the Thames River—it's home to the U.S. Coast Guard Academy and one of Connecticut's finest private educational institutions, Connecticut College. Where Rte. 213 intersects with Ocean Avenue, detour for a moment with a right turn, which leads down to the city's southernmost point. Here you'll find **Ocean Beach Park** (1225 Ocean Ave., 860/447-3031 or 800/510-SAND, www.ocean-beach-park.com), Connecticut's last remaining Coney Island-style seaside amusement park, complete with a boardwalk, triple water slide and pools, playgrounds, arcade, snack vendors, and mini-golf center (open 9 A.M.–11 P.M. daily, Memorial Day–Labor Day, $12 parking on weekends, $8 on weekdays, $15 for holidays and major concerts; entrance fee is $4 adults, $3 children). There are no major rides or roller coasters, but this is still a great place to come with a group of friends or a pack of wild kids on a weekend—there's plenty to keep everybody busy, and a nice stretch of beachfront, too.

From the park, follow Pequot Avenue east along the shoreline and up alongside the west bank of the Thames River; you'll see a large lighthouse sitting at the mouth of the river and the industrial eastern shoreline of Groton across the way. This neighborhood is where playwright Eugene O'Neill grew up, and the setting of his most famous work, *Long Day's Journey Into Night*. His

# NEW LONDON, GROTON, AND MYSTIC

boyhood house, **Monte Cristo Cottage** (325 Pequot Ave., 860/443-0051) is now a museum (open 10 A.M.–5 P.M. Tues.–Sat., 1–5 P.M. Sun. mid-June–Labor Day, 1–5 P.M. on weekends Labor Day–late Oct., $5).

Pequot Avenue and then Shaw Street lead north to Bank Street, onto which a right turn leads into downtown New London. This historic shipbuilding and whaling center looks worn in places, but there are a number of great old buildings, many that have been—or are being— restored. Additionally, a handful of good eateries and shops have opened on or near the city's two main commercial thoroughfares, Bank Street and State Street, which intersect near the City Pier. Still, it will take considerably more work, time, and investment for New London to realize its full potential.

The street layout downtown is quirky and engaging, a pod of crooked and often narrow lanes that was established well before the American Revolution; the neighborhood is fronted on the east by rail tracks and the Thames River.

Take the time to examine storefronts, building facades, and rooflines—for New London is a lesson in New England architecture. Fortunately, classics like the 1888 H. H. Richardson–designed **Union Station** have resisted attempts at demolition or modernization thanks to the efforts of the area's many dedicated preservationists. On Bank Street, the magnificent 1921 **Capitol Theater** is in the midst of restoration. Other notable buildings worth admiring as you walk around town include the **Soldiers-Sailors Monument** at the foot of State Street; the 21 classic Greek Revival homes currently under renovation along Starr Street; the H. H. Richardson–designed **New London Public Library,** which was built in 1892; the imposing wood-frame **State Court House** at the top of State Street; and **Ye Antientest Burial Place,** on Hempstead Street, which served the city from the 1650s through the late 1700s. Also be sure to get a look, and possible a visit inside, the **New London Maritime Museum** (150 Bank St., 860/447-2501, open 1–5 P.M. Wed.–Fri. and Sun., 10 A.M.–5 P.M. Sat., $5), which is inside the 1833 Customs House and was designed by Robert Mills (of Washington

Monument fame) and recently given a $1 million restoration. This superb example of Federal architecture is noted for its vaulted ceilings, heartpine floors, and flying staircase. It still contains houses of the U.S. Customs office, making it the oldest continuously operated customs house in the country. The Maritime Museum contains exhibits pertaining to the infamous *Amistad* incident (the 53 kidnapped Africans aboard that ship ended up in New London after the *Amistad* grounded off Montauk Long Island in 1839). You'll also learn about Connecticut's long history of submarine manufacturing.

On the same stretch as the graveyard, the **Hempsted Houses** (11 Hempstead St., 860/443-7949 or 860/247-8996, open afternoons Thurs.–Sat. mid-May–mid-Oct., $5) comprise two early examples of residential architecture. The original main house dates from 1678 and was built by the father of shipbuilder and farmer Joshua Hempsted, who with journals documented life in this house for nine generations. Next door is a 1759 house built by Joshua's grandson; it's one of the few 18th-century stone houses in southern New England.

Just around the corner, guided tours of the **Shaw-Perkins Mansion** (11 Blinman St., 860/443-1209, open 1–4 P.M. Wed.–Fri. and 10 A.M.–4 P.M. Sat., $5) illuminate New London's legacy as a major trade and mercantile center during the 1800s. The building was used as Connecticut's naval war office during the American Revolution, and many artifacts and furnishings date to this important period.

A short drive south, via Howard Street, leads to one of the region's top new attractions, **Fort Trumbull State Park** (90 Walbach St., 860/444-7591, http://dep.state.ct.us/stateparks, free), which was constructed in the 18th century and for more than a century protected New London's harbor and the Thames River. From the 1950s through the 1980s, the fort became a Cold War research facility, housing the state-of-the-art Naval Undersea Warfare Center—here sonar and periscope technology and submarine antennas were tested. Grounds and parking open daily 8 A.M.–sunset; there's also 24-hour pedestrian access for fishing enthusiasts and others want-

downtown New London

ing to walk along the pier and waterfront. The former barracks contain a visitor center with exhibits detailing the fort's history.

At this point, it's best to get in your car and head west from downtown on Broad Street (via State), making a right turn on Williams Street and following it north under I-95 toward the campuses of Connecticut College and the Coast Guard Academy. Edging the campus of Connecticut College is the **Lyman Allyn Art Museum** (625 Williams St., 860/443-2545, http://lymanallyn.conncoll.edu), whose collection of more than 30,000 objects highlights the American impressionism movement that was so key to the late–19th- and early–20th-century arts scene in Connecticut. The museum also houses galleries devoted to contemporary, modern, and Early American painting and regional decorative arts. Outside the museum is the Children's Art Park, an interactive walk past engaging sculptures and labyrinthine art installations (open 10 A.M.–5 P.M. Tues.–Sat, 1–5 P.M. Sun., $5).

A short distance beyond the museum is the sweeping 750-acre **Connecticut College Arboretum** (Williams St., 860/439-5020, http://arboretum.conncoll.edu, open dawn–dusk daily;

tours once a week May–Oct, call for times; free), which was begun by the college in 1931 and is as much a place to scamper about and get some exercise as it is a great horticultural learning facility and conservation center. There are four main components to the plant section: the Native Plant Collection, which contains nearly 300 varieties of indigenous trees, shrubs, and woody vines; the Caroline Black Garden, a survey of ornamental trees and shrubs from around the world; the beautifully landscaped grounds of the Connecticut College Campus; and a greenhouse. In May, come to see the colorful dogwood and azalea trees abloom; June is ideal for mountain laurel, and in July, note the fine collections of giant rhododendron, sourwood, and sweet pepperbush. Much of the grounds comprise wetlands, including a salt marsh, a maple bog, and a small pond. A visit here offers a tranquil break from the bustle of downtown New London.

At the arboretum is the **Science Center of Eastern Connecticut** (33 Gallows Ln., 860/442-0391, www.scec.conncoll.edu, open 10 A.M.–6 P.M. Tues.–Sat., 1 P.M.–5 P.M. Sun., $6), where about 100 interactive stations offer visitors a chance to learn about everything from creatures of the forest

© ANDREW COLLINS

## EUGENE O'NEILL

Eugene O'Neill was born in New York City in 1888. Here at Monte Cristo Cottage—during summers at least—he was raised by his dysfunctional and loutish father, James, who earned some fame as a traveling actor best known for his *Count of Monte Cristo.* Hence the cottage's name. Fall through spring, the family largely moved about the country, as James O'Neill's jobs required extensive travel.

Eugene O'Neill set several plays in New London, including *Ah, Wilderness!,* whose lead character was based upon the editor of the *New London Telegraph* who had been O'Neill's boss when he worked as a reporter for the daily. *Long Day's Journey Into Night* earned O'Neill posthumous acclaim—he determined that the work should never be made public during his lifetime, and so it finally made it to Broadway in 1957, four years after the playwright succumbed to pneumonia. Indeed, this starkly moving and deeply sorrowful study of a family's various weaknesses and addictions is closely autobiographical, and O'Neill's own adult life continued the sad legacy. Two of his three marriages failed, and two of his three children met early deaths—one by a drug overdose and the other by suicide. Only his daughter, Oona, lived into old age, but she was estranged from her father for having married a man many years her senior—Charlie Chaplin.

and sea to the world of science. There are additional trails here, oriented more toward kids and families, plus a large picnic grove.

Right by the intersection of Williams and Mohegan Avenues, you'll come to the home of the **United States Coast Guard Academy** (31 Mohegan Ave., on Rte. 32, just off I-95, 860/444-8501, www.cga.edu, campus visitor's center and museum open daily) which was begun in 1876. At that time instruction was entirely aboard the cutter ship, *Dobbin,* but the academy broke ground in 1932 on the western shores of the Thames River, constructing this handsome campus and making New London its home. Presently, students train for their careers fighting oil spills, enforcing immigration and customs laws, and conducting dangerous search-and-rescue missions in classrooms as well as on the school's training ship, the *Eagle.* The academy grounds are freely accessible to the public, and you can wander about the grounds admiring the campus and the *Eagle* (call for visitor hours, 860/444-8270) or inspecting the **Coast Guard Museum** at Waesche Hall (860/444-8511). Here you'll see more than 6,000 nautical artifacts and works of maritime art, including about 200 ship models.

Note that from here you have the option of following Rte. 32 north a few miles to Norwich to continue touring the inland half of the Thames River (by the way, it's pronounced "thaymes" here in Connecticut). Otherwise, hop onto I-95 and cross the Thames, immediately leaving the Interstate via exit 86 for the city of Groton, New London's considerably more industrial urban neighbor.

## GROTON TO STONINGTON
### Groton

For centuries, the hilly riverside land now occupied by Groton was a valuable hunting land, over which Pequot Indians frequently found themselves in battle—initially rebuffing the attacks of Narragansetts from the east, and later English settlers, who developed a trading post here in 1649. The jaunty terrain accounts for Groton's unpredictable layout—streets climb diagonally over hills, dead-end, and flow into one another. Fishing and shipbuilding fed Groton's early coffers, and several hundreds of local men set sail to points throughout the Caribbean, South America, and Africa through the 1700s and 1800s.

Throughout the 20th century, Groton has maintained its ties with the sea by becoming the world's foremost producer of submarines. No tour is complete without a visit to the **Historic Ship *Nautilus* and Submarine Force Museum** (Naval Submarine Base, exit 86 from I-95, follow signs, 860/694-3174 or 800/343-0079, www.ussnautilus.org, open 9 A.M.–5 P.M. Wed.–Mon., 1–5 P.M. Tues., closed Tues. Nov.–mid-May, free). Visitors actually board and explore the U.S.S *Nautilus,* the world's first nuclear-powered submarine and the first ship to

THE CONNECTICUT COAST

reach the North Pole. You can visit the crew's quarters and even stare through a periscope. Other exhibits include an interactive computer that sheds light on how exactly a submarine operates; a replica of the *Turtle,* the world's first submarine (which was invented in nearby Essex by David Bushnell during the American Revolution); and two small theaters that show films on submarine history and technology.

From the sub base, drive south along the shoreline of the Thames, beneath I-95. At the corner of Bridge and Thames Street, you'll pass beside the **U.S. Submarine World War II Veteran's Memorial** (860/399-8666), where a black marble wall lists the many servicemen who perished in submarines during World War II. The wall also has plaques naming each of the 52 boats lost. Continue south along Thames Street along the river, passing through the west side of downtown Groton, for a short distance, making a left turn onto School Street and then a right onto Monument. You'll soon come to **Fort Griswold Battlefield State Park** (Monument St. and Park Ave., 860/445-1729, www.revwar.com/ftgriswold, park open dawn–dusk daily, monument and museum open in summer 10 A.M.–5 P.M. daily, free), the exact spot of the Colonial fort where 85 American militiamen were slaughtered by the British army in a lopsided 1781 battle. A 135-foot-tall monument marks the site and interprets the battle with a series of plaques; you can ascend the 166 steps to the top of the obelisk for fine views of the Thames River Valley.

Norwich-born Benedict Arnold, the former Revolutionary War general who switched allegiances during the war, cost the men their lives. The former commander of Fort Griswold, Arnold led a vast contingent of redcoats in the capture of New London, from which he oversaw the British attack of Groton. It's said the Brits were particularly vicious in their takeover of Groton—when the American commander, Lieutenant Colonel William Ledyard, surrendered his sword with the realization that he and his inexperienced troops couldn't possibly hold the fort, the receiving British officer promptly plunged the weapon back through Ledyard's heart. Perhaps this was an act of retribution on the part of the Brits, whose own acting commander had been felled earlier by Ledyard's servant, an African American named Gordon Freeman (Arnold stayed safely behind and watched from the banks of New London). In any case, the British brutally took Groton, sacking many of its homes. You can also tour the **Ebenezer Avery House** (860/445-1729, limited hours, free), a center-chimney Colonial built in 1750 by a naval ensign—it served as a military hospital following the debacle of 1781.

Return to Thames Street and continue your drive south along the river, past the massive Pfizer Pharmaceutical plant, and eventually make a left turn onto Shennecossett Road, which leads pass the campus of UConn Avery Point. Since 1972, **Project Oceanology** (860/445-9007, www.oceanology.org) has served essentially as a classroom on the water, visited by students and teachers during the school year and the general public in summer for 2.5-hour journeys. Aboard you'll have the chance to assist in trawling for marine life, test seawater for pollution, analyze mud and sand samples, and learn how computers interpret data about the ocean. Two fiberglass boats accommodate up to 50 passengers.

## Groton Long Point

Continue east from the campus, making a left onto Brandegee Avenue and then a right onto Poquonnock Road; continue east until joining with U.S. 1, and then make a right turn a couple miles later onto Groton Long Point Road (Rte. 215). This leads into one of the most impressive coastal residential neighborhoods in the state, Groton Point, whose picturesque streets are lined with mostly brown-shingle Nantucket-style houses staring out over Long Island Sound. There's just one way onto Groton Point, via a narrow causeway, past the Yankee Fisherman restaurant.

## Noank

When you cross back over the causeway and drive back toward the way you came, make a right turn onto Elm Street (Rte. 215) and follow the road into the amazingly well-preserved

© ANDREW COLLINS

**downtown Mystic**

Colonial fishing village of Noank, a sleepy little place if ever there was one. Noank has several marinas, a famous seafood restaurant—Abbott's Lobster in the Rough—and a tiny commercial district with a few shops and basic eateries. It has limited hours, but the **Noank Historical Society** (108 Main St., 860/536-7026) has a curious collection of maritime memorabilia and local bits of history and lore.

## Mystic

From Noank, continue up Rte. 215 a couple of miles to reach downtown Mystic, which is most closely associated with the Mystic Seaport maritime museum, but is itself an extremely pretty and engaging Victorian village. There are a number of fine shops in downtown Mystic, plus a slew of restaurants, coffeehouses, and ice-cream parlors—and it's great fun simply to stand on the drawbridge over the Mystic River and admire the boats on either side await their turn to pass. A fire in 2000 took out several buildings along Main Street, and it isn't clear as of press time what will be built in their place. Also memorable is actually watching the drawbridge open for passing boats—the draw span rises to an enor-

mous height. The **Mystic Art Association** (9 Water St., 860/536-7601, www.mystic-art.org, open 11 A.M.–5 P.M. daily, $2 donation suggested) mounts contemporary works—many of them with a maritime theme—in its three galleries.

Cross the bridge and make a left onto Holmes Street and then another left. Like Colonial Williamsburg in Virginia, or Plimoth Plantation in Massachusetts, **Mystic Seaport** (75 Greenmanville Ave., 860/572-5315 or 888/9-SEAPORT, www.mysticseaport.org) masterfully re-creates an entire 19th-century community—it contains one of the world's greatest maritime museums and one of Connecticut's greatest treasures. The grounds and shops are open 9 A.M.–5 P.M. daily April–October, 10 A.M.–4 P.M. daily November–March, daily admission is $17, with discounts for kids and for ordering tickets online.

The museum was created in 1929 out of the remnants of important shipyards along the Mystic River. It has grown steadily over the years with the acquisition of vintage sailing craft, the establishment of one of the world's foremost maritime libraries and research centers, and its on-going shipbuilding and restoration programs, which are carried out in the shipyards.

The tradition of shipbuilding in Mystic dates from the 1600s, and some 600 vessels were built here between the American Revolution and the creation of Mystic Seaport. Whaling and shipping were major elements of the local economy, and Mystic Seaport occupies former shipyards once run by the Greenman brothers and Charles Mallory. Few communities produced more ships than Mystic during the early 19th century, but here as elsewhere, the tradition slowed considerably following the Civil War (for which Mystic shipyards produced a number of steamboats) and eventually petered out by the early 1900s.

The old-fashionedness of Mystic Seaport will forever be one of its great draws, even in this age when kids are usually not excited about an attraction unless cutting-edge technology is involved. The 17-acre compound of 60 buildings and historic vessels sits on a beautiful broad point on the east bank of the scenic Mystic River, just a few hundred yards north of downtown shops and restaurants and a couple miles north of Long Island Sound. The wood-frame buildings effectively re-create a 19th-century seaport village, the very kind that thrived along the southern New England coast in towns like Essex, New London, Newport, Salem, and Fall River. There's a shipsmith shop, cooperage, sail loft, mast hoop shop, one-room schoolhouse, grocery shop, chapel, hardware store, an 1870s oyster house brought here from New Haven, and a transplanted lifesaving station brought here from Block Island (Rhode Island).

Within the village, docents lead tours; demonstrate various chores, crafts, and vocations of the era; and regale visitors with tales and historical tidbits. Horse-drawn carriages traverse the dirt lanes through the village, which is alive with flower gardens spring through early fall. Seasonal events, from Chowderfest to musical performances, are held throughout the year.

Whaling was a major aspect of this region's history, and a highlight of a visit to Mystic Seaport is stepping aboard the *Charles W. Morgan* (1841),

*Whaling was a major aspect of this region's history, and a highlight of a visit to Mystic Seaport is stepping aboard the* **Charles W. Morgan** *(1841), the last surviving wooden whaler in America.*

the last surviving wooden whaler in America. Other vintage tall ships include the 1882 full-rigged *Joseph Conrad,* a Danish training ship that is today used in the seaport's educational programs, and the *L. A. Dunton,* a 123-foot fishing schooner that dates from 1921 and is the site of cod salting and splitting demonstrations, anchor-raisings, and other intriguing activities. The 1908 *Sabino* was built in East Boothbay, Maine, and is the last of America's wood-hulled, coal-fired, steam passenger ships. Cruises of varying lengths (with separate fees) ply the Mystic River and venture out into the sound.

You can also rent a small rowboat or sailboat from the museum's boathouse, which you can then take for a sail down along the Mystic River. Lessons are available, or you can venture out on one of the many guided tours offered throughout the day. Mystic Seaport also has full docking facilities, so you can actually sail right up and visit via your own boat (reservations required).

The latest and most prominent shipbuilding project at Mystic Seaport is the freedom schooner *Amistad,* which launched in 2000. The $3.1 million, 129-foot vessel is a replica of the one detained during the late 1830s in a tale of controversy regarding the fate of the 53 illegally captured Africans aboard. The ship now sails about the United States acting as an educational ambassador on behalf of Connecticut and the struggle for civil rights.

The maritime galleries at Mystic Seaport are famous, holding a vintage small craft collection of some 400 vessels that is superior to any in the United States, plus thousands of ship models, figureheads, sailor's crafts and arts, and paintings. Mystic Seaport has been a leader in preserving not only early ships themselves, but also the fast-fading traditions of early shipbuilding. Visitors can watch ongoing restorations at the shipyard, which comprises carpenters' shops, metal and paint shops, and an immensely powerful lift dock.

Other attractions include a planetarium, where visitors learn how sailors traditionally navigated using the solar system; a children's museum; and an extensive (and first-rate) collection of stores that include the world-renowned Maritime Gallery at Mystic Seaport, a print shop, a bake shop, and a bookshop; and a full-service restaurant, the Seamen's Inne.

From the seaport, Greenmanville Avenue leads north to a more recently developed part of town—right by exit 90 of I-95—where you'll find the stores of Olde Mistick Village and the Mystic Factory Outlets, as well as the **Mystic Aquarium** (55 Coogan Blvd., exit 90 from I-95, 860/572-5955, www.mysticaquarium.org, open daily year-round, call for exact hours, $16). There are some 6,000 creatures at this impressive aquarium. Many exhibits have been added in recent years. There's a 30,000-gallon exhibit with bonnethead sharks, which contains 500 of what are described as the most exotic and beautiful species in the world. You'll also see jellyfish, dolphins, 1,000-pound beluga whales, African penguins, and sea lions.

Head back down Greenmanville Avenue. For a change of pace from some of the area's more commercial attractions, make a left turn onto Mistuxet Avenue and a second left to reach the

**Denison Homestead Museum at Pequotsepos Manor** (120 Pequotsepos Rd., 860/536-9248, limited hours, open mid-May–mid-Oct., $4). It's a formidable 1717 center-chimney house that's furnished with antiques and heirlooms from several generations of the Denison family. The museum neighbors the **Denison Pequotsepos Nature Center** (109 Pequotsepos Rd., 860/536-1216, open daily, $4), a 125-acre preserve crossed by about seven miles of trails. There's also a natural history museum and a bookstore.

## Stonington

Follow U.S. 1 east to U.S. 1A and then south into little Stonington, which was settled by a family from the Plymouth Colony in 1649 and then grew over time into a trading post and busy Colonial shipping, whaling, and shipbuilding center. During the great industrial age of the 19th century, Stonington acted as the terminus of the newly built coast railroad; from trains cargo was moved onto steamships, which sailed to any number of exotic places. The village has changed little, seemingly, in appearance over the past century, as it's still lined with Colonial and Victorian

© ANDREW COLLINS

**Stonington village**

houses, from immense sea captains' mansions to smaller bungalows. Perhaps no other community in Connecticut captures the spirit of coastal New England as well as Stonington.

Nearly sold for subdivision a few years back, the **Captain Nathaniel B. Palmer House** (N. Water and Palmer Sts., 860/535-8445, www.stoningtonhistory.org/palmer.htm, open 10 A.M.–4 P.M. Tues.–Sun. May–Nov., donation requested) now houses the Stonington Historical Society and is a fine example of the 1850s mansions built with the wealth of maritime traders and explorers. Appropriately, a grand widow's walk extends across the roofline. It was aboard the 47-foot sloop *Hero* that the 21-year-old explorer, Nathaniel B. Palmer—along with his brother Alexander—set out on a mission to find new seal rookeries and along the way identified an as-yet unchartered piece of land—a place we now call Antarctica. The Palmers built this 16-room mansion in 1852 on Pine Point, which afforded fine views of the area. The beautiful woodworking attests to the wealth of these men; inside also hang portraits of the Palmers and their families, plus a considerable trove of memorabilia pertaining to their maritime exploits.

If you'd sailed to the eastern tip of Connecticut in about 1830, on a clear night some 10 miles out you'd catch the flicker of a lighthouse in the distance, now Stonington's **Old Lighthouse Museum** (7 Water St., 860/535-1440, open 10 A.M.–5 P.M. daily July–Aug., donation suggested). The 30-foot stone tower in which parabolic reflectors broadcast the glow from 10 oil lamps is formidable, standing importantly over pebbly DuBois Beach. In 1889, a beacon was built on the new breakwater at the fore of Stonington harbor, thus rendering the old lighthouse superfluous. The Stonington Historic Society took residence in 1927, and has displayed the everyday tools and belongings of area farmers, fishers, shipbuilders, and merchants ever since in six austerely decorated rooms. In one, a substantial dollhouse contains miniatures.

About five miles north of the village (just follow Main Street across Rte. 234 until it becomes Taugwonk Rd.), **Stonington Vineyards** (523 Taugwonk Rd., Stonington, 860/535-1222, www.stoningtonvineyards.com) is a relatively small but prolific facility set on 12 gorgeous, rolling acres. The winery tour here is one of the better ones, and there's also a small art gallery worth checking out after you take a moment to sample some wines. The vineyard is open daily.

A short drive away in North Stonington, the **Jonathan Edwards Winery** (74 Chester Maine Rd., 860/535-0202, www.jedwardswinery.com) is one of Connecticut's younger, but already most popular, wineries. Set in a dramatic barn and farmhouse with 48 acres of rolling grounds, this winery is unusual in that it produces wines using Napa Valley grapes, which it buys from top California vineyards. Eventually, plans are to start growing Connecticut grapes for wine production, but the vineyards here are still a bit to young for this purpose. Guests can tour the winery and burgeoning vineyards, bring a picnic lunch to enjoy on the grounds, and, of course, buy bottles of the chardonnays, white zinfandels, zinfandels, merlots, syrahs, and cabernet sauvignons.

## SHOPPING

In North Stonington, **Raspberry Junction** (417 Rte. 2, 860/535-8410) is a vast treasury of crafts from across America, from baskets and pottery to hang from your kitchen rafters to carved wooden birdcages to hang outside your porch door. It's a barn full of goods that will keep the Martha Stewart in you busy for the better part of an afternoon. Crafts demonstrations are frequently given.

Just off I-95 is Connecticut's version of Sturbridge Village, **Olde Mistick Village** (860/536-4941, www.oldmysticvillage.com), a re-created 1700s village comprising about 60 shops (or "shoppes" in the village's folksy, and cloying, vernacular) offering the usual touristy goodies, but also some very interesting arts and crafts. At the "meetinghouse," church bells chime every 15 minutes and weddings are held regularly. A duck pond makes for a favorite visit among kids, while walkways throughout the village are lined with fragrant floral gardens and shrubbery. By the vintage water wheel and the Victorian gazebo, storytellers and musicians are typically on hand to entertain. This is good, old-fashioned family entertainment—the village motto is "easy to get to . . . hard to leave" but could just as easily be "you can never have too many scented candles." Several restaurants are based here, including the phenomenally popular Go Fish and a reputable steak house, the Steak Loft. Just across the street from Olde Mistick Village are the **Mystic Factory Outlets** (Coogan Blvd., 860/443-4788) a 24-store collection of national-brand retailers. Book browsers should pop inside **Bank Square Books** (53 W. Main St., Mystic, 860/536-3795), an excellent independent general-interest store.

Although it underwent an ambitious remodeling in 1999, the **New London Mall** (Frontage Rd., just off I-95 by the bridge over the Thames River, New London, 860/442-3111, www.newlondonmall.com) is a fairly ordinary midrange facility anchored by **Office Max** and **Marshalls.** Considerably more impressive in the eyes of most retail junkies is the nearby **Crystal Mall** (Rte. 85, exit 92 from I-95, 860/442-8500, www.crystal-mall.com), which has a big ol' food court and several prominent anchor stores including **Macy's, JCPenney, Filene's,** and **Sears.**

Stonington's quaint Colonial village is one of the top centers for antiquing in coastal Con-

necticut—there are about 10 shops, many of them specializing in maritime art and collectibles, along Water Street, beginning around the village green and continuing south. There is also a bunch of great shops—from antiques stores to frame shops to clothiers—around downtown Mystic, particularly west of the drawbridge. And of course, don't overlook the many shops that are a part of Mystic Seaport.

Pick-your-own farming is popular for apples at **Willow Spring Farm** (1030 Noank-Ledyard Rd., Mystic, 860/536-3083) and for apples, peaches, strawberries, blueberries, and pumpkins at **Scott's Yankee Farmer** (436 Boston Post Rd., on U.S. 1, East Lyme, 860/739-5209).

## RECREATION
### Bicycling
The southeastern shoreline is prime cycling territory, as it's relatively flat and offers some beautiful rides, especially through Groton Long Point, Noank, Mystic, and Stonington on the east side of the region, and through Old Lyme, Niantic, and Waterford on the west side. Several shops in the area rent bicycles, including **Bicycle Barn** (1209 Poquonnock Rd., Groton, 860/448-2984;

© ANDREW COLLINS

**boats in Stonington Harbor**

also in Niantic at 7 Hope St., 860/739-2453); and **Mystic Cycle Centre** (42 Williams Ave., 860/572-7433).

## Golf

Popular area golf courses include **Shennecosset** (Plant St., Groton, 860/445-0262), and **Pequot Golf Club** (127 Wheeler Rd., Stonington, 860/535-1898), which both have fairly challenging 18-hole courses, and **Elmridge Golf Course** (227 Elmridge Rd., Pawcatuck, 860/599-2248), which has 27 holes.

## Hiking

Several of the state parks mentioned above have good trails for hiking, although most of Connecticut's best and most extensive trail networks lie inland away from the congested coastline. Still, you'll find trails at **Rocky Neck State Park** in Niantic, and **Harkness Memorial State Park** in Waterford. In Stonington, birdwatchers and outdoors enthusiasts will find plenty to keep them occupied at **Barn Island State Wildlife Management Area** Palmer Neck Rd., Stonington. Another good spot for both hiking and beach activities is **Nehantic State Park** (Rte. 156, Lyme, 860/434-7733).

## Horseback Riding

**Trail Blazers at the Stable** (711 Stonington Rd., Stonington, 860/535-2962) offers guided trail rides through the wooded countryside; no experience is required.

## ENTERTAINMENT AND NIGHTLIFE

At Connecticut College in New London, **Palmer Auditorium** (270 Mohegan Ave., 860/439-ARTS) presents an esteemed series of classic music, dance, and jazz concerts throughout the school year. World-renowned artists have been drawn here. The restored art deco **Garde Arts Center** (329 State St., New London, 860/444-7373 or 888/ON-GARDE) is a major regional performance venue, hosting big-name musicians and bands as well as Broadway shows, a cabaret series, family-oriented entertainment, and a prestigious film series shown on one of the largest screens in the county. This 1,500-seat former vaudeville house is also home to the **Eastern Connecticut Symphony Orchestra** (860/443-2876). In Waterford, an acclaimed music series is held on the manorly grounds of **Harkness State Park** (860/442-9199 or 800/969-3400, July–Aug.).

New London and Mystic are the area's main nightlife centers, with the latter having the strongest draw among tourists. There you can go for laughs at **Treehouse Comedy Club** or musical comedies at the **Odyssey Dinner Theater,** both of which are at the Best Western Sovereign Hotel, Rte. 27, Mystic, 860/536-7126. There's live music most nights at **Trader Jack's** (14 Holmes St., New London, 860/572-8550). **41° North** (21 W. Main St., 860/536-9821) is a laid-back smoky tavern with decent burgers and a crowded singles scene.

In New London, the **Bulkeley House Restaurant and Pub** (111 Bank St., 860/443-5533) is in a red, 1790s Colonial with twin chimneys—it's an appealing spot for a drink or to hang with locals; basic American fare is served, too. The **Bank Street Roadhouse** (36 Bank St., 860/443-8280) hosts live blues and rock on weekends, while **Bank Street Café** (653 Bank St., 860/444-1444) presents various music genres throughout the weekends. One of the longest-standing performance spaces in the region, **El n' Gee Club** (86 Golden St., 860/437-3800) books innovative and offbeat bands, including some national acts.

In Waterford, the **Post Road Brewing Co.** (49 Boston Post Rd., on U.S. 1, 860/442-1200) is an English-inspired brewpub with a second-floor game area with backgammon, chess, and such. New London has a pair of gay clubs, **Frank's** (9 Tilley St., 203/443-8883) and a friendly little storefront lounge called **Heroes** (33 Golden St., 860/442-HERO).

## FESTIVALS AND EVENTS
### Spring and Summer

Crustacean lovers flock to **Lobsterfest** (Mystic Seaport, 860/572-5315 or 888/9-SEAPORT), a weekend-long late-May celebration where eating is but one of many family-oriented activities—this is one of the many festivals and concerts held at Mystic Seaport year-round; call for a full list or visit www.mysticseaport.org.

Groton's U.S. Naval Submarine Base is, appropriately, the site of **Subfest** (exit 86 from I-95, 860/694-3238) a Fourth-of-July-weekend celebration with entertainment and activities aboard the *Nautilus* submarine—one imagines that submarine sandwiches must figure into the fun at this event. Later in the month, come to the North Stonington Grange Fair Grounds for the **Agricultural Fair** (860/535-2877). Downtown New London comes alive each summer to partake of **SailFest,** a lively celebration in mid-July that includes a the arrival in the harbor of several vintage tall ships, the largest fireworks display in New England, live music, and many other family- and adult-oriented activities. Boating—and seafood—enthusiasts may want to head to Stonington Village in late July to partake of the **Blessing of the Fleet** at the town dock (860/535-3150). The **Midsummer Festival** (Lyme Academy of Fine Arts, 84 Lyme St., Old Lyme, 860/434-5232) draws culture vultures and kids, too, with everything from an arts festival to a petting zoo and pony rides. The **Mystic Outdoor Art Festival** (860/572-9578) takes over historic downtown Mystic in early August; fans of nautical and maritime painting shouldn't miss this one.

### Fall and Winter

Early September's **Boats, Books, and Brushes** (860/443-8332) is great fun—this three-day event showcases vintage schooners and celebrates the region's literary and arts heritage with storytelling, arts exhibits, and performances. In October, towns throughout the region celebrate **Eastern Connecticut Walking Weekend** with a variety of outdoors events timed perfectly to coincide with peak foliage-watching; for information, call 860/963-7226. During the holiday season, Mystic kicks into gear with the **Festival of Lights** (860/536-4941), which sees the aquarium, Olde Mistick Village, and other area attractions decked with luminaria. On New Year's Eve, **First Night Mystic** (860/536-3575) comprises a variety of festivities and live performances at locations throughout the historic downtown.

## ACCOMMODATIONS

While you'll find quite a few decent motels and chain properties in southeastern Connecticut, this area offers so many characterful and intriguing country inn experiences that it's a shame to stay some place bereft of history and character. Furthermore, rates are relatively steep here in summer whether you stay at a chain or an inn. That said, a few of the better chain properties are described below, along with a considerable number of inns. (In fact, there was room to include only a sampling of the many fine B&Bs and historic accommodations in greater Mystic; check out **www.visitmystic.com** to get a sense of others in this area.) Summer—and even spring and fall—really can fill up in these parts, so it pays to plan and book ahead whenever possible. Remember also that off-season rates, especially January–March, drop sharply—as much as 50 percent—and many places close down for a few weeks or months during the slower periods.

### Hotels and Motels

**$150–250:** The **Marriott Mystic Hotel and Spa** (625 North Rd./Rte. 117, Groton, 860/446-2600 or 800/228-9290) is the newest luxury property in southeastern Connecticut. It's a lavish 285-room, six-floor property with top-notch facilities. A major draw is the exclusive Elizabeth Arden Red Door Salon, a handsome full-service spa offering a wide range of treatments. Rooms have work desks with lamps and upscale furnishings, and other hotel facilities include a full-service restaurant, room service, a coffee shop, business center, indoor pool, health club, whirlpool, and sauna.

The **Mystic Hilton** (20 Coogan Blvd., 860/572-0731) is the most luxurious of chain hotels in town. A drawback to some is being up by I-95, but on the other hand, the shops of Olde Mistick and various outlet complexes, plus the aquarium, are within a walk of the hotel. And downtown Mystic is just a short drive from this 184-room redbrick property. There's a very nice indoor pool and fitness center, and the restaurant is extremely good.

The 80-room **AmeriSuites** (224 Greenmanville Ave., on Rte. 27, 860/536-9997 or 800/833-1516) is ideal for families, as all rooms have sitting areas, kitchenettes, and plenty of room to spread out. Another excellent option for longer stays is the relatively new **Marriott Residence Inn** (40 Whitehall Ave., 860/536-5150 or 888/824-2822, www.wghotels.com/ribmmystic), an all-suite property with an indoor pool, exercise room, grocery-shopping service, and units with full kitchens and separate living areas.

Long one of the top accommodations choices in southeastern Connecticut, the **Inn at Mystic** (U.S. 1 at Rte. 27, 860/536-9604 or 800/237-2415, www.innatmystic.com) sits high on a 15-acre bluff overlooking Mystic Harbor and Long Island Sound. The 67 rooms are spread among several buildings, ranging from newer spacious motel buildings to a vintage gatehouse with antiques-filled suites to a 1904 Colonial Revival inn where Lauren Bacall and Humphrey Bogart once honeymooned. Quite a few rooms have wood-burning fireplaces and whirlpool tubs, and there's tennis and walking trails on property. Intriguing packages are offered throughout the year, making this a more affordable option than you might expect. The inn's Flood Tide restaurant is one of the best in town, especially during weekend brunches.

**$100–150:** Another fine option is the **Best Western Sovereign Hotel Mystic** (9 Whitehall Ave., 860/536-4281 or 800/780-7234), which is just a few blocks from Olde Mistick, the aquarium, and the outlet shops and has shuttle service to both Foxwoods and Mohegan Sun casinos. An exercise room, game room, kids' playground, and indoor heated pool make it a popular spot among families. There's also a Ground Round restaurant on the premises.

The **Whaler's Inn** (20 E. Main St., 860/536-1506 or 800/243-2588, www.whalersinnmystic.com) consists of both Victorian buildings and a nicely maintained motor court within steps of the shops and bustle of downtown Mystic. It's a great all-around property, and although most rooms are in the newer motor court, they're all furnished tastefully with four-poster beds, wingback chairs, and Colonial-style furnishings. The on-site restaurant, Bravo, Bravo, is one of the best in region; there's also a bagel-and-coffee shop.

It's hard to miss Groton's **Thames Inn and Marina** (193 Thames St., 860/445-8111); apparently the owners are trying to set some sort of record for having the rustiest sign in America—at this point, it's almost charming. Fortunately, rooms are nice, and the staff is too. The fact that rooms have fully equipped kitchens is a plus for families or long-term visitors, and the hotel is on a relatively pleasant stretch of the Thames River. There are 20 boat slips with power and water, too, at the marina.

Just off I-95 by the Coast Guard Academy, Connecticut College, and downtown New London, the **Holiday Inn** (360 Bayonet St., 860/442-0631 or 800/HOLIDAY) is a pleasant upscale property with 136 rooms. Furnishings are typical of this genre, but fairly new and well taken care of. There's a pool, exercise room, restaurant, and sports bar on the premises. Parents of students at area colleges and tourists alike also favor the 120-room **Radisson New London** (35 Governor Winthrop Blvd., 860/443-7000 or 800/333-3333), a full-service hotel with an indoor pool and a decent restaurant.

**SpringHill Suites by Marriott** (401 N. Frontage Rd., Waterford, 860/439-0151 or 888/287-9400, www.springhillsuites.com) is an ideal choice if you're planning a longer stay. Each unit has a well-stocked kitchenette, one or two beds and pull-out sofa, complimentary Continental breakfast, free local calls, data ports, and a good work desk. Facilities include a pool, hot tub, and exercise room. The hotel is right off I-95, convenient to New Haven and to the shore communities nearby.

**$50–100:** The **Niantic Inn** (345 Main St., Niantic, 860/739-5451, www.nianticinn.com) is one of the better midpriced lodgings in coastal Connecticut—it's an easy walk from the beach and the many shops of this seaside community within the town of East Lyme. All of the 24 rooms are full 400-square-foot suites with kitchenettes, climate control, and tasteful, modern furnishings.

## Country Inns and Bed-and-Breakfasts

**$150–250:** No hotel in downtown Mystic has a more alluring setting than the intimate and luxurious **Steamboat Inn** (73 Steamboat Wharf, off W. Main St., Mystic, 860/536-8300, www.visitmystic.com/steamboat), whose 10 expansive rooms overflow with elegant light-wood furnishings, floral bedspreads, and TVs hidden inside large wooden armoires. Six rooms have fireplaces, all have whirlpool baths, and several rooms look directly over the Mystic River.

Much of the land surrounding the **Old Lyme Inn** (Lyme St., exit 70 from I-95, 860/434-5352, www.oldlymeinn.com), an 1850 working inn of 300 acres, was truncated when I-95 was constructed just south of the main building in the 1950s. Then, in the following decade, a fire swept through and destroyed much of what remained. Finally, in 1976, the graceful but neglected building was purchased and fully restored, its staircases and walls rebuilt from top to bottom. Today's inn, which was bought and heavily refurbished by new owners in 2001, looks better than ever, and a large row of trees blocks the

Inn at Stonington

noise and views of the nearby Interstate. Rooms are done with a tasteful assortment of Empire and Victorian pieces; all have phones and TVs, and some have canopied beds. There's a fine restaurant on the premises, and rates include a country-style Continental breakfast.

Many travelers will appreciate the theme of **Antiques & Accommodations** (32 Main St., North Stonington, 860/535-1736 or 800/554-7829, www.antiquesandaccommodations.com), a stunning Victorian house in the heart of a picturesque village center that's a short drive from Mystic, Stonington village, and the casinos. This big 1861 B&B is decked in fabulous antiques (collected by the owners on countless trips to Great Britain). Next door, a smaller 1820s center-chimney cottage contains a few more rooms. All are beautifully decorated, and a stay here includes one of the better breakfasts in southeastern Connecticut—crab soufflé and banana waffles are a couple of favorites.

At **High Acres B&B** (222 Northwest Corner Rd., North Stonington, 860/887-4355 or 888/680-7829, www.highacresbb.com) you can actually join your hosts for a horseback ride along one of this 150-acre property's many groomed trails. Accommodations are in a lavishly decorated 1740s colonial on a meadow-crossed estate; there are four large guest rooms with private baths, and a full country breakfast is presented.

A stunning cross between a small luxury hotel and a charming country inn, the 18-room **Inn at Stonington** (60 Water St., 860/535-2000, www.innatstonington.com) opened in 2001, and has quickly set the new standard for deluxe accommodations in southeastern Connecticut. The main building sits on a wharf overlooking Skipper's Dock restaurant, and many rooms have sensational harbor views—and some have balconies; a second neighboring building contains several more guest rooms. Although it's a new construction, the inn has classic detailed molding and Greek Revival influences and styles typical of Stonington's many 18th- and 19th-century mansions. Bathrooms are spacious with whirlpool hot tubs, separate showers, and high-quality bath amenities. Rooms have fireplaces but are all decorated differently, some with Asian and African touches,

THE CONNECTICUT COAST

© ANDREW COLLINS

**Lighthouse Inn, New London**

others with a more traditional New England aesthetic—lavish custom-made beds with carved headboards, recessed lighting, high chests with drawers, and high-thread-count linens are typical. Guests can arrive by boat, using the inn's 400-foot deepwater dock. A late-afternoon wine-and-cheese reception is held daily, and Continental breakfast is included. This is the only accommodation in downtown Stonington village.

**Randall's Ordinary** (Rte. 2, just north of I-95, exit 92, North Stonington, 860/599-4540, www.randallsordinary.com) captures the spirit of early Colonial Connecticut better than any hostelry in the state. Set on 250 wooded acres, this 1680s building has preserved many early traditions, including open-hearth cooking. There are a few rooms on the second floor of the main building, all with austere but romantically authentic furnishings, including antique canopy beds, antique rockers and dressers, hand-woven blankets, and fireplaces in each room. Another 12 rooms are inside a dramatic 1819 barn. A favorite accommodation, especially if it's a very special occasion, is the Silo Suite, which has a fireplace, Adirondack birch bed, and two-person whirlpool tub. The inn is owned by Foxwoods Casino.

**$100–150:** A courtly Greek Revival mansion on three tree-shaded acres just north of downtown, the **House of 1833** (72 N. Stonington Rd., Mystic, 860/536-6325 or 800/FOR-1833, www.houseof-1833.com) ranks among the most luxurious accommodations in the area. Even so, rooms (all with private bath) begin at only around $100. You'll find both antiques and new pieces here, but most exude a sumptuous Victorian feel; guests also have use of a large and impressive landscaped pool, a Har-Tru tennis court, and several 18-speed bicycles. Hosts Carol and Matt Nolan serve an extravagant two-course full breakfast.

For sheer history, you might want to consider the rambling, gambrel-roofed **Adams House** (382 Cow Hill Rd., Mystic, 860/572-9551, www.adamshouseofmystic.com), a lovely 1750s structure still with many of its original architectural details, including a fireplace-warmed dining room (and two guest rooms with fireplaces), plus a mix of fine antiques. All six rooms have private baths, and a separate guest house has two more rooms.

The **Queen Anne Inn** (265 Williams St., New London, 860/447-2600 or 800/347-8818, www.queen-anne.com) is a perfect example of the architectural style for which it's named, and sits on the edge of a historic neighborhood that has unfortunately been bisected by an I-95 overpass. Still, this mustard-yellow and red house cuts a regal figure. There are nine rooms on three floors, including an especially romantic Tower Suite fashioned out of the turreted top floor, with its own kitchen. All rooms have antiques, and many reveal such original details as dark paneling and rustic fireplaces.

Built in 1901 by industrialist Charles Strong Guthrie, the **Lighthouse Inn** (6 Guthrie Place, New London, 860/443-8411, or 888/600-5681, www.lighthouseinn-ct.com), was originally a private mansion called Meadow Court and stood on 12 acres fronting the Thames River and Long Island Sound. The famed Olmsted brothers originally laid out the grounds. Today, most of the acres have been developed into a suburban neighborhood, and the massive old house now operates as a handsome 50-room property with upscale furnishings and views of the water from some rooms (27 rooms are in the mansion itself, while a carriage house contains another 23 rooms, and a studio can sleep six comfortably). The on-site restaurant, Timothy's, is one of the best in New London, and there's swimming in Long Island Sound a stone's throw from the front door.

The **Bee and Thistle Inn** (100 Lyme St., Old Lyme, 860/434-1667 or 800/622-4946, www.bee-andthistleinn.com) ranks among the most lavish and finely appointed country hotels in the state. This classic yellow gambrel-roofed 1765 Colonial sits on five and a half impeccably maintained acres of tree-shaded lawns and gardens alongside the placid Lieutenant River. A sweeping carved staircase leads through the center foyer into the upper floors, which contain 11 antiques-filled guest rooms of varying shapes and sizes—there's also a romantic cottage with a kitchen and fireplace. There's an outstanding restaurant here, too.

**Another Second Penny Inn** (870 Pequot Tr., Stonington, 860/535-1710, www.second-penny.com) is a striking, wood-frame 1710 Colonial farmhouse. The three guest rooms are spacious and have fireplaces, whirlpool tubs, four-poster beds, and mostly Federal and Georgian-style antiques. An exquisite five-course breakfast is included. It's just three miles from downtown Mystic.

## Campgrounds

There's overnight camping at **Rocky Neck State Park** (Rte. 156, Niantic, 860/739-5471) where you'll find 165 sites, showers, and a small restaurant and snack bar. Popular commercial campgrounds in the region include **Camp Niantic by the Atlantic** (Rte. 156, Niantic, 860/739-9308) with 76 sites; **Seaport Campground** (Rte. 184, Old Mystic, 860/536-4044) with 130 sites; and **Highland Orchards Resort Park** (Rte. 49, North Stonington, 860/599-5101 or 800/624-0829), which has 260 sites and a free weekend shuttle that runs back and forth to Foxwoods Casino. All three have camp stores, bath facilities, and the sorts of amenities you'd expect at a large-scale facility.

## FOOD

You'll do well to visit southeastern Connecticut on an empty stomach, as excellent restaurants proliferate. The seafood shanties that are a fixture for the full length of the coastline tend to have more authentic and secluded settings in these parts, in many cases down narrow village streets overlooking the water. Several of the many hotels have notable restaurants, and the tourist buzz of Mystic accounts for that area's bounty of dining options. What the area lacks, at least compared with the central shore and New Haven, are restaurants specializing in distinctly ethnic cuisine, as is true of eastern Connecticut on the whole.

### Upscale

Just up the road from Old Lyme's art museums are two venerable inns. The **Bee and Thistle Inn** (100 Lyme St., exit 70 from I-95, Old Lyme, 860/434-1667, $21–30) is the more formal and dramatic of the two, a gambrel-roofed 1750s house with delightful gardens surrounding it. The kitchen presents arguably the finest contemporary cuisine of any restaurant in southeastern Connecticut. The menu changes seasonally, but has featured a crab-and-gruyère tart over creamed spinach; Thai green curry scallops served with sugar-snap peas, julienned red peppers, baby corn, and jasmine rice.

Across and slightly down the road, the **Old Lyme Inn** (Lyme St., 860/434-5352, $21–34) has a venerable dining room renowned for both classic and cutting-edge Continental fare, including a starter of pepper-crusted rare tuna with pickled ginger and wasabi mayo, and entrées such as pan-seared rainbow trout with fresh asparagus and Portobello risotto, and an asparagus-Cointreau coulis; and gnocchi with with fresh spring peas, artichoke, spring onions, and a roasted-tomato chardonnay sauce. Exceptional wine list.

Dinner at North Stonington's **Randall's Ordinary** (Rte. 2, just north of I-95, exit 92, 860/599-4540, prix fixe $39) harkens back to the very earliest Colonial times; meals are cooked in deep cauldrons and Dutch ovens over an open hearth and served in a spare (in that Puritanical sort of way) dining room inside a 1685 house, where on many nights a harpist plays music from the Colonial era. Note the trap door leading to an old root cellar, which once harbored runaway slaves during the house's tenure as a stop on the Underground Railroad. In the tap room off the main dining room, port, Madeira wine, and hot-mulled cider are available. Recipes, some of which actually come from the records of the inn's original 18th-century proprietors, are authentic to the Colonial period: sage-roasted capon, and Nantucket scallops are possibilities—dinner is a prix fixe affair with your choice of entrée plus wonderful soups and sides like potato-leek pie and butternut-squash soup. At lunch, try the local seafood stew, which is lightly seasoned and simmered slowly in a heavy cast-iron kettle. The waitstaff is clad in period costumes from the 17th and 18th centuries.

**Flood Tide** (U.S. 1 and Rte. 27, 203/536-8140, $22–34), the acclaimed restaurant at the Inn at Mystic, is high on a hilltop, from which commanding views of Long Island Sound are had—understandably, the setting is popular during the day, and brunch is an especially popular scene. The Flood Tide churns out fine classic Continental cuisine, including pepper-seared tornadoes of beef with roasted shallot–bourbon cream, served with gorgonzola polenta rounds, fire-roasted sweet red peppers, and crisp haricots verts. Desserts are lusty and dramatic.

## Creative but Casual

Romantic and affordable, Stonington's **Water Street Café** (142 Water St., 860/535-2122, $7–20) serves wonderfully eclectic and consistently delicious food from a frequently changing repertoire. Grilled lamb loin paillard with watercress, fried capers, and a creamy mint vinaigrette, and warm duck salad with an asparagus and sesame-orange dressing are a couple of popular standbys, but there are always intriguing specials, too. (Note also the tuna tartare appetizer with ponzu sauce, the chili, and burgers.) The dining room has but a handful of tightly spaced tables (it can be near impossible to get a table on a busy night), a small bar, and soft live music many nights—it's especially inviting on a cold winter night. Another gem of a restaurant in Stonington, **Noah's** (113 Water St., 860/535-3925, $12–20) presents a fairly short and simple menu of daily entrées, including char-grilled salmon with dill butter. But check out the daily list of some 15 specials, which might include grilled spice-rubbed mako shark with mango-lime relish. Occupying adjoining storefronts, the right-hand dining room is also an art gallery; both spaces are eminently charming and have wooden booths and tables.

**Boom** (194 Water St., Stonington, 860/535-2588, $15–20) has garnered tremendous praise from area food critics; this unprepossessing space overlooks a sprawling marina and boatyard in Stonington village. Most of the tightly spaced tables face the water, which is a plus—as is the reasonably priced and generally tasty New American cooking, such as sweet potato ravioli with grilled chicken and sage cream sauce. However, service ranges from haughty to airheaded, portions are somewhat small, and the decor—outside of the great views—isn't particularly noteworthy. See for yourself if Boom deserves its thunderous applause. There's a second Boom in Westbrook (Brewer's Pilot Point Marina, 63 Pilot's Point Dr., 860/399/2322).

Not by any stretch is **Bravo, Bravo** (Whaler's Inn, 18 E. Main St., 203/536-3228, $18–25) your ordinary hotel restaurant—this highly respected purveyor of contemporary Northern Italian fare could easily stand on its own in any setting in Connecticut. Walk through the front door, and you'll be nearly bowled over by the palpable aroma of garlic and spices—closely spaced tables crowd the hardwood floors, the front ones with sidewalk views through large plate-glass windows. The menu changes often, but might offer seafood sausage stuffed with lobster and scallops, served over caramelized shallots in a red wine and vanilla sauce; veal ravioli served with marinara, mushrooms, and goat cheese; or Maryland crab cakes topped with a rich lobster chive sauce. The sort of restaurant downtown New London badly needed for so many years, **Timothy's** (Lighthouse Inn, 6 Guthrie Place, New London, 860/443-8411, $17–27) opened downtown in the late 1990s, moved in 2002 to the Lighthouse Inn, and has impressed everybody with its combination of efficient but easygoing service and creative but accessible cooking. Among the excellent entrées, pan-seared Portabello mushroom, spinach, capers, sundried tomatoes, artichoke hearts, garlic, and a white wine butter sautéed and served with fettuccine is a winner. There's also a lavish Sunday brunch.

A reliable, convivial longtime favorite, the **Daniel Packer Inne** (32 Water St., Mystic, 860/536-3555, $16–24) occupies a characterful white 1756 gambrel-roof house in the heart of Mystic. There's both a pub and a somewhat more formal dining room, and in either you can sample consistently good lobster rolls, goat cheese salad, rack of lamb with a wild strawberry demiglace, and fresh Stonington scallops sautéed with shallots and lemon and finished with spring truffles, sweet-cream butter, and fresh chives.

A terrific new eatery in New London, **La Vie En Rose** (130 Pequot Ave., 860/444-8860, around $25 prix fixe) is helmed by the former chef of the famous Wild Boar in Nashville; in fact, he's also cooked privately for a who's who of celebrities. In this modest bistro in up-and-coming New London, he prepares surprisingly affordable contemporary French fare, such as slow-cooked center-cut sea bass Provençal with diver scallops served over pesto risotto; and a napoleon of roasted vegetables with a fresh–fava bean sauce and a potato-crisp cake. There's also a very nice á la carte lunch menu.

A short drive from the museums and historic district of Old Lyme, **Anne's Bistro** (Old Lyme Marketplace, Halls Rd., on U.S. 1, 860/434-9837, $13–24), which began in the late 1970s as a catering business, has evolved into a wonderful full-scale restaurant. A subtly creative menu of American and Continental favorites is presented, from triple mushroom risotto to salmon baked with a fresh herb crust and served with horseradish sauce. There's always a fresh catch of the day, whose preparation runs according to available produce and ingredients. Hanging plants and colorful artwork brighten the setting.

## Pizza, Pub Grub, and Seafood

Things might have been very different for **Mystic Pizza** (56 W. Main St., 860/536-3700 or 860/536-3737, $6–17, large pies $10–17) had screenwriter Amy Jones not poked her head inside this otherwise unprepossessing family-run parlor in the center of town. But she did. And in 1988, the motion picture *Mystic Pizza* opened, helping to launch the careers of Julia Roberts, Annabeth Gish, and Lili Taylor. Much of the movie was filmed around town—now the restaurant is regionally famous and wildly popular. As for the pizza itself: not bad, but by no means the best in a state famous for it. Still, specialty combos like barbecue chicken and "seafood delight" pies always seem to satisfy. Traditional seafood platters, steaks, and pastas are also served. **The Recovery Room** (445 Ocean Ave., 860/443-2619, $6–12) serves out-of-this-world pizza and very good pastas, too. Among pizza lovers, this place is absolutely worth the trip from anywhere. In case you're wondering about the name, it's in homage to Lawrence & Memorial Hospital, across the street. A long list of both red and white pizzas includes many great toppings. The Gorgonzola with sweet red and yellow peppers, roasted garlic, and olive oil is an outstanding white pie, while you won't go wrong with the red-sauced sausage cacciatore pizza with crushed-plum tomatoes, fresh Italian sausage, chopped garlic, basil, and oil.

You may have to wait a bit for a table, at least on weekends, at **Paul's Pasta Shop** (223 Thames St., Groton, 860/445-5276, $6–10), a cramped but spirited restaurant on the ground floor of a Victorian house near the Thames River. Homemade pastas and sauces are sold by the pound, or stay and savor sandwiches of hot eggplant and provolone, great meatball grinders, or deliciously prepared specialties like linguine primavera and spaghetti with sausage and peppers. This is one Italian restaurant that's resisted come-and-go cooking trends, proving that when fresh ingredients are used, traditional recipes shine.

**Abbott's Lobster in the Rough** (117 Pearl St., Noank, 860/536-7719, $8–18) handles the art of lobster dinners as well as any seafood restaurant on the Atlantic seaboard. Picnic tables are set up on a dock and inside a screened-in porch facing Long Island Sound. You can't get closer to eating fish fresh out of the sea, short of actually wading into the water. Area birds know about Abbott's, too—signs warn you not to leave your food unattended or a seagull may swoop in for it. The truly ambitious usually order the complete lobster feast, comprising a bounty of chowder, shrimp, steamers, mussels, and lobster. Other delights include the quarter-pound lobster rolls and quahogs with clam stuffing. Open daily May through Labor Day and weekends thereafter until Columbus Day.

**Go Fish** (Coogan Blvd., Mystic, 860/536-2662, $10–22) is one of the newer seafood specialists in a town that's known for them, but this dining accessory to quaint Olde Mistick Village has a few twists. First, there's a huge sushi bar with a full selection of vegetarian and seafood pieces. Second, the menu in the expansive and colorful main dining room is one of the longest you'll find, with every permutation of fishy fare you can imagine, from traditional saffron bouillabaisse to hearty lobster ravioli. You can also just sit at the raw bar and munch on cold-water crab claw with mustard sauce and cherrystone and littleneck clams on the half shell. With high-decibel energy, this is a good choice when you have kids or a large group.

**Seamen's Inne** (135 Greenmanville Ave., 860/536-9649) is a Southern-themed bit of kitschy fun in Mystic, perhaps best known for its country breakfast buffets of Southern fried chicken, cheddar grits, candied yams, and such along with Dix-

ieland music. The place overlooks the Mystic River. Dinner often features wild game, plus the expected (and tasty) seafood chowders, fresh lobster, broiled fish, and other seafood favorites.

A fixture by the shore in the summer community of Niantic since 1929, **Constantine's** (252 Main St., Niantic, 860/739-2848, $6–17) keeps customers happy by serving dependable and huge portions of Cajun chicken Caesar salad, sea scallops alfredo, barbecued baby back ribs, and fresh swordfish. The staff couldn't be friendlier, and many tables in this casual family-style place look out toward the sound.

In the same vintage redbrick complex as Margaritas, **Voodoo Grill** (12 Water St., Mystic, 860/572-4422, $8–17) specializes in Cajun, Southwestern, Creole, and barbecue.

**Dad's** (147 Main St., Rt. 156, Niantic, 860/739-2113, $5–12) is a summer-only seafood spot overlooking the harbor and the rail track that separates Rte. 156 from the sound, ideal for lobster rolls, seafood platters, and burgers.

Out on a pier jutting into Stonington Harbor, you can't beat the setting at **Skipper's Dock** (66 Water St., 860/535-8544, $8–18), and many fans say you can't beat the quality of seafood either. Many tables sit right on the water at this festive post-beach hangout that's set on stilts in the water in a characterful weathered building. If you think scoring a table is tough at Abbott's on a summer weekend, give the **Yankee Fisherman** (937 Groton Long Point Rd., 860/536-1717, $9–22) a look. It, too, is frantically popular, both for its fresh seafood dinners and its charming location on the causeway leading to Groton Long Point.

By Mystic's famous drawbridge, **S & P Oyster Co.** (1 Holmes St., 860/536-2674, $13–29) has pleasant red-walled dining rooms facing directly onto the Mystic River. Oysters stuffed with lobster, bacon, and Gorgonzola are a local specialty, but also consider seafood lasagna, calamari salad with a wasabi-ginger vinaigrette, and a T-bone steak and grilled, garlic-shrimp platter. For lunch you might try the oyster grinder with Gorgonzola and sautéed onions and peppers. The food tends to be rather rich, the staff friendly and enthusiastic. In short, this is a dependable fish house.

In East Lyme, check out the **Flanders Fish**

Skipper's Dock restaurant, Stonington

**Market & Restaurant** (22 Chesterfield Rd., 860/739-8866, $7–20), where you can buy fine takeout fare or eat it here. It's a simple place, as a local seafood place should be. If you want a delicious lobster dinner minus the high costs and touristy trappings, settle in for a meal at the enchantingly down-home **Bank Street Lobster House** (194 Bank St., 860/447-9398, $10–18). It's the real thing; an excellent choice for a lobster dinner that's less touristy and pricey than some of the places around Mystic. The food is simply out of this world, and a deck out back overlooks the New London harborfront.

## Mexican

The expected watered-down Mexican fare at **Margaritas** (12 Water St., Mystic, 860/536-4589, $9–17), part of a regional chain, is compensated for by the restaurant's inviting location inside the stately old redbrick Exhibition Hall building, just up from Main Street. On the other hand, you can sample remarkably authentic and by all accounts terrific regional Mexican fare at **Zavala** (2 State St., New London, 860/437-1891, $11–20). The restaurant was opened in 2002 by the owners of a previous restaurant in Lower Manhattan, which closed

following the September 11 terrorist attacks. In this new spot, near New London's train station, you can try such creative fare as blue-corn-crusted calamari with jalapeños; sautéed snapper Vera Cruz–style with onions, tomatoes, capers, and olives; and roasted pork loin smothered in a salsa verde with tender cactus. It's a rarity in Connecticut to find such deftly prepared Mexican cooking.

## Asian

**Bangkok City** (123 State St., New London, 860/442-6970, $7–17) could stand a makeover, but most regulars agree it's a good bet for reasonably authentic Thai fare, from deep-fried whole red snapper with garlic and chilies to breaded frogs legs sautéed with basil leaves and peppers. Just down the street, **Little Tokyo** (131 State St., 860/447-2388, $8–16) is a petite Japanese restaurant that serves very good sushi, teriyaki, and the like.

## Quick Bites

Say what you will about the "wrap" craze of recent years, there's an unusually good purveyor of these burrito-crêpe knockoffs in Mystic: **Under Wraps** (7 Water St., 860/536-4042, under $7) is tucked away inside a nifty old gray house, with a dining room containing art deco accents. The jambalaya wrap is especially tasty.

**Mystic Drawbridge** (Main St. at the bridge, 860/536-7978) claims to make the best ice cream in town—be the judge. A cone here does surely hit the spot on a sunny afternoon, and this cozy parlor sits right on the west bank of the Mystic River, with a few outdoor seats directly facing the quaint bascule drawbridge. Pastries, coffees, and sweets are also available.

In Old Lyme, **Hallmark** (113 Shore Rd., Rte. 156, 860/434-1998, under $5) is a cute drive-in with the usual array of ice cream, sandwiches, and burgers—a good place to take the kids after subjecting them to art appreciation at the area museums.

**Sea Swirl** (30 Williams Ave., Mystic, 860/536-3452, $4–10) is a cozy seafood shack with a few picnic tables in front and more off to the side. This is one of the most popular seafood counters along the shore, and devotees swear it offers the freshest seafood. Excellent scallop rolls, lobster rolls, clam strips and fritters, fried chicken, and kielbasa hot dogs are served.

An inviting lunch spot on busy Bank St. in New London, **Anastacia's** (64 Bank St., 860/437-8005, under $7) serves a nice mix of chowders and soups, leafy salads, and delicious sandwiches.

## Java Joints

The **Yellow House Coffee & Tea Room** (149 Water St., Stonington, 860/535-4986), inside a smart Victorian house by the Stonington village common, serves excellent sandwiches, freshly made Portuguese bread, tempting sweets, and about 30 homemade soups. Summer crowds quench their thirst (and winter crowds warm up) at **Green Marble Coffee House** (8 Steamboat Wharf, Mystic, 860/572-0012), which has a wide selection of teas, too. **Mugz** (42 Bank St., New London, 860/442-1684) is a cute place that's popular with Connecticut College students and serves tasty soups and sandwiches. There's also an art gallery onsite. It has a breezy deck overlooking the Thames River.

## Gourmet Goods and Picnic Supplies

In downtown Niantic, the **Bake House** (289 Pennsylvania Ave., 860/739-9638) is your source for vanilla muffins, cherry cheese croissants, soft chewy cookies, and fresh bagels. You can also get excellent (and big) sandwiches made with fresh-baked breads. Similarly delicious goodies, plus a nice range of sandwiches and other savory lunch fare, make the **Village Bake House** (500 Long Hill Rd., Groton, 860/445-8292) appealing. Drop by **Mystic Market East** (63 Williams St., 860/572-7992) for outstanding prepared food, sandwiches, and desserts to go, plus gourmet groceries. Offerings include toffee-chip cookies; grilled chicken sandwiches with sun-dried tomatoes, lettuce, chipotle mayo, and rosemary focaccia; and salads of fresh greens, goat cheese, roasted spiced walnuts, dried cherries, and garlic croutons. You'll find a handful of tables, but most patrons buy their meals and take them elsewhere—to the beach, perhaps.

# INFORMATION AND SERVICES

## Visitor Information

This region is served by the **Southeastern Connecticut Tourism District** (470 Bank St., P.O. Box 89, New London, CT 06320, 860/444-2206 or 800/TO-ENJOY, www.mysticmore.com). You can also grab brochures and ask questions at the **Mystic & Shoreline Visitor Information Center** (Olde Mistick Village, 860/536-1641). On the Web, www.visitmystic.com is a useful site with links to numerous attractions, B&Bs, and other useful sites.

## Getting Around

A car is the best way to get around, although it is possible to see a bit of Mystic and New London by taking Amtrak or Greyhound to the area and exploring on foot. Mystic is especially walkable, and some accommodations are within walking distance of attractions and restaurants. You can reach the area from eastern and western shore points via I-95, and the slower and more congested U.S. 1, and you can get here from Norwich and the Quiet Corner via I-395.

# The Connecticut River Valley

The Connecticut River Valley encompasses the heart and soul of the state—it's where indigenous life thrived for thousands of years, and it's also the region first visited and soon after settled by Europeans. For the purposes of this book, the region comprises all of the communities within the eastern and western geological walls of the Connecticut River Valley, a huge area that's tremendously varied historically, physically, and culturally.

Hartford, the state capital, contains many of the area's most popular attractions, plus a flurry of restaurants and performing arts venues. It's a tough old town that has experienced a number of setbacks in recent years, most prominent of which was its near theft of pro-football's New England Patriots franchise from Massachusetts—at the last minute, the Patriots' owners bailed on Connecticut, leaving area boosters and politicos embarrassed and hurt . . . and the city's image, yet again, stained.

This rough-and-tumble river city, however, has shown plenty of character in the face of its

Essex Marina

CONN. RIVER VALLEY

To Storrs

To Springfield

MASSACHUSETTS
CONNECTICUT

West Stafford

Shenipsit State Forest

Soapstone Mountain

Somers Mountain Museum

Somers Historical Museum

Somers

Shallowbrook Equestrian Center

North Central Tourism Bureau

Enfield Shakers Historic District

Martha A. Parsons House

Enfield

Taylor Rd.

King House Museum

Suffield

Phelps-Hathewey House

New England Air Museum

Bradley Int'l Airport

Old New-Gate Prison and Copper Mine

Tariffville

Luddy-Taylor Museum

Noden-Reed House and Barn

Connecticut Trolley Museum

Windsor Locks

East Windsor Hill

Wood Memorial Library

Oliver Ellsworth Homestead

Windsor Historical Society

Loomis-Chaffee School

Huntington Museum

Windsor

Bloomfield

Salmon Brook Settlement

McLean Game Refuge

Granby

Enders State Forest

Great Pond State Forest

North Granby

Phelps Tavern Museum

Simsbury

Heublein Tower

Talcott Mtn. State Park

The Living Museum

4-H Farm Resource Center

Science Center of Connecticut

HARTFORD

West Hill Historic District

West Hartford

Noah Webster House

Hill-Stead Museum

Avon

Simsbury Commons

Unionville

Westfarms Mall

Farmington

Miss Porter's School

Sessions Woods Wildlife Management Area

Nassahegan State Forest

Burlington Trout Hatchery

Canton Historical Museum

Canton Green

Canton

Collinsville

New Hartford

Stratton Brook State Park

Roaring Brook Nature Center

Farmington River

Tunxis State Forest

East Hartland

Barkhamsted Reservoir

Saville Dam

Ski Sundown

Lake McDonough

Barkhamsted

To Riverton

To Burlington

Tolland

Rockville

Crystal Lake

Nellie McKnight Museum

Ellington

Vernon

South Windsor

Wickham Park

Buckland Hills Mall

Manchester

Case Mountain Park

Cheney Homestead

Rentschler Field

East Hartford

Webb-Deane-Stevens Museum

Glastonbury

Wethersfield

Fish Family Farm

Bolton

Gay City State Park

Andover

Connecticut River

# THE CONNECTICUT RIVER VALLEY

CONN. RIVER VALLEY

© AVALON TRAVEL PUBLISHING, INC.

various debacles. Plans continue unabated to landscape and restore access to downtown's riverfront, improve the notoriously weak public school system, restore the local economy, and continue with plans for Adriaen's Landing, a full-blown convention-arts-sports-and-entertainment center by the river.

The towns north of Hartford have grown into busy bedroom suburbs since the 1970s, but they're historically known for their tobacco crops—much of the area remains agrarian in character. The northwestern suburbs that make up the Farmington River Valley possess the character and, in many places, the wealth common in Fairfield County's Gold Coast; in these parts, you'll also find some of New England's best opportunities for angling and river rafting.

The true geographical center of the state, which sits mostly west and south of Hartford, is a jumble of historic factory towns that played a pivotal role in America's industrial revolution, and the tight-knit residential communities often populated by immigrants who first worked the region's manufactories during the latter half of the 19th century. Steep, high ridges extend through this part of the state clear up into the Farmington River Valley, making this area popular among hikers.

South of Hartford, the Connecticut River itself jogs slightly in an easterly direction and resumes its course down through a part of the state that has somehow resisted the strident invasions of suburban housing, superhighways, and corporate office parks. Indeed, the lower Connecticut River Valley looks like a vision of the state a century ago, complete with wedding-cake Victorians set on bluffs overlooking the river, a vintage rail line that offers sightseeing excursions, and a bevy of little shops that sell the kinds of furnishings and decorative arts that probably graced the first Sears & Roebuck catalog. Vintage B&Bs and fine restaurants are the norm in these parts.

With I-91 spearing the valley and allowing traffic to pass it by at breakneck speed, it's not surprising that many people have driven through this area without ever pausing and taking the time to appreciate its considerable virtues. As you approach this fast-growing and rapidly changing part of the state, make a point of sticking with the quietest and sleepiest of surface roads. You'll no doubt come away with a new and unexpected sense of both Hartford and the entire river valley.

## A FEW PRACTICALITIES
### Media
The daily *Hartford Courant* (860/241-6200, www.ctnow.com) was begun in 1764 as the *Connecticut Courant*. It rapidly developed the largest circulation among newspapers in the original colonies, and it is today the nation's oldest newspaper in continuous publication. The *Hartford Advocate* (860/548-9300, www.hartfordadvocate.com) is the region's arts-and-entertainment weekly. A very good resource for arts, entertainment, and nightclubs, it's written with a definite iconoclastic sensibility. The monthly *Metroline* (860/570-0823, www.metroline-online.com) is based in Hartford, but serves the entire state's (and western Massachusetts's) gay and lesbian communities.

Serving the northern part of the river valley, the *North Central News* (860/698-9328, www.northcentralnews.org) is a free monthly with arts, entertainment, events, and features.

### Tours
A great number of tours touch on different parts of the Connecticut River Valley, and in just about every way imaginable, whether from the basket of a hot-air balloon or from the deck of a vintage riverboat.

Just before you cross the Rte. 82 drawbridge from Haddam to East Haddam, you'll pass the marina and restaurant for **Camelot Cruises** (1 Marine Park, Haddam, 860/345-8591 or 800/522-7463, www.camelotcruises.com), which offers 2.5-mile excursions on 400-passenger ships up and down the river. Many involve lunch or dinner, and might include an Agatha Christie–style murder mystery, New Dixieland jazz, or an all-day cruise to Long Island.

At Hartford's Riverfront Plaza, from May through October, the three-deck *Mark Twain* riverboat offers Connecticut River cruises, and from Charter Oak Landing, the *Lady Fenwick*

Cruises up and down the Connecticut River offer sightseeing opportunities, often in conjunction with other entertainment—from meals to murder-mystery theater to live jazz.

does the same. Lunch, weekend brunch, sunset cocktail, and evening music cruises are available. Contact **Mark Twain Cruises** (exit 27 from I-91, turn left at the ramp and follow signs to the park, 860/526-4954 or 877/658-9246, www.deepnavigation.com). The same company also offers fall foliage cruises, on the *Becky Thatcher,* from Middletown down and then back up the Connecticut River—these four-hour sails depart on weekends at noon all through October and are definitely a time to have your camera with you. And from mid-June through Labor Day, Mark Twain Cruises' *Aunt Polly* offers cruises of the Lower Connecticut River out of Essex Harbor, and also out by the lighthouse off Old Saybrook. A number of additional cruises are available, including winter "eagle watching" cruises from mid-January through mid-March (Saturdays) out of Essex.

Flight-seeing excursions are another tour option. One of the most innovative flight-seeing companies is **Chester Charter** (Chester Airport, 61 Winthrop Rd., 860/526-4321 or 800/PLANES-1), which takes passengers on trips inside fully restored 1941 Boeing Stearman open-cockpit biplanes—you get to wear the helmet and goggles, so you can fully act out any Red Baron fantasies you might have.

In Plainville, **Interstate Aviation** (Robertson Airport, 62 Johnson Ave., 860/747-5519) offers

passenger rides over the area, as well as flight instruction and charter services.

Of the many hot-air balloon companies, **Berkshire Balloons** (Southington, 203/250-8441, www.berkshireballoons.com) offers some of the best tours throughout the region. You can also combine a hot-air balloon ride with a stay at a bed-and-breakfast. Another operator is **Balloon Rides by Castle View** (Cheshire, 203/272-6116, www.castleviewballoons.com). With both tours, reservations are strongly advised—the farther ahead you book the better chance you'll get the date that interests you.

Farmington also has very good companies that offers excellent trips along Farmington River Valley: **Kat Balloons** (860/678-7921) and **A Windriders Balloon** (314 South Rd., 860/677-0647).

If you'd rather keep your feet on the ground, you might want to try a narrated bus tour instead. **Heritage Trails** (860/677-8867, www.charteroaktree.com) has been conducting tours of Hartford and the Farmington River Valley since 1983; tours depart daily in comfortable 10-passenger minibuses, and guests are treated to a colorful, personable, and informative commentary on what they are passing. There are stops for photo opportunities, but otherwise passengers do not leave the vans. Tours pick up at several downtown Hartford and Farmington area hotels (call for details). Tours of Hartford take two hours and cost $20 per person, covering dozens of sites from Bushnell Park and the Mark Twain House to the riverfront.

Other excursions include the guided **Farmington Evening Dinner Tour,** during which guests enjoy a meal inside a 1789 house that once served as a tavern and inn; price including dinner is $34.95 per person, and this tour lasts 3.5 hours. The **Amistad Sites Bus Tour of Farmington** includes 20 sites that played an important role in the Amistad rebellion (most of them homes where 37 Africans resided for several months until they were freed following their 1841 trial and returned by ship to Africa). This tour costs $20 per person and lasts about 90 minutes. In the fall consider the **Halloween Graveyard Tour** (which includes dinner at an old inn), during which you'll wander through two ancient Colonial graveyards;

$34.95 per person. Several additional tours are available, and reservations are required.

And if you *really* want to keep your feet on the ground, **Hartford Guides Historic Walking Tours** (860/522-0855) is a nonprofit group that offers excellent and informative downtown excursions led by highly knowledgeable guides. Good for individuals or groups, tours are given daily and last 2.5 hours; a nominal fee is requested. You can also call this company with general questions about sightseeing and exploring the city—they're very helpful.

## Getting There

East–West I-84 and North–South I-91 intersect in downtown Hartford, making it easy to drive here and to other towns in the Connecticut River Valley from Boston, New York City, Springfield, and other major regions in the Northeast. Exit signs from both I-91 and I-84 are clearly marked for downtown and also for a number of major city attractions. Rather oddly, no Interstate highway has ever been built to join Hartford with its nearest fellow New England capital city, Providence, Rhode Island. Years ago, plans called for I-84 to connect the two cities (which are just 73 miles apart), but the route was changed to run in a northeasterly direction, eventually joining with I-90 in Massachusetts. The easiest route to follow between the two cities (and also to reach Willimantic and other central-eastern Connecticut towns) is to take I-84 a few exits east of Hartford to I-384, and follow this east to U.S. 6, a surface road that eventually leads to Providence.

An extensive network of interstate-train-and-bus providers serves the Connecticut River Valley. The region is also served by Bradley International Airport. Nearly a dozen chain motels and hotels are by the airport; they are ideal if you need to catch an early morning flight.

# Hartford

## Destination Hartford

Hartford is working hard to remake its image. The trend toward urban downtown renaissances swept America throughout the mid-1980s and into the 1990s, as one-time disasters like Cleveland, Baltimore, and Providence stepped forward and rebuilt their infrastructures, basing their strategies on preservation, user-friendliness, reduced crime, jointly funded private and public investment, and mixed-use neighborhood redevelopment. Hartford is relying on these same principles to reinvent itself and, just maybe, to show up the media. In recent years, the media has knocked the city a bit, especially concerning the controversial Adriaen's Landing development and the infamous 1999 rejection of Hartford as the new home of football's New England Patriots.

Economically, Hartford has been slow to recover from the malaise of the 1980s. Quite a few major Hartford-area companies have completed major layoffs or downsizing programs during the past few years, and still others have moved out of the area entirely. A high dropout rate plagues the city's public school system, and Hartford is among the poorest cities in the nation, one of only a handful of major metropolitan areas to experience population decline in the 1990s. The problems are not unlike those found in other major cities, but further complications exacerbate them here.

The white flight that emptied many cities' coffers during the 1950s and 1960s stung Hartford equally hard, but the manner in which the region's wealthier satellite suburbs abandoned the city was, as it has been all over Connecticut, acute and remarkable. Not only did middle- and upper-class professionals cease living in Hartford, they stopped visiting entirely—tending instead to frequent Boston or Manhattan for short trips.

Today's Hartford is a mix of good and on-the-rebound. The city bustles during weekdays, but remains quiet most nights. Downtown is a virtual graveyard on Sundays, when most businesses and eateries are closed—although several museums remain open and relatively uncrowded, making it a nice time to visit the Wadsworth Atheneum or Mark Twain House. As recently as the late '90s, Hartford suffered from a dearth

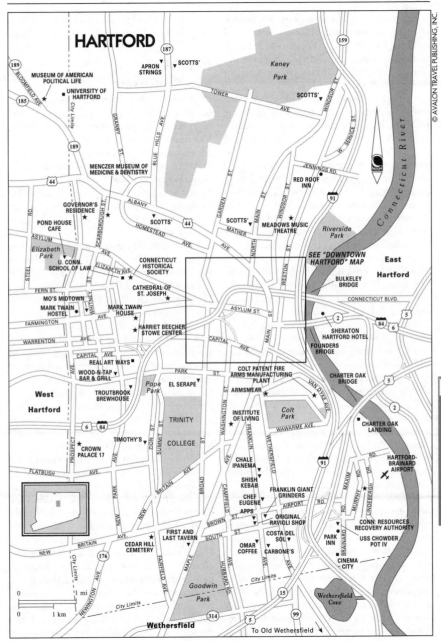

**HARTFORD**

Keney Park

SCOTTS'

APRON STRINGS

MUSEUM OF AMERICAN POLITICAL LIFE

UNIVERSITY OF HARTFORD

TOWER AVE.

SCOTTS'

Connecticut River

JENNINGS RD.

RED ROOF INN

MENCZER MUSEUM OF MEDICINE & DENTISTRY

ALBANY

GOVERNOR'S RESIDENCE

POND HOUSE CAFE

SCOTTS'

SCOTTS'

MEADOWS MUSIC THEATRE

Riverside Park

Elizabeth Park

U. CONN. SCHOOL OF LAW

HOMESTEAD AVE.

CONNECTICUT HISTORICAL SOCIETY

SEE "DOWNTOWN HARTFORD" MAP

East Hartford

MO'S MIDTOWN

CATHEDRAL OF ST. JOSEPH

BULKELEY BRIDGE

MARK TWAIN HOSTEL

MARK TWAIN HOUSE

ASYLUM ST.

CONNECTICUT BLVD.

FARMINGTON

HARRIET BEECHER STOWE CENTER

SHERATON HARTFORD HOTEL

WARRENTON

CAPITAL AVE.

FOUNDERS BRIDGE

REAL ART WAYS

WOOD-N-TAP BAR & GRILL

PARK

EL SERAPE

COLT PATENT FIRE ARMS MANUFACTURING PLANT

CHARTER OAK BRIDGE

**West Hartford**

TROUTBROOK BREWHOUSE

Pope Park

ARMSMEAR

Colt Park

TIMOTHY'S

TRINITY COLLEGE

INSTITUTE OF LIVING

WAWARME AVE.

CHARTER OAK LANDING

CROWN PALACE 17

HARTFORD-BRAINARD AIRPORT

FLATBUSH

CHALE IPANEMA

SHISH KEBAB

FRANKLIN GIANT GRINDERS

CHEF EUGENE APPS

CONN. RESOURCES RECOVERY AUTHORITY

ORIGINAL RAVIOLI SHOP

USS CHOWDER POT IV

FIRST AND LAST TAVERN

COSTA DEL SOL

PARK INN

CEDAR HILL CEMETERY

OMAR COFFEE

CARBONE'S

CINEMA CITY

0    1 mi

0    1 km

Goodwin Park

Wethersfield Cove

**Wethersfield**

To Old Wethersfield

© AVALON TRAVEL PUBLISHING, INC.

**CONN. RIVER VALLEY**

of hip restaurants and nightclubs, but this has changed markedly. But although dining and clubbing have picked up downtown, Hartford lacks the exciting and desirable shopping options a city needs to attract suburbanites for weekend outings.

Throughout the 1980s and early 1990s, Hartford gained notoriety for both drug and gang problems, but even then crime rarely affected the heart of downtown or any of the visitor-oriented neighborhoods. Recently, homicide, violent crime, and gang activity have dropped precipitously, and once–drug-infested areas have been cleaned up largely through the self-policing efforts of concerned neighborhood groups. Hartford is a safe city to walk and drive in, and it should only continue to improve in terms of visitor-friendliness as its various revitalization plans unfold.

As for the city's second-city status relative to New York City and Boston, both about 90 minutes away, Hartford may never compare with these urban superpowers in terms of clout and cachet. But it is a legitimate urban destination, and it has the potential to develop into a thriving midsize city—such as Baltimore, Providence, and Connecticut's most notable urban success story, New Haven.

A walk through downtown reveals an aesthetically pleasing streetscape, with brilliant Bushnell Park surrounded by a mix of historic and contemporary blocks. At the same time, some shoddy urban renewal projects (Constitution Plaza and the Civic Center leap immediately to mind) and poor planning have resulted in the dismantling of countless architectural wonders and charming historic streets.

It's only slightly ironic that Hartford was the first city in America with a permanent public planning agency, established in 1908. The agency's early philosophy rested on a number of very sound tenets, including the recognition of Connecticut River as the city's foremost natural resource. But after perennial springtime flooding escalated to tragic proportions during the mid-1930s, Hartford turned its back on the river, building dikes and eventually an Interstate highway that effectively cut the people off from the water. Major steps have been taken to reconnect downtown

with the river, and the construction of Adriaen's Landing should further help this process along.

## HISTORY
### Rival Settlements
Hartford, as with all of central Connecticut, was occupied chiefly by Sequin Indian tribes for centuries before European settlers began establishing settlements across the region. The Sequins formed a league of tribes under one chief, and the tribes that lived in what is now Hartford included Podunk, Poquonnuc, and Suckiaug Indians. The name *Connecticut* is a variation on Quonitockut (meaning "Long Tidal River"), which is how the tribes referred to what we now call the Connecticut River.

Dutch explorer Adriaen Block (after whom Rhode Island's Block Island is named) navigated the Connecticut River in 1614, and in 1633 fellow Dutchmen established a trading post called Huyshope, which means "House of Hope." This was the inspiration for the name of the present-day street that runs nearest the original encampment (just south of the point where the Park River—now covered by city streets—empties into the larger Connecticut River, and north of the old Colt Armory). That very year, the Dutch found themselves almost immediately outnumbered by various bands of British colonists from such Massachusetts settlements as Plymouth, Watertown, Dorchester, and New Town (which would later be renamed Cambridge).

History may paint an uneasy relationship between the indigenous inhabitants and the white Europeans, but the tensions between the Dutch and the English were themselves noteworthy. There's considerable debate over the origins of the nickname for New Englanders, "Yankee," but some trace it to attitudes of Hartford's early Dutch traders toward the acquisitive and aggressive Puritans from Massachusetts. The Dutch called them Jankes (pronounced "YAHN-kess"), a colloquial term for robbers or thieves, and so this moniker apparently stuck. The Jankes won out, too, as by 1654 the Dutch abandoned their interest in the Connecticut River Valley and shut down the trading post.

# THE LEGEND OF THE CHARTER OAK

The royal charter that governor John Winthrop secured for Connecticut recognized the colony as consisting of 21 towns, 15 from the original Hartford Colony and 6 from New Haven. The rivalry between these two factions continued over the next three centuries, and remains strong today. In fact, the state's legislative body met alternately in Hartford and New Haven until 1875, when a state referendum decreed Hartford the state's sole capital.

In 1687, another shift in British rule again threatened Connecticut's independence. Charles II died, and was succeeded by his brother, James II. Ever the autocrat and bureaucrat, the new king decided it was about time to consolidate these uneasily maintained colonies under the aegis of one formal Dominion of New York and New England, with one royal governor, Sir Edmund Andros. All of the neighboring states gradually abandoned their patents and charters but for Connecticut, which stalled and held out until finally Governor Andros and 75 of his regents paid a personal visit to Hartford and its governor, Robert Treat.

At Sanford's Tavern on King's Highway (now Main Street, about where the Wadsworth Atheneum stands), Andros met with Treat and demanded the surrender of Connecticut's charter. Treat and an array of speakers rebuffed the royal governor's entreaties for the better part of the day, before finally darkness fell upon the October afternoon and candles were lit to continue the discussions.

The story about what happened next has been told countless times and in countless ways, but suffice to say, the next series of events might very well have formed the basis for an Agatha Christie

mystery. During a brief pause in the discussions, some say just as the last colonist gave one final heartfelt speech in the name of the colony's independence, the candles were suddenly extinguished and the room instantly fell pitch black. Had the room remained aglow, the charter would surely by now have passed hands from Treat to Andros; but in the darkness, the document was stolen away (reportedly by Captain Joseph Wadsworth) from the premises and buried within the trunk of Hartford's most enormous oak tree—forever known as the Charter Oak.

Of course, this rebellion of sorts was symbolic at best. Andros left without the paper he came for, but he nevertheless incorporated Connecticut within the Dominion of New York and New England—diplomatically, however, he included Treat on his advisory council.

Connecticut has enjoyed independent state rule for the entire duration of its political formation, excepting the two years during which James II ruled the British Empire. England's Glorious Revolution of 1689 ended the King's controversial regime, and Parliament replaced him with his Protestant daughter, Mary, and her husband, William of Orange. The Dominion of New York and New England came to an abrupt end, and Andros was called back to England. Connecticut's legislature voted immediately to return to the rule of the original charter, and the state was governed exactly according to the salvaged charter until a new constitution was revised during the Constitutional Convention of 1818 (the revised version of that year remains the oldest extant state constitution in America).

## The World's First Constitution

Hartford is generally thought to have been the first permanent community in the state, although colonists first situated themselves in Windsor, slightly north, and Wethersfield, slightly south, in 1633. Unfortunately for these transplants, the lot of them failed to endure the winter of 1634, retreating downriver to regroup at the new military post, Saybrook. Most of these families returned eventually to Massachusetts. In 1635, a lasting settlement finally put roots in the region; a group of 50 men,

women, and children from New Town established a village just north of Huyshope.

The following spring, the minister of New Town, Thomas Hooker, led his entire congregation here. It's believed the city is named for the hometown (Hartford, England) of Hooker's assistant, the Reverend Stone, who led the first group of New Town Congregationalists in 1635. By 1638 the three towns of Hartford, Windsor, and Wethersfield had developed into one colony, led by Hooker and under whose guidance the settlement's most respected legal mind, lawyer

Roger Ludlow, drew up a document of self-rule called the Fundamental Orders.

The Orders were ratified by the General Court of Hartford in 1639, the three towns thereby forming "one publik State or Commonwealth," and thus was born the world's first constitution. Its creation explains Connecticut's nickname (printed on each license plate), "The Constitution State."

## A New Legacy:
## Insurance and Industry

Throughout the 18th century, Hartford had developed into one of the New World's great port cities. A fleet of ships moved goods in and out of the city via the Connecticut River, but the War of 1812's shipping embargo devastated the city's maritime commercial viability. That aspect of the economy would never fully recover, but this event did force Hartford to look elsewhere to spur its economy. What would take place over the next 140 years, from the 1820s through the 1960s, would be the emergence of Hartford into one of the nation's great manufacturing centers and into the insurance capital of the world.

The city's shipping concerns actually planted the seed for the growth of the insurance industry, as Connecticut River trade fostered the city's growth as a banking center, and financial concerns began to realize the need for some sort of policy to cover shipping losses. Shipping died out with the advent of rail transport, but the idea of insurance caught on, and Hartford concentrated on insuring against fire and, eventually, against accident, life, and liability.

The city's rise in insurance coverage is said to date from the great fire of New York City in 1835, when 700 buildings were destroyed. The loss totaled $20 million, and Hartford Fire Insurance Company was responsible for handling just $64,000 in claims. But company head Eliphalet Terry traveled immediately to New York following the calamity, positioned himself atop a soapbox, and loudly proclaimed that all policyholders would be paid immediately—indeed, he is said to have begun writing checks on that very day. Word of the prompt and dramatic manner in which the company handled the claims spread faster than the fire itself, and soon

major businesses from all over the country were rushing for coverage by Hartford companies. In 1906, Hartford insurers paid out an aggregate $15 million in claims to cover the San Francisco earthquake and fire, proving yet again their ability to come through in the most desperate times.

Though the city has long been best known for insurance, Hartford was a manufacturing giant during the 19th century, with prosperity peaking during the late Victorian age. The region developed early on: America's first commercial woolen mill was set up by Jeremiah Wadsworth in 1788; its famed Connecticut Brown fabric was used in President Adams's 1789 inaugural attire.

Independent-spirited Connecticut led the nation in patents per capita from 1790 through the early 20th century, and much of this pioneering activity centered on Hartford. Samuel Colt invented the revolver; his munitions armory along the banks of the Connecticut River—near the old Dutch Huyshope settlement—revolutionized the gunmaking industry, earned tremendous revenues, and employed thousands of workers.

Successes such as Colt's continued throughout the 19th century. The Austin Organ Company built pipe organs. The United States Rubber Company led the way in rubber tires and produced the very first pneumatic tires. The Fuller Brush Company opened a factory in the northern end of town, near the Connecticut River. It grew to become the largest brush factory in the world, its products sold door-to-door by young men, in the great tradition of Yankee peddlers. Capewell Horsenails Inc. produced the nails in horseshoes; it moved from Hartford to Bloomfield in 1985 but remains the world's largest horse-nail supplier. Gold beating developed into a major industry in Hartford; in fact, the 440 square feet of gilt atop the State Capitol was beaten locally.

The first bicycle manufactured in this country, the Columbia Bicycle, was produced in Hartford in 1878 by the Pope Manufacturing Company. The same Pope factory began manufacturing rather cumbersome and expensive Columbia Electric Phaetons around the turn of the 20th century—it was one of the nation's earliest automobiles. Soon after the Whitney Steam Car

Company joined the market, and for a few years Hartford was the center of America's auto industry—car traffic in greater Hartford actually developed to the point in 1901 that some of America's earliest speed limits were posted. Alas, both the steam and electric cars proved impractical and were obsolete by the end of the decade.

Longer-term success was enjoyed by a pair of young and ingenious machine-shop experts named Pratt and Whitney, who carved out a successful living building the machine tools required by factories for mass production. Pratt & Whitney helped revolutionize manufacturing by creating a near-perfect standard-measuring machine in 1885, which gave us the first "standard inch." Their greatest accomplishments, however, came with the their success building aircraft engines—today, planes flying from every airport in the world do so with parts and engines manufactured in greater Hartford.

By the turn of the 20th century, Hartford was one of the wealthiest cities in America, leading the nation in insurance and the production of machine tools, firearms, typewriters, pay phones, electric switches, bicycles, and countless other innovations and machines. It was also an arts and cultural center, with several publishing houses and a community of artists and literati in the West End of the city led by Mark Twain and Harriet Beecher Stowe. By now more than half of its residents were foreign-born, and the population stood at about 80,000. The once white and conservative old New England city had changed, having developed a vibrant African American community and several Jewish neighborhoods. More than a quarter of the city was Roman Catholic by 1900, and in 1902 Hartford truly renounced its blue-blood roots by electing a labor populist, Ignatius Sullivan, as mayor.

Even after insurance and manufacturing had begun to dominate the city's economic base by the early part of the 20th century, Hartford continued to prosper as a vast tobacco and agricultural market into the middle of the 20th century, as crops from neighboring towns passed through the city en route to other parts of the country. Hartford continued to function as a provisions center for many years to come.

Following World War II, though, Hartford began to experience many of the ills that plagued cities across America and especially the Northeast. Cheaper labor and production costs in the South and Midwest lured many factories out of town, and a residential movement out of the inner city and into the suburbs grabbed hold of Hartford. The population dropped from 164,000 in 1935 to about 130,000 by the early 1990s, and various civic attempts to reinvent the city failed on nearly every level.

However, with a brighter economy, serious efforts were made to reform the city's public education system, and to redevelop the city's waterfront. Hartford looks forward in the coming years to confounding its critics and staking its claim as one of the new millennium's urban success stories.

# DOWNTOWN HARTFORD SIGHTS
## Upper Main Street and the Old State House

For hundreds of years, Hartford's focal point has been the **Old State House** (800 Main St., 860/522-6766, www.ctosh.org, open 10 A.M.–4 P.M. weekdays, 11 A.M.–4 P.M. Sat., $5), which commands a regal presence over Thomas Hooker Square, at the corner of Main and State Streets. From this point, no downtown Hartford site is more than a 15-minute walk away.

This 1796 structure is the nation's oldest still-standing statehouse, the site of such landmark events as the *Amistad* and Prudence Crandall trials, and home to a museum of curiosities that contains—among other odd lots—a two-headed calf. An additionally intriguing, if less outlandish, draw is the restored senate chamber, in which hangs one of Gilbert Stuart's famed portraits of George Washington. The present building (earlier "meetinghouses" stood on this site beginning in 1635) was the first major design of America's earliest prominent architect, Charles Bulfinch, who is best known for his Massachusetts State Capitol building overlooking Boston Common and for his redesign of the U.S. Capitol after the British burned it during the War of 1812.

Bulfinch's statehouse didn't always look as elaborate as it does today: the distinctive balustrade was added in 1815, the cupola in 1827, and the clock in 1848. The legislature met in this building until the early 1870s, when a statewide vote named Hartford the sole capital of Connecticut (up to this point, the legislature had convened on alternating years in New Haven). The plan also called for the construction of a more substantial capitol building overlooking nearby Bushnell Park, and so this dignified structure became known forever after as the Old State House.

Interest in preserving the building's legacy waxed and waned during the next century. In the 1870s a massive Victorian wedding cake of a post office was built, dominating the statehouse's eastern entrance until it was razed in the 1930s. Consistent with the city's ridiculous planning principles of the 1960s and 1970s was a brilliant proposal to knock down the Old State House and put up a parking garage. Fortunately, citizens and some powerful civic leaders protested, and ultimately plans were made to fully restore the statehouse to its current glory—the renovation was completed in the mid-1990s.

Walk north along Main Street, Hartford's first legitimate thoroughfare—named originally King's Highway—and you'll soon pass by one of New England's most distinctive structures, the **Richardson Building** (942 Main St.), which is still sometimes referred to by its previous name, the Cheney Building. It was the first commercial undertaking of the legendary architect H. H. Richardson (after which the style Richardson Romanesque is named). This elaborate sandstone building, noted for its high Romanesque arched windows and central glass-roofed atrium, was built in 1876 and initially housed retail, office, and residential tenants, making it one of the nation's first multi-use buildings.

Construction was financed with the fortunes accrued by the Cheney brothers from nearby Manchester, whose prodigious mills once produced the nation's finest silk. For much of the 20th century the retail space was occupied by the tony Brown-Thomson department store, and then the G. Fox Department Store, which also occupied the massive 11-story 1918 structure to

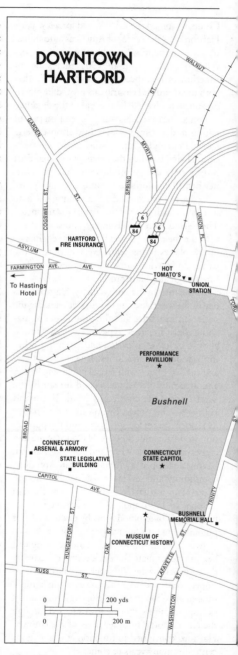

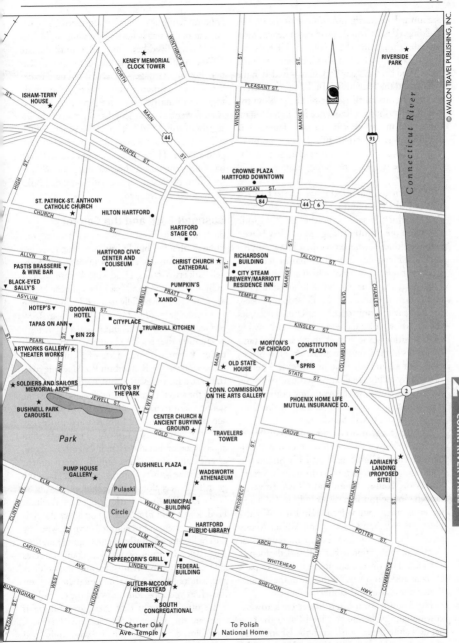

© AVALON TRAVEL PUBLISHING, INC.

CONN. RIVER VALLEY

the immediate north, now known as the G. Fox Building. Alas, Hartford's retail prominence plummeted throughout the 1960s and 1970s; G. Fox—which had been to Connecticut what Macy's had been to New York City—folded in the 1980s, and the Richardson Building struggled to secure tenants until rather recently. Now the building has shops, a Residence Inn hotel, restaurants, and many other businesses. The G. Fox Building was converted into the new home of Capital Community-Technical College in 2001, which gave the neighborhood another shot in the arm.

Walk across Main Street to see **Christ Church Cathedral** (Main and Church Sts., 860/527-7231), which is said to be the oldest Gothic church in the country (designed by New Haven architect Ithiel Towne, who is best known for his successful engineering of romantic covered wooden bridges, many of which still span New England rivers). The parish was founded in 1762 and is now the home of the Episcopal Diocese for the State of Connecticut. The church occupies the site known originally as Sentinel Hill, owing to its position some 70 feet above sea level (and the banks of the Connecticut River, a few blocks east). For a glimpse of the magnificent interior, marked by richly detailed carved oak paneling, drop by the church weekdays during normal business hours, or attend mass (at noon Mon.–Sat., 8 A.M. and 10:30 A.M. Sunday).

Continue north over I-84, and Main Street eventually joins a six-way intersection with Albany Avenue, High Street, and Ely Street. On your right, at the corner of Main and Ely Streets, stands the **Keney Memorial Clock Tower,** a French Gothic-inspired tower built in 1898 and patterned after Tour St-Jacques in Paris. Wealthy Hartford merchants Henry and Walter Keney erected this dramatic 135-foot memorial to their mother, in recognition of her selfless dedication as a parent. The tower rises above a 1.5-acre park of lawns and shrubbery, on the site of the original Keney homestead and family business.

Head south onto High Street back toward downtown; just before you hit I-84, at the corner of Walnut Street, you'll reach the **Isham-Terry House** (211 High St., 860/247-8996, open by appointment only, donation requested). The occupants of this stately house, sisters Julia and Charlotte Isham, lived here from 1896 until the late 1970s, their "union" constituting the quintessential "Boston marriage"—a term often used to describe two women (often sisters) who reside together unmarried for a seeming eternity. The Ishams went to great lengths to preserve the integrity of this 1854 Italianate Victorian, which still retains its original gaslight fixtures and stained-glass accents. The rest of the neighborhood, alas, has failed to retain its historic integrity, making the efforts of these two preservation-minded ladies all the more appreciated.

## Bushnell Park and the Capitol

Back on High Street, cross over I-84 and continue south a few blocks until you reach Asylum Street. This puts you at the corner of one of Bushnell Park's two flanks. Head a block west (to your right, if facing the park), past the Parkside Hotel, to glean a look at the fully restored **Union Station** (1 Union Place, 860/247-5329). Built in 1889 by George Keller, and rebuilt in 1914 following a devastating fire, it's based on a station in Hannover, Germany, and made of local Portland brownstone in the Richardson Romanesque style; tracks are now elevated, but used to run right along the street. Like so many city landmarks, the station was threatened with demolition some years ago but was saved and fully restored in the late 1980s; it now houses not only Hartford's train and bus station but also a handful of offices, shops, eateries, and music clubs. Similar entertainment and nightlife activity dominates Union Place, the gentrified street alongside the station.

Back at **Bushnell Park,** fringed by Asylum, Ford, Jewell, and Elm Streets, you'll face the gently sloping stretch of tree-dotted lawn crowned by the ebulliently captivating State Capitol building. The park comprises two halves, about 19 acres apiece, bisected by Trinity St. and the Soldiers and Sailors Memorial Arch, which are both on the left as you look south toward the capitol.

It's often thought that these graceful green acres are the design of the esteemed Frederick Law Olmsted, a Hartford native who landscaped such landmarks as New York's Central Park and

© ANDREW COLLINS

**The 1878 State Capitol crowns spectacular Bushnell Park.**

Boston's Back Bay Fens. In fact, however, Olmsted assumed only an advisory role, being a good friend of the park's champion and brainchild, the Reverend Horace Bushnell. A respected civic leader and minister, Bushnell had for years rued this noxious section of downtown Hartford, which by the mid-1800s consisted of rail tracks, freight yards, slag heaps, hacked-up tenements, a roiling river of waste, and rank industrial ruins Charles Dickens might have dreamt up.

Bushnell convinced the city legislature to put forth a public ballot on whether to create a green space on the site of this industrial morass, and in 1854 the citizens of Hartford voted to establish the first municipally funded public park in the United States. A Swiss-born botanist, Jacob Weidenmann, actually laid out and designed the space. His success was rewarded ultimately with an appointment to Olmsted's landscaping firm, and Weidenmann moved on to create such gems as Congress Park in Saratoga Springs, New York, and the Capital Grounds in Des Moines, Iowa.

You'd never know it today, but Weidenmann's plans called for the Little River (later rechristened the Park River, but also called both the Hog and rather poetic, Meandering Swine River) to play a central role in Bushnell Park's look, spanning the waterway with scenic bridges and lining it with pleasant walkways. Sadly, following the devastating flood of 1936, city planners opted

to cover the river beneath city streets and buildings, and so it's no longer visible today. That is, unless you contact Huck Finn Adventures, a canoe and rafting outfitter in the suburb of Canton that offers underground canoe excursions along the Park River; they run directly beneath the city and Bushnell Park.

Of course, the park is ideally appreciated above ground. Brown-baggers lunch here daily, and locals and visitors cavort about the grassy slopes and beneath the boughs of shade trees. Festivals and events draw crowds to Bushnell Park throughout the year, beginning with the First Night New Year's celebrations. The **Performance Pavillion** (860/543-8570) hosts everything from Monday-night jazz concerts in July to various events and fundraisers, including gay pride (late June) and the American Cancer Society's five-mile walk (in late October). An excellent way to become acquainted with Bushnell Park is to get a copy of *Leaflet*, a twice-annual newsletter detailing activities, events, and resources in the park; contact the **Bushnell Park Foundation** (P.O. Box 31173, Hartford, CT 06106, 860/232-6710, www.bushnellpark.org).

One notable characteristic of the park is its bounty of war memorials, some of them surrounding the grounds of the State Capitol. You can't miss the towering 116-foot-tall **Soldiers and Sailors Memorial Arch** (Trinity St., 860/232-6710), which was erected of Portland brownstone in 1886 and honors the several thousand Hartford residents who fought in the Civil War—note the battles depicted in the arch's terracotta frieze. Free tours of the arch are given at noon on Thursdays, May–October.

Up the hill, the **Connecticut State Capitol** (210 Capitol Ave., 860/240-0222) is one of the strangest such buildings in the country, a somewhat jarring but undeniably exuberant amalgam of architectural styles. The prevailing influence is Gothic. The building is distinct, it certainly couldn't be called boring, and most Hartford citizens adore it (secretly, if not openly). Architect Richard Upjohn's 1873 design drew harsh criticism from the public and the news media, especially his initial plan for a central clock tower. Midway through construction, the project was suspended, and the clock tower idea was scrapped in favor of the 12-sided gilded dome you see today. In 1878, the capitol opened its doors to the legislature. Final cost: $2.5 million.

One thing we don't see today is *Genius of Connecticut,* a statue of a winged goddess that once stood rather precariously atop the dome. The lady was dethroned in the late 1930s for fear that a strident storm might knock her from her perch and imperil human life below; she was unceremoniously melted down for scrap metal and used in the war effort. A full-size replica of *Genius* now stands in the building's Rotunda, safely out of harm's way, although plenty of loyalists still await the day that she's returned to her proper perch high above Hartford.

The League of Women Voters sponsors several free tours weekdays (except Sunday), year-round (and also on Saturdays in summer), during which visitors are regaled with tales of the capitol's history and inner workings, tidbits about the state legislature, and glimpses of the Hall of Flags and quite a bit of grand statuary (including *Genius*); the capitol's interior fully lives up to its flamboyant exterior, complete with polished granite columns, stained-glass windows, and an atrium ceiling with hand-stenciled gilt leaf. The state's legislative body is considerably less scintillating, but you are welcome to observe it, when in session, through public galleries.

The state senate's offices are just west on Capitol Avenue, beyond the highway ramps leading to and from I-84. The bulky contemporary **State Legislative Building** is no match for the capitol, but just beyond stands the impressive **Connecticut Arsenal and Armory,** at 360 Broad Street, a massive 1909 building in which an entire blimp was built for the U.S. Navy during World War I. Designed by the esteemed local architect Benjamin Wistar Morris, the armory replaced an old railroad roundhouse and is currently the site of many events and galas.

Across Capitol Avenue from the capitol is the Connecticut State Library, in which you'll find the **Museum of Connecticut History** (231 Capitol Ave., 860/757-6535, open 9 A.M.–4 P.M. weekdays, free). A daunting Italian Renaissance structure created in 1910 by Donn Barber (of Travelers

Tower fame), the library contains astoundingly comprehensive research and reference collections open (not on loan, however) to the public. The museum's greatest draw is its irreplaceable collection of Colt firearms (numbering about a thousand) and artifacts relating to the munitions manufacturer's illustrious career. Also here are the state's original 1662 charter (yes, the one alleged to have resided secretly for a bit inside the massive oak tree of legend), the official portraits of the state's governors, and some excellent changing exhibits.

At this same intersection of great civic pride stands **Bushnell Memorial Hall** (166 Capitol Ave., 860/246-6807, www.bushnell.org), which presents about 300 works of theater, opera, and dance annually. The 1930 building, built of redbrick and limestone, is a National Registered Landmark, its ornate art deco interior known for its exquisite sconces and lighting fixtures. Already the size of the Met in New York City, the Bushnell added an adjoining $30 million, 950-seat theater in 2001. A landscaped breezeway connects the newer wing to the original building.

Saunter back down toward Bushnell Park, along Trinity Street, and turn east at the Soldiers and Sailors Memorial. You soon may hear carnivalesque pipe organ music emanating from an enormous, characterful wooden shed with a radiant band of stained glass. Therein revolves the **Bushnell Park Carousel** (860/246-7739, open 11 A.M.–5 P.M. Tues.–Sun., May–mid-Oct.), a 1914 Stein & Goldstein merry-go-round (the chirping Wurlitzer organ dates from 1925). This clattering contraption and its 48 horses were meticulously restored in 1974, and at 50 cents per ride, it's one of the great entertainment bargains in Connecticut.

You might then stroll around the small lake beyond the carousel, or walk across to the southern edge of the park, where you'll come upon a working Tudor-style pumping station that, believe it or not, houses art installations. The 1947 **Pump House Gallery** (860/543-8874, open 11 A.M.–2 P.M. Tues.–Fri., weekends by appointment, free) exhibits primarily the creations of local artisans. There's also a seasonal café here, the **Pump House Grill,** run by the folks at Vito's on the Park (see the Food section). It's open only in the warmer months and has outdoor seating, making it a great way to enjoy the park's scenery and a light meal simultaneously.

Amid the various buildings and landmarks dominating Bushnell Park, take care to appreciate the trees—for they represent no mere mélange of typical New England species, but rather a carefully thought out arrangement of both common and exotic trees, ranging from familiar species of maple, oak, walnut, sycamore, birch, and ash to more exotic Chinese toon, bald cypress, and Kentucky coffee tree. Enthusiasts of flora should arrive armed with the *Bushnell Park Tree Walks* brochure, which presents a detailed self-guided tour of the grounds, identifying some 50 of the park's 125 species (there are about 600 trees altogether). These illustrated tracts are available from tourist offices or by sending a SASE to DEP Maps and Publications, 165 Capitol Ave., Room 555, Hartford, CT 06106.

## The Civic Center and Trumbull Street

Exit the park just east of the carousel and turn north up Ann Street; you'll pass by the magnificent **Goodwin Hotel,** 1 Haynes St., built in 1881 in the Queen Anne style. Although the building was gutted in the 1980s, a luxury hotel now rises from its meticulously restored facade. Directly across Asylum Street, from the hotel, you simply cannot miss the monolithic concrete leviathan before you, better known as the **Hartford Civic Center and Coliseum** (bounded by Ann, Church, Trumbull, and Asylum Sts., 860/249-6333, www.hartfordciviccenter.com). This stark, grim mess occupies an entire city block and connects to the north, via an enclosed pedestrian bridge, to an enormous parking garage and the Hilton Hotel. Just beyond the hotel, sitting astride I-84, is a bizarre user-unfriendly park that looks a bit like a prison recreation yard. This entire stretch of ill-conceived urban renewal is an eyesore, although the Hilton is well run and very nice inside.

The Civic Center was eyed largely through rose-colored glasses upon its 1975 opening. One guidebook of that period noted that with "the creation of the glamorous Civic Center, Hartford is now almost as busy after dark as during daylight hours." Indeed, the Civic Center has long hosted a slew of big-name performers and popular sports teams, and during these events there has always been a nice buzz about the neighborhood surrounding it. However, the center's Hartford Whalers skipped town in 1997, and the construction of the Meadows Music Theatre and, eventually, Adriaen's Landing, has many wondering if the Civic Center has run out of reasons for being. And no matter the building's initial reception, few would call it glamorous today.

Currently, concerts and exhibitions take place here from time to time, although many events now occur at the Connecticut Expo Center and many concerts are held at some of the region's newer venues. Call Ticketmaster, 860/525-4500, for ticket information. The center also hosts games played by the **Hartford Wolf Pack** (860/548-2000, www.hartfordwolfpack.com), minor league ice hockey. In January 1978 a blizzard dumped many tons of wet snow on the Civic Center; the roof collapsed and took two years to be replaced. Fortunately, the disaster occurred in the early morning, several hours after a crowded basketball game, and so there were no injuries.

Neighboring the Civic Center to the west is the Victorian brownstone **St. Patrick-St. Anthony Catholic Church** (Church and Ann Sts., 860/756-4034, open mornings daily, free), which was completely restored inside and out in 1988. The original 1829 church on this site (the current one dates from the 1870s) housed the first Roman Catholic parish in the state. To the east, Trumbull Street borders the Civic Center and is, more than Main Street, Hartford's center of corporate goings-on. The street is lined with office towers, as well as a handful of trendy eateries and shops (some of them set in striking early-20th-century buildings). At the corner of Trumbull and Church Streets is the **Hartford Stage Company** (50 Church St., 860/527-5151, www.hartfordstage.org), a contemporary theater designed in 1977 by Robert Venturi.

Culture vultures should make a point of dropping by the **Greater Hartford Arts Council** (45 Pratt St., 860/525-8629, www.connectthedots.org), a one-stop for information on local arts and culture; you can also pick up a map that covers downtown's 20-block Arts and

CONN. RIVER VALLEY

## ADRIAEN'S LANDING

The comprehensive plan for Hartford's new and dramatic riverfront redevelopment, Adriaen's Landing, was unfurled in 1998. Since that time, the project's focus has shifted on several occasions, and the project has stalled on several occasions, mired in a depressing morass of bureaucracy, finger pointing, conflict, and delay. One constant has been the goal of building the largest convention center between New York City and Hartford, and it does finally appear that this structure will open in 2005.

At one time it looked likely that Robert Kraft would bring his New England Patriots football team to Hartford. Alas, he reneged on this deal, leaving an excited Gov. John Rowland and others largely behind the effort to woo the team red in the face, with both anger and embarrassment. Other controversies have concerned the very name of the project—some critics have lobbied to change the name to an eminently more recognizable Twain's Landing.

Plans for the conception of the project have called for everything from a 44-foot-long full-size replica of Adriaen Block's Dutch ship, *Onrust*, looming over a massive maritime museum and river aquarium to a village of specialty shops, movie theaters, nightclubs, and restaurants set along a re-created waterway. Many of these plans have been scrapped. What does appear to be a sure thing is the 550,000-square-foot Connecticut Convention Center, on which construction began in fall 2002.

The facility is going up right along the river-

Entertainment (A&E) District, identifying the sites of restaurants, clubs, performance halls, parking garages, and the like.

Opposite the Civic Center to the south (just east of the Goodwin Hotel) is **CityPlace,** 185 Asylum St., a 1983 office complex comprising 18-story and 38-story towers that share a three-story atrium. Some critics fault CityPlace for being bland and unimaginative, but it nonetheless possesses more personality and command than the Civic Center. The loftier of the towers is Hartford's tallest building.

Continue south along Trumbull to Pearl Street, the site of a pair of respected art spaces. A right turn from Trumbull leads to the **Artworks Gallery** (233 Pearl St., 860/247-3522, open Wed.–Sat., free), the oldest artists' cooperative in the state, which hosts juried art competitions and poetry readings and is home to the Contemporary Sculptors Guild.

Leading south from Pearl Street is one of Hartford's most charming and best-hidden thoroughfares, tiny **Lewis Street,** which is still partially lined with the fine redbrick Federal-style buildings that once spanned its entire length (several of these early 1800s beauties were torn down to make way for office and parking facilities). At the end of Lewis Street, turn left onto Gold Street, which leads up the hill from the edge of Bushnell Park to Main Street. Long ago, Gold Street was a seething den of prostitution and other illicit dealings, but it's been cleaned up considerably today.

### Lower Main Street and the Wadsworth Atheneum

As you approach Main, you'll notice on your left the tall, intricate triple-tiered spire of **Center Church** (675 Main St., 860/249-5631, open 11 A.M.–2 P.M. Wed.–Fri., or by appointment, free), a magnificent 1807 cathedral patterned after London's St. Martin-in-the-Fields and filled with stained-glass designed by Louis Tiffany. This Congregational church is home to the oldest parish in Connecticut, established by Thomas Hooker in 1632. Behind it is Hartford's **Ancient Burying Ground** (860/722-6490), the city's oldest cemetery, with about 400 sites dating from 1640 to 1803—some of the state's earliest figureheads and leaders are buried here, although many of the original brownstone grave markers are faded and no longer readable. After years of neglect, the burying ground was rehabilitated a century ago; its magnificent Gold St. fence and gate (1898) were designed by the famous firm of McKim, Mead & White.

An interesting time to view the burying ground and the church is on a sunny midday, when the

front, between I-91 and Columbus Boulevard, right on the eastern edge of downtown. It will connect with the walkway to the river as well as to a brand-new Marriott Hotel, which is also slated to open in the next couple of years. Based on early drawings and blueprints, the convention center looks like will be impressive, if monolithic. It should drum up plenty of convention business for the city, create as many as 2,000 long-term jobs, and pour plenty of cash into Hartford's diminishing coffers.

Alas, where Adriaen's Landing originally was expected to contain a museum, amusements, sports facilities, shops, and other forms of entertainment that appeal both to residents and leisure visitors, the current scenario—a convention center and business

hotel—appears, thus far anyway, to hold little appeal except for corporate travelers and convention attendees. Some critics of the building also note that its design may encourage its visitors to drive into Hartford, park, enter the building, and leave the same way they came—never really interacting with downtown.

It also appears that there will be a residential component to Adriaen's Landing, in the form of condominiums and/or apartments. And right across the river in East Hartford, Rentschler Field Stadium (built in 2003) is now the home for UConn football games. As of this writing, there remain plans to build some restaurants and other amusements at Adriaen's Landing, but it's not yet clear what form these will take.

reflection of the neighboring Gold Building office tower, to the immediate north, paints the church and its spire in a fanciful pattern of dappled yellows and golds. The Gold Building itself draws a mix of reactions; not everybody loves the gold glass cladding of this chunky 1970s skyscraper. Do drop by the building's lobby, however, to visit the **Connecticut Commission on the Arts Gallery** (755 Main St., 860/566-4770, open weekdays, free), which displays the works of contemporary Connecticut artists who have received fellowships from the commission.

Across Main Street is the building most easily identified with Hartford's compact, but elegant skyline, the 527-foot-tall **Travelers Tower** (Main St. and Athenaeum Square, 860/277-0111). Completed in 1919 (it was then the tallest building in New England) and designed by Donn Barber, this 34-story tower is faced in pink granite and crowned with an 81-foot-tall pyramidal copper cupola, which is lighted at night and visible from miles in all directions. The building's observation deck offers fine views and is open weekdays May–October.

On the same side of Main, a block south of Travelers Tower, is one of the oldest museums of art in America, the **Wadsworth Atheneum** (600 Main St., 860/278-2670, www.wadsworth-atheneum.org, open 10 A.M.–5 P.M. Tues.–Fri.,

10 A.M.–5 P.M. weekends, $9, free until noon Sat.), which was established in 1842. The building consists of three parts, with the original 1842 main building on your left as you face it—this crenellated Gothic Revival structure was designed by Ithiel Towne. To the right, with the handsome stained-glass windows, is the grand Colt Wing, designed in the early 1900s by Benjamin Wistar Morris. To the right of that is the 1910 Morgan Memorial Wing (a gift of Hartford's most successful financier, J. P. Morgan). The Wadsworth was named for and founded by Daniel Wadsworth, a descendant of one of the city's earliest and most prestigious families. His father, Jeremiah Wadsworth, was visited many times by George Washington. The site of Wadsworth's large Georgian-style stable is just across Athenaeum Square, the barn having been relocated to the town of Lebanon some years ago, where it now sits beside the house-museum that was once the home of Colonial governor Jonathan Trumbull.

The Wadsworth is perhaps best known for its changing exhibits, several of which have stolen thunder from the top art museums in Boston and New York City. But the permanent collection deserves equal praise, comprising some 50,000 works and spanning 5,000 years. Highlights include the collection of *Elizabeth Eggington,* the oldest dated American portrait; the Egyptian, Greek, and Roman bronzes; the Renaissance and baroque paintings; the French and American impressionist collections (featuring works by a number of Connecticut artists); and an exhaustive assemblage of Pilgrim Century American furniture and decorative arts. An excellent sampling of Hudson River School paintings is appropriate given that one of that movement's leaders, Frederic Church, was a native of Hartford and a good friend of Daniel Wadsworth. Also highly relevant to Hartford's history is the exhibit of art and artifacts known as the Amistad Collection, which concerns the lives and contributions of African Americans from the slave period to the present.

The Wadsworth's **Museum Café** (860/728-5989) is just off the lobby and makes an outstanding spot for lunch; unfortunately, you must pay admission to the museum to access the café. Note that there are tentative plans for the Wadsworth to undergo a major renovation and expansion in mid-2004–2006, which may result in restricted hours; be sure to check ahead before planning your visit. As you walk out of the Wadsworth and continue south on Main Street, take note of the enormous steel sculpture *Stegosaurus,* created by late artist and Litchfield County resident Alexander Calder. Across the street, at 555 Main, is dreary **Bushnell Plaza,** another of Hartford's more disheartening attempts at urban renewal. This headquarters of the Metropolitan District Commission, which oversees the region's water supply, manages to suck the life out of a significant chunk of Main Street—the plaza's construction required the demolition of Mulberry Street, which once contained a colorful bevy of coin, stamp, and hobby shops.

Back on the east side of the street is the city's grand 1915 **Municipal Building** (550 Main St.), a late Georgian-style beauty whose stunning lobby can be appreciated with a quick peek inside. Contained within are the offices of Hartford's City Hall. Continue south taking note of the recently expanded **Hartford Public Library** (500 Main St., 860/543-8628, open daily Oct.–May, closed Sun. June–Sept.), which is built astride an 1834 stone bridge (whose details are barely visible today) that once spanned

the Park River. It now crosses the Whitehead Highway, which today sits atop the covered river, extending from I-91 at exit 29A beneath Prospect and Main Streets, and ending near the southeast corner of Bushnell Park.

Another clunker of a building, the bland-looking 1960s **Federal Building** (450 Main St.), dominates the block immediately south of the library; appropriately, this unsympathetic-looking building houses such bureaucracies as the IRS and the FBI. Across Main is the **Central Baptist Church,** 457 Main St., an imposing white church dating to the early 1800s.

Hartford has been called a transient city, but one family occupied the **Butler-McCook Homestead** (396 Main St., 860/522-1806 or 860/247-8996, open 10 A.M.–4 P.M. Wed.–Sat., 1–4 P.M. Sun., $5) from its 1782 construction until 1971, nearly 200 years. The last remaining McCook left the house and many of the family's possessions as a museum, which has been carefully maintained by the Connecticut Antiquarian & Landmarks Society. Inside you'll find an unusual collection of Japanese armor, fine American paintings, antiques, and Victoriana. Across Main Street is yet another early 1800s church, **South Congregational** (307 Main St.), whose parish dates from 1670.

From the east side of Main, between the Federal Building and Butler-McCook, walk east along Sheldon Street to Prospect to see another of the city's few remaining 18th-century structures, the 1788 **Amos Bull House** (59 S. Prospect St., 860/566-3005). This wood-shingle, gambrel-roofed house with a brick facade now houses the Connecticut Historical Commission.

Back at Main, south of Butler-McCook, turn left to reach Connecticut's first synagogue, the **Charter Oak Avenue Temple** (21 Charter Oak Ave., 860/249-1207), which houses the Charter Oak Cultural Center. Contrary to the state's reputation as a tolerant and progressive haven for outsiders, Connecticut's state constitution denied non-Christians the rights to worship openly or own property for the purposes of religious assembly and burial. Jewish immigrants, then, were nonplussed to arrive in Connecticut and find themselves discriminated against. The legislature finally reformed the constitution in 1843, but it was another 30 years before the Beth Israel Jewish congregation had raised sufficient funds to buy land and construct the Charter Oak Avenue Temple. They moved to West Hartford in 1935 and sold the building to, interestingly, a Baptist congregation, which remained there until 1972, at which time plans were drawn up to raze this historic structure.

The Charter Oak Temple Restoration Association formed a few years later, and fought successfully to save and restore the building, establishing a cultural center within its walls. Today, you can tour the interior, which consists of the former sanctuary (containing exhibits on the immigration of Jews to Connecticut, the life they adapted to once here, religious life in 19th-century Hartford, stained-glass and stencil decoration, architecture, and ritual and reform). The former school and community room is now a small art gallery and theater offering international programming, from Brazilian folk dancing to African American history exhibits. Open weekdays (gallery Tues.–Fri.); free.

Just east of here a 1906 granite column marks the site of the famed **Charter Oak.** The tree, 33 feet in circumference, blew down in a storm in 1856—it was believed by then to have been more than 1,000 years old. It's not hard to imagine how a charter, or a set of encyclopedias for that matter, could have been stashed inside so massive a tree. It is alleged that countless items have been fashioned out of the tree, and the WPA guide to Connecticut offers a wonderful quote from Mark Twain, claiming to have witnessed "a walking-stick, dog collar, needle-case, three-legged stool, bootjack, dinner table, tenpin alley, toothpick, and enough Charter Oak to build a plank road from Hartford to Salt Lake City."

## The Riverfront Recaptured

Since a floodwall was erected during the early 1940s in an effort to keep the volatile Connecticut River from overstepping its bounds, city streets have remained dry and safe from disastrous rains. The only real access until recently was via Riverside Park, north of downtown, a pleasing expanse of waterside greenery that could only be reached easily by car, via either I-91 or an unpleasant morass of streets in one of the city's ugliest industrial neighborhoods, North Meadows.

Activity in the downtown Front Street neighborhood, which was nearest the walled-off river, greatly diminished in the decades following the construction of the floodwall. Parts of the neighborhood were razed in the 1950s for construction of the Founders Bridge, which connects State Street via Rte. 2 over the Connecticut River to East Hartford. State Street begins at Main Street, beside the Old State House; it used to run to a wharf along the river, where, until service ceased in 1931, steamships carried passengers to and from New York City.

In the late 1950s, Front Street and its nearby side streets were bulldozed to make way for a massive and aesthetically depressing urban renewal project called Constitution Plaza, which now occupies the swath of land from State Street north for a few blocks. In the 1960s, the construction of elevated I-91 further sealed the river off from the city—you could no longer walk to its banks from downtown.

For all practical purposes, Hartford was landlocked from the 1930s until recent times, the Connecticut River's many attributes forgotten by residents unable to see and walk alongside it. With the abandonment came a lack of interest in keeping the river clean, and so throughout much of the 20th century the waters dirtied and failed to support the diverse ecosystem that thrived here prior to the industrial revolution. Only since the mid-1980s has a serious effort been made to reunite the Connecticut River with the city of Hartford, and only in 1999 was the connection finally realized.

The drive to reclaim the Connecticut River began in the 1980s with the formation of **Riverfront Recapture** (1 Hartford Square W, Hartford, CT 06106, 860/713-3131, www.riverfront .org). This nonprofit organization has cleaned up the river; established walkways from downtown to the river, across the river, and along both sides of the riverbanks; and operated three parks along the river's banks: Riverside Park and Charter Oak Landing in Hartford, and Great River Park in East Hartford. Positive results began occurring with great speed. Many goals have already been reached, and others shall unfold over the coming years.

There is now a great deal of activity along the river. From spring through fall events range from a summer music series to movies shown "under the stars." Fishing and boating tournaments are often held along here, and excursion cruises now run spring through fall up and down the river.

Currently, a visit to the riverfront and the neighborhood nearest it will allow you to take full advantage of completed improvements, while giving you a glimpse of what lies ahead. You can also walk through the intriguing, if not entirely appealing, blocks that have been developed into Constitution Plaza and into several other modern office projects. The best place to begin a tour of the area is behind the Old State House, at Main and State Streets.

Walk east along State, down the hill, and on your left you'll see the ambitious but underutilized **Constitution Plaza,** which dominates the blocks north and east of here clear to the junction of I-84 and I-91, a mangle of highway interchanges and exit ramps. Constitution Plaza, described optimistically in one brochure as a "uniquely landscaped plaza," won a number of design awards following its $40 million construction in the early 1960s. It consists of concrete walkways and courtyards towered over by boxy high-rises. Its enthusiastic reception has dampened considerably over the years, partly because architectural and urban planning principles have changed dramatically, and partly because the complex has since its inception been isolated from the rest of downtown. Constitution Plaza was expected to spark an urban renaissance and curtail the bleeding of post-World War II Hartford's wounded spirit—its initial positive impact was, instead, short-lived. Eventually, this complex will be connected to Adriaen's Landing. Perhaps then, a new generation of planners can improve on its layout, design, and effect upon the immediate neighborhood.

A concrete pedestrian bridge crosses south from Constitution Plaza over State Street to the world's first two-sided building, the 1960 headquarters of the **Phoenix Home Life Mutual In-** surance Company, 1 American Row. Glass panels curve around each side of the building to form a perfect ellipse; this sleek and imaginative design gives it the profile of a large fish.

Phoenix Home's grounds, which are atop a concrete landscaped plaza above State Street and Columbus Boulevard, connect via yet another pedestrian bridge to the new stepped terrace that crosses I-91 and leads directly down to the Connecticut River. The adjoining Terraces amphitheater accommodates up to 2,000 spectators, who can now watch sailing regattas, water-skiing, and other river activities, as well as enjoy concerts held on a stage at its base. A bulkhead called State Street Landing provides access to excursion boats and water taxis, including a Connecticut River cruise boat, the aptly named *Mark Twain.* For the first time in more than six decades, visitors enjoy passenger service along the river. Eventually, a promenade will continue from the stepped terrace clear across Founders Bridge, making it easy for walkers, joggers, and cyclists to access the river walks on both sides.

Following the construction of this walkabout came the creation of a riverside trail from here to grassy, tree-shaded 61-acre **Riverside Park** (Leibert Rd. off Jennings Rd., exit 33 from I-91, 860/713-3131), which has rope courses, picnic areas, softball and cricket fields, and summer music concerts. The park offers easy access to the river and is home of the Riverfront Recapture Community Boating Program. Eventually, the walk is expected to run another five miles north to the mouth of the Farmington River, in Windsor.

The best river access south of downtown is from **Charter Oak Landing** (exit 27 from I-91, turn left at the ramp and follow signs to the park, 860/713-3131). This park has a dock, a public boat launch, walking trails, and picnic areas.

## SOUTHERN HARTFORD SIGHTS

Once you get beyond downtown, you'll need a car to explore the rest of Hartford. If you've explored some of the sights along or near the southern end of Main Street, such as Butler-McCook Homestead and the Charter Oak Avenue Temple, you might consider continuing south to see the vestiges of the Industrial age around the city's Colt Park, the historic mansions lining Wethersfield Ave., the close-knit Italian neighborhood in the city's South End, and the classic collegiate-Gothic campus of Trinity College.

## Colt Village and Park

From the intersection of Charter Oak Avenue and Main Street, head east along Charter Oak, until it curves around and becomes Van Dyke Avenue. This leads into a strangely alluring industrial area dominated by Colt Village—the spot marks the approximate area along the Connecticut River at which Dutch settlers established the Huyshope trading post during 1630s.

Often cited as America's first true industrial park, munitions baron Samuel Colt's eponymous village once comprised a chunk of streets extending from the Connecticut River to Van Block Street, the eastern border of what is now Colt Park. The still-commanding **Colt Patent Fire Arms Manufacturing Plant** (Van Dyke Ave. at Sequassen St., 860/722-6514, open for tours by appointment) anchored this Victorian compound of workers' houses and factory buildings (many still standing), a wharf and ferry facilities (now gone, the riverfront cut off from the neighborhood by I-91), and a community center called "Charter Oak Hall" (now gone, burned during the Civil War—allegedly by Southern arsonists).

Crowning the dramatic factory is a distinctive and restored blue onion dome studded with gold-colored stars. The dome was inspired by Colt's tours of Russia and Turkey. The building dates from 1855 (although it was rebuilt largely in 1864 following a devastating fire) and now stands nearly vacant, but for a handful of artists' studios and apartments. Firearms have not been manufactured here in many decades, and preservationists are considering ways to restore the structure and possibly convert a portion of it into a Colt Firearms museum.

Considerable legend surrounds Colt's revolver, an invention he patented in 1839, and which earned him instant fame and fortune. Legend has it that Colt conceived of the revolver while working as a young man aboard a merchant ship; inspired by the workings of the ship's wheel, he

carved a revolving gun cylinder out of a block of wood. And so the arms-manufacturing industry the world over was soon revolutionized.

From the Colt Armory, retrace your steps back along Van Dyke to Charter Oak Avenue, and make your first major left onto Wyllys Street. Along here stands the richly ornamented **Episcopal Church of the Good Shepherd and Parish House** (155 Wyllys St., 860/525-4289, open by appointment). This high-Victorian Gothic 1868 church was designed by Edward Tuckerman Potter (of Mark Twain House fame). Samuel Colt's wife, Elizabeth, commissioned the red- and yellow-sandstone structures: the church notable for its steep, patterned slate roof and the parish house designed vaguely to resemble a ship—a nod to Colt's love of sailing.

Continue on Wyllys Street a couple blocks, making a left onto Wethersfield Avenue; immediately ahead, on the left-hand side of the street, you'll see what remains of the great and vast Colt estate, **Armsmear** (80 Wethersfield Ave.), a lavish Italianate mansion that dates from 1857 and has been called the greatest and most dramatic home ever built in Connecticut (some might dispute that claim, considering the gaudy mansions of P. T. Barnum in Bridgeport—none of which still stand, however). The estate originally comprised a lake and fountains, a half-mile-long greenhouse, elaborate sculpture gardens, rustic bridges, and a deer park, plus a fine view of the Connecticut River and Colt Village. Mrs. Colt stipulated in her will that the estate be used as a residence for "widows and orphans of Episcopal clergy and other refined and educated gentlewomen," so the building is not open to the public.

This stretch of Wethersfield contains several elegant old homes, most of them built by the many benefactors of Hartford's Victorian industrial preeminence. A short distance north of Armsmear is the formal entrance of **Colt Park** (860/543-8876), which was established in 1905 as a memorial to Samuel Colt. Visitors can enjoy the basketball courts and baseball, soccer, rugby, and other sports fields.

Back on Wethersfield Avenue, turn right and then back to the left at the major (and confusing intersection) of Maple Avenue, Park Street,

# SAMUEL COLT

Considerable legend surrounds the famous Colt revolver, an invention Samuel Colt patented in 1839 and which earned him instant fame and fortune. It's said that Colt dreamt up the revolver idea while working as a young man aboard a merchant ship: he observed the workings of a ship's wheel and managed to carve a revolving gun cylinder out of a block of wood. The arms-manufacturing industry the world over was forever revolutionized.

Samuel Colt is probably best remembered locally less for his successes in the field of weapons manufacturing than for his unbelievably grand and garish mansion, Armsmear. It's one of the most

© ANDREW COLLINS

CONN. RIVER VALLEY

**Inspired by travels in Russia and Turkey, Samuel Colt set an eye-catching onion dome atop his 1855 Colt Patent Fire Arms Manufacturing Plant, where thousands of workers manufactured Colt's eponymous guns for years. Today, it's home only to a smattering of apartments and artists' studios.**

flamboyant monuments of personal wealth created in the United States prior to the Civil War, and one that preceded the "cottages" Vanderbilt and friends constructed in Newport. Many speculate that Colt based the plans for the house on Queen Victoria's Osborne House, which she had commissioned in 1846 on the Isle of Wight. Colt's own residence, fit for a king, went up 11 years later in 1857.

Colt's lavish Italianate residence has been called the greatest and most dramatic home ever built in Connecticut (some might dispute that claim, considering the gaudy mansions of P. T. Barnum in Bridgeport—such as the 1849 Iranistan—but none of these still stand). It utilized design elements from both the Mediterranean and the Far East, and such rare-for-the-day technologies as indoor plumbing. Furnishings were imported from eastern Asia, and no expense whatsoever was spared.

The estate originally comprised a lake and fountains, a half-mile-long greenhouse, elaborate sculpture gardens, rustic bridges, and a deer park, plus a fine view of the Connecticut River and Colt Village. Mrs. Colt stipulated in her will that the estate be used as a residence for "widows and orphans of Episcopal clergy and other refined and educated gentlewomen," and so the building is not a museum per se, but is occasionally opened to the public for tours, by appointment only. Samuel Colt had few years to enjoy this palace; he died of pneumonia in 1862 at the age of 47.

His wife, Elizabeth, lived for another 40 years, never remarrying and continuing to run his company with a deft hand. She was a premier patron of the arts, with strong ties to painters, sculptors, and other creative souls. Her connections accounted for much of Armsmear's artistic touches, including a superb gallery of fine arts, and she is remembered today for having been one of the greatest philanthropists Hartford has ever known.

Wethersfield Avenue, and Main Street. You want to make the sharp 135-degree turn onto Maple, and then make your immediate left onto little one-way **Congress Street,** where gas lamps and cobblestone walks mark a wonderful little historic district of Italianate redbrick and brownstone two-family houses. The founders of Pratt & Whitney once lived along this street. Plans in the 1960s called for razing the block, but, thankfully, preservationists led by the Hartford Architecture Conservancy fought to keep the street intact.

At the end of Congress, turn left onto Morris Street and then right again back onto Wethersfield Avenue (you've basically driven a small triangle, beginning and ending at Colt Park), which you should follow south for a couple miles. This dull stretch through a not-too-thrilling part of town leads to Airport Road, onto which a left turn leads to Brainard Airport and several bland industrial parks. **Hartford-Brainard Airport** (Lindbergh Dr.), is the second oldest municipal airport in the nation and is now used for corporate charters, sightseeing companies, and private planes. In 1927 a throng of about 25,000 spectators gathered to watch Charles A. Lindbergh return to American soil following his historic solo transatlantic flight to Paris.

One attraction near the airport that is little written about, but quite worthy of a visit (especially if you've kids in tow), is the museum at the **Connecticut Resources Recovery Authority** (211 Murphy Rd., 860/247-4280, open noon–4 P.M. Wed.–Fri. Sept.–June, 10 A.M.–4 P.M. Tues.–Sat. July–Aug., free), which is dedicated to educating the public about the tremendous benefits of effective recycling and solid-waste management. This 6,500-square-foot facility contains surprisingly captivating exhibits explaining the recycling process and how these raw materials are used; also, from a mezzanine you can watch the machinery recycle bottles, cans, and plastic containers.

## The South End

Back on Airport Road, cross back under I-91 and continue through the intersection with Wethersfield Avenue; make your first right onto Franklin Avenue, which marks the spine of the city's Little Italy. There are plenty of tempting restaurants

and pastry shops to visit along here, with most of them clustered within a few blocks of the intersection of Franklin Avenue and South Street.

Head west along South Street to reach the southernmost of the city's emerald-green spaces, **Goodwin Park** (Maple Ave. and South St., 860/543-8876). This serene, rolling sanctuary offers a fitness trail, sports fields, paddle-tennis and tennis courts, volleyball, playgrounds, and a spray pool. Across from the park's western border is the dignified entrance to **Cedar Hill Cemetery** (254 Fairfield Ave., 860/956-3311), which was established in 1864 and landscaped by Bushnell Park architect Jacob Weidenmann, who is also one of many important Hartford residents interred here. Others marked by the burial ground's many tall monuments and headstones include Samuel and Elizabeth Colt, Horace Wells (little-known developer of anesthesia), and J. P. Morgan (the noted industrialist). You can pick up a brochure listing prominent gravesites at the main gate.

## Trinity College and Environs

Head north of the cemetery along Fairfield Avenue, crossing New Britain Avenue and continuing along Zion Street, a neighborhood known locally as Behind the Rocks. On your right you'll come to the Summit Street entrance to the campus of **Trinity College** (300 Summit St., 860/297-2001, www.trincoll.edu, campus tours by appointment). Now secular, Trinity was formed in 1824 as an Episcopal college (it was known during its earliest years as Washington College) and stood then on what is now the site of the State Capitol (which explains why Trinity Street bisects Bushnell Park, and not Trinity's campus). It moved in 1872 to Gallows Hill, the highest point in Hartford, so-named for having been the former site of the city's public executions.

The campus now comprises 100 leafy acres bounded by Summit, Vernon, and Broad Streets and New Britain Avenue. Its distinguishing feature is the tall 1932 English Perpendicular Gothic-style chapel, whose spire is visible from all over the city, most obviously as you approach Hartford from the west on I-84 (look to your right as you pass exit 45); the chapel adjoins a peaceful cloister on its south side. Architect

William Burges designed the chapel and the school's many other Oxford-inspired structures, which are set around a magnificent square. This grouping of Gothic beauties is known as the "Long Walk," and indeed, you should take your time strolling in their imposing shadows. If you have time, drop by Trinity's **Austin Arts Center** (860/297-2199, www.austinarts.org, limited hours, open daily), which mounts fine arts exhibits throughout the school year and also presents live entertainment. Also on campus is the art-film theater **Cinestudio** and the well-stocked **Gallows Hill Bookstore.** Presently, Trinity is in the midst of a major campus renovation, including the recent construction of new dorms and academic buildings, as well as redesigned walkways and outdoors areas. Near-term projects include a state-of-the-art library addition and restoration of Trinity College Chapel; long-term changes include a new hockey rink, art history galleries, and expansion of Austin Arts Center. Expect to see the campus buzzing with activity until at least 2010.

A couple blocks east of Trinity, via Vernon Street, make a right onto Washington Street, where you'll come upon the 35-acre **Institute of Living** (400 Washington St., 860/545-7000, open by appointment), a stunningly landscaped compound whose grounds, main mansion, and outbuildings were designed as a collaborative effort by such notables as Calvert Vaux, Frederick Law Olmsted, Jacob Weidenmann, George Keller, and numerous others. The institute opened at the turn of the 20th century as a remarkable and humane experiment in psychiatric care—up to this point the mentally ill were typically cared for in harsh and dreary asylums. On weekdays, you can stop at the guard's booth for permission and instructions on how to tour the grounds.

Head north on Washington Street, making a left on Park Street, to reach another of the city's great crowns of greenery, **Pope Park** (Park St., 860/543-8876). This 89-acre plot was given to the city in 1898 by Colonel Albert A. Pope, whose nearby Pope Manufacturing Company was famous for its Columbia Bicycles (and later for building electric automobiles). Not far from the capitol and the southern edge of downtown, this

neighborhood has long been known as **Frog Hollow,** and it occupies an illustrious place in the city's industrial history. Throughout this neighborhood during the late 19th century, such manufacturing giants as Weed Sewing Machines (which became the Pope Company), Underwood Typewriters, Pratt & Whitney, and Sharps Rifles lined Capitol Avenue and the streets around it.

# WEST END HARTFORD SIGHTS

The West End is easily accessed from Pope Park and the Frog Hollow neighborhood. Just get to the intersection of Capitol Avenue and Broad Street, and head north on Broad under I-84 to Farmington Avenue, the West End's main commercial spine. Or, from downtown, head west on Asylum Street (which becomes Asylum Avenue west of downtown), passing over I-84, until you reach Farmington Avenue. Most of the West End's points of interest are along either Farmington or Asylum, which diverge in a westerly direction from their intersection just beyond I-84.

## Lord's Hill

This area, at about where Farmington and Asylum Avenues meet, was once known as Lord's Hill and consisted of several regal buildings, some of which were destroyed to make way for I-84, which now cuts along the base of the hill. One of the greatest of those demolished was the George Keller-designed Hartford Public High School, a grand turreted affair that went up in 1870 and was razed in 1963.

Asylum Avenue was originally called the Litchfield Turnpike, but was renamed in honor of the Connecticut Asylum for the Education and Instruction of Deaf and Dumb Persons, the first such institution in America. It stood atop Lord's Hill before moving to West Hartford (and being renamed the American School for the Deaf) in 1919. Today, Lord's Hill is dominated by the headquarters of the **Aetna Insurance Company** (151 Farmington Ave., 860/273-0123, tours by appointment); this grand complex dates from the 1930s and is considered to be the largest Colonial-style building in America.

Across the street you'll detect the high spires of

the **Cathedral of St. Joseph** (140 Farmington Ave., 860/249-8431, open daily, free tours by appointment), which is notable for its 26 enormous stained-glass windows and for the world's largest ceramic mural, *Christ in Glory*. The present structure, although vaguely art deco in style, was actually built between 1958 and 1962. It replaced what had been one of New England's most elaborate cathedrals, an ornate 1877 creation designed by the same architect as New York City's St. Patrick's. It took 25 years to build, but just one evening—New Year's Eve, 1956—to burn completely (in a freak fire).

Just northeast of here, on the site of the original Connecticut Asylum, stands the elaborate headquarters of **Hartford Fire Insurance** (690 Asylum Ave., not open to the public). Founded in 1810, this is the oldest insurer in the state (and third-oldest in America); its present main building, noted for its gracious domed roofline, dates from 1921, although the entire complex now encompasses several structures, including a 22-story office tower that went up in the 1960s. The Pulitzer Prize–winning poet Wallace Stevens toiled for years as an executive with the company—very few of his colleagues ever had any knowledge of his literary life, and very few of his readers had any knowledge of Stevens's white-collar workaday life.

## Nook Farm

From here, head back down to Farmington Avenue and drive a few blocks west to reach the Nook Farm neighborhood, which in the late 1800s constituted one of New England's greatest literary communities. Harriet Beecher Stowe, William Gillette (the Shakespearean actor who later built Gillette Castle, in East Haddam), and Mark Twain were among the best-known residents. Indeed, one of the state's most treasured landmarks is the 19-room **Mark Twain House** (351 Farmington Ave., 860/247-0998, www.marktwainhouse.org, hours vary, so phone ahead, open daily May–Oct. and Dec., closed Tues. Jan.–Apr. and Nov.; one-hour tour only, $9), which is getting a lot of attention these days, especially after the publicity generated by the 2001 release of the Ken Burns PBS docu-

mentary on the author. Mark Twain (whose birth name was Samuel Langhorne Clemens) commissioned architect Edward T. Potter to construct this opulent Victorian home in 1874; he lived here with his family during the prime of his literary career (until 1891), during which he penned such classics as *The Adventures of Tom Sawyer, Adventures of Huckleberry Finn, The Prince and the Pauper, Life on the Mississippi,* and *A Connecticut Yankee in King Arthur's Court.* From this house, Twain submitted the first-ever typewritten manuscript, *Tom Sawyer.* The interior, designed largely by Louis Comfort Tiffany, has been meticulously restored and includes many of the author's original furnishings and belongings. Much of the work on the house has already been completed; opened in recent years to the public, for instance, were the drawing room, a spare bedroom, and a butler's quarters. Future projects include restoring many of the wall coverings, upholstery, and furnishings; opening a state-of-the-art resource center in the basement, where visitors can study and discuss Twain's ideas and characters on computers; and a 35,000-square-foot visitors center that shall be behind the carriage house—this center will hold a library, galleries, a theater, an a lecture space. The building was scheduled to open in fall 2003.

Nearly across the street is the **Harriet Beecher Stowe Center** (73 Forest St., 860/522-9258, www.harrietbeecherstowecenter.org, open daily June–early Oct. and Dec., Tues.–Sat. otherwise, $6.50, which includes admission to both houses), an 1871 Victorian "cottage" in which the author of *Uncle Tom's Cabin* lived from 1873 until her death in 1896. Guided tours offer a glimpse into Stowe's abolitionist politics and other novel notions about social reform, and reveal how sharply Stowe's taste differed from her neighbor's, Mark Twain. Her furnishings tend to be comfortable and quite modern for the times, rather than showy. Outside the house are perfectly preserved period gardens, and also on the grounds is the 1882 **Katharine S. Day House,** a considerably more lavish Victorian that was purchased in 1939 by Stowe's granddaughter, Katharine Day. The home now serves

## MARK TWAIN

In the eyes of the many fans of such literary classics as *Tom Sawyer* and *Huckleberry Finn*, Mark Twain (1835–1910) is closely associated with the home of his early years, the Mississippi River town of Hannibal, Missouri. But from 1871 to 1891, he resided in the mansion that now preserves his legacy in Hartford's West End. He spent the final few years of his life on a magnificent estate called Stormfield, in the northern Fairfield County town of Redding—alas, it burned to the ground many years ago.

Born Samuel Clemens in Florida, Missouri, in 1835, Twain (as we'll call him here, although he used both names throughout his life) spent his childhood in Hannibal, but had embarked on an itinerant career as a newspaper journalist by the time he reached his late teens.

For a period of about 15 years, he lived in such varied locales as Cincinnati, Ohio; Hawaii; Keokuk, Iowa; New York City; San Francisco; Virginia City, Nevada; and Washington, D.C. And he first earned a widespread name for himself with the publication of *Innocents Abroad* in 1869.

It is in the house at Nook Farm, on Farmington Avenue, that Twain facilitated a great literary community of the day, and also penned the majority of his most famous works. He also raised three daughters there—Susy, Clara, and Jean—with his wife, Olivia Langon Clemens. After living in Connecticut for nearly two decades, Twain then traveled abroad for 10 years, living in Austria, England, France, Italy, and several other countries at various times.

BOB RACE

as a library, whose focus is cultural and family history, 19th-century American literature, social reform, and women's history. It also contains rooms decorated in period style.

Just down the street, at 133 Hawthorne Street (near the corner of Forest) is the private home in which Katharine Hepburn grew up.

Back on Farmington Avenue, continue west a couple blocks, making a right onto Sherman Street. This neighborhood is filled with the Victorian residential architecture typical of Nook Farm, and you'll find quite a few notable examples of the Gothic, Stick, and Queen Anne styles on these blocks. A glaring but quite handsome exception to this rule is the **Hartford Seminary** (77 Sherman St., 860/509-9500, www.hartsem.edu), a minimalist 1981 structure created by Richard Meier, the man best known for Los Angeles's new Getty Center. The seminary used to be across the street, occupying the 20-acre campus of 1920s Gothic school buildings that now houses the **University of Connecticut School of Law** (55 Elizabeth St.,

860/570-5100, www.law.uconn.edu). This campus is patterned after Magdalen College at England's Oxford University.

Just east of campus, beyond where Elizabeth Street intersects with Asylum Avenue, is about where the North Branch of the Park River empties into pipes and meanders in an easterly direction below Bushnell Park and downtown before emptying into the Connecticut River. The South Branch remains uncovered and flows down beside the Mark Twain House, under I-84, through Pope Park, and eventually into West Hartford.

### Elizabeth Park and Environs

At the aforementioned intersection of Elizabeth and Asylum you'll find the **Connecticut Historical Society** (1 Elizabeth St., 860/236-5621, www.chs.org, open noon–5 P.M. Tues.–Sun., $6), which contains a research library and a museum offering regularly rotating temporary exhibits. The society was founded in 1825, and the permanent collection includes an especially impressive assortment of 17th- and 18th-century Connecticut decorative arts. The library contains a tremendous genealogical collection, ideal for native Nutmeggers looking to trace their roots. This society occupies a grand 1928 home that once belonged to Curtis Veeder, who invented the rotary counting device, which he adapted into the speedometer now used in automobiles. In 2000, the society announced tentative plans to move into a brand-new state-of-the-art space on Zion Street, near Trinity College. The 115,000-square-foot building would be designed by world-renowned architect Frank Gehry (famous for the Guggenheim Museum in Bilbao, Spain, and dozens of notable contemporary houses and buildings in greater Los Angeles). This move won't take place until 2007 or so at the earliest.

Head west on Elizabeth Street to reach one of the most beautiful (and overlooked) rose gardens in America, **Elizabeth Park** (Prospect and Asylum Aves., 860/231-9443, www.elizabeth-park.org, open daily year-round, greenhouses open 8 A.M.– 3 P.M. weekdays). Laid out in 1897 by the firm of Hartford native Frederick Law Olmsted, this oval 2.5-acre park is the nation's first municipally owned rose garden, and it contains some 15,000 bushes, encompassing more than 800 varieties. A rose festival is held here in June, but any time from May through October is ideal for seeing the roses in full bloom, along with an annual tulip garden, perennial and rock gardens, and flowering shrubs. There are also sports fields and tennis courts at this 102-acre park, part of which lies in West Hartford, and in warm weather, a series of outdoor concerts is held. In winter, the park's pond is popular for ice-skating. The **Pond House Cafe** (860/231-8823) at Elizabeth Park has one of the region's most appealing settings. In case anybody thinks there's yet another connection here to the Colts, Elizabeth Park was actually named by Charles Pond, who left his estate to the city with the specification that it be turned into a horticultural park and named for his wife, Elizabeth.

The neighborhood north of Elizabeth Park is the city's most prestigious; Prospect Avenue and Scarborough Street, along with several neighboring streets, are studded with grand homes from the early part of this century. It's a pretty spot for biking, strolling, or driving around. Just north of Elizabeth Park is the 1909 **Governor's Residence** (860/524-7356, one-hour tours 10 A.M. Tues.–Wed., by appointment only, Jan.–June and Sept.–Oct. free), which has been home to the state's first families since 1945.

In this same neighborhood is Hartford's quirkiest attraction, the **Menczer Museum of Medicine and Dentistry** (230 Scarborough Street, 860/236-5613, www.library.uchc.edu/hms, open 9:30 A.M.–4:30 P.M. weekdays, free). A curious house with nine rooms filled with medical and dental instruments that date from the 18th to 20th centuries—some of the devices quite painful and unpleasant looking—the Menczer pays special homage to the life of Horace Wells, the Hartford resident who developed anesthesia. This accomplishment may not sound as important as the invention of the telephone or the automobile, but anybody who's ever undergone surgery may readily appreciate what the experience might have felt like had Wells not found a medical use for nitrous oxide ("laughing gas") in 1844. Apparently, there was a dark side to Wells's experimentation; he's alleged by some to have experienced a Jekyll-and-Hyde transformation into a serial killer under the influences of the gas. The constant trials with the drug seem likely to have contributed to his death at the early age of 33.

## SHOPPING

One major thing missing from downtown Hartford is an appealing and vibrant retail base. Downtown is mostly filled with prosaic workaday businesses, from wig shops to occupational-uniform stores to delis. For boutiquing, residents head to West Hartford's or Glastonbury's downtown, and for major mall browsing, they favor either Westfarms Mall in Farmington or Buckland Mall in Manchester.

A few of the city's museums have first-rate shops, including the Wadsworth Atheneum, the Old State House, the Mark Twain House, and the Connecticut Historical Society. On Trinity College's campus, you'll find an excellent selection of academic and popular works at the **Gallows Hill Bookstore** (860/297-5231).

A great stop for bric-a-brac is the **Hartford Flea Market** (380 Market St., 888/445-6543, www.hartfordfleamarket.com, open weekends Apr.– Dec.) where a litany of vendors sell crafts, antiques, cosmetic, clothing, and other goods.

## RECREATION
### Along the River

One fine byproduct of the renewed interest in the Connecticut River has been the establishment of the **Riverfront Recapture Community Rowing Program** (1 Hartford Square W, Hartford, CT 06106, 860/713-3131, www.riverfront.org). Anyone over 14 and able to swim is welcome to enroll in rowing and canoeing classes (both sweep and sculling programs are offered), which are held twice a week from early June through early October. This is a very popular program, and a terrific way to build your rowing skills while also working toward the betterment of the community. To reach the Riverside Park, take exit 33 from I-91, follow Jennings Road toward the river, turn right onto Leibert Road, and watch for park entrance signs.

Riverfront Recapture also administers both Charter Oak Landing and Riverside Park, as well as the cycling and walking pathways that now or will soon line both banks of the Connecticut River.

### Golf

Hartford has a couple of fine public 1920s-era municipal golf courses at Goodwin and Keney Parks. **Keney Golf Course** (280 Tower Ave., 860/525-3656) is a tight par-70 course that was restored a few years ago; **Goodwin Park Golf Course** (1130 Maple Ave., 860/956-3601) comprises a short nine-hole par-35 and a comparatively more challenging, but still basic, par-70 18-holer.

### City Parks

The city has long been known for its great parks, many of which are detailed, under their respective neighborhoods, in the Sights sections above. These include Bushnell, Colt, Elizabeth, Good-

win, and Pope Parks. Another one, at the north end of the city, with especially good recreational facilities, is **Keney Park** (Tower Ave. and Garden St., 860/722-6506), which has a swimming pool, tennis and basketball courts, and various playing fields (including a cricket round). It's home to the Hartford mounted police and stables.

### Spectator Sports

Hartford's NHL hockey team, the Whalers, left the city in 1997, but you can still watch minor-league hockey's **Hartford Wolf Pack** (860/548-2000, www.hartfordwolfpack.com), which plays at the Hartford Civic Center all winter long.

Golf fans head to nearby Cromwell each July to watch top pros compete in the PGA's **Greater Hartford Open** (860/522-4171, www.ghogolf.com).

A new football stadium, **Rentschler Field,** was built in 2003 just across the river from Hartford, on the former site of Pratt & Whitney airfield in East Hartford. It's a stunning stadium, with seating for about 40,000 fans. For ticket and schedule information concerning UConn football games at Rentschler field, contact the UConn Ticket Office (860/486-2724 or 877/AT-UCONN, www.uconnhuskies.com).

## ENTERTAINMENT
### Theater

Founded in 1964, the nationally acclaimed **Hartford Stage Company** (50 Church St., 860/527-5151, www.hartfordstage.org) offers six plays per year (Sept.–June), including both new innovative works and classic dramas, as well as various discussions and seminars with playwrights and directors. The company performs in a dramatic (but not universally admired) building designed in 1977 by the noted contemporary architect Robert Venturi. Hartford Stage's former home was an old Sears & Roebuck garage on Market Street; it was razed to make way for Northeast Plaza. (Evening shows are held Tues.–Sun., with matinees Wed. and Sun. and sometimes on Thurs. and Sat.)

**TheaterWorks** (233 Pearl St., 860/527-7838) is an off Broadway-style theater that's vastly underrated considering the high caliber of its mostly contemporary, avant-garde, and experimental productions; performances are evenings Tuesday–Saturday, and matinees are on Sunday. The city's top non-equity performance space is the **Producers Guild** (Wallace Stevens Theater, 690 Asylum Ave., 860/528-2143); it presents a wide-range of high-quality plays featuring local actors, and ticket prices are quite reasonable.

## Music and Dance

One of the leading performance venues in the northeast, the stunning **Bushnell Memorial Hall** (166 Capitol Ave., 860/987-5900, box office open 10 A.M.–5 P.M. Mon.–Sat., noon–4 P.M. Sun.) has been dazzling Hartford audiences since 1930. A full repertoire of Broadway hits and top classical and dance groups come here regularly. The Bushnell is also the regular home of the **Connecticut Opera** (860/527-0713, www.connecticutopera.org), and the **Hartford Symphony** (860/244-2999, www.hartfordsymphony.org), which also sponsors the **Classical Conversations** series (860/246-6807), affording visitors a chance to learn about the lives of noted composers. The most economical way to enjoy the greatest variety of performances is to subscribe to a series; several flexible subscription plans are offered, where you can mix and match events from different genres (e.g., see a mix of music, theater, and dance performances). Another Bushnell feature is the **Connecticut Forum** (860/509-0909, www.ctforum.org), an engaging lecture series that draws in scholars, educators, and other noteworthy speakers.

In northern Hartford's industrial area you'll find **Meadows Music Theatre** (61 Savitt Way, 860/548-7370, www.meadowsmusic.com), a highly successful outdoor and indoor performing arts venue that has already hosted R.E.M., Michael Bolton, Elton John, and other major performers. Monday nights in July and August, you can come to Bushnell Park to hear the **Hartford Jazz Festival** (860/233-5105). **Summer Wind Performing Arts Center** (40 Griffin Rd. N, Windsor, 860/687-9836 or 800/477-6849, www.tickets.com) is the newest concert venue in the Connecticut River Valley, a lovely outdoor space with seating for 1,500 under a canopy and 4,500 on the lawn. Jazz, opera, R&B, and soul are among the offerings.

## Film

Hartford's major multiscreen movie theater is **Cinema City** (235 Brainard Rd., 860/549-0030), down near Brainard Airport. The relatively new **Crown Palace 17 & Odyssey Theatre** (New Park Ave., off Exit 44 of I-84, 860/236-6677, www.crowntheaters.com) is a magnificent 17-screen cinema with a five-story IMAX-style theater. Founded in 1975, **Real Art Ways** (56 Arbor St., 860/232-1006, www.realartways.org) offers cutting-edge cinema in the way of nightly after-work movies. It's the state's most respected spot for contemporary film, and it also has a 5,000-square-foot gallery space renowned for its provocative installations. Another fun place to catch cerebral flicks is Trinity College's **Cinestudio** (300 Summit St., 860/297-2463, www.cinestudio.org.), which presents an intriguing mix of vintage movies, new indies, and film festivals—there's balcony seating, too.

# NIGHTLIFE

Several of the restaurants detailed below are also popular spots for bending the elbow. You'll never go wrong with either the food or the blues music at **Black-Eyed Sally's** (350 Asylum St., 860/278-7427).

## Brewpubs

Head to the **Trout Brook Brewery** (45 Bartholomew Ave., 860/951-1680) to play pool, watch sports on TV, on hang out with a raucous collegiate crowd. Downtown's City Steam Brewery Cafe is home to the **Brew Ha Ha** comedy club (942 Main St., 860/525-1600), and also has a pool and games area, live music many nights, and its signature brewed-on-site ales and stouts.

## Singles Haunts

Fairly lively singles joints include **Pig's Eye Pub** (356 Asylum St., 860/278-4747), which is attached to Black-Eyed Sally's and has a nice patio;

**88 Pratt Street** (88 Pratt St., 860/522-7623), which is close to the Civic Center and popular after sporting events and concerts; and the nearby **Scarlett O'Hara's** (59 Pratt St., 860/728-8290), which frequently offers live music and acoustic jams—it's a nice place to come with friends or in hopes of meeting new ones.

## Gay Bars and Clubs

**Polo Club** (678 Maple Ave., 860/278-3333) is a loud, lively gay bar with stage and drag shows and general dancing among the patrons when drag acts aren't performing. **Chez Est** (458 Wethersfield Ave., 860/525-3243) is a longtime men's disco and club.

## Hangouts

The food at **Coach's Sports Bar** (187 Allyn St., 860/525-5141) is nothing special, but this is a nice spot to congregate before, during, or after sporting events. **Arch Street Tavern/Café 85** (85 Arch St., 860/246-7610) is a handsome brick space that cultivates a dressy after-work following, serves a nice selection of comfort foods and great beer, and offers live music some nights—it's on the edge of the new Adriaen's Landing development. The **Half Door** (270 Sisson Ave., 860/232-PUBS) is a lively, warmly furnished Irish Pub that hosts live Irish music many evenings.

## Live Music and Clubbing

The **Brick Yard** (113 Allyn St., 860/249-2112) is one of the city's top rock venues, booking both local and national acts. A very respected live music venue for rock, alternative, and other regional and some national bands is the **Webster** (31 Webster St., 860/525-5553, www.webstertheatre.com). At trendy Pastis restaurant, the **Rhythm Room** (201 Ann St., 860/278-8852) presents live jazz most nights and is a swank place for cocktails.

## FESTIVALS AND EVENTS

### Summer

Held in Elizabeth Park late in each June, **Rose Weekend** (860/242-0017) is the perfect time to see the garden's stunning collection of roses in their peak bloom. Also in mid-June, let your

taste buds warm to the **Taste of Hartford** festival (860/728-3089). Over the Fourth of July, enthusiasts of the city's newly restored waterfront enjoy live music and fireworks at **Riverfest** (860/713-3131).

### Fall

At the end of September, Bushnell Park hosts the **African-American Parade/Sharpe Rib Burn-off/Rally & Bazaar** (860/242-1734), a multifaceted affair with a procession of floats and bands (beginning at Bushnell and ending at Keney Park) and a sizzling rib cook-off. Mid-October sees the **Greater Hartford Marathon** (860/652-8866), which includes 26.2-, 13.1-, and 3.1-mile runs for adults and kids. In mid-November, shoppers seek out holiday-gift ideas at the **Fall Home Show** (860/563-2111). It's held at the Connecticut Expo Center, which later in the month hosts the **International Auto Show** (860/246-6566, see the Expo Center website, www.ctexpocenter.com, for a full list of events held there throughout the year).

### Winter

Hartford has never been shy about celebrating the coming of winter and the December holidays. Constitution Plaza's **Festival of Light** (860/525-8629) kicks off with the day-after-Thanksgiving kindling of some 200,000 lights in the form of angels, bells, and other fanciful shapes. The lights remain aglow each night until January 6. Other holiday-minded events include two **Christmas Crafts Expos** (Connecticut Expo Center, 860/653-6671, on consecutive weekends in early Dec.); the Wadsworth Atheneum's week-long **Festival of Trees** (860/278-2670); the **Holiday Light Fantasia** (Goodwin Park, 860/343-1565), which celebrates Chanukah, Kwanzaa, Christmas, New Year's, and Three Kings Day with beautiful lights, lasting from late November through early January; and New Year's Eve's traditional **First Night** celebration (860/728-3089).

### Spring

In early March, the Connecticut Expo Center hosts the **Original Connecticut Home Show** (860/563-2111), which for more than a half-century has given the public a glimpse at new and innovative products and design ideas for the home. The **Connecticut Spring Antiques Show** (207/767-3967), held in late March at the Connecticut Expo Center, is well respected for its major representation of Early American furniture and decorative arts.

## ACCOMMODATIONS

Hartford's hotel scene has changed a great deal in recent years, with several properties changing names and some new ones opening. Still, there aren't a ton of options right in the city itself. In the downtown area, you'll find some upscale business hotels, and on the city's northern and southern fringes, just off I-91, there are some budget properties, but they vary greatly in quality and all suffer from rather drab industrial settings. If you're trying to save money and you don't mind a 10- to 25-minute drive, you'll find a better range of inexpensive chain hotels in the towns north and south of Hartford along I-91, especially Enfield, Windsor Locks (by the airport), Wethersfield, and Rocky Hill.

### Downtown

**$150–250:** The centrally located **Goodwin Hotel** (1 Haynes St., 860/246-7500 or 800/922-5006, www.goodwinhotel.com) looks and feels like the distinctive first-class hostelry it's long aspired to be—for a while there, the dull guest rooms failed to match the character of the hotel's vintage 1881 Queen Anne exterior. Rooms now have tastefully sumptuous furnishings, from chintz floral bedspreads to striped white-and-green drapes; some have sleigh beds, and a few suites have loft sleeping areas—it's not hard to understand why this is a top choice of visiting celebrities. Voicemail, data ports, and all the expected amenities of the modern working world keep business travelers pleased and weekday rates high—beginning around $200 for standard rooms. Weekends, however, are a relative bargain starting at under $100 (sometimes well under, depending on specials and packages). Off the lobby, a spectacular barrel-vaulted atrium regularly hosts glamorous soirees and wedding fêtes, and Pierpont's restaurant serves fine

Continental and regional American fare ($14–26)—although the food and service have received mixed reviews in recent years. There's also a full health club.

Although it's primarily geared toward convention groups and meetings, the elegant **Hastings Hotel** (85 Sigourney St., 800/569-4115, www.dolce.com) does book rooms to individuals when there's availability. There's a full gymnasium and fitness center, steam rooms and saunas, and 271 comfortable, upscale rooms. The hotel is on the west side of downtown, close to many restaurants and attractions. Downtown's newest hotel, the **Marriott Residence Inn** (942 Main St., 860/524-5550 or 800/331-3131) opened inside the historic Richardson Building in 2001. Studio, one-, and two-bedroom suites are available, each with fully equipped kitchens, living and dining areas, and work desks. These spacious units are great if you're staying for more than a few days; guests can take advantage of a complimentary grocery-shopping service, an exercise room, and free breakfast each morning. There are shops and restaurant's on the buildings ground floor.

**Hilton Hartford** (315 Trumbull St., 860/728-5151 or 800/HILTONS, www.hartford.hilton.com) is a grand, towering business-oriented hotel central to just about every attraction in downtown Hartford, and although the exterior is a bit dull, the Hilton sparkles from the inside. There are nearly 400 rooms, a full business center, a restaurant and sports bar, room service, a health club and indoor pool with sauna and whirlpool, and a coin laundry. The **Crowne Plaza Hartford Downtown** (50 Morgan St., 860/549-2400 or 800/2-CROWNE), an 18-story property just north of I-84, underwent a massive top-to-bottom refurbishment not long ago, and it now looks and feels first-class. There are 350 rooms, and facilities include a restaurant and lounge, pool, and fitness room.

Although it's technically across the river in East Hartford, the **Sheraton Hartford Hotel** (100 E. River Rd., 860/289-9703 or 800/325-3535) is a very short drive or cab ride from everything Hartford has to offer—it's a short walk from the restored Connecticut riverfront. Although the exterior of this recently renovated midrise dates from an architecturally uninspired time, the interior sparkles with handsome rooms that have ergonomically correct work areas and lots of room to spread out. There's a business center, indoor pool, fitness center, restaurant, and a lounge with live jazz many nights.

### Elsewhere

**$50–100:** Look past the bland industrial setting south of downtown and the similarly uninspired facade: The **Park Inn** (185 Brainard Rd., 860/525-9306 or 800/670-7275) is one of the city's better under-$75 sleeps. These units have adjoining sleeping and sitting areas divided by archways, and there's plenty of space to spread out. There's a pool and exercise room on the premises. The USS Chowder Pot IV seafood restaurant is next door, as is a multiplex cinema.

North of downtown, and just off I-91 at exit 33 (convenient to the Meadows Music Theater), the **Red Roof Inn** (100 Weston St., 860/724-0222 or 800/THE-ROOF) compares favorably with the Park Inn, except that rooms are standard size. The "business kings" cost a few bucks more and are slightly larger than normal with big 25-inch TVs and writing desks; all rooms are clean with simple, but with well-kept furnishings, and guests get a free daily newspaper and free local calls. There's a fax and copy service on the premises, plus both a McDonald's and Burger King adjacent (so you can host your very own battle of the burgers in your room). Be aware that this semi-industrial area is dreary.

**Under $50:** If you're on a budget and don't mind simple accommodations, consider staying at the **Mark Twain Hostel** (131 Tremont St., Hartford, 860/523-7255), a clean and safe place in the pleasant west end of town, near the Mark Twain museum and several good restaurants. There's 24-hour access, laundry facilities, a fully equipped kitchen, and common rooms; it's just $18 nightly, and major credit cards are accepted. Another good choice for students and budget travelers is the 158-room **Greater Hartford YMCA** (160 Jewell St., Hartford, 860/522-4183, www.ghymca.org), which is right across from the Hartford Civic Center.

## FOOD

With politicians and business leaders always pressing for stylish venues for hobnobbing and deal-making, Hartford has no shortage of excellent restaurants, the top three or four among the finest in the state. At the next tier, the city has lively bistros, trattorias, and cafés of good to excellent quality but still trails the suburbs (especially the Farmington River Valley and Glastonbury) in this mid- to upper-priced genre of restaurants when it comes to consistency and ambience. The city's greatest strength lies in its variety of ethnic eateries, especially those in the South End, whose Little Italy is the second-most-respected in the state (trailing only New Haven).

### Downtown

**Upscale:** The flagship of a highly trendy greater Hartford mini-empire (other Max restaurants are in Avon and Glastonbury), **Max Downtown** (CityPlace, 185 Asylum St., 860/522-2530, $19–33) is a dashing space descended upon regularly by the city's power brokers and deal makers. Framed by tall windows, amber chandeliers, and color-splashed murals, this slick dining room offers first-rate New American fare. Consider coconut-crusted shrimp with Asian cabbage slaw and wasabi-coriander vinaigrette, or grilled double-cut pork chops with fresh corn polenta and black bean salsa. Nine-to-fivers cut loose after work with cigars and martinis in the adjacent GarBar.

From the valet parking to the judicious use of surreal lamps and artsy mirrors, the ultra-chic **Trumbull Kitchen** (150 Trumbull St., 860/493-7417, $6–20) feels more L.A. than Hartford, hence the difficulty you can sometimes expect scoring a table. It's worth persevering, though, for the chance to sample the tasty cooking at this tapas-style restaurant that features a variety of small plates, salads, and pizzas, plus a handful of more substantial (but still moderately priced) dishes. Highlights include Atlantic salmon with a spicy coconut curry, goat cheese–stuffed figs with prosciutto and balsamic vinegar, hoisin-roasted chicken salad, and the steamed clam, bacon, mozzarella, and fresh basil pizza. Grazing is the way to do things here.

For a slightly quieter and more intimate meal, try **Low Country** (391 Main St., 860/524-1508, $9–19), an upscale restaurant that serves outstanding cuisine of the South, with an emphasis on coastal Carolinian fare. Jazzy piped-in music sets the tone for purloo (rice, shrimp, grilled andouille, sausage, and chicken), deep-fried catfish with grits and pecan butter sauce, and fried chicken and waffles with maple syrup. The servers are deft and gracious, though a little poky some nights. Occupying the former lobby of the 1875 Hotel Capitol, Low Country blends African sculptures, gilt-frame mirrors, and exposed brick for a subtly striking appearance. There's a swish cocktail bar in back.

The popular steakhouse chain, **Morton's of Chicago** (30 State House Sq., 860/724-0044, $19–35), has a relatively new location in downtown Hartford; as you might guess, it's a favorite haunt of politicos and corporate bigwigs. Whole-baked Maine salmon, double filet mignon with Béarnaise sauce, and steak au poivre are favorite dishes at this courtly, masculine restaurant.

**Creative but Casual:** Of Hartford's new-style Italian eateries (as opposed to the many excellent traditional-style spots on Little Italy's Franklin Avenue), **Peppercorn's Grill** (357 Main St., 860/547-1714, $16–22) consistently offers the best food, most adept service, and happiest ambience—laid-back but dapper, with a nice bar that's perfect if you're dining alone. Standouts from the extensive menu include grills like medallions of Atlantic monkfish served over a ragout of cranberry beans, mushrooms, and spinach with a rosemary scented shrimp sauce, to intensely flavorful pastas. Drawing a young music-loving crowd, **Black-Eyed Sally's** (350 Asylum St., 860/278-7427, $10–20) emulates the blues and jazz clubs of Memphis and New Orleans with live music and portraits of music icons (including a classic Elvis on black velvet). The food reveals Southern influences (hickory-smoked meats, jambalaya, catfish, sweet-potato shrimp cakes, bourbon pecan pie), but plenty of eclectic pastas and grills are offered, too.

Black-Eyed Sally's is near Goodwin Park and another favorite of urban hipsters, **Hot Tomato's** (1 Union Place, 860/249-5100, $15–23), a boisterous spot fashioned out of the western wing of historic Union Station. The kitchen doles out massive portions of sauce-smothered pasta, chicken, and seafood, including pasta per Elvis (curly noodles baked with smoked bacon, caramelized onions, and a rich cheese sauce) and chicken pesto with homemade ricotta gnocchi. It's a tad pricey considering the lackluster (but friendly) service and mediocre wine selection, but there's no denying that people have fun here, from families with kids to couples on first dates. If the weather's cooperating, grab a seat on the terrace and enjoy the fine park views. **Pastis Brasserie & Wine Bar** (201 Ann St., 860/278-8852, $13–21) effectively captures the homey welcoming ambience of an authentic Parisian bistro, complete with beautiful moldings and wainscoting and a long snazzy zinc bar. Dishes like steak frites, foie gras ravioli, cassoulet, and mussels are prepared with the deft touch that good, simple Gallic fare requires, and the handsome wine list is mostly French.

Sample delectable Tuscan-inspired platters of salad, meat, cheese, panini sandwiches, biscotti, and other light bites at the slick new **Bin 228** (228 Pearl St., 860/244-9463, $13–21), an intimate eatery whose exposed-brick walls are lined with wine bins. There's a great selection of wines, nearly two dozen of them available by the glass.

One of the city's most acclaimed restaurants of recent years, **Spris** (10 Constitution Plaza, 860/247-7747, $11–25), serves first-rate contemporary Italian fare. A lengthy menu includes thin-crust pizzas (try the mare e monti, topped with shrimp, calamari, porcini mushrooms, and red sauce), pastas, and meat and fish grills. Grilled sirloin strips over a bed of arugula with a rosemary sauce is a satisfying entrée. It occupies the former studio of the defunct Gayle King TV show with panoramic views of Constitution Plaza. It's close to the riverfront and many downtown attractions. **Hotep's** (283 Asylum St., 860/548-1675, $14–23) offers a wonderfully eclectic menu of Caribbean, South American, and Latin American cuisines. Rather oddly, the interior has a vaguely Egyptian theme, with decorated elements from that country. There aren't too many menu items of Middle East origin, but everything served is quite good: yucca-crusted grouper served with coconut-pumpkin and shrimp ragout, scallion essence, and raita; a starter of baby-goat ravioli with shaved pecorino cheese; or cedar-wood-roasted mango and sorrel-painted salmon with tangerine rice.

**Steak, Pizza, Pub Grub, and Seafood:** The whimsically decorated brewpub **City Steam Brewery and Café** (942 Main St., 860/525-1600) is a maze of stained glass, exposed purple air ducts, and carved wooden staircases set in the historic Richardson Building in the heart of downtown. The vaguely German-influenced menu offers hearty favorites like chicken-sausage sandwiches with grilled onions and brewers mustard, plus a nice range of handcrafted brews. It's one of the few city center eateries open for lunch on Sunday. For the best downtown pizza, try **Vito's by the Park** (26 Trumbull St., 860/244-2200, $12–19, large pies $15–19), a bubbly European-inspired trattoria with French doors overlooking Bushnell Park and live Big Band music some nights. The D'Estate pie—topped with summer squash, fresh asparagus, and tomatoes—is a winner, as are any of the deep-dish stuffed varieties. Many traditional Italian dishes are also offered: cioppino, ziti with broccoli and

sausage, and several veal and beef dishes. For late-night dining, the **Wood-n-Tap Bar & Grill** (99 Sisson Ave., 860/232-TAPS, $8–23) is a great option for a snack or a meal; it has free parking, too. Chicken tenders, burgers, pizzas, pastas, steaks, and barbecue chicken are served.

**Polish:** In 1999, food-writing wonders Jane and Michael Stern, who live in Connecticut, wrote an almost lyrical reflection for *Gourmet* on the **Polish National Home** (60 Charter Oak Ave., 860/247-1784, $6–15). Consequently, this seeming model of simplicity has become one of the hottest tickets in town. Amid the swirl of neon beer signs and photographs of famous Polish sons, you can order delicious food like *kapusta* (a soup of cabbage, carrots, pork roast, and sausage), *placki* (potato pancakes with applesauce and sour cream), kielbasa sausage, and heavenly pierogis. On Sunday nights, the place is the home of *Polka Party,* a radio show on WRYM (840 AM) that's been going strong since the 1930s.

**Quick Bites:** West Hartford's delightful Tapas has a second spot in downtown Hartford, **Tapas on Ann** (126–130 Ann St., 860/525-5988, $8–15), where you'll find just a smattering of tables and chairs but plenty of great food (all

## LITTLE ITALY

Guess what? New York City's once-famous Little Italy currently comprises a block of Mulberry Street, the rest of it having been consumed by an ever-expanding Chinatown. In Boston, the once close-knit and Italian North End still has a few good restaurants, but it is now a yuppified and pricey neighborhood with no distinct ethnic identity. Where have all the great Little Italys gone?

Well, Connecticut has a pair of gems. New Haven's centers on Wooster Street, a short ways east of the village green, and is lined with exceptional restaurants—including Frank Pepe's, the home of America's first pizza pie. Several fine eateries along here are detailed in the New Haven section of the Connecticut Coast chapter.

Hartford's Little Italy may be slightly less known

than New Haven's, but you'll find a dizzying array of outstanding restaurants here, most of them along Franklin Avenue, where restaurants line both sides of the street, mostly from the 400 block south. You won't go wrong at any of these places. **Carbone's** (588 Franklin Ave., 860/296-9646, $17–26) is easily the star of the show—the perennial winner of newspaper polls and a darling of restaurant critics. Some locals suggest, quietly, that while Carbone's is quite nice it's perhaps a tad overrated and overpriced. At the other end of the spectrum, the **Original Ravioli Shop** (499 Franklin Ave., 860/296-1330) is an inexpensive spot for authentic groceries and handmade pastas; it also has its own small dining room and is perfect if you'd like a relatively quick taste of the neighborhood. In terms of value, quality, and service, **Chef Eugene** (428 available to go): mini pizzas such as the Basque, with herbed garlic sausage, brie, ricotta, mushrooms, and sundried tomatoes; chicken, pork, and veggie souvlaki; and seared salmon sandwiches topped with fresh lime-yogurt cilantro salsa.

**Java Joints:** Across from the Civic Center, **XandO** (103 Pratt St., 860/244-8233) is a remarkably homey coffeehouse (serving booze, too) with a handsome curved wooden bar, a timber-beam ceiling, ocher walls, leaded-glass windows, and a cozy balcony. Sip chai teas, vanilla lattes, or mocha martinis, or choose from the extensive by-the-glass wine list. Beware, it can get a bit smoky in here. Around the corner, **Pumpkin's** (54 Pratt St., 860/278-1600) offers hefty sandwiches, light snacks, and great coffees.

## Trinity College and the South End

**Brazilian:** A mix of locals and suits flock to **Chale Ipanema** (342 Franklin Ave., 860/296-2120, $13–23) for Brazilian-Portuguese fare, from bouillabaisse to *feijoada* to squid in a delicious brown sauce. In one of the two snazzy dining rooms that make up this town house restaurant, a band plays samba music on weekends.

**Afghan:** A few doors down the street, the aroma of coriander, bay leaves, and cardamom wafts from the front door of **Shish Kebab** 360 Franklin Ave., 860/296-0301, $11–17), the only Afghan restaurant in Connecticut. One imagines the owners gave it such an unadventuresome name in hopes of attracting novices to this splendid cuisine that shares characterics with Turkish, Indian, and several Middle Eastern cultures. Kebabs are indeed a mainstay, as is *kabeli palow*, a moist rice dish heaped with seasoned almonds, raisins, and carrots, served with vegetables and sautéed chicken or lamb. A soul-warming side of pumpkin puree goes well with any dish, as does the remarkably ungreasy starter of vegetable samosas. It's not on the menu, but be sure to request a dish of tangy homemade yogurt to ladle over your bread, or virtually any food you order. This place is top-notch.

**Spanish:** A block east of Franklin, **Costa del Sol** (901 Wethersfield Ave., 860/296-1714, $15–24) is a sophisticated Spanish restaurant, takeout shop, and specialty food store. You'll find their cold and hot tapas are extremely true to Spanish tradition (cured ham, artichoke hearts and white asparagus with vinaigrette, grilled squid with fried garlic), along with traditional paellas (including a vegetarian version) and grills.

Franklin Ave., 860/296-4540, $10–18) is the neighborhood's surest bet. The dining room on the ground floor of this modest house is simple and unmemorable, but the staff treats everybody like a member of the family, and the kitchen specializes in both the familiar (fettuccine carbonara and veal Sorrento) and the unusual. Typically enticing dishes are shrimp *karshere* (in a liquor cream sauce with bacon and roasted peppers) and veal Maryanne (with olives, mushrooms, sundried tomatoes, and a wine-and-cream sauce with a touch of marinara). Many locals swear that **Franklin Giant Grinders** (464 Franklin Ave., 860/296-6574, under $7) serves the best sub sandwiches in Connecticut— they're incredibly huge and filling.

It's a few blocks away from Little Italy proper (near Trinity College), but the always-packed **First and Last Tavern** (956 Maple Ave., 860/956-6000, $8–15) produces pizza (large pies $14–22) on par with any parlor in Connecticut. Regulars tear with delight upon biting into the piquant puttanesca pie, with tomatoes, olives, capers, anchovies, and spicy hot peppers. Other Italian favorites, from capicolla grinders to shrimp scampi, round out the menu. Wherever you take lunch or dinner, save room for the neighborhood's pièce de résistance, **Mozzicato de Pasquale's Bakery and Pastry Shop** (860/296-0426). This bright, spacious showroom for sweets is lined with shiny glass counters, racks piled high with Italian butter cookies, rum-soaked ricotta-filled babas, and castle-like wedding cakes. At one end, a row of vats spill over with freshly made gelato. A trip here will satisfy even the most severe sugar addict.

**Mexican:** Maybe the best Mexican food in town is served at a tiny hole-in-the-wall on Broad Street called **El Serape** (931 Broad St., 860/547-1884, $4–8), where fresh ingredients and old-fashioned recipes produce vibrant platters of tamales and tacos.

**Creative but Casual:** A stone's throw from the campus of Trinity College, **Timothy's** (243 Zion St., 860/728-9822, $5–10) is an art-filled storefront café typically buzzing with live music and invigorating conversation. The menu is remarkably eclectic, with many veggie dishes; burgers; Tex-Mex options like an enchilada filled with fresh sweet potatoes, tomatillos, and herbs; and grilled tuna in a tamari-ginger sauce (for just $9) with salad and mashed potatoes. Clearly, this place is trying to keep impoverished students from going hungry; even if you could afford to pay a little more, you'd be hard-pressed to find better food in a more inviting ambience. **Apps** (451 Franklin Ave., 860/296-2777, $8–32) specializes in tapas and has a sexy martini bar. A wide range of tasty foods are served, including gazpacho with lump crabmeat and topped with cumin crème fraîche; goat cheese fondue with chervil, green apple, and flat bread; and grilled Portobello mushrooms with sage, cherry tomatoes, and pine nuts. A few entrée portions are also offered. There's live music many nights.

**Java Joints: Omar Coffee Company** (555 Franklin Ave., 860/296-6627) is fun for a cup of great coffee—this is a sunny storefront coffeehouse in Hartford's Little Italy. There are a few seats inside, but it's more a place to pick up a drink during a stroll along Franklin Avenue. There's a nice selection of pastries, too.

## The West End

**Creative but Casual:** Set in a ripe-for-gentrification warehouse district just off I-84 (exit 46), the **Troutbrook Brewhouse** (45 Bartholomew Ave., 860/951-1680, $5–14) occupies an enormous industrial building refitted with several dining areas. A general sports theme prevails, with games shown on large-screen TVs, ranks of pool tables in one of the side bars, and live music offered many nights. The menu (which

has loads of kids' choices) offers a typically tasty array of comfort foods: wraps and sandwiches (try the Cajun crawfish salad variety for something a bit out of the ordinary), baby back ribs, a steak-and-clams casino combo, and plenty of smoked and barbecued items.

The **Pond House Cafe** (1555 Asylum Ave., Hartford/West Hartford border, 860/231-8823) occupies a charming building and location in genial Elizabeth Park, site of the noted rose gardens. The creative menu blends traditional French cuisine with nouvelle ingredients—you might start with duck consommé with fresh ginger and scallions, followed by grilled pheasant stuffed with nut-and-dried-fruit risotto and served with a raspberry vinaigrette. The Pond House Cafe, as the name suggests, overlooks a rippling pond and is particularly enjoyable for a meal when it's light outside and you can appreciate the scenery through the large windows.

**Quick Bites:** Something of a neighborhood legend, **Mo's Midtown** (25 Whitney St., 860/236-7741) is a plant-filled hole-in-the-wall diner in the historic heart of the West End. Tourists, truckers, and students feast side-by-side on pancakes, tuna melts, and other diner favorites. **Alchemy Juice Bar & Cafe** (203 New Britain Ave., 860/246-5700) is a pleasant cyber lounge and health-food eatery that offers smoothies, juices, and light snacks.

## Elsewhere

Hartford's Blue Hills area, a 10-minute drive north of downtown, is the home of a vibrant West Indian (mostly Jamaican) community. There's a small chain of Jamaican bakeries, all in this north side of the city, called **Scotts'**, with branches at 801 Windsor St., 860/243-2609; 1344 Albany Ave., 860/247-3855; 1711 Main St., 860/246-6599; and 630 Blue Hills Ave., 860/243-2609. Or consider **Apron Strings** (675 Blue Hills Ave., 860/243-9494, $4–9) where curried goat, oxtail, and kingfish await hungry diners. A second branch of Apron Strings is in the downtown Richardson Mall, at 942 Main Street, 860/549-4212, serving delicious Jamaican food closer to the heart of the city.

Not far from Brainard Airport, the **USS**

**Chowder Pot IV** (165 Brainard Rd., Hartford, 860/244-3311, $8–24), a branch of the popular Branford seafood restaurant, is decked in nautical kitsch and serves as a regular venue for the audience-participatory show *Joey & Maria's Comedy Wedding*. This corny extravaganza is presented about twice monthly (call at least two weeks before you're hoping to attend, as it books up early). The food itself is dependable and fresh, if not especially imaginative.

## INFORMATION AND SERVICES

### Visitor Information

Pamphlets, brochures, and tourism information are available through the **Greater Hartford Tourism District** (31 Pratt St., 4th Fl., Hartford, CT 06103, 860/244-8181 or 800/793-4480, www.enjoyhartford.com). There is also an information kiosk at the **Civic Center Mall** (Center Court, Trumbull and Asylum Sts., 860/275-6456) and there's also a staffed visitor center at the Old State House.

### Getting Around

**CTTRANSIT,** with an information booth at State House Square on Market Street (860/525-9181, www.cttransit.com), provides local bus service along 30 routes in Hartford, Farmington, West Hartford, and Wethersfield. The basic fare is $1, and some routes do not operate nights, Sundays, and holidays. It's definitely best to phone ahead to plot out any bus trips.

It's far more practical to use a car around Hartford, even though one is not needed to see most of the major downtown attractions. Hartford is not a difficult city to drive in, and it sits at the junction of two major Interstates, North–South I-91 and East–West I-84. Even with a few confusing intersections and one-way streets, traffic is neither horrendous nor exceedingly aggressive, and street parking is not hard to find outside of

© ANDREW COLLINS

On Main Street today, the stately triple-tiered spire of Hartford's 1807 Center Church (modeled on London's St.-Martin-in-the-Fields) is offset by more contemporary structures.

the city center. Within the city center, Hartford has some 20,000 parking spaces, from garages to metered spots. You can pick up an A&E District map from **Greater Hartford Arts Council,** which shows locations of garages and lots. Rates aren't bad, usually $1–4 hourly, $2–20 daily. Special events rates average $3–10.

As in any major city, it's best to remove valuables from your car seats and lock everything up whenever you leave your car; that said, car theft and related vandalism are considerably less common in Hartford than in Boston, New York City, or other major northeastern cities.

CONN. RIVER VALLEY

# Farmington River Valley

The Farmington River Valley, a swath of scenic heavily wooded towns extending in a northwesterly direction from Hartford, offers a little of everything Connecticut is known for excepting a shoreline (unless you count the banks of the meandering river). Upscale countrified suburbs like Avon, Farmington, and Simsbury offer the chic shopping, deluxe country inns, and hot restaurants more often associated with Fairfield County, not to mention several well-endowed historical societies and house-museums. West Hartford possesses the urban edge of neighboring Hartford, minus the traffic, concrete, and office towers. Farther west, former mill villages like Unionville and Collinsville have hulking and well-preserved redbrick Victorian factory buildings overlooking the trout-rich Farmington River—many of these now contain antiques shops. And in the farthest and highest reaches of the valley, rural upland communities like Barkhamsted, Burlington, Canton, Hartland, New Hartford, and Riverton give visitors a sense of the rugged terrain of the neighboring Litchfield Hills, but are within an easy drive of Hartford.

The Farmington River is one of the most dramatic waterways in New England, and so beautiful that in 1994, Congress designated 14 miles of the river's west branch as the National Wild and Scenic Rivers System. Otters, bald eagles, and other relatively rare wildlife inhabit the river, and Atlantic salmon are going to be reintroduced to the river in the near future.

The valley actually has two branches of the Farmington River running through it. The west branch begins at the West Branch Reservoir on the Colebrook (Litchfield County) and Hartland (Hartford County) town lines, a few miles south of the Massachusetts border. It runs south, passing through the village of Riverton, the American Legion State Forest in Barkhamsted (where it joins with a small eastern branch of the Farmington River, which flows south from Barkhamsted Reservoir), the town of New Hartford, the Collinsville section of Canton, eastern Burlington, and the Unionville section of Farmington, be-

fore it meets with the main branch of the Farmington River in Farmington (roughly behind Miss Porter's School). From here, the Farmington completely changes course, running north through Avon and Simsbury, then coursing over the Metacomet Ridge in Tariffville and then flowing eastward straddling the Bloomfield and Granby town lines before pushing through Windsor and emptying into the Connecticut River.

## WEST HARTFORD TO FARMINGTON
### West Hartford
West Hartford, in part because it bears the name of that sprawling city it borders, lacks some of the cachet of the more exclusive suburbs west of Hartford. For this reason, it's something of a well-kept secret, known among outsiders primarily for its enormous upscale shopping mall on the southwestern edge of town, just off I-84. A more thorough investigation of the vibrant downtown commercial district and several neighborhoods of noteworthy Colonial Revival architecture reveals West Hartford's true charms.

More than any other border community, West Hartford blends—culturally and geographically—imperceptibly with Hartford proper. Most of the main east–west thoroughfares in West Hartford—Farmington Avenue, Park Street, New Britain Avenue—extend from Hartford. The former is unquestionably more urban in appearance, and more densely settled, but West Hartford offers many similarities. And some of the major area attractions—Mark Twain House, Harriet Beecher Stowe House, and the Science Center of Connecticut—are close to the border of these two municipalities. There's the buzz of the city here, to some extent, but the pace is quieter than in Hartford, and you can find plenty of open green spaces. There is a strong presence of several ethnic groups, and the businesses lining Farmington Avenue reflect the variety of the population, particularly from a culinary standpoint.

From Hartford, enter West Hartford by driving west out of town on Farmington Avenue (Rte. 4). About a mile after crossing the border, turn left onto Trout Brook Drive and you'll see, on your immediate left, one of the top kids' attractions in the region, the **Science Center of Connecticut** (950 Trout Brook Dr., 860/231-2824, www.sciencecenterct.org, open Tues.–Sun.). The Science Center consists of changing interactive touch-friendly exhibits and both planetarium and laser shows. A computer lab, wildlife sanctuary, marinelife touch-tank, and several innovative technological exhibits are among the most popular draws. A massive whale sculpture greets visitors—you can actually walk inside the whale and look around. Various admission packages are offered, ranging from $6 for the exhibits to $11 for a combo ticket to the shows and exhibits (with discounts for children).

From here, a short detour leads you to the University of Hartford, which straddles the Hartford and West Hartford borders at the northern end of town. Head north on Trout Brook Drive, turning right onto Albany Avenue (U.S. 44) and then left onto Bloomfield Avenue (Rte. 185). Signs for the entrance to campus will appear soon after the intersection, on your right.

One rapidly growing museum in greater Hartford is the University of Hartford's **Museum of American Political Life** (200 Bloomfield Ave., West Hartford, 860/768-4090, www.hartford.edu/polmus, open 11 A.M.–4 P.M. Tues.–Fri., noon–4 P.M. weekends, closed Sundays in summer, donation requested), which contains memorabilia, exhibits, and documents tracing the history of American politics and elections. Inside you'll find a trove of buttons, banners, medals, ribbons, and pieces of glassware and pottery used in past presidential races. Primary exhibits trace the right to vote and how rights have been extended over the years, often through vigorous battles on the part of minority groups; how politicians have crafted their images throughout history to jibe with public

expectations; the history of presidential elections; and an always timely discussion of the Presidency and the Press. You'll also find 14 first ladies' gowns, including those of Mrs. Washington, Mrs. Lincoln, and Mrs. Grant.

Back on Farmington Avenue, continue west over Trout Brook and within a half mile you'll find yourself planted firmly in the midst of West Hartford's intriguing downtown, a favorite of window-shoppers and café aficionados. It's rather ironic that the growth of the shopping mall and upscale shopping centers at Corbins Corners on the edge of West Hartford ultimately shattered Hartford's retail base and yet did virtually nothing to diminish the downtown retail center of West Hartford itself.

*The Farmington River is one of the most dramatic waterways in New England, so beautiful that in 1994, Congress designated 14 miles of the river's west branch as the National Wild and Scenic Rivers System.*

At the heart of downtown, LaSalle Road and Farmington Avenue form a T-shaped throng of tree-shaded wide redbrick sidewalks lined with old-fashioned streetlamps and storefronts of every ilk, from upscale chain to local one-of-a-kind boutique—nearly 150 shops in all. A block east of LaSalle, Main Street is similarly appealing for several blocks south. A remarkable cross-section of people swarm West Hartford's downtown retail district, as diverse and people-watching-worthy as any such neighborhood in Connecticut. Three times weekly, from early spring through October, a farmers market takes place at the corner of LaSalle and Arapahoe Roads.

A short drive south along South Main Street from the commercial district leads to the **Noah Webster House and Museum of West Hartford History** (227 S. Main St., West Hartford, 860/521-5362, http://noahwebsterhouse.org, hours vary, so call ahead; open year-round, $5), which is set at the childhood home of America's premier lexicographer. Now sitting on a sliver of the 120-acre farm that once surrounded it, this restored 18th-century house contains period furnishings and artifacts illustrating the life of Noah Webster, the man who created America's very first dictionary—several early editions of the dictionary are also displayed. A renaissance man, Webster was also a farmer, lawyer, school-master, legislator, and patriot. This restored 18th-century red saltbox is in the heart of one of West Hartford's trademark all-American suburban neighborhoods, and so architecture buffs might want to explore the neighboring streets.

Back in the center of town, continue west on Farmington Avenue (Rte. 4) to reach Farmington. Along the way, you might want to motor through the **West Hill Historic District,** a planned 1920s upscale community built on the site of Cornelius J. Vanderbilt's estate. On 25 half-acre sites stand homes that were built by some of Hartford's top architects; they range in style from Colonial Revival to English Tudor. Most have steep slate roofs and stucco or masonry construction. From downtown, you can get a nice look at this neighborhood by driving or bicycling west on Farmington Avenue, turning north onto Mountain Road, and taking any of the side roads between here and Albany Avenue (U.S. 44).

## Farmington

Of the towns in this region, Farmington has begun to look the most like an edge city, with invasive highway development and sleek industrial parks dominating the southeastern side of town. It was not developed as a planned suburb the way that West Hartford was, but it has grown into a busy commuter town in recent decades. This has resulted in great prosperity, but also in the loss of the easier pace that characterized the town before this century, when it was a leading farming and merchant center. Its Colonial business success is evidenced by the great number of elegant old homes set around town. Much of the rolling farmland and country estates that sat on either side of the Farmington River fell into the hands of developers during the latter part of this century, and have now been subdivided and suburbanized to the detriment of Farmington's character. There are relatively few areas where you can get out of your car and stroll among shops and eateries, although the grand neighborhood anchored by the exclusive Miss Porter's prep school for girls remains walkable and alluring.

As you enter town along Rte. 4, make a left turn (south) onto Main Street (Rte. 10), and

you'll immediately enter an impressive neighborhood of clapboard Colonial and Victorian homes. The blocks on your right contain the campus of **Miss Porter's School,** the quintessence of New England prep academia, where a young Jacqueline Bouvier (the future Mrs. John F. Kennedy) studied as a teenager. This prim-and-proper girls' school comprises a fine collection of grand white Colonial buildings, which tumble down a slight hill to the banks of Farmington River, where the waterway's west and main branches meet. Shortly past the campus, you'll come upon the first of three historic attractions in this neighborhood, the **Day-Lewis Museum** (158 Main St., 860/678-1645, seasonal hours, free), which houses an archaeology collection owned by Yale University, and which abuts an ancient dig.

Backtrack a few blocks up Rte. 10, making a right onto Mountain Road, and then make a left onto High Street to reach the 1720s **Stanley-Whitman House** (37 High St., 860/677-9222, www.stanleywhitman.org, open year-round with seasonal hours, $5), a remarkably well-preserved early New England home notable for its overhanging second story, which typifies houses of that period, as well as its medieval-influenced windows.

The most remarkable **Hill-Stead Museum** (35 Mountain Rd., 860/677-9064 or 860/677-4787, www.hillstead.org) is just up the street (open 10 A.M.–5 P.M. Tues.–Sun. May–Oct., 11 A.M.–4 P.M. Tues.–Sun. Nov.–Apr., $9 for admission to the house, grounds are free). The owner and co-designer of this 1901 mansion, Theodate Pope Riddle (1867–1946), stipulated upon establishing her estate as a museum that none of its paintings or furnishings should ever be lent to another museum—and this is no ordinary assemblage of art and antiques. Works by Monet, Manet, Degas, Whistler, and Cassatt hang on these walls—two of Monet's haystacks bracket the living room, which is also filled with priceless antiquities, including fine Chinese porcelains and Japanese woodblock prints. The rambling 14-room house sits on 152 acres of rolling fields and woodlands, and visitors are welcome to laze about on the meadow below the house (once

Hill-Stead Museum, Farmington

Ms. Pope's six-hole private golf course) or wander through the sunken garden laid out by famed landscape architect Beatrix Farrand. Pope was the daughter of a wealthy Ohio industrialist; Stanford White codesigned the house with her, and modernist and postmodernist architect Philip Johnson is her second cousin. Indeed, she lived a long and fascinating life, having survived the sinking of the *Lusitania* and having opened and designed the now-renowned Avon Old Farms prep school in 1920.

### Unionville

Back on Rte. 4, continue west through Farmington's small downtown and past restaurants and small shopping centers into the Unionville section of town. As you motor along, you'll see the river on your left; and in the center of this mill village, at the intersection of Rte. 177, you'll find a smattering of antiques shops and some fine old industrial buildings. Continuing west on Rte. 4 leads you along an especially scenic stretch of river, and then at the intersection with Rte. 179, a left turn enables you to continue on Rte. 4 into the quiet, sparsely developed town of Burlington.

### Burlington

This is a fairly quiet community, with little to see or do except for some nice hiking at Sessions Woods Wildlife Management Area and in Nassahegan State Park, which is also the home of the **Burlington Trout Hatchery** (34 Belden Rd., just south of Rte. 4, 860/673-2340, open to the public 8 A.M.–3:30 P.M. daily, free). There's a nature trail

here, and you can see where some 90,000 pounds of trout are raised each year to be released into ponds, rivers, and streams across the state.

## CANTON TO SIMSBURY
### Collinsville

Back at the intersection of Rtes. 4 and 179, follow the latter along the Farmington River, crossing it as you enter the town of Canton. This section of town comprises the busy Victorian mill town of Collinsville, named for Samuel Collins, who opened one of the world's leading ax and ax-handle manufacturing companies here inside the hulking old buildings that overlook the river. Tiny Collinsville, whose redbrick mills were once alive with commerce and industry, today looks and feels like it was created for people to laze away their Sundays. Both the residential and industrial Victorian architecture, some of it fronting the Farmington River, are magnificent; many structures now contain antiques shops. There's also a gem of a little town green, around which many of the village's historic structures are set. And you can relax for hours at **Gertrude and Alice's,** a quirky literary coffeehouse fashioned out of the old rail station.

Just steps away is the **Canton Historical Museum** (11 Front St., 860/693-2793, www.cantonmuseum.org, open 1–4 P.M. Wed.–Sun., $4), which chronicles the history of the Collins Company and displays many of old tools, as well as exhibits on Canton's history. Although many of Connecticut's historical museums focus on the state's Colonial past, this one is chiefly Victorian in nature, as Canton wasn't actually incorporated until 1806. The re-created general store and post office, the fine 19th-century farming equipment, and the excellent research library make this a worthwhile stop.

### Canton

From Collinsville, you can drive in either of two directions to gain two very different senses of Canton. If you bear left as you head north of the village and continue onto Rte. 179, you'll hug the Farmington River for a bit longer. You'll cross the Albany Turnpike (U.S. 44), and eventually

CONN. RIVER VALLEY

pass through the Canton Center Historic District, a roughly 500-acre patch of early 19th-century houses and mostly open space that retains a rural ambience no longer the rule in this fast-growing suburb of Hartford. On Rte. 179, you'll eventually pass through the similarly charming village of North Canton, before moving through the bucolic eastern halves of the towns of Barkhamsted and Hartland. Here you'll cross over some high ridges, pass beside several old farmsteads, and go through a few chunks of forest—this is one of the region's least known scenic drives, so you'll encounter little traffic.

Conversely, if you bear right on Maple Street as you leave Collinsville, you'll soon join with the Albany Turnpike (U.S. 44) where it passes through the more modern side of Canton, which is dominated by shopping centers containing increasingly high-end and sophisticated shops and eateries. In the center of this district you'll come upon the **Canton Artists Guild** (Canton Green, Albany Tpke., U.S. 44, 860/693-4102, open Wed.–Sun. March–Dec., free), a mid–18th-century building containing three fine art galleries, which stage impressive shows throughout the year.

Make a left onto Lawton Road, opposite where Rte. 177 intersects with U.S. 44 from the south, to reach Canton's excellent **Roaring Brook Nature Center** (70 Gracey Rd., 860/693-0263, www.roaringbrook.org, open Tues.–Sun. year-round, also Mon. in summer, $3), a state preserve where you can see live animals, wildlife dioramas, and an Indian longhouse. There are also five miles of nature trails.

## Avon

From Canton, U.S. 44 leads east into Avon. What we now call Avon was referred to as Nod in 1666, when settlers first developed it, allegedly calling it by abbreviation of its longer name, Northington District (of Farmington). Winter privileges were granted soon after, meaning the residents of Nod were permitted to build their own meetinghouse, instead of requiring the growing number of residents to schlep all the way to Farmington on blustery, wintry Sundays. In many cases, this initial recognition of independence eventually paved the way for a town to break off and incorporate as its own entity. In Avon's case, this indeed happened, but not until 1830.

As you cross the Avon town line, make a right turn onto Rte. 167 and follow it south nearly back down to the Farmington border; at the intersection with Harris Road, you'll find yourself in the heart of the **Pine Grove Historic District,** which includes the Pine Grove Schoolhouse and five homes built prior to 1865. Anchoring the district is the **Pine Grove Schoolhouse,** on Rte. 167, an 1865 one-roomer that was in use until 1949 and is operated by the **Avon Historical Society** (860/678-7621). Inside the little building you'll find original bolted desks, hand slates dating from 1900, and textbooks that go back as far as the 1920s. The society also administers **The Living Museum** (8 E. Main St., in the center of town, at the junction of Rte. 10, U.S. 44, and U.S. 202), a second former 19th-century schoolhouse, and the **Mariam M. Hunter History Room** (296 Country Club Rd., just off Rte. 167, north of the Pine Grove Historic District), a repository of local historical documents and books at the Avon Public Library, filled with information on the town history. Admission to these three buildings is free, but hours are highly limited, so phone ahead.

Go back up Rte. 167, turn right back onto U.S. 202/44, and you'll pass the posh Farmington Valley Mall, which is on the Avon and Simsbury line. From here, proceed into Avon's neat and gentrified town center, a highlight of which is the **Farmington Valley Arts Center** (25–27 Arts Center Ln., Avon Park N, 860/678-1867), which comprises 20 studios of working potters, painters, jewelers, and all other kinds of artists. It's set inside a complex of brownstone buildings that once housed a safety-fuse manufacturer. If you continue east along U.S. 44/Rte. 10, you'll pass by some of the hottest restaurants and fanciest shops in the area. Cross over the main branch of the Farmington River (which by now has wended its way back north again from Farmington), before U.S. 44 and Rte. 10 split at the Avon Old Farms Inn.

Follow Rte. 10, which leads back down to

## HEUBLEIN TOWER: A LITTLE PIECE OF THE TYROL IN TALCOTT MOUNTAIN STATE PARK

As you drive north on U.S. 202/Rte. 10, look right across the Farmington River plain, and high above you'll see Talcott Mountain. It's not a mountain per se, but a thousand-foot-tall span of the Metacomet Ridge, which runs clear from New Haven to Massachusetts. You may do a double-take when you first spot the tower perched on the edge of the ridge, watching imperiously over these scenic river towns. What you're looking at is the 165-foot-tall Heublein Tower, inspired by Tyrolean castle architecture and the goal of virtually every hiker who tackles the blue-blazed trails crossing through Talcott Mountain State Park.

The simple and pleasant 1.5-mile trail to the base of the tower can be crowded on weekends, but it requires little planning, and it's an easy enough adventure even for young kids. The exterior and cupola of the tower were completely restored to their former glory in the winter of 1998–1999, and visitors can ride an elevator to the lofty observation area (which was used as the building's ballroom when this structure was used as the private summer home of its builder, liquor importer Gilbert Heublein). From the top, views stretch to Long Island Sound to the south and New Hampshire's Mount Monadnock to the north.

Heublein Tower, Simsbury

© ANDREW COLLINS

Intrigue has surrounded the tower since its construction in 1914. On one occasion, Gilbert Heublein was showing off his 2,000-watt spotlight to a few guests, when the light aroused the attention of local authorities. Quickly, the rumor spread that Heublein was sending secrets to German submarines in the Atlantic during World War I. In 1944, the now-defunct *Hartford Times* bought the place and used it for important functions and glamorous soirees, one of which was attended by General Dwight D. Eisenhower shortly before he announced his presidential candidacy.

The simplest trail to the tower is reached via the signed parking area off Rte. 185, which runs east toward Bloomfield from U.S. 202/Rte. 10. Follow the blue-blazed Metacomet Trail 1.5 miles to the base of the tower; it's a steep trail in places, but it levels out midway up the hill, where it runs along Metacomet ridge. The trails are open 8 A.M.–sunset year-round, and the tower is open 10 A.M.–5 P.M. Thurs.–Sun. spring–fall. For further information, call the ranger's office (860/677-0662) or contact the State Parks Division of the Bureau of Outdoor Recreation (Connecticut DEP, 79 Elm St., Hartford, CT 06106, 860/424-3200, http://dep.state.ct.us/rec/parks.htm).

Farmington. On your left, note the campus of the fine prep school Avon Old Farms, whose medieval-like Cotswold-inspired design can be attributed to the school's founder, Theodate Pope Riddle (of Hill-Stead museum fame).

U.S. 44 runs east over Talcott Mountain into West Hartford—shortly after you enter West Hartford you'll see signs for the parking for the blue-blazed Metacomet Trail, which is a long but very scenic way to reach the Heublein Tower in Simsbury.

## Simsbury

On U.S. 202/Rte. 10 (a.k.a. Hopmeadow St.), head north and you'll find yourself in the midst of the **Simsbury Center Historic District,** a seven-block corridor filled with fascinating residential and commercial structures, some of which date to the 18th century. The highlight of this area, which is home to some fine old inns and several great restaurants, is the Simsbury Historical Society's **Phelps Tavern Museum and Homestead** (800 Hopmeadow St., U.S. 202/Rte. 10, 860/658-2500, www.phelpstavernmuseum.com, open noon–4 P.M. Tues.–Sat., $6). It comprises roughly a half-dozen structures including a 1740 one-room schoolhouse, a 1771 homestead, a 1795 Cape-style cottage with herb garden, an 1880s carriage house, a 1970-built replica of a 1683 meetinghouse, and outbuildings including an ice house and a barn. Costumed docents lead tours through this complex, which is operated by the town's historical society (founded in 1911). This is an excellent way to see Simsbury's 325-year history come to life.

**Flamig Farm** (7 Shingle Mill Rd., Simsbury, 860/658-5070, www.flamigfarm.com) is a great stop for kids. This educational farm has a petting zoo, horse and carriage carriage rides, pumpkin picking, pony rides, and other agricultural fun.

North of downtown Simsbury, Rte. 315 leads east over the northern stretch of the Metacomet Ridge into an odd little throwback to Victorian times, Tariffville, around which the Farmington River flows. A carpet mill was begun here in 1827, and the small network of streets contains a number of fine Victorian buildings.

# NEW HARTFORD TO HARTLAND
## New Hartford

The least developed part of the Farmington River Valley is its western fringe, along the west branch of the Farmington River. To explore this area, follow U.S. 44 west from Canton into New Hartford, a quaint Victorian village nestled in the shadows of 800-foot Jones Mountain. You'll find a few simple business concerns here and some fantastic Victorian architecture, but little else. What this area is best known for is its scenic biking and country-driving roads. One great route to follow is Rte. 219 north from the center of New Hartford, alongside the lower portion of Barkhamsted Reservoir. You'll pass the **Lake McDonough Recreation Area** (860/379-3036 or 860/379-0038), with a boat launch ($4 fee) on your left, and just a bit farther north, you'll see Ski Sundown on the right. Various rowboats and paddleboats can be rented here, and activities include hiking, fishing, and picnicking on the grounds. Parking costs $4.

## Barkhamsted

Once you cross the Barkhamsted town line, at Rte. 318, turn left and drive across Sayville Dam, from which you'll enjoy great views of the reservoir. There are parking areas on either side, and the east side of the dam is marked by a dramatic stone turret tower. From the parking areas, you can also get a great sense of this beautiful stone-arch dam.

A short distance west of the reservoir, a right turn on Rte. 181 leads you north through Barkhamsted Center and along the eastern edge of Peoples State Forest, an expanse laced with many excellent hiking trails. On your right, you'll occasionally glimpse the long Barkhamsted Reservoir, which extends north from Sayville Dam to nearly the Massachusetts border. Or, back on Rte. 318, continue a little farther west and turn right on River Road, which winds along the west branch of the Farmington River. You'll see **Peoples State Forest** (E. River Rd., 860/379-2469) on your right and the American Legion State Forest on your left. Just as you enter the Peoples State Forest, you'll notice the Forest Ranger Headquarters and the parking area ($5 fee on weekends, Memorial Day–Labor Day). From here, there's access to the Farmington River for boating and fishing, and at the park, you'll also find a nature museum, hiking trails, and—in winter—great cross-country skiing.

## Riverton

East River Road leads through the state forest to the village of Riverton, which is geographically and aesthetically more like one of Litchfield County's quaint, anachronistic Colonial villages than it is like any other communities in the Farmington River Valley. Life moves slowly in what is literally a "river town." You might munch on a scoop of ice cream at the Village Sweet Shoppe or mingle among the locals at the Riverton General Store, which occupies the ground floor of a stately white Italianate Victorian.

The **Hitchcock Chair Factory** (Rte. 20, 860/379-4826, open daily) is this otherwise-sleepy hamlet's great claim to fame, and indeed the shop is open to visitors not just for shopping, but to see how these chairs have been made since Lambert Hitchcock opened his factory in 1818. The factory building is a long, sweeping, pale gray, brick building with red trim, beside which is an old Colonial house that acts as a furniture showroom. Windows from inside the factory overlook the river juncture of the Farmington with the Still River. It's certainly a far cry from picking out furniture at some bleak suburban shopping mall.

Soon after opening his factory, Hitchcock became a household name. He's best known for his chairs, which were seated with rush, cane, or solid wood, painted, and embellished only slightly with frilly gold stenciling. You can still watch woodworkers at the factory, who will discuss the technique of building these chairs as you watch them. A survey of the factory's classic, sturdy, and elegant furniture is found inside the **Hitchcock Museum** (860/379-4826, seasonal hours), in what used to be the Old Union Church (ca. 1829), a hand-cut granite structure that also contains other Colonial and Victorian painted furniture.

Opposite the chair factory, and across the Farmington River, is the 1796 Old Riverton Inn, which was a stopover for stagecoaches throughout the 1800s and continues to welcome weary travelers today.

## Hartland

Head north from Riverton on Rte. 20 (or, if you came by way of Rte. 181 in Barkhamsted, continue north, as it will eventually meet with Rte. 20) into one final super-sleepy and wonderfully picturesque town, Hartland. The town is essentially split in two by the Barkhamsted Reservoir—just a tiny, tiny strip of land, between the tip of the reservoir and the Massachusetts border, connects West Hartland and East Hartland. Much of both sides of Hartland is dominated by Tunxis State Forest.

As you're driving along Rte. 20 in a northeasterly direction from West Hartland, keep an eye out for Milo B. Coe Road, a left turn shortly after you enter the forest. In the "ya never know what you're gonna find" category is this winding, wooded road, which wends up a couple miles toward the state border. After passing a pair of gorgeous old farmhouses, and after a ways through the woods, on your right you'll come to a small, simple, stone obelisk. The writing on it has largely eroded at this point, but a sign beside it offers a clear rendering of this memorial's purpose: "Milo B., son of Harlow and Mary Coe, died October 18, 1854, age 11 years. He was found dead in front of this monument supposed to have fallen from a cart in which he was riding and instantly killed." A tender and awkwardly worded testimony to a long-ago tragedy, these stone markers were actually rather common in the 18th and 19th centuries to mark sad passings, and although most have now fallen, some do still stand here and there. Not more than a tenth of a mile north, the pavement ends and another small granite marker dating from 1906 marks the Connecticut-Massachusetts border.

## SHOPPING
### Pick-Your-Own Farms

Just north of the Avon Old Farms Inn, **Pickin' Patch** (Nod Rd., north from junction of U.S. 44 and Rte. 10, 860/677-9552) is one of the state's longest-running family-operated farms, dating from 1666. You can pick your own fruits and vegetables in season at this gorgeous property abutting the Farmington River. Hayrides are offered in spring and fall, and you can cut your own Christmas tree in December.

## Mall Crawls

You'll find one of the more impressive shopping malls in the state just off I-84 (exit 40), on the borders of Farmington, West Hartford, and Newington, at **Westfarms Mall** (Rte. 71, 860/561-3024), which is anchored by Nordstrom, Lord & Taylor, Filene's, Filene's Men's Store & Furniture Gallery, and JCPenney—it's also home to a franchise of the popular Rainforest Cafe theme restaurant. Across the street and all along Rte. 71, you'll find several more outdoor shopping centers—this is a retail mecca. U.S. 44/202 in Avon, near the Canton border, is dominated by the **Simsbury Commons** (Borders, Bed Bath & Beyond, and others) and several other strips of major shops and some popular chain eateries.

## Downtown Shopping Districts

West Hartford has a wonderful downtown retail core. There's quite a bit of parking along the street and a large garage on Main Street, just south of Farmington Avenue. Possibilities among the dozens of mostly owner-managed shops include **Barker Animation** (60A LaSalle Rd., 860/232-8666), a cousin of the comic and collectibles museum in Cheshire. Students in the acclaimed art department at University of Hartford often drop by **Ava Art** (151 New Park Ave., 860/656-0425) to stock up on supplies. Fine used books, including a great collection of first editions, are found at **Brick Walk Bookshop** (966 Farmington Ave., 860/233-1730), which borders the critically lauded contemporary fine arts gallery **Paesaggio** (860/233-1932). West Hartford's other major spot for fans of literature is **The Jumping Frog** (141 South St., 860/523-1622), which carries nearly 100,000 titles. Bead-crafters satisfy their yearnings at **The Beadoir** (951A Farmington Ave., 860/231-8755).

## Antiques

The state's largest antiques show is held each June at the **Farmington Polo Grounds** (508/839-9735). Richard Wacht's **Canton Barn Auction Gallery** (75 Old Canton Rd., 860/693-0601) is a big deal around these parts. On Saturday nights, you can come to enjoy chocolate-pecan or apple pie (plus a whole bunch of additional great varieties) while browsing the goods, and then enjoy the auction. This is one of the most interesting forms of shopping, nibbling, and people-watching in all of Connecticut. Nearby **Collinsville Antiques** (1 Main St., Collinsville, 860/693-1011) is a hatchet and ax factory that's been converted to house several dealers. **Antiques on the Farmington** (218 River Rd., Unionville, 860/673-9205) is a popular multi-dealer shop.

## Miscellany

The hempy and happy **Trading Post** (221 Albany Tpke., Canton, 860/693-4679) specializes in head-shop stuff, CDs, and 1960s-vintage clothes—a trip here may rekindle some of the "trips" you had as a teenager.

# RECREATION

## Bowling

In Simsbury, bowling has come back into vogue at **Blue Fox Rock & Bowl** (1603 Hopmeadow St., U.S. 202/Rte. 10, 860/658-4479). The renovated space, formerly known as Simsbury Lanes, is hip and funky—what swing dancing is to clubbing, this place is to bowling. The neon-streaked interior, strobe lights, and rock music make for great fun.

## Cross-Country Skiing

**Winding Trails Cross Country Ski Center** (50 Winding Trails Dr., 860/677-8458, www.windingtrails.com) has 12 miles of groomed trails set across 350 wooded acres. Both beginners and experienced skiers are welcome; the cost is $8 for adults, and season passes are available. Ski lessons, 200 sets of rental skis and boots, and a lodge with snack bar are available.

## Downhill Skiing

New Hartford's **Ski Sundown** (126 Ratlum Rd., Rte. 219, 860/379-SNOW, www.skisundown .com) has 15 trails open day and night, including grades for all levels of ability.

## Golf

There's ample opportunity to test your skills at **Tunxis Plantation Country Club** (87 Town Farm Rd., Farmington, 860/677-1367), which comprises a pair of 18-hole courses and a nice nine-hole course. Another beauty is **Simsbury Farms Golf Club** (100 Old Farms Rd., West Simsbury, 860/658-6246), an 18-hole course surrounded by local orchards. Arguably, the most challenging of the area is **Blue Fox Run** (65 Nod Rd., Avon, 860/678-1679), whose course meanders alongside the Farmington River.

## Hiking

In Northwest Simsbury, there's light hiking at **Great Pond Forest,** signposted from Great Pond Road, a left turn from Fire Town Road, which runs north from Rte. 167 just west of Rte. 10/US 202. At the end of the dirt road into this 280-acre forest of tall pine trees, there's a parking lot and a sign detailing the few trails through this peaceful bit of woodland. In an hour, you can easily circumnavigate the Lilliputian lily pond for which the park is named.

Another fine hiking spot is along the Metacomet Ridge, via either Penwood State Park or its neighbor, **Talcott Mountain State Park.** The best-known point along the trails through here is **Heublein Tower** (see the sidebar "Heublein Tower"), but for a more serious hike approach from the parking lot by the signposted Hartford Reservoir No. 6 off U.S. 44 (in West Hartford, just east of Avon). From here, walk north a short way on the dirt road and you'll meet with the ubiquitous blue-blazed **Metacomet Trail,** which hugs the reservoir's western shore before heading west and climbing steadily some 700 feet toward the ridge. It's a good three miles to Heublein

## RIVER EXCURSIONS

**H**uck Finn Adventures in Collinsville (860/693-0385) is best known as a canoe outfitter and tour operator, but this fine establishment can also set up bike, kayak, and cave exploration excursions. The company works with both the Farmington River Watershed Association and Hartford's Riverfront Recapture to help preserve and maintain the waterways on which it offers its tours, and it's a real friend of Connecticut's environment. Trips for families, a couple of friends, large groups, or just you (or you and your dog) can be arranged, with as much or as little guidance as you require. The bulk of the canoe excursions are along the Farmington River, from several different locations; this is a fairly calm and peaceful river, where swimming is encouraged (you might also take to the river by wooden or rubber raft). Adventurers, however, will find some outstanding whitewater rapids, most notably at Tariffville Gorge in the Tariffville section of Simsbury. The duration of trips varies greatly, and shuttles run about every 20 minutes to return you to your point of embarkation. There are also catamaran canoes, which are ideal for travelers who use

wheelchairs or might have other disabilities that prevent them from easily taking to the river.

Huck Finn also arranges hikes around the Farmington River Valley, up to Talcott Mountain, and to Heublein Tower, and rents all-terrain bicycles. Prices vary greatly according to the tour and whether you're merely renting a bike or boat or using a guide; the shuttle service is free (although tips are greatly appreciated).

Another great way to experience the Farmington River is on a river tube, which you can rent from **Farmington River Tubing,** 860/693-6465. The cost includes rental of the river tube, a life jacket, and return shuttle bus. It's a 2.5-mile ride down the river, including three sets of rapids; the ride begins at Satan's Kingdom State Recreation Area.

**Main Stream** (860/693-6791, www.mainstreamcanoe.com) also offers canoeing and kayaking trips through the region, and is an excellent resource for boat rentals and instruction, as is **Collinsville Canoe & Kayak** (Rte. 179, Collinsville, 860/693-6977, www.cckstore.com), which has rentals and instruction.

Tower via this route, and you can either return the same way or continue north and work your way back down the eastern side of the reservoir (a total of 8.5 miles).

The western edge of the river valley is home to some excellent and fairly strenuous hiking, as it's here that you enter the beginning of the Litchfield Hills. The blue-blazed **Tunxis Trail** edges its way north from Plymouth (in Litchfield County), east into Burlington, and along the twisting so-called Mile of Ledges. The trail continues well north to 1,100-foot Johnnycake Mountain before turning west into Harwinton and meandering back down to its origin in Plymouth. This nearly 10-mile trail isn't for beginners, but it can be a wonderfully rewarding trek. Several points offer trail access: Leave from the parking area off East Church Road (a right turn from Rte. 72 about 2.5 miles north of U.S. 6) or, from Bristol, follow Hill Street north from U.S. 6 (west of Rte. 69) for three miles (it will become Chippens Mill Road once you enter Burlington) and turn left on Greer Road, which leads to the trail.

The Tunxis Trail continues well north through western Hartford County and is particularly popular in the rural towns of Barkhamsted and Hartland, where there are several legs of the trail, including one that climbs into **Tunxis State Forest** and passes over a few mountains, offering nice views back down toward Barkhamsted Reservoir.

Some of the most rugged and beautiful hiking trails in the state pass through Barkhamsted's **Peoples State Forest**. From the junction of Rtes. 318 and 181, turn north up East River Road, which runs along the east bank of the Farmington River. As you enter the boundary of the state forest, fork right onto Green Woods Road and stop at the wonderful old stone museum built in the 1930s by the Civilian Conservation Corps; it looks like something you'd expect to find in the heart of the Adirondacks. Another option is to park at the picnic area on East River Road and hike up the short blue-blazed trail to the museum (this is sometimes preferable, as parking along Green Woods Road is limited). Miles of very good and well-maintained trails wind through this park, and the steep and hilly northwestern reaches harbor some wonderful overlooks, which peer down over the

winding Farmington River and toward the Colonial village of Riverton.

In Burlington, **Sessions Woods Wildlife Management Area** (Milford St., Rte. 69, south of Rte. 4, 860/675-8130, http://dep.state.ct.us/burnatr) has two self-guided trails (three miles and 0.6 mile), which offer wildlife and ecology demonstrations. Trails pass through a beaver marsh and lead to a waterfall and an observation tower.

## Ice-Skating

Victor Petrenko, Scott Davis, and Ekatarina Gordeeva are among the stars on ice who utilize the town's **International Skating Center of Connecticut** (1375 Hopmeadow St., U.S. 202/Rte. 10, Simsbury, 860/651-5400, www.iscskate.com). This world-class facility hosts Olympic-level skating shows, and visitors are welcome to watch the stars practice (phone ahead for details). Year-round, the public is also welcome to come for skating.

## ENTERTAINMENT AND NIGHTLIFE

All summer long, the **Centennial Theater Festival** (995 Hopmeadow St., U.S. 202/Rte. 10, Simsbury, 860/408-5303, www.ctfestival.org) highlights professional theater, music, and dance.

## FESTIVALS AND EVENTS

In mid-June and late August, treasure-hunters convene for the **Farmington Antiques Weekends** (Polo Grounds, Town Farm Rd., 317/598-0012). Simsbury's **Septemberfest** (860/651-7307) draws fans of used book sales, road races, and live music. Later in the month, the residents of Canton pay homage to the ax-manufacturer after whom Collinsville village is named, with **Sam Collins Day,** which is run by the Volunteer Fire Department (Canton Springs Rd., 860/693-7841). Highlights include food stalls, children's activities, and a birdhouse auction. In early October, West Hartford hosts the **Pumpkin Festival** (Westmoor Park, 119 Flagg Rd., 860/232-1134), which features square-dancing, cider making, and marshmallow roasts.

# ACCOMMODATIONS

Lodgings in the Farmington River Valley run toward the high-end, a mix of truly historic and made-to-look-historic inns and midsize hotels. Most of these places are in the towns close to Hartford, such as Farmington and Simsbury, which have a strong corporate presence and so gear themselves largely to business travelers by week and leisure travelers on the weekends. In the western and northern reaches of the area, there is an alarming dearth of options. You may want to consider basing yourself in eastern Litchfield County, if B&Bs are your thing, or in the towns of Plainville or Southington, if you're seeking a nearby inexpensive property.

## Hotels and Motels

**$150–$250:** The upscale, 98-room **Simsbury Inn** (397 Hopmeadow St., U.S. 202/Rte. 10, Simsbury, 860/651-5700 or 800/634-2719, www.simsburyinn.com) is a thoroughly modern hotel with a courtly Georgian-style brick facade that evokes the charms and history of the region, with its smartly decorated Colonial-style rooms and two excellent restaurants. The more formal of the two, Evergreens, serves nice if conservative Continental and American fare ($18–28), while the pub offers lighter fare (mostly under $10), such as baby back ribs and New England seafood bisque. With room service, business amenities, tennis, and a gorgeous indoor pool, this inn appeals heavily to a corporate clientele, although the competitively priced weekend packages pull in a share of folks touring the area. The inn is part of a local hotel group that also includes the **Farmington Inn** (827 Farmington Ave., Farmington, 860/269-2340 or 800/648-9804, www.farmingtoninn.com), a slightly smaller property that looks from the outside like a spruced up motor court but possesses a quite handsome interior. Rooms have a mix of antiques and reproduction antiques and fine landscape paintings—the bathrooms are particularly spacious and attractive. Rates often dip below $150 during less busy times.

Whatever your reason for visiting the region—business or pleasure—the immaculate **Avon Old Farms Inn** (Rte. 10 and U.S. 44, 860/677-2818, www.avonoldfarmsinn.com) is arguably the best of the members of this hotel group. There's been a house on this setting since the 1670s, and descendants of the first landowners operated what is now the Avon Old Farms Restaurant as a country inn beginning in 1923. Now, the main house with its seven dining areas is solely the restaurant, while accommodations are in the elegant and nicely integrated modern building across the busy road. Rooms possess the expected Colonial spirit, and some 400 watercolors depicting local landscapes decorate both guest and public spaces. There's a pool, coffee bar, sauna, and exercise room on the premises, and one of the area's better golf courses is across the street.

**$100–150:** Marketing heavily to business travelers and extended-stay clientele, the efficiently run **Centennial Inn** (5 Spring Ln., Farmington, 860/677-4647 or 800/852-2052, www.centennialinn.com) is nonetheless an excellent choice even for short-term visits, especially for families or groups of friends traveling together. The bright and airy accommodations basically look like high-grade Colonial-style condos, with cathedral ceilings and skylights, loft bedrooms, living rooms with working fireplaces, and fully equipped kitchens. If you'd prefer self-catering and independence, and you don't require the facilities of a large hotel, this place is perfect.

**$50–100:** Popular with parents of prep school kids and outdoors enthusiasts keen to hike or cross-country ski at the many nearby parks and forests, the condo-like **Iron Horse Inn** (969 Hopmeadow St., U.S. 202/Rte. 10, Simsbury, 860/658-2216 or 800/245-9938, www.ironhorseofsimsbury.com) has 27 efficiencies with self-catering—ideal for long-term stays. Guests have use of an outdoor pool and sauna. A midrise economy hotel with an unspeakably bland exterior but a golden location, the **West Hartford Inn** (900 Farmington Ave., West Hartford, 860/236-3221 or 877/782-2777, www.westhartfordinn.com) tends to book up well ahead on weekends, owing to its nice rates and clean—although characterless—rooms. It's steps from the Science Center of Connecticut and a two-block stroll from West Hartford's intriguing little shopping district—ideal if you're not planning to spend much time in your room.

## Country Inns and Bed-and-Breakfasts

**$150–250: Merrywood** (100 Hartford Rd., Rte. 185, Simsbury, 860/651-1785, www.merry-woodinn.com) is set on five beautiful, evergreen-shaded acres fringing the western slope of Talcott Mountain. The setting alone makes staying here a special experience, but the grand Colonial Revival house is equally noteworthy. It has been decorated with a sensible mix of fine antiques, plus the sorts of luxuries both business and leisure travelers will appreciate: cable TV and VCRs; mini fridges stocked with complimentary snacks, beers, and soft drinks; phones with data ports—one suite even has a whirlpool tub and private steam bath. There's also a pool outside. Rates include afternoon tea, often set before a roaring fireplace, and an especially impressive full country breakfast. This is a first-rate B&B in every sense of the word.

The brick gambrel-roofed **Simsbury 1820 House** (731 Hopmeadow Rd., Rte. 10/US 202, Simsbury, 860/658-3023 or 800/TRY-1820, www.simsbury1820house.com), listed on the National Register of Historic Places, is in the center of town, within walking distance of several good restaurants and Phelps Tavern Museum. The main building is a fine early 19th-century mansion that was in the same family until the 1940s and was fully restored in the late 1980s. Many of the 34 rooms are in a more recent wing that dates from 1890, but all are furnished in period style and have such modern amenities as private baths, phones, cable TV, and climate control; some have balconies or nonworking fireplaces. And a separate carriage house has several additional rooms, including some especially nice split-level suites with whirlpool tubs. The 1820 Cafe serves a light lunch and dinner, as well as the breakfast included with the rate. The hostelry is owned by the same family behind the Simsbury, Farmington, and Avon Old Farms inns.

**$100–150:** Across the road and the west branch of the Farmington River from the Hitchcock Chair Factory, the 1796 **Old Riverton Inn** (Rte. 20, 860/379-8678 or 800/EST-1796, www.rivertoninn.com) is a wobbly, old, pale-gray building whose rather simple rooms contain a smattering of antiques, their mix of carpets, rugs, and floral wallpapering a patchwork of styles. The place is eclectic and fun, as you'd expect an old inn to be—decidedly not fancy, but entirely memorable and pleasant. Rooms have private baths and cable TV but are otherwise rather old-fashioned. A suite has a working fireplace.

Simsbury's new accommodation is the **Linden House** (288–290 Hopmeadow St., 860/408-1321, www.lindenhousebb.com), an imposing Queen Anne Victorian mansion with six lovely guest rooms, four with fireplaces and all with phone, cable TV, and private bath. Rooms contain an eclectic mix of antiques, and each is done in a different color scheme. A Continental breakfast is included.

## Campgrounds

There's great camping in the northwestern reaches of the Farmington River Valley, including the 30-site **Austin F. Hawes Memorial Campground** at the American Legion State Forest, Barkhamsted, 860/379-0922, once the sacred hunting grounds of the region's Tunxis Indians. It's on the west side of the Farmington River (with the 3,000-acre Peoples State Forest on the east), ideal for canoeing and fishing enthusiasts, and the sites sit in a deep evergreen forest.

## FOOD

This is one of Connecticut's most sophisticated regions when it comes to eating out, with a high number of chic bistros and cafés serving the towns in the eastern Farmington River Valley, closest to Hartford. Even in the more remote and quiet villages, like New Hartford and Riverton, you'll find a smattering of very sophisticated restaurants.

## Upscale

One of the first restaurants to bring healthful contemporary cuisine to greater Hartford, **Ann Howard's Apricots** (1593 Farmington Ave., Farmington, 860/673-5403, $18–30) remains a trendsetter and an always-stellar source of fine dining. A trademark dish offered in this antiques-filled dining room is herb-crusted roast rack of New Zealand lamb with caramelized shallots and roasted red bliss potatoes. Downstairs, a low-keyed British-style tavern presents a lighter menu ($8–14) that includes meatloaf, oven-baked Maine crab cakes, and roast breast of chicken stuffed with spinach, mushroom, and asiago cheese.

**The Grist Mill Cafe** (44 Mill Ln., Farmington, 860/676-8855, $13–28) has developed into one of the finest restaurants in the state. The setting, overlooking a wide expanse of the Farmington River just down the hill from Miss Porter's School, makes it a hit with couples seeking romance and locals looking for a quiet alternative to the noisy see-and-be-seen spots strung throughout Hartford and the lower Farmington River Valley. Excellent, uncomplicated contemporary American fare, such as peppercorn steak with merlot sauce and braised veal chop with roasted vegetables, is joined by a variety of pastas. This immaculately restored 18th-century mill contains two distinct dining areas: a small, smart-but-casual café and a more formal restaurant; both have clear, crisp views overlooking the river.

Sometimes an amazing setting can be a curse, a reason for so-called culinary connoisseurs not to take a restaurant seriously. Such is perhaps the case with the **Hop Brook Tavern** (77 West St., Rte. 167, Simsbury, 860/651-7757, $16–25), a restaurant fashioned out of a burly old red gristmill on a waterfall, with rustic beamed dining rooms and many tables with enchanting views. The food here is excellent, creative, and somewhat underrated—it's even reasonably priced, considering the setting. For a starter, you might go with a fresh conch salad with a sweet Vidalia onion marmalade. A nice entrée is the walnut-crusted pork loin, served with a maple demi-glace and steamed asparagus over a bed of apple-mashed potatoes. Completing this superior vision of fine dining is a well-chosen wine list.

Look no farther than the **Old Riverton Inn** (Rte. 20, Riverton, 860/379-8678, $11–19) to satisfy your yearnings for a truly traditional old New England dining experience. The low-beamed ceiling and white-paneled walls retain the Colonial flavor of this 200-year-old tavern. The menu offers no surprises, just tried-and-true regional favorites like Yankee pot roast, roast pork loin with applesauce, and the occasional nod across the Atlantic, like stuffed sole with Béarnaise sauce.

The 1750s **Seasons at the Avon Old Farms Inn** (Rte. 10 and U.S. 44, Avon, 860/677-1651, $17–27), across busy Rte. 10 from the hotel of the same name, presents a first-rate menu of creative New American fare, such as rack of lamb with mango and fresh mint barbecue sauce or pan-seared sea bass with a tangy citrus sauce and a banana mash and sweet potatoes. Whereas so many old country inns rest on their laurels and priceless setting (there are seven dining areas—one a former blacksmith's shop—filled with antiques, dried flowers, and wide-plank crooked floors), Seasons also presents memorable cooking that could stand up anywhere. Weekend brunches are one of the restaurant's strengths, owing particularly to the table of amazing desserts.

## Creative but Casual

Vintage posters neatly framed, mustard walls, varnished woods, and a smart and simple storefront give **Arugula** (953 Farmington Ave., West Hartford, 860/561-4888, $15–23) a rather Parisian sensibility, but the menu clearly pays homage to a full range of Mediterranean nations and perhaps one or two in the Far East. Consider saffron couscous with roast chicken; wild mushroom rosemary lasagna; and a filet mignon of tuna with ginger-mustard glaze and warm roasted eggplant. It's quiet and homey enough for a date, and sophisticated enough for entertaining clients. The locally famous Max restaurant cartel furthered West Hartford's reputation as a trendy culinary hub when it opened **Max's Oyster Bar** (964 Farmington Ave., 860/236-6299, $16–27), a riotously noisy, always jam-packed, and rather pricey place in the town's hopping restaurant district. Oysters may be the signature draw, but Max's offers an impressive range of seafood entrées with creative preparations, from the Maine lobster pan-roast with garlic-mashed potatoes, fennel, and sweet-chile sauce to pistachio-crusted salmon over Belgian endive salad with roasted beets and a grapefruit vinaigrette.

One of the area's most respected Vietnamese-trained chefs, who's also responsible for the Bamboo Grill in the same shopping center, not long ago expanded his horizons by opening **Buon Appetito** (50 Albany Tpke., U.S. 44/202, Canton, 860/693-2211, $14–24), a diminutive storefront trattoria with an astoundingly varied menu. Consider pasta *giobatto* (hot sausage, veal, and chicken sautéed with tomatoes, mushrooms, scallions, leeks, and hot peppers with a marsala-deglazed spicy tomato sauce and fresh rosemary served over herb fettuccine) or a "create your own dish," which entails beginning with pasta and adding any variety of vegetables, seafood, and chicken. Soft-shell crabs are available in season.

Overshadowed by the dozens of celebrity-patroned eateries in the heart of Litchfield County, **Chatterley's** (2 Bridge St., New Hartford, 860/379-2428, $13–16) offers excellent regional American fare, with entrées typically costing about $5 less than you'd pay for the same kind of cooking in name communities like Woodbury and Litchfield. A real cornerstone of this picturesque Victorian village, the place consists of a romantic dining room with arched windows and a green-and-plum color scheme, and a more casual—at times raucous—saloon in an adjoining room with TVs over the bar. In the former, you might try goat-cheese ravioli with caramelized onions, grilled chicken, and Italian parsley, or spice-rubbed ribeye steak with Roquefort shallot butter. The saloon has burgers, soups, and lighter stuff. It's all good, and the welcoming zero-attitude service is a tremendous plus.

A highly trendy addition to the buzzing restaurant scene in West Hartford, the **Elbow Room** (986 Farmington Ave., 860/236-6195, $8–22) is both a suave cocktail bar and an eclectic affordable restaurant with simple light fare (homemade potato chips, ahi burgers, ribs) to more substantial contemporary American chow. A great place to bring a date, and not an unlikely venue to meet your next one.

Helping solidify West Hartford's place as one of the state's top towns for eating out, **Restaurant Bricco** (78 LaSalle Rd., West Hartford, 860/233-0220, $15–25) presents outstanding Mediterranean cuisine that stands out when so much of this genre of cooking sounds the same from place to place. Top choices include the wood-fired pizzas (try the one with sundried tomatoes, Coach Farm goat cheese, roasted garlic, and red onion); the grilled diver sea scallops spiedino with braised Swiss chard, cannellini bean ragout, and apple-smoked bacon are a treat, as is risotto with shaved black truffles, chanterelle mushrooms, and red-wine veal glaze. The postmodern interior is striking, the noise level high but invigorating, and the staff hip but friendly. Bricco's proprietor, Billy Grant, rather recently opened **Grant's** (977 Farmington Ave., West Hartford, 860/236-1930, $14–22) just around the corner. By all accounts, Grant's is just as wonderful, its menu borrowing a bit more from France, but still offering the same style of cuisine as Bricco. Fried oysters in artichoke aioli, followed by filet mignon topped with jumbo shrimp of sautéed spinach are a couple of better dishes here. The scene is hip and trendy, the decibel level high.

Legions of prep school parents take their kids out to **Max a Mia** (70 Main St., U.S. 44/Rte. 10, Avon, 860/677-MAXX, $11–25), a chic contemporary Italian eatery in the heart of Avon. Like its Hartford counterpart, this place is dashed and splashed with vibrant colors and abuzz with the din of happy diners. Through the excitement, the staff remains remarkably courteous and affable, the food consistently on the mark. The trademark "stone pies" are a delight (consider the one with sweet fennel sausage, roasted garlic, broccoli rabe, wild mushrooms, marinara, and mozzarella), as are any of the dozen pasta dishes and such grills as brick-roasted half-chicken with oven-roasted vegetables and mashed potatoes. This sort of hearty fare only works if the produce and ingredients are farm fresh, and at Max a Mia, this is a sure bet.

Modestly decorated yet remarkably inviting—and very reasonably priced, considering the excellent food—**Metro Bis** (928 Hopmeadow St., U.S. 202/Rte. 10, Simsbury, 860/651-1908, $15–20) is a neat intimate place with recessed lighting, curtain valances, and simple wooden floors—an ambience that allows the remarkably tasty and colorful food to take center stage. The eclectic cooking ranges from chili-seared catfish with with curried split green peas, Serrano ham, and a roasted red pepper broth to grilled tandoori-marinated leg of lamb with braised lentils, cucumber tzatziki, crispy pappadum and Manchurian sauce.

A branch of the popular Waterbury-based chain, with additional outposts in Woodbury and Wethersfield, the **Carmen Anthony Fishhouse of Avon** (Shops at River Park, 51 E. Main St., U.S. 44, 860/677-7788, $20–30) is a loud, popular spot with pricey, but generally good—if not stellar—steaks, and chops; many of the preparations are Italian-influenced.

A sister restaurant of the acclaimed Peppercorn's Grill in Hartford, **Piccolo Arancio** (849 Farmington Ave., Rte. 10 at Rte. 4, Farmington, 860/674-1224, $14–23) serves the same brand of very fine country-contemporary Italian fare, a bounty of wood-fired pizzas, pastas, risottos, and grills—including grilled mustard-crusted pork tenderloin with caramelized onions. It's adjacent to the Farmington Inn.

## Steak, Pizza, Pub Grub, and Seafood

**Dakota** (235 W. Main St., Avon, 860/677-4311, $12–27) is much loved for its prime rib, top sirloin, live Maine lobster, and grilled chicken and shrimp dinners; prices are quite reasonable, too, for this sort of fare. The setting is an almost kitschy lodge-like building that evokes the spirit of Grand Teton National Park in Wyoming (well, in a ersatz way) with a distinctive fieldstone chimney, antlers twisting in all directions, and fine lodge-pole woodwork. This place is an absolute mad scene on weekends and pretty crowded any day of the week.

Avon's **First and Last Tavern** (26 W. Main St., U.S. 44, 860/676-2000, $10–16 for large pies) is set in a saltbox Colonial with a long rambling dining room behind it; it's huge and can accommodate many more people than its cousin in Hartford—it's a little less characterful out here, but the pizzas and pastas are still delicious.

In West Hartford, **Harry's** (1003 Farmington Ave., 860/231-7166, $12–17 for large pizzas) might just lay claim to Connecticut's most delicious white clam pizza. A contemporary space with wooden booths and framed photographs—it looks like an art gallery gone pizzeria—the place specializes in crisp-crust pizzas with fairly typical (but fresh) toppings, none too unusual except for the peculiar yet ubiquitous marriage of pineapple and Canadian bacon. There are two more branches in Avon, one on W. Avon Road, 860/675-8883, and the other at Avon's Riverdale Farms shopping center, U.S. 202/Rte. 10, 860/409-0707. Next door to Harry's is its much-touted rival, **Luna Pizza** (999 Farmington Ave., West Hartford, 860/233-1625, $11–15 for large pizzas). Both are outstanding, and Luna offers a very nice antipasto, as well as some pies with slightly more jazzy toppings: consider the white pizza with salmon, mozzarella, capers, Bermuda onions, and herbs. The setting of charmingly warped wooden floors, pale blue pressed-tin ceilings and walls, marble tables, and brass sconces lends it more character than Harry's, but Luna's definitely has the more brash and cool waitstaff. Luna is also growing quickly, with additional locations in Cromwell, Glastonbury, Plainville, and Simsbury.

Set in a vintage rail station and infused with a cozy tavern ambience, **One-Way Fare** (4 Railroad St., Simsbury, 860/658-4477, $5–13) has both indoor and deck seating and is a favorite locals' hangout for unpretentious comfort fare like cranberry chicken salad, sautéed trout, and pastrami and Swiss on rye. On cold nights, you might dive into the rich cheese fondue, which serves two to four.

Far less heralded among Hartford-area pizza experts is a little underrated gem in the rather remote Tariffville section of Simsbury called **Elizabeth's** (32 Main St., 860/651-4214, $8–20, large pizzas $15–17). This smart and sophisticated pizza and pasta place is inside a rustic storefront on Main Street—seating is in large upholstered booths. The pies here tend toward complicated and therefore filling (a large one can easily feed three or four): Best bets are chicken pesto or the Mediterranean (with plum tomatoes, Calamata olives, feta cheese, and garlic).

The pastas range from basic shells with meatballs to a knockout dish of sea scallops, sundried tomatoes, capers, and olive oil over linguine.

## Asian

The food at **Green Tea** (1067 Farmington Ave., Farmington, 860/678-8880, $8–16), a rustic-feeling restaurant with varnished wood walls and pitched ceilings, rates about as well as any Chinese food in greater Hartford. The menu is predictably lengthy, naming all the usual seafood, beef, poultry, and veggie dishes plus some rather elaborate specialties like boneless strips of braised duck sautéed with snow peas, bok choy, water chestnuts, and mushrooms with a spicy sauce. A handful of "weight watchers" dishes satisfy health-conscious diners.

West Hartford has a handful of noteworthy Chinese restaurants—locals have long favored **Butterfly's** (831 Farmington Ave., West Hartford, 860/236-2816, $8–16), which is quite good and often has live piano entertainment.

Sushi is a specialty of the Farmington River Valley: There are no fewer than four outstanding sushi restaurants in this region. Top accolades go to **Toshi** (Riverdale Farms, 136 Simsbury Rd., Rte. 10/US 202, Avon, 860/677-8242, $9–20), which ranks among the best Japanese restaurants in the state—it's arguably *the* best. The sushi is sublime, the rolls inventive (sour plum and Japanese yam; soft-shell crab with avocado), and the broiled beef tenderloin-and-shrimp combo renowned. Pluses are the warm airy dining room with track lighting and two levels of seating, and the friendly informative servers. Others in the area that earn similarly high marks for cuisine and ambience include **Japanica** (270 Farmington Ave., Farmington, 860/677-5633); **Murasaki** (10 Wilcox St., Simsbury, 860/651-7929); and **Osaka** (962A Farmington Ave., West Hartford, 860/233-1877).

One of the better Thai restaurants in the state, **Lemon Grass** (7 S. Main St., West Hartford, 860/233-4405, $8–13) does this piquant and often complex style of Asian cuisine justice, offering about 15 veggie dishes (try the sautéed crispy tofu with carrots, peanuts, onions, and sweet potatoes or the semi-sweet pineapple-fried rice), several curry dishes, and some rather elaborate items like grilled swordfish topped with shrimp and clam curry sauce, snow peas, bell peppers, baby corns, and basil. The neat, uncluttered dining room is warmed with soft lighting and smiling servers.

Canton's **Bamboo Grill** (50 Albany Tpke., U.S. 44/202, 860/693-4144, $10–15) is top in the area for Vietnamese food—a traditional house dish is fried whole flounder with a hot and spicy sauce. It's BYOB, and the decor is simple and unmemorable.

As is true at many of Connecticut's Indian restaurants, the food at **Taste of India** (139 S. Main St., West Hartford, 860/561-2221, $10–16) is well-prepared, but the seasonings are extremely mild (you'll need to request extra heat, but the gracious staff is very good about accommodating special requests or bringing extra sides of certain dishes). Nearly all of the curry dishes cost under $10; a house specialty is chicken *paatia,* a curry of mango and tomatoes with a bit of sugar, lemon juice, and traditional herbs and spices. The delicious onion *kulcha* bread is stuffed with fresh onions, green chilies, and green coriander. Offering a mix of northern (which is what you'll mostly find in America) and exciting southern Indian dishes, Simsbury's **New India** (1416 Hopmeadow St., U.S. 202/Rte. 10, 860/408-9001, $8–18) is a neatly decorated eatery near the center of town. Among the dishes you'll be hard-pressed to find at other Indian eateries in the region is *masala dosa* (potatoes, lentils, and spices wrapped in rice pancakes and served with a coconut chutney). Good old tandoori chicken is just as well-prepared here.

## Mediterranean

**Tapas** (1150 New Britain Ave., West Hartford, 860/521-4609, $7–16) is a nutty place, as evidenced by a note in the menu about the origin of tapas: "In the Mediterranean centuries ago,

CONN. RIVER VALLEY

Spaniards covered their vessels of wine with pieces of bread to discourage UFO's from landing on their grape as they wandered." Okay. The food is truly out of this world: spanakopita; an "almost famous" Greek salad; sweet South Bay clams reduced with garlic, white wine, olive oil, and herbs, baked over ricotta and topped with mozzarella and Parmesan cheese—virtually every Mediterranean culinary style is represented. You can watch the chefs at work from the cozy dining room (you can actually smell their creations from about six blocks away) or sit on the ambient covered patio painted with purples, blues, and floral designs. Note that there's no freezer on the premises, a way of letting you know that every morsel of food here is fresh as can be.

## Mexican

**Margarita's** (144 Albany Tpke., U.S. 44, Canton, 860/693-8237, $7–15) is one of the very, very few Mexican restaurants in the state that actually serves memorable food, offering plenty of Tex-Mex kick (as opposed to chain-restaurant blah), although still somewhat Americanized. The seafood quesadilla (shrimp, sole, crab) is rich and satisfying, as is the biting salsa that comes with your pre-dinner chips—it's redolent of cumin. The namesake drink is managed as competently here as anywhere in the state, and there are two bright dining areas—an upstairs cantina with sofas and lounging space, and a more traditional downstairs space splashed in cheerful reds, yellows, and blues. Service is friendly, if a bit absent at times.

## Quick Bites

**A Trifle More than Truffles** (Canton Village Shopping Center, 220 Albany Tpke., U.S. 44, Canton, 860/693-3799) is a cozy bakery, candy shop, and coffeehouse in Canton Village, in the center of town. The shop, filled with delicious sweets and goodies, also has ample seating. The food is a work of art, and there's a laundrette next door, in case you wish to combine laundry with pigging out. (There are additional branches in Avon at 369 W. Main St., 860/677-1784, and in West Hartford at 29 S. Main St., 860/521-6544.)

In Simsbury, the **Perfect Pear Café** (532 Hopmeadow St., Rte. 10, 860/651-7734, $8–14) is a cute and cheerful eatery serving three meals a day. You might sample Belgian waffles with vanilla-bean whipped cream at breakfast; the Perfect Pear salad of poached pear, goat cheese, and toasted pine nuts over mixed greens with honey-lime dressing at lunch; and similarly creative fare at dinner. West Hartford's **A. C. Petersen Farms Restaurant** (240 Park Rd., 860/233-8483, $4–9) is a great pick for casual diner-style cooking, from burgers to tuna melts. But the real draw here is the outstanding ice cream, which has been famous in Connecticut for generations.

## Java Joints

Along West Hartford's shop-filled Main Street, **Peter B's** (860/231-9390) is the place to lounge away a weekend afternoon, complete with chess, newspapers, and conversation. The gelatos here are a nice treat. One of the more innovative coffeehouses in the area is **Perfect Blend Café** (1086 New Britain Ave., West Hartford, 860/570-0010), which really fulfills several roles: boutique, restaurant, live music hall, and multicultural social center. The Georgian-style brick mansion in which it's located was rescued from disuse and restored elegantly, so that today you can drop by for coffee or a glass of wine, shop for jewelry or period furniture upstairs, or perhaps catch live jazz or folk on Friday and Saturday nights. The Sunday brunches are a big hit. You can take a break from antiques shopping in Collinsville at **Station House Coffee Bar** (2 Front St., 860/693-0600).

## Gourmet Goods and Picnic Supplies

In West Hartford, the lively market and eat-at-the-counter café **Tangiers** (668 Farmington Ave., 860/233-8168) offers a wide range of Middle Eastern and Mediterranean foods, including Lebanese, Greek, Turkish, Moroccan, Israeli, and Armenian. The restaurant serves gyros, falafel, and such, but you can get virtually any kind of Middle Eastern ingredient to take back home. **Kane's Meat Market** (1310 Hopmeadow St., U.S. 202/Rte. 10, Simsbury, 860/651-0614) is famous for its slow-cooked ribs, which are sometimes cooked up at a makeshift barbecue in the parking lot.

## INFORMATION AND SERVICES
### Visitor Information
Most of the towns in this region are served by the **Greater Hartford Tourism District** (31 Pratt St., 4th Fl., Hartford, CT 06103, 860/244-8181 or 800/793-4480, www.enjoyhartford.com). Exceptions are Barkhamsted, Hartland, New Hartford, and Riverton, which are handled by the **Litchfield Hills Travel Council** (Box 968, Litchfield, CT 06759, 860/567-4506, www.litchfieldhills.com).

### Getting Around
Highway access to the Farmington River Valley is via either I-84, which has exits for Farmington and West Hartford at the southeastern edge of the area, or Rte. 8, which has exits for New Hartford at the northwestern edge. It's also easy to get here by following Rte. 20 west from Windsor Locks, U.S. 44 west from Hartford or east from Winsted, or U.S. 202 south from Granby or east from Torrington.

## Tobacco Country

*Broad, level tobacco fields stretch out on either side of U.S. 5 through a region renowned as the heart of the wrapper-leaf tobacco-producing industry. In the spring, the tobacco plants are started in cold frames and brought to fair size under glass. The fields are carefully prepared, harrowed smooth as the chocolate frosting on a cake, and marked in geometry patterns so that the rows can be cultivated two ways, either lengthwise or across the field. Tobacco "setting," the transplanting of the plants to the fields, is done with a two-wheeled combination drill and water cart, behind which two men ride on small seats. These men, holding "flats" or trays of plants on their knees, drop a plant every time an indicator "ticks," and regulate the flow of water and fertilizer into the drills. In late August and September, when the rich aroma of the leaf fills the air, hundreds of men and women work swiftly to harvest and cure the crop.*

This passage, excerpted from *Connecticut,* a 1938 guidebook on the state compiled by the Works progress Administration, described what was by the Depression a century-old annual rite, like oystering off the coast of Norwalk or manufacturing hardware in New Britain. Broadleaf tobacco was farmed as far south as Portland, Connecticut, and as far north as southern Vermont, but the most intense farming was along the

river valley between Hartford and lower Massachusetts, in a group of towns that were nearly all once a part of the state's earliest settlement, Windsor.

Tobacco and the tradition of smoking was as foreign as corn and wild turkeys to the earliest settlers, and as with these other products, it was the Native Americans who introduced white men to this abundant crop. The settlers noticed that the local Indians smoked tobacco in pipes, but it wasn't until Israel Putnam—later to become famous as a general in the American Revolution—observed the regional customs of the Caribbean during a 1760s voyage that the notion of rolling the leaves into cigars was introduced to Connecticut.

By the early 1800s, tobacco farming had developed locally into a cottage industry, but the variety of tobacco that thrived in this soil and climate differed from what had become a major crop in North Carolina and Virginia by this time. Connecticut tobacco was acceptable for smoking locally, but was ill-suited as a serious export crop, given its comparatively inferior grade. However, the wide sturdy leaves of Windsor-area tobacco were perfect for use in cigar wrappers and in the ties used to bind them.

And so the state's tobacco country excelled throughout much of the 19th century, before losing ground to advancements in tobacco farming on the Indonesian island of Sumatra, where the sultry climate produced a better product than in Connecticut. The ever-ingenious Nut-meggers, already quite famous for their techno-logical acumen, retaliated by creating a way to develop a cut of tobacco leaf that would compare favorably with that grown in more humid parts of the world. The valley's farmers began en-meshing their field with long low tents of muslin netting, which indeed trapped the moisture and created a better, lighter leaf.

The boom lasted a couple of decades; by 1921, there were 31,000 acres (just under 1 percent of the total acreage of Connecticut) of tobacco fields in the state. But several factors precipitated a de-cline in the state's most significant cash crop: Cuba and Florida developed into the preemi-nent producers of cigars, and new cigar-making technology made the reliance on tobacco leaves for binding the cigars unnecessary. The land north of Hartford is also quite valuable, and so the acres of farmland—once studded with long red or brown tobacco-curing barns—have largely given way to suburban housing and office parks. A significant chunk of tobacco crop was also plowed over to make way for Bradley Interna-tional Airport in Windsor Locks.

Today, if you ask residents in this area, you'll learn that nearly all of them either worked or had friends or family members who toiled after school or during the summer on tobacco farms. The high labor demands during the crop's heyday also lured immigrant workers to the region from the West Indies, which today accounts for the substantial presence locally of Jamaican descendants. There are still a hand-ful of commercial farms, whose cumulative acreage is a little under 2,000 acres (and falling). Along several back roads in the area you'll still pass alongside rows of old tobacco barns, but many of them are now abandoned or used for other purposes.

As it relates to the state's history, Connecti-cut's Tobacco Country is both colorful and im-portant—a part of the state where it's still very easy to see how the land shaped the people, and the people in turn reshaped the land. As a tourist destination, this is one of the least-visited parts of the state. The terrain is less dramatic than in the hills or along the coast, and this stretch of the

Connecticut River is somewhat marred by the presence of I-91, whereas the lower valley (south of Middletown) remains bucolic to this day.

Of course, there are benefits to touring this underappreciated country. The costs of rooms at the few country inns and at area restaurants pale in comparison with the more touristy parts of the state. Despite the suburbanization of the towns nearest the river, communities 10 miles on either side—like Granby, Ellington, and Somers—have a wealth of unspoiled forests and state parks, perfect for hiking. This is also one of the earliest-settled parts of the state, and for this reason it's home to a slew of remarkable house-museums, most of them with highly limited hours. But phone ahead, mention that you're in-terested in dropping by and taking a tour, and your request will almost certainly be met with unabashed enthusiasm.

# WESTERN TOBACCO COUNTRY
## Bloomfield
The Tobacco Country towns unfold north of Hartford, beginning with the suburb of Bloom-field. From Hartford, follow Rte. 189 north—you'll pass the dramatic 1920s Gothic campus of St. Thomas Catholic Seminary on your imme-diate left, just across the Bloomfield town line—until you reach the peaceful town center, at the intersection of Rte. 178. Bloomfield, originally the western edge of Windsor, has a decidedly all-American feel to it, right down to the enor-mous 1860s Congregational church overlooking the town green. Continue north on Rte. 189, passing briefly through the old mill village of Tariffville and the western edge of East Granby into Granby proper.

## Granby
Granby, a part of Simsbury until it branched off and incorporated in 1786, is one of the least de-veloped towns in greater Hartford, retaining its rural character and largely wooded countryside. Much of the southern end of town is dominated by the **McLean Game Refuge** (Rte. 10/U.S. 202, 860/653-7869), a 2,500-acre nature pre-

CONN. RIVER VALLEY

serve established in 1932 by former U.S. Senator George P. McLean as a place where local wildlife could be free to roam unfettered by overbuilding and human interference. Many miles of trails traverse this park; hunting and fishing are prohibited. The trails are detailed on a map by the parking area, just off Rte. 10/US 202. Not far from the park's entrance, the **Salmon Brook Settlement** (208 Salmon Brook St., U.S. 202/Rte. 10, 860/653-9713, 2–4 P.M. Sun., mid-May–mid-Oct., $2) is administered by the Granby Historical Society. The settlement comprises several 18th- and 19th-century buildings, including the one-room Cooley School (1870); the 1732 Rowe House, which is the town's oldest standing structure; a 19th-century tobacco barn; and a Colonial shoemaker's shop.

Similarly agrarian is the town's cousin, East Granby (reached via Rte. 20), which is still the home of a few farms. It's better known, however, as the site of America's earliest copper mine, which eventually became the nation's first federal prison, **Old New-Gate Prison and Copper Mine** (Newgate Rd., north from Rte. 20, East Granby, 860/653-3563, www.chc.state.ct.us/old_new.htm, $4). At press time, state tourism budget cuts had forced the museum to close indefinitely; call ahead to confirm if it's open. This is a fascinating attraction whose legacy raises a couple of good questions: Why is it the "Old" *New*-Gate Prison? And how is one site both a prison and a copper mine?

For starters, the facility began as the Simsbury copper mine in 1707. For the next six decades mostly immigrant workers toiled below ground mining ore that produced anywhere from 10–50 percent copper. Eventually, better sources of copper were discovered elsewhere, and the mine's profitability diminished to the point that in 1773 the land was converted into New-Gate Prison (named for the infamous Newgate prison in London, England). For a time the prisoners were required to continue mining copper, and when this endeavor finally ended once and for all, their toil turned to manufacturing nails, shoes, and similar such implements. During the Revolutionary War, troublesome Tories and captured British prisoners of war were confined here. Over the course of its 42-year run, New-Gate incarcerated 800 prisoners.

New-Gate sits on the western lower slope of Peak Mountain, which is a continuation of the Metacomet Ridge (a.k.a. Talcott Mountain) in Simsbury (it carries clear into Massachusetts, where the same ridge is known as Mt. Holyoke and Mt. Tom up in the Pioneer Valley). The prison is built into the side of a hill, down which lead a few hiking trails. The base of the western prison wall, next to which you'll also find a handful of picnic tables, offers great views of the western hills. Every so often the silence is broken by a jet zooming overhead to the east, having just taken off from nearby Bradley Airport. Visitors can explore the mine, the cells in which prisoners slept at night (in total darkness), the old guard house, and various aboveground ruins. Note that it's quite chilly down in the cells (about 40°F), so a warm jacket or sweater is recommended, even when the air above ground is mild.

## Suffield

From East Granby, follow Rte. 187 north into the similarly rural community of Suffield. Here, turn right onto Rte. 168 and continue east through the rolling farmland and past dozens of Colonial houses to the pretty town center of Suffield. In these hills, Simon Viets opened the nation's very first cigar factory, at the corner of Ratley Road and Spruce Street (off Rte. 187 at the northern end of town). Among the many fine old homes standing in town is one of the state's most impressive house-museums, the 1761 **Phelps-Hatheway House** (55 S. Main St., Rte. 75, 860/247-8996, seasonal hours, open mid-May–mid-Oct., donation requested). The structure's immense side wing is one of the earliest examples of Classical Revival in the Connecticut River Valley, and the lovely formal gardens sparkle throughout spring and summer; a 300-year-old sycamore tree shades the grounds. The interior of the house remains as sumptuous as when wealthy merchant Oliver Phelps lived here—note the 1790s hand-blocked French wallpapering and well-preserved moldings. A bit farther down the street is the **King House Museum** (232 S. Main St., Rte. 75, 860/668-5256, limited hours), a 1764 center-chimney Georgian Colonial, known for its embroidered bed linens, fine doll collection,

## "THE NOTCH"

Suffield, along with Enfield and Woodstock to the east, were originally settled as part of Massachusetts. Early Massachusetts land surveyors incorrectly set the border at a point some eight miles south of where it should have been. Disputes about how to resolve this situation continued over the next hundred years, with a variety of attempts at compromise thwarted by stubborn minds on both sides of the issue. In 1749, the residents of the three towns thumbed their noses at the high taxes and strong-arming government of Massachusetts and opted to secede and reincorporate in the Nutmeg State. This move was contested bitterly by Massachusetts, but a compromise was finally achieved that accounts for that funny little indentation in Connecticut's northern border, between Suffield and North Granby. In this largely undeveloped "notch," the village of Gillette Corner, Massachusetts, is one of the only spots in the United States where a community is bordered on three sides by a state other than its own.

antique bottles, and memorabilia concerning the state's tobacco industry. Many of the early antiques were built in the Connecticut River Valley.

### Windsor Locks

From Suffield's town center, continue south on Rte. 75 toward Windsor Locks. As you approach the border, on your right you'll see Bradley International Airport and the signs leading to the **New England Air Museum** (Rte. 75, Windsor Locks, 860/623-3305, www.neam.org, open 10 A.M.–5 P.M. daily, $8). This is a relatively unheralded attraction, considering that it's one of the most substantial aviation museums in the country, and it contains enough airplanes and well-executed exhibits to keep even the casual observer intrigued for a few hours. Maintained by the Connecticut Aeronautical Historical Association, the museum comprises two large exhibition buildings (one on civil aviation and the other on military planes), plus a huge yard out back full of vehicles awaiting restoration. All

told, there are more than 130 aircraft on display, ranging from the 11th plane engine built by the Wright Brothers to an A-10 Warthog used in Desert Storm.

One of the most prized aircraft is a VS-44 Flying Boat (the last surviving of three created by nearby aviation pioneer Igor Sikorsky before he turned his efforts principally to the creation of helicopters), a versatile plane designed to land and function on the water. Plans are underway to build another exhibition building at the museum, specifically to house the Flying Boat. Most intriguing perhaps is the Silas Brooks Balloon Basket (ca. 1870)—the oldest aircraft artifact in the United States. "Open Cockpit Days" are held throughout the year, allowing visitors to climb inside certain planes. You can also examine closely dozens of engines, Jeeps, weapons, artifacts (among them an original page from the log of Amelia Earhart's ill-fated final voyage), uniforms, and photographs, including a wealth of memorabilia relating to a century of military campaigns in which air combat has played a vital role. A small theater shows movies and videos on a variety of topics, and one poignant display chronicles the 1979 tornado that ripped through this facility, destroying 30 aircraft and shutting down the museum for two years. A bookstore offers a wide selection of models, toys, and books related to aviation.

Appropriately, the air museum is on the grounds of New England's second-largest air facility (after Logan in Boston), **Bradley International Airport,** which sits over what was once a huge tract of tobacco farms and covers parts of East Granby, Suffield, and Windsor Locks (its official address is the latter community). The airport was named not—as some might imagine—for some important aviation or government official, or for the distinguished U.S. General Omar Bradley, but for a little-known military pilot named Eugene Bradley, who crashed and died on this site during a routine takeoff in 1941. At that time, the airstrip had recently opened as a World War II air force base; it also housed German prisoners for a time. After the war, however, it sat largely abandoned until the state seized the land and

CONN. RIVER VALLEY

developed it into a commercial airport in 1950. The facility continues to grow each year, as terminals are expanded or added and new airlines and routes secured.

Although the airport has provided the town with considerable fame, much of Windsor Locks exists out of the shadows of overflying aircraft—a bustling Connecticut River town with the greatest evidence of industry found in any town in the Tobacco Country. Indeed, because of the power generated by the river's Enfield Rapids, quite a few mills thrived in the eastern section of town during the 19th century. Most of the manufacturing base has dried up, but evidence of these buildings and the working-class community that built up around them lies east of the airport, along Rte. 140 near the banks of the Connecticut River. A good place to learn about the area's history is the **Noden-Reed House and Barn** (58 West St., off Rte. 140, 860/627-9212 or 860/623-6686, seasonal hours, open May–Oct., free). It's a 22-acre farmstead with an 1826 brick barn and period-furnished 1840s Victorian house. The barn is one of New England's few remaining brick ones, and the interior is filled with vintage carriages, old farming implements, and hatchets and spears used to cultivate tobacco. It is often said that America's first true Christmas tree was decked out on this site. In 1777, a young Hessian mercenary who had fought in the Revolutionary War lived in a cabin on this property, as a boarder of the family who owned the farmstead. A laborer on the farm, Henrick Roddemore, erected and trimmed a Christmas tree his first winter here, in 1777.

## Windsor

From this part of town, turn south along Rte. 159, which meanders south largely along the west bank of the Connecticut River and into the town that best defines this region: Windsor. (The area originally included the land that now makes up Bloomfield, South Windsor, East Windsor, Windsor Locks; parts of Vernon and Ellington; and the southern tips of Somers, Enfield, Suffield, East Granby, and Granby!). These days, a quick drive through this busy river town may reveal what appears to be a modern and rather typical-

looking New England suburb, complete with blocks of 20th-century homes and numerous corporate parks. But Windsor is where English settlers, invited by the area's Native Americans, first settled Connecticut in 1633—few towns have played a more pivotal role in the state's history.

Although Roger Sherman, framer of the 1639 Fundamental Orders of Connecticut, is Windsor's best-known historic figure, a close second belongs to the distinguished statesman who once resided at the **Oliver Ellsworth Homestead** (778 Palisado Ave., Rte. 159, 860/688-8717, seasonal hours, open mid-May–mid-Oct., $2). Ellsworth was instrumental in drafting the U.S. Constitution; he served as a U.S. senator and was later appointed U.S. Chief Justice by his good friend, President John Adams. Both Adams and George Washington were guests in this 1740 house, which contains among other priceless artifacts a tapestry presented to Ellsworth by Napoleon in 1803, as a show of appreciation for the diplomat's efforts in establishing a treaty between France and the United States.

The drive farther south along Rte. 159 actually reveals a good bit of the city's legacy, lined as it is with dozens of 18th-century homes and one 17th-century house. The red gambrel-roofed 1640 Lt. Walter Fyler House, along with the three-story redbrick 1765 Dr. Hezekiah Chaffee House, makes up the **Windsor Historical Society** (96 Palisado Rd., Rte. 159, 860/688-3813, open 10 A.M.–4 P.M. Tues.–Sat., $3). Both houses are filled with some of the finest and most elegant antiques of any museums in the region, and the society also maintains an excellent genealogical library. The Hezekiah Chaffee House contains 15 rooms and shows many of the early medical instruments of its owner, Dr. Chaffee. Call ahead to learn about some of the intriguing changing exhibits staged here.

The historical society overlooks the northern of Windsor's two village greens, the Palisado, which is named for the small fort built here by the settlers in 1637 to protect them from attacks by the Pequot Indians. The Pequots were enemies of the Podunks, who invited the settlers here in the first place. These first settlers were Puritans from Dorchester (of the Plymouth Colony), who set-

## AMY ARCHER-GILLIGAN: ANGEL OF MERCY, OR THE REAL "OLD LACE"?

Just north of Windsor's Broad Street Green, at 37 Prospect Street (now a private residence), Mrs. Amy Archer-Gilligan operated a nursing home until she was arrested in 1916 for poisoning residents. This angel of mercy, as she claimed to represent herself, was charged with five counts of murder, but it's thought that as many as five *dozen* met their fate here. An ulterior motive? Well, it does happen that many of her boarders paid their way into the home by signing over their life-insurance policies to their entrepreneurial host. Mrs. Archer-Gilligan's misguided attempts at euthanasia were later developed into the droll play and Cary Grant film *Arsenic and Old Lace*. Mrs. Archer-Gilligan was ultimately convicted on one count of murder, for which she was sentenced to life in a mental institution; she died there in 1962, at the ripe old age of 89.

tled at this area just north of where the Farmington River (then called the Tunxis, after the native tribes who lived near its source) enters the Connecticut. Although many in the original Windsor colony headed back to Massachusetts during the very cold first winter, a few stayed behind to oversee the livestock and maintain the settlement. Thus, it's somewhat open to interpretation whether Windsor is to be credited with having been the state's first lasting settlement, as some argue that because most of the group left during the first winter it wasn't "lasting" at all. In any case, Windsor became, along with Hartford and Wethersfield, the foundation for Connecticut. Walking tours of the original Palisado neighborhood are offered by the Windsor Historical Society on Thursdays and Fridays; call for details and times.

The second green, just a short distance south along Broad Street, is steps from the 300-acre campus of prestigious **Loomis-Chaffee School** (Batchelder Rd., 860/687-6000, www.loomis.org), which was founded as the Loomis boys' prep academy in 1914. Chaffee School for girls was added in

1926, and in 1970, the schools were combined. Former governor Ella Grasso, the first elected female U.S. governor, is among the school's many successful graduates.

Just south of the town center on the Windsor Town Green, the **Huntington Museum** (298 Broad St., 860/688-2004, www.huntingtonmuseum.org, open 10 A.M.–4 P.M. Thurs.–Sat., noon–4 P.M. Sun., $6) opened in 2001 inside a gorgeous 6,500-square-foot mansion. Rotating art exhibits change throughout the year. This stunning Edwardian mansion was built in 1901, inspired by Mark Twain's house in Hartford and also many of the opulent mansions of Newport. It's noted for its fine original woodwork, 12-foot ceilings, and stained-glass windows.

From Windsor Center, turn up Rte. 75 and, after crossing I-91, make a left onto Day Hill Road. Here you'll get a dramatic illustration of how the nature of the northern Connecticut River Valley has changed from agrarian to corporate. Thousands of acres of tobacco fields have been converted into corporate "parks" and executive "campuses," now sheltering such business giants as Konica and Kaiser Permanente. It seems the prototypical farming community of the 1800s has been replaced with the prototypical business community of the 2000s. At the end of Day Hill, turn right onto Prospect Hill Road, which leads to Lang Road. To learn more about the industry for which this region is best known, stop by the **Luddy-Taylor Connecticut Valley Tobacco Museum** (Northwest Park, 145 Lang Rd., Windsor, 860/285-1888, seasonal hours, open March–mid-Dec., free). Set appropriately inside an old tobacco curing barn, with both modern and old-fashioned equipment, various old photos, and documents. The museum is part of 473-acre **Northwest Park** (860/285-1886, http://northwestpark.org, open dawn–dusk year-round, nature center open 9 A.M.–5 P.M. Mon.–Sat., free), which includes an animal barn, more than 10 miles of hiking and cross-country skiing trails, and a nature center and library. The trails actually pass by several of the few remaining barns in an area where they once proliferated, and one trail runs alongside the Farmington River, which is dammed off and called Rainbow Reservoir at this point. This is a remarkably verdant and engaging bit of natural terrain in a part of the state where open spaces are fast disappearing. Prospect Hill continues back to Rte. 75, which leads south back to Windsor Center.

# EAST OF THE RIVER

## South Windsor

From Windsor Center, on the west side of the river, continue down Rte. 159 to I-291, and take the Interstate east over the Connecticut River to South Windsor, exiting at U.S. 5 (the first exit), a wide, dull commercial street lined with businesses and shops. For a more appealing drive, make your first left onto Chapel Road and then a right onto Main Street, which parallels U.S. 5 in direction and contrasts sharply with it in ambience (Main Street captures the 18th- and 19th-century architecture and spirit of Windsor). On your right, as you drive up Main just past Chapel, you'll see behind the homes an entire field of tobacco crops and several dilapidated brown tobacco barns behind them. This leads to one of the most comprehensive sources of the region's Native American history, the redbrick hip-roofed **Wood Memorial Library** (783 Main St., 860/289-1783, seasonal hours, free). This privately funded facility opened in 1926 to promote the understanding of the "Northeastern Woodland Indians" that once thrived throughout what is now New England. In addition to exhibits and documents on this topic, this neoclassical library contains mounted birds, Early American antiques, and some 10,000 volumes on a variety of topics—there are especially good adult and kids' fiction sections.

Main Street continues north through the pretty East Windsor Hill section of South Windsor before you must turn onto Sullivan Avenue (the road otherwise dead-ends), right by the Watson House. Then make a left onto U.S. 5, where the road continues over the border into the town of East Windsor (unquestionably, all the various Windsors in these parts are confusing).

East Windsor Hill is one of the prettiest spots in the valley, a tiny community of tobacco farms, red barns, and stately old homes. Right by the East Windsor Hill post office, Ferry Lane leads down to the Connecticut River. There's no water access here, just a plaque marking the site of the first ferry to run across the Connecticut River. It was operated by John Bissell beginning in 1641—he opened it as a means to get his cattle back and forth across the river, and the ferry continued to operate for many years. The pretty white house at the end of this lane dates from 1658 and has had many uses since, including shop, inn, and even a poor farm in the 1920s.

## East Windsor

After about four miles on U.S. 5, you'll come upon Rte. 140, from which a left turn leads below I-91 and into East Windsor's historic Warehouse District. Named in early Colonial times for being the point where goods brought up the river by ship were warehoused until transferred (by oxcart or by flat boat, depending on the water conditions and the size of the cargo) either around or over the troublesome Enfield Rapids section of the river.

A top attraction among both kids and adults is the **Connecticut Trolley Museum** (58 North Rd., Rte. 140, just east of I-91 and U.S. 5, East Windsor, 860/627-6540, www.ceraonline.org, seasonal hours, open spring–fall, $6), which provides rides on restored streetcars through three miles of scenic countryside. Directly behind the Trolley Museum is the 8,000-square-foot **Connecticut Fire Museum** (860/623-4723, seasonal hours, open Apr.–Oct., $2), which contains antique fire equipment dating to the 19th century, including an 1894 fire sleigh, and numerous fire engines manufactured throughout the 20th century.

## Enfield

U.S. 5 continues north into the town of Enfield, which was once a rural tobacco town but is now, owing to the intrusion of I-91, a middle-class suburb of both Hartford and Springfield (Massachusetts), the latter just 10 miles up the road. U.S. 5 (Enfield Street) contains some very elaborate and attractive old mansions dating from the late 1700s through the early part of the 20th century.

# PAUL ROBESON

The privately owned mansion at 1221 Enfield Street (U.S. 5), which is not open to the public, once belonged to one of the true renaissance men of the 20th century, the singer, actor, athlete, and outspoken political activist Paul Robeson. He is, unfortunately, often remembered more for his unconditional support of the Soviet Union and Joseph Stalin than for his many accomplishments. But in historical hindsight, many people now recognize the good in Robeson's ideals and interests, if not necessarily agreeing with his unyielding support of communism (contrary to popular belief, he was never a member of the Communist Party).

Robeson first gained notice as an all-American football player and Phi Beta Kappa student at Rutgers. After earning a law degree from Columbia, Robeson—who was black—almost immediately resigned from the first law firm to hire him after a white secretary refused to take dictation from him. A year later, in 1924, Robeson began his stage career in Greenwich Village, debuting in Eugene O'Neill's *All God's Chillun Got Wings,* and in his first film, *Body and Soul.* He also began singing in concert halls at around this time, earning rave reviews that lead to starring roles in London's West End in *Show Boat* and on Broadway in *Porgy and Bess.*

In 1934, the acclaimed filmmaker Sergei Eisenstein invited him on a journey to the Soviet Union—Robeson would say later that the Russians treated him like a man and appreciated his musical and acting talents without consideration of his race. Already accomplished in Eastern European folk singing, Robeson fell in love with Russian culture and music, and he began increasingly to speak out favorably on behalf of communism and Soviet causes. In 1940, Robeson moved into the gracious mansion on Enfield Street, where he lived for the next 13 years. It was during this time that he came under increasing scrutiny from the FBI, petitioned major league baseball to end its ban on African American ballplayers, and was misquoted—allegedly—as saying that American blacks would never fight in a war involving foreign interests. This comment drew the ire of many black leaders, and soon his concerts were being protested by angry mobs and canceled by promoters afraid of the negative publicity his presence could generate.

The final three decades of Robeson's brilliant life were marked by intense public criticism, deep depression, and personal angst. After speaking out against the Korean War, Robeson was banned from television and his passport was confiscated. The virulent witch hunt conducted during the early 1950s by the House Un-American Activities Committee ultimately sank Robeson's already listing career, and revelations in the late 1950s of the Stalin regime's many crimes against humanity sent this troubled figure into a severe funk. He lived largely as a recluse over the next two decades, dying in 1976 at the age of 78.

For a small town with no major sightseeing attractions, Enfield is unusual in its rich and varied history, much of which you can learn a thing or two about at the **Martha A. Parsons House** (1387 Enfield St., U.S. 5, 860/745-6064, seasonal hours, open May–Oct., $1). The 1787 house was originally a parsonage for the Congregational church, and it belonged to the same family until the 1960s. Ms. Parsons was born here in 1869, along with her two sisters. She was unique for her time, being relatively (and independently) wealthy. All three sisters worked their entire lives and never married, and Martha became a business executive at Landers, Frary, & Clark, a manufacturing concern in New Britain. She started as a secretary, but became the company's executive secretary in 1912, a position traditionally held in those days by men—she actually signed all of her business correspondence M. A. Parsons so as not to reveal her gender. Martha Parsons broke through the glass ceiling, and how!

She lived in New Britain during these years, but moved back to the house in Enfield upon her retirement and lived there until her death in 1962, before which she established that the house should be opened as a museum. A nice thing about a home owned by three unmarried women is that virtually all of the original furnishings remained here (with no heirs to receive them). Another great asset of the house is the original woodblocked wallpaper (ca. 1800), which was typically expected to last for no more than 40 years, but is still plainly visible—if a bit ragged—200 years after its creation. The Washington Memorial design of this paper (the statesman died in 1799) was popular during this period, but this is the last existing example of its kind. Remarkable furnishings throughout the home range from a 1740 Windsor chair to a pair of cherrywood Chippendale side chairs to some locally produced Shaker furnishings contained in an upstairs bedroom.

Nearby, the **Old Town Hall Museum** (1294 Enfield St., U.S. 5, Enfield, 860/745-1729, limited hours, free) has vintage clothing, farm implements, and exhibits on the Hazard gun-powder factory and Enfield's Shaker Village (more on this below), including a horse-drawn Shaker hearse. It's a good place to learn about the mill-working community that thrived here until the early part of the 20th century.

## Thompsonville

From U.S. 5, Rte. 190 leads into the Thompsonville section of town (around exit 47 of I-91), named for the operator, Orin Thompson, of one of America's first carpet mills (ca. 1828). The mill once prospered here (actually on the west side of town, near the river). East of Thompsonville, the Hazardville section of Enfield (around Rtes. 190 and 192) comprises a historic district set around what was, during the early 19th century, the Hazard Powder Company—some of the facility's early buildings still stand. Gun, not talcum powder, was manufactured here and then shipped to quarries throughout the state. It was a dangerous business, and many of the powder-makers lost fingers, limbs, or worse during their stressful careers.

In northeastern Enfield, at the intersection of Taylor and Shaker Roads (where Rte. 220 turns sharply north toward the Massachusetts border), there once existed the only community of **Shakers** in the state of Connecticut. Joseph Meacham founded the settlement in 1780, where it thrived until 1915; remaining members moved to settlements in Pittsfield, Massachusetts, and New Lebanon, New York. The Shakers were one of

the first groups to practice forest conservation, this at a time when nearly all of Connecticut's woodlands had been stripped for farming or for lumber to fuel mills and factories. They reforested their land, and in 1802 Enfield's Shakers came up with the now commonplace notion to package seeds in envelopes. The Shakers also practiced feminism, pacifism, and abolitionism long before these ideas were popular, and they harbored many fugitive slaves prior to the Civil War, including Sojourner Truth. The Shakers' land and buildings now serve a "community" of a very different sort: the minimum security Osborn State Prison Camp. It says a bit about the industry of the Shakers—and the lack of industry of the rest of society—that only supervised prisoners (with no choice but to toil) seem suited to carry out the work ethic established by the original community. Some of the old buildings are south of the prison, preserved in the Enfield Shakers Historic District, although none are open to the public.

## Somers

Follow Taylor Road south to Rte. 190 and continue east into Somers, one of the most picturesque and undeveloped towns in an already picturesque and sleepy region. A drive through this town of rolling farms and woodland reveals the transition from the Connecticut River Valley's fertile lowlands to the eastern uplands, which reach some 1,300 feet near Somers's eastern border. Route 190 passes first through the old mill community of Somersville, where history seekers will appreciate the **Somers Historical Museum** (11 Battle St., Somers, 860/763-2578, open only by appointment). A short distance north of Rte. 190, on the eastern side of town, the **Somers Mountain Museum of Natural History and Primitive Technology** (332 Turnpike Rd., Somers, 860/749-4129, www.somersmountain.org, open by appointment, $2), displays arrowheads from every state, an authentic wigwam, buckskin clothing, and other Native American handiwork. Some artifacts date back 10,000 years. It's been a museum since the 1930s, but was originally operated by its founder, James F. King, as also a trading post of sorts (he died at age

91 in 1986). It had been an "Indian" museum during its heyday, when this topic was treated with perhaps a slightly pejorative mentality quite typical of that time. It fell largely into disuse for a few years after his death, and was brought back to life in 1993 by concerned volunteers who also recognized a need to rethink the museum's treatment of indigenous cultures. Inside are stone tools, projectile points, jewelry, dolls, weaponry, and other artifacts of Native American culture. The museum also offers excellent educational workshops on ancient lifestyles and traditions. There's a small but nicely outfitted shop where you might buy drums, Native American flutes, pottery, and other items.

The southeast part of Somers, reached by taking Rte. 83 south and making a left onto Parker Road, leads to **Shenipsit State Forest/Soapstone Mountain,** which also falls in northeast Ellington and western Stafford Springs. If **mountain biking** is your passion, it's worth making a trip here, where twisting dirt, gravel, and paved roads lead through 6,100 acres of this densely wooded forest to 1,075-foot Soapstone Mountain. At the top of this relatively undervisited peak, you'll find a small grove of picnic tables, a massive weather station, and an easily climbed wooden observation tower. From the tower's top deck, you'll be treated to views of Springfield and the Pioneer Valley, plus miles of northern Connecticut farmland that once yielded the state's greatest cash crop, tobacco. Bring a pair of binoculars with you—on the clearest days you can see the nation's most-climbed peak, Monadnock Mountain in New Hampshire.

Bikers should note that there's no designated parking at Parker Road, but it's safe to park along the side of the road (shortly after you turn on to it from Rte. 83). From here, begin your bike ride 1.2 miles up Parker Road (the last third is rough and unpaved), turning left at the four-way intersection (onto Soapstone Mountain Road) and continuing another 1.3 miles to reach the short paved turnoff for the tower. For information on the hiking trails and other good biking roads in the park, phone the ranger's office at Shenipsit State Forest, 860/684-3430.

## Ellington

Back on Rte. 83, head south into Ellington, a quiet rural town whose main attraction is Crystal Lake, in the east end of town, which is surrounded by a slew of summer cottages and has a small public beach. In the center of town, Ellington's Federal-style 1812 **Nellie McKnight Museum** (70 Main St., 860/871-0459, limited hours) contains artifacts relevant to both the original Native American and Colonial inhabitants of the region.

# SHOPPING
## Pick-Your-Own Farms

As you might predict given the region's fertile terrain, farms raising all manner of produce and flowers thrive throughout Tobacco Country—although at none, in case you're wondering, can you come and roll your own cigars. Stop by the **4-H Farm Resource Center** (Simsbury Rd., Rte. 185, Bloomfield, 860/242-7144) to visit with barnyard animals, watch farm demonstrations, pick out a Christmas tree, and pick apples and raspberries. In northern Windsor, just off Rte. 75, **Brown's Harvest** (60 Rainbow Rd., 860/688-0266) has pick-your-own strawberries and pumpkins, and hayrides are offered at various times throughout the year.

You can pick flowers, fruits, and vegetables at Enfield's **Easy Pickin's Orchard** (46 Bailey Rd., near Rte. 190/191, 860/763-FARM) and in the fall you might paint pumpkins or make your own scarecrow. Or take a look at a real dairy farm, **Collins Powder Hill Farm** (9 Powder Hill Rd., 860/749-3416, open for tours by advanced request), which also makes its own ice cream and sells compost and, if you happen to be in the market for one, Holstein cows. A couple miles east, in Somers, **Pleasant View Farm** (452 South Rd., Rte. 83, 860/749-5868) has pony and hayrides, miniature golf, and a weekend flea market—a great outing for kids and adults. Nearby, **Kassandra—Herbs Unlimited** (54 Springfield Rd., Rte. 83, 860/749-0839) is a source of fresh and potted herbs, essential oils and capsules, and naturalist books and gifts. In Ellington, **Johnny Appleseed's Farm** (Rte. 83, 860/875-1000) contains hundreds of acres of pick-your-own peaches and apples. Near South Windsor's East Windsor Hill neighborhood, the **Wagon Shed Nursery** (155 Griffin Rd., 860/289-7356) sells not only Christmas trees but all kinds of holiday trimmings and goodies—it's a full-service gardening center year-round. Appropriately, the first decorated and illuminated Christmas tree in America was put up by Hendrick Roddemore of Windsor Locks in 1777.

## Antiques

In Enfield, **Treasure Hunters** (543 Enfield St., 860/253-9343) is a multi-dealer complex. You'll find a mix of antiques, crafts, home furnishings, dolls, and collectibles at the several shops comprising Granby's **Old Mill Pond Village** (U.S. 202/Rte. 10, 860/653-3433).

## Garden Gifts

**Revay's** (266 North Rd., East Windsor, 860/623-9068) carries a huge selection of garden accessories and gifts, much of it contained within a 40,000-square-foot greenhouse; there's also a Christmas shop with ornaments and holiday items.

# RECREATION
## Boating

There are public boat launches (with parking) along the Connecticut River in Enfield on Parson Road, a bit northwest of I-91 (exit 46, to U.S. 5 north), and in Windsor on E. Barber Street, off Rte. 159 (just south of the I-291 bridge overpass). In Ellington, there's parking for 15 cars along the west side of 200-acre Crystal Lake (on Rte. 30), where water-skiing, canoeing, and other light boating are quite popular.

## Bowling

The **Bradley Bowl** (129 Ella Grasso Tpke., Rte. 75, 860/623-2597) is a frequent stop on the Pro Bowlers' Association (PBA) tour and a favorite local bowling venue.

## Golf

Popular area courses, all of them with below-state-average greens fees, include **Airways Golf Course** (1070 S. Grand St., West Suffield,

860/668-4973) an 18-hole par-71 that's rather flat and without many hazards, but is still considered a decent challenge. A bit tougher is 7,000-yard **Cedar Knob Golf Course** (Billings Rd., Somers, 860/749-3550), an 18-hole, par-72 known for its large greens, and **Tradition Golf Course** (147 Pigeon Hill Rd., Windsor, 860/688-2575), a tricky and watery 18-hole, par-71 course.

## Hiking and Cross-Country Skiing

You'll find a wildlife sanctuary, trail, and waterfalls at **Enders State Forest** (Barkhamsted Rd., Rte. 219) in the western edge of Granby. Near the center of town, not far from this historic Salmon Brook Settlement (the name of this area when it was a part of Simsbury), are two adjoining hiking spots: **McLean Game Refuge** (Salmon Brook Rd., U.S. 202/Rte. 10, 860/653-7869), known for its bird-watching and cross-country skiing trails; and the 114-acre **Salmon Brook Park** (U.S. 202/Rte. 10, 860/653-2538), with trails, a playground, and a swimming pond.

Heublein Tower is the most notable (albeit man-made) feature along the 40-mile traprock ridge that runs in a northerly direction through the western side of the Connecticut River Valley. In the northern part of the state, it's traversed by the blue-blazed **Metacomet Trail** (and is called the Metacomet Ridge, after the noted and doomed Native American warrior, King Philip, also known as Metacomet). The trail can be accessed at numerous state parks in the area, including Talcott Mountain State Park, which is described above. Another popular route is through **Penwood State Park,** 860/566-2304, which straddles the Simsbury/Bloomfield border and begins just north of Talcott Mountain State Park, off Rte. 185 (midway between its junction with Rte. 10/U.S. 202 and Rte. 178)—there's a parking lot on the north side of the road. There are hiking, biking, and cross-country skiing trails at this 800-acre park. If you follow the Metacomet Trail through the park, you'll wind up at a lookout tower called The Pinnacle, from which you can see outstanding views of the area—this hike is just under five miles round-trip from the parking area.

Another way to tackle this ridge is to head up near Old New-Gate Prison in Granby to **Peak**

**Mountain.** The blue-blazed Metacomet Trail is accessed here from Newgate Road, just a short way north of Rte. 20 (as though heading toward the prison); there's room for a few cars to park along the side of the road. This is a four-mile round-trip hike along the traprock ridge; it overlooks the prison site in some places. This ridge marks a common flight path to nearby Bradley International Airport, so your peace and quiet will be disturbed often by the roar of engines, but you'll also get a remarkably close look at these planes.

One of the best trail systems in the greater Hartford region is **Windsor Lock Canal** (Canal Rd., off Rte. 159, Windsor Locks, 860/627-1420), a level 4.5-mile trail for bikers and walkers along the Connecticut River and the historic canal. (The canal opened in 1829 to bypass the Enfield Rapids). The four locks of this 70-foot-wide waterway once accommodated 60-ton ships en route to Springfield—prior to its construction, ships had to stop at Warehouse Point in East Windsor (across the Connecticut River). Their cargoes were then loaded by oxcart over this stretch. The method proved cumbersome and inefficient, and for a short time the canal provided a fine alternative. Successful completion of a railroad to Springfield rendered the canal obsolete by 1845. To enjoy this hike, begin at the canal where it's crossed by the Rte. 140 bridge over the Connecticut River, in Windsor Locks at Rte. 159. Or begin up in Suffield, where there's a parking lot on Canal Street, just off Rte. 159 south of its junction with Rte. 190. As you wander down alongside the river, you'll see the fearsome and formidable Enfield Rapids, and realize instantly why ships were unable to pass over them.

### Polo

Lest you think polo is relegated to the posh towns of Greenwich and New Canaan, Somers is in fact the site of a premier facility, the **Shallowbrook Equestrian Center** (247 Hall Hill Rd., Rte. 186, 860/749-0749), which has the largest indoor polo arena in the nation. The U.S. Polo Association stages tournaments here (open to the public), and American Horse Shows Association events are also presented here year-round.

## FESTIVALS AND EVENTS

One of the state's most prominent agricultural fairs, the **Four Town Fair** (56 Egypt Rd., off Rte. 83, 860/749-6527) takes place in Somers in mid-September; activities include demonstrations and contests, horse shows, a chicken barbecue, live entertainment, rides, and the like. For more than a century, the **Wapping Fair** (Rye Street Park, 860/644-8989) has been going strong each September in South Windsor, complete with fireworks, carnival rides, and agricultural exhibits and contests. The juried annual **Suffield Crafts Fair** (860/668-5767) is held at the historic Phelps-Hatheway House in mid-September. The weekend before Halloween is a hugely popular family-oriented event at **Old New-Gate Prison** (860/653-3563), including a torchlight mine tour, storytelling, cookie decorating, and live music and dancing.

In early December, historic house museums in several towns in the Tobacco Country are opened to the public for **Holidayfest** (860/763-2578 or 800/248-8283); each home contains seasonal displays, and various events are tied into this engaging celebration. In March, July, and November in North Granby, the **Quilt Happening and Sale** (Lost Acres Orchard, 860/653-6600) offers demonstrations and discussions on quilting, with both new and old pieces for sale.

## ACCOMMODATIONS

Hartford's northern suburbs, especially the corridor on either side of I-91, are packed with chain properties, from the usual budget motels to a few higher-end options close to Bradley Airport. The best of the bunch are noted below, based as much on pleasant locations as on the facilities themselves. For this reason, only one airport hotel, the particularly inviting Sheraton, is included—there's really no appeal in staying at one of the places by Bradley, unless you need to be near the airport to catch an early flight. Most of them (including Ramada Inn, Baymont Inn, Days Inn, Doubletree Hotel, Fairfield Inn by Marriott, Holiday Inn, Homewood Suites, and Motel 6) line a bland and overbuilt strip of Rte. 75.

## Hotels and Motels

**$150–250:** Far superior to what you'll typically find at an airport, the **Sheraton Bradley International Airport Hotel** (Bradley Airport, 860/627-5311 or 800/325-3535) towers directly above the main terminal, and is so pleasant that even long-term visitors have been known to choose this over the hotels in downtown Hartford and the 'burbs. Expect to find a bright, helpful staff and warmly decorated rooms, plus a well-maintained pool and health club. If you like watching planes land and take off, this is the ideal hotel for you.

Another of the excellent properties near the airport, the **Bradley International Airport Doubletree** (16 Ella Grasso Tpke., Windsor Locks, 860/627-5171 or 800/222-TREE) is a midrise 200-room hotel with upscale furnishings, friendly service, a concierge level with its own private lounge, and a very nice restaurant off the lobby. There's also an indoor pool and fitness center, and the hotel is set slightly down Rte. 75 from the hubbub of fast-food restaurants and rental-car agencies, but it's still just 10 minutes from the airport.

One of the newest hotels in the upper Connecticut River Valley, the **Hartford/Windsor Marriott Airport** (28 Day Hill Rd., 860/688-7500 or 800/228-9290) has a convenient yet picturesque location on a knoll over I-91. This upscale 300-room hotel includes 75 concierge-level units, which have their own lounge and business services. All guests can use the 24-hour business center, enjoy free transportation to and from the airport (a 10-minute drive), free parking, a 24-hour snack-gift shop, and room service. There's an indoor pool, fitness center, and a full restaurant and lounge.

**$100–150:** The **Marriott Residence Inn** (100 Dunfey Ln., 860/688-7474 or 800/331-3131) is a good choice for longer stays; each units has a fully equipped kitchen and separate sitting area. The penthouse units have upstairs sleeping lofts. Just down the hill from the Hartford/Windsor Marriott, the top-notch **Courtyard by Marriott** (1 Day Hill Rd., Windsor, 860/683-0022 or 800/321-2211) is utilized primarily by business travelers at the countless corporate parks nearby.

Rates vary dramatically according to the season, and can be quite reasonable on winter weekends. There's a health club and indoor pool, and the location is convenient to Hartford, the airport, and all area attractions.

The **Radisson Hotel Springfield-Enfield** (1 Bright Meadow Blvd., 860/741-2211 or 800/333-3333), an attractive 176-room full-service midrise hotel with a pool and a restaurant, is your best bet in Enfield and is ideal if you plan on spending time in both the Hartford and Springfield areas. There's a restaurant and lounge, indoor pool, and exercise room.

**$50–100:** The moderately priced **Baymont Inn & Suites** (64 Ella Grasso Tpke., Windsor Locks, 860/623-3336 or 877/229-6668) offers lots of in-room perks: coffeemakers, voicemail, free local calls, irons and boards, recliner seats, pay movies and in-room games. Suites have microwaves, refrigerators, and pull-out sofas. It's one of the best airport hotels for the buck. The tip-top **Hampton Inn** (2168 Poquonock Ave., Windsor, 860/683-1118 or 800/HAMPTON) sits just off U.S. 20, a short drive from the airport. Facilities include a fitness center, indoor pool, and hot tub, and several suites have whirlpool tubs, microwaves, and mini-refrigerators.

Central to the whole area, **Holiday Inn Express** (260 Main St., East Windsor, 860/627-6585 or 800/HOLIDAY) is close to Bradley, and the Trolley Museum. The very nice rooms were renovated in 1998, and the excellent Continental "breakfast bar" offers Belgian waffles and such. The staff is professional and helpful, and there's an exercise room on the premises.

**Under $50:** Enfield has the two cleanest and best-maintained budget accommodations in the area—they're across the street from each other in the Thompsonville section (just off exit 47 of I-91), adjacent to a shopping center with a multiplex theater, supermarket, and a couple of cheap and casual chain restaurants. The **Motel 6** (11 Hazard Ave., Rte. 190, 860/741-3685 or 800/4-MOTEL-6) has clean rooms in a Colonial-style building. The **Red Roof Inn** (5 Hazard Ave., 860/741-2571 or 800/THE-ROOF) is usually a tad more expensive (pending availability), but, in addition to standard rooms, Red Roof offers roomy business kings with work stations and recliner seats.

## Country Inns and Bed-and-Breakfasts

**$100–$150:** Anchoring the East Windsor Historic District (a mile east of the Connecticut River), the imposing 1788 three-story **Watson House** (1876 Main St., South Windsor, 860/282-8888) might remind you of the grand Georgian Colonials of Salem, Massachusetts. The twin-chimneyed, pale gray, Palladian-style home served as a stop on the Underground Railroad. Today, it's an inn comprising three suites with lavish sitting areas and four still-large standard rooms; all accommodations have working fireplaces, and two of the rooms possess what is believed to be original wallpapering. The front rooms look out upon the quaint village store and post office and beyond, toward gorgeous old red barns and tobacco fields. Full breakfast included.

Sitting on six pastoral acres near the McLean Wildlife Refuge and Salmon Brook Settlement, the **Dutch Iris Inn Bed & Breakfast** (239 Salmon Brook St., Granby, 860/653-9091 or 877/280-0743, www.dutchirisinn.com) occupies a handsome 1812 Colonial and has four guest rooms; full breakfast is included.

**$50–$100:** Among the evidence of Somersville's 19th-century industrial prowess are a number of old factories and warehouses, near which stands the stately **Old Mill Inn** (63 Maple St., off Rte. 190, Somersville, 860/763-1473). Stephanie and Jim D'Amour offer six guest rooms in this stately old house; each room is outfitted with robes and down comforters. Common amenities include an antiques-filled parlor with fireplace, a small exercise room, a sundeck, a telescope ideal for stargazing, and a common lounge with cable TV and a wet bar. Wander amid the maples towering over the grounds to access the inn's frontage along the Scantic River; here you'll find a hammock, swing, picnic table, and a canoe for guest use. A full breakfast is included.

In Enfield, the **Benjamin Lord House** (154 Pearl St., 860/745-7005), an 1876 Queen Anne Victorian, has three comfortably furnished rooms. Elegant furnishings fill the house, along with five ornamental fireplaces, leaded transom windows, and stained-glass. Each room has a TV/VCR and phone. Rates include a healthful Continental breakfast.

## FOOD

This part of the state offers mostly simple and unpretentious family-oriented restaurants, and fast-food places catering to the suburbanites and office workers who tend to live and work in these towns. The I-91 corridor (especially along U.S. 5) contains most of this development, while the more rural communities of Grandy, Ellington, Somers, and Suffield have but a smattering of dining options.

### Upscale

It's hard to tire of restaurants set in converted historic mills, especially when they're as nicely done as the **Mill on the River** (989 Ellington Rd., South Windsor, 860/289-7929, $11–20), complete with a covered pedestrian footbridge over a ferocious waterfall and Connecticut's oldest (Indian-built) dam, situated on the Podunk River. This is the region's star culinary setting, and although the filling German-Continental food—Jaegerschnitzel, Viennese goulash soup, chicken Cordon bleu—is fine, it's not reason alone to visit. Brunch here is a local pastime, and at all meals many of the regulars are inclined to get a bit dressy (although nearly casual attire is just as appropriate).

A sprawling Colonial-style house with dining in several rooms, a gazebo in warm weather, and a somewhat formal interior, **Nutmeg Manor** (297 S. Main St., U.S. 5, 860/627-7094, $13–25) sits right on the East Windsor and South Windsor border. It's a favorite spot for weddings and formal parties, and the kitchen does a nice job with its menu of such sophisticated Continental fare as grilled monkfish with a roasted shallot au jus and orzo or Angus-grilled sirloin with Saga blue cheese and bordelaise sauce, and nut-crusted salmon with apple-mint risotto.

One of the few somewhat dressy restaurants in the region, the **Somers Inn** (585 Main St., Rte. 190, Somers, 860/749-2256, $17–26, presents a fine but woefully predictable menu of Continental and American favorites, including whole broiled or boiled lobster, steak au poivre, and chicken cordon bleu. The setting, an elegant and relaxing white Colonial building in the town's pretty historic center, helps distract from food and service that are merely ho-hum.

## Creative but Casual

The **Blue Goose** (16 S. Main St., Rte. 187, East Granby, 860/653-4488, $11–17) is a handsome and homey restaurant minutes from Bradley Airport, yet located on a quiet woodland road. Top choices from the menu of classic well-prepared American and Continental fare include chicken, roasted shallots, butternut squash, spinach, and apples tossed with angel hair pasta, or scrod stuffed with delicious crabmeat. **Tosca** (68 Bridge St., Suffield, 860/668-0273, $15–24) serves excellent Northern Italian fare in a cozy, intimate dining room tucked inside a small strip mall. Sautéed shrimp with mushrooms, sundried tomatoes, spinach, and roasted peppers over penne pasta; and a starter of yellowfin tuna tartare are both noteworthy.

## Steak, Pizza, Pub Grub, and Seafood

In downtown Bloomfield, **Calamari's** (39 Jerome Ave., 860/243-2757, $13–19) stands out among area eateries for its stellar fresh seafood and lighthearted nautical decorating motif, ranging from the usual buoys and nets hanging from the walls to the front walk lined with powder-white sand and various seashells and detritus. Checkered tablecloths inside complete the "in the rough" ambience of this restaurant-cum-fish market. All manner of fish is served as you request it: fried, grilled, baked, broiled, or sautéed. Or consider the chef's specialty of fresh fish of the day lightly blackened, with oysters and shrimp in a cilantro-and-garlic wine sauce. Calamari's has an equally fine sister branch in South Windsor, 1750 Ellington Rd. (Rte. 30 at Rte. 194), 860/644-6901, and the same folks also own and operate the nearby Mill on the River and Jonathan Pasco's.

A favorite for lunch, dinner, or happy hour among the employees of the several industrial parks in this area where the borders of Bloomfield, Windsor, and Tariffville meet, **Cheffries** (1936 Blue Hills Ave. Ext., Rte. 187, North Bloomfield, 860/285-8666, $13–21) is a friendly American restaurant in an airy contemporary building. Typical are steak, ribs, stuffed chicken and mushroom gorgonzola, baked scrod, and clams casino.

In a glorious painstakingly restored 1784 house on U.S. 5, **Jonathan Pasco's** (131 S. Main St., East Windsor, 860/627-7709, $14–21) makes for a nice meal perhaps after checking out the nearby Trolley Museum or hiking in Somers or Ellington. Jonathan Pasco, a Revolutionary War hero, built and lived inside this house, and the restaurant still displays a smattering of artifacts pertaining to his life. There are two menus—a bar list, featuring fried calamari (excellent), onion rings, and burgers; and a more substantial menu, where seafood is clearly king: consider redfish lightly blackened and topped with shrimp, scallops, and leaf spinach in a mornay sauce, or seafood gemelli with sautéed shrimp, scallops, lobster tail, red peppers, portobello mushrooms, broccoli, and a light lemon cream sauce.

## Ethnic Fare

In a simple and spare room at the South Windsor Town Center shopping complex, little **Higashi** (1735 Ellington Rd., Rte. 30 at Rte. 194, 860/644-7788, $9–15, most sushi rolls under $4), has good if strictly by-the-book sushi, but some extraordinary hot entrées, such as blackened tuna, deep-fried breaded oysters, and green mussels in a special house sauce. The popular Indian restaurant in West Hartford, **Taste of India** (216 Broad St., 860/688-8333, $8–16) opened a bright and attractive branch in Windsor not long ago.

**Guadalajara Grill** (9 Bank St., Granby, 860/844-0066, $8–14) offers a mammoth menu of both traditional and more inventive Mexican favorites. Avocado tostadas, chicken carnitas, mussels criolos (steamed with chopped Spanish onions, cilantro, garlic, and lime juice), and grilled red snapper topped with fresh salsa and octopus and prawns rank among the favorite dishes. This is not your usual Americanized-Mex—many of these recipes are authentic to regional Mexico. The dining room is large and warmly decorated.

The Suffield Inn is a long, rambling structure that resembles an enlarged version of one of the area's ubiquitous tobacco barns, but painted white and with a redbrick facade. It no longer lets rooms, and the accommodations have been turned into apartments. Another surprise is the inn's restaurant, **International Churrasquiera** (94 Mountain Rd., Suffield, 860/668-0219, $10–16), which specializes in the hearty spicy fare of South America— dishes like bean casserole Braziliera with beef and Portuguese sausage; and pork Alentajana and clams, sautéed in a spicy brown sauce. It's a low-key locals' hangout with a lively ambience and friendly servers—half the space is a cozy pub, and historic photos line the hallway behind the dining room.

## Java Joints

The **Beanery** (697 Poquonock Ave., 860/688-2224) is a little white brick café in northern Windsor off I-91, a bit south of the airport (nice if you need to kill some time before a flight). There's a small dining area inside and several outdoor tables with umbrellas, nestled beneath a grove of trees. Coffees, tasty lunch fare, desserts, and pastries are served. In Granby, **Elements** (561 Salmon Brook St., Rte. 10, 860/653-0009) offers live music on weekend evenings and serves creative, light fare throughout the day: coffees, teas, sweets, panini sandwiches, salads, and wraps.

## Quick Bites

Fans of good old-fashioned all-American fun can never seem to get enough of **Bart's** (55 Palisado Ave., Rte. 159, Windsor, 860/688-9035), a deli and bait shop by the Farmington River that's been serving up delicious hot dogs and fried fish

to a few generations of Windsor residents. Special theme nights (country line-dancing, 1950s car-cruising) are held in summer, and there are picnic tables by the riverbanks. You can even fish in the river with equipment from Bart's—note that shad season is April–June. The *Hartford Courant* recently let the world in on what had been one of the valley's greatest little dining secrets, a kitschy little burger-and-dog stand called **Carville's Ranch House** (27 Windsor Ave., Windsor, 860/522-2266, food under $6), which is decked out in neon Wild West–inspired signage and has only a few outdoor tables and a big takeout counter. Messy chili dogs, fried clams, and fries are among the favorite dishes.

**Country Diner** (111 Hazard Ave., Enfield, 860/763-5338, $5–12) has great breakfasts and is packed most weekend mornings. This cheerful, sunny spot is great for any meal (open only certain nights for dinner; call to check).

# INFORMATION AND SERVICES

## Visitor Information

Towns in this region are served by the **Greater Hartford Tourism District** (31 Pratt St., 4th Fl., Hartford, CT 06103, 860/244-8181 or 800/793-4480, www.enjoyhartford.com).

## Getting Around

I-91 cuts through the heart of Tobacco Country and provides easy access to the region's towns. Particularly scenic routes include Rte. 189, which runs north from Bloomfield through East Granby and into Granby; Rte. 190, which runs east from Suffield through Enfield to Somers; and Rte. 140, which runs east from East Windsor through Ellington.

## The Heart of Connecticut

Although Hartford is often thought, even by its own residents, to sit at the geographic center of Connecticut, the city is in fact on the northern fringes of the true heart of the state. At the core of Connecticut rests a clutch of communities that's often bypassed by visitors, one that's characterized by its unpretentious and welcoming residents, rich manufacturing and mercantile history, and reasonably priced accommodations and restaurants. From any town in the region, you're within an easy 60- to 90-minute drive of any point elsewhere in the state, making this an ideal area in which to base your explorations of Connecticut.

Interestingly, Connecticut's "heartland" is something of a microcosm of America's—it's obscured by its very centrality. Just as people identify the United States chiefly with its coasts and mountains, observers and residents alike do the same when discussing Connecticut. You'll first hear about the beach communities fringing Long Island Sound and the verdant beautiful hills of Litchfield and Putnam Counties before anybody lets you in on the many attributes of central Connecticut.

Although much of the region is heavily suburbanized, and in places urbanized, the heart of Connecticut contains several parks with challenging and rewarding hikes, as well as some of the best golfing in the state. Cities like New Britain and Middletown are fast revitalizing their downtowns, drawing fans of myriad ethnic cuisines from near and far. Wethersfield's historic district possesses the greatest cache of preserved pre-1850s homes in Connecticut, and Glastonbury is a hotbed of sophisticated restaurants and beautiful countryside. And throughout this area, there are legacies of its role in America's industrial revolution, from retrofitted redbrick factory buildings to restored spans of the old Farmington Canal.

## WETHERSFIELD TO BERLIN
### Wethersfield

With nearby Hartford and Windsor, Wethersfield was one of Connecticut's earliest permanent settlements, and it possesses one of the best-preserved historic districts in America, including some fine house-museums. If you're interested in historic houses and streets, you'll want to dedicate an entire day to strolling through Old Wethersfield.

From Hartford, follow Wethersfield Avenue (Rte. 99) south into Wethersfield. Much of the town has grown up in recent years into a busy, if in places overdeveloped, suburb, and Rte. 99 is mostly the domain of vapid shopping centers. But make a left turn onto Church Street, and you'll find yourself transported back into Colonial Connecticut. Broad, Main, and the other side streets in this village of large clapboard homes with steep roofs and immense chimneys make for some of the nicest sidewalk strolling in the area. It's hard to believe that such a picturesque and peaceful neighborhood could exist surrounded by modern suburbia, but Old Wethersfield is actually as authentic a slice of early New England as any in Connecticut, containing more than 200 pre-1850 buildings.

A good place to begin your explorations of the village is the **Wethersfield Historical Society** (150 Main St., 860/529-7656, www.wethhist.org, open 10 A.M.–4 p.m. Tues.–Fri., free) in one of the neighborhood's newer buildings (time is relative, after all)—the Federal-style, 1804 Old Academy. Inside, you'll find a first-rate research library and archives. The society also operates the Wethersfield Museum inside the Victorian **Keeney Memorial Cultural Center** (200 Main St., 860/529-7656, open 10 A.M.–4 P.M. Tues.–Sat., 1–4 P.M. Sun., $3). It contains a museum shop, and presents changing historical exhibits throughout the year, in which furniture, paintings, and other artifacts are shown. A small visitor center offers information on area attractions, plus restroom facilities.

You can then visit the society's **Hurlbut-Dunham House** (212 Main St., open 10 A.M.–4 P.M. Wed.–Mon., May–Oct., $3), a brick Georgian Colonial mansion that was given an Italianate makeover in the mid-19th century. Notable are its fine furnishings and such details as Rococo Revival wallpapering and Gothic-style fireplaces. A final piece in the historical society's group of buildings is the **Cove Warehouse Maritime Museum** (Main St. at Warehouse Cove, open 10 A.M.–4 P.M. Sat., 1–4 P.M. Sun., mid-May–mid-Oct., $1), a gambrel-roofed, wooden barn-like structure containing a wealth of maritime memorabilia. The warehouse overlooks the many sailboats and pleasurecraft moored in Wethersfield Cove, where maritime trade flourished from the town's earliest settlement until the War of 1812 and the industrial revolution largely diminished the Connecticut River's maritime importance.

The oldest house in the district open to the public dates from 1720. The postmedieval-style **Buttolph-Williams House** (249 Broad St., 860/529-0460 or 860/247-8996, open 10 A.M.–4 P.M. Wed.–Mon., May–Oct., $5) is notable for its small casement windows and hand-hewn overhanging second floor. Inside is an excellent collection of period antiques.

Wethersfield was once known throughout America for onion farming, and it also grew to become one of the country's leading seed suppliers. **Comstock, Ferre & Co.** (263 Main St., 860/571-6590 or 800/733-3773, www.comstockferre.com) is the oldest continuously operating seed company in America, having opened its doors in 1820. It's still a fine nursery, and the National Historic Landmark buildings make for a great look into the past. Nearby is the not-quite-so-ancient Charles C. Hart Seed Company.

One of the more innovative approaches to local history has been instituted by the keepers of the **Webb-Deane-Stevens Museum** (211 Main St., 860/529-0612, www.webb-deane-stevens.org). There are three neighboring late-1700s houses, each of which has been preserved to show the different careers and lifestyles of its original occupants: merchant Joseph Webb, diplomat Silas Deane, and leatherworker Isaac Stevens. In the Webb House, murals painted by Wallace Nutting, noted curator and collector of Americana, were recently uncovered after about a century hidden behind wallpaper. Among the depictions is the time that Comte de Rochambeau and General George Washington convened in the parlor to plan out the im-

pending Battle of Yorktown (during which the Continental Army prevailed triumphantly). The museum is open 10 A.M.–4 P.M. Wednesday–Monday May–October, 10 A.M.–4 P.M. on weekends November–April, and admission is $8 for all three houses, or $3 to tour just one house.

If you, or more likely your kids, are feeling a bit antsy at this point from having toured too many historic homes, you might run over to nearby **Wethersfield Nature Center** (30 Greenfield St., 860/721-2953, open 10 A.M.–4:30 P.M. Mon.–Thurs., 10 A.M.–1 P.M. Sat.), a 120-acre nature park with hands-on exhibits, a log cabin, a library of botany, and a park with reptiles, mammals, and birds.

A little-known fact is that a tiny sliver of Wethersfield exists on the east side of the river, snug between the borders of East Hartford and Glastonbury—it's inaccessible by road and there's nothing to see here, but it's an odd bit of local trivia. Most residents of the Connecticut River Valley think that Haddam is the only town with land on both sides of the river.

## Newington

Neighboring Newington is also a heavily developed bedroom community. There is a pair of historic house-museums in town, the **Enoch Kelsey House** (1702 Main St., Rte. 176), and the **Kellogg-Eddy House** (679 Willard Ave., Rte. 173); both have limited, seasonal hours and are best visited by appointment, 860/666-7118. To reach them from Wethersfield, drive west from Rte. 99 along Rte. 287 into Newington, crossing U.S. 5/Rte. 15.

## New Britain

From Newington, follow Rte. 175 west into one of 19th-century America's great manufacturing centers, New Britain, which is better known these days for its outstanding museum of American art. Like so many of the state's once-thriving industrial cities, New Britain fell hard during the second half of the 20th century and has begun to rise a bit from the ashes. A $30 million courthouse opened in downtown in 1998, and several streets have been cleaned

© ANDREW COLLINS

**New Britain Museum of American Art**

up and revitalized recently. Minor league baseball has become a popular spectator sport.

New Britain was at the forefront of the industrial innovation; nearly 1,500 patents were awarded here during the 19th century, for any number of products we take for granted today, from the important—artificial limbs, cash registers—to the mundane (the invention of the lemon squeezer leaps to mind). New Britain was one of the earlier American cities to institute a city water-and-sewage system, open a library, and develop an urban park. It also developed the state's first graded school system and founded it's first "normal school" (teacher's school), which was established here largely because of the city's centrality and strong transportation ties during the middle of the 19th century. The State Normal School eventually grew into Central Connecticut State University.

New Britain today is a city of steeples, mostly stone, masonry, and redbrick churches catering to the population's deep ethnic religious roots (predominantly Catholic). Downtown, which extends from the intersection of West Main and Main Streets, is fairly mixed as far as success in raising its visitor friendliness. The area's architecture

reveals a good bit of the city's industrial heritage. Many of the factories and offices constructed during the 1800s and early 1900s still stand, alongside early–20th-century apartment buildings and quite a few of the mansions that captains of industry constructed with their enormous spoils. A drawback is the lack of a decent retail base, and the area could stand an infusion of vibrancy.

The **New Britain Downtown District** (860/225-5507 or 860/225-3901) publishes and distributes a *New Britain Architectural Walking Tour* pamphlet, which observes the city from three distinct perspectives: "People Make the City" concentrates on a residential neighborhood that fringes southwestern downtown, and includes residential structures ranging from an 1830 Greek Revival at 25 S. High Street (the oldest surviving building in the downtown area) to an immense Gothic Revival mansion built in 1860 by the head of the Stanley Rule and Level Company. "The Heart of the City," as the name suggests, shows off central New Britain's mix of well-preserved municipal and commercial structures (the 1910 post office at 120 W. Main St.; the Streamline Modern 1950s Miss Washington Diner on the corner of

CONN. RIVER VALLEY

Main and Washington Sts.; the McKim, Mead & White–designed 1883 Italianate-Gothic City Hall; the 1911 neoclassical Elks Club at 30 Washington St.; and an austere row of four art deco commercial buildings along W. Main St.). Lastly, "The City Expands: An Early 20th Century Commercial Street" gives a small sampling of two- to three-story buildings that reflect how an increasing dependence on automobiles influenced the urban planning and design of the city; these buildings are along Main Street, just south of Walnut Street. In the heart of all of this touring is Central Park, a triangular park dominated by a 1900 Beaux Arts/neoclassical obelisk memorializing soldiers who lost their lives in the Civil War.

The city's nickname, Hardware City, is due to the many tool-manufacturing concerns that have prospered here during the past 150 years. Best known are the Stanley Works (bolts, chisels, hammers, levels, screwdrivers), Landers, Frary & Clark (bread mixers, cutlery, geiger counters, irons, meat grinders, stoves), the Fafnir Bearing Company (bearings for everything from jet engines to agricultural equipment), American Hardware (keys, locks, mailboxes), and North & Judd (bridles, saddlery hardware, spurs, stirrups). For a chance to see many of these early industrial artifacts, and to learn a bit about the local firms that produced them, stop by the **New Britain Industrial Museum** (185 Main St., 2nd floor, 860/832-8654, www.nbim.org, open 2–5 P.M. weekdays, free).

There's also a local history room on the second floor of the nearby **New Britain Public Library** (20 High St., 860/224-3155, ext. 16, www.nbpl.lib.ct.us). Just down the street, the **New Britain Youth Museum** (30 High St., 860/225-3020, www.newbritainyouthmuseum.org) has changing cultural and historical exhibits; toys and games; crafts and after-school activities; and free admission. It's a great way to keep your kids busy and interested should you find yourself having an otherwise slow day. The museum has a second location in the Kensington section of neighboring Berlin, at **Hungerford Park** (191 Farmington Ave., Rte. 372, 860/827-9064, open 11 A.M.–5 P.M. Tues.–Fri., 10 A.M.–5 P.M. Sat., fall–spring; 10 A.M.–5 P.M. Tues.–Fri. summer), where kids

can enjoy a nature center replete with exotic animals and reptiles, as well as a wildlife rehabilitation center. The park also has nature trails, a pond observation station, gardens, and wildflower meadow. It's just a few minutes' drive south of the New Britain town line.

One downtown neighborhood that's taken serious steps to turn itself forward is **Arch Street,** the spine of a largely Hispanic community. It's a modest street with mostly the usual workaday stores and businesses, but some fine early–20th-century architecture and urban streetlife make it a standout. Storefronts have been spruced up along here, new parking lots added to encourage visitors, and a few antiques shops have opened.

A newer, though quite modest, attraction is the **New Britain Police Museum** (125 Columbus Blvd., 860/826-3066, www.newbritainpolice.org), which contains memorabilia documents, weapons, and other ephemera related to the police. It's generally open Saturday mornings, and admission is free, but it's best to call ahead first.

On the pretty west side of downtown, you'll find arguably the most underrated cultural attraction in Connecticut, the **New Britain Museum of American Art** (56 Lexington St., 860/229-0257, www.nbmaa.org, open noon–5 P.M. Tues.–Fri. and Sun., 10 A.M.–5 P.M. Sat., $4). It was founded in 1903, and has developed a permanent collection of more than 5,000 works. Represented are the Colonial period, the Hudson River School, the American impressionists, the bronzes of Solon Borglum, and the Ash Can School. Particularly noteworthy are the murals of WPA artist Thomas Hart Benton—they comprise what was originally a seven-panel mural cycle called *The Arts of Life in America,* which was commissioned in 1932 by the Whitney Museum for its Reading Room. Five of the panels are located here at the museum, and each depicts different aspects of Americana.

Artist Sol LeWitt has also lent the museum some 300 works. Other artists represented in the permanent collection—the lists is a veritable "who's who" of American visual-arts excellence—include sometime Connecticut impressionists Childe Hassam, J. Alden Wier, Mary Cassat, and Willard Metcalfe; WPA painter John Steuart

Curry; modern artists Grant Wood, Marsden Hartley, Joseph Stella, Lee Krasner, Robert Motherwell, Andrew Wyeth, and Georgia O'Keeffe (with a wonderful New York City landscape from the 1930s); early portraitist Gilbert Stuart; and early Connecticut luminaries George Caitlin (of Litchfield), Ralph Earl (of Bolton), and John Trumbull (of Lebanon). There's also a painting by onetime Hartford resident and Hudson School notable Frederic Church of West Rock, in New Haven, as it appeared in 1849. Exhibits change often and highlight new artists or show the works of other collections.

The first Fridays in July and August offer "Cafe on the Park," a popular program with food and art discussion. The museum is on a pretty tree-lined street that runs into gently undulating **Walnut Hill Park,** which is surrounded by striking old homes and is an ideal spot for jogging, cycling, tennis, or simply lying about.

North of downtown, across the Rte. 9 underpass, is Broad Street, the city's old Polish enclave. Stroll along this street and you'll walk by great bakeries and delis, plain brick and clapboard facades, and family-run stores with Polish names—it's a way to gain a real sense of the city's old-world ties. This old Polish community is steeped in history and looks like something you'd expect to find in the Greenpoint section of Brooklyn.

The northeastern end of New Britain is more residential and pleasant to walk through, with many early–20th-century Colonial Revival homes that will remind you of the neatly planned early suburbs of nearby West Hartford. This is where you'll find the modern campus of **Central Connecticut State University (CCSU),** whose **Copernican Observatory and Planetarium** (1615 Stanley St., 860/832-3399) possesses one of the largest public telescopes in the country. Special programs are held throughout the year, and regular shows take place at 8:30 P.M. Fridays and Saturdays; special kids' shows are held at 7 P.M. on Fridays and at 1:30 P.M. on Saturdays ($4).

Across Stanley Street from the university is sprawling **Stanley Quarter Park** (451 Blake Rd., 860/826-3360), with a small pond and walking trails, most of it heavily wooded. Lots and lots and lots of geese and ducks call the placid pond

home, and visitors can rent aqua cycles and paddleboats to explore the waters. There is also a children's fishing pond, playground, jogging tracks, an outdoor ice-skating rink, the largest public inline-skate park in New England, and other recreational facilities.

If you've an interest in World War II history, be sure to stop by the **National Iwo Jima Memorial Monument** (exit 29 from Rte. 9, Iwo Jima Memorial Expressway, to Ella Grasso Blvd., just east of CCSU, 860/666-5521, www.webtravels.com/iwojima.com), a 40-foot monument unveiled on February 23, 1995, the 50th anniversary of one of the most dramatic, momentous, and tragic trials of World War II. Nearly 7,000 American soldiers gave their lives during this bloody battle, and here a flame burns 24 hours a day, 365 days a year, to remember their valiant efforts. If you've seen the historic Joe Rosenthal photo of the raising of the U.S. flag at Iwo Jima (it's also been depicted on a postage stamp), you'll fast recognize the bronze statue capping the monument; it was erected in the exact image of the photograph. The battle actually spanned a full month, but the flag raising took place on February 23, the fifth day of combat.

## Berlin and Kensington

South of New Britain, the town of Berlin (whose pronunciation, as opposed to that of the capital of Germany, rhymes with Merlin) is best known for helping develop central Connecticut into a base for metals manufacturing.

From New Britain, follow Rte. 372 southeast (you'll pass the New Britain Youth Museum at Hungerford Park, described above, shortly after entering town) through the Kensington section of town. At the corner of Main and Peck Streets, the **Berlin Historical Society Museum** (860/828-5114, open 1–4 P.M. Sat. Apr.–Dec.) has changing exhibits on the area's early industries. Just before you reach the Wilbur Cross Highway (U.S. 5/Rte. 15), you'll enter Berlin's **Worthington Ridge Historic District.** Notable sites here include the 1833 Berlin Academy (now the Berlin Free Library, 860/828-3344), the 1850 Berlin Congregational Church, and the 1774 Worthington Meetinghouse.

# PLAINVILLE AND BRISTOL

## Plainville

Due west of New Britain is Plainville, which, as the name suggests, is pretty plain; a semi-industrial town in the center of the state, at the crossroads of heavily trafficked stretches of I-84 and Rte. 72, so that rumbling superhighways seem to cross at so many points.

Like several towns in this part of the state, Plainville was originally part of neighboring Farmington; it was actually the last one to secede and form its own town, in 1869. The Pequabuck and Quinnipiac rivers flow through this town whose name aptly fits its geographical profile—a broad plain. The Pequabuck is a branch of the Farmington River, while the Quinnipiac's source is in Plainville—it flows all the way to Long Island Sound. This is an uncommonly flat community, and at 9.6 square miles, it's one of the smallest towns in the state. Although a town of modest attractions, many of its earliest buildings still stand, among them the 1789 Cooke's Tavern (which is still a popular restaurant, now called J. Timothy's). Shoppers will appreciate the fact that Plainville is one of the better sources of antiquing in greater Hartford, with a small district of shops centered around the intersections of West Main (Rte. 372) and Whiting Streets, right near the town hall.

Other remnants of the area's history are scattered about town. On Rte. 10, you'll see three original milestone markers that were erected in the 1700s to tell travelers (in Roman numerals) how many miles they were from Hartford. They stand at the corners of Betsey Road, Rte. 372, and in front of Woodmore Village. On Broad Street, the 1874 Torrant School was converted—with outstanding attention to historic preservation and detail—into an apartment dwelling in 1983; it had functioned continuously as a school for nearly a century. A particularly interesting historic structure is the Stockinette Knitting Mill, a huge brick mill dating from 1850 (although the current structure was just one component of the complex and dates from 1877). This textile mill, at 58 W. Main Street, produced the "union suit," underwear worn by soldiers both in the Civil War and World War I. The building currently serves the needs of Nutmeg Television Studios, 860/793-2552, but visitors are welcome to drop by.

*On Rte. 10, you'll see three original milestone markers that were erected in the 1700s to tell travelers (in Roman numerals) how many miles they were from Hartford.*

For the best glimpse into local history, visit the **Plainville Historic Center** (29 Pierce St., just off Rte. 372, east of Rte. 177, 860/747-6577, limited hours) where you'll find rooms decorated from various periods, materials and a diorama pertaining to the Farmington Canal, a nature room with a Birdarama, a barn and tool collection, and a "children of yesteryear" room. Also noteworthy is the **Plainville Public Library** (56 E. Main St., Rte. 372, 860/793-1446) that contains, among other oddities, a collection of 500 bird eggs amassed by former governor and Plainville resident John H. Trumbull (it's on the basement level). Here local historian Ruth Hummel has done a tremendous job organizing the town's history and developing many tours—definitely stop by and ask her questions if you have an interest in the town's (or even the region's) history.

Though not as extensive nor as well-known as Lock 12 Historical Park in nearby Cheshire, Plainville does have its own preserved span of the Farmington Canal, which ran through the town from 1828 through 1848. Head south of downtown to **Norton Park** (Washington St., Rte. 177, 860/747-6577) to see the 700-foot section of canal that has been restored to its original proportions (36 feet wide at ground level, 4 feet deep, and 20 feet wide at the bottom), complete with its berm and tow path. Norton Park is named for John Norton, a leading Civil War abolitionist. A plaque marks the site of Norton's homestead (109 E. Main St.); it was a stop on the Underground Railroad.

CONN. RIVER VALLEY

North of downtown, Rte. 177 leads to the town's best spot for hiking and observing wildlife. In 1989, roughly four acres of wetlands were designated **Tomasso Nature Park** (Granger Ln., near Robertson Airport, 860/747-6577). Here, you can observe speckled and bull frogs, snapping turtles, garter and northern watersnakes, woodchucks, muskrats, white-tailed deer, green-backed and great-blue heron, and countless other mammals and birds. There are trails through the park, and a helpful brochure that's written with both kids and adults in mind. The municipal Robertson Airport, incidentally, is the state's oldest airport (1911), 860/747-5519.

## Bristol

From Plainville, Rte. 72 leads into the small but busy city of Bristol, which many locals consider as much a part of the Litchfield Hills as they do greater Hartford—indeed, it bridges these two regions and also shares many traits with towns in the adjoining Waterbury area. Bristol is hilly and quite green, with some choice parkland, especially in the western half of town; yet it shares the industrial history that characterizes other towns in central Connecticut and greater Waterbury.

Indeed, Bristol—with its Litchfield County neighbors to the west, Plymouth and Thomaston—stood at the heart of America's clock-making history during the early 19th century. This legacy is chronicled with great panache at one of the state's more remarkable attractions, the **American Clock and Watch Museum** (100 Maple St., just south of U.S. 6, in the center of town, 860/583-6070, www.clockmuseum.org, open 10 A.M.–5 P.M. daily April–Nov.; 10 A.M.–5 P.M. Fri.–Sat., 1–5 P.M. Sun. in Dec.; $5). Within the walls of this 1801 house (and the two large adjacent additions) are some 3,000 timepieces, many of them manufactured locally, with others from all over the world. In fact, this is the largest collection of timepieces in the world—nearly half of its items are on exhibit at any given time. In a front parlor, you'll see the desk of former clockmaker Eli Terry, after whom Terryville is named. The hundreds of clocks gong and ding on the hour (within a few minutes of each other), meaning that noon is a particularly striking, if you'll pardon the pun, time to visit.

From the center of town, head south on Rte. 69, making a left onto Rte. 72, to reach another of Bristol's more idiosyncratic draws, the **Carousel Museum of New England** (95 Riverside Ave., Rte. 72, 860/585-5411, www.thecarouselmuseum.com, open daily Apr.–Nov., Thurs.–Sun. Dec.–March, $5), which contains dozens of antique carousel characters and historic artwork from carousels—an appropriate tribute given the presence of nearby Lake Compounce amusement park, which has a 1911 carousel. There's a second branch in Mystic.

Back on Rte. 69, continue south to the **H. C. Barnes Nature Center** (175 Shrub Rd., off Rte. 69, 860/585-8886, open Wed.–Sat. year-round, Sun. spring–fall., trails open daily, center admission $2), a 70-acre nature center with marked trails, a small nature library and interpretive center, and animal exhibits.

From Bristol, Rte. 229 leads south into Southington. Along this drive, as you near the Southington border, two things stand out. On your left is a bunch of big satellite dishes marking the grounds of cable television's ESPN Headquarters and broadcast studios—this sports television empire continues to grow and grow, to the point that ESPN's corporate campus looks almost like a city within a city.

Then on your right, in the near distance, are the rides of 100-acre **Lake Compounce** (822 Lake Ave., off Rte. 229, Bristol/Southington line, 860/583-3300, www.lakecompounce.com) that has been entertaining families for longer than any amusement park in the nation (having opened in 1846). Each summer, legions of kids and adults come to test out the twisting water slides and roller coasters (plus 30 more rides), the vintage 1911 carousel, the dance reviews, the lakeside sandy beach, and other such adventures and diversions. Tickets cost about $30 for adults, $22 for kids, and $17 for senior citizens. The park is open almost daily June–Aug., and with more limited hours (mostly on weekends and holidays) in May, September, and October.

# SOUTHINGTON TO MERIDEN

## Southington

At 40 square miles, the southwestern Hartford suburb of Southington is one of the largest towns in the state. Once a part of Farmington, it broke away in 1779, eventually taking the name South Farmington, which in time became shortened to "South'ington." Factories and mills went up beginning in the late 1800s, although the town was never industrialized to the extent that New Britain and Waterbury were.

There are a couple of appealing historic districts in Southington, including the **Plantsville** section of town, where you'll find an antiques district centered around the corner of W. Main and S. Main (Rte. 10) Streets, right by exit 30 of I-84. Here, it seems that every one of the old brick buildings is either an antiques store or a rather rowdy tavern. The village is set around a hulking old concrete factory and possesses a vintage blue-collar charm similar to Putnam, in northeastern Connecticut.

A short distance north, the **Barnes Museum** (85 N. Main St., Southington, 860/628-5426, limited hours, or by appointment free), originally named the Bradley Homestead, dates from 1836 and retains its original architectural details except for some evidence of remodeling in the early part of the 20th century. Solid oak floors and woodworking fill much of the house, which contains historic diaries, photos, magazines, and books. Also downtown, the **Southington Historical Center** (239 Main St., 860/621-4811, call for details) occupies the town's former library, a stately early–20th-century structure that frequently offers exhibits and lectures.

## Marion

Many interesting buildings lie at the southwestern end of town, in the **Marion Historic District,** off Rte. 322 just west of I-84. From downtown, you can also reach it by following W. Main Street from Plantsville. Go beneath the I-84 overpass until the street turns into Marion Avenue. Many of the homes along Marion and the side streets date to the 19th and late 18th centuries.

## Milldale

Head east of Marion on Rte. 322, through the Milldale section of town, and you'll soon spot the **Southington Drive-In** (935 Meriden-Waterbury Tpke., Rte. 322, 860/628-2205), which has been showing movies since 1955. It's one of only about 100 drive-ins still in operation throughout America. Off to the east, at the Meriden, Southington, and Berlin border, you'll see West Peak Mountain interrupting this mostly flat landscape.

## Cheshire

From Southington, Rte. 10 leads south into one of the prettiest communities in central Connecticut; Cheshire is notable for its wealth of pick-your-own farms and nurseries. The town is convenient to New Haven, Hartford, and Waterbury, and therefore an ideal choice among commuters. Great care has been taken to conserve the town's agrarian heritage, and you'll find several parks, trails, and preserves. It's not a hotbed of culture or retail activity, which is fine with most of its residents, but plans are underway for a regional shopping mall and a hotel-convention center. Whether a town so pleasant will benefit or be ruined by such a venture remains to be seen.

The center of Cheshire, where Rtes. 10, 68, and 70 intersect, comprises one of the more engaging historic districts in Connecticut—and also one of the more underrated. There are some 25 noteworthy structures here, many of them dating from the mid- to late 1700s. Many are private homes, but the exteriors are quite easy to see from the street. The Cheshire Historical Society occupies the 1785 **Hitchcock-Phillips House** (43 Church Dr., 860/272-2574, tours of the period-decorated house are offered 2–4 P.M. Sun. Sept.–May). The garden behind the house is of particular note.

A short way north of downtown is yet another fanciful and rather quirky museum, the **Barker Character, Comic & Cartoon Museum** (1188 Highland Ave., Rte. 10, 860/699-3822, www.barkermuseum.com, open 11 A.M.–5 P.M. Tues.–Sat., free). It contains an astounding collection of comic strip, western, TV, and advertising character memorabilia. Values of the items are

© ANDREW COLLINS

**Lock 12, along a restored stretch of the Farmington Canal, Cheshire**

given for each exhibit, but none of these products are for sale. Herb and Gloria Barker, who personally collected this stuff over more than 20 years, simply want to give visitors a sense of what some of these seemingly trivial items are worth today—in some cases, it's quite a lot of money. The little museum is crammed with oddities, including original production cels and drawings of Disney characters, Scooby-Doo, and the like; Wonder Woman cake pans; Donny and Marie Osmond string puppets; Dukes of Hazzard and Sonny & Cher action figures; Smurfs plastic figurines; Mork & Mindy board games; a 1950s-era can of Donald Duck grapefruit segments; a Planter's Peanut Butter Maker; and just about anything else you can recall from your childhood. Outside, human-size cutouts of various cartoon characters are set around the property, which also has picnic tables, and a speaker plays favorite tunes of the era. At the time of this writing, the museum is undergoing a major expansion.

A short drive south of downtown is one of

the state's more innovative attempts at historic preservation, involving not a building but a stretch of the Farmington Canal, which was built in 1827 and operated until the mid-1840s. Canals were big business in the 1820s and 1830s, but their successes were few and rather short-lived owing to railroad expansion. The Farmington Canal was part of a waterway that extended from New Haven north to the Pioneer Valley city of Northampton, Massachusetts. The entire canal was completed in 1835. Barges, about 75 feet long, were used to haul up to 25 tons of goods. Upkeep of the canals was expensive, and this, along with the advent of railroads, contributed to the demise of the Farmington, which lost money every year it was in operation. The National Park Service took to restoring the locks of the Farmington Canal in 1975, and work began on Lock 12, here in Cheshire. Today, at **Lock 12 Historical Park** (487 N. Brooksvale, Rte. 42, 203/272-2743), you'll find the lock gates and a lockkeeper's house, plus a museum that was once a carpenter-blacksmith shop and was moved here from another site. Inside, the museum, dioramas, photos, and documents trace the life of the canal (a more thorough interpretation is found at the Plainville Historical Center, described above). A helicoidal bridge spans the canal, and picnic areas abound. The grounds are open daily; the museum has limited hours, mostly weekends spring through fall. Today, you can also bike or hike along the now-paved canal path that runs through the park and continues at least a mile north of it and nearly eight miles south into Hamden.

The nearby Cheshire Land Trust-operated **Roaring Brook Park,** on Roaring Brook Road (continue west of Lock 12 along Rte. 42, turn right onto Mountain Rd., and make a left onto Roaring Brook Rd.), hugs the slopes of West Mountain and consists of an old mill site, 80-foot cascades, a gorge, and several marked hiking trails. Woodcock, owls, deer, rabbits, and other wildlife make their homes throughout the park and in a separate wildlife preserve, access to which is restricted.

Another great spot for hikers and outdoors enthusiasts is the **Riverbound Farm Sanctuary** and **Nature Center** (1881 Cheshire St., 203/634-1911, center open third Sun. of the month Apr.–Nov., grounds open dawn–dusk daily year-round), which is operated by the Quinnipiac Valley Audubon Society. Here in an 1814 farmhouse is a nature center, and crisscrossing this 23-acre wildlife preserve are two hiking trails. There's also a butterfly garden.

## Meriden

Due east of Cheshire is a city that still has a fairly long way to go in terms of revitalizing itself, but it was once the center of New England's silver-producing industry. Silver City, as Meriden is known, actually had its own Silver Museum until 1996, when it closed from a lack of funding. The collection was moved to Wallingford. Currently, efforts are underway to tear down some of the old silver-manufacturing buildings, many of which have toxic soil underneath left over from the chemicals used to produce silver. It's a massive project that will take some time, and until this happens, efforts to reseed downtown with new industry and retail remain slow.

One of the few areas where things are looking up, at least slightly, is along W. Main Street, where redbrick sidewalks and old-fashioned street lamps have been installed and several historic building facades have been restored. Also, northeast of downtown, the gambrel-roofed **Solomon Goffe House** (677 N. Colony Rd., exit 7 from I-691, 203/634-9088, limited hours) is a period-furnished 1711 home, the oldest in Meriden—a point easily illustrated if you have the chance to walk across the original floorboards. It's open to the public by appointment and for special events, which are led by period-dressed docents and range from soap-making and peach-preserving sessions to Christmas candlelight tours and house-trimming parties.

Meriden's major highlight is 1,645-acre **Hubbard Park** (203/630-4259), which also straddles the borders of Southington and Berlin. It comprises the Hanging Hills and West Peak mountains in its remote northern reaches and sparkling 6.5-acre Mirror Lake in its lower 118-acre section, which was laid out in the 1890s by the Olmsted Brothers architectural landscaping

firm. The park, whose entrance is off W. Main Street (Rte. 322), offers a wealth of diversions. Visitors pop in to enjoy the children's playground, municipal swimming pools and tennis courts, picnic areas, and park benches overlooking Mirror Lake. There's also a bandshell, where concerts are held from time to time.

A more strenuous option is to hike from the parking area at Mirror Lake (a sign shows a map of the park's trails) for 1.5 miles up to Castle Craig, a turn-of-the-20th-century, Arts & Crafts–style stone turret perched high above the south face of the Hanging Hills. It's easily visible (as are a few television and radio antennas) from the park's lower section, and also along I-691, which cuts through the park. Although not a long hike, it does rise from about 300 to 1,000 feet above sea level during the course of its climb, part of which is along a pedestrian bridge over I-691. If you'd simply like to enjoy the view from Castle Craig without enduring the hike, you can drive up the park road (open 10 A.M.–5 P.M. daily spring–fall), a favorite of local bicycling enthusiasts. From the tower lookout, you'll spy (if the visibility is good) Heublein Tower in Simsbury and several other peaks to the west and south. Once at the top, you'll see a large parking lot—the park ranger usually starts turning visitors away at around 4:30 P.M.

## MIDDLETOWN

Follow I-691 east from Meriden until it changes from a limited-access highway into two-lane Rte. 66, in the small town of Middlefield. The town has some excellent hiking areas and a popular downhill ski center, but otherwise lacks much to see or do. This road will soon lead into the river city of Middletown.

Some have described Middletown as distinctly Midwestern looking, with its broad Main Street peering down at a wide stretch of river, a span that indeed looks as though Mississippi riverboats should be plying it. But Middletown has long played a prominent role in Connecticut's history, early on as a wealthy merchant city, and over the years as a university hub and busy industrial center.

During the second half of the 18th century, Middletown was the wealthiest of the state's towns, named for its highly strategic position midway along the Connecticut River between Hartford and Saybrook. Ships carried goods between Middletown and the West Indies, and all vessels passing through town stopped to pay duties at the city's customs house. Evidence of early mercantile success appears in the form of the many large homes around town and the large brownstone commercial structures—many of which used to house banks—along Main Street.

The city's industrial prowess can be traced to the pistol factory established here during the American Revolution by Simeon North, who (along with Eli Whitney of Hamden) helped bring about the industrial revolution by developing a means of mass-production through interchangeable parts in 1813. North's pistols armed the first U.S. army, thus ensuring Connecticut's place over the next two centuries as America's munitions store. Typewriters, rubber goods, silks, and silverware are a few more of the goods that were fashioned here for many years.

Today's Middletown is less industrial than in the past, but it still has a close-knit Italian American community with ties to the city's manufacturing heyday, plus substantial numbers of Asian, Hispanic, and African American residents. Towering prominently over its skyline is one lone and somewhat undistinguished-looking 12-story skyscraper, which accommodates the Middlesex Assurance Company. A more striking landmark is the grand **Arrigoni Bridge,** which crosses the river, connecting Middletown with Portland (it had a feature role in the Billy Joel music video for the song "River of Dreams").

Along a Main Street wide enough to hold an Interstate highway are rows of shops; many have recently been given face lifts. While it has successfully resisted the temptation to turn out its locally owned businesses, downtown has never quite lived up to its full potential. But the future looks promising, as Middletown attempts to attract the sorts of businesses that will give it the retail cachet of West Hartford or, more appropriately, Northampton, Massachusetts. Northampton makes the most of its proximity to Smith College, and Middletown is

similarly the site of **Wesleyan University** (High St., 860/685-2000) whose 1830s campus rises several blocks and about 150 feet above Main Street.

Founded in 1831 by Methodists (although admission has never been linked to its religious affiliation), Wesleyan brings its own iconoclastic brand of scholarship to this otherwise conservative city, and not all the locals appreciate the sometimes politically charged and countercultural students. But Wesleyan sponsors countless arts festivities and has helped enliven the town's once-flagging restaurant and nightlife scene.

The school's grounds, like those of so many traditional New England liberal arts colleges, are dotted with standout examples of architecture, the best of which date from the mid-1800s to the mid-1900s. Buildings follow no dominant scheme, but call on a variety of eras and cultures: Tudor, Greek Revival, and Mediterranean Villa. In total, they make for a rewarding stroll. When school is in session, you can observe an eclectic and spirited student body whose diversity, to use that clichéd recruiting buzzword of recent years, jibes appropriately with the varied campus aesthetic.

Among the notable structures is 1828 **Russell House** (350 High St.), whose hefty yet graceful Corinthian columns attest to its classic Greek Revival design—it's been a part of Wesleyan since the 1930s. Another is the remarkable 1928 Renaissance Revival **Olin Library,** which was designed by Henry Bacon (of Lincoln Memorial fame) and, upon Bacon's untimely death, executed by the famous firm that employed him—McKim, Mead & White. In 1983, the library was expanded rather ingeniously: A greater structure of a similar style was built around the original, so that the one fits within its successor. It's a beautiful building, and the public is welcome to poke around inside.

In fact, much of Wesleyan is accessible to visitors—in winter, you might do as the students do and toboggan and sled down Foss Hill toward the playing fields surrounded by imposing administrative buildings. Come and stargaze in the Van Vleck observatory, or go skating at Wesleyan's rink. The school has an excellent fine arts and performing-arts reputation, which can be appreciated by visiting the **Center for the Arts,** 860/685-2500, which comprises the Mediterranean Revival Davison Art Center and the Zikha Gallery's works of contemporary sculpture, painting, and photography.

Another of the school's arts assets, a short drive south of campus, is **Wesleyan Potters** (350 S. Main St., 860/344-0039, open Tues.–Sat., free), a renowned school and cooperative gallery of handcrafted pottery, weaving, and other fine works—tours of the studios are available, and many items are for sale in the gift shop.

Back along Main Street, a start in the right direction toward rejuvenating Middletown has been the funky and engaging **Main Street Mall**, which contains a handful of offbeat stores and eateries. In general, Main Street is looking better and more vibrant than it has in years, with several new restaurants having opened, and many either abandoned or dowdy storefronts having been spruced up and rented to new shops and businesses. Also relatively new and quite popular is **Kidcity** (119 Washington St., Rte. 66, 860/347-0495, www.kidcitymuseum.com, open 11 A.M.–5 P.M. Sun.–Tues., 9 A.M.–5 P.M. Wed.–Sat.), a hands-on interactive museum geared toward youngsters ages six months to 10 years (and accompanied by at least one adult). Various rooms on two floors allow children to pretend to crew a clipper ship or to create their own movies in a state-of-the-art video theater. First-floor exhibits (one based on a farm, another on a ship) are geared toward the under-five crowd, while second-floor exhibits (on global music, inventing, and such) cater to kids ages 6–10. Rather unusually for a children's museum, admission of $3 is charged for adults and $5 for kids. The museum occupies the 1835 Camp-Sterns House, which was the convent for St. Sebastian's church for several decades.

In the other direction is the 1810 **General Mansfield House** (151 Main St., 860/346-0746, limited hours, phone ahead). It's named for Civil War hero General Joseph Mansfield, who resided here and was killed in battle at Antietam. It's one of the few historic houses in the state with a tie to the Civil War, as it contains many pieces from that period.

Connecticut is well known for its submarine history, as the first such vehicle was invented in Essex in the late 18th century, and the modern submarine industry blossomed in Groton. Here in Middletown, you can learn a great deal about these sleek underwater boats at the **Submarine Library Museum** (440 Washington St., 860/346-0388, seasonal hours, free).

A couple blocks down from Main Street, the Connecticut River wends alongside Rte. 9 and the edge of this small city. Here, Harbor Park has a riverfront setting on the Connecticut, and an old yacht club now houses the Harbor Park Restaurant, which serves fairly basic food but is a great place to enjoy the views. Across the river from Middletown, Rte. 66 leads over a great old bridge to the quiet town of Portland, a largely undeveloped chunk of Connecticut River Valley, whose eastern reaches are dominated by the presence of Meshomasic State Forest.

## CROMWELL TO EAST HARTFORD

### Cromwell

North of Middletown, Rte. 99 leads into tiny Cromwell, a modern suburb well known as the site of a long-running PGA golfing event, the **Greater Hartford Open**. Cromwell was the northern end of Middletown, before breaking off and incorporating in 1851. Cromwell is also the home of a rather unusual attraction, **Amy's Udder Joy Exotic Animal Farm Park** (27 North Rd., 860/635-3924, open April–Oct., $3). It's on the western side of town, just off I-91 at exit 21. Explore more than 50 indoor and outdoor animal exhibits, where you'll see both native and exotic animals, including wallabies, emus, four-toed pygmies, tarantulas, and hedgehogs. Many of these animals can be handled, with supervision, in the petting zoo, and young ones can also enjoy pony rides ($2).

### Rocky Hill

Back on Rte. 99, continue north into Rocky Hill, where a left turn onto West Street leads to 63-acre **Dinosaur State Park** (400 West St., one mile east of exit 23 off I-91, 860/529-8423, www.dinosaurstatepark.org, park grounds open

CONN. RIVER VALLEY

© ANDREW COLLINS

**The ferry across the Connecticut River from Rocky Hill to Glastonbury is the oldest continuously operated ferry service in the United States.**

9 A.M.–4:30 P.M. daily; exhibit center open 9 A.M.–4:30 P.M. Tues.–Sun., kids $2, adults $5). Here, a geodesic dome covers some 500 Jurassic-period dinosaur tracks—visitors can make plaster casts of the fossils (call the park to learn what casting materials you'll need to bring). Dioramas show the environment in which these tracks were made and depict the Connecticut River Valley as it would have appeared in the late Triassic period.

Throughout the 1800s, workers at brownstone quarries along the Connecticut River continued to stumble upon remarkably well-preserved dinosaur fossil tracks, most of which were eventually sold or given to museums around the world. But none of these finds compares with the mother lode of fossils uncovered in Rocky Hill during routine construction in 1966. Hundreds of dinosaur tracks were found preserved in sandstone, Jurassic imprints dating back some 200 million years. This is the largest dinosaur site in North America, and it's covered under a geodesic dome, so that visitors can ogle these fossils year-round, regardless of weather conditions. The grounds of the state park should not be overlooked; there's a 300-foot-long swamp boardwalk and several nature trails and picnic sites. In addition to the grounds and the dinosaur center, the casting area is open 9 A.M.–3:30 P.M. daily May–October.

Like Wethersfield to the north, Rocky Hill has given way largely to industrial parks and suburban housing over the years, while at the same time possessing a district of some of the oldest homes in the state. From Rte. 99, turn right onto Rte. 160, where signs lead east toward the ferry across the Connecticut River to Glastonbury. But instead of heading for the ferry, make an immediate left onto Old Main Street, along which you'll pass by dozens of these venerable old Colonials (most of them with new ranch houses squeezed between them—but you can still get a nice feel for how things were by driving through).

If you have a little extra time, arrange for a visit to the 1803 **Academy Hall Museum** (785 Old Main St., 860/563-6704, www.rockyhill-history.org), home of the Rocky Hill Historical Society (seasonal hours). Many years ago the academy operated a navigational and maritime school for budding sea captains.

Back at Rte. 160, the road winds down to a leafy green park fronting a placid stretch of the Connecticut River that looks about as one imagines it must have when Adriaen Block charted its course in 1614. These days, in season (7 A.M.–6:45 P.M. weekdays, 10:30 A.M.–5 P.M. weekends, May–Oct., $5 for car and driver, $1.75 per each additional passenger), a small ferry boat runs automobiles back and forth from a little terminal beside the park (which has benches and picnic tables) across the river from Rocky Hill to Rte. 160's continuation in Glastonbury. It's the oldest continuously operating ferry in America, having been established in 1655. If it's winter, and you'd like to continue this tour by moving along to Glastonbury, head back to Rte. 99 and continue north into Wethersfield, where Rte. 3 leads across the William H. Putnam Bridge across the river.

## Glastonbury

Whether by ferry or by bridge, once you reach Glastonbury, head south on Main Street (Rte. 17) into South Glastonbury. This is the distinctly more rural half of this large upscale community, long a popular town among Hartford banking and insurance executives. At the junction of Main Street (Rte. 17) and Ferry Street

(Rte. 160), you'll come upon the **Welles-Ship-man-Ward House** (860/633-6890, seasonal hours) a 1755 house-museum notable for its unusually large kitchen fireplace and its small collection of horse-drawn vehicles.

Continue north back up Rte. 17 to reach the **Connecticut Audubon Society's Holland Brook Nature Center** (1361 Main St., Glastonbury, 860/633-8402, www.ctaudubon.org, open 1–5 P.M. Tues.–Fri., 10 A.M.–5 P.M. Sat., 1–4 P.M. most Sundays, $1 for the discovery room), which has exhibits and wildlife mounts (plus several small live animals), a butterfly garden, bird-feeding stations, and a great diorama on the Connecticut River's ecosystem. Nature trails at neighboring 48-acre Earle Park lead through a forest of beech, tulip, silver maple, and red oak trees clear to the Connecticut River. The town's **Museum on the Green** (1944 Main St., 860/633-6890) has been fashioned out of the old 1840s town hall and contains information and artifacts on local history (seasonal hours).

## East Hartford

Route 2 leads north from Glastonbury into the heavily industrialized city of East Hartford, best known as the home of Pratt & Whitney Aircraft, which has its very own private airfield—it's actually larger than Hartford's municipal airport, Brainard, back across the river.

## SHOPPING
### Middletown

Like its counterpart in New Haven, **Atticus Bookstore** (45 Broad St., 860/347-1194) is a well-stocked, inviting shop with a knowledgeable staff and a hip little café that's usually abuzz with literary chatter. The **Main Street Mall**, formerly called the Clocktower Shops, has an array of cool stores. Across the way, **Amato's Toy & Hobby** (395 Main St., 860/347-1893; also 283 Main St., New Britain, 860/229-9069) is a good old-fashioned toy store, packed with models, miniature trains, and other great stuff that will bring a smile to anybody's face, young or adult. Fine pottery and crafts are sold at the **Wesleyan Potters Gallery** (350 S. Main St., 860/344-0039).

### Pick-Your-Own Farms

In South Glastonbury, **Rose's Berry Farm** (295 Matson Hill Rd., off Rte. 17 via Foote St., 860/633-7467) has a country store, December Christmas Shop, summer–fall Sunday breakfasts, and pick-your-own fruits and vegetables, including strawberries, raspberries, blueberries, and pumpkins. Arguably, Connecticut's grandfather of pick-your-own farms is Middlefield's **Lyman Orchards** (Rtes. 147 and 157, 860/349-1793), a 1740s farmstead set around a magnificent Gothic and Italianate mansion. Here, you can pick many varieties of strawberries, blueberries, peaches, nectarines, pears, raspberries, tomatoes, corn, apples, and pumpkins. The place is also famous for its apple pies. Call the orchard's produce hotline, 860/349-1566, for the latest scoop on which fruits and veggies are available when. Adjoining the orchard is a pair of top-flight golf courses. **Hickory Hill Orchard** (351 S. Meriden Rd., Cheshire, 203/272-3824 or 203/272-6593) has special events on weekends in the fall, hayrides, a pumpkin patch, baked goods, pick-your-own fruits, Christmas shop, and such. There's also a gourmet foods gift shop with British-style baked goods, cottage pies, and sweets. **Bishop Farms** (500 S. Meriden Rd., Cheshire, 203/272-8243) is a 200-year-old farmstead with farm animals, antiques, a fruit winery, and a dried-flower shop.

### Antiques, Arts, and Crafts

**Bovano of Cheshire** (830 S. Main St., Cheshire, 203/272-3200) has for more than four decades developed a reputation for its enameled metals, including candle bobeches. Painstaking skill is required to make them, and you can visit the store and ask questions of the knowledgeable staff. It's tucked behind Sweet Claude's ice cream. In Plainville, the **Old Stadium Antiques Mall** (361 New Britain Ave., 860/410-1081) presents the wares of about 30 antiques and crafts dealers. You'll find another excellent multi-dealer setup at the **Plantsville General Store Antique Center** (780 S. Main St., Rte. 10, 860/621-5255), which also has about 30 dealers selling everything from '50s kitchen appliances to Depression era glass.

## Shopping Malls

The best of the malls in the area are in the Farmington River Valley, but shoppers will find a nice array of midrange stores at **Westfield Shoppingtown Meriden** (470 Lewis Ave., the Lewis Ave. or Chamberlain Hwy., exit from I-691, 203/235-3343, www.westfield.com), which is anchored by Filene's, JCPenney, Sears, and Lord & Taylor.

# RECREATION

## Baseball

Connecticut was largely without a strong fan base for minor league baseball for many years. But recently, as major league baseball has rubbed some fans the wrong way with its high salaries, egomaniacal players, and costly tickets, a few minor league affiliates have made a splash here. In New Britain, an American League's Minnesota Twins' double-A affiliate, **Rock Cats,** make their home at New Britain Stadium (Willowbrook Park, S. Main St., exits 24 and 25 from Rte. 9, 860/832-4518, www.rockcats.com), with a season running April–August. In addition to the fact that the management of the Rock Cats has done a nice job endearing the team to the local community, the players themselves are young, talented, and clearly eager to make a good impression and work their way up to triple-A ball—and eventually, if all goes well, to the major leagues. There's a nifty fireworks display after every Friday home game.

## Family Amusements

On the chance you've tended to poo-poo the challenges of miniature golf, you need to pay a visit to **Safari Golf** (2340 Berlin Tpke., Berlin, 860/828-9800), which has garnered all sorts of awards and kudos over the years for its exotic jungle theme—note the abundant use of replica exotic animals: giraffes, zebras, gorillas, and rhinoceroses. The three-tier Kilimanjaro final hole is daunting.

**Lake Compounce** (see Exploring in Bristol, above) is the oldest amusement park in the country.

## Hiking

Fringing the Middletown border, Middlefield's **Wadsworth Falls State Park** (860/566-2304) is one of Connecticut's favorite spots for hiking, freshwater fishing, and swimming, and on a sunny weekend afternoon the popularity will be apparent from the numbers of visitors. The entrance and parking lot are just off Rte. 157, and a sign shows trails and locates bathhouses, picnic tables, and fireplaces. The most popular route is the trail to the dashing waterfalls along this stretch of the Coginchaug River—it's about a two-hour, three-mile (round-trip) hike. There are two sets of falls: the Little Falls, which are less than a mile in, and the great Wadsworth Falls, which are at the southwestern end of the park, near paved Cherry Hill Road.

The good old **Metacomet Ridge,** which is covered above in the Tobacco Country and Farmington River Valley sections, passes through the heart of the state, too. One of the best-known places to experience it is along **Mt. Higby,** where it is traversed by the blue-blazed Mattabesett Trail. Access is from Rte. 66 in Middlefield, near the Meriden border (just east of exit 18 from I-91)—there are parking areas on the north side of the road and also by Guida's Drive In. Like other mountains along the range, Higby is not shaped like a knob, but is a high ridge, and this rugged trail entails a vertical climb of more than 1,000 feet. At the summit, you'll see New Haven's skyline, Sleeping Giant, and the sprawl and industry of Meriden. Higby's west face is a steep cliff, so exercise caution near the edge. It's possible to hike it a little more than three miles to where the trail actually crosses I-91 at exit 20, in Middletown. From there, the trail meanders west into Meriden's Giuffrida Park and then winds north into Berlin, where it finally ends on Spruce Brook Road (just east of Rte. 15/U.S. 5, the Wilbur Cross Hwy.).

You can also follow the Mattabesett Trail south from Mt. Higby, crossing Rte. 66 and heading down around Black Pond. The trail then runs south, straddling first the Meriden-Middlefield border then the Wallingford-Durham border, then turning east through northern Guilford and Madison, before turning north back into Durham, passing east through Millers Pond State Park, into Haddam, and then terminating at **Seven Falls,** at the Haddam-Middletown border. There are access points throughout all of these towns (detailed in the Connecticut Forest and Park Association's *Connecticut Walk Book*—see Suggested Reading in the back of this book). The Seven Falls section of the Mattabasett comprises a series of blue-blazed loop trails, which vary from 2.5 to 8 miles round-trip and so can be easily explored or provide a more challenging hike. Parking for the hike is just off Rte. 154, south of the Middletown border (you'll see signs for the trail). This is a complex system of trails, so it's not a bad idea to consult the trail book before setting out.

Another stretch of the Metacomet Ridge can be hiked at Berlin's **Ragged Mountain Memorial Preserve.** It's reached via West Lane, a left turn from Rte. 71A, about two miles north of its intersection with Rte. 364. A favorite spot in the state for rappelling, this 563-acre preserve is also home to a well-marked nine-mile loop trail rising some 1,000 feet, rewarding hikers with views down over Wasel Reservoir and many miles of central Connecticut's river valley.

Another favorite is 884-acre **Hurd State Park** (off Rte. 151, in the Cobalt section of East Hampton, 860/526-2336), which offers hikers the opportunity to walk down along the eastern shore of the Connecticut River. There are a few good trails here, some with as dramatic a vertical drop as 600 feet—it's steepest nearest the river, where precipitous hills climb down to the shoreline. In winter, cross-country skiers favor the park. Split Rock Trail leads to a ledge offering views 200 feet down to the river. The strange old village of Cobalt,

## GOLFING IN THE HEART OF CONNECTICUT

In a state where golfing enjoys an extremely high level of popularity, it's not too surprising that the densely settled center of the state has among the highest number of public courses—everything from challenging, and frustrating, 18-hole layouts to easy par-three executive facilities. Note that if your own game is driving you slightly crazy, you might learn a few things watching the pros battle it out at the **Greater Hartford Open,** 860/522-4171, which is held at the end of June or early July each year at the spectacular Tournament Players Club at River Highlands, Rte. 99, Cromwell. Alas, this course is not open to the general public for playing. Also, as of this writing, the tournament was seeking a new sponsor, so there's a slight question as to its future in Connecticut.

Adjacent to the 18th-century Lyman farmstead, **Lyman Orchards Golf Club** (Rte. 157, Middlefield, 860/349-1793) comprises two challenging 18-hole courses, one designed in the late 1960s by Robert Trent Jones and the second created in 1994 by golfing great Gary Player. This is a high-profile course with among the highest greens fees of any public course (motorized carts are also required on the Player course)—book well ahead if you want to play this one on a weekend.

In the Kensington section of Berlin, **Timberlin Golf Club** (330 Southington Rd., 860/828-3228) ranks in the minds of many locals as the top public course in the state—it's a medium-length course that doesn't look especially challenging or even interesting, but it's nicely maintained and often less crowded than hot spots like Lyman Orchards and Stanley Golf Course.

Of city courses, **Stanley Golf Course** (245 Hartford Rd., New Britain, 860/827-8570) does a fine job masking its proximity to urbanity, with a challenging 6,700-yard 18-holer and a short and tight par-35 nine-holer. Others on this side of the river include 18-hole **Pine Valley** (300 Welch Rd., Southington, 860/628-0879); 18-hole **Rockledge Country Club** (289 S. Main St., West Hartford, 860/521-3156); nine-hole **Rolling Greens Golf Course** (600 Cold Spring Rd., Rocky Hill, 860/257-9775); and the well-maintained 18-hole **Hunter Golf Course** (688 Westfield Rd., Meriden, 203/634-3366).

Portland has some fine public courses, including 18-hole **Portland Golf Club** (169 Bartlett St., 860/342-6107), which is known for its finely tuned greens and fairways, and 18-hole **Quarry Ridge** (9 Rose Hill Rd., 860/342-6113). The latter course has wonderful views over the Connecticut River. Up in Glastonbury, nine-hole **Minnechaug Golf Course** (16 Fairway Crossing, 860/643-9914) is best known for its eighth hole, whose green is surrounded completely by water.

CONN. RIVER VALLEY

which is named for the cobalt mine that once prospered here, has other fine hiking opportunities. The southern tip of Meshomasic State Forest marks the beginning, locally, of the **Shenipset Trail**, which is the eastern Connecticut River Valley's counterpart to the more famous Metacomet Trail. It, too, runs much of the length of the state, in a northerly direction. To reach this stretch, turn left (north) onto Depot Hill Road, at the junction of Rte. 66 and Rte. 151 (just after you pass from Portland into East Hampton). Make a right onto Gadpouch Road and park right by the trailhead for this blue-blazed trail. It's possible to hike clear through Portland to the Glastonbury border from here—a distance of several miles. But a fairly short and moderately steep jaunt takes you up the side of Great Hill, which offers fine views up and down the Connecticut River, as well as of Great Hill Pond just down below.

### Linear Parks

Hikers, bikers, runners, and cross-country skiers can take advantage of the **Farmington Canal Linear Park** (Rte. 42, 203/272-2743), an eight-mile paved "rails to trails" park that follows the route of the defunct Farmington Canal and is attached to Lock 12 Historical Park. Plans are for this park eventually to extend all the way south through downtown New Haven and along the shore to West Haven, and all the way north up into the Farmington River valley, perhaps eventually connecting all the way to Northampton, Massachusetts.

### Skiing

**Mount Southington** (396 Mount Vernon Rd., off exit 30 from I-84, 860/628-SNOW or 800/982-6828, www.mountsouthington.com) offers day and night downhill skiing November–April. There are 14 trails, ranging from easy to most difficult, and six lifts, plus lessons, rental equipment, children's programs, racing programs, and a halfpipe for snowboarding. You can hit the slopes day or night, and lift rates are quite reasonable, just $30 for an adult all-day weekend or holiday ticket. This 50-acre ski facility is one of the best in the state, and it has greatly expanded in recent years to include sledding and snow tubing.

## ENTERTAINMENT AND NIGHTLIFE

### Bars and Clubs

Wesleyan students in search of good beer favor **Eli Cannon's** (695 Main St., 860/347-ELIS). You can drink from a vintage barber's chair. More than 100 bottled selections join 25 on tap, many of them microbrewed. Head to **The Cellar** (39 New London Tpke., Glastonbury, 860/652-8337) for live rock music. Southington is home to Connecticut's premier country-western dance and live-music club, the **Cadillac Ranch** (45 Jude Ln., just off exit 31 of I-84, 860/621-8805), which also serves light food. There are line-dancing lessons most evenings; call for details. Fans of the genre congregate regularly in Plainville at **Starstruck Karaoke** (317 Farmington Ave., 860/747-8805).

### Arts and Culture

In New Britain, the **Hole In The Wall Theater** (10 Harvard St., 860/229-3049) offers six theatrical productions, some of them quite cutting edge, on Fridays and Saturdays much of the year. You can also catch plays Sept.–June at the **Repertory Theatre of New Britain** (23 Norden St., 860/223-3147, www.nbrep.org). In summer, jazz, blues, country, folk, and children's concerts are held at the Miller Band Shell in New Britain's leafy **Walnut Hill Park** (Park Place, 860/224-9161). In Berlin, the **Connecticut Cabaret Theatre** (31–33 Webster Mill Plaza, 860/829-1248, www.ctcabaret.com) stages professional musicals and comedies on weekend evenings; you can bring your own dinner, snacks, and drinks, and limited food is available there.

Middletown is the site of the oldest and largest children's theater in the state, the **Oddfellows Playhouse Youth Theater** (128 Washington St., Rte. 66, 860/347-6143), which presents plays year-round. One of the more cerebral and inventive options for a night on the town is to pop by the **Buttonwood Tree** (605 Main St., 860/347-4957, www.buttonwood.org), a performance space with offerings ranging from poetry readings to acoustic music. You're welcome to hang out, play board games, or read. Wesleyan

University is an excellent source of inexpensive and often very good performing arts presentations—the **Center for the Arts** (High St., 860/685-3355) sponsors dance, theater, film, and world music performances at a number of campus venues. Downtown Middletown recently saw the opening of a new multiscreen cinema, the **Destinta Theatre Complex** (49 College St., just off Main St., 860/346-4000), which also has a Mexican restaurant on-site. **Park Road Playhouse** (244 Park Rd., West Hartford, 860/586-8500, www.parkroadplayhouse.org) presents about five plays throughout the year, generally tried-and-true classics, but also some contemporary works.

## FESTIVALS AND EVENTS

Late April marks the annual **Meriden Daffodil Festival** (Hubbard Park, 203/630-4259), which includes food, rides, a parade, fireworks, and music; approximately 60 varieties of daffodils are displayed. **Liberty Bank Middletown Road Races** hosts 10K running and wheelchair races in Middletown each September, 860/347-6924. Fireworks, a road race, and crafts characterize the fun at the late-September **Cromwell Riverport Festival** (West and Main Streets, 860/635-2690).

In Rocky Hill, the young and the old come for food and steamboat and carnival rides to the **Ferry Park Family Festival** (Rte. 160, Rocky Hill, 860/258-2772). Cheshire is a lively place to be in mid-September, when the **Junior Women's Club Arts and Crafts Festival** (203/272-0101) is held on the town green. Around the same time, about 250 juried artists present their wares at Glastonbury's **On the Green Art and Craft** (Main and Hubbard Streets, 860/657-2321).

Early October is the **Berlin Agricultural Fair** (Beckley Road, 860/828-4280), with tractor pulls, flowers displays, horse shows, and the like. For the first week of October, numerous events in Southington make up the **Annual Apple Harvest Festival** (860/628-8036). New Britain presents an impressive **Antique Auto Show** (Klingberg Family Center, 370 Linwood St., 860/224-9113), which also entails dancing, historical displays, and such. In late October, Meri-den's **Meet the Artists & Artisans Show** (Meriden Square, 203/874-5672) allows visitors to mingle with artisans at a juried presentation of their works. Bristol is home to a hearty **Mums Festival** (860/589-4826 or 860/584-0625), which runs from late September through early October and includes horsebacking riding, pumpkin painting, cider milling, and a costumed-pet parade.

For several days in early December, East Hartford lights up for the **Annual Holiday Festival** (860/528-1458), which is kicked off with a tree-lighting ceremony and continues with children's activities, caroling, theater, crafts shows, and Santa parties.

## ACCOMMODATIONS

You'll find dozens of chain hotels in central Connecticut, many of them relatively new and catering to the many business travelers who frequent office parks in Rocky Hill, Cromwell, and other towns near Hartford. Many of these places offer great deals on weekends, when business travelers aren't around. And as of this writing, an upscale 100-room hotel, the Inn at Middletown, was under construction on Middletown's Main Street, inside the historic National Guard Amory close to Wesleyan University. The hotel will have a full-service restaurant, fitness center, and several two-room suites.

### Hotels and Motels

Virtually all of the 30 motels on the Berlin Turnpike, from Meriden to Newington, are seedy and strange, Berlin's Hawthorne Inn being the lone exception. It's a shame more of these haven't been properly maintained and pleasantly developed; they mostly date from the mid-1930s, 1940s, and 1950s, and some of them are very interesting-looking from the outside, or at least possess a certain camp factor. Many of them have reasonably clean rooms and even bright well-kept exteriors, but they exist mostly for prostitution or for transient living and don't possess a great deal of appeal for vacationers. Many have engaging motifs and names that conjure up images of sylvan New England motels. Some are listed in local and state tourism brochures, which by no means grants them any real degree of legitimacy. A tour of them might prove interesting; perhaps the state should buy them all up and create a linear motel park. The bulk is in Meriden, up by the Berlin town line, and in Newington. Unless you're feeling very adventuresome and you're on the tightest of budgets—avoid them. Backpackers looking for an authentically twisted experience might relent and give them a shot.

**$100–150:** Most of the places in central Connecticut where you might actually want to stay are fairly ordinary chain properties. At the upper end is one of the nicest of the upscale business hotels in central Connecticut, the 250-room **Hartford Marriott Rocky Hill** (Corporate Ridge, 100 Capital Blvd., 860/257-6000 or 800/228-9290). Here you'll find a decent restaurant, a beautiful indoor pool, a very nice health club with whirlpool, and bright new rooms. The location in a corporate park off I-91 may sound ominous, but this is a new development that's nicely landscaped and heavily wooded—a surprisingly nice setting. Best of all, from here it's a 10-minute drive on the highway to downtown Hartford and just 15 minutes south to New Haven or the Essex/East Haddam area, making this a great base for exploring the entire region. Excellent weekend packages make this an affordable retreat for most budgets.

In Meriden, the **Ramada Plaza Hotel** (275 Research Pkwy., 203/238-2380 or 800/2-RAMADA) is a fine chain business hotel marred only by its corporate park locale. But hey, the rooms are clean and bright, the location convenient to all of central Connecticut and the lower valley. Facilities include an indoor pool and fitness center. Another excellent business hotel with leisure-friendly weekend rates is the **Radisson Hotel and Conference Center** (100 Berlin Rd., Rte. 372, Cromwell, 860/635-2000 or 800/333-3333). It's an airy light-filled hotel with Colonial-reproduction furniture, spacious rooms with work desks and in-room coffeemakers, a polished restaurant, and a full state-of-the-art fitness center complete with an indoor pool. The **Holiday Inn** (4 Sebethe Dr., 860/635-1001 or 800/935-4016) is another reliable midpriced option in Cromwell. It has 145 rooms, a restaurant, and an indoor pool. Both of these properties are convenient both to Hartford and Middletown.

A nice clean motor lodge on a relatively peaceful stretch of the Berlin Turnpike (a.k.a. Wilbur Cross Pkwy.), the **Hawthorne Inn** (2421 Wilbur Cross Pkwy., U.S. 5/Rte. 15, Berlin, 860/828-4181) is probably best known for its exceptional steak-and-seafood restaurant in the adjacent building. Rooms at this mock-Tudor property have dark floral drapes and bedspreads, giving them more warmth than most chain properties, and there's a nice exercise room and outdoor pool. The same family has operated this place since the 1940s, and the eye for detail and hospitality definitely shows.

Although the hotel itself is perfectly adequate, clean, and modern, the **Radisson Bristol** (42 Century Dr., 860/589-7766 or 800/333-3333) should be considered only as a backup to the Holiday Inn Express. It's situated amid a bleak industrial park, and the common areas and restaurant-bar are sterile and lack personality. Facilities include an indoor pool, sauna, and exercise room. One plus, however, is that you may bump into pro athletes and sports personalities visiting ESPN studios. The **Residence Inn by Marriott** (778 West St., Southington, 860/621-4440 or 800/331-3131, www.waterfordhotelgroup.com) has 94 suites, many with fireplaces and all with full kitchens. It's perfect for longer stays.

**$50–100:** Of midrange chain properties, Meriden's **Hampton Inn** (10 Bee St., 203/235-5154 or 800/HAMPTON) stands out for its comfy contemporary rooms, free local calls, and a top-notch staff—you won't find a better hotel in this price range in the state. **Holiday Inn Express** (120 Laning St., Southington, 860/276-0736 or 800/HOLIDAY, www.whghotels.com/hiesouth) is one of the best under-$100 properties in the state, with upbeat and cheerfully decorated rooms with white-tile baths, sofas, and tasteful decorating. There's a pool, and some of the rooms have whirlpool tubs. It's on a bluff overlooking I-84, beside Brannigan's Ribs.

The **Ramada Inn Plainville** (400 New Britain Ave., 860/747-6876 or 800/446-4656, www.ramadact.com) has nicely done rooms with coffeemakers, hairdryers, and irons and boards. It's well-managed, and has a fun little restaurant specializing in pubby English fare, a dance club that's actually been known to draw locals, and a nice pool.

Middletown is strangely lacking in nice economical accommodations, but a short drive across the river yields one of the best deals in the Connecticut River Valley, the 47-room **Riverdale Motel** (1503 Rte. 66, Portland, 860/342-3498), a red-roofed, white-clapboard building on a quiet stretch of highway, close to the fine golf courses and myriad hiking opportunities of Portland, East Hampton, and Haddam Neck.

**Under $50:** You'll find several fine budget-oriented properties in these parts. The **Cheshire Welcome Inn** (1106 S. Main St., Rte. 10, Cheshire, 203/272-3244 or 877/646-4309, www.cheshirewelcomeinn.com) is a nice budget option with everything from tasteful basic units to efficiencies to a few vanity suites (one has a red heart-shaped tub). It was recently renovated and is set well away from busy Interstates at the south end of town. The **Motel 6** (1341 Silas Deane Hwy., Rte. 99, Wethersfield, 860/563-5900 or 800/4-MOTEL-6) is a super-clean and fully modernized budget property in a two-level Colonial-style building. The **Travelodge** (30 Laning St., Southington, 860/628-0921) has nicely kept rooms and is another of the better budget options around. Also reliable for budget travelers is the **Motel 6** (625 Queen St., Rte. 10, Southington, 860/621-7351 or 800/4-MOTEL-6). For proximity to Middletown and low prices, it's hard to beat the **Super 8** (1 Industrial Park Rd., Cromwell, 860/632-8888 or 800/800-8000), where rates include a Continental breakfast.

## Country Inns and Bed-and-Breakfasts

**$100–150:** The rambling **Chimney Crest Manor** (5 Founders Dr., Bristol, 860/582-4219, www.bbonline.com/ct/chimneycrest) is a dramatic, 32-room Tudor-style mansion with a memorable red slate roof—a complete departure from the fussy little Colonial B&Bs that dominate so much of Connecticut. Rooms here are massive and striking, with eclectic furnishings

that give the place a whimsical and romantic flair. A cherry-paneled library is one of the fine common rooms, the 40-foot-long Garden Suite was once a ballroom, and the Master Suite looks big enough for you to throw your very own private ball. The most recent addition is a spa suite with a full whirlpool soaking tub. Many rooms look east into the Farmington River Valley.

**Brianna's House** (52 Vine St., New Britain, 860/229-4262, www.briannasbnb.com) opened recently in downtown New Britain, just a block from the wonderful art museum and Walnut Park, in the Walnut Hill District. Rooms in this 1880 Queen Anne Victorian have a homey mix of vintage furnishings picked up mostly at New Britain antiques shops—each has a private bath. Proprietor Larry Knee is gregarious and chatty, and he knows a great deal about New Britain; he'll also happily pick up guests at the train station in New Haven, by advance request. An excellent fresh-made breakfast is included.

**$50–100: Udderly Woolly Acres** (581 Thompson St., 860/633-4503), in unspoiled eastern Glastonbury, has far more than an unusually charming name to its credit. This 1830 Greek Revival farmhouse overlooks a 20-acre farm of sheep, goats, and geese; you can sample fresh vegetables, eggs, milk, cheese, and other local products during the full breakfast included with your stay. This is an especially appropriate option for families, as the owners welcome kids and encourage them to explore the farm.

In the heart of Old Wethersfield, the **Chester Bulkley House B&B** (184 Main St., 860/563-4236) offers five graciously furnished rooms (three with private bath) in a stately 1830 Greek Revival house. The full breakfast is substantial enough to let you skip lunch. **Butternut Farm** (1654 Main St., Glastonbury, 860/633-7197, www.butternutfarmbandb.com) is a 1720s farmhouse whose property includes a menagerie of farm animals. There are five guest rooms with wide-plank floors and antiques, and this characterful old house also contains original wide-brick fireplaces, pumpkin pine floors, and wood paneling. It's a remarkable work of restoration, in a memorable setting that will have you feeling you're miles from Hartford. Full breakfast is included.

CONN. RIVER VALLEY

# FOOD

Encompassing a broad range of landscapes and terrains, this section of the state comprises an equally varied selection of culinary offerings. High population density has resulted in large numbers of restaurants, and the number of pronounced working-class ethnic enclaves has given the heart of Connecticut many excellent purveyors of Italian, Polish, and certain Asian cuisines. New Britain is one city where you're apt to find great variety, Middletown is another.

## Upscale

Glamorous **Brix** (1721 Highland Ave., Rte. 10, 203/272-3584, $18–26) is Cheshire's respected contribution to central Connecticut's upscale restaurant scene. The menu borrows heavily from Northern Italy, with respectable renditions of veal osso bucco and, for dessert, tiramisu, but some of the fare lacks the finesse that has clearly gone into decorating this sleek, elegant space. Furthermore, service can be uneven on busy nights. The restaurant at the nicely run motel-style **Hawthorne Inn** (2387 Wilbur Cross Hwy., U.S. 5/Rte. 15, Berlin, 860/828-3571, $13–29) is locally renowned for perhaps the best prime rib around, plus remarkably fresh and well-prepared seafood like baked stuffed lobster and broiled swordfish. There's dinner and swing dancing some nights, and despite the banquet-hall ambience, the place is tastefully decorated through and through. Another of the area's successful "Max" restaurants, **Max Amore** (140 Glastonbury Blvd., Somerset Square, Glastonbury, 860/659-2819, $13–22), has made a reputation for delicious oak-grilled steaks and seafood entrées, plus a wide selection of freshly made pastas paired with creative ingredients.

For months, curious passersby watched as a dramatic 1787 Georgian mansion in Old Wethersfield underwent a thorough makeover. Power lunchers and parents of Wesleyan students favor the elegant confines of **Tuscany Grill** (600 Plaza Middlesex, Middletown, 860/346-7096, $9–22), once the soaring ceilinged foyer of the Middlesex Opera House. Tuscany succeeds with a range of contemporary Italian dishes, from sliced pan-seared breast of duck with wild mushroom risotto and an apricot demi-glace to a host of brick-oven pizzas. The pastas all come in entrée and appetizer portions.

## Creative but Casual

A standout in little Plainfield is **The Cottage** (427 Farmington Ave., Rte. 10, 860/793-8888, $13–25), a highly underrated restaurant with a provocative global-inspired menu that sets it apart from other eateries in the region. The cooking here changes weekly, but on a lucky visit, you might enjoy smoked pork chops with a potato pancake and maple-apple-ginger glaze. Or the house specialty dessert, hot apple fritters dusted with cinnamon sugar served with ice cream and melted caramel (it's hard to think of a better way to finish off a meal on a blustery fall evening). The setting is a modest house not far from the Farmington border. A similarly appealing Plainville option is **Confetti!** (393 Farmington Ave., Rte. 10, 860/793-8809, $10–22), which serves upmarket American fare and seafood.

The vegan **It's Only Natural** (386 Main St., Middletown, 860/346-9210, $10–14) excels where many vegetarian restaurants fail: The food on the plate really looks and tastes as good as it sounds in the menu. Savor mushroom and sauerkraut pan-sautéed pierogis with apple butter, tofu sour cream, caramelized onions, and brown rice, or spicy Cajun tempeh with a roasted red pepper sauce. The addictive sweet potato fries come with a delicious smoked-ketchup dip.

**Main & Hopewell** (2 Hopewell Rd., South Glastonbury, 860/633-8698, $15–24) is a vibrant jazz (on weekends) bistro with stellar contemporary Italian and American cooking, such as tender poached calamari or fettuccine with shrimp, lobster, and Manila clams in a lobster-tomato broth. Pan-seared duck breast topped with sweet-onion marmalade and potato salsa is another dish that gives a sense of the kitchen's talents.

# NEW BRITAIN'S EDIBLE POLISH LEGACY

New Britain is well-regarded for its variety of ethnic eateries, but it's probably best known for Polish cuisine, an outgrowth of the pronounced community of immigrants who settled here from Eastern Europe in the late 19th and early 20th centuries to work the city's many machine-tools manufactories.

There are two primary clusters of Polish eating, the first being just north of downtown along Broad Street, principally on the two blocks between Grove and Washington Streets. Here you'll find **Cracovia** (60 Broad St., 860/223-4443), a full-service cheerfully decorated restaurant known for its home-style lunches and dinners, and also groceries and Polish bakeries that specialize in authentic foods. Another excellent option near the same neighborhood is **Larosa's** (146 East St., 860/225-6187). The other section is just south of downtown along S. Main Street, below Franklin Square, from about Ellis to South Street. The most notable of these is **Fatherland Restaurant** (450 S. Main St., 860/224-3345), whose dining room is filled with photos of favorite Polish national figures, including musicians Chopin and Liszt. At all of these restaurants, entrées typically cost $5–12.

Polish food tends to be hearty and soul-satisfying, utilizing many ingredients found most often in cooler climates: potatoes, cabbage, peas, pork, lamb, veal, and such. Pierogis, little doughy dumplings that can either be fried or boiled, are highly addictive: they typically come with fillings like potatoes, sauerkraut, mushrooms, and cheese, along with sides of sour cream and applesauce. Another favorite delicacy is the blintz, a rolled crêpe-like confection filled with farmers cheese, sour cherries, blueberries, or apples, and usually rolled in powdered sugar. Very often, cheese blintzes come smeared in plum butter. Or sample the *nalesniki*, golden pancakes served with homemade cottage cheese.

Roast pork with caraway seeds, breaded pork chops, and veal stew are classic Polish entrées, while pickled beets or borscht—the traditional Polish soup—are classic starters, as is beef-and-barley soup. And then there are the kielbasa sausages, spliced down the center. They're traditionally made of pork, and may be prepared either smoked or grilled, heavily spiced or not. *Golabki*, cabbage stuffed with a mix of rice, pork, and beef and slathered in tomato sauce, is another standard, as are tasty stuffed bell peppers.

## Steak, Pizza, Pub Grub, and Seafood

Middletown's Italian community is about as pronounced as any in Connecticut, and the local dining scene reflects this. Many locals swear by **Cantina Cafe Ristorante** (74 Court St., 860/704-0000, $11–16), which is in the quirky, if not especially inviting, basement of the downtown Sons of Italy Hall. The menu offers few surprises, which is fine if authentic home-style Italian cooking is your desire: grilled shrimp pancetta and veal piccata are typical. Another acclaimed choice for traditional Italian fare is **Elizabeth's Bar & Restaurant** (825 Cromwell Ave., Rte. 3, Rocky Hill, 860/721-6932, $12–22), where veal marsala, New York strip steaks, and fried calamari are prepared to perfection.

**Brannigan's** (176 Laning St., Southington, 860/621-9311, $8–23) smells the way a rib joint should smell, like meat that's been slow-smoking in homemade barbecue sauce for hours on end. The ribs here are superb, although locals in the know are quick to point out that this is a fine place for seafood, steaks, and other hearty American fare. In season, there's dining on a patio.

Other places get most of the attention when it comes to pizza in greater Hartford, but **Krys's Italian Restaurant** (83 W. Main St., Southington, 860/628-4321, large pies $10–14) might just bake the finest white clam pies in the region. This is a very simple family-style parlor amid the mix of antiques shops and old-time taverns in the Plantsville section of town. Equally impressive and somewhat unheralded is **Bella Pizza & Restaurant** (512 High Rd., Berlin, 860/829-0002, large pies $10–14) in the Kensington section of Berlin.

This neighborhood eatery has outstanding pies, delicious calzones, and a terrific by-the-glass selection of wines that sets it apart from the others in the area.

**J. Gilbert's Wood-Fired Steaks** (185 Glastonbury Blvd., Glastonbury, 860/659-0409, $12–30) draws raves for its Jamaican jerk chicken, grilled corn and chicken tortilla soup, and—of course—fine steaks, like a 24-ounce porterhouse with a veal, butter, and merlot sauce. This is also a place for sophisticated cocktails. A household name among carnivores, the national chain **Ruth's Chris Steak House** (2513 Berlin Tpke., Rte. 5/U.S. 15, Newington, 860/666-2202, $18–34) has a popular branch in these parts. The cuts of steak are bold and beautiful, and they come with a choice of several great kinds of potatoes, from lyonnaise to steak fries.

Cromwell's easygoing **J.T.'s Roadhouse Grill** (36 Shunpike Ave., 860/635-6294, $8–16) has tasty finger foods, pub grub, and great Black Angus steaks. The service is friendly, the prices reasonable. In 2000, the **First and Last Tavern** (220 Main St., 860/347-2220, $12–17, large pies $15–22) opened inside the new police station building in downtown Middletown. By all accounts, the delicious pizzas here are just as good as those served at the Hartford original—the shrimp scampi pizza is a favorite. Don't overlook the long list of grinders, pastas, and salads, too. The ambience is clubby and inviting, the brick walls crammed with vintage black-and-white photos of Connecticut.

## Asian

A relative newcomer on the Japanese-food scene is **Sapporo** (1295 Silas Deane Hwy., Rte. 99, Wethersfield, 860/721-8477, $8–19), whose specialties in addition to sushi and sashimi include stir-fried tofu and a delicious house duck.

For the best Thai food in the lower valley, check out **Thai Gardens** (300 Plaza Middlesex, Middletown, 860/346-3322, $8–14), which offers a fairly typical assortment of particularly well-prepared dishes, such as pineapple paradise (red curry with shrimp, bamboo shoots, coconut milk, green beans, pineapple, and sweet basil). It's a pretty space with booth seating.

**Golden Sun Lao-Thai** (1219 Burnside Ave., U.S. 44, East Hartford, $7–14) is just over the Manchester border in a shopping center. The dining room is sedate and attractive, with faux-stucco walls. But the real draw here is the outstanding Thai and Lao cuisine. Four styles of soft-shell crab are offered in season (the "rainbow" version with mushrooms, silver noodles, red and green peppers, and a coconut curry is perhaps the best). Another specialty is beef macadamia. From the Laotian side of the menu, consider *larb kai,* ground chicken breast tossed with roast-rice powder, lime juice, red onion, scallion, cilantro, mint, and fresh herbs.

Regulars drive from all corners of the state to sample some of Connecticut's best gourmet Chinese fare at the simply and aptly named **Great Taste** (597 W. Main St., 860/827-8988, $7–19), an elegant yet unassuming restaurant in New Britain. All the usual standbys are offered, but you'll also find some intriguing specials like Neptune's Nest, with jumbo shrimp, scallops, and king crab marinated with vegetables and a spicy white sauce and served on a crisp "nest" of noodles; and the house-sizzling steak.

## Mexican, Southwestern, and Latin American

Few Hartford-area restaurants have opened with faster acclaim in recent years than **Bamboleo** (2935 Main St., Glastonbury, 860/657-9251, $15–24), a snazzy—and noisy—restaurant opened by the folks beyond Hartford's and New Haven's popular Hot Tomato's Italian eateries. Part of the appeal is simply the bustling ambience, trendy bar, and great cocktails, but Bamboleo also turns out some quite decent cooking, such as braised pork shank with a sweet-and-hot mango-habanero glaze. There are also six types of ceviche available; you could easily make a meal of these.

It's nearly in Haddam, at the very southern end of Middletown, where you'll find excellent Southwestern and Mexican cooking at **Coyote Blue Tex Mex Cafe** (1960 Saybrook Rd., Rte. 154, 860/345-2403, $7–14). The desert combo (spinach and feta quesadilla, cheese and scallion enchilada, bean burrito, guacamole, sour cream, and rice) is one of the more satisfying offerings—the food is sometimes authentic, sometimes not, but it all has a nice bite to it, and the ingredients are fresh. Margaritas here are among the best in the region, served in thick Mason jars. This delightful sleeper is way south of town on the Haddam line. In Southington, **El Sombrero** (151 Queen St., 860/621-9474, $7–14) has decent, but predictable Mexican fare that can be spicy if you ask for their outstanding hot sauce (infused with chipotle peppers).

### Other Ethnic Fare

Polish food may be New Britain's culinary calling card, but this patchwork of ethnic enclaves scores high marks for a number of differing cuisines. For instance, **East Side** (131 Dwight St., New Britain, 860/223-1188, $6–14) prepares schnitzels, sauerbraten, and potato pancakes that will leave you temporarily immobilized, but very happy. Head over the Cheshire and you'll find hearty, well-prepared Austrian fare at the **Watch Factory** (122 Elm St., 203/271-1717, $10–18), which is set inside a complex of engaging shops across from the town hall. The kitchen here favors traditional country-style recipes, but often adds contemporary twists.

### Quick Bites

One of the region's great family traditions, often tied in with hiking, swimming, or cross-country skiing at one of Middlefield's excellent outdoors venues, is a meal of burgers, fries, and fresh-made ice cream at **Guida's Drive In** (Rte. 66, Middlefield, 860/349-9039, under $8).

With a repertoire of a few hundred possible soups, **Vermont Gourmet** (63F Hebron Ave., Glastonbury, 860/659-2695, under $8) is a terrific spot for light bite—you'll also find sandwiches, salads, and such. **Blackie's Hot Dog Stand** (2200 Waterbury Rd., Cheshire, 203/574-9153) is the stuff of cult status, a neon-shrouded roadhouse just off I-84 with stools and booths for seating, and the juiciest hot dogs around slathered with a variety of artery-hardening toppings. It's a great building, an odd little converted garage with a pair of octagonal turrets and distinctive neon signs. Open late is the knockout neon-and-steel

© ANDREW COLLINS

In Cheshire, Blackie's hot dogs inspire an ardent following.

**Olympia Diner** (414 Berlin Tpke. U.S. 5, Newington, 860/666-9948, $3–10), where heaps of pancakes slathered in eggs and bacon will clog your arteries but warm your soul, and the usual burgers, Greek salads, and such round out the long and impressive menu. Late at night, it's an absolute pageant of people-watching.

**O'Rourke's Diner** (728 Main St., Middletown, 860/346-6101, $5–8) is a local legend, famous across New England for its mix of traditional greasy spoon fare prepared to perfection, as well as more innovative offerings. Brunch is the toughest time to score a table—the staff knows the regulars, even the semi-regulars, by name, and on less-crowded days the place feels like some kind of communal kitchen, with family members bantering back and forth. The tiny dining area features leatherette booths with seats a distinctly retro shade of olive green and the usual Formica counters. The menu goes on and on. An omelette with roasted portobello mushrooms, brie, and asparagus is a nice variation on eggs Benedict. Open early (4:30 A.M.) but closed in the early afternoon, so dinner is not offered.

In summer (it's closed the rest of the year), it's worth the trip down to a little side alley off Washington Street, right before it meets with Rte. 9, to sample the addictive lemon, watermelon, almond,

**CONN. RIVER VALLEY**

and other ices at **Vecchitto's Lemon Ice** (323 DeKoven Dr., Middletown, no phone).

Another great option for similar fare is **Mortensen's Restaurant and Ice Cream Shop** (3145 Berlin Tpke., Newington, 860/666-8219), an old-school parlor that's a favorite with families. If Fido is feeling a little peckish, bring him over to **Praline's** (1143 Meriden/Waterbury Rd., Southington, 860/621-4823; 1245 E. Main St., Meriden, 203/237-4303; and 1179 Farmington Ave., Berlin, 860/828-3626). Here you'll find, among the delightful array of ice creams and sweets for people, a concoction called Milk Bone ice cream. Another contender in central Connecticut's best ice cream sweepstakes is **Sweet Claude's** (828 S. Main St., Cheshire, 203/272-4237), set in a quirky old Victorian house not far from the Lock 12 Historical Park. The "adult" flavors include a knockout version accented with Kahlua.

In Old Town Wethersfield, steps from the many historic museums in this charming neighborhood, **Main Street Creamery** (217 Main St., 860/529-0509) is a handsome storefront café with tables and chairs set out along the broad redbrick sidewalk. It's an idyllic spot for fresh-made ice cream and other sweets. For a tasty lunch in the same neighborhood, head to the **Spicy Green Bean Deli** (285 Main St., Wethersfield, 860/563-3100, under $9), a diminutive café and market with outstanding veggie chili and some delicious, hefty sandwiches and salads. There's outdoor seating, too.

The locally famous drive-in **Frankie's** (1195 Farmington Ave., U.S. 6, Bristol, 860/584-9826, under $10), whose flagship branch is down in Waterbury, is also in Bristol, on the east end of town (right by the Farmington border). Nearby, **Vita's Italian Market and Deli** (562 Farmington Ave., Bristol, 860/582-0440) sells obscenely huge grinders, pizzas by the slice, and other hearty and filling fare, plus gourmet Italian groceries. The first Connecticut branch of the fanatically popular **Krispy Kreme** (2909 Berlin Tpke., Newington, 860/666-9948) chain opened not too long ago—by the time you read this book, there will no doubt be others. But for now, donut

lovers from all over the state are flocking to Newington for these heavenly sweets.

## Java Joints

As you might expect where a university is present, Middletown has a strong coffeehouse scene, anchored by the eclectic café at **Atticus Bookstore** (45 Broad St., 860/347-1194). **Klekolo World Coffee** (181 Court St., Middletown, 860/343-9444) is another funky spot for an espresso, and it's also a popular venue to hear poetry readings and folk music. In New Britain's restored Arch Street area, **Vintage Coffee** (61 Arch St., 860/225-0211) sells hot coffee, but also offers sandwiches, bagels, and other light fare. It's attached to a multi-dealer antiques shop and set inside a historic downtown building. **Caffe del Mondo** (550 N. Main St., 860/621-9977) is a cheerful spot in Southington for java; there's live entertainment many nights.

## Gourmet Goods and Picnic Supplies

In Middletown's Main Street Mall, you'll discover a huge selection of gourmet goods and whole foods, plus natural soaps, holistic medicines, and vitamins, at the spacious and attractive **It's Only Natural Market** (386 Main St., 860/346-9210). **Urban Oaks** (225 Oak St., New Britain, 860/223-6200) is an organic market that's only open to the public on Saturdays, when regulars flock here from all over to sample the house-baked pastries, fresh produce, and coffees. It's a great stop if you're visiting the New Britain Museum of American Art.

# INFORMATION AND SERVICES
## Visitor Information

Most of the region is served by the **Greater Hartford Tourism District** (31 Pratt St., 4th Fl., Hartford, CT 06103, 860/244-8181 or 800/793-4480, www.enjoyhartford.com). Contact the **Litchfield Hills Travel Council** (Box 968, Litchfield, CT 06759, 860/567-4506, www.litchfieldhills.com) for the latest information on Bristol.

## Getting Around

Given its location in the center of the state, it's extremely easy to both reach and navigate the heart of Connecticut from anywhere else in the state. The major Interstates of I-84 (which passes through Cheshire, Southington, Plainville, New Britain, and East Hartford) and I-91 (which hits Meriden, Middlefield, Middletown, Rocky Hill, and Wethersfield) are easy connections. Route 9 runs along the west side of the Connecticut River, through Middletown and Cromwell, before cutting west through the region. I-691 is a major east–west route from Middletown through Meriden to Southington and Cheshire. Route 72 connects Bristol and Plainville with New Britain, Newington, Berlin, and Cromwell. Route 2 pierces East Hartford and Glastonbury, with Rte. 17 cutting down toward Portland and East Hampton before cutting back into Middletown. And U.S. 5 (the Berlin Tpke.) runs north–south from Wethersfield through Newington, Berlin, and Meriden.

# The Lower Connecticut River Valley

Given that southern Connecticut is far more populated and developed than the northern interior, it may come as some surprise that the stretch of the Connecticut River Valley that looks and feels the most as it did 200 years ago is the lower span—the towns south of Middletown to the shoreline. Only East Lyme and Old Saybrook, which are at the mouth of the river and are covered in the Coastal Connecticut chapter, look at all modern, and even they have a bounty of historic homes and quiet streets.

Edge your way up the western shore of the river and you'll come upon the Colonial shipbuilding village of Essex, where the British burned the town's commercial fleet during the War of 1812. Continue on through two hotbeds of Victorian trade and manufacture, Deep River and Chester, and then to the quiet town of Haddam—the only town in the state whose residents live on both sides of the river and have to drive through neighboring towns to reach the other side. Farther west, Killingworth and Durham are rural towns where family farms still play a significant role in the local economy.

Drive up the east side of the river from East Lyme and you'll encounter an even more authentic slice of the past, from Lyme, which has but a handful of traffic lights and businesses, to East Haddam, whose riverside village was a popular resort among the steamboat set during the mid-19th century—several towering Victorians, including the restored Goodspeed Opera House, stand guard over the community.

## HADDAM TO CHESTER

### Higganum

A good way to conquer the lower Connecticut River Valley is to begin in Middletown and work your way down toward the coast. Follow Rte. 154 south and you'll quickly pass into the tiny Higganum section of Haddam, where at Rte. 81 (Killingworth Road), there are a few local shops and stores. If you're an enthusiast of afternoon teas and fine gardens, follow Rte. 81 south about 2.7 miles south of where it passes under Rte. 9 to Brault Hill Road. A right turn leads up to **Sundial Gardens** (Brault Hill Rd., 860/345-4290, www.sundialgardens.com, gardens open daily, $2), a remarkable old homestead that hosts a full afternoon tea on Sunday from January through mid-October (reservations required). The beautifully groomed grounds consist of distinct gardens laid out with designs from different periods, from the 16th century to the present. A highlight is the topiary garden with a fountain. There's also an herb shop, gourmet foods, and, from just after Thanksgiving until Christmas Eve, a Christmas shop.

### Killingworth

After leaving the gardens, you can return to Higganum the way you came or, for a scenic side trip back to town, turn right onto Rte. 81 and continue south into Killingworth, a heavily wooded town even less developed than the towns along the river. Killingworth, by the way, was named Kenilworth originally. You know how people sometimes grow up with peculiar nicknames derived from a sibling's inability to pronounce the given name correctly? This sometimes happens to the names of towns, too.

## Durham

Numerous patches of Cockaponset State Forest, several of them laced with trails, are found across town. Turn right onto Rte. 148 and follow it to Rte. 79, where a right turn leads into Durham, the site of one of the best-attended agricultural fairs in Connecticut. Named Cogingchaug by its earliest indigenous inhabitants, which translates roughly (and unflatteringly) to "Long Swamp," the town looks a bit more promising today—indeed, it's developed considerable cachet in recent years for being a pretty, relatively underdeveloped community within easy commuting distance of New Haven, Middletown, Hartford, and even Waterbury.

A great lesson in humility was learned by the early Congregational settlers of Durham. The community at that time split into two rival factions, each determined to build a taller and more prestigious church than the other. For some time, the race escalated, and the spires of the respective buildings were thrust higher and higher—the costs grew, too, so that each congregation ultimately ended up borrowing money to achieve its lofty aim. South Church won. In 1842, as if borrowing a page from the very finest works of Greek mythology, a violent storm roared through Durham and toppled the steeple, which plunged like a dagger through the roof of the building.

In the charming center of town you'll find a smattering of appealing shops, most within a short walk of the town green, on which the aforementioned aggie fairs are held. It's one of the region's prettiest greens, surrounded by lovely old Colonial and Victorian buildings. At the south end of the town center, where Rtes. 79, 77, and 17 meet, a right turn onto Higganum Road (which turns into Candlewood Hill Road at the Haddam border) will

lead you back to Haddam and the intersection of Rtes. 154 and 81.

## Haddam

Haddam prospered originally from shipbuilding and various merchant concerns, as did so many other towns along this stretch of the Connecticut. Follow Rte. 154 south into Haddam proper to **Haddam Meadows State Park** (860/566-2304), with great views of the river. This 175-acre park has a few playing fields, but makes a great stop whether you're out for a game or not. Picnic tables overlook the river, and boat launches are available. Across the river is another chunk of Haddam, which is rather strange as you can't reach it except by crossing the river to East Haddam and driving north a good ways to "re-enter" Haddam. For many years, the Haddam Connecticut Yankee Nuclear Power Plant on the eastern shore supplied the region with electricity, and Haddam with tremendous tax revenue, but the plant was decommissioned in the late 1990s, and there's now considerable debate over what to do with the old hulking monolith.

Opposite the park entrance, slightly down Rte. 154, is the historic town hall at Rte. 154 and Walkley Hill Road. The **Thankful Arnold House** (Hayden Hill and Walkley Hill Roads, 860/345-2400, open for tours, but limited hours or by appointment). This gambrel-roofed 1794 house is the base of the Haddam Historical Society and a good place to learn of the community's 300-year history. A garden beside the house raises produce and flowers that would have been common at a homestead during Colonial times.

## East Haddam

From the south end of Haddam, Rte. 82 leads over the Connecticut River via a handsome old drawbridge into East Haddam, whose Victorian Village is set on a low bluff overlooking the river. The most prominent feature here is **Goodspeed Opera House** (860/873-8668, www.goodspeed.org), a magnificent 1876 structure built by a local shipping magnate named William H. Goodspeed. Free tours (call ahead

© ANDREW COLLINS

**old rail station, Haddam**

for a schedule) are offered June–Oct. on Saturday and Monday, and visitors are welcome to wander the glorious grounds, where picnicking is encouraged.

A four-story Second Empire wedding cake with turrets, a mansard roof, and lavish details consistent with Victorian excess, the opera house enjoyed a great first several decades, but fell to disuse by the middle of the century and was all set for demolition by 1958. During a time remarkably bereft of preservation-minded forces, locals nevertheless banded together and saved the place; a few years later it was buzzing with top-flight musicals. The theater seats 360 in grand style, and a long, winding staircase marks the entrance to the lobby. A classy old bar of walnut and brass overlooks the river, and Victorian wallpapering completes the fanciful look. Down the hill and fronting the river is a steamboat passenger terminal, where cruises from Essex debark. And within steps of the building are a few eateries and quaint shops.

East Haddam has several historic districts and

is a fine place for country driving and biking (although it's quite hilly, so be prepared for some hard pedaling). From the area around Goodspeed, follow Rte. 82 east, making a right onto River Road. Follow this winding way until you see signs for one of the most peculiar attractions in Connecticut, **Gillette Castle State Park** (see the sidebar "The House that Sherlock Holmes Built").

From the park, continue south on River Road to Rte. 148, just down a steep incline from Gillette Castle. A left turn will lead you to the small aforementioned ferry terminal, where it's possible from spring until early fall to take your car across the river to Chester—the ferry service here dates from 1769. For more touring of this stuck-in-time community, head east on Rte. 148 until it meets back with Rte. 82. (Note along the way the turn for Joshuatown Road, on your right, which leads to Selden Road, the turnoff for Seldon Neck State Park, a small island in the Connecticut River that can be explored only by boat.)

CONN. RIVER VALLEY

## THE HOUSE THAT SHERLOCK HOLMES BUILT

**G**illette Castle State Park, a 184-acre wooded ridge offering spectacular views over the Connecticut River, was once the estate of the great 19th-century stage actor William Gillette, who earned great acclaim for his stage portrayals of Sherlock Holmes.

Gillette was an eccentric with perhaps more than a passing desire to be noticed, and he designed an enormous 24-room fieldstone castle—it took five years to build at a cost of more than $1 million—and filled it with curious furnishings, which you can now observe today largely as they were left. The actor died in 1937, and left a will stipulating that "the property not fall into the hands of some blithering saphead who has no conception of where he is or with what surrounded." Gillette wanted his lifelong project to be preserved, and to this end the state took over and developed it into a state park in 1943.

He also created a working three-mile-long miniature railway, which is no longer operative, though you can walk along the old rail bed of what Gillette called the Seventh Sister Shortline (so named because the property is situated upon the southernmost of seven hills, known as the Seven Sisters, which flank the eastern banks of the lower Connecticut River). There's even a small stone rail terminal, Grand Central Station, and one trail passes through an old rail tunnel. In fact, the grounds are laced with nature trails and picnic groves (there's a seasonal snack bar on the premises), and the views of this especially pristine turn in the river are outstanding. Spring through fall, you'll see the little auto ferry chugging back and forth across the river, from Chester to the landing just below the castle, in the village of Hadlyme (which straddles the border of the two towns for which it is named, East Haddam and Lyme). Gillette Castle (67 River Rd., 860/526-2336), which underwent a massive restoration completed in spring 2003, is open daily Memorial Day to Columbus Day, and weekends thereafter until Thanksgiving. Admission is $5. The park grounds are open daily year-round.

## Lyme and Hamburg

If you were to continue east on Rte. 82, you'd eventually hit Rte. 156, which passes down through Lyme alongside a handful of horse farms, bringing you to East Lyme. Along the route you'll pass a wide expanse of the Eight Mile River, fringed by the quaint village of Hamburg. The river drains into Hamburg Cove, part of the Connecticut River, and is one of the state's great places for spotting wildlife—including bobcats, otters, red foxes, great horned owls, American bald eagles, and other animals that have become increasingly uncommon elsewhere in heavily developed southern New England. The **Eightmile River Watershed Project,** 860/345-4511, works to protect this gorgeous and diverse landscape, more than 80 percent of which remains heavily forested. If you're interested in learning how to help balance the growth of this region with its preservation, this is an excellent resource.

## Moodus

Follow Rte. 82 north to Mt. Parnassus Road,

make a right, and follow until it becomes Millington Road and eventually takes you to one of the region's favorite places for hiking, **Devil's Hopyard State Park,** in the eastern side of town. Along Millington Road, you'll also drive through the **Millington Green Historic District,** a small community of preserved 18th-century homes.

Back at Rte. 82, follow it north, but rather than returning the way you came, to East Haddam, continue north at Rte. 151 into another of East Haddam's funny little villages, Moodus. Fronting the lovely town green in Moodus is the **Amasa Day House** (Rtes. 149 and 151, 860/873-8144 or 860/247-8996, seasonal hours, open late May–mid-Oct., $3), which was constructed in 1816 and purchased at auction by Amasa Day in 1843—it fetched a princely $3,000. Inside are three generations of Day furnishings and antiquities.

From here, drive south along Rte. 149, which curves back down along the Connecticut River to Goodspeed Opera House. Shortly before you reach Rte. 82, you'll notice tiny **St.**

**Stephens Church,** behind which is the **Nathan Hale Schoolhouse,** 860/873-9547, where the Revolutionary War hero taught briefly as a young man. In the belfry of St. Stephens there's a Spanish bell that was allegedly cast in A.D. 815, although many scholars doubt that it's anywhere near this old. On Rte. 82 is the relatively new home of the **East Haddam Historical Society** (264 Town St., 860/873-3944, limited hours), which contains period clothing, photographs, a fascinating model of the Goodspeed Opera House, and many other exhibits.

## CHESTER TO ESSEX
### Chester
From East Haddam, take either the ferry or Rte. 82 back across the river to visit Chester, whose quaint downtown centers around the intersection of Rte. 148 and Main Street. It's one of the area's best spots for shopping and dining. It's also home to the unique **Connecticut River Artisans Cooperative** (5 W. Main St., 860/526-5575), an exceptional contemporary and traditional gallery presenting the work of several locals.

Chester, a picturesque Victorian river town, is a great place to grab a bite to eat. It sits on a stretch of the Connecticut River named by the Nature Conservancy as one of "the last great places on earth." A little town of 3,500, it was a key ship-building and light, water-powered manufacturing center until the 20th century, but is now fairly quiet and perfectly preserved, its main street alive with intriguing little shops that are mostly inside 19th-century buildings.

From Chester, drive south along Rte. 154 into **Deep River,** which is less quaint than neighboring Chester and Essex, an almost hardened little river community with remnants of Victorian industry.

### Essex
Continue south into Essex, a small town justly renowned for its shipbuilding heritage. In summer, the town's riverside marinas, which now occupy the sites of several prominent Colonial and Victorian shipbuilding concerns, glow with colorful sailboat and pleasurecraft activity. In the book *100 Best Small Towns in America,* written in 1996 by Norman Crampton, Essex was named the number one small town in the nation. In-

downtown Chester

deed, life here appears to be quite idyllic—the historic downtown seems like a Hollywood set for a movie about Colonial times, with rows of restored clapboard buildings.

Probably the best way to get a sense of alluring Essex is to head into the delightful historic village, which is signposted from Rte. 154. You can learn a great deal at the **Connecticut River Museum** (67 Main St., 860/767-8269, www.ctrivermuseum.org, open 10 A.M.–5 P.M. Tues.–Sun., $5), which traces both the Dutch and English settlers who originated explorations of the river. The museum opened in the mid-1970s and comprises two historic buildings five miles north of where the river opens into Long Island Sound. It's an ideal spot for picnicking and bird-watching. Inside an 1870s steamboat warehouse you'll find a permanent collection of ship models and maritime artifacts and detailed exhibits on the entire length of the river, from Long Island Sound to lower Quebec. A highlight is a full-scale working reproduction of America's first submarine, *The Turtle,* which was constructed in hopes that it would be the Continental Army's "secret weapon" during the American Revolution. Another display illuminates the history of Connecticut's first warship, the *Oliver Cromwell,* built in Essex in 1776. There's also an exhibit illustrating Ivoryton's history as the nation's foremost producer of ivory piano keys.

A great way to spend a day getting to know the river is to combine your visit to the Connecticut River Museum with a tour on the **Essex Steam Train and Riverboat Ride** (1 Railroad Ave., 860/767-0103, www.valleyrr.com). The ride begins on a vintage train and runs from Essex north through Deep River, from which passengers have the option of returning by train or continuing via an old-fashioned steamboat to just below the Goodspeed Opera House in East Haddam. Back in the vintage station, the Depot Mercantile Company sells local products, railroad memorabilia, books, and artifacts. Special events, from music concerts to weekends when a historic red caboose is added to the run, are held throughout the year. There are runs on Presi-

dents and Easter weekends, Wednesday–Sunday in spring and fall, daily in summer, and then Friday–Sunday from Thanksgiving weekend to just before Christmas. The fare is $18.50 for adults for the combined train and boat ride, $10.50 for the train only.

## Ivoryton

On the western side of Essex, Rte. 602 leads into historic Ivoryton, named for the proliferation of ivory imported here back when Essex was a major merchant port. At one point, the vast majority of the ivory from Zanzibar made its way here. A memorable museum here is the **Museum of Fife & Drum** (62 N. Main St., 860/767-2237 or 860/399-6519, open weekends in summer, by appointment other times), which traces the nation's history of marching parades from the Revolutionary War to the present. This curious collection, a half mile north of the Ivoryton Playhouse, has a large main room with a music library, which is also where music presentations are offered. Inside are wooden drums and fifes, uniforms, and flags, plus photographs of drum corps of yore. One drum is believed to have been played at the Battle of Bunker Hill, while others saw action in the Civil War. The collection of fifes is equally prodigious. The museum is a favorite stop for kids and also for visiting members of drum corps from around the world.

# SHOPPING
## Chester

If Stickley furnishings are your thing, you must not miss **Ye Olde Tyler Merchant House,** at the junction of Rtes. 154 and 82 (Haddam, 800/613-0105), whose fine furnishings from the Arts and Crafts movement are rivaled by few such shops.

Chester is best known for its clutch of fun shops, many of them specializing in antiques and crafts. Just park along Main Street, and you'll find a couple hours' worth of browsing, including **Ceramica** (36 Main St., 860/526-9978), known for its handcrafted Italian tableware; **One of a Kind Antiques** (21 Main St.,

© ANDREW COLLINS

**Connecticut River Museum, Essex**

860/526-9736), which specializes in period American and British furnishings, plus estate jewelry; **Sarah Kate** (29 Main St., 860/526-3811), a smart women's clothier; and **Souleiado** (14 Main St., 860/526-1480), whose offerings range from French country furnishings to imported Simon Pearce glassware. If crafting is important to you, consider a visit to the **Chester Book Co.** (28 Ferry Rd., 860/526-9887), which specializes in crafts books. Local art is shown at **Chester Gallery** (76 Main St., 860/526-9822). Trish Ginter of **Lucille's Bridal Finery** (4 Water St., 860/526-3999) custom-designs stunning silk gowns, headpieces, and garters.

### Essex

Essex has a smattering of shops in its historic downtown. It's an appropriate setting for one of the state's top sources of books on maritime and nautical history, **Clipper Ship Bookstore** (12 N. Main St., 860/767-1666), and **Hastings House Antiques,** which specializes in Oriental scrolls and screens, plus a wide array of home and decorative arts. Delftware and fine European and American paintings are sold at **Bonsal-Douglas** (1 Essex Square, 860/767-2282). There

are about a dozen additional specialties shops, most of them on Main Street, whose wares range from the usual (rubber stamps, cards) to the more intriguing (nautical artifacts and gifts, handcrafted toys). Also drop by the **Essex Art Association Gallery** (10 N. Main St., 860/767-8996) that shows a wide variety of media.

## RECREATION
### Golf

The lower valley is without many golfing opportunities, but in the Moodus section of East Haddam is the short 18-hole **Leisure Resort at Banner** (10 Banner Rd., 860/873-9075).

### Hiking

There are miles of trails in the western reaches of the lower Connecticut River Valley, mostly running across the 15,000 acres of **Cockaponset State Forest,** which comprises patches of woodland throughout mostly Chester, Durham, Haddam, and Killingworth. The largest tract falls between the northern border of Chester and southern edge of Haddam, encompassing Pattaconk and Turkey Hill reservoir. The Cockaponset

CONN. RIVER VALLEY

Trail, which can be tackled as one 10-mile loop or via a series of simpler loops, is accessed via the **Lake Pattaconk State Recreation Area,** off Cedar Lake Road, which runs north from Rte. 148 and just west of Rte. 9 (exit 6). There's a beach here, which also makes it a nice spot for swimming.

Quite near the center of quiet Killingworth, you'll find a slice of Cockaponset State Forest that abuts **Chatfield Hollow State Park** (860/663-2030), one of the lesser-used hiking venues in the lower Connecticut River Valley. The main entrance and parking area is on the north side of Rte. 80, about a mile west of its junction with Rte. 81; the park is also accessible from its northern end, off dirt Abner Lane, which is just south off of Rte. 148. Once here, you'll find a large area for swimming, fishing, and picnicking at Schreeder Pond, which is close to the park entrance and can be quite popular on summer weekends, but is still relatively free of overcrowding. A handful of good trails circumnavigate the park, crossing over a few mildly steep ridges in places and revealing some nice thickets of mountain laurel.

Perhaps best appreciated as a fine source of bird-watching, East Haddam's 860-acre **Devil's Hopyard State Park** (366 Hopyard Rd., 860/873-8566) is pierced by the thundering Eight Mile River, whose 60-foot waterfalls and adjoining mill ruins are a favorite point of exploration. This is an extensive and well-maintained member of the state park system, with camping, shelters, fireplaces, picnic areas, and excellent hiking trails. There are several good routes to the park (one of which is detailed in the East Haddam section). The most straightforward is to follow Rte. 82 as it runs along the Lyme and East Haddam border, just past Rte. 82. Make a left onto Hopyard Road and follow it right to the heart of the park.

## ENTERTAINMENT AND NIGHTLIFE
### Arts and Culture
The **Goodspeed Opera House** (860/873-8668, www.goodspeed.org) presents touring productions of nationally acclaimed major musicals, with a season running April–December. While performances are held Wednesday–Sunday, note that several local restaurants offer excellent pre-theater dinner specials on Wednesday and Thursday (call the theater for details). There's also a second facility, the **Norma Terris Theatre** (N. Main St., Chester, 860/873-8668), which is geared more toward new shows, emerging musicals, and world premieres.

A great summer stock venue is the **Ivoryton Playhouse** (103 Main St., 860/767-8348 or 860/767-7318), which also hosts a year-round children's theater and a variety of concerts.

## FESTIVALS AND EVENTS
In late May, the steamboat *Lady Fenwick* makes its annual **Northwest Passage** cruise, 860/526-4954, an all-day jaunt from the foot of Main Street in Essex up the Connecticut River to Hartford. In mid-June, the Essex Steam Train and Riverboat company presents the **Hot Steamed Jazz Festival** (800/348-0003) at its historic rail depot at 1 Railroad Avenue. In mid-July, about 2,000 marchers from about 70 fife-and-drum corps take part in the **Deep River Ancient Muster** (Devitt's Field, off Rte. 154, 860/526-1255).

Come early fall, the Connecticut River Museum stages the **Traditional Vessels Weekend** (860/767-8269), three days of boat races and maritime festivities. Later in the month, crustacean devotees might want to check out the **Chester Rotary Club Annual Lobster Fest** (Chester Fairgrounds, Rte. 154, 860/526-2122). Also at the end of the month, the largest "aggie" fair in Connecticut, the **Durham Fair** (860/349-9495) gears up at Durham Fairgrounds—internationally known music performers are typically are part of the festivities. Around Columbus Day weekend, **RiverFest** (Connecticut River Museum, 67 Main St., Essex, 860/767-8269) is one of the most popular events in the lower valley. Rowing fans won't want to miss the **Head of the Connecticut Regatta,** a 3K rowing race staged at Middletown's HarborPark, 860/346-1042.

Over the Presidents' Day weekend, the Connecticut Audubon Society sponsors the **Connecticut River Eagle Festival** (800/714-7201,

© ANDREW COLLINS

Griswold Inn, Essex

www.ctaudubon.org/eagle.htm), a free event (the only part charged for was an optional boat ride along the river where participants reported seeing dozens of bald eagles). The festivities include live entertainment, food, interpretive displays, and ice-carving demonstrations. In early February, Chester has a **Winter Carnivale** (860/526-2077) complete with an outdoor ice-carving competition and shop and gallery receptions.

## ACCOMMODATIONS

In keeping with the peaceful and low-key spirit of the region, the lower Connecticut River Valley is virtually without motels and chain properties; however, Old Saybrook fringes Essex and has several such accommodations. What you will find in these parts is a handful of historic inns, among the most characterful in the state. Similarly, both Old Saybrook and East Lyme have more of the same and are good bases from which to approach the lower valley.

### Hotels and Motels
**$100–$150:** The family-operated **Sunrise Resort** (Rte. 151, Moodus, 860/873-8681 or 800/225-9033, www.sunriseresort.com) has long

been a fixture of the lower valley, offering a something-for-everyone peaceful getaway with the sorts of diversions and activities that keep both adults and kids happy. On 400 acres you'll find a massive pool, tennis, mountain biking, horseback riding, hot tubs, softball and basketball courts, dancing and live music, mini golf, and boating along the Salmon River. A team of social directors plans out the day's activities, and many meals are set around corny but fun themes (think Hawaiian luau). Accommodations include meals and most activities; additionally, day visitors may pay to come for meals and to enjoy the grounds; call for details.

### Country Inns and Bed-and-Breakfasts
**$150–250:** A newcomer compared with the Griswold (see below), Ivoryton's **Copper Beech Inn** (46 Main St., 860/767-0330 or 888/809-2056, www.copperbeechinn.com) was once the seven-acre estate of one of the village's wealthy ivory merchants, Mr. A. W. Comstock (as in Comstock Piano Keys, which were produced here). You get a nice bit of the area's history staying here, not to mention some of the most beautiful accommodations in the state. New owners took over the property in 2002 and have given it

CONN. RIVER VALLEY

a much-needed top-to-bottom restoration. Only a few of the rooms are in the main house, which is also the site of the first-rate restaurant; nine others are in a dramatic carriage house with cathedral ceilings and a more contemporary, though still soothingly countrified, look—the bathrooms have large whirlpool tubs. Two rooms have private sundecks. A particularly nice draw here is the lavishly landscaped and heavily shaded grounds.

The handsome **Gelston House** (8 Main St., Rte. 82, East Haddam, 860/873-1411, www.gelstonhouse.com) looks more than a little like its neighbor, the Goodspeed Opera House. This dramatic 1850s structure, crowned with a magnificent white cupola, has led a colorful life, having harbored rumrunners during Prohibition, and having served as an enlistment center during the Civil War. Today, it's known throughout the region for its superb restaurant, but don't overlook the six lavish guest rooms, some with views of the opera house and the river, all with cable TV, private baths, and ornate Victorian furnishings.

A longtime favorite, the **Inn & Vineyard at Chester** (318 Main St./Rte. 148, 860/526-9541 or 800/949-7829, www.innatchester.com), was bought and virtually reinvented in 2003 as a new luxury country hotel and spa. All 43 rooms were remade with deluxe furnishings and updated amenities, and the property's ten wooded acres have been laid out with groomed hiking trails. High-speed wireless Internet access is available in rooms and throughout the grounds and public areas, and rooms also have cordless phones equipped with voicemail. The spa offers every imaginable treatment, and as of press time, the inn is continuing to renovate and upgrade. The main restaurant, set inside an 18th-century barn, serves sterling contemporary American cuisine, while the less formal Jack's Bar and Grill specializes in single-malt scotches and lighter fare.

Stay at the six-room Federal-style **Bishopsgate Inn** (Goodspeed Landing, East Haddam, 860/873-1677, www.bishopsgate.com), which was built in 1818 by a wealthy merchant and shipbuilder, and you'll awaken each day just steps from the Goodspeed Opera House, the delightful Landing Market Cafe, and the more formal Gelston House. In fact, everything you could

possibly require for a sumptuous and memorable weekend away from home you'll find within walking distance of this splendid inn, whose rooms are done with pencil-post feather beds, Early American repro antiques (plus quite a few authentic pieces), and one room with a private sauna. This option is less expensive than some of the larger country inns in the lower valley, not because the rooms are any less gracious, but simply because it's a smaller spot with fewer facilities—it's really quite a good value.

**$100–150:** Quiet Killingworth is the appropriate setting for so bucolic and inviting an accommodation as the **Acorn B&B and Antiques** (628 Rte. 148, 860/663-2214, www.acornbedandbreakfast.com), a cheerful two-guest room Cape on a countrified plot of mature oak trees. A brick back patio leads to an in-ground pool, near which is a relaxing hot tub. Common areas are furnished with Arts and Crafts furnishings from the Old Hickory Company.

Whether or not it's truly the nation's oldest continuously operating inn, as the owners claim, is hardly important; the **Griswold Inn** (36 Main St., Essex, 860/767-1776, www.griswoldinn.com) is ancient, and set along a flawlessly beguiling stretch of historic Essex's Colonial Main Street. You expect horse-drawn carriages to clatter along outside the front door. Rooms reflect the age of the place in both good and sometimes not-so-good ways—the "Gris" exudes ambience, but is not especially cutting edge (no TVs in guest rooms) or luxurious, and so shouldn't be considered if a Ritz-Carlton sort of experience is what you're seeking. But all do have phones, and some have fireplaces.

Highly romantic inns are very much a theme of the lower Connecticut River Valley, and Deep River's **Riverwind** (209 Main St., 860/526-2014, www.riverwindinn.com) pulls this theme off as well as any. Its eight guest rooms (one of them a full suite) and several warm common areas are replete with antiques and collectibles—there's nothing spare about Riverwind. A very fine full breakfast is served. New owners bought the place in summer 2002, and they have done a great job carrying on the inn's tradition of warm hospitality.

Only one accommodation in Chester allows

you to be within walking distance of the wonderful shopping and dining downtown. That is **123 Main Street** (123 Main St., 860/526-3456, www.123main.net), a yellow Victorian farmhouse whose sweeping porch and lawn look directly into the village. Five guest rooms have polished hardwood floors, period-style wallpapering, and a smattering of antiques. Two rooms share a bath, and these can be booked together—nice if you're traveling with children (kids over 10 are welcome). Full breakfast is included on weekends, Continental the rest of the time.

## Campgrounds

**Devil's Hopyard State Park** (366 Hopyard Rd., East Haddam, 860/873-8566) is among the most enchanting parks for camping in the state, its 21 sites within an earshot of the pacifying roar of 60-foot Chapman Falls. Contact **Gillette Castle State Park** (860/526-2336) for reservations and information on the two scenic campgrounds in Haddam and East Haddam along the Connecticut River. One campsite is upriver along the banks of **Hurd State Park** (Rte. 151, East Hampton, 860/526-2336) and the other is at the accessible-only-by-water Selden Neck State Park, which is just south of Gillette.

## FOOD

There aren't a whole lot of restaurants in the lower valley, but those you do find rank among the most romantic and appealing, although in some cases expensive, in the state. Some of the favorites are inside country inns, while others occupy vintage buildings in the quaint villages of East Haddam and Chester. There are no ethnic eateries in these parts, but given the wealth of such restaurants in nearby Middletown and Old Saybrook, nobody seems to miss them. Simpler and less expensive fare is found at a handful of traditional pub-style taverns dotting the region.

### Upscale

**Sage on the Waterfall** (129 W. Main St., 860/526-9898, $14–25) offers a range of contemporary American food, plus lighter fare such as burgers and lobster rolls. Fashioned from a sprawling 19th-century brush mill, it's reached via a covered footbridge over roaring cascades. Evergreens tower over the property, and a fireplace and friendly staff warm the inside.

The luster of the **Copper Beech Inn** (46 Main St., 860/767-0330, $24–36) is as visible from the building's immaculately restored 1880s gabled exterior as it is from the superbly understated service. And then there's the truly exceptional food, thanks to a change in ownership in 2002. Consider fillet of sole stuffed with a purée of Nantucket Bay scallops and served with a sublime lobster-ginger sauce; or the dessert classic of caramel-apple pie, served with house-made Calvados ice cream. A wonderful bright solarium off the dining room is ideal for pre- or post-dinner drinks. This is the sort of place where you might pop the big question over dinner—and you might just want to spend your wedding night at the inn.

In a wonderfully decadent 1853 Victorian, just steps from the Goodspeed Opera House, theater-goers and gourmands alike can't seem to fuss enough about the fine Continental cuisine of the **Gelston House** (8 Main St., Rte. 82, East Haddam, 860/873-1411, $16–27), whose dining areas include a spacious sun porch with views of the Connecticut River. Dishes like lobster and scallop-stuffed haddock in a white wine sauce as well as duck roulade with lentils set the tone for a romantic first-class dining experience. There's both a formal restaurant here and a tavern serving lighter cuisine.

The three-story **Griswold Inn** (36 Main St., Essex, 860/767-1776, $14–26) has been a fixture of this Colonial river village for well over 200 years, and the menu offers up a number of dishes that might very well have been available on opening night: a mixed grill of fresh, farmer's, and smoked country sausages with sauerkraut and German potato salad (okay, maybe if there were Hessian soldiers present that night), and traditional—absolutely delicious—New England chicken pot pie. More contemporary offerings include potato-crusted boneless trout with a sundried tomato cream sauce and spit-roasted duckling with a dried-cherry port wine sauce, but this cuisine rarely strays from a traditional course and is sometimes criticized for being old hat. Nonetheless, the place is always packed and ready to show visitors a rollicking good time—there's live banjo, jazz, and swing music nightly. One dining room is fashioned out of an old covered bridge that was imported from New Hampshire, and a tap room dating to 1738 was originally a schoolhouse.

More than a few dining critics have called **Restaurant du Village** (59 Main St., 860/526-5301, $22–33) the finest French restaurant in Connecticut, and so you might be surprised upon your first visit to discover a dining room that is homey and unprepossessing, reminiscent of a country farmhouse in Aix-en-Provence. The food is similarly without pretensions: snails Alsatian, broiled with a garlic-parsley sauce; half-duckling roasted crispy with an orange and lemon sauce and a balsamic reduction, medallions of filet mignon with black truffle sauce. If these dishes sound uncomplicated, it's because they're not—purists will find little fault with this eatery in quaint downtown Chester.

## Creative but Casual

**Fiddlers** (4 Water St., Chester, 860/526-3210, $16–22) has a tasteful dining room with a few nautical paintings, and serves tantalizing high-quality seafood, from oyster stew, conch fritters, whole steamed lobsters, and bouillabaisse.

An urbane, minimalist bistro with narrowly spaced tables and etched-glass wall dividers, **River Tavern** (15 Main St., 860/526-9417, $17–23) is something of a counterpoint to Chester's very high quaintness factor. The short but sweet menu offers many nightly specials, such as grilled, brined fresh mackerel with tomato purée and lemon; and roast herb-stuffed chicken with apple-and-leak puree and crisp potato tart. There's also a great selection of single malts and small-batch bourbons.

## Steak, Pizza, Pub Grub, and Seafood

The **Pattaconk 1850 Bar & Grille** (33 Main St., Chester, 860/526-8143, $6–17) is an authentic locals' hangout—complete with extensive glowing beer signage—in a town that's known more for its quaint and rather upscale eateries. The menu is immense, ranging from

traditional Italian and American fare, with an emphasis on seafood (baked stuffed sole, seafood primavera), to burgers, clam pizzas, deli sandwiches, and a nice Cobb salad. In East Haddam, folks gather for nachos, Philly cheesesteaks, London broil, shrimp scampi, and other basic comfort foods at **Hale & Hearty** (381 Town St., Rte. 82, 860/873-2640, $8–16). It has a tavern on one side and a slightly more formal, though still very relaxed, dining room on the other. Both rooms are warmed by fireplaces, and so a relaxing and convivial atmosphere makes this a nice spot for unfussy food—it's great for kids, and close to Gillette Castle and Goodspeed Opera House. Killingworth's **Country Squire** (243–247 Rte. 80, east of Rte. 81, 860/663-3228, $7–19) is housed in an 18th-century building, and offers traditional American cuisine in a handsome, if slightly heavy-handed atmosphere.

A great find if you have kids in tow or are simply looking for a casual affordable meal, the noisy but fun **Oliver's Taverne** (124 Westbrook Rd., Rte. 153, Essex, 860/767-2633, $8–22) has great lunch deals. Nightly, you can expect great sticky baby back ribs and other down-home fare.

The **Black Seal** (15 Main St., Essex, 860/767-0233, $7–16) offers standard pub fare and a nice range of beers—it's a fun place to gather with friends. A strangely alluring little spot by Midway Marina, along the Connecticut River, is the **Blue Oar** (16 Snyder Rd., Haddam, 860/345-2994, $10–16). It's little more than a shanty, with seating on a porch or at picnic tables—about as pure a riverside dining experience as you'll find in southern New England. The staff is low-key and friendly—you must bring your own wine or beer, no credit cards are accepted, and the john is in the adjacent marina. What makes this place a winner is fresh-as-the-day seafood, much of it prepared with creative sauces and sides. Good bets include mussel bisque, steamed clams, and grilled salmon. Call ahead before eating here, as hours vary and the place is closed during the winter.

In Higganum's town center, the gambrel-roofed **Glockenspiel** (26 Killingworth Rd., Rte. 81, 860/345-4697, $12–22) serves traditional, if heavy, German and American fare, such as Wiener schnitzel, sauerbraten, and knockwurst.

© ANDREW COLLINS

Queen of Tarts bakery, Chester

## Quick Bites

In culinarily bereft Deep River (there just aren't many restaurants here compared with neighboring river towns), a simple but fun option for breakfast or lunch is the **Whistlestop Cafe** (108 Main St., 860/526-4122, under $8), a tiny clapboard building set amid the old brick factory buildings that dominate the northern part of Rte. 154.

## Java Joints

**Queen of Tarts** (16 Main St., Chester, 860/526-5024) serves very good pastries and sweets, and is also a good source for coffees and snacks. It's one of a handful of good lunch options in downtown Chester. **Essex Coffee and Tea Company** (51 Main St., 860/767-7804) is a cozy white clapboard café across from the Griswold Inn in downtown Essex, a short walk from the town

pier and Connecticut River Museum. Scones, pastries, iced and hot drinks are the bill of fare.

## Gourmet Goods and Picnic Supplies

In the heart of Chester's old-fashioned downtown, another possibility for outstanding picnic fare is the very rustic **Wheatmarket** (4 Water St., 860/526-9347), a cozy gourmet market that can make you a picnic basket to go from shelves piled high with delectables. **Simon's Marketplace** (17 Main St., Chester, 860/767-1452) is a great source of gourmet foods, sandwiches, deli items, and gifts. It's sort of an idealized country store. The soups and specials change daily. In Essex, you can pick up gourmet sandwiches, prepared salads and foods, and first-rate cheeses and pátés at **Olive Oyl's Carry-out Cuisine** (77 Main St., 860/767-4909).

## INFORMATION AND SERVICES
### Visitor Information

Most of the towns in this region are served by the **Greater Hartford Tourism District** (31 Pratt St., Hartford, CT 06103, 860/244-8181 or 800/793-4480, www.enjoyhartford.com). The one exception is Lyme, which falls within the **Southeastern Connecticut Tourism District** (470 Bank St., New London, CT 06320, 860/444-2206 or 800/TO-ENJOY, www.mysticmore.com).

### Getting Around

The quickest way to get from town to town along the west side of the valley is via Rte. 9, which runs from Middletown to Old Saybrook, passing through Haddam, Chester, Deep River, and Essex. Arterial east–west state roads lead from this limited-access highway to East Haddam (and then Lyme), Durham, and Killingworth. A more scenic way of taking in the area is along Rte. 154, which hugs the river's western shore most of the way down.

# The Western Hills

North of the immediate coastal slope, Connecticut is divided geologically into three parts: the Connecticut River Valley, which dominates the state's midsection, and the eastern and western hills, which ascend precipitously on either side of this basin. In these western hills, which take in all of Litchfield County and the northern halves of Fairfield and New Haven Counties, the terrain is more severe and dramatic than in the state's eastern hills. Both sides are sparsely settled (given Connecticut's overall population density), especially the farther north you go, but the western hills are within easy driving distance of New York City. This proximity to a metropolis known for its high-profile celebrities and executives has had a profound effect on tourism here.

Hundreds of big-name actors, musicians, artists, directors, newscasters, writers, and other media personalities either own homes in Connecticut's western hills or vacation here regularly. For every one famous face that frequents these parts, perhaps 20 not so recognizable but still well-heeled captains of industry reside here. You can live in rural Litchfield County and still drive into New York City within a couple of hours, and down to coastal Fairfield County in even less time. For many people, this region offers rural yet sophisticated living, along with easy access to America's largest and most exciting metropolitan area.

© ANDREW COLLINS

West Cornwall's covered bridge

The region's proliferation of padded wallets and demanding consumers has infused what may on the surface look like a rustic and even primitive landscape with a high number of big-ticket restaurants, elegant antiques shops, and fine country inns. Ten-acre 18th-century farmsteads routinely sell for $1 million in towns like Washington and Norfolk, and yet the cost of living in these parts is not high when compared with posh Fairfield County. The closer you get to Fairfield County, a commuter belt rife with corporate headquarters, the greater the number of suburban-looking neighborhoods and correspondingly higher real estate costs.

One section that acts as a foil to greater Litchfield and northern Fairfield County is the Naugatuck River Valley, a string of largely depressed industrial towns that make for interesting exploring, but lack the amenities, upscale eateries and shops, and conspicuous charm of the rest of the western hills. Contrary to what you might expect, however, there are abundant and rewarding opportunities for hiking, horseback riding, skiing, and mountain biking throughout the entire region, from the more densely populated lower Naugatuck and Housatonic River Valleys right up into the Litchfield Hills.

Connecticut's shoreline seems to garner more attention, but the western hills comprise some of New England's most picturesque and captivating landscapes. A tour through this area, perhaps beginning in Ridgefield and weaving northward through New Milford, Kent, Cornwall, Washington, Woodbury, Litchfield, and then finally Norfolk, is a journey that reveals Connecticut's considerable appeal better than any other.

## A FEW PRACTICALITIES
### Media
There are several small regional weekly papers serving towns in Litchfield County, the most prestigious and comprehensive being the *Litchfield County Times* (860/355-4121, www.countytimes.com), which provides witty commentary, colorful interviews, and solid news reporting on

## SMALL-TOWN NEWS (WITH BIG-TIME NAMES)

*Litchfield County Times Monthly* (860/355-4121) may seem—upon first glance—like any other local-features monthly produced in any other rural part of the world. It's filled with current arts and entertainment information on the county, as well as some well-written features and historical stories. But read it a bit more closely and you'll start noticing that it's filled rather often with names of famous actors, artists, and writers.

It's published as part of the weekly *Litchfield County Times*, which is one of the more colorful little newspapers you'll ever lay eyes on. Stories range from the usual small-town scuttlebutt to rather discreet celeb gossip, which is fairly easy to come by in these parts. A typical front page in the late 1990s, for example, detailed the sale of the home of director Mike Nichols and television news journalist Diane Sawyer to international clothier William Rondina (owner of the Carlisle Collection). The same paper had a personable appreciation of local resident "Sandy Calder" (better known to you and me as sculptor Alexander Calder, who lived in Litchfield County until his death in 1976). Another account, of a debate on a local country club's petition for the right to siphon water from a local lake, quoted remarks for and against at the local town meeting. One by one, a local realtor, veterinarian, teacher, and so on gave his or her thoughts, culminating in an ironically soft-spoken objection by the playwright (and vitriolic AIDS- and gay-rights activist) Larry Kramer.

Such detailed glimpses into the lives of world-renowned figures are casually interspersed with pieces about local book sales and real estate news and school board elections, in such a way that one is made constantly aware that Litchfield County is all about small-town living, but also about the big-time personalities who seek it. The tone of the newswriting always underplays the fame of its subjects, as if to say, "Look, these people just happen to be our neighbors." But Litchfield residents are unquestionably proud of their celebrity by association and, discreet as they may claim to be, rarely pass up an opportunity to name names.

THE WESTERN HILLS

THE WESTERN HILLS

MASSACHUSETTS
CONNECTICUT

NEW YORK
CONNECTICUT

West Hartland
West Hartland
Riverton
West Branch Farmington River
New Hartford
Bakersville
New Hartford

5 mi

5 km

Colebrook Reservoir
West Branch Reservoir
West
Winsted
Colebrook
Winchester Center
Highland Lake
Burr Pond State Park
Paugnut State Forest
Sunnybrook S.P.
Harwinton

Litchfield-South Roads Historic Distric
Roraback Wildlife Management Area
Northfield Brook Lake
Thomaston Dam
Northfield

HITCHCOCK CHAIR MUSEUM
SOLOMON ROCKWELL HOUSE
COLEBROOK HISTORICAL SOCIETY
Colebrook

GREENWOODS THEATRE
Norfolk
NORFOLK HISTORICAL SOCIETY MUSEUM

Dennis Hill State Park

TORRINGTON HISTORICAL SOCIETY
Torrington

ACTION WILDLIFE FOUNDATION
Goshen
GOSHEN HISTORICAL MUSEUM

TAPPING REEVE HOUSE
Litchfield
Bantam Lake
SANDY BEACH
Humaston Brook State Park

Campbell Falls State Park
Haystack Mtn. State Park

Canaan

LAND OF NOD WINERY

Cornwall Hollow
Tyler Lake
Dog Pond
Woodridge Lake
WHITE MEMORIAL FOUNDATION
Bantam
Upper Shepaug Reservoir
H.O.R.S.E. OF CONNECTICUT
Woodville

O'HARA'S LANDING
Taconic
Twin Lakes
Salisbury

MUSIC MOUTAIN
Falls Village
Lime Rock
WEST CORNWALL COVERED BRIDGE
Cornwall
MOHAWK SKI AREA
Mohawk State Forest
Housatonic Meadows State Park
Warren
HOPKINS VINEYARD
Lake Waramaug

HOLLEY HOUSE MUSEUM
LIME ROCK PARK
West Cornwall
Housatonic River
Kent Falls State Park

Bear Mountain
Mt. Frissell
Lakeville
Twin Lakes

BEARDSLEY GARDENS
Sharon
SHARON AUDUBON CENTER
Cornwall Bridge
SLOANE-STANLEY MUSEUM & KENT FURNACE
Kent
Mount Bushnell S.P.
Macedonia Brook State Park
Macedonia

GAY-HOYT HOUSE MUSEUM
SHARON PLAYHOUSE

To Hartford

To New Haven

Wolcott

Bethany

69

Waterbury

69

TROLLEY STOP
LUNCHEONETTE
AND GENERAL STORE

63

Woodbridge

67

15

34

68

Beacon
Falls

8

Seymour

115

GENERAL DAVID
HUMPHREY'S HOUSE

VINTAGE
MOTOR CARS

To Bridgeport

THOMASTON
OPERA HOUSE

262

Waterbury

8

73

262

Oakville

63

Naugatuck

Naugatuck
State Forest

CATNIP ACRES
HERB NURSERY

Oxford

SEYMOUR
ANTIQUES CO.

Ansonia

Derby

Shelton

108

Morris

Thomaston

109

Black Rock
State Park

63

Watertown

WATERTOWN
HISTORICAL
SOCIETY MUSEUM

Lake
Quassapaug

Middlebury

63

GOLDEN AGE OF
TRUCKING MUSEUM

84

Osbornedale
State Park

34

110

SHELTON HISTORY
CENTER

Huntington

Morris

61

Bethlehem

PARADISE
VALLEY FARM

61

6

Woodbury

64

QUASSY
AMUSEMENT PARK

6

Southford Falls
State Park

SCHREIBER'S
FARM

River

STEVENSON
DAM

188

Kettletown
State Park

Indian Wells
State Park

JONES FAMILY
FARMS

FLANDERS
NATURE CENTER

BELLAMY-
FERRIDAY HOUSE

ABBEY OF
REGINA LAUDIS

132

GLEBE HOUSE
HURD HOUSE

317

172

South
Britain

CHURAEVKA
VILLAGE

Lake Zoar

LAKE ZOAR
WILDLIFE AREA

34

111

TWOMBLY NURSERY

Monroe

Stepney

GUNN MEMORIAL
LIBRARY & MUSEUM

109

Washington

47

PAINTER
RIDGE

WOODBURY
SKI AREA

67

Southbury

Housatonic

MCLAUGHLIN VINEYARDS

Sandy
Hook

302

Huntington
State Park

59

New Preston

River

Marbledale

202

WASHINGTON
ART ASSOCIATION

STEEP ROCK
RESERVATION

SILO

INSTITUTE FOR
AMERICAN INDIAN
STUDIES

199

Shepaug

Roxbury

67

Bridgewater

BRIDGEWATER
GENERAL STORE

133

THE BROOKFIELD
CRAFT CENTER

25

Newtown

84

6

Putnam
Memorial
State Park

53

Bethel

Danbury

107

Redding

58

Topstone
State Park

Gaylordsville

BULLS BRIDGE
COVERED BRIDGE

Northville

NEW MILFORD
HISTORICAL
SOCIETY

New Milford

67

SUNNY VALLEY
PRESERVE

7

202

Brookfield

Candlewood
Lake

7

To Norwalk

37

Sherman

SHERMAN
PLAYHOUSE

37

Squantz Pond
State Park

39

39

New
Fairfield

39

37

6

202

84

Ridgefield

35

CONNECTICUT

NEW YORK

55

22

THE WESTERN HILLS

© AVALON TRAVEL PUBLISHING, INC.

N

Litchfield and surrounding towns. *The Voice* (860/738-4026, www.thevoicenews.com) effectively captures the often strong libertarian views of the northwest hills—this Winsted-based alternative newsweekly offers insightful and provocative articles, plus a nice roundup of area goings-on, dining, shopping, and such. *The Register Citizen* (860/489-3121, www.registercitizen.com) is the daily paper covering Torrington and Winsted. The *Greater New Milford Spectrum* (860/354-2273, www.spectrum.newmilford.com) covers New Milford and the surrounding area with a weekly paper.

## Tours

There really aren't any guided-tour companies covering northwestern Connecticut, but a handful of outfitters listed below give special-interest tours, such as hot-air balloon rides.

Running flight-seeing tours out of Oxford's little airfield is **Capital Aviation** (Waterbury-Oxford Airport, 288 Christian St., Oxford, 203/264-3727 or 800/255-3727).

For a hot-air balloon adventure through the Housatonic River Valley, contact **Steppin' Up Balloons** (258 Old Woodbury Rd., Southbury, 203/264-0013), which has sunset and sunrise flights over the region. Reservations are required. Oxford's **Gone Ballooning** (5 Larkey Rd., 203/888-1322) offers flights over the Naugatuck and lower Housatonic River Valleys, as well as

into the southern Litchfield Hills. **Aer Blarney Balloons** (860/567-3448, www.aerblarney.com) is another reliable outfitter for ballooning.

**Loon Meadow Farm** (860/542-6085, http://loonmeadowfarm.com) has been offering horse-drawn hayrides through town for many years. Hot-mulled cider and a bonfire are enjoyed afterward. (To get there, take Maple Avenue, which becomes Lovers Lane, travel north from the village green in Norfolk for about two miles, and Loon Meadow Drive is on the right). In North Terryville, the very southeastern Litchfield Hills, **Wood Acres Farm** (68 Griffin Rd., 860/583-8670, www.woodacresfarm.com) also offers hay, sleigh, and carriage rides.

## Getting There

East–West I-84 and north–south Rte. 8 are the region's major limited access highways. A number of state roads also connect the region with other parts of the state, New York's Hudson River Valley, and Massachusetts's Berkshires.

An extensive network of interstate train and bus providers serves the western hills. Of particular note, is the convenient Metro-North train service from New York City to both Danbury and Waterbury. The region is also served by Bradley International Airport. Somewhat farther afield, but still convenient to the area, are New York City's JFK and La Guardia airports, and upstate New York's Westchester and Stewart airports.

# Western Litchfield County

Northern New Englanders often scoff at the notion that Connecticut is anything more than a big sprawling suburb of New York City. Let them wallow in their ignorance, for the western reaches of Litchfield County offer a near-perfect vision of rugged and unspoiled countryside. The tortuous Housatonic River dominates the landscape, entering the state in Canaan, on the Massachusetts border. It winds down through evergreen forests, under covered bridges, and beside bucolic Colonial hamlets where time has stood still (except to allow for the latest culinary and home-furnishing trends—okay, so New York City isn't so far away).

Although New Milford, at the lower end of the region, teems with chain department stores and fast-food restaurants, the rest of western Litchfield County is largely without such vagaries. Compared with the eastern half of the county, detailed later in this chapter, the western hills are considerably less populated and developed. It isn't necessarily more charming in these parts, just more rural. And the hills rise a bit higher and the temperatures dip lower. This is the only part of the state whose flora and fauna bear similarities to the upper elevations of western Massachusetts and even lower Vermont.

downtown New Milford

The villages on this side of the county are strung largely along U.S. 7 and its intersecting routes—there are no limited-access four-lane highways through here, and it can take a good while longer to drive among points than you might imagine simply by consulting a map. This slight matter of inconvenience is a good thing, of course, an incentive to slow down, breathe in the crisp air of the Berkshire foothills, and admire scenery you may never have dreamed existed within the border of one of America's smallest and heavily developed states.

## NEW MILFORD TO WASHINGTON

### New Milford

As you drive up busy U.S. 7/202 beside massive shopping centers and discount superstores, you may feel as though you've crossed the threshold of a sprawling suburb, but much of New Milford is rural and spread out, despite its tremendous growth in recent decades. This dull stretch of U.S. 7/202 functions as the supply depot for much of Litchfield County and neighboring New York State, and it's the final spate of commercialism you'll encounter as you enter the western Litchfield Hills.

At the center of New Milford, U.S. 202 and U.S. 7 split. This tour follows U.S. 202, but you can just as easily skip over it and follow U.S. 7 along the winding Housatonic River into Kent, which is described below. This is supposed to be a scenic drive, although there's relatively little to see along the way, except for one of the state's two covered bridges still open to auto traffic, which is on Bulls Bridge Road just west of U.S. 7, in the tiny village of Bulls Bridge.

At the intersection of U.S. 7/202, follow U.S. 202 over the Housatonic River and into New Milford's idyllic downtown, along the state's longest town green (at a full quarter mile). This seems fitting, as New Milford is actually the largest town in the state, at 64.4 square miles. Residents of the coastal community of Milford settled this land in 1703, hence the name, and Colonial statesman Roger Sherman operated a law office facing the green.

The city has been very aggressive about preserving and beautifying this lovely downtown, making it one of the region's favorite destinations for browsing and walking around. Just off the green, Bank Street is lined with great restaurants and one-of-the-kind boutiques and shops, plus a magnificently restored art deco movie theater. New sidewalks have laid down, utility

© ANDREW COLLINS

wires buried out of sight, and Victorian-style gas lamps, park benches, and ornamental trees added, making this a thoroughly gratifying spot for exploring. Future plans call for landscaping the downtown side of the Housatonic River, so that visitors will have incentive to wander along its banks—there's presently no easy or attractive access to the river from the retail area.

A nice thing about downtown New Milford is that while it's quite pretty, it's also a real working community, with everyday shops and concerns that help remind you you're in an authentic small town—it hasn't been overly gentrified or riddled with characterless chain stores (á la Gap).

At the northern end of the green, you'll find the **New Milford Historical Society** (6 Aspetuck Ave., 860/354-3069, www.nmhistorical.org, limited hours, May–Oct., $3), which also houses some exhibits in the restored Richard Booth Hall, a tiny clothing store at the turn of the 18th century on the village green (the building is back on the green, after having been moved a couple times). Exhibits include an antique toy collection, portraits of early New Milford families, and historical gardens. The society itself is based in the 1800 Knapp House, and also maintains an

1843 one-room schoolhouse and the 1820 Litch-field County First Bank.

If cooking and crafting are your interests, make a detour north along U.S. 202 from the center of town to reach the **Silo** (44 Upland Rd., New Milford, 860/355-0300 or 800/353-SILO, www.thesilo.com), operated by Ruth Henderson, the wife of former bandleader Skitch Henderson. Apart from being a shop where you can pick up all kinds of gourmet goods and cookery, the Silo offers cooking classes and seminars, many of them led by some of the region's many talented chefs. There's also an art gallery here, which presents rotating exhibits. The Silo also offers cooking programs geared toward kids, and the shop sells toys and games that appeal to youngsters.

## Bridgewater

Back at the south end of the town green, follow U.S. 202 (Bridge Street) down the hill and turn right onto Rte. 67, which continues south a few miles into Bridgewater, an unobtrusive town ideal for country driving or biking. Turn right (south) onto Rte. 133 (N. Main Street), and you'll enter the tiny village, which consists of lit-

Bridgewater village

tle more than the **Bridgewater General Store,** out of which America's very first mail-order business was begun in the 1850s by Charles B. Thompson. Continue down Rte. 133 to reach a picturesque stretch of the Housatonic River, where there's parking and a boat launch. Return back up the road a mile or so and make your first right onto Wewake Brook Road, following it north until it intersects with Minor Bridge Road, onto which you'll turn right.

## Roxbury

From here, Minor Bridge Road crosses over the Shepaug River and enters the similarly scenic and uncommercial town of Roxbury, home to more actors, writers, and other celebrities than you can shake a stick at.

Turn left on South Street and follow it right into the center of town (making a left onto Rte. 67), which consists of neatly tended old Colonial and Victorian houses, plus one antiquated single-standing complex of shops that includes a gas station (with old-fashioned pumps), a general store, a realtor, and a post office. A right turn onto Rte. 67 out of the general store leads to Rte. 199, which makes for a scenic drive by several old farmsteads north into Washington.

Or, a longer but even more dramatic option is to turn left from the general store and then left again onto Rte. 317, Good Hill Road. Arthur Miller still lives along this handsome street in a 1783 Colonial that he once shared with his wife, Marilyn Monroe, and Alexander Calder lived just around the corner until his death in 1976. As you rise up a "good hill" a little more than 2.5 miles from the center of town, make a left turn onto Tophet Road (note the little makeshift airstrip on your right, at the intersection). Great views from this grassy ridgeline extend to Woodbury to the east and Roxbury to the west.

Follow Tophet Road north, bearing left after 1.5 miles onto Gold Mine Road, and continue straight ahead when this turns into Painter Ridge Road, about 1.5 miles after that. This road rewards you with outstanding views of the countryside, and you'll immediately come to understand why this is called Painter Ridge. Eventually, the route passes through a couple of intersections (follow the signs for Washington) and intersects with Rte. 47, onto which a left turn takes you into Washington.

## Washington

Every October, thousands of travelers motor through this area for one singular but immensely satisfying reason: to watch northwestern Connecticut's breathtaking bounty of deciduous trees shed its leaves with all the panache of a Broadway chorus line. It's no secret that the courtly town of Washington has long staged one of the region's best leaf-peeping productions. Sugar maple, scarlet oak, honey locust, red maple, hickory, beech, birch, and elm—count on these broadleaf beauties for a good show.

This scenic slice of Connecticut woodland has developed into a smart, sophisticated cultural crossroads in recent years. A half dozen or more area restaurants serve the caliber of cuisine that makes even nationally known dining critics sit up and take notice. The acclaimed Washington Art Association mounts and sells the work of dozens of local artists—and this part of Connecticut teems with talented sculptors, painters, illustrators, and craftspeople. You can take fine arts classes at the association and fascinating crafts and Native American history classes at the Institute for American Indian Studies, in the southern end of town. Intriguing bookstores, clothes boutiques, and antiques shops also proliferate here. Watching the leaves turn in the fall still holds the keen interest of most visitors, but these days this pastime is merely one of Washington's many draws.

Washington was originally called Judea, when the First Congregational Church went up on the town green in 1741—one of the highest-elevation greens in the state, by the way. There's a post office near this peaceful patch of grass, along with a little old general store. If it all sounds like a scene from a coffee-table book on New England, it should—Washington has been in plenty of those.

As you enter town on Rte. 47, you'll pass the landscaped entryway to the Mayflower Inn, one of New England's most prestigious hostelries and immediate evidence of Washington's cachet as one of Connecticut's most desirable little towns.

On your left are the imposing buildings of the **Gunnery Prep School;** across the road are the school's sports fields and various school buildings. The Gunnery was founded in 1850 by F. W. Gunn, and is one of a few such private institutions of learning that have existed here. The Mayflower occupies the grounds of the old Ridge School. Not far away, the prestigious **International College of Hospitality,** which provides many of the staff at the Mayflower and other prestigious inns throughout New England, occupies the grounds of a former prep school. And on the remote west side of town is yet another prep school, Rumsey Hall.

This neat and beautifully preserved village sits on a hill overlooking the stately Tudor-style Gunnery School, anchored by a classic Congregational church and numerous Colonial homes fronted by white-picket fences. The history of this lovely town is traced through exhibits at the **Gunn Memorial Library & Museum** (5 Wykeham Rd., just off Rte. 47 and across from the Gunnery, 860/868-7756, www.biblio.org/gunn, limited hours, donation suggested). The museum has both a 1781 Colonial house and a small stone library built in 1908. The house contains antiques and historical documents, and the library has an extensive collection of historical and genealogical books. Some of the interesting collections here include tools, quilts, needlework, pewter, paintings by local artists, and autographs of George Washington and other dignitaries of the day.

Right at the campus of the Gunnery, Rte. 199 leads south from Rte. 47 about 1.5 miles to Curtis Road, where a right turn leads to the **Institute for American Indian Studies** (38 Curtis Rd., 860/868-0518, open daily but closed Mon.–Tues. Jan.–Mar., $5). Exhibits identify where native people thrived in Connecticut and where, sadly, European colonization resulted in Indian suppression, and in many places eradication—with so many museums and historical societies throughout the state focusing on Connecticut's post-1500s history, the IAIS provides a valuable and provocative perspective. Nature trails extend behind the property, one passing through a newly restored, re-created Alongkian Village, which is anchored by a bark-clad longhouse. The gift shop here is spacious and well-stocked, and dinosaur bones were recovered on this site in the 1950s.

## Washington Depot

Back on Rte. 47 in the hilltop center of town, continue down this road about a mile and you'll reach the community's commercial hub, Washington Depot, which is centered at the intersection of Rtes. 47 and 109. Here, you'll see the uncharacteristically large and commanding brick town hall and various interesting shops and a few eateries—the great flood of 1955 destroyed many of the buildings, which explains why the depot has a somewhat newer feel than Washington proper up the hill. It's a small enough area for walking, and bibliophiles should be certain to browse the shelves of the **Hickory Stick Bookshop.** Art lovers will want to see the gallery at the **Washington Art Association** (860/868-2878, www.washingtonart.org, open daily), adjacent to the town hall at Bryan Memorial Plaza. The association was established in 1952 and has grown to become one of the most respected regional art showcases around, showing exhibitions of both local and national artists throughout the year. Anybody with a yen for browsing will find several more curious stores within walking distance.

If you're looking for a chance to stretch your legs, either hike the aforementioned IAIS trails down to Steep Rock Reservation (a 15-minute ramble) or make the 10-minute drive by way of Washington Depot. At the entrance to **Steep Rock Reservation** (off River Rd., 860/868-9131, open daily dawn–dusk), a nonprofit, locally operated land trust of unspoiled woodland, mounted boxes by the two main parking areas contain maps detailing a few two- to four-mile trails. Some of these reach elevations of nearly 800 feet, and other less strenuous ones run alongside the rocky Shepaug River. A bike trail parallels the river, over what used to be the train tracks of the Shepaug Railroad. The railroad passed through Washington Depot en route to Litchfield from the early 1870s to the 1930s—

so tortuous was this route that the train's engine, so the local stories go, often met the caboose on the railroad's sharpest curves.

### New Preston

From downtown, follow Rte. 109 west a short way, but where this marked state route makes a sharp left, continue straight instead up Baldwin Hill Road and continue until you reach U.S. 202; go straight across the intersection and turn onto Rte. 45, which leads into New Preston, a compact village of colorful clapboard Victorian buildings that buzzed with sawmill and carriage-factory activity 150 years ago. Today, it buzzes with the chatter of antiques and home-furnishings aficionados. This is the part of town where you might notice a celebrity out browsing fancy furnishings and housewares. Several businesses overlook the roaring waterfalls of the Aspetuck River, where light industry once thrived.

### Lake Waramaug

Route 45 continues up just a short distance to rippling Lake Waramaug, which looks a bit like a scene from the Swiss Alps, surrounded as it is by green hills and a mix of vacation cottages and country farmhouses and estates. On the southwestern shore be sure to stop and admire the several grand Victorians (including the elegant Hopkins Inn) atop the grassy bluff across the lake. At the northwestern tip, pull over at **Lake Waramaug State Park** (30 Lake Waramaug Rd., 860/868-2592), where you can scamper along the beach and, if the weather is suitable, set up a meal at one of the many lakeside picnic tables. On the north shore of the lake, up Hopkins Road and behind the grand Hopkins Inn is the **Hopkins Vineyard** (25 Hopkins Rd., 860/868-7954, www.hopkinsvineyard.com), a 30-acre vineyard and winery with tastings daily May–Dec., and on weekends and some weekdays Jan.–Apr. (when it's best to call ahead). Guided tours are given on weekend afternoons at 2 P.M. In all, it's about eight miles around the lake, and you'll end up back on Rte. 45, a bit north of where you left it to begin circumnavigating the lake.

## KENT TO CORNWALL

### Warren

Continue up Rte. 45 into quiet Warren, an almost entirely residential and quite rural Colonial hamlet best known for its handsome Congregational church, which stands over the tiny village center. Turn left in Warren onto Rte. 341, a winding hilly road that rolls down into one of the highest-profile towns in Litchfield County: Kent.

## MERWINSVILLE: THE RISE AND FALL OF A WAY-STATION

In the direction of Kent via Bulls Bridge, U.S. 7 passes through a small village called Gaylordsville, which has an old tavern that's open to the public only by appointment. The Merwinsville Hotel (Browns Forge Rd., 860/350-4443) opened in 1843 and long ago ceased operation, but it still contains many antiques and artifacts. The place was opened by an entrepreneur, who built the hotel right where the new Housatonic Railroad was planned and refused to sell right-of-way land to the rail company unless it agreed to (a) use his hotel as a meal stop and (b) name the station after him—hence, Merwinsville. The hotel's fortunes began to slide, and in 1915, the aged owner of the ticket office, faced with the possibility of being replaced by a younger worker, threatened to stop allowing trains to use his station unless his job was preserved. The railroad responded by building a new station next door and renaming the stop Gaylordsville.

A consortium of preservationists and concerned neighbors now operates the hotel as a museum, and has renovated much of it while continuing to raise funds to complete the job. Here, too, is the **Gaylordsville Historical Society** (860/354-5986), in the old Brown's Forge just down the street.

## Kent

Bordering New York state, bisected by the roaring Housatonic River, and surrounded by high stony ridges that make for great hiking (including a stretch along the legendary Appalachian Trail), Kent also has a trendy downtown of urbane shops. You can walk the whole run of businesses along Main Street (U.S. 7), which begins at Rte. 341 and continues for about a third of a mile north. Housed in both Victorian wood-frame buildings and newer Colonial-style shopping centers, you'll find a quirky little record shop, an excellent bookstore, world-renowned (that's right, *world*) art galleries, and a few good clothiers, plus a series of inviting spots for snacking.

The sprawl along U.S. 7 in New Milford has ever so slowly crept into town in the way of a few condo clusters and modern shopping plazas, but Kent achieves a pleasing balance, offering enough diversions to keep visitors and residents busy for an afternoon, while still retaining its historically intimate Colonial scale. Across the Housatonic from downtown is the

remains of the Kent Iron Furnace, which produced pig iron for 70 years in the 19th century

riverside campus of Kent Prep School. If you head south along U.S. 7, you'll enter the Bulls Bridge section of town, which is described with New Milford, above.

Head north of downtown Kent on U.S. 7 for about a half mile and look for the signs for the **Sloane-Stanley Museum and Kent Furnace** (U.S. 7, 860/927-3849, open 10 A.M.–4 P.M. Wed.–Sun. mid-May–Oct., $3). With its rugged ridgelines and tree-studded landscape, Kent may not look today like an especially industrial landscape, but in Colonial times, the land in these parts was commonly used for mining and manufacturing. This museum honors the state's early mining and labor tradition in two ways. First, you can tour the museum, the brainchild of Eric Sloane, a local artist, writer, and tool collector who lived from 1905 to 1985 and donated his tremendous cache of early tools for exhibition at the museum. The Stanley Works, the renowned New Britain tool-manufacturing concern, provided this land and the building to house the tools. Sloane focused especially on handmade pieces, many used for wood- and metal-crafting. A small, rough-hewn, shingle-roof cabin stands next to the main museum; Sloane built this in 1974 based on descriptions in a wood-backed leather 1805 diary he found that belonged to a local toolmaker named Noah Blake. The decor and exhibits in the cabin illustrate the conditions under which craftsmen labored in the Colonial age.

A second feature of this site is the long-dormant but nicely preserved Kent Iron Furnace, whose granite block arch sits just behind and below the museum. This furnace produced pig iron for some 70 years commencing in the early 19th century. Currently, plans are underway to restore the furnace and clear the area where outbuildings once stood and a mill-race flowed.

**Kent Falls State Park** (860/927-3238) is north of here, right off U.S. 7, and is easily accessed for swimming, fishing, camping, and hiking. The two waterfalls in this park are a favorite photo op, and a path runs alongside them, allowing you to look at the cascades from several angles.

© ANDREW COLLINS

**West Cornwall's covered bridge**

## Cornwall Bridge

Cornwall is due north of Kent, and from where Rte. 45 joins it for about 12 miles north to Rte. 112, U.S. 7 is one of the prettiest stretches of river road in New England. Two sections of the 50-square-mile town of Cornwall lie along the river, the southernmost being Cornwall Bridge, which is named for the long, wooden-covered bridge that spanned the river before the terrible flood in 1955 ripped it to shreds. Now a high, modern, and not particularly charming bridge carries traffic along U.S. 7 over the river, where you'll pass briefly into the very edge of Sharon. Here you'll find the entrance to **Housatonic Meadows State Park** (860/927-3238 or 860/672-6772), and you'll begin to notice fly-fishing outfitters and businesses along the road. A trail at Housatonic Meadows runs high into the hills and joins with the Appalachian Trail, or you can camp, fish, or picnic down along the river.

## West Cornwall

Drive a bit farther north along U.S. 7, taking in the excellent views of the Housatonic, and you'll enter West Cornwall. This charming village is reached by following Rte. 128 east across the river, through a long, magnificent, barn-red covered bridge built by the renowned architect and bridge engineer Ithiel Town in 1864. West Cornwall is a picturesque enclave of both Colonial and Victorian buildings, with a few excellent crafts and antiques shops and a couple of good restaurants.

## Cornwall

Continue up into the hills along Rte. 128, into the heart of Cornwall—where James Thurber once owned a home, as have such celebrities as Whoopi Goldberg, Michael J. Fox, and Sam Waterston. The Van Doren family (of *Quiz Show* scandal fame) resided here for many years. Cornwall was also the site of a foreign mission school for the "education" of indigenous residents of the Sandwich Islands (now Hawaii) during the early 1800s.

This is some of Connecticut's most rugged and heavily forested terrain—it feels almost as though it's in the heart of the Berkshire Mountains in nearby Massachusetts. In the center of the village, which is no more substantial or developed than the sections of Cornwall along the Housatonic, you'll see the

THE WESTERN HILLS

sloping hillside of the Mohawk Ski Area, which adjoins Mohawk State Forest—one of the best hiking venues in the county.

Cornwall was home to Connecticut's only tract of native original pines and hemlocks (most dating back some 300 years), but a tornado ripped through in 1989 and tore most of them down just like that. You can still see evidence of this freak occurrence today along Rte. 4 at the edge of Cornwall, near the ski area. From here, you can either return to U.S. 7 via Rte. 128 and continue north along the river toward Falls Village and Canaan, or you can continue following this tour by heading east on Rte. 4, which brings you back to Cornwall Bridge, crosses U.S. 7, and continues up a winding beautiful hill into Sharon.

## SHARON TO SALISBURY
### Sharon

Continue up Rte. 4 to reach the 860-acre **Sharon Audubon Center** (325 Rte. 4, 860/364-0520, www.ctaudubon.org, open daily, $3), a vast sanctuary containing some 11 miles of hiking trails, wildflower and herb gardens, and an excellent little bookshop and library. In the main interpretative building are exhibits on the Litchfield Hills ecosystem.

From the nature center, continue along Rte. 4 into the town center, the western side of which touches the New York village of Amenia. Turn right onto Main Street (Rte. 41) once you hit town, and note the beautiful old Colonial mansions on both sides of the street. Among them is the **Gay-Hoyt House Museum** (18 Main St., 860/364-5688, www.sharonhist.org, 1–4 P.M. Tues.–Fri., free), a 1775 house containing 18th- and 19th-century furnishings, a textile collection, children's exhibits, and art and photography installations. The house itself is a red-brick twin-chimneyed Colonial with a lawn that slopes down to the Sharon green. Nearby is **Beardsley Gardens** (157 Gay St., Rte. 41, Sharon, 860/364-0727, www.beardsleygardens.com), which has gardening and design workshops and sells thousands of plants and accessories.

### Lime Rock

From Sharon, follow Rte. 41 north into the Lakeville section of Salisbury, turning right onto Rte. 112 for a quick detour down to **Lime Rock Park** (860/435-5000 or 800/RACE-LRP, www.limerock.com), a racetrack and also one of 20 racetracks that is the site of the acclaimed **Skip Barber Racing and Driving School** (800/221-1131, www.skipbarber.com). Throughout the year, the quiet of this peaceful section of town is interrupted by the hum of automobile engines—celebrity drivers like Paul Newman, Jerry Seinfeld, and Tom Cruise have driven here. Seasonal events are sometimes held at the racetrack, such as the Annual Dodge Vintage Festival each September, when old-fashioned sports cars take to the track for a swap meet. Actual races are held from about May through October.

In Lime Rock, head to **White Hollow Farm** (U.S. 7 and Rte. 112, 860/435-0382), which has a dramatic corn maize open daily from Friday–Sunday, mid-August–October Admission to wander through this sprawling maze is $7 per person.

### Lakeville

Return to Rte. 41 and continue north by the sprawling campus of Hotchkiss prep school, and down along the shore of Lake Wononskopomuc (not to be confused with Lake Wononpakook, which is just south of campus), which is a couple hundred yards from the village of Lakeville, where Rte. 41 and U.S. 44 meet. This section of Salisbury comprises the **Lakeville Historic District** and is where the state's first blast furnace stood, built in 1762 on the site of a former iron forge. This furnace played a vital role in the American Revolution, producing munitions, cookery, and other metalware for the troops. In 1844, Alexander Holley opened the state's first cutlery and pocketknife factory—the dramatic 1866 redbrick Holley Manufacturing Building now contains offices.

Open to the public is the **Holley-Williams House Museum** (15 Millerton Rd., Rte. 41/U.S. 44, 860/435-2878, seasonal hours, free), which was built in 1768 but added to significantly in 1808, thus accounting for its hybrid Federal and Classical Revival appearance. The museum dis-

Salisbury village

## Salisbury

Drive east along Main Street (Rte. 41/U.S. 44) into the three-block Salisbury Historic District, one of the most scenic in the northwestern part of the state, where about 30 mostly 19th-century buildings make up a small-town commercial center. The 1800 **Federal Congregational Church** is of particular note, with Palladian windows in the tower an open octagonal belfry. Also notable are the **Bushnell Tavern,** parts of which date to 1746 (and the rest to 1790), and the **Scoville Memorial Library** (1891), a gray limestone building. The rambling White Hart Inn presides over the scene. Route 41 runs north a few miles to the Massachusetts border, and is the best way to access hiking trails for Connecticut's highest summit, Bear Mountain, and the stretch of the Appalachian Trail that passes over it.

## FALLS VILLAGE AND CANAAN
### Falls Village

From Salisbury, continue east on U.S. 44 and then turn right onto Rte. 126, a twisting country road leading south into Falls Village. Here, in the early 1930s, America's oldest continuing summer chamber music festival was established, the now highly acclaimed **Music Mountain.**

This is a great spot for fishing, as Rte. 126 passes alongside the Hollenback River, which feeds into the Housatonic—the Nature Conservancy recently established a preserve along here. The Hollenback is calm and lined with dense forest, making it a wonderful stretch for canoeing and an easy place to spot wildlife and flora. This is particularly appropriate, given that well-known naturalist and writer Hal Borland lived in and wrote about this area for many years. The tiny center of Falls Village is an unspoiled hamlet in the New England tradition.

If you've got kids who love cats, or you love them yourself, you might stop by **The Last Post** (call for directions, 860/824-0831), a retirement home in the country for kitties. Ani-

cusses not only the Colonial manufacturing history of Lakeville, but also how families lived during the 19th century, with particular focus on the role of women. Exhibits discuss the lives and thoughts of prominent women of the day, including Susan B. Anthony, Elizabeth Cady Stanton, and Litchfield County's own Harriet Beecher Stowe. Light is shone upon the role women played in the abolitionist movement and the Civil War, and on the battle for suffrage. You can also sneak a peek at the seven-hole outhouse, which had a hole for each member of the family.

Beside the Holley House, in its neighboring carriage house, is the little-known **Cannon Museum** (860/435-2878, seasonal hours, free). The iron furnaces of Mt. Riga produced cannons for the Americans during the Revolutionary War, and right across the street from the Holley House was a small cannon factory. The Cannon Museum aims its exhibits, so to speak, toward a younger audience, but adults will probably get a kick out of this place as well.

mals are never put down here and are free to live out their lives, although visitors interested in adopting them are very welcome. Still, even if you don't want a cat of your own, or perhaps if you miss yours back home, you can stop by and play with the more than 350 felines, who live in a big house with many rooms and ladders and have a five-acre fenced-in yard for exploring.

## Canaan

Route 126 joins with U.S. 7, onto which a left turn leads north back up to U.S. 44 in the bustling, by regional standards, town of Canaan, which has had a rather rough go of things the last few years (or decades). Downtown, the heart of which is along Main Street where U.S. 7 and 44 join for a stretch, has a number of turn-of-the-20th-century storefronts, quite a few either vacant or in need of a little sprucing up. One pleasant development involved the 1923 Colonial movie theater, which faced potential demolition after its owner passed away in 1997. Fortunately, a group of some 140 concerned locals banded into a nonprofit group and began working to restore the Greek Revival building in which this theater, with its 32-foot-wide screen, is located.

The outlying community of Canaan, and its sister town, North Canaan, are mostly forest and farmland, popular areas for country driving and biking. From the center of Canaan, U.S. 44 leads east into Norfolk, which begins the tour of the eastern Litchfield Hills.

There is one worthwhile detour for wine enthusiasts: Intimate, relatively young, and lesser-known among Connecticut's vineyards (which is why a number of visitors have taken a shine to it), the **Land of Nod Winery** (99 Lower Rd., East Canaan, 860/824-7340, open Fri.–Sun. or by appointment) already produces commendable chardonnays and pinot noirs aged in barrels made of local oak. The winery also produces a light raspberry wine. Visitors are welcome for a look around during the day. You can also sample these wines at the pub in the Wake Robin Inn in Salisbury.

# SHOPPING

By a hair, the eastern half of Litchfield County is better for shopping than this side, as there's simply less commercial development, even in the way of antiques shops, in the western Litchfield Hills. Nevertheless, there's plenty of browsing for fine old furnishings, collectibles, and books. And there are a number of intriguing clothiers and specialty shops, particularly in Kent, New Milford, New Preston, and Salisbury—all four are towns where you can park the car or lock up the bike and spend the better part of an afternoon strolling among the shops. There are no malls or concentrations of chain shops in this area; however, U.S. 7 in the lower half of New Milford has all the usual super discount stores you might need for basic goods, camping and outdoors gear, and whatnot.

## Kent

About a dozen fine art galleries in Kent present just about every conceivable kind of art, from 15th-century drawings to the finest contemporary pieces. Most are on or just off Main Street (U.S. 7), and especially notable ones include the **Bachelier-Cardonsky Gallery** (860/927-3129); the **C & J Goodfriend Gallery** (860/927-1300); and the **Paris-New York-Kent Gallery** (860/927-4152). The **Heron American Craft Gallery** (16 N. Main St., Kent, 860/672-4804) specializes in jewelry and arts from different regions of the country.

There are also about a dozen antiques dealers in town, including the **Kent Antiques Center** (Main St., 860/927-3313), a cooperative of several dealers. **B. Johnstone & Co.** (25 N. Main St., 860/927-1272) specializes in antique china and cutlery, custom-made couture furniture and clothing, and bath and body items. **House of Books** (Main St., 860/927-4104) is an excellent, atmospheric, independent bookstore with a nice selection of regional books, history, and serious fiction. **Pauline's Place** (U.S. 7, 860/927-4475) has a very good reputation for its remarkable selection of antique and estate jewelry. You can also have your pieces repaired here. **R. T. Facts** (22 S. Main St., 860/927-1700) is an emporium of garden and architectural objects and decorative items. It's great fun to rummage through. **Foreign Cargo Kent** (Main St., 860/927-3900) is owned by a woman who has lived all over the world and has an eye for fashion, jewelry, and decor from far-flung places.

## New Milford

Shops along Bank Street include **Focal Point** (36 Bank St., 860/335-0081), which offers painted furniture, whimsical garden and home decor, and wrought- and cast-iron items. Looking for the daily newspapers from Paris, San Francisco, or Rome? **Archway** (64 Bank St., New Milford, 860/355-1557) carries about 2,500 periodicals, plus fine imported pipes and cigars.

## New Preston

**J. Seitz & Co.** (9 E. Shore Rd., 860/868-0119) overlooks a dramatic waterfall and is filled with a mix of newer and older pieces, many Southwestern and Western; some wonderful clothing for men and women; excellent upholstered chairs; and fine pillows and linens. This is a favorite shop of Litchfield County celebrities, and has been featured in many magazines. A 5,000-square-foot basement level showcases more substantial furnishings, rugs, and such. Right next door is a small gallery of exquisite French interior design elements and antiques called **French Window.** The inviting **Judy Hornby Gallery** (13 E. Shore Rd., 860/868-0501) contains a vast selection of mostly French furnishings from the 1700s to the 1960s, from inexpensive accents to high-end tables and chairs; it's also an art gallery. The fine jewelry, set with gems and pearls, at **Crowe Jewellers** (13 E. Shore Rd., 860/868-6611) is custom-crafted by owner Sean Gilson.

## Washington Depot

**Seraphim** (2 Titus Rd., 860/868-1674) is a luxuriant clothier selling chenille sweaters, romantic dresses, flannel pajamas, jewelry, and other fine women's apparel. For antiques, **Stock in Trade** (U.S. 202, Marbledale, 860/868-5090) has a nice selection of English country and American pieces, plus fly-fishing and golf collectibles. The rambling **Tulip Tree Collection** (Rte. 47,

860/868-2802) displays an enormous selection of home furnishings, from antiques to newer pieces—plus upholstery, rugs, and accessories.

## Elsewhere

One of the better sources of fine art in the region is up in Sharon, at **Garuda Gallery** (Rte. 41, 860/364-5883). **Cornwall Bridge Pottery** (West Cornwall, Rte. 128, 800/501-6545) is a well-visited landmark whose kiln and studio you can tour. In the same village, the whimsically named **Wish House** (413 Main St., 860/672-2969) stocks fun gifts, inspired children's toys and games, clothing for all ages, and other artful odds and ends. You'll find one of the larger selections of vintage furnishings at the **Salisbury Antiques Center** (46 Library St., 860/435-0424).

**Sweethaven Farm** (Academy St., 860/435-6064) is a cute house just off Salisbury's Main Street, where you can buy gifts, exquisite herbal floral wreaths, and other lovely items for home and garden. In Falls Village, **Rustling Wind Creamery** (164 Canaan Mountain Rd., east of Rte. 63, 860/824-7634 or 860/824-7084), known for its horseback riding (see below), also produces fine goat cheeses, special soaps, sweaters, and many other creative products. It's a bit off the beaten path, but a wonderful place for a visit; just call ahead first to confirm hours and directions.

In downtown New Milford, **Blast from the Past** (17 Church St., 860/354-3517) sells antiques and just old stuff from the past century or so, including kitchenware, old records, furniture, Christmas collectibles, and just about anything else you'd expect to find in a pack rat's attic.

# RECREATION

## Boating, Canoeing, and River-Rafting

**Clarke Outdoors** (U.S. 7, West Cornwall, 860/672-6365, www.clarkeoutdoors.com) is a highly reputable source for its canoe, kayaking, and renting supplies and tours along the Housatonic River. Mark Clarke has won national canoe races and definitely knows what he's doing. Beginner, advanced beginner, and intermediate kayaking lessons are offered, plus excellent canoe "clinics," whitewater instruction, and tours. Just about anything you can do in a boat on the Housatonic River, the staff can help you with.

## Downhill Skiing

The **Mohawk Ski Area** (Cornwall, 860/672-6100 or 860/672-0161, www.mohawkmtn.com) is a respectable facility, proof that Connecticut does have some quite decent day slopes. There's a full rental shop, a ski school, and more than 100 acres of groomed ski trails. Several lifts service about 25 (nearly half of them lighted) trails, of varying difficulty.

## Fishing

An excellent source for fly-fishing in these parts is **Housatonic River Outfitters** (24 Kent Rd., U.S. 7, Cornwall Bridge, 860/672-1010, www.dryflies.com), which is based in an interesting old building near the covered bridge in West Cornwall. Inside is a full range of equipment and fishing accessories. Also available are guided fishing trips and casting lessons. Another excellent outfitter is **Housatonic Meadows Fly Shop** (13 U.S. 7, Cornwall Bridge, 860/672-6064, www.flyfishct.com), an authorized Orvis dealer that also acts as a half-day and full-day guide service.

There's great fishing at **O'Hara's Landing** (Twin Lakes Rd., Salisbury, 860/824-7583), where salmon, bass, trout, perch, pickerel, and bluegill swim in the clear blue Twin Lakes. You can launch a boat or rent one from O'Hara's, which also has a casual lakeside restaurant. Sailing and water-skiing are also available, and all equipment can be rented.

## Golf

There aren't a huge number of golf courses in the area, but you'll find a pretty nice one at **Candlewood Valley Country Club** (401 Danbury Rd., U.S. 7/202, 860/354-9359) in New Milford. It has received a great many renovations and makeovers in recent years.

## Hiking

In New Milford, the Nature Conservancy's **Sunny Valley Preserve** (8 Sunny Valley Ln., 860/355-3716) consists of 11 distinct tracts

of preserve, the headquarters of which are based at the old Sunny Valley Farm, west of U.S. 7 and about midway between the Housatonic River and Candlewood Lake. There are very good hiking trails here, as there are at some of the preserve's other tracts (which fall in both New Milford and Bridgewater). These include Cedar Bridge and Silica Mine Hill (both along the eastern banks of the Housatonic down near where it's known as Lake Lillinonah), as well as nearby Rocky Hill, Iron Ore Hill, and Schaghticoke Farm. Wolfit Mountain is another good hiking spot. You could easily spend a week checking out the many different parts of Sunny Valley Preserve. **Steep Rock Preserve** in Washington is another invigorating spot for a forest ramble.

**Macedonia Brook State Park** (159 Macedonia Brook Rd., Kent, 860/927-4100 or 860/927-3238) has 2,300 acres of excellent and challenging hiking along ridgelines offering fabulous views of the region and access to the Appalachian Trail. More than 13 miles of trails cut over these steep rocky hills, and novice hikers might want to head elsewhere, as a familiarity with rugged terrain is strongly advised.

Northwestern Connecticut sees 52 miles of the **Appalachian Trail**, part of which climbs over 2,300-foot Bear Mountain, the highest point in the state. All but a tiny stretch of the trail passes through national and state forestland, and Connecticut is attempting to pick up the final couple of acres. Rattlesnakes have reportedly become a presence on the trail, and you may also see a variety of other wildlife, including the occasional bear. The rattlers, incidentally, are not aggressive, and just need to be viewed from a distance to be dealt with safely. There are simple shelters along the trail for camping—seven lean-tos and 12 campsites. Fires are prohibited, and water should be treated before consumption.

The Appalachian Mountain Club maintains the trail, sometime putting in more than 7,000 hours per year to do so. The terrain along the Appalachian is quite rugged in many places. A Boy Scout troop from Sherman cleared much of the Connecticut span of the trail back in the 1930s, although most of the trail as we know it today follows a somewhat different path (it's constantly being shifted and reworked). The trail enters the state along the New York border in Kent, just northwest of Bulls Bridge. It hugs the western banks of the Housatonic River for some way north, past Cornwall and into Falls Village, where it crosses the river to the east bank. It then crosses back over and continues at a northwesterly pace to Bear Mountain, and finally Massachusetts.

**Bear Mountain** makes for an outstanding day hike. There's always a congregation of hikers at the peak of the trail, which affords magnificent vistas of the surrounding area, so keep in mind that this is a less-than-ideal choice if you're seeking solitude. Furthermore, overuse has led to increased erosion of the trail, and the volunteers who maintain this hiking territory are always seeking help. Still, this makes for a challenging and scenic adventure, especially if you can get out here on a weekday. The elevation of 2,300 feet may not sound exceptionally high, but due to the considerably lower elevation of the neighboring terrain, the views are not bad.

### Horseback Riding

Just off U.S. 202, in the Woodville section of Washington, is **H.O.R.S.E. of Connecticut** (43 Wilbur Rd., 860/868-1960, www.horseofct.org, open Fri.–Sun. year-round), a nonprofit organization that rescues stray horses and provides homes for them. You can stop by to see and feed the horses, take a tour of the property, and arrange for trail rides by advance reservations.

In Falls Village, **Rustling Wind Stables** (164 Canaan Mountain Rd., east of Rte. 63, 860/824-7634, Tues.–Sun. year-round by appointment) offers English- and Western-style trail rides.

## ENTERTAINMENT AND NIGHTLIFE

You don't come to this part of Connecticut with high hopes of partying, but there's a smattering of drinking holes, mostly at restaurants mentioned below. Particularly happening with the late-night crowd are the Bistro in New Milford, the G. W. Tavern in Washington, The Pub in Norfolk, the Irish pub at Lakeview's Wake Robin Inn, and

the Tap Room at the White Hart Inn in Salisbury.

Like the Yale Summer Music program in Norfolk, **Music Mountain** (Gordon Hall, Rte. 63 near Rte. 126, Falls Village, 860/364-2084, or, on concert days, 860/824-7126, www.music-mountain.org) continues to operate as a source of extremely high-caliber music in a remote village in the woods—it began in 1930. The season typically features string quartets, and there are always some interesting variations and unusual works presented.

After having been closed for a period, the **Sharon Playhouse** (Rte. 41, 860/364-SHOW, www.triarts.net) came back in 2001, and now offers two or three summer-theater productions each season, typically musicals and light comedies.

## FESTIVALS AND EVENTS
### Winter and Spring

During the month of December, there's an **Annual Christmas Show & Sale** (4 Bryan Plaza, 860/868-2878) held in Washington Depot; more holiday festivities commence around the **Covered Bridge Christmas** celebrations on Rte. 128 in West Cornwall's pretty village. In mid-February, alpine enthusiasts flock to Salisbury to observe the **U.S. Eastern Ski Jumping Championships.** Come to the shores of Lake Waramaug to watch area prep school teams crew—this goes on mostly through the month of May.

### Summer and Fall

An **Arts and Crafts Fair** (Bridgewater Fairgrounds, Rte. 133, 860/354-1509) keeps shoppers happy in early June. Arts and crafts, food stalls, and entertainment are the draw along the town green in late July during **New Milford Village Fair Days** (Main St., 860/350-6080). The old rail track and station in the center of town are the site of the **Canaan Railroad Days** in mid- to late July. In August, a large **Arts and Crafts Fair** is held on the green in Sharon. Late August sees the annual **Bridgewater Country Fair** (Bridgewater Fairgrounds, Rte. 133, 860/743-0546), which features three days of tractor pulls, oxen pulls, agricultural competitions, arts and crafts, and entertainment. A **Storytelling Festival** takes place at Washington's Institute for American Indian Studies the weekend after Thanksgiving.

## ACCOMMODATIONS

This part of the state has some of the most romantic inns in New England, ranging from luxurious high-end resorts to reasonably priced B&Bs with both private and shared baths. There are accommodations in towns throughout the region, but you'll find the greatest numbers of them around Lake Waramaug in Washington, in downtown New Milford, and up in Salisbury.

Most of the lodgings described below have at least three or four rooms, and are staffed daily year-round. Dozens of smaller, informally operated B&Bs dot Litchfield County, too, but it's best to book these through the area's very good reservation service: **Nutmeg B&Bs** (860/236-6698).

### Hotels and Motels

**$150–250:** The **Interlaken Inn** (74 Interlaken Rd., Lakeville, 860/435-9878 or 800/222-2909, www.interlakeninn.com) is a full-scale resort on 30 acres near Hotchkiss prep school and Lime Rock racetrack, and within a few minutes' drive of the great hiking and fly-fishing for which the northwestern corner is known. Many of the 83 rooms and suites, decorated with English country–style fabrics and furnishings, have fireplaces, and guests have the use of a chip-and-putt golf course, outdoor pool, tennis courts, racquetball court, and full fitness center. The resort property also hugs the shore of Lake Wononskopomuc, and there's swimming plus boats available for guests. The inn's restaurant, Morgan's Grille, is a trusty option with a refined menu of black Angus steaks and fresh seafood.

**$100–150:** Rooms at the **Fife & Drum** (53 N. Main St., Kent, 860/927-3509, www.fifendrum.com) are in a rustic two-story building across the parking lot from the restaurant of the same name. The eight Colonial-style rooms have separate outdoor entrances, air-conditioning and ceiling fans, clean baths with upscale soaps and hair dryers, and pretty furnishings, including some four-poster beds

and cheerful floral-print drapes and bedding. There's a nice gift shop, too.

An innovative use of space and one of the more moderately priced accommodations in the region, the **Heritage Inn** (34 Bridge St., New Milford, 860/354-8883, www.heritageinnct.com) was fashioned out of an 1870 wood-frame tobacco warehouse—there's even a vintage tobacco press on the front porch to help tell the story of the building's history. The family-owned hotel is run with a light and friendly touch (a note to guests "encourages" check-in after 2 P.M. and check-out at 11 A.M., language that captures the management's courteous philosophy). Rooms are fairly simple and cheerfully decorated, and a full hot breakfast is included. This hotel is not related to the Heritage Inn resort in Southbury, but it's owned by the same folks who run the Twin Tree Inn in nearby Brookfield.

Another great accommodation in New Milford is the **Homestead Inn** (5 Elm St., 860/354-4080, www.homesteadct.com), which consists of a main 1850s house and an additional motel-style unit that dates from the 1930s, plus a separate cottage. Each option has its advantages, and all rooms are very nicely kept, with a mix of antiques and reproductions. Guests have full use of the homey common rooms, which have two fireplaces, plus various porches and gardens. All rooms have private baths, phones, and cable TV, and Continental breakfast is included.

As far as motor courts go, the **Inn at Iron Masters** (229 Main St., Lakeville, 860/435-9844, www.innatironmasters.com) is the best option in the region. This one isn't cheap, either, but the rooms at this nicely landscaped property truly are impressive, with upscale Colonial-style furnishings and scads of amenities (hair dryers, climate control, coffee/tea service, etc.). In fact, the only thing about this place that puts it in the category of motor court is its architecture—you'll feel as though you're at a country inn once you're inside your room. Continental breakfast is included.

The **Sharon Motor Lodge** (Rte. 41, 860/364-0036) is in an excellent location in the heart of the beautiful village of Sharon, set back from the road down a long, almost regal, drive. The grounds are shaded by trees and have an Olympic-size outdoor pool, but the rooms are rather ordinary, especially considering the rates, which climb well over $100 nightly on peak weekends.

## Country Inns and Bed-and-Breakfasts

**Over $250:** One of the most exclusive country inns in the United States, the **Mayflower Inn** (Rte. 47, Washington, 860/868-9466, www.mayflowerinn.com) is really more like a luxury hotel on an extremely intimate scale than the sort of rambling rustic hostelry more typical of the region. There are just 26 rooms, but there's also a full fitness center, heated pool, tennis, game room, and one of the best restaurants in Litchfield County. Once the site of the Ridge prep school, which was built in 1894, the double-gambrel-roofed wood-frame building was converted into an inn back in the 1920s, but fell to disuse over the years before being essentially reconstructed in 1992. The owners are serious art collectors and have furnished the public areas with fine 18th- and 19th-century paintings. The grounds consist of 28 acres of rhododendrons, maples, stone walls, and streams, and are a pleasure to saunter about on. No expense was spared on these rooms, which are filled with large marble baths, Frette linens, Regency-striped wallpapers, and four-poster canopied beds.

**The Boulders Inn** (Rte. 45, New Preston, 860/868-0541 or 800/455-1565, www.bouldersinn.com), run for many years by Kees and Ulla Adema, is a dramatic shingle-style house dating to the 1890s, with several outbuildings behind it. In 2002, the Ademas sold the grand property to a new innkeeper, Martin O'Brien, who has set about updating the inn and making it even more lavish than it was. A major makeover was conducted throughout the winter of 2002–2003, and the entire place now has the ambience of a luxury Rocky Mountain lodge, with earthy tones, and a mix of craftsmen-style furniture, period antiques, and country accents. Rooms are spread throughout the historic main lodge, the several cozy cottages (all with fireplaces), and a drop-dead gorgeous carriage house containing the most lavish suites (all have DVD-stereo systems, dual phones, voicemail, and high-speed internet), most with deep soaking tubs and stone fireplaces. Little expense has been spared. The inn sits on a lawn overlooking Lake Waramaug, and it's home to one of Litchfield County's best restaurants.

One of the top new properties in the county, the sumptuous **Huckleberry Inn** (219 Kent Rd., Warren, 860/868-1947 or 866/868-1947, www.thehuckleberryinn.com) occupies a meticulously restored late–18th-century house with original wide-plank chestnut floors, original woodwork, and hand-hewn beams. There are just three guest rooms, along with a cozy cottage outfitted with a marble steam shower, heated marble bathroom floor, a cobblestone fireplace, and a full kitchen. All rooms have VCR-stereo systems, but the ambience and museum-quality antiques faithfully recall the past. In-room massage can be arranged. A substantial breakfast is included.

One property that faded steadily during the latter half of this century, to the point of utter disrepair in the early 1990s, was the **Birches Inn** (233 W. Shore Rd., New Preston, 860/868-1735 or 800/LAKE-INN, www.thebirchesinn.com). It sits on the shore of Lake Waramaug, set back on a rise from the water. Fortunately, new owners completely renovated the place in the mid-1990s, turning it into a one of the area's most appealing accommodations. There are eight antiques-filled rooms, five in the main inn and three down along the shore, the latter with secluded decks overlooking the water. The restaurant here is outstanding.

**$150–250:** Depending on the style of accommodation you choose, the **White Hart Inn** (Village Green, Rte. 41 and U.S. 44, Salisbury, 860/435-0030 or 800/832-0041, www.whitehartinn.com) suits most budgets and tastes, and is therefore an excellent base for exploring the extreme northwestern corner of the state. There are 26 rooms; those in main building are rather small but have nice new bathrooms. Accommodations in a separate building behind the inn are quite a bit larger, though less quaint. All contain reproduction Colonial antiques and are nicely maintained, but the White Hart does appear to have lost some of its luster in recent years and could stand a light makeover. A highlight

© ANDREW COLLINS

**Lakeville's Wake Robin Inn**

is the long front porch with wicker furnishings, a favorite place to people-watch in summer.

Purchased by new owners Michael Bryan and Shaffin Shariff in 2002, the stately **Wake Robin Inn** (Rte. 41, Lakeville, 860/435-2515, www.wakerobin.com) has received a much-needed infusion of energy, and is presently undergoing a complete makeover. Already, the 24 rooms in the historic 1896 main inn have been redecorated, as has the fireplace-warmed lobby and a convivial Michael Bryan's Irish pub. The pub is open late, and serves both traditional pub fare and some more creative and substantial specials. The inn is fast becoming a hit with both locals and guests, in part because of the Wake Robin's easygoing but highly efficient staff. Down the hill from the main hotel, a smaller row of motel-style units is open April–November; it's a popular choice with families (rooms can be connected), and it's also pet-friendly (by arrangement). This hilly, wooded property has a pair of nature trails. A rarity for a property this large: full breakfast in included on weekends, and Continental breakfast on weekdays.

**$100–150: Hilltop Haven B&B** (175 Dibble Hill Rd., West Cornwall, 860/672-6871, www.hilltopbb.com) was built in the 1930s on 800-foot Dibble Hill. The 63-acre compound is run by innkeeper Everett Van Dorn, and it's by far one of Litchfield County's most charming B&Bs. From the wraparound front porch you have views of the Berkshires in Massachusetts and Taconic Mountains in New York, and a five-foot stone fireplace warms the inviting living room. Additionally, a beautifully restored historic cabin with a kitchen and a redwood hot tub, situated on a babbling brook—once an old sawmill site—makes for about as romantic a retreat as you'll find in this area. Convenient both to Mohawk Mountain and the great fishing and canoeing of the Housatonic, the **Cornwall Inn** (270 Kent Rd., U.S. 7, Cornwall, 860/672-6884 or 800/786-6884, www.cornwallinn.com) offers casually elegant accommodations in an 1820s building. It has been an inn since 1871, but a more recent overhaul gave this property a stylish new feel. That historic building has six rooms, and there are another eight in a newer lodge next door. Each room has cedar-post feather beds, cable TV, data ports, and air-con-

THE WESTERN HILLS

ditioning. There's also a full-service restaurant with a delightful setting.

The Housatonic Fly Shop (see Fishing, above) operates the **Housatonic Meadows Lodge** (13 U.S. 7, Cornwall Bridge, 860/672-6064, www.housatonicmeadowslodge.com)—in fact, the fly shop shares the property. Not surprisingly, it's a popular choice among fishing enthusiasts, but this 1780 house, with five large guest rooms that share three baths, is a nice option no matter your interests. Rooms have quilted bedspreads and simple, homey, yet tasteful furnishings.

**$50–100:** Within steps of the town green and downtown shops is the economical **Barton House B&B** (34 East St., U.S. 202, New Milford, 860/354-3535), an 1850s Colonial-style house whose rooms each have a private bath, TV, fresh flowers, and are filled with antiques. Although there's a busy grocery store directly beside the property, the backyard rolls down toward a brook and is peaceful and quiet. A common room has a piano, and books fill the library.

A short drive or a beautiful 10-minute walk from Lake Waramaug is **Constitution Oak Farm** (36 Beardsley Rd., Kent, 860/354-6495, oakfarm@aol.com), a quirky old house (the marker outside says 1833, but it looks to be at least 200 years old) with wide-plank floors, an eclectic mix of antiques and older pieces, furnishings upholstered in every pattern imaginable, and floral wallpapers—it's sort of a busy decorating theme, and this is neither a prim nor fancy place. Rates are extremely reasonable.

The **Hopkins Inn** (22 Hopkins Rd., 860/868-7295, www.thehopkinsinn.com) might be the greatest bargain in Connecticut, offering guests a chance to encamp inside a gorgeous 1847 Federal-style farmhouse on a hill high above Lake Waramaug, many of whose rooms offer panoramic views of the countryside. On summer and fall weekends, it's important to book well ahead, as this place fills up fast. Rooms are small and simple (this is a former boarding house), and some share baths. But they have pretty chenille bedspreads, country antiques, and large windows that let in plenty of light. Best of all, there's a fine restaurant downstairs and a winery out back.

## Campgrounds
**Macedonia Brook State Park** (159 Macedonia Brook Rd., Kent, 860/927-4100 or 860/927-3238) has among the most scenic campsites in Connecticut, set in groves of tall shade trees. It's an ideal spot if hiking is on your agenda, as the park is laced with excellent trails. Up in Canaan, **Lone Oak Campground** (U.S. 44, East Canaan, 860/824-7051 or 800/422-2267, www.loneoakcampsites.com) has a host of daily programs for both kids and animals—this is really more of a camping resort, with swimming pools, movies, an arcade, a nightclub, and stocked fishponds.

There's also excellent camping at the **White Memorial Foundation Campgrounds** (U.S. 202, Litchfield, 860/567-0089), which has a pair of sites—one looks directly over the lake and accommodates both tenters and RVers, and another is in a wooded plot and handles only tenters. Another excellent camping spot with water views is **Lake Waramaug State Park** (30 Lake Waramaug Rd., 860/868-2592) in Washington. There's great swimming here and very nice (but not cheap) restaurants nearby. **Housatonic Meadows State Park** (U.S. 7, Cornwall Bridge, 860/672-6772 or 860/927-3238) has pine-shaded campsites for both tents and RVs, right by the trout-filled Housatonic River.

## FOOD

Excellent restaurants abound throughout Litchfield County, and the trend toward increasingly innovative cooking continues unabated, as hot new eateries seem to open up in these parts every few months. Washington and Lake Waramaug have the lion's share of sophisticated eateries, with quite a few in Salisbury and New Milford. Kent, strangely, doesn't have many new restaurants of great interest, but it's a wonderful town for snacking—just stroll along Main Street to check out the handful of businesses specializing in everything from truffles to takeout sushi to homemade ice cream.

### Upscale
As restaurants at country inns go, **The Boulders** (Rte. 45, New Preston, 860/868-0541, $21–30)

THE WESTERN HILLS

is one of the best in Connecticut. Contemporary fare like house-made pheasant tortellini in a mushroom broth with shaved fennel, bacon lardoons, and parmesan; and beef short rib ragout with grilled broccolini, soft saga blue cheese–polenta, crispy smoked shallots, and roasted-carrot coulis, are always outstanding. In warm weather, take a seat on the stepped terrace, which looks out toward the lake.

Another stellar hotel restaurant is the **Mayflower Inn** (Rte. 47, Washington, 860/868-9466, $21–32), whose dining room can be a bit formal for some tastes, but is worth putting up with if you're seeking some of the best contemporary American cooking in the state. World-beat influences are evidenced in dishes like grilled swordfish with black bean–whipped potatoes and a mango salsa. The sugar cookies are out of this world.

An advantage to dining at the **White Hart Inn** (Village Green, Rte. 41 and U.S. 44, Salisbury, 860/435-0030, $12–25) is that you have three distinctly different dining rooms to choose from, and the menu (the same one is used in all three spaces) has both light and less expensive fare, such as grilled portobello sandwiches with goat cheese and roasted red peppers, and more serious and filling dishes like grilled Porterhouse with bourbon stilton-sauce served with mashed potatoes. You can dine in the more formal American Grill; the rustic Tap Room, with a fireplace, wooden floor, and creaky old tables; or the garden room, which is filled with sunlight during the day, but feels sort of Holiday Inn-ish. Overall, the Tap Room offers the coziest ambience. Both service and food quality can be uneven at times, but this is generally a safe bet for a very nice meal.

For many years the **Fife & Drum** (53 N. Main St., U.S. 7, 860/927-3509, $13–30 on the main menu, $6–12 on the tavern menu) has been a fixture on Kent's sophisticated but countrified Main Street. Inside is a traditional New England–style dining room with rustic booths—it's an inviting if unadventuresome space, and the same could be said about the menu, although traditionalists adore such classics as flambéed roast duckling, and châteaubriand béarnaise for two. A tavern menu

offers inexpensive and tasty burgers, salads, burritos, wraps, and the like. The highlights at Fife & Drum are the award-winning wine list (distinguished by *Wine Spectator*) and the live piano music presented nightly by owner and former conductor for the likes of Peggy Lee and Frank Sinatra, Dolph Traymon.

The specialties at the **Hopkins Inn** (22 Hopkins Rd., New Preston, 860/868-7295, $17–26) are authentic Austrian and Swiss cooking, and the seating is in a great rambling old dining room with views down the hill toward Lake Waramaug (which, of course, looks as though it's smack in the middle of the Alps, thus adding a further sense of authenticity to the cuisine). Try the sweatbreads Viennese-style, or the salmon with herb butter.

The menu at **Adrienne** (218 Kent Rd., U.S. 7, New Milford, 860/354-6001, $17–27) changes often, but is always tremendously eclectic and interesting, one month featuring portobello mushrooms layered with grilled and roasted vegetables, a tomato-orange sauce, and crisp potatoes, and another offering roasted filet mignon on a potato cake with ratatouille and spinach hollandaise. Asian, Mediterranean, and Eastern European influences are evident in the food, but the dining room is thoroughly New England, set on the ground floor of an 18th-century farmhouse with creaky wide-plank floors, four fireplaces, and pretty gardens in back.

Dinner at the **Birches** (233 W. Shore Rd., 860/868-1735, $15–26), one of several fine inns overlooking Lake Waramaug, is one of Connecticut's surest bets for exquisite contemporary fare—and at prices quite reasonable when compared with similar-caliber eateries in the neighborhood. The menu changes often, but may feature pork chops with roasted plums, garlic-mashed potatoes, and lightly creamed spinach; or grilled salmon in corn husks with snow peas, haricot verts, and a risotto cake. The starter of diver scallop wrapped in mesquite smoked salmon with tobiko caviar créme is a classic. Despite the fabulous setting—many tables look through large windows toward the lake—and stylish ambience, the staff runs the Birches without the slightest air of snobbery.

## Creative but Casual

A simply decorated storefront eatery on Canaan's lovably raffish Main Street, **The Cannery** (85 Main St., U.S. 44 and 7, Canaan, 860/824-7333, $17–25) has been serving cutting-edge internationally influenced American food for longer than most in Litchfield County, and the quality remains remarkably high. Warm calamari salad with fennel vinaigrette is a pleasing way to begin a meal; rack of lamb with cannellini bean stew makes a hearty entrée, especially on a cold night.

A welcome antidote to the vast slew of urbane but often-times sterile new restaurants invading the countryside is the warm, happily untrendy **G. W. Tavern** (20 Bee Brook Rd., Rte. 47, Washington, 860/868-6633, $8–22). The tavern serves excellent and filling fare at reasonable prices, offering both pub favorites (fish and chips, meatloaf) and some stellar contemporary dishes, including excellent salmon cakes, fresh baked cod whose preparation changes seasonally, and frequent wild game specials. Numerous ales, porters, and lagers are on tap, plus there's a good wine list. The G. W. has two dining rooms, a more informal one facing a fireplace, and another in back with windows overlooking Bee Brook (there are also a few outdoor tables). It's open late and has a fun and lively staff—a great spot simply for mingling at the bar.

Just up the street, the **Bistro Cafe** (31 Bank St., 860/355-3266, $12–20) was one of the first restaurants to serve exciting cuisine in New Milford's revitalized downtown. The cooking here reflects Asian, Mediterranean, and regional American influences, including a terrific crispy goat cheese and potato tart appetizer with smoked-tomato jam and baby greens, and entrées like chicken pad thai with fried tofu, chopped scallions, and toasted peanuts, and oven-roasted pork loin with Southwestern-style smoked pepper demi-glace and black bean salad. The warmly lighted dining room has high ceilings and a casual but elegant ambience. Service can be uneven, but it's always friendly.

Amid the bevy of upscale antiques shops in New Preston, **Oliva** (East Shore Rd., Rte. 45, 860/868-1787, $13–23) offers an always-interesting slate of Northern Italian and Mediterranean dishes, including outstanding pizza (arguably the best in Litchfield County), plus Moroccan lamb stew and a brilliant antipasto consisting of unusual imported cheeses, vegetables, and fine prosciutto. Dining is in a tiny nook with exposed brick and a slate floor, and there are one or two tables on a terrace.

The **Boathouse at Lakeville** (349 Main St., 860/435-2111, $10–27) offers some of the best—okay, only—sushi in northwestern Connecticut, along with a menu of fine regional American cooking, including outstanding seafood. Start off with Maryland crab cakes or smoked trout pâté, before moving on to Chilean sea bass with lemon-caper butter or Bass Ale–braised baby back ribs with house-made barbecue sauce. The sushi menu includes such inspired creations as the Salisbury roll, with tuna, salmon, smelt roe, and avocado. The airy and contemporary dining room, with canoes and crew boats hanging from the rafters, is warmed by a fireplace in winter. Having moved from its original location in Sharon to Lakeville in 2001, **West Main** (8 Holley St., 860/435-1450, $17–26) continues to serve first-rate contemporary American and Mediterranean fare, such as delicious Tuscan white bean soup. Grilled spiced pork loin with green apple–red onion jam is a favorite entrée. There's dining on a patio in summer.

After closing for a short time, the wildly popular **Doc's Restaurant** (62 Flirtation Ave., New Preston, 860/868-9415, $14–21, pizzas $9–13) reopened in the same itsy-bitsy space overlooking Lake Waramaug. This place has long been famous for its thin-crust pizzas (such as the *biancaneve*, topped with ricotta, mozzarella, and garlic), but don't overlook the extensive menu of traditional Italian grills: *melanzane repieni* (rolled eggplant with ricotta and mozzarella, baked in marinara sauce with penne), *gamberoni Siciliana* (pan-seared jumbo shrimp with white wine, capers, onions, garlic, plum tomatoes, and oregano), etc. The current Doc's is less famous than the original, but it's still very popular—and the tiny dining room fills up fast on weekends.

## Steaks, Pizza, and Pub Grub

Even a handful of the region's transplanted Southerners have given their approval to the slow-cooked, Texas-style barbecue prepared at **The Cookhouse** (31 Danbury Rd., U.S. 7, New Milford, 860/355-4111, $8–24), a massive barn-like structure with two levels of seating under a high pitched ceiling—the layout is ideal when live comedy or music is presented, which is often on weekends. Specialties include "slo-smoked" prime rib, wild turkey shepherd's pie, smoked chicken and black bean quesadillas, and steak fries the size of cigars. The **Marble Dale Pub** (U.S. 202, New Preston, 860/868-1496) is a relaxed spot popular for its lobster specials and very good burgers—plenty of locals (even some high-profile ones) come here when they're looking for homey ambience and un-complicated food.

The rambling white **Bulls Bridge Inn** (333 Kent Rd., U.S. 7, Bulls Bridge, 860/927-1000, $10–17) serves traditional American fare, such as baked jumbo shrimp with crabmeat stuffing, and herb-roasted turkey with apple stuffing and cranberry sauce. The former post office and general store, which was a stagecoach stop in the late-18th century, anchors this sleepy village. The historic tap room is a favorite spot for mingling with locals over fine ales and noshing on Cajun chicken sandwiches, fried mozzarella, and smoked salmon.

The relatively new **Upper Crust** (373 Litchfield Rd., U.S. 202, 860/350-0006, large pies $12–18), just across from the Silo cookery shop, serves some of the best pizzas around. It's set inside a cheerful little white farmhouse in the rural north end of New Milford. Favorite pies include the prosciutto and fig topped with gorgonzola, fresh arugula, and balsamic vinaigrette; and the fresh clam and applewood-smoked bacon. You can also build your own salad from a long list of intriguing ingredients (roasted beets, calamata olives, shaved fennel, toasted walnuts, and so on).

At the newly refurbished Wake Robin Inn, **Michael Bryan's Irish Pub** (Rte. 41, Lakeville, 860/435-2000, $7–14) serves well-prepared comfort foods—Guinness beef stew, beer-battered fish and chips, country pâté, and salmon cakes. The cozy dining area is convivial and inviting, and the staff friendly. It's one of the better places in Litchfield County for locals, weekenders, and visitors from afar to mix and mingle.

## Ethnic Fare

This isn't much of an area for exotic cooking, but you will find one of the state's best Mexican restaurants, **Salsa** (54 Railroad St., 860/350-0701, $8–16) in downtown New Milford. A trip to this small storefront eatery will transplant you to New Mexico—delicious green chile stew is a specialty, and the chips come with your choice of three fresh salsas (tomatillo, chipotle, and habanero). The menu offers mostly American-style versions of Mexican fare, some New Mexican and others Arizonan or Texan —fajitas, sour cream chicken enchiladas, and roasted vegetable burritos, for instance. Serves beer and wine only.

## Quick Bites

A gleaming stainless-steel diner with an art deco design, the **Collin's Diner** (Main St., Canaan, 860/824-7040, under $10) has been doling out hearty egg breakfasts, sandwiches, and blue-plate specials since the early 1940s.

In Sharon, locals congregate regularly at the **Country Corner Tavern** (Rte. 41, 860/364-0070, under $10), a sunny little family restaurant in the town's sole shopping center; try to get a seat, especially if there are just one or two of you, at the vintage green wooden counter. Barbecue ribs and black-bean burgers are among the yummiest offerings from a menu with all the typical diner favorites.

For delicious ice cream, wander by the old Kent train station, site of **Stosh's** (38 N. Main St., 860/927-4495), which has some of the best sweets around (many of the area's best restaurants serve Stosh's ice cream for dessert). In New Milford, consider completing your walk around downtown with a big ice-cream sundae at **Sprinkles** (60 Railroad St., 860/355-1664).

As you drive or stroll through the quaint covered bridge in West Cornwall, consider dropping by the **Wandering Moose Cafe** (Rte. 128, 860/672-0178, $8–15), if you're in the mood for a snack. This homey diner serves particularly good breakfast, lunch, and—on weekends—dinner.

## Java Joints

Anchoring New Milford's bustling downtown is **Bank Street Coffee** (56 Bank St., 860/350-

8920), a sunny storefront café with several tables by the window; light snack foods are offered in addition to coffee drinks. For both ambience and decadent drinks and sweets, the region's best coffeehouse is the **Kent Coffee Company** (Main St., 860/927-1445), a homey—if slightly raggedy—storefront spot with delicious coffee concoctions, like bianca latte (hot white chocolate topped with whipped cream), fine teas, and melt-in-your-mouth truffles.

Salisbury's **The Roast Coffee House** (860/435-0600, 20 Main St.) is a dapper little place for latter, tucked down an alley behind the town pharmacy on Main Street. The sweet but simple **Nine Main Bakery and Deli** (Main St., New Preston, 860/868-1879) is a cheerful bakery in a Victorian house in New Preston. It's good for a coffee break while antiquing, and serves chunky oatmeal-and-chocolate-chip cookies, muffins (the cherry-pecan variety is delicious), chai tea, and sandwiches.

### Gourmet Goods and Picnic Supplies

Kent's **Stroble Baking Company** (Main St., 860/927-4073) has wonderful baked goods and takeout, including a sushi platter ($9 per dozen pieces). An exquisite patisserie and chocolatier that also added a more substantial café in 2003, **Belgique** (U.S. 7 and Rte. 341, Kent, 860/927-3681) is a must-see for any serious food lover. It's set inside a quaint little house in downtown Kent, and it sells simply superb hand-made chocolates, real Belgian hot chocolate, artful cakes, and savory sandwiches and gourmet goods.

Salisbury's **Thyme-Enz Harvest Bakery & Prepared Foods** (10 Academy St., 860/435-1302) has both eat-in and takeout delights, from heavenly butter cookies to designer pizzas to bountiful salads and sandwiches. In Bridgewater, the **Village Store** (27 Main St. S, Rte. 133, 860/354-2863) has a wonderful bakery with handmade doughnuts and scones, plus a deli with homemade salads, pastas, and daily lunch specials. **Egg & I Pork Farm** (355 Chestnutland Rd., Rte. 109, New Milford, 888/265-7675, www.eggandiporkfarm.com) supplies many of the top restaurants with its delicious meats, particularly smoked bacon and country hams. You

can buy its stuff retail by dropping in, calling, or ordering from the website. In Washington Depot, **The Pantry** (Titus Rd., 860/868-0258) stocks gourmet foods, prepares tasty sandwiches, and sells a vast array of cookery and food-related gifts.

The cakes and sweets produced at **Matthews 1812 House** (250 Kent Rd., U.S. 7, 860/672-0149 or 800/662-1812, www.matthews1812 house.com) have been featured on TV and in articles. This very special bakery does a brisk mail-order business, but you can also drop in to sample the award-winning candies, dessert sauces, fruit-and-nut cakes, and other delectables.

In Salisbury, **Harney & Sons Fine Teas** (23 Brook St., 860/435-5050 or 800/TEA-TIME, www.harney.com) is well-known for its tea importing business, and it supplies teas to fine restaurants and luxury hotels all over the country, offering some 200 varieties through mail order. There's a tea-tasting room here, and you can buy all the tea accoutrements you'd ever want.

## INFORMATION AND SERVICES

### Visitor Information

All but one of the towns in this region are served by the **Litchfield Hills Visitors Bureau** (Box 968, Litchfield, CT 06759, 860/567-4506, www.litchfieldhills.com). The exception is Bridgewater, which is served by the **Housatonic Valley Tourism District** (30 Main St., Box 406, Danbury, CT 06810, 203/743-0546 or 800/841-4488, www.housatonic.org).

### Getting Around

U.S. 7 is the main north–south road through western Litchfield County; U.S. 202 branches off from U.S. 7 in New Milford and leads through Washington, before cutting into the eastern half of the county. And U.S. 44 is the main east–west route from the northwestern corner of the region to the east. Several state routes also cut east to west, and virtually all of these roads are picturesque, winding, and hilly. It's tempting to glance at the magnificent scenery as you motor about the dramatic western reaches of Litchfield County, but bear in mind that many of the roads twist sharply, and careful attention is required to drive them. Traffic is never too bad, except perhaps on weekends in summer and fall when enthusi- asts of country roads chug along, often well below the speed limit—try to let others pass by you if your goal is more to see the sights than to get somewhere fast.

## The Eastern Litchfield Hills

The towns comprising the eastern band of Connecticut's Litchfield Hills are a far more eclectic jumble than those to the west. Overall, this northwest corner of the state is known for its bucolic vistas and sleepy villages unencum- bered by suburban sprawl and other common vagaries. But Southbury bridges rural Litch- field County with the bedroom communities and somewhat haggard mill towns of north- ern New Haven County, where it's situated. And the county seat, Litchfield—one of the most impressive New England villages you'll ever find—nudges up against industrial Tor- rington, the only true city covered in this sec- tion. Likewise, quiet and picturesque Norfolk has the old mill town, Winsted, as its neighbor. These contrasts give the region an eclectic per- sonality, so you never quite know what to ex- pect as you pass from town to town.

Sunday drivers in search of picture-book views will find that the eastern Litchfield Hills offer plenty of great vistas, but just as many gritty, and often fascinating, reminders of the state's rich industrial history. The area is not, however, inherently less interesting or less rife with shopping and culture than western Litch- field County. As noted above, Litchfield is the region's heart and soul, and will certainly re- quire a full roll of film to immortalize in your scrapbook. Woodbury, to the south, has more antiques stores per capita than any town in New England. Perfectly preserved villages like Bethlehem, Morris, and Goshen seem cen- turies behind the rest of the state. And the harder-edged communities of Torrington and Winsted are not without their charms, despite the fact that many traditional guidebooks ig- nore them.

## NORFOLK TO WINSTED

### Norfolk

Norfolk, although it had considerable water- power, was never developed either agriculturally or for manufacturing purposes because of its rugged high-hill terrain; it's the most mountain- ous town in Connecticut. The community was one of the last in the state to be settled (in the 1740s), and it was developed gradually over the next few decades into a proper village—but it has remained bucolic and rather placid since its inception. A few mills operated on the rivers running through town, but they petered out eventually, and some dairy farms have contin- ued to thrive over the centuries, but they repre- sent a small cottage industry.

There aren't many historical notes linked to Norfolk, except for one tale of generosity dating from the American Revolution. Norfolk was not among several northwestern Connecticut towns to contribute men to Ethan Allen's famed Green Mountain Boys—but records show that while en route from Hartford to the Berkshires, an expedi- tion of 16 men lost a horse while passing through this difficult territory, and one of Norfolk's more patriotic townspeople contributed his own to assist in what became the first taking of a British fort.

Norfolk remained secluded from the rest of the state for most of its first 150 years; finally, in 1871, a railroad was built linking the Housatonic and Naugatuck lines. This brought a new generation of visitors into town, and toward the end of the late- 19th century Connecticut industrialists began to build summer homes in Norfolk, taking advantage of the cool climate and beautiful scenery. In 1899 the summer-long Norfolk Music Festival was begun, and it's still going strong today.

# UNITED WE STAND, DIVIDED WE MOVE THE CHURCH BACK AND FORTH

The village of Colebrook is today anchored, as are so many small Connecticut towns, by a glorious white Congregational church. But the site of this particular church was determined almost entirely by accident, rather than sound planning. A rushing stream called Mill Brook bisects the town and effectively separates it into upper and lower sections. These two halves, comprising northern Colebrookers and southern ones, fought bitterly over where to build the first meetinghouse, as churches were called in Colonial times.

After much bickering, it was decided that the church would be erected a scant few hundred yards south of the brook. The location issue, however, which was frequently at the crux of civic controversies during Connecticut's earliest years, did not fade away easily. For the most part, northern Colebrookers refused to attend the church or help find it a preacher.

In the early 1790s, soon after the church was completed, the two sides finally reached an agreement to move the controversy-plagued church, using 150 pair of oxen, to a point slightly *north* of Mill Brook. The first attempt failed, after a substantial exertion of manual and animal labor had moved the building a few hundred feet but failed to edge the structure beyond the brook. Another costly and laborious attempt was mounted the following year. It too failed. For a dozen years, stubborn worshipers continued to battle back and forth, with the southern Colebrookers insisting that the church be returned to its original location and the northerners just as adamantly demanding that it be lifted the final 100 yards over Mill Brook and into their jurisdiction. It's said that a fair number of residents grew so dissatisfied with the failure of Colebrook to resolve this issue that they washed their hands entirely of the Congregational Church and converted to Baptism.

Ultimately, some 15 years after the argument began, the remaining hapless parishioners decided to move the building. It had stood all this time on a temporary and very poor building site, but it was finally moved to a suitable and permanent plot of land—within a stone's throw of where it was constructed in the first place.

Norfolk remains one of Connecticut's most captivating settings, and there are several fine country inns here. Development has been kept to a minimum, and the village green looks today as one might imagine it a century ago—you can't park directly by the green, but there are spots along Maple Avenue near the town hall and down off U.S. 44 by the Pub restaurant.

Arranged around the green are the **Norfolk Historical Society Museum** (860/542-5761, open weekend afternoons late May–mid-Oct., and by appointment), the **Norfolk Chamber Music Festival** headquarters, the town library, an imposing Congregational church with a four-tier clock tower and a massive spire, and the Yale University summer school of music (which is related to the festival). The striking **Norfolk Library** is a peculiar edifice at the north end of green, with red scalloped siding, a turret, and a stone-faced ground floor. Another oddly charming building is **Apple House,** a whimsically designed shingle-style Victorian, which was purchased in 1998 by a couple of New York theater producers who have restored its original architectural elements—including its distinctive turret—to open it as the summertime **Greenwoods Theatre.**

The huge three-story Victorian **Battell-Stoeckel House,** on whose grounds the Chamber Music Festival and Yale summer school of music are located, is one of several fine homes around the green. A long driveway leads down to the Music Shed, a long, low, rambling redwood-shake structure where the concerts are given summerlong. The grounds are ideal for strolling or picnicking.

The green itself is sloped slightly and dotted with tall elegant shade trees, a fine war memorial, and at one end a distinctive cement fountain designed by Stanford White and executed by Saint Gaudens—here there are elaborate old antique lampposts and an ornate bench—it's a perfect place to sit and take in the scene.

THE WESTERN HILLS

A 10-minute drive south of the green is **Dennis Hill State Park.** At the top of a long sweeping drive is a rounded-off bald hill and a sprawling stone house with a low sweeping roof. A wooden stairwell winds up the exterior of the building and up to the roof, from which amazing views are had of the Litchfield Hills, the Berkshires in Massachusetts, and the Taconic range in New York state. The house, alas, has been vandalized a bit over the years, as the interior stands open (there are no doors or panes of glass in the window frames). It's interesting to imagine what it might have looked like set up properly and furnished. The hill is at 1,627 feet above sea level.

## Winchester Center

As you head back up Rte. 272 toward the green, note Winchester Road on your right. A turn here presents you with an interesting and scenic detour into the sleepy village of Winchester Center, which has a tiny green that could best be described as unimproved since Colonial days (hence its considerable charm). A sign by the green indicates how much a carriage would have been charged upon passing over the old Waterbury Turnpike when it opened in the late 1890s.

Technically, the incorporated town of Winchester takes in all of the city of Winsted, and encompasses a large chunk of land bounded by Colebrook, Norfolk, Goshen, Torrington, and Barkhamsted. But when people talk about the northern and most heavily populated half of town, they generally refer to it as Winsted. The southern half of town, however, where the lamp museum is, is a sparsely populated patch of woodland and farms, with several ponds and one large lake, a few chunks of state parkland, and one of the least modernized town centers in the state.

## Haystack Mountain and Campbell Falls

Drive west on Rte. 263, and make a right turn back onto Rte. 272 to return to the Norfolk town green. Back at the green, Rte. 272 leads north (breaking off to the right from U.S. 44) and up to **Haystack Mountain State Park.** Just past where U.S. 44 branches off to the west, take a left on Haystack Mountain Road to reach the parking area for hiking and to reach the 35-foot observation tower, which on a clear day yields views as far as Long Island Sound. Continue up Rte. 272 to reach **Campbell Falls State Park,** an even more secluded park that touches the Massachusetts border. For a scenic detour around the park, as you head up Rte. 272 take a left on Ashpohtag Road, a quick right onto Bald Mountain View Road, and follow this as it winds below Bald Mountain, the highest peak in Norfolk. This road will eventually meet with Tobey Hill Road, where a right turn leads to Campbell Falls.

## Colebrook

Back at the Norfolk town green, head east on U.S. 44 a short distance and then make a left onto Rte. 182; this road winds for a few scenic miles into the middle of Colebrook, which has the third-lowest population density of any town in the state. Now a remarkably remote and quiet town that looks as though it should be in rural northern Vermont, Colebrook began quietly, but eventually developed into one of the county's most prosperous agricultural communities.

Colebrook's quaint village center today consists of a modest town hall, a small historical society set in a Colonial house, a tiny post office, a wobbly old pale yellow general store, and the magnificent white Greek Revival Congregational Church of the Wildwood (the current one dates from 1842 and replaced the aforementioned original on the same site), all set around a small green. The **Colebrook Historical Society** (Rte. 183, 860/379-3142) has ongoing exhibits and is usually open weekends in summer (or by appointment). Social activity here revolves around the steps of the post office or outside the general store, and northern and southern Colebrookers now appear to get along okay (see the sidebar "United We Stand").

Much of Colebrook is dominated by woodland administered by the Algonquin State Forest, a vast and dense tract of pristine undeveloped land. From the village green, you can drive through the heart of it by taking Rte. 183 north. Take your very first right onto School House Road, and continue east until the paved surface gives way to a rutted dirt road that winds alongside a rambling stream before eventually intersecting with Sandy Brook Road (there's no street sign, but it's your only option). At this T intersection, make a right; Sandy Brook Road winds through the forest, paralleling Sandy Brook. This is ideal territory for mountain biking, and you'll also see a few fishermen, spring through fall, casting a line into this waterway. Sandy Brook Road ends at Rte. 8, just north of the Winchester border and a bit south of the Colebrook Reservoir and the Massachusetts border. Wooded hills surround this large reservoir, and there's a high dam at the southeastern end of it. Non-motorized boating is permitted here, and there's a launch right off Rte. 8.

Another scenic drive is simply to follow Rte. 183 north from the village green for a few miles into Sandisfield, Massachusetts; or, in North Colebrook, make a left from Rte. 183 onto Church Hill Road and follow it into northern Norfolk, where it becomes N. Colebrook Road, passes by a handful of placid ponds, and branches off onto several smaller lanes. If you stay on course or bear left at any major intersections, the road you choose will eventually join back with either U.S. 44 or Rte. 272, both of which lead into the heart of Norfolk.

## Winsted

From Colebrook, head south on Rte. 8 (or, if coming directly from Norfolk, east on U.S. 44) and you'll quickly enter the bustling community of Winsted, which most people think of as its own entity but is in fact, politically speaking, a city within the incorporated town of Winchester. It was established in the early 1770s along the Mad River, which provided power for early industries. Whereas Winchester is rural and has no business concerns to speak of, Winsted is a working-class mill town whose Main Street (U.S. 44) is lined with turn-of-the-20th-century brick storefronts and workaday businesses. You'll find greasy spoon diners, pool halls, hardware stores, pharmacies, and several churches, including St. Joseph's, the first Catholic church to serve northwestern Connecticut. Winsted looks like the set of an old Frank Capra movie; it is neither run-down nor gentrified, it's simply stuck in time.

The sight of a few teenagers in modern attire mingling outside the Gilsam Cinema could just as easily be a scene from the movie *Pleasantville*.

The rush of the Mad River can be heard along Main Street, and you can easily imagine how this fast-moving river could have once supplied power to a host of saw- and gristmills, noxious tanneries, and noisy factories. Among the wares that once came out of Winsted are cheese boxes, pocket- and table knives, cut nails, iron wire, scythes and hoes, carriages, clocks, and all manner of early machinery. Iron forges, which processed the ore of nearby Salisbury and Kent, cast a glow here between 1795 until the 1850s. A woolen cloth mill opened here in the 1780s.

Winsted's commercial productivity slipped steadily during the Depression and more severely on the heels of World War II, but the town has largely been spared the scars of urban renewal that blight a few sections of Torrington, to the immediate south. Overall, this is a well-preserved downtown with one of the broadest Main Streets in the state, from which fine views are to be had of the rolling green hills. It's not as quaint as most of Litchfield County, but Winsted does possess a simple, nostalgic charm.

Town planners are currently working on ways to improve downtown, to clean up some of the grittier spots without entirely erasing Winsted's character. One proposal is to create a median along Main Street, which would enhance the appearance and promote safety for pedestrians. Additionally, some 30 of the least distinguished houses and apartment buildings may be razed in hopes of attracting developers.

Running along the south side of Main Street, by the Mad River, is Riverfront Park, which consists of a forested walkway along much of the river and is connected to Main Street via a pedestrian bridge. It's worth passing over the bridge and staring down at the typically mild current, remembering that this seemingly tepid waterway has been known to live up to its name. During the Great Flood of 1955, which ravaged much of lower-lying Connecticut, dozens of homes and businesses were destroyed when the Mad River rose to many feet above its normal level.

At the west (Norfolk) end of Main Street,

Lake Street rises up a steep incline to 1,400-acre Highland Lake, which is situated immediately above the community—it's a pretty body of water with many homes and weekend cottages (quite a few belonging to urban dwellers down in Waterbury, New Haven, and Bridgeport) surrounding the long meandering shoreline, which is divided into the First, Second, and Third bays, with the former being just above downtown. There's a boat launch at First Bay.

Just south of Lake Street, as you cross the Mad River from downtown, a left turn onto Prospect Street leads to the **Solomon Rockwell House** (225 Prospect St., 860/379-8433, limited hours, free), an 1813 Classical Revival mansion that houses exhibits, documents, and furnishings relevant to Winsted's and Winchester's history. Soaring Ionic columns dominate the front entrance. You may notice the resemblance to Solomon Temple in Woodbury; both buildings were designed by Colebrook's self-taught architect, Captain William Swift. The Rockwells were heavy into the early iron industry, where they accrued their fortunes. The rooms are not furnished as they were originally but contain a great variety of paintings, artifacts, and treasures culled from throughout the region.

At the east end of Main Street (the junction of Rte. 8 and U.S. 44), you'll discover Winsted's town green, which would be more picturesque but for the abundance of rather ugly buildings around it—this section of town could use some sprucing up. The green has a massive Civil War monument in the middle of it—while Winsted was developed long after the American Revolution, it did contribute the very first regular Civil War enlistee from the state of Connecticut, Samuel B. Horne. Despite what sits around it, the green itself is long and pleasant, frequently the site of concerts and local gatherings.

## TORRINGTON AND HARWINTON

### Torrington

You can hop on the limited access highway, Rte. 8, to reach the next town on this tour, Torrington, or head south out of downtown Winsted on Rowley Street, which eventually turns into Torrington Road (and then Winsted Road) and parallels Rte. 8.

With a population of 35,000 and a somewhat heavily developed downtown, Torrington is Litchfield County's one, albeit small, metropolis. It's a fairly depressed city that has had a difficult time economically in recent decades. The heart of downtown has quite a few vacant storefronts (the retail occupancy rate is about 25 percent), although there have been a few recent efforts to develop the city. The **Nutmeg Conservatory for the Arts** bought 60–62 Main St. in 1998, and the art deco **Warner Theatre** continues to be a great asset. Real estate here is extremely inexpensive, and it's hoped that the low prices and potential for rejuvenation will lure investors to this city, which has an enviable setting—just minutes from well-to-do tourist-popular towns like Litchfield and Norfolk.

Unfortunately, Torrington has happily courted major chain stores like Wal-Mart, Rite Aid, and Kmart over the years, and these stores are in shopping centers on major roads leading out of downtown, which has tended to hurt local businesses in the city center. The one major shopping plaza in the center of downtown faces, and thus mars the appearance of, the town green, as does a nearby high-rise housing project. It's a shame that the more appealing downtown structures, like the neoclassical **Torrington Library**, are overshadowed by so many aesthetically degrading ones.

Another aspect of downtown that could stand improvement is the treatment of the Naugatuck River, which originates in northern Torrington and flows right through town in a most undistinguished manner. The river has been cleaned of its pollutants in recent years, and now it would be nice to see the riverfront landscaped a bit.

Torrington was laid out in 1732, and in the 1750s its future as an industrial center was secured when a mill was established on the West Branch of the Waterbury River—many more manufacturing concerns would follow, from brass foundries to clockmakers to lock factories. The Wrightville section of town was laid out in 1852 for the workers of the local scythe factory. An

## TORRINGTON AND THE CIVIL WAR

Gail Borden wasn't the only resident of Torrington whose actions would figure prominently in the Civil War. In 1837, several citizens met to set up an antislavery society. But, upon searching for a gathering place, they found that every church and meeting hall in the region turned them away for fear that pro-slavery forces might retaliate. Finally, a local townsman offered his barn, and a meeting was held on a bitter January day. A drunken mob soon assembled outside the barn in hopes of rattling those in attendance, and as a small riot ensued, the meeting disbanded. But the group continued to find new places to conduct their meetings, despite facing ridicule from many of their friends and fellow citizens and expulsion in many cases from their churches. One most dedicated of these antislavery activists was a solemn man named John Brown—the very same John Brown whose abolitionist showdown at Harpers Ferry, West Virginia, would result in his hanging in 1859.

industrious man by the name of O. L. Hopson invented a swagging machine in 1866, which made it possible to mass-manufacture needles.

One of the more interesting developments was a settlement called Burrville, in the northeastern section of town. A few small factory shops opened in the 1820s, at first making hammers, bricks, and light tools, and then a tannery was created. In 1851, one of the Burrs, after whom the village was named, dammed the river west of the village and built a reservoir (now Burr Pond) that became known by all for its pristine waters and beautiful setting. These factors attracted an entrepreneur named Gail Borden to Burrville. For some time, he had been experimenting with the idea of condensing milk by preserving it with sugar, and a need for the purest possible source of water to perfect this process drew him here, where he developed a small factory on the reservoir.

Borden struck success in Burrville, and his invention of condensed milk is sometimes credited with having nourished the Union to victory

over the Confederacy in the Civil War. Borden eventually moved his operations to Dutchess County, New York, and the remains of his Burrville factory burned in a fire in 1877. Today, the site of the Borden condensed milk factory is preserved in the form of **Burr Pond State Park** (385 Burr Mountain Rd., 860/482-1817). The wooded perimeter of the 90-acre pond for which the park is named makes for a wonderful hike; in warm weather, you can swim on the pond, and in winter, bring along your ice skates. There are also 40 basic campsites.

In addition to the **Warner Theatre** (68 Main St.), several fine art deco and turn-of-the-20th-century buildings sit along Torrington's Main Street, chief among them the mustard yellow **Yankee Pedlar Inn**—a creaky old hotel with a disproportionately large, almost kitschy, red sign on the roof. Other notables include city hall, a traditional, columned, redbrick building; the First Congregational Church, whose cornflower-blue doors and Gothic stone arches depart from the white clapboards of churches in neighboring towns; and the red-turreted **Torrington Historical Society—Hotchkiss-Fyler House** (192 Main St., 860/482-8260, open 10 A.M.–4 P.M. Tues.–Fri., noon–4 P.M. weekends, Apr.–Nov. and mid-Dec.–Dec. 31, $3), which is one of the better house-museums in Litchfield County. The Society contains a period-furnished parlor, living room, library, dining room, and other parts of a typical 1900s mansion. Constructed at the turn of the 20th century, the building contains marvelous stenciling, fine woodworking and moldings, and a very nice collection of art—every architectural ornament of the period seems to have been incorporated into the exterior design. An adjacent carriage house contains an operational machine shop called **Hendey Machine Tools,** a tribute to a real company that operated in Torrington from 1870 to 1954. A 1930s Hendey lathe, shaper, and milling machine on exhibit in this shop, which allows a nice glimpse into the industrial history of Torrington.

### Harwinton

Torrington's neighbor to the southeast is a little town called Harwinton, whose name is a derivation of the three communities from which its first settlers hailed: Hartford, Windsor, and Farmington. For many years, it was supposed that Harwinton was the source of vast and profitable lead deposits; how this rumor began is anybody's guess, but after a couple of centuries of digging, not an ounce of lead has ever surfaced.

A couple of parts of Harwinton have been named historic districts, including the Litchfield–South Roads Historic District, where the early part of town was settled in 1745. Here, just east of where Rte. 4 branches off toward Torrington from Rte. 118, are several Federal houses, a historic former tavern, the 1909 neoclassical Hungerford Memorial Library, the 1916 Harwinton Community Hall (notable for its massive Gothic Revival tracery window), and the original meetinghouse. A mile east of town center is the Burlington–Harmony Hill Roads Historic District, which is more agrarian in feel and contains many fine old homes.

Follow South Street from Rte. 4 to reach one of the lesser-publicized sanctuaries in the region, the **Roraback Wildlife Management Area,** which at 2,000 acres is the largest wildlife management area in Connecticut. Mink, otters, turkeys, foxes, bobcats, great horned owls, and yellow warblers are but a sampling of the fauna living in this diverse habitat consisting of forests, grasslands, fields, wetlands, and ponds. The property, which used to be Valley View Farm and was owned by politician J. Henry Roraback (who entertained the likes of J. Edgar Hoover and Calvin Coolidge at the farm—bet those gatherings were a gas), was willed by his legacies to Connecticut in 1982. The 13-room Victorian main house still stands on the property and is used as offices by the State DEP; also on the property is a 73-foot-tall windmill dating to 1936 (it's restored, but no longer functional). Visitors can wander about and photograph or observe the wildlife, fish in the ponds and streams, and ride horseback on several gravel roads. In season, there is also hunting for deer, turkey, small game, and waterfowl.

## LITCHFIELD, BANTAM, AND GOSHEN

Litchfield is synonymous with Colonial Connecticut, owning one of New England's most gracious elm-shaded greens and preserving countless examples of grand 18th-century architecture. Today, a living museum with fancy shops and sophisticated restaurants, Litchfield was a prosperous Colonial trading center and played a valiant, behind-the-scenes role in the American Revolution.

Settlers largely from Hartford, Windsor, and Wethersfield purchased this land in 1715 from Potauck and Bantam Indians. By 1720, Litchfield had been laid out into 57 lots of approximately 15 acres apiece; the first courthouse, school, and Congregational church were erected around a common (village green) by the middle of that decade. Like most commons, Litchfield's was used early on for cattle grazing, but eventually developed into a hub of social activity.

Litchfield's first few decades were unnerving for its new inhabitants, owing to frequent skirmishes and confrontations with the Native American population; many neighboring tribes were quite hospitable to the settlers, but others attacked and harassed residents of the largely agrarian community. In 1751, Litchfield was named the county seat, winning a hotly contested battle for the position over neighboring Goshen, the true geographical center of the county.

During the American Revolution, Litchfield distinguished itself on many fronts. The future American statesman, Aaron Burr, visited in 1773 to stay with his sister Sarah and her new husband, the justice Tapping Reeve. For the next two years, Reeve taught the anxious young Burr everything he could about the ways of politics and justice. In July 1775, Burr left Litchfield to begin his esteemed military and political career, but he continued to call Litchfield home until moving back to New York City in 1780. Reeve, perhaps pleased with the success of his first student, opened America's first formal law school in 1784; the Tapping Reeve (or Litchfield Law) School thrived well into the 19th century, turning out some of this country's most brilliant legal minds.

Only a few weeks before Burr enlisted to fight in the American Revolution, a brazen young military colonel named Ethan Allen, who was born in Litchfield in 1737 (although he grew up largely in nearby Cornwall and Salisbury), led his troop of cocky "Green Mountain Boys" on a surprise raid of the Brits's Fort Ticonderoga, on Lake Champlain in upstate New York—this was the first successful capture of a British flag by American forces. Dozens of the Green Mountain Boys hailed from Litchfield County. In fact, the very following day, Colonel Seth Warner of nearby Roxbury commanded the defeat of the Brits at Crown Point, thereby securing the whole of Lake Champlain.

Litchfielders quickly developed a reputation for fierce patriotism and loyalty: In January 1776, countless townsmen enlisted to defend New York's Fort Washington. Upon hearing the call for enlistees sent out by Captain Bezaleel Beebe, many residents literally sprinted to the village green in fear that sufficient troops might be rounded up before they arrived. Alas, the fort was lost to the British, and of the 36 Litchfield enlistees, only six returned home alive, the majority of the dead having failed to survive the inhumane prison conditions of their captors.

From 1775 through 1780, Litchfield's secure and almost impenetrable inland location made it an ideal supplies and munitions store for

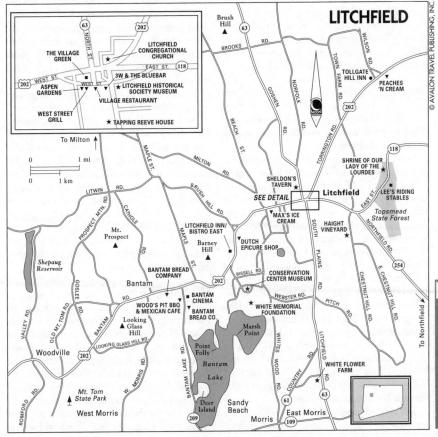

THE WESTERN HILLS

Washington's troops. Residents contributed to the effort in some astonishing ways: General Oliver Wolcott, for example, supplied the troops with exactly 42,088 lead bullets. The source of these bullets was deliciously ironic: A few years before the war, a towering equestrian statue of King George III was erected on Bowling Green, at the southern tip of British-occupied New York City. So many unsympathetic rebels vandalized this effigy of their enemy that a law was finally passed outlawing the desecration of statues in New York City.

It seems the law was taken rather lightly, according to a report in the *New Hampshire Gazette* of July 11, 1776: "Last Monday evening the Equestrian Statue of George III, with tory pride and folly raised in the year 1770, was, by the Sons of Freedom, laid prostrate in the dust—the just desert of an ungrateful tyrant." Lead being a hot commodity of the day, the statue was chopped up and moved piecemeal in an oxcart some 100 miles to Litchfield, where General Wolcott's wife, children, and a few neighbors melted down the pieces and transformed them into patriot bullets. Untold British troops were felled, ironically, with the so-called melted majesty of their toppled king.

In the wake of the town's contribution to American independence, local merchant Julius Deming helped secure Litchfield's commercial success by establishing a strong merchant trade program with China. The next 50 years of successful international shipping marked Litchfield's golden era, when immense mansions popped up one after the other and the population swelled—by 1820, Litchfield had nearly 5,000 residents (compared with just 4,000 in Hartford and about 6,000 in New Haven). The advent of westward expansion and rail transportation in the middle of the 19th century soon spelled the end of Litchfield's boom. The slow and tortuous Shepaug railroad did connect Litchfield to points south in 1872, but by then much faster and more efficient lines had been built along the neighboring Housatonic River Valley to Canaan and the Naugatuck River Valley through Torrington and Winsted.

The railroad was abandoned in the late 1930s, but by now, Litchfield's merit as a resort desti-

rural lane in Litchfield County

nation had been realized. Because the industrial revolution skipped over Litchfield, its verdant farmland and Colonial patina had been effectively preserved. Artists, writers, industry heads, and wealthy families began spending their summers here, and with the age of automobile travel, there soon evolved a new breed of Litchfielder: the weekend visitor.

Today, Litchfield remains a quiet village with big-city culture and considerable celebrity. Antiquers, Revolution history buffs, hikers, foodies, and curiosity seekers visit through the spring, summer, and fall—increasingly, winter is also gaining in popularity. Development in town is constant but stable, and Litchfield has nowhere near the unmanaged commercialism of many other Colonial New England towns. Quite a few locals protested when a branch of the upscale women's clothier Talbot's opened on the precious village green, but Litchfield's historic integrity and neighborly demeanor continue, for the most part, unabated.

## The Village Green

Litchfield's village green, at the confluence of North, East, South, and West Streets (a.k.a. Rte. 63 and U.S. 202) gets fancier each year. As the traffic has increased, one- and two-hour (unmetered) parking limits have been established; the police are very quick to ticket offenders. The popular shopping area extends a few hundred feet below the green, along the west side of South Street, and for about a quarter mile along West Street, which fringes the green. You'll find upscale boutiques, antiques shops, and a few acclaimed restaurants (most notably the West Street Grill) along this stretch.

South Street bisects the long and oft-photographed green, which is decked with war memorials and gardens. Tall trees shade the many picnic tables, and an information booth with brochures anchors the green. You may be surprised to see that few examples of authentic Colonial architecture line the green; two fires in the late 1800s destroyed most of the white clapboard buildings, and no less handsome Italianate and Victorian structures, mostly in redbrick and granite, have been erected in their place.

## North Street

The homes lining North and South Streets, on either side of the green, are some of New England's most impressive. It's definitely worth walking a half mile or so up and down each street. The first structure you'll note upon crossing U.S. 202, on the left-hand corner of North Street, is the **Litchfield Correctional Center,** which was built as the county jail in 1811 (on the site of the previous one). It's Litchfield's oldest standing government building. People often make fun of the fact that the jail abuts the First National Bank of Litchfield, which was built in 1814 and is still operating.

The previous town jail held some fairly infamous prisoners, including the English mayor of New York City, David Matthews, who was sent here following his arrest on June 21, 1776. Later on, he was joined by Ben Franklin's only son, William, the loyalist governor of New Jersey, who spent two years here. After he was released, William left America for England. The elder Franklin, horrified that his son should desert and take up arms against the cause for which he staked his life, held William in low regard for the remainder of his years.

As you continue up North Street, you can't miss the mansard-roof mansion, the former **Sheldon's Tavern,** 73 North St. (now a private residence). Built as a hostelry in 1760, the tavern hosted George Washington during one of his half dozen visits to Litchfield; it was later owned by James Gould, who co-operated the Litchfield

Law School with Tapping Reeve. Washington's aide, Alexander Hamilton, stayed with him that night—Litchfield resident Aaron Burr would kill Hamilton in a duel some years later.

Continuing up the street, you'll pass the site of Reverend Lyman Beecher's old home (the house has since been moved nearby). Beecher took his preaching position in Litchfield in 1810; his son, Henry Ward Beecher, went on to become a respected preacher. His daughter, born in 1811, a diminutive charge of energy named Harriet, went on to champion an end to slavery. Abraham Lincoln mused, upon being introduced to Harriet Beecher Stowe, how nice it was to meet the little lady who started the Civil War. Indeed, her 1852 novel *Uncle Tom's Cabin* fueled antislavery sentiments throughout the North. The controversial abolitionist John Brown was born in the neighboring town of Torrington, only a decade before Stowe.

Just up the street, a plaque marks the site of the **Pierce Academy,** which was established in 1792 as America's first school for girls; some 3,000 women passed through its doors during its 40-year tenure.

## South Street

Back at the village green, head to the corner of South and East Streets to visit the **Litchfield Historical Society Museum** (860/567-4501, www.litchfieldhistoricalsociety.org, open 11 A.M.–5 P.M. Tues.–Sat., 1–5 P.M. Sun. Apr.–Nov., $5 includes admission to Tapping Reeve House), which has both changing and permanent exhibits and is the most comprehensive facility in the county and one of the best in New England.

Continue down South Street, past the enormous stone **St. Michael's Episcopal Church,** and you'll soon reach little Wolcott Avenue. Opposite this intersection, you'll see the **Tapping Reeve House** (860/567-4501, open 11 A.M.–5 P.M. Tues.–Sat., 1–5 P.M. Sun., Apr.–Nov., free with paid admission to Litchfield Historical Society Museum), an impressive yellow Georgian Colonial with a long white picket fence and a tree-shaded front yard; it's now a museum detailing the history of Tapping Reeve's law school.

Reeve moved to Connecticut in 1772, began his tutorial of Aaron Burr in 1773, started giving informal lectures in 1782, and officially opened his school two years later. Over the next 50 years, more than 1,000 students graduated from the Litchfield Law School, including 130 future U.S. senators and congressmen, three supreme court justices, and countless other dignitaries and educators. Famous alums include statesman John C. Calhoun, inventor Sydney E. Morse, educator Horace Mann, lexicographer Noah Webster, and painter and Litchfield native George Catlin (who later spent time traveling with, living among, and depicting Native Americans on canvas). Reeve, despite being something of an absent-minded professor, was a great legal mind, an early champion of women's rights, and a U.S. Supreme Court justice from 1798 to 1814.

Across the street is the oldest of the mansions in town, the now-private **Oliver Wolcott House,** where all of those patriot bullets were fashioned out of a statue of King George III. George Washington was a guest of Wolcott in 1780, the second time he spent the night in Litchfield. The next morning he continued on to West Point, where General Washington would learn of Benedict Arnold's treason. Wolcott served a great political and military career, serving as major general of the Connecticut militia, signing the Declaration of Independence, and serving as state governor until his death in 1797.

Farther south, you'll pass the town's library; beyond that, at the corner of Old South Road, is the tiny cottage where Ethan Allen is alleged to have been born.

## West of the Village Green

West of the green, at the end of the row of shops, you'll see a small, ornate, Gothic Victorian wooden church. From here, you can drive along U.S. 202 west toward Bantam, passing the most commercial section of town, where several contemporary strip malls compete for your shopping dollars. Longtime visitors to Litchfield may remember the grand Kilravock Inn, which stood at the corner of Brush Hill Road (a little more than a mile west of the village green) and U.S. 202; alas, the inn burned down a while back.

Continue a couple of miles to reach Connecticut's largest nature preserve, the 4,000-acre **White Memorial Foundation** (860/567-0857, www.whitememorialcc.org); take White Hall Road from U.S. 202, midway between the villages of Bantam and Litchfield. The preserve was established in the early part of this century by brother and sister Alain and Mary White, whose parents had summered in Litchfield in the 1860s. Alain and Mary began purchasing the land in 1908, and they left the entire expanse as a nonprofit conservation and recreation center in 1913 (they went on to begin Connecticut's state park system and donated thousands more acres throughout Litchfield County to this cause). The Whites are a prominent early Connecticut family (White Street, in Danbury, is named for them).

This is one of New England's leading preserves, an outstanding facility in every regard. A highlight is the **Conservation Center Museum,** which contains extensive rotating and permanent exhibits detailing the region's natural history, as well as a library and gift shop. The dioramas and extensive taxidermy are both interesting and useful for getting a sense of how the local topography and ecosystem have evolved since the Ice Age. The exhibits in the nature center are remarkable, detailed, and beautifully presented. If the Museum of Natural History in New York City is many, many times bigger, it could be argued that this compact but attractive center is more user-friendly and just as informative when it comes to flora and fauna of the Northeast. The museum, really one of the state's best, also contains large maps of the trails and the property, and great geological displays.

The extensive grounds are crossed by 35 miles of trails (including six miles of the Mattatuck Trail, which traverses the county before joining the Appalachian Trail in Cornwall), some for cycling and others for horseback, foot, or, in winter, cross-country skiing. One of the best features is the expansive wetland area, through which a wooden boardwalk has been laid out, allowing you to study this habitat up close. The foundation is also a bird-watchers' paradise, with 30 observation platforms set up at the Holbrook Bird Observatory, allowing you to view the more than 240 species common to the area; a platform also overlooks Bantam Lake, which has a fine trail running alongside it. None of these trails are very hilly, and some, such as the nature trail that begins close to the museum and brushes down close to the Bantam River, are fairly short and can be done on a whim. Bobcats, beavers, and coyotes are among the many critters you might see wandering across this property, although certainly deer and raccoons are more common. The museum ($4) and the grounds (free) are open year-round.

### Bantam

Part of incorporated Litchfield, the village of Bantam was named by the Potauck Indians who once lived on this turf. White settlers first arrived in the early 1800s, when the residents of Litchfield, to the east, discovered the fine potential for hydropower along the Bantam River. Early industrialists dammed the river in several places, turned nearby Bantam Lake into a valuable reservoir, and proceeded to construct successful flour, cotton, and gristmills, as well as a first-rate carriage factory.

Bantam retains a somewhat rural, working-class feel, and is without question the least chichi section of Litchfield, which is not to say it isn't a pleasure to visit. The manufacturing interests have all but dried up, but the industrial past has been ingeniously preserved, as most of the hulking redbrick buildings now house multi-dealer antiques centers and artisans workshops. One popular small-town attraction is the **Bantam Cinema** (Bantam Lake Rd., Rte. 209, between U.S. 202 and Bantam Lake, 860/567-0006), housed inside a historic red carriage barn.

West of Bantam near the Washington border, 233-acre **Mt. Tom State Park** (U.S. 202, 860/868-2592) has a large pond popular for non-motorized boating (no trailers allowed; you can bring boats only on the roof of your car), fishing, and swimming, or in winter ice skating. The real treat here, however, is hiking to the summit of 1,325-foot Mt. Tom, which is crowned with a 30-foot stone observation tower built in 1921. The tower provides amazing views of the countryside in every direction—on the clearest of days you might be able to see Long Island Sound to the

south. The oak- and birch-covered trail to the top ascends about 400 feet in elevation and is about 1.5 miles long. The area's original Bantam Indians hunted these grounds, and communicated with neighboring tribes by sending smoke signals from the summit. There's no better spot when the foliage is turning in early October.

### Milton

The frozen-in-time village of Milton, in the northwest corner of Litchfield, offers cyclists and drivers some of the most scenic touring in Connecticut—a rugged landscape studded with Colonial homes and interwoven with stone walls. You can reach Milton from Litchfield several ways. Here are two particularly memorable ones: From the village green, head west on U.S. 202 a little more than a mile; make a right onto Brush Hill Road; continue until you reach Maple Street, onto which you'll make a right turn. Continue until you reach Milton Road, onto which you make a left turn; the Milton village green lies about a half mile ahead. Or, from the Litchfield village green, head west to Bantam, passing through the center of the village. Make a right onto Cathole Road, which is a short way beyond the Carriage Factory Antiques Center; continue north until you reach a T-intersection (Litwin Road); turn left, and then make an immediate right onto Headquarters Road, which leads to the village green. By bike, either of these trips will require some climbing uphill; on the plus side, once you're off U.S. 202, you'll encounter very little auto traffic.

Settled in 1795, Milton now consists of a pair of churches dating back to the early 1800s, a small meetinghouse, and several Colonial farmsteads; there are no shops or businesses—not even a post office, and many of the roads remain unpaved. It actually feels strange to drive so modern a contraption as an automobile through this anachronistic hamlet where horse-drawn carriages seem more appropriate.

The green itself is stark and treeless, with white clapboard homes and dark, rough-hewn bars lining its triangular perimeter. The two churches, rarely glimpsed by tourists, are a couple of the finest specimens, from an architectural perspective, in the state. On the north side of the green, the Trinity Episcopal Church wears a simple white facade, contrasted dramatically with its rows of tall, Gothic, stained-glass windows. A couple hundred yards west is the classic, wind-worn First Congregational, which is almost entirely without ornamentation.

At this point, you may opt to head directly up to Goshen, which is just over the Milton border. To do so, head up Shearshop Road, which begins at the northwest corner of the green; this road quickly devolves into a rather bumpy dirt road that winds through some majestic woodland and past a few horse farms. It eventually intersects with the paved Milton Road; bear left and continue up the road until you eventually hit Rte. 4 (the Sharon Tpke.). A right turn takes you to the traffic circle in Goshen's center, at the intersection with Rte. 63.

## East of the Village Green

Eastern and western Litchfielders once competed fiercely with each other on virtually every level. Today, East Litchfield enjoys a quieter, more residential feel than the western half of town, which is anchored by busy U.S. 202; there is little shopping in East Litchfield.

At the eastern border of the village green, U.S. 202 east veers off to the left (toward Torrington), and Rte. 118 bears to the right into East Litchfield. The eastern Litchfield Hills' only winery, the **Haight Vineyard** (Chestnut Hill Rd., follow signs from intersection of Rte. 118 and U.S. 202, 860/567-4045, www.haightvineyards.com) was opened in 1978, the first in the state—it was opened just after Connecticut legalized wine-producing by passing the Farm Winery Act. The fertile grounds rise above the Bantam River and produce fine chardonnay, ries-

## LITCHFIELD'S BELEAGUERED FIRST CONGREGATIONAL CHURCH

Even if this is your first time to Litchfield, you may recognize the hulking white First Congregational Church, at the northeast corner of the green—a rendering of it appears in virtually every coffee-table book ever created about New England. Although stately, it's not more impressive than at least a couple dozen other white churches in Connecticut. But its majestic setting is unrivaled. Interestingly, Litchfielders haven't always appreciated its considerable grace. The 1828 church (the parish dates to 1721) was desanctified, desteepled, and relocated around the corner in 1873, and a considerably more elaborate gothic Victorian was erected in its stead. For the next half century, the original church served as a dance hall, a movie theater, and a roller rink.

In the 1920s, however, a Colonial Revival movement took hold, giving rise to a local movement to restore the structure to its original use and location. Its majestic steeple and detailed interior were meticulously re-created, and the tall white pillars were added. The poor old gothic impostor was unceremoniously demolished.

That wasn't the first time Litchfield Congregationalists had battled over whether to preserve tradition or follow the trends of the day. In the early 1800s, during Reverend Lyman Beecher's 16-year spell as local preacher, more and more churches (particularly those in American cities) began using iron heaters during winter church services. A pro-stove contingent began lobbying for the addition of a stove to the Litchfield church. A fierce debate ensued for some time, with antistovers claiming that sanctity could never be upheld in a heated church. Finally, one September Sabbath, the prostovers got their wish and were permitted to place a heater in the sanctuary. When the congregation filed in, not surprisingly, most of the antistovers reacted with anger and displeasure, wiping the sweat off their brows and removing layer after layer of warm clothing. It's said that one woman even fainted from heat exhaustion. At the end of the service, the weary pro-stover responsible for the new heater walked purposefully past the perspiring antistove contingent and placed his hand directly onto the allegedly sizzling stove. Much to the embarrassment of the melodramatic naysayers, it became suddenly clear that the stove had never been lit. With that, the controversy died down once and for all.

ling, seyal blanc, and marechal foch varietals. Free tastings and tours are given daily. The owners have a second winery and a wine education center in Olde Mistick Village in Mystic (860/572-1978).

Back on Rte. 118, continue past Rte. 254 a short distance, make a right onto East Litchfield Road, and then another right onto Buell Road. You'll find yourself in the middle of **Topsmead State Forest** (860/567-5694), a pristine 511-acre woodland ideal for cross-country skiing and sledding in winter and hiking year-round. The land was owned originally by the Chase family (of the long-successful Chase Brass Company, in Waterbury). In 1972, heiress Edith Chase, a dedicated Connecticut preservationist, passed away and left her 1925 Cotswold-inspired "cottage" (really a mansion, designed by renowned architect Richard H. Dana) to the state for all to enjoy. In summer, on the second and fourth Saturdays of every month, tours are given of this bluff-top manor house. One of Topsmead's most popular trails runs through a 40-acre wildflower preserve.

In the 1950s, Montfort Missionaries built the 35-acre **Shrine of Our Lady of the Lourdes** (Rte. 118, 860/567-1041, grounds open May–Oct., outdoor mass is held 11:30 A.M. Sun., holy hour is at 3 P.M.), using a "simple picture postcard" of the original grotto in Lourdes, France, as their only blueprint. Today, all are welcome to roam the grounds. If you have a Harley, or some other form of two-wheeled, motorized transportation, drop by the **Blessing of the Motorcycles,** held every May.

## Northfield

In southeastern Litchfield, Northfield is a small village that, like Milton at the opposite end of town, is rarely heard from these days; an excursion here makes for a picturesque drive. The town prospered in the mid-19th century, when about 75 skilled workers and their families settled here from Sheffield, England, to work in the now long-gone Northfield Knife Company. For years, its cutlery was famous throughout America and Europe.

Here's a scenic loop through Northfield: Head east from the Litchfield village green on Rte. 118, turning right onto Rte. 254 (Northfield Road). Follow this past old farmsteads and Colonial homes into the tiny village center, the crux of which is at Main Street and Knife Shop Road. (Every May on the Saturday of Mother's Day weekend, a well-attended flea market takes place on the Northfield village green, the proceeds of which benefit the town's historical society.) Turn left onto Knife Shop, then make a quick left on Newton Hill Road, which you can follow back up north a couple miles. At Marsh Road, take a left, then a right onto Buell Road, on which you'll pass East Litchfield's Topsmead State Forest.

## Goshen

Like Litchfield, its neighbor to the south, Goshen was settled and soon-after incorporated in 1720. The two towns paralleled each other in growth and agricultural development for about 30 years, and Goshen might very well have surpassed Litchfield in wealth and prestige, had the latter not been chosen over it as the county seat in 1751.

Today, Goshen is without so much as a major grocery store, and it's hard to believe it could have ever held a candle to Litchfield. In fact, Goshen continued to prosper as a farming town throughout the late 18th and early 19th centuries. In 1780, Goshen had a population of 1,500 (about half that of Litchfield), but the town shrank dramatically to just over 600 residents by the 20th century. Goshen never laid claim to much in the way of manufacturing; however, it did earn kudos as one of young America's leading cheese producers. It's believed the town's cheese factory, established in 1845, was the nation's first. Although dozens of the old dairy farms have closed since the 1950s, Goshen retains a handful of them today.

Although Goshen is an attractive, hilly town to drive or ride through, you'll find few attractions here. Near the quaint (and some might say dangerous) traffic circle in the village center (the intersection of Rtes. 63 and 4), you'll find a few buildings of historic note. Just south of the circle, the **Goshen Historical Museum** (21 Old Middle Rd., Rte. 63, 860/491-9610, open by appointment year-round and on Saturday afternoons in July and August; free) is housed in the old Eagle Academy building, which was established in 1823.

A few doors closer to the green, you'll see the towering spire of the **Goshen Congregational Church,** from which Hiram Bingham took charge of a group of U.S. missionaries in the early 1800s to spread Christianity among the inhabitants of the Sandwich (now Hawaiian) Islands. For this reason, a Hawaiian state flag is flown here year-round; inside, you can look over documents and illustrations detailing the expedition. Bingham, by the way, later became famous as the first explorer to reach the Machu Picchu ruins in Peru in 1911. His descendants operate a B&B and horse farm in the town of Salem. Architecturally, Goshen's most curious structure is the **Old Town Hall,** on the northeast side of the traffic circle. This 1895 Victorian is recognizable by its strange little shingled cupola.

Near the center of town, little **Dog Pond** is an ideal spot for a canoe ride; from the junction of Rtes. 63 and 4, head west on Rte. 4, take a quick left onto West Street and bear right onto Town Hill Road, which leads to the dirt boat launch. Larger and also popular for boating, **Tyler Lake,** which is stocked for fishing, is reached by taking Rte. 4 west to Tyler Heights Rd., on your right.

The **Action Wildlife Foundation** (337 Torrington Rd., Rte. 4, 860/482-4465, www.actionwildlife.org, open 10 A.M.–5 P.M. Wed.–Sun. Apr.–May, 10 A.M.–5 P.M. daily June–mid-Dec., $5) is a must-see for nature and animal lovers. This former dairy farm on 116 acres has been turned into an unusual game park, in which more than 100 animals representing some 35 species of exotic animal live in habitats that closely resemble the wild. Visitors can walk freely along trails through the park, often getting very close looks at the llamas, Asian water buffalo, emus, elk, bison, and other animals. There's also a petting zoo with pot-bellied pigs, miniature donkeys, pygmy goats, and Shetland ponies; and a museum with taxidermy exhibits of many other animals you might never otherwise see up close.

# MORRIS TO SOUTHBURY

## Morris

Morris is a small wooded town immediately south of Litchfield; it was the site of one of the nation's first preparatory schools to accept both boys and girls, the Morris Academy, which was established by a hero of the Revolutionary War, James Morris. An early graduate was John Pierpont (class of 1804), the grandfather of Hartford philanthropist J. Pierpont Morgan. The school is now long gone, and Morris the town is named for its benefactor.

From Litchfield, you reach Morris by heading south out of the center of town on Rte. 63, and then turning right onto Rte. 61, which cuts directly through the town center. Or, from Bantam, head south on Rte. 209, which winds alongside the western shore of sparkling Bantam Lake and intersects with Rte. 109. Deer Island juts into Bantam Lake from Rte. 209, and you'll see quite a few summer cottages on the island and along Rte. 209, plus a small marina and boat launch. It's neither as pretty nor as dramatic as Lake Waramaug in nearby Washington, but it's a fine lake for boating, water-skiing, or taking in the views of the Litchfield Hills and the White Memorial Foundation, which fringes the northeastern shore of the lake.

Once you've made your left turn onto Rte. 109, make a left turn shortly after onto E. Shore Road to reach **Sandy Beach** (E. Shore Rd., 860/567-7550 or 860/567-5387, staffed weekends Memorial Day–June, daily July–Labor Day, $5 for vehicles, $1 for walkers or cyclists), a pleasant stretch of Bantam Lake shoreline with bathhouses, a canoe launch, lifeguards, and a snack bar.

## Bethlehem

From Morris's simple town center, at the junction of Rtes. 109 and 61, continue south on Rte. 61 to Bethlehem, site of a popular agricultural fair each September (you'll see the fairgrounds on your left shortly after you cross the town border). Bethlehem is not unlike Morris, in that it's peaceful and quiet, having been isolated from the area's primary transportation routes since its incorporation in 1787.

The striking 1740s Colonial Bellamy-Ferriday House was once home to America's first divinity school.

However, this village is unique in Litchfield County in that it has no zoning laws, and it's a relatively easy commute to the city of Waterbury, which is about 15 miles to the southeast. The east side of town has been gradually suburbanized since the 1980s, and observers in this region sometimes look at the future of Bethlehem to get a better sense of how the Litchfield Hills may develop over the next few decades, and to see whether zoning regulations should be imposed in an effort to preserve the local character.

Although there's nothing to stop a major business park or a sprawling subdivision from setting down near the village center, Bethlehem remains fairly sleepy and quite pleasant to look at. A green at the intersection of Rtes. 132 and 61 is dotted with leafy trees and surrounded by historic homes.

The north end of the green is bordered by a long picket fence and rows of narrow evergreens—these mark the property line of the **Bellamy-Ferriday House** (9 Main St., Rte. 61, 860/266-7596, 11 A.M.–4 P.M. Wed., Fri., and weekends May–Oct., $5), an imposing three-story 1740s Colonial that received a considerable Federal-style makeover in the early-19th century; note the elaborate dentils, quoins, and pillars set around the exterior. The zealous preacher, Joseph Bellamy—a devotee of fire-and-brimstone minister Jonathan Edwards—operated America's first divinity school out of this building during its early years. Today, the house

and its outbuildings are open to the public and contain furnishings that span the buildings' history. Behind the house is a formal 1920s parterre garden, and beyond that a small nature preserve crisscrossed by stone walls and nature trails. You'll see a mix of hardwoods, conifers, and nut trees planted over the generations, and you'll stroll through a lovely apple orchard. Few house-museums in Litchfield County offer such an inviting balance of man-made and natural features.

## Woodbury

The most direct way to reach Woodbury from Bethlehem is via Rte. 61 to U.S. 6; the most scenic is Rte. 132 to Rte. 47, which takes you through the Victorian village of Hotchkissville and eventually down to U.S. 6 as well.

Woodbury was the first village settled by European explorers in this region—settlers acquired a deed from the native Pootatucks living here on April 20, 1659. The original township consisted of a plot of land roughly the size of Litchfield County today, extending east to west from the Naugatuck to the Housatonic River, and north to south from what is now Southbury to about Bantam Lake.

Woodbury was settled out of a "major" religious schism among the residents of coastal Stratford, a dispute surrounding the "Halfway Covenant" system of church membership. This is a highly complicated and, by today's standards, seemingly pedantic argument over how one became a true member of the church; the old camp believed in putting members through an intense examination involving church law, biblical knowledge, and enough grilling to render most of those tested doctoral candidates in theology by today's standards. The dissenters felt that this system was one of exclusion, and so after many years of bickering moved on to create their own church in northern Stratford. In 1672, many relocated to Woodbury, believing it to be the only way to resolve the dispute; the provision to settle a new town had been set up by Governor Winthrop. Woodbury was so-named in 1674, and a road down to Stratford was constructed a few years later. It is often said that many of the new settlers came not because of religious dissent, but simply for the prospects of better land and new opportunity.

The early settlers faced the trials of King Philip's War in 1675. Woodbury has long had a tradition of supplying more than its due share of troops for war, a tradition that began during King Philip's War and continued through the French and Indian Wars, both wars with Great Britain, and the Civil War. Also, about half of the men who aided Colonel Ethan Allen in the 1775 raid on Fort Ticonderoga hailed from Woodbury. During the fateful year of 1776, about one in five Woodbury (which then consisted of today's Bethlehem, Southbury, and Roxbury) residents were fighting in the War of Independence at any given time.

It is believed that Woodbury was home to the colony's very first clothier, Abraham Fulford, whose "fulling mill" was laid out in the early 1700s near the East Sprain, or East Meadow Rocks. But for the most part this was an agrarian community, excepting a few moderate-sized woolen mills and a successful knife-making operation in the Hotchkissville section of town.

Where Bethlehem has no zoning, Woodbury is curious in that its zoning bylaws were set up to encourage people to run businesses out of their own homes (a highly unusual circumstance in Connecticut—and in most American communities). This factor, combined with the area's rich history, bounty of Colonial homes, and fine scenery, has attracted dozens of antiques dealers, making this one of the nation's premier antiquing centers. Of the 40-odd antiques shops, many are along north–south–running Main Street (U.S. 6), but quite a few more are along Main Street's various off-roads in old farmsteads and classic 18th-century houses. Many of these places do not keep regular shop hours, so it's advisable to phone ahead to set up an appointment

## AMERICA'S EPISCOPAL CHURCH

Opposite the Masonic Hall on Woodbury's U.S. 6, Hollow Road meanders down past a few prestigious 18th-century homes to the pale gray 1750 **Glebe House** and adjacent **Gertrude Jekyll Garden** (203/263-2855). The Episcopal Church, the American version of England's Anglican Church, was born in this large hybrid saltbox and gambrel-roofed Colonial in 1783. On this date, 10 American-Anglican priests met secretly in the living room of their host, the Reverend John Rutgers Marshall, and nominated the nation's first Anglican bishop, Dr. Samuel Seabury.

In those days, Anglicans faced many obstacles. The close of the Revolutionary War had recently resulted in America's independence, and the Anglican churches in the New World found themselves in a precarious position—still bound by the authority of England's Anglican Church, but cut off from the mother country politically. Furthermore, Anglicans on U.S. soil were largely despised, or at the very least mistrusted, by the Congregational majority.

At that time, any person who aspired to serve as an Anglican priest had to travel to England to receive his orders—an extremely expensive and time-consuming process that threatened the very existence of the Anglican Church in America. Woodbury's Reverend Marshall had been the most recent Anglican priest to undergo this ordeal, and at his home this small cabal gathered to appoint a local bishop who could thenceforth ordain priests on U.S. soil. Upon his nomination, Dr. Seabury traveled to Aberdeen, Scotland, in 1784, where he was consecrated and then returned to the United States to carry out his service and carry on the tradition of the Episcopal Church.

The Glebe House now contains early period furnishings, as well as documents that relate to the story of the Episcopalians. The house opened to the public in 1925, making it one of the first house-museums in America.

On the grounds of Glebe House is a garden designed by the renowned British horticulturist Gertrude Jekyll. It's the only such garden in the country; she never so much as set foot in Woodbury—the garden was designed from blueprints she made for the house in the 1920s, but for some reason were never carried out. In the late 1970s, her plans were discovered, and in 1990, the garden was created according to her original design.

or request a catalog. Some of the major establishments with regular hours are detailed below in the Shopping section.

Although small-scale, home-based businesses thrive here, Woodbury has taken strict steps to keep chain stores, gaudy signage, and fast-food restaurants away—it remains a picturesque and remarkably well-preserved Colonial town, and because it's just five miles north of I-84, it's one of the most accessible Litchfield-area communities.

In northern Woodbury, just a short ways past the main town center, there's a triangular grass sliver of town green that's the prettiest of Woodbury's three commons—it has benches and a white gazebo, and it's a nice place to stop and have a break. There are a few nice antiquaries just off this green, plus two of the town's old churches. At the northern end is the gracefully dilapidated Canfield Pharmacy, a tan 1868 Victorian that doesn't seem to have changed (or enjoyed a paint job) in many years. It's said that Marilyn Monroe used to hang out here while her husband, Roxbury's Arthur Miller, completed his errands around town (this story, by the way, is told about the pharmacies in just about every town bordering Roxbury!). Sadly, a fire gutted the interior of the building in 1998, and the future of the pharmacy (and its classic soda fountain) is still in question.

At the south end of downtown Woodbury is the creaky old **Curtis House** inn, a quirky old place that claims to be the oldest continuously operated hostelry in Connecticut (as does the Griswold Inn in Essex). It's not fancy, but it offers a pretty good 1950s-retro spin on Colonial New England—the sort of place you might imagine a big family piling into in one of the *Mr. Blandings Builds His Dream House* genre movies from years past, back when northwestern Connecticut was a rural backwater.

The Curtis House marks the southern end of Woodbury's historic center. A drive or bicycle ride north reveals no fewer than five towering, mostly 19th-century (the Catholic church dates from 1903) white clapboard churches, many handsome old houses, and an imposing Greek Revival Masonic Hall (King Solomon Lodge). The hall (427 S. Main St.) sits on a 30-foot rocky bluff on the west side of the street. It's said that during the 1700s, long before the hall was built, parishioners were called to the then-nearby Congregational church by the beating of a drum atop this stone plateau.

Across the way, Hollow Road also is the site of the 1680s **Hurd House,** a center-chimney, early-Georgian Colonial—originally a saltbox, but the rear was altered. For many years the former blacksmith shop (at 15 Hollow Road) was operated next door by the Skelly family, which owned the Hurd House from the mid-19th century onward. This is the oldest structure in Litchfield County.

Appropriately close to the Glebe House (see the sidebar "America's Episcopal Church") and up on Main Street is **St. Paul's** Episcopal church (ca. 1785), which is nearly across from the library—it's simple and compact with a squared-off spire. It is inappropriately located, however, adjacent to the town's ancient Congregational burial ground (which is next to where the town's first Congregational church once stood). No doubt spinning in their graves are hundreds of anti-Anglican residents, who died well before the Episcopal church was established here. Now the two burial grounds have more or less merged.

Just south of the historic section of town, at the intersection of U.S. 6 and Rte. 64, a culinary boom has sprouted, with about a dozen restaurants currently vying for your appetite. Some have been around for years, but a few bona fide culinary stars have emerged over the past decade.

## Hotchkissville

Hotchkissville is just a blip, no shops or public buildings, and although there are quite a few old homes, it really only merits a pass-through on Rte. 132. This undertraveled road from Bethlehem passes several farmsteads and some great old homes. It's a far less cutesy and gentrified stretch of no less authentic historic buildings. At one time, the American Shear and Knife Company—Woodbury's longest running and most profitable factory—stood in the center of Hotchkissville (from 1850 until it burned in 1914), an immense red-brick structure with a billowing smokestack. This was once a successful, self-sustained industrial village with its own shops and school; it's named for the Hotchkiss brothers, a couple of early factory owners.

For a scenic detour and a chance to enjoy an outstanding nature center, as you're heading up Rte. 132 from Hotchkissville hang a right onto Brushy Hill Road; follow this to Flanders Road, where a left turn leads to the **Flanders Nature Center** (203/263-3711, www.flandersnature-center.org). This is a fine preserve with a nature store, trails through fields of wildflowers, a grove of nut trees, and ponds and bogs. The center's offices are inside a well-preserved 1786 Cape-style farmhouse, one of the finest late–18th-century buildings in the area. Classes and events are held here and in the adjoining studio, and it's well worth phoning ahead for a list of topics (perhaps organic art or stargazing). In winter, the center produces its own maple syrup, and visitors are welcome to come observe this process in Flanders's sugarhouse—it's one of the most engaging of the nature center's many excellent programs, and kids particularly enjoy this one (see the special topic). Trails lace the former Van Vleck Farm, now the center's nature sanctuary—a particularly nice one runs beside a large marsh. Each trail has a different theme based on what you're likely to see during your hike: the Old Orchard Trail, Wilderness Trail, Geology Trail, and so on.

If you continue north on Flanders Road, you'll pass the **Abbey of Regina Laudis** (203/266-7637, www.abbeyofreginalaudis.com, open 11 A.M.–4 P.M. daily). It's on some 350-wooded acres and maintained according to "the principles of traditional Benedictine stewardship and contemporary ecological awareness." The abbey was founded in 1946. You can listen to the nuns sing Gregorian chants every morning at 7:45, and also visit the abbey's dairy farm, carpentry and blacksmith shops, pottery kilns, and gift shop, which sells pottery, herb teas and perfumes (made with herbs grown on the property), and jams and jellies. An 80-figure crèche resides inside a rustic old barn. The 40 nuns at Regina pray seven times daily and once in the middle of the night. 1950s starlet Dolores Hart aburptly retired from Hollywood in the early 60s and moved to the abbey, where she is now prioress.

## Southbury

From downtown Woodbury, follow U.S. 6 south a few miles to reach Southbury. Just as you cross the border, you'll come to an impressive stretch of Colonial houses both along U.S. 6 and also on a parallel crescent called Mansion House Road, which is separated from U.S. 6 by a grassy hill. A plaque marks the spot where General Jean Baptiste Count de Rochambeau and his French troops marched en route to Yorktown, Virginia, in 1782. Across the street is a small Colonial graveyard, Stiles Memorial Cemetery—it's a characteristically charming spot.

In fact, Southbury was ceded from Litchfield County many years ago, and this rapidly growing town is now a part of northern New Haven County. It very much retains the character and spirit of other communities in the northwestern hills—the major difference is that when I-84 was constructed in the 1970s, Southbury's sleepy downtown took on a somewhat suburban feel, complete with shopping centers and a massive IBM office building right off the highway.

Another significant change was the construction of Heritage Village, a 2,600-unit retirement community on a wooded hill in the center of town; fortunately, it has an attractive design, and the condos are shrouded by trees and shrubbery to such an extent that the whole complex fits in rather well with the rest of the town. The Colonial house that now serves as a community center once belonged to entertainer Victor Borge and, before that, to the Americana collector and photographer Wallace Nutting, who went on to live in Webb House in Wethersfield.

Like many towns in the region, Southbury was begun as a spin-off from a larger community, in this case Woodbury. As more and more settlers built homes in the southern reaches of Woodbury, the need for "winter privileges" arose (in winter, a group of homeowners too far from the main parish could hire a minister to preach out of their homes while the weather remained uncooperative). After several years, around 1732, the residents were permitted to build their own meetinghouse—this parish soon began to burst at the seems, so that the residents in the western reaches of the southern reaches of Woodbury went through a similar rally for their own parish. In 1775, such a meetinghouse was erected—now the Congregational church of South Britain. Southbury finally incorporated as a town in 1787.

Before I-84 was built, most of the area's commercial activity surrounded the tiny village of **South Britain,** on the west side of Southbury, situated along Rte. 172. South Britain is a pleasant anachronism consisting of a couple white churches, one neatly preserved and the other rather dilapidated, plus a popular general store. It's on the other side of town from Heritage Village and IBM and all the development, and so it has a feel more characteristic of Roxbury, which borders Southbury to the northwest.

It's easy to forget it, but the Housatonic River forms Southbury's western border—it's not easily accessed and plays no central role in town, and so it often seems as though the river never touches the town. But drive over on I-84 to the final exit in Southbury and then up the river road by the massive Connecticut Light and Power station, and you'll come to Shepaug Dam, where there's a bald-eagle observation area—pamphlets provide all sorts of information about the birds.

Not far from here is **Churaevka Village** (Rte. 172 at I-84—follow Main Street east parallel to I-84 and make a right onto Russian Village Road), a small community of Russian families who were among the Czarists who fled from the mother country following the Russian Revolution. Led by Count Ilya Tolstoi, they settled in this little neighborhood anchored by a tiny Russian Orthodox chapel with an onion dome, and their families have continued to live here ever since.

**Kettletown State Park** (Kettletown Rd., 203/264-5169 or 203/264-5678), at the southern tip of Southbury, is a remote patch of woodland on an inlet of the swift-moving Housatonic River, a short ways south of I-84. There's excellent fishing and swimming from the shore, and the park also has 72 campsites (with very limited facilities). To reach it, take exit 14 from I-84; south of the highway, the road forks, with a left onto Georges Hill Road leading you on a long, winding journey to the park. Bearing right onto Lakeside Road leads down to the smaller **Lake Zoar Wildlife Area,** which has a boat launch on the

Housatonic (which, at this span of the river, is called Lake Zoar, a man-made expanse of the river created when the Housatonic was dammed.

## SHOPPING

If shopping is more than an incidental pastime for you, you could easily spend a full week exploring the shops of Litchfield, and a second week in Woodbury. These two towns have dozens of excellent antiques shops, plus a great many boutiques selling everything from pewter mugs to handmade dolls. The other towns in the eastern Litchfield Hills all have a handful of appealing shops, but Litchfield and Woodbury are clearly the stars of the show.

### Pick-Your-Own Farm

Depending on the season, you'll find fresh fruit, corn, greens, pumpkins, and other delicious goods at the **Berry Farm** (Southbury, 264 Crook Horn Rd., off Rte. 67, just west of U.S. 6, 203/262-6000). The farm also throws seasonal events, such as hayrides through the pumpkin patch; call for details.

### Litchfield

Litchfield is one of the region's top antiques centers. Most of the shops are close to the village green, in the village of Bantam, or along U.S. 202 between these two points. Near the green, **Jeffrey Tillou Antiques** (39 West St., 860/567-9693) is a long-popular purveyor of 18th- and 19th-century American art and paintings. Check out the impressive selection of furnishings, glassware, and garden accessories at **The Workshop Inc.** (West St., 860/567-0544). On U.S. 202, by the entrance to the White Memorial Foundation, **Linsley Antiques** (499 Bantam Rd., 860/567-4245) has three floors of country English furniture, with an emphasis on pine, oak, mahogany, and walnut pieces.

**Gooseboro Brook Antiques** (38 Old Turnpike Rd., 860/567-5245) handles stoneware, clocks, quilts, copper, and many unusual primitive collectibles. **The Old Carriage Shop Antiques Center** (U.S. 202, 860/567-3234) is inside the Flynn & Doyle Carriage and Sleigh

THE WESTERN HILLS

# MAPLE SUGARING AT FLANDERS NATURE CENTER

Frosty winter mornings are a favorite time for such griddle-born delicacies as pancakes, French toast, and waffles, and so the consumption of maple syrup—ersatz and otherwise—is at its peak. Have you stood lately in the aisle of Super Stop & Shop deliberating over which brand to buy? The difference in price between any of the myriad imitation syrups and the few pure ones is dramatic—a 24 oz. container of the real thing typically commands $9 or $10, while the same bottle of Log Cabin or Mrs. Buttersworth sells for about $3. Is it not extravagant to invest so much in this simple condiment whose only ingredient is the sucrose secreted naturally by the *Acer saccharum*, better known as the American sugar maple? It all tastes pretty much the same, doesn't it?

In a word, no—no more than frozen fish sticks taste pretty much the same as fresh sockeye salmon. Golden virgin maple syrup, with its faintly smoky caramel overtones and subtle soul-warming bouquet, tastes far superior to the impostor, a runny amalgam of high-fructose corn sweetener, potassium sorbate, food dye, fenugreek, and a motley array of lab-crafted flavor additives. Try a taste test at home and see for yourself. Better yet, spend an afternoon at a Connecticut sugarhouse—March is the prime time to watch a maple-sugaring demonstration. An ingredient that enhances the flavor of every food is toil, and your taste buds cannot discern this meaningful component of maple syrup without first observing the process by which it is gathered, distilled, and bottled.

Although far more prevalent in Vermont and New Hampshire, maple-syrup operations abound across Connecticut. Those open to the public range from pick-your-own farms, whose efforts turn to sugaring during this otherwise barren and bitter season, to educational nature centers that allow visitors an up-close look at syrup-making. An ideal venue for witnessing this rite of winter is the Flanders Nature Center, in Woodbury. Bill Akins, the volunteer maple-sugaring guru at this first-rate 1,300-acre facility, is modest about the crucial role he plays at Flanders: "All I do is take sap that contains 1 or 2 percent sucrose from a tree and boil it until it's 66 percent sucrose. That's all there is to it." But just as there's a science to producing the juiciest heirloom tomatoes or raising the finest rose gardens, there's a noble, labored art behind the production of one simple gallon of maple syrup.

The syrup operation at Flanders has been going strong since 1966, and is open to the general public on weekends about 3–5 P.M., late February–end of March. The season is fixed not by the center but by the true general manager of New England's maple-syrup harvest, Mother Nature. During a good year, there's sugaring for six or seven weeks. A bad season might yield but a couple good weekends. What conditions make for the best sugaring? No two experts agree, although there's a general consensus that snow underfoot and crisp winter nights followed by sunny days 10–15°F above freezing make for the most consistently high output.

During a visit to Flanders, you'll want to park along Cowles Road (call for directions) and hike for a few minutes to the rickety red-clapboard sugarhouse, amid a grove of mature maple trees—any such concentration of the species is called a sugar bush. You'll be greeted by a trained interpreter, who leads you with a small group deeper into the sugar bush, where you'll be regaled with tales about maple-sugaring history. Next, you'll see each stage of syrup production, from collecting sap to pouring finished syrup into the containers in which they're sold.

Indians native to New England first learned to tap maples as a source of sweetener for food. During particularly harsh winters, they subsisted solely on maple sugar. The Indians passed the tradition along to the earliest European settlers, and the methods have been handed down—and occasionally improved—each generation since. Bill Akins and his team still rely mostly on the same simple tools and time-honored traditions that residents of the Connecticut countryside have been using for centuries.

Whatever the exact tools and techniques you apply, extracting sap from a maple tree (a gallon of pure syrup likely requires the sap of two or three trees) is a painstaking, time-consuming process. The tree (finding a healthy mature sugar maple is paramount) is first tapped—that is, a tiny hole is drilled at a slightly upward angle to a depth of at least two inches. A narrow spout called a spile is hammered into the hole, through which the juice empties into a covered five-gallon galvanized metal bucket hung from the tree.

Depending on conditions, the bucket may take from a day to some weeks to fill. The guides sometimes let visiting children gather one of the partially full buckets and help carry it over to the 250-gallon holding tank in the bed of Bill Akins' pickup truck—one of the aforementioned "improvements" upon Colonial sugar-making. (Bill also uses a power drill to tap the trees. He may be a hard worker, but he's no dummy.) When the tank is full, Akins backs his truck up to the sugarhouse and empties the sap through a velvet filter into a pair of 500-gallon stainless-steel boiling tanks.

It takes many hours to reduce roughly 50 gallons of this viscous sap down to a gallon of pure maple syrup. In the Flanders sugarhouse, this boiling is done in an enormous wood-burning furnace called an evaporator, which sits below the holding tanks and receives the sap through a narrow metal tube. No matter how much Akins insists the process is uncomplicated, the series of tanks, tubes, and heaters used to transport, filter, and reduce the sap

is formidable. As is the amount of time he spends stoking the fire so that it burns at just the right temperature (about 218°F—the necessary boiling point to produce maple syrup) throughout the entire process.

Flanders, a nonprofit nature center, helps fund its maple-sugaring demonstrations by bottling and selling the syrup it produces—it also distributes a free pamphlet describing how to attempt maple sugaring at home, using trees in your own backyard and some fairly basic household tools and materials: a hot stove, a large pot for boiling, and a candy thermometer. Even if you have these items, a healthy dose of patience and a zest for honest hard work are additional requirements.

The back page of the pamphlet also lists about a half dozen tempting maple-syrup recipes—from an elaborate Vermont maple cake to a batch of maple popcorn that even the culinarily challenged can master (see below).

To witness maple-sugaring at Flanders is to experience one of the few extant practices of New England's earliest history. Now, back at the grocery store, aisle 6: Aunt Jemima or the real thing? Is there even a choice?

### Maple Popcorn

2 c. granulated sugar
2 c. maple syrup
1 t. vinegar
2 T. butter
1 c. chopped peanuts
4 quarts popcorn

Combine sugar, syrup, and vinegar and cook over low heat, stirring until sugar dissolves. Cook to 275°F on candy thermometer. Remove from heat and add butter; stir until melted. Add peanuts and pour over popcorn, blending well.

Co.'s 19th-century redbrick building, and shows pieces from more than 20 dealers. **Rico Kennedy Gallery** (931 Bantam Rd., Bantam, 860/567-2649) presents fine Latin-American art, both contemporary and classic.

The **P. S. Gallery** on the Green (860/567-1059), is another of Litchfield's renowned spaces, where some of the state's top artists present their work. The **McKnight Gallery** (27–29 West St., 860/567-5571) is run by artist Thomas McKnight, who in 1994 was commissioned to create the Clintons' official White House Christmas card; his dynamic, vibrant paintings are lauded worldwide. And the **Alison Palmer Studio and Gallery** (931 Bantam Rd., Bantam, 860/567-1966) is worth a stop—it's set in the old switch factory building. Palmer's whimsical ceramics and crafts are featured.

**Barnidge & McEnroe** (7 West St., 860/567-4670) is a fine, general independent bookseller, with a strong selection of children's books, cooking, crafts, fine and performing arts, local history, and travel. For used titles (including many fine antiquarian books and postcards), stop by **John Steele Book Shop** (15 South St., 860/567-4670), a few doors down.

You'll find warm outdoor apparel, men's and women's country clothing, and warm blankets at **Gilyard's Outfitters** (1062 Bantam Rd., U.S. 202, 860/567-9885).

West of the village green, the **Susan Wakeen Doll Company** (425 Bantam Rd., 860/567-0007) sometimes opens its workshop for tours or special events; year-round, you can browse her exquisite handmade creations. The handwoven works at **Tina's Baskets** (3 West St., 2nd floor, Litchfield, 860/567-0385) dazzle just about everybody who walks in—owner Tina Puckett weaves traditional, sculptural, and free-form baskets.

South of the village green is the remarkable mail-order nursery **White Flower Farm** (two miles north of Morris on Rte. 63, 560/567-8789 or, for mail order, 800/503-9624, www.whiteflowerfarm.com, open mid-Apr.–mid-Dec.). The farm has rows upon rows of marvelous flower and shrub gardens. Parking is just north of the main store, a short ways past Esther's Road, which is just north of the farm. You can

walk the 25-acre grounds, which include dozens of gardens showing off forsythia, rhododendrons, azaleas, roses, and hundreds of perennials and shrubs. All of the grounds are open to the public, and you're encouraged to walk up to the friendly employees tending the grounds and ask questions. This is a great way to learn about gardening while you shop.

## Norfolk

**Joseph Stannard Antiques** (Station Place, U.S. 44/Rte. 272, 860/542-5212) is Norfolk's leading dealer, specializing in 18th- and 19th-century French furniture and art. Local craftspeople regularly present their eclectic wares at the **Norfolk Artisan's Guild** (U.S. 44, 860/542-5487), which is well respected throughout New England.

## Woodbury

**West Country Antiques** (Rte. 47, 2 miles north of Main St., 203/263-5741) also carries gorgeous furnishings imported directly from France. Another major purveyor of French pieces is **Country Loft Antiques** (557 Main St. S, 203/266-4500), whose spread comprises two barns and a 17th-through 19th-century farmhouse. **David Dunton** (Rte. 132, 203/263-5355) is one of the country's leading dealers of American Federal antiques and paintings.

Occupying the grounds of a restored silk mill, **Grass Roots Antiques** is a collective of seven dealers offering an assortment of antique furniture and collectibles. **Wood & Palette** (139 Main St. N, 203/263-6492) is strong on frames and art restoration, as well as an eclectic array of furniture and collectibles.

**Wayne Pratt** (346 Main St. S, 203/263-5676) is a highly esteemed dealer of fine American antiques—it's one of the most famous antiques shops in the state. For more than 100 years, **Hamrah's, Inc. Oriental Rugs** (115 Main St. N, 203/266-4343) has offered an amazing selection of Asian rugs—it's on the scale of a museum. The **Lighting Barn** (271 Washington Rd., 203/263-0010) specializes in period sconces, chandeliers, and lamps; it is also expert on repair and rewiring of old fixtures. **B. Bourgeois** (270 Main St., U.S. 6, Woodbury, 203/263-

7770) has beautiful French and other European pieces displayed in a lovely old house in the center of town. Offering a rather different take on the usual European and American pieces, **Eleish & Van Breems Antiques** (487 Main St. S, 203/263-7030) features decorative accessories, furniture (and reproductions), and garden elements with a focus chiefly on Scandinavia and Northern Europe.

An impressive, rambling compound on the Nonnewaug River, the esteemed collection of formal and country American and British furniture, **Mill House Antiques** (1068 Main St. N, 203/263-3446) claims the largest selection of Welsh dressers in the state, plus an extensive array of formal dining room tables. The main building is the old Burton's Mill (ca. 1835), which is in the heart of Minortown. There's been a mill here since the 1780s. The mill was the largest in Woodbury, ceasing operation in 1952. Mill House is the largest antiques shop here and was the first in town.

**Monique Shay Antiques and Design** (Hidden River Farm, 920 Main St. S, 203/263-4597) is known for its French-Canadian farmhouse antiques, especially pine armoires and cupboards. A bit off the beaten path (this one is not far from the Flanders Nature Center), **Robert S. Walin** (547 Flanders Rd., 203/263-4416) deals primarily in American formal and folk pieces. It's housed in a 1759 Colonial.

A golf driving range most of the week, the plot of land just south of the several shopping centers near the junction of U.S. 6 and Rte. 64 is transformed into the **Woodbury Antiques & Flea Market** (203/263-2841, 7 A.M.–3 P.M. Sat.). **Merry-Go-Round of Fine Crafts** (319 Main St. S, 203/263-2920) frequently has artisans appear to demonstrate their skills; a diverse assortment of crafts are sold here, from folk dolls to wooden jewelry to calligraphy. All are handcrafted by Connecticut residents. The works of more than 150 artisans are also represented at **Handcrafter's Haven** (40 Main St. N, U.S. 6, 203/263-2111). The small but well-stocked **Woodbury Pewter Factory Outlet** (860 Main St. S, 800/648-2014) offers factory seconds (virtually indistinguishable from those pieces that pass muster, and sold at a considerable discount) in lamps, mugs, candlesticks, and other decorative arts. Definitely the most charming toy store in the area, **Geppetto's** (682 Main St. S, U.S. 6 and Rte. 64, 203/266-4686), has Steiff, Corolle, North American Bears, Good Kruger, and other top-name toys, plus games, puzzles, and arts and crafts galore.

The **Beaux Arts Gallery** (495 Main St. S, 203/264-9911) is one of the most important galleries in the eastern Litchfield Hills, with a knowledgeable and friendly staff; this is a great place to pick up advice and information about both established and up-and-coming artists, as well as to have your old works restored, reframed, or preserved. If you're in search of a fine art restorer, try the **Vigues Art Studio** (203/263-4088). There are a few good rug merchants in town, one of the best being **Des Jardins Oriental Rugs** (289 Main St. S., 203/263-0075), which specializes in Oriental, art deco, folk, French country, formal English, and many others. **Forge & Anvil** (442 Main St., 203/263-7442) crafts hand-wrought iron furniture and accessories.

## Elsewhere

Harps, dulcimers, and psalteries are handmade at **Folkcraft Instruments** (High and Wheeler Sts., Winsted, 860/379-9857), where folk music and books are also sold. The staff can also teach you how to play these instruments. **Laurel City Coin** (462 Main St., Winsted, 860/379-0325) is one of the county's foremost dealers in coins, jewelry, and estate gold and silver.

Torrington isn't a fine arts center like some of its neighbors, but you can check out **Artwell** (51 Water St., 860/482-5122), which has some dynamic exhibitions.

## RECREATION
### Downhill Skiing

Downhill enthusiasts can test their abilities at the **Woodbury Ski Area** (Rte. 47, near the Woodbury–Roxbury–Washington town lines, 203/263-2203, www.woodburyskiarea.com), a popular operation for day and night skiing, with a chairlift, surface lifts, and 14 trails. The shop offers rentals, and snowboarding is available. More than 20 miles of cross-country trails are adjacent to the property.

## Golf

Torrington has a fairly simple nine-holer, **Eastwood Country Club** (1301 Torringford West St., 860/489-2630), which also has public tennis courts and a swimming pool. The area's other option also has nine holes: **Stonybrook Golf Club** (263 Milton Rd., 860/567-9977) in Litchfield. But this steep, hilly course is in magnificent condition and offers a considerable challenge.

## Hiking

Many of the state parks and attractions detailed earlier in this chapter make for outstanding hiking excursions. Adjoining the **Bellamy-Ferriday House** is a wonderful 90-acre preserve that comprises former farmland allowed to grow dense with white pine, walnut, and hemlock trees and bushes of lilac and forsythia. You access the main trail encircling the preserve via the parking area north of the house; don't use the driveway to the house, which is off Rte. 61, but rather the small lane off Munger Lane, which runs parallel to Rte. 61 to the west.

At **Mt. Tom State Park,** the 1.5-mile yellow-blazed Tower Trail leads up a dirt road, then up a steady grade to the peak of little Mt. Tom. You'll eventually come to an old stone lookout tower, to which wooden steps lead 30 feet to the observation area. In the distance, you'll see much of the Litchfield, Morris, and Washington countryside—including more than a few church spires.

**Dennis Hill** and **Haystack Mountain State Parks** in Norfolk; **Burr Pond** in Torrington; and **Kettletown State Park** are all terrific places for a ramble. But the mother of all hiking venues in the region may be the 4,000-acre **White Memorial Foundation** in Litchfield, which contains dozens of well-marked, captivating trails.

## Horseback Riding

Horseback-riding enthusiasts can take advantage of the many bridle trails traversing Topsmead, and at the White Memorial Foundation, by contacting **Lee's Riding Stables** (57 E. Litchfield Rd., off Rte. 118, 860/567-0785), which arranges guided trail rides. Children can enjoy pony rides. This is one of the longest-running stables in the state, and the hosts are extremely friendly and helpful.

## ENTERTAINMENT AND NIGHTLIFE

Litchfield County is not a major destination for night-crawlers, but there are a few more spots in the eastern hills than in the west. Notably, some of the restaurants covered below have a busy bar following, including Julio's in Southbury, the Pub in Norfolk, and the Village Restaurant in Litchfield. **Shadrach's** (Heritage Inn, Heritage Rd., Southbury, 203/262-8062) is a tap room meant to evoke Colonial times, with a long list of microbrewed beers and a light bar menu.

The **Bantam Cinema** (Bantam Lake Rd., Rte. 209, Bantam, 860/567-0006, www.bantamcinema.com) is a tiny one-screen place, but it usually shows great films—new releases, but often with an artsy bent. The snack bar sells heavenly imported chocolate candy bars. The redbrick art deco **Gilson Cinema** (354 Main St., Winsted, 860/379-6069) is a favorite destination in this region that's fairly starved for arts and entertainment. You can come here with friends or to meet them, as it's not only a movie theater but also a small café. There are two screens, showing mostly current releases; the smaller upstairs theater shows some very progressive arts films, too.

© ANDREW COLLINS

**Housed in a former carriage factory, Bantam Cinema boasts an artsy roster of films, plus fine imported chocolate at the snack bar.**

## CONNECTICUT'S WINE TRAIL

There are 10 wineries in Connecticut, and the number seems to grow by one every couple years or so. The Connecticut Wine Trail is rather idiosyncratic and hardly famous beyond the region, which means it gives the average connoisseur a chance to spend a bit of time in the various tasting rooms and often enjoy extremely personable and knowledgeable tours of each facility. The majority of these wineries sit on beautiful grounds, many of which have hiking trails, picnic grounds, and other ancillary features. It wasn't even until 1978 that the state passed a law allowing vineyards to produce wine commercially.

Most of the wineries are open year-round on weekends and at least Wednesday–Sunday during the warmer months (about Apr.–Oct.). Hours can vary, however, and many of these sites are fairly secluded, so it pays to phone ahead and check that somebody will be there and able to help you when you're planning on coming.

The larger wineries produce as many as 7,000 cases of wine annually, while a few smaller ones produce only a few hundred. Even a larger winery in Connecticut is relatively small, however, when compared with commercial wineries in places such as California, Washington, and the North Fork of Long Island. The latter has rapidly become the East Coast's top winemaking region (it's very easy to reach this area from Connecticut, either by driving around Long Island Sound or by taking the ferry from New London or Bridgeport). Anybody who has ever gone winery-hopping out in California, however, can attest to the fact that many of those large commercial

wineries are lined up along the highway like used-car dealers. In Connecticut, you may not enjoy the cachet of visiting Mondavi or Sterling Vineyards, but you might also appreciate the contrasting personal attention and genuinely unique surroundings of each local vineyard.

You can obtain information on many of the wineries at www.ctwine.com, or call the Connecticut Wine Trail, 860/267-1399.

### Connecticut Wineries

**Chamard Vineyards,** 115 Cow Hill Rd., Clinton, 860/664-0299, www.chamard.com

**DiGrazia Vineyards,** 131 Tower Rd., Brookfield, 203/775-1616, www.digrazia.com

**Haight Vineyard,** 29 Chestnut Hill Rd., Litchfield, 860/567-4045, www.haightvineyards.com

**Heritage Trail Vineyards,** 291 N. Burnham Hwy., Lisbon, 860/376-0659, www.heritagetrail.com

**Hopkins Vineyard,** 25 Hopkins Rd., New Preston/Lake Waramaug, 860/868-7954, www.hopkinsvineyard.com

**Jonathan Edwards Winery,** 74 Chester Maine Rd., North Stonington, 860/535-0202, www.jedwardswinery.com

**McLaughlin Vineyards,** Albert's Hill Rd., Sandy Hook/Newtown, 203/426-1533

**Priam Vineyards,** 11 Shailor Hill Rd., Colchester, 860/267-8520, www.priamvineyards.com

**Sharpe Hill Vineyard,** 108 Wade Rd., Pomfret, 860/974-3549, www.sharpehill.com

**Stonington Vineyards,** 523 Taugwonk Rd., Stonington, 860/535-1222, www.stoningtonvineyards.com

Litchfield has an excellent variety of locally produced entertainment, most of it conducted through **Litchfield Performing Arts** or LPA (860/567-4162, www.litchfieldjazzfest.com), which sponsors classical concerts, dance, and theater at various venues, including the First Congregational Church.

The world-renowned **Norfolk Chamber Music Festival** (Rte. 272 and U.S. 44, northwest corner of village green, 860/542-3000, www.yale.edu/norfolk) is an ongoing feature in this arts-minded community. Concerts are held

throughout the season, drawing top chamber groups both internationally and domestically. The event typically includes a picnic on the Ellen Battell Stoeckel Estate's 70 placid acres. You can visit the art gallery and simply enjoy the grounds. This is one of the most unusual experiences in New England. In Norfolk, the **Greenwoods Theatre** (20 Greenwoods Rd. W, U.S. 44, 860/542-0026, www.greenwoodstheatre.com) occupies a historical building that had faced demolition until a pair of New York theater producers bought and rehabilitated the space in

1999. The summer-stock theater presents five works each season.

The 1931 **Warner Theatre** (69 Main St., 860/489-7180, www.warnertheatre.org), which recently underwent a massive renovation, is as striking an example of art deco as you'll find in these parts, with a marquee that juts out over Main Street. Regional theater, from Shakespeare to contemporary works, is performed throughout the year; the Warner also draws nationally known musicians and concert groups. In its heyday, Torrington had three grand theaters, but the Strand burned and the Palace was closed down.

## FESTIVALS AND EVENTS

### Summer

June is a big month of celebration in Litchfield; artists display their works during the **Gallery-on-the-Green** (860/567-8504) in the middle of the month. Around the same time, the **Litchfield Hills Road Race** (860/567-8504) draws runners from all over the state, and many from points even farther beyond. Later in the month, gourmands delight in the foods displayed at **A Taste of Litchfield Hills** (Haight Vineyard, 860/567-4045), a weekend-long festival for eating. Many of those beautiful homes along North and South Streets are opened for your viewing during the **Litchfield Open House Tour** (860/567-9423), held in mid-July.

In August 1996, Litchfield Performing Arts sponsored the town's first **Litchfield Jazz Festival,** now held at the Bethlehem Fairgrounds. The two-day event drew a range of impressive performers and has continued to be one of the best music festivals in Connecticut. In July and August, **Summer Concerts** (860/567-9527) is held on the Litchfield village green from 7–9 P.M. on Wednesday evenings. The **Morris Bluegrass Festival** (Morris Memorial Park, 860/567-3066 or 860/567-0270) takes place in August; contests are held in traditional, trick, bluegrass, mandolin, and a host of other techniques and genres. The Woodbury Library hosts the **Sunset Sounds Summer Concert Series** (library lawn, Main St., U.S. 6, 203/263-3502 or 860/723-8010), featuring an eclectic bunch of regional musicians—

from folk singers to jazz artists—who perform weekly at 7 P.M. The **Connecticut Agricultural Fair** is held at Goshen fairgrounds in July.

In August, there's the **Norfolk Weekend 'Round The Green** (860/542-6942), when local authors (and there are quite a few prominent ones) host a book signing, the library has a book sale, and the Congregational church has a fair. Crafts are sold on the green, and there's usually a major event in the Music Shed. The Goshen fairgrounds are the site of the **Litchfield County 4-H Fair** (860/567-9447), held in mid-August. The **Litchfield Grange Fair** is held at the Grange Hall on U.S. 202 the last Saturday in August. The Woodbury Volunteer Fire Department and Ambulance Association throws a four-night **Carnival** at Hollow Park in late August, with rides, music, food, and festivities. Also in August, Haight Vineyard hosts the **Crafts of the Litchfield Hills** show.

### Fall and Winter

Over Labor Day weekend, travelers come from all over New England to attend the **Goshen Agricultural Fair** (Rte. 63, just south of Rte. 4, 860/491-3655), which originated in 1912 and is one of best such fairs in New England. And at the end of September, the **All Breed Dog Show** (860/485-9642) is held at the fairgrounds. In early October, the grounds host the **Scottish Festival** (860/456-8733), and later in the month is **A Fall Carriage Rally** (860/589-6293).

The **Harwinton Fair** (Locust Rd., 860/485-1821) is another of the region's very good agricultural fairs, with wood-chopping contests, a blacksmith shop, and the usual demonstrations and contests; it's held in early October. The **Litchfield Post Card Show** (860/589-6984) is held in the town's firehouse on U.S. 202 annually in late September. The White Memorial Foundation (U.S. 202, 860/567-0857) hosts an educational **Family Nature Day** the fourth Saturday in September. The **Litchfield Arts & Crafts Show,** at the Middle School (U.S. 202, 860/567-0820) is held the second weekend of October.

It's only appropriate that the little town of Bethlehem would host the **Christmas Town Festival** (Rtes. 61 and 132, 203/266-5557) in eight buildings near the town green. Here you'll see arts and crafts exhibitions and food booths, and you can have your holiday cards sent from the post office with Bethlehem postmarks. In mid-December, you get a second crack at the **Litchfield Open House Tour;** during this time, many of the town's beautiful homes are decked for the holidays.

## ACCOMMODATIONS

As the eastern Litchfield Hills are more densely populated than the western reaches of the county, and because a semimajor highway (Rte. 8) passes through the region, you'll find quite a few more chain accommodations and larger hotels than you will to the west. Norfolk and Litchfield both have many country inns, however, and you'll also find a smattering of intriguing historic B&Bs throughout the area.

Most of the lodgings described below have at least three or four rooms, and are staffed daily year-round. Dozens of smaller informal B&Bs operate in Litchfield County, too, but it's best to book these through the very good reservation service, **Nutmeg B&Bs** (860/236-6698).

Note that one reputable Litchfield-County hotel is not listed below: the Tollgate Hill Inn (www.tollgatehill.com) was purchased by new owners after having sat dormant for two years. If all goes well, this venerable Colonial property and its charming restaurant will be restored to their full potential by 2004. There has also been some talk of Holiday Inn opening a hotel in Winsted, on the lake above downtown, but details are elusive at this time. Finally, the owners of Vermont's famed Pitcher Inn are scheduled to break ground in 2003 on a new luxury hotel in the quiet town of Morris—this will be, like Washington's Mayflower Inn, a member of the highly prestigious Relais et Chateaux hotel group.

### Hotels and Motels

**$150–250:** The **Litchfield Inn** (U.S. 202, Litchfield, 860/567-5358 or 800/499-3444, www.litchfieldinnct.com) is a reproduction (and quite new) Colonial-style inn, whose guest rooms are nonetheless quite charming and decorated with a period look. The loca-

tion, along a busy commercial stretch, is less than rustic, but the staff is courteous and helpful, and the addition of an excellent new restaurant, Bistro East, has helped improve the experience. Some of the 30 rooms have VCRs and fireplaces. It's a good choice if you prefer modern to old-fashioned.

**The Heritage** (Heritage Village, 522 Heritage Rd., Southbury, 203/264-8200 or 800/932-3466, www.dolce.com) is a modern, full-scale hotel-and-conference resort in the heart of the retirement village in Southbury. Despite this setting, the hotel caters to all ages. The clientele is quite diverse, from young weekending couples to business travelers. The 163 rooms are pleasantly furnished with Colonial-influenced reproductions, and are typical of any nice chain hotel—rooms come with cushy extras like two phones, irons and boards, and coffeemakers. But the main reason to stay here is to take advantage of the considerable amenities: nine holes of golf, an indoor pool, health club, lighted tennis, racquetball, and massage and spa treatments. There are a couple of good restaurants, including the Eight Mile Brook Steakhouse, and the hotel's location by the Pomperaug River is appealing, even though it anchors a large condominium village.

**$100–150:** Convenient to the Litchfield Hills, Waterbury, and central Connecticut, the **Southbury Hilton** (1284 Strongtown Rd., just off exit 16 of I-84, Southbury, 203/598-7541 or 800/774-1500) is a fairly typical but pleasant U-shaped low-rise business hotel with an indoor pool, whirlpool, and fitness center.

**$50–100:** Built in 1891, the **Yankee Pedlar Inn** (93 Main St., Torrington, 860/489-9226, www.pedlarinn.com) has been steadily improved in recent years. A reasonable attempt has been made to keep rooms classy and pleasant, as they are done with Hitchcock furnishings and Colonial prints; most have four-posters or canopy beds and other such touches. The public rooms are pleasantly old-fashioned. And although nature and beautiful scenery aren't right outside the door, they're only a short drive away. All of the 60 rooms have private baths, phones, and cable TV, and there's a dependable eatery on the premises, **Conley's Pub and**

**Restaurant,** $8–18, which also has a lighter and less-expensive pub menu.

The **Days Inn** (395 Winsted Rd., Torrington, 860/496-8808) is a very good option among the handful of chain hotels in Northwestern Connecticut—and it's only a bit pricier than the Super 8. Rooms have large TVs and new carpeting and bedspreads, although they could go a little easy on the air-freshener. Many suites have whirlpool tubs.

A nicely kept budget option in a dull location (nevertheless very convenient for exploring eastern Litchfield County and both the Naugatuck and Farmington River Valleys), the Torrington **Super 8 Motel** (492 E. Main St., U.S. 202 at Rte. 8, Torrington, 860/496-0811 or 800/800-8000) has clean rooms with new and tasteful furnishings, including large TVs and nice little print drawings of Colonial towns on the walls. It's a step above some of the dumpy little independent motels in the region.

## Country Inns and Bed-and-Breakfasts

**$150–250: Angel Hill** (54 Greenwoods Rd. E, Norfolk, 860/542-5920, www.angelhill.com) consists of two guest rooms and two suites in an 1880 country house. It's furnished with high-style Victorian antiques, and a housekeeping suite occupying the second floor of an old carriage house, with a kitchen and such (you're still welcome to complimentary breakfast in the main house on Saturday and Sunday mornings), which can be rented nightly or for about $550 weekly. Each room has a theme: one overlooks an orchard, and has a fireplace and canopy bed; another is a cottage suite with two rooms, one with a dining table and a double whirlpool tub (this one is particularly romantic).

You'd expect a town bursting at the seams with top-quality restaurants and antiques shops to have plenty of B&Bs, but Woodbury sorely lacked accommodations until several years ago, when the **Longwood** (1204 Main St. S, Woodbury, 203/263-3067, www.longwoodcountryinn.com), then called the Merryvale, came onto the scene (a few smaller properties have since come and gone). This is an elegant attractive option, with five op-

ulently decorated Victorian guest rooms tucked inside an unpretentious-looking late-18th-century farmhouse, which was fully restored in the 1990s, but has received some major upgrades even since then. The very talented innkeeper makes all her own bedspreads and does a wonderful job decorating these exquisite rooms, some of which have romantic canopy beds, fireplaces, or whirlpool tubs. The verdant grounds are a pleasure to walk around, and the tasty hot breakfasts add a memorable touch to the experience. There's also a very good restaurant, Coriander.

**$100–150:** Henry and Diane Tremblay's **Manor House** (Maple Ave., Norfolk, 860/542-5690, www.manorhouse-norfolk.com) is one of the most wonderful inns in New England, and with some rooms starting at $125, it's within reach of many budgets. Their 1898 Bavarian Tudor inn was built by Charles Spofford, who designed London's subway system; his friend Louis Tiffany contributed 20 stained-glass windows to the parlor. Rooms vary greatly in size and look; many are tucked below romantic pitched ceilings. One room has its own private wood-paneled elevator and a private sundeck, a few others have fireplaces, and all are filled with warm down comforters and flannel sheets. Perfect year-round, the Manor House is especially fine in fall and winter, when a fire roars in the parlor and a hot, filling breakfast awaits you each morning.

**$50–100:** The **Dutch Moccasin** (51 Still Hill Rd., Bethlehem, 203/266-7364) has a great bit of historical lore behind its name: the original structure was built in the 1700s by Dutch traders, who did business with the area's local Indians. This cozy gambrel-roofed house still has many original details: chestnut interior beams, wide-plank oak and pine floors, and four stone fireplaces (some of them in guest rooms). There are six rooms and a suite, all decorated with an early Colonial look that includes Hitchcock chairs, hand stenciling, and period antiques; the least expensive rooms share a bath. Full breakfast is included.

A short drive (or moderate walk) from the village green, the **Mountain View Inn** (67 Litchfield Rd., Rte. 272, Norfolk, 860/542-6991, www.mvinn.com) is the only accommodation in town with its own restaurant. This Victorian B&B, with inviting fireplaces in the common areas, is decorated in period style, with brass four-poster beds; some rooms share baths. Full breakfast is included, and packages are available that include a four-course dinner as well.

The ancient **Curtis House** (506 Main St., U.S. 6, Woodbury, 203/263-2101) has been in existence as a hostelry since 1753, and it appears that most of the rooms were last renovated in about 1953. As you walk through the building, floorboards caw, pipes gurgle, and heaters sputter—this is not a luxurious place, but it does have plenty of character. Plus a handsome old restaurant that serves very traditional New England fare (Yankee pot roast, roasted leg of lamb with mint jelly, lobster Newburg, and such). Some rooms share a bath, and they do have canopied beds and a smattering of antiques (or in many cases, simply old pieces). The place was renovated top to bottom in 1900 for a then-astounding $400, and it appears the management has easily recouped this investment over the years. A more recent revamping saw the sprucing up of the decor and the addition of cable TV to each room.

### Campgrounds

North of downtown Winsted, close to Riverton, the **White Pines Campsite** (232 Old North Rd., 860/379-0124 or 800/622-6614) is a popular and social spot, ideal for families. There's a swimming pool and a small pond, a game room and recreation hall, a playground, general store, and regularly scheduled activities for kids and adults.

Straddling the Goshen-Litchfield line in a particularly beautiful and remote part of the area, **Hemlock Hill Camp Resort** (Hemlock Hill Rd., 860/567-2267, www.hemlockhillcamp.com) is one of Litchfield County's most extensive camping facilities. Sites are shaded by an immense grove of pine trees, and guests have the use of two pools, a hot tub, miniature golf, and a snack bar. It's a fairly social spot, popular with families and geared strongly to RVers. It's a short drive from here to the Mohawk State Forest.

Actually in Goshen, **Valley in the Pines** campground (Lucas Rd., 800/228-2032) is just up the road from Hemlock Hill, with 33 extremely secluded and shady sites.

The **White Memorial Foundation** has two campgrounds; Point Folly is the best of the two, with about 50 tent and RV sites set along a narrow peninsula jutting into Bantam Lake and allowing water views from most any angle. The other option, Windmill Hill, has about 20 shaded tent sites and is inland on a gentle slope.

## FOOD

As in western Litchfield County, this part of Connecticut is renowned for its outstanding restaurants, the best known centered in the towns of Litchfield and Woodbury. Because the population density is slightly higher in these parts, you'll also find a greater number of inexpensive family-style restaurants and diners, but this is still largely a region without ethnic eateries—you'll have to slip down to Waterbury or Danbury for those.

### Upscale

Rustic Tuscan trattorias have come and gone through Connecticut, but **The Venetian** (52 E. Main St., Torrington, 860/489-8592, $13–20) has resisted the temptation to go trendy. For years, two dramatic murals have overlooked a dining room of satisfied patrons feasting on traditional Italian favorites—veal osso bucco with risotto, Caesar salad tableside, grilled eggplant with fresh basil and olive oil, and sautéed portobello mushrooms with prosciutto and melon. Many of Litchfield County's first- or second-generation Italians know the Venetian is the spot for a taste of home.

Many consider James O'Shea's **West Street Grill** (43 West St., Litchfield, 860/567-3885, $19–29) the father of this region's culinary rebirth. There was a handful of important, formal restaurants in Litchfield County prior to West Street's opening in the late 1980s, but this small, cozy storefront eatery brought the inventive, New American regional style of cooking (already so popular in Manhattan, and spawned by such California luminaries as Alice Waters, Jeremiah Towers, and Wolfgang Puck) to the Litchfield Hills. Since that time, many competitors have opened (and many older establishments have gone New American), but the West Street Grill remains strong, offering such favorites as Parmesan aioli grilled peasant bread and grilled sirloin steak with buttermilk onion rings and garlic-mashed potatoes. The prices have risen gradually over the years, but you can still enjoy a full dinner for two with wine for roughly $100—not bad considering that similar meals in Manhattan go for at least $150. Have fun gawking at the visiting celebs.

Esteemed chef Carole Peck, one of the first graduates of the Culinary Institute of America, helped bring outstanding cooking to the antiques shoppers of Woodbury by opening her **Good News Cafe** (694 Main St. S, 203/266-4663, $17–30 in the dining room, $7–15 in the café) in 1993. With both a formal dining room and a simpler and more affordable café (ideal for lunch or late coffee and dessert), the Good News hits all budgets and several tastes. On either side you'll be treated to some of the best cooking on the eastern seaboard. The menu changes seasonally, but wok-seared shrimp with new potatoes, calamata olives, and a garlic aioli is one of the classics, as are a sinfully rich lobster macaroni with provolone and truffle oil, rich crab tacos, and an array of delicious and creative fish grills paired with tempting sauces. Service is highly adept and generally quite charming, and the wine list is exemplary. The desserts are also notable, and include key-lime cheesecake with a chocolate cookie–crumb crust, cherry compote, and candied macadamia nuts.

The stately, if rather formal, dining room at the Longwood country inn in Woodbury, **Coriander** (1204 Main St. S, 203/263-7005, $18–24) presents an often-changing menu of haute contemporary American and Continental fare. You might begin with baked brie wrapped in phyllo dough with pommery mustard and apricot-fig chutney, before moving on to grilled marinated duck breast with cranberry-corn relish and a port-wine demi-glace.

## Creative but Casual

An admirable, lower-profile competitor of the Good News Cafe is **John's Cafe** (693 Main St. S, Woodbury, 203/263-0188, $16–26), which oc-cupies an intimate, simple space that once contained short-order burger and chops restaurant. This subtle New American eatery, decorated with a few modest French country antiques, conjures up delicious cornmeal-crust pizzas (about $10) and hearty such as grilled Atlantic salmon with sautéed spinach and corn-tomato compote, and pork chops (from Connecticut's Egg & I Pork Farm) with gratin potatoes, broccoli rabe, Portobello mushrooms, and gorgonzola-onions. There's a great selection of mostly California wines (plus an interesting beer list, but no liquor) and scrumptious desserts, too (consider the chocolate pot de crème with caramelized bananas and whipped cream). The once-tiny restaurant underwent a much-needed expansion in 2003.

Inside the Litchfield Inn, and run by the owners of New Milford's Bistro Cafe, **Bistro East** (U.S. 202, 2 miles west of Litchfield's village green, 860/567-4503, $16–21) delivers excellent globally inspired bistro fare, from gingered, sesame-seared Maine salmon with jasmine rice and Asian-style stir-fry vegetables to macadamia-crusted chicken and crispy coconut shrimp with a pineapple stir-fry and coconut rice. The blueberry crème brûlée makes an outstanding dessert. The wine list is one of the most extensive in the county.

The somewhat cloyingly named **3W & the bluebar** (3 West St., Litchfield, 860/567-1742, $17–26) can be forgiven, because it's a warm and engaging space, and the kitchen turns out very good food. There's a full sushi menu and sushi bar, where you can try lobster tempura rolls and tender diver scallop sushi by the piece. The rest of the storefront dining room with exposed-brick walls consists of small, cozy tables with candles on them. On the main menu, you'll find the emphasis is on seafood and both Asian and Latin American ingredients: recommended are the steamed potato dumplings with spinach, lemongrass, and goat cheese with a Thai basil sauce; and black-sesame-seared tuna with bok choy, smoked-scallion vinaigrette, and citrus-zest jasmine rice. Attached is a small bakery and coffeehouse that's only open during the day.

## Steak, Pizza, Pub Grub, and Seafood

After the Carmen Anthony Steakhouse enjoyed

great success in Waterbury, the owners opened **Carmen Anthony Fishhouse** in 1998 (757 Main St. S, U.S. 6, 203/266-0011, $18–28), and it has been a huge hit in Woodbury's little pack of great restaurants. This is a big place with a few rambling dining rooms—so big that the staff has a tendency to slip up when things get busy. However, the quality of the fish, as well as the several good cuts of steak, is extremely high. Most of the fish entrées can be ordered grilled, poached, broiled, or blackened, and several are also offered with more creative accompaniments, such as sea bass with a spicy sauce of chopped tomatoes, hot peppers, capers, calamata olives, and a garlic basil sauce.

**Jessie's** (142 Main St., Winsted, 860/379-0109, $11–18) is noted for its extremely friendly staff, its charming location in a restored Greek Revival house on Main Street, and the fresh ingredients its chefs use to prepare the traditional Italian fare, from baked lasagna to veal parmigiano. It's a very nice spot for a casual meal. Pizza is available on Fridays and Saturdays only.

**The Pub** (Station Place, U.S. 44, Norfolk, 860/542-5716, $7–18) is no ordinary pub—it's actually two excellent restaurants inside one dark, inviting space of a landmark 1902 building near the town green. One half of the menu does harken back to Norfolk's simpler days, when everybody in town dropped in after hunting or hiking for burgers and beer (more than 150 kinds), but another section shows off inventive, eclectic fare and exotic imported brews. Note also the wonderful apple crumble for dessert. The atmosphere is warm, cozy, and dark—not unlike a British pub.

The **Village Restaurant** (25 West St., Litchfield, 860/567-8307, $15–22 in dining room, $6–11 in pub) holds its own against some of the fancier eateries nearby, offering a more expensive Continental and New American menu in one dining room, and a casual pub menu (great burgers) in the other. Grilled Norwegian salmon with a mustard-cream sauce and herb-encrusted pork chops with a sweet Calvados sauce are some of the best dishes.

In summer, patrons crowd the outdoor brick patio of casual **Aspen Gardens** (51 West St., 860/567-9477, $7–17), a festive Greek- and Italian-influenced American eatery overlooking Litchfield's village green. From the lengthy menu, order the savory spinach pie or the rich shrimp scampi, or try a burger, pizza, or plate of fish and chips. The kitchen also presents a long list of familiar appetizers, such as buffalo wings, garlic bread, and nachos. There's booth seating inside, too.

Fans of outdoor grilling have long flocked to the **Charcoal Chef** (670 Main St. N, U.S. 6, Woodbury, 203/263-2538, $5–15), which is up near the Bethlehem border and looks much as it probably did when it opened in 1956. This casual but attractive roadhouse with comfy tables and a diner-style counter serves up hefty platters of char-grilled ham steaks, chili burgers, cube steaks, swordfish, rainbow trout, and other choice meats, along with deep-fried seafood platters. A wide range of sandwiches is also available, and milk shakes and ice-cream sundaes are offered for dessert.

Southbury's smart, but casual **Julio's** (220 Main St., 203/264-7878, $8–17) serves some of the best wood-fired pizzas in the region, plus wonderful salads and fresh pastas (a delicious gnocchi dish, whose preparation changes seasonally, is sometimes on the menu). This is a smart, warmly furnished, and consistently outstanding take on the getting-boring tradition of affordable family-oriented Italian restaurants, which proliferate across Connecticut. Service is friendly, there's a great yet affordable wine list, and everything is made fresh from scratch. This place is fanatically popular, so make reservations on weekends.

If you're tiring of healthful, froufrou, so-called new New England cuisine, dig into the juicy Texas-style brisket and ribs at **Wood's Pit B.B.Q. & Mexican Cafe** (123 Bantam Lake Rd., Rte. 209, 860/567-9869, $7–15), where chef Paul Haas cooks authentic, spicy food from the Deep South, and even deeper south, Mexico. It's right beside the Bantam Cinema.

In Harwinton, near the Burlington town line, is a modest little airport with a similarly modest little restaurant called the **Landing Zone Grille** (525 Burlington Rd., 860/485-2733, $9–18), which has developed a semi-cult following for its zippy Cajun-influenced American chow, including alligator tenders, chicken wings (offered with any of six special sauces), barbecue bourbon-marinated ribs with vinegar chips, and juicy burgers.

## Ethnic Fare

Inexpensive and mild (i.e., intended for gringos) Mexican food is presented nightly at **Señor Pancho's** (Union Square shopping center, Main St., Southbury, 203/262-6988; also U.S. 202, Litchfield, 860/567-3663, $7–15), a popular family-style place with excellent salsa, margaritas, and some of the friendliest waiters in the state. Gets pretty noisy on weekends, but always a lot of fun.

Adding a much-needed entry into the foreign-eating market is Southbury's **Empire Szechuan** (775 Main St. S, 203/262-1998, $8–18), serving excellent Chinese food, with especially good shrimp specials and some fairly spicy items. There's also a full sushi bar with a very good selection of maki and nigiri. The slick setting, with soaring ceilings and tall windows, is a departure from the cramped and kitschy Chinese restaurants that typify much of suburban Connecticut.

## Quick Bites

For casual, diner-like American comfort food (in huge portions), try **Leo's** (7 Poverty Rd., Bennet Square, Southbury, 203/264-9190, $4–13), which has a complete dinner special for around $10 if you dine between 4:30 and 6 P.M. There's a second branch in nearby Middlebury, near the Waterbury border, at 800 Straits Tpke., 203/598-7505, and another one on Rte. 25 in Newtown, near the Monroe border, 203/426-6881. All of them make terrific breakfast fare, too. If you're looking for late-night eats in the region, head to Torrington's **Twin Colony Diner** (417 E. Elm St., 860/482-5346, under $12), which is open 24 hours and has the standard enormous diner menu.

Woodbury isn't all about fancy and frilly restaurants—there's ample opportunity for light and delicious eating. You can pick up wonderful pastries (try the fresh fruit tarts), cider bread, macaroons, carrot cake, croissants, and heavenly biscuits at **Ovens of France** (Sherman Village, 660 Main St. S, U.S. 6, 203/263-2540). In the same shopping center is the **Sandwich Construction Company** (670 Main St. S, U.S. 6, 203/263-4444). It's a rather bare-bones little deli

that produces big sandwiches with fresh, top-of-the-line ingredients—a specialty is the sweet Jack Daniels barbecue with cheddar cheese.

Greek-influenced **Constantine's** (1143 Main St. S, U.S. 6, Woodbury, 203/263-2166, $7–12) is packed many nights with locals fond of the filling, old-fashioned Italian and Greek food, from broiled lamb chops, veal marsala, and poached salmon. The roadhouse setting and doting waitresses complete the picture.

A true throwback to old-fashioned luncheonettes, **Phillips Country Kitchen** (740 Main St. S, Woodbury, 203/263-2516, $2–6) prepares the best doughnuts in town, plus inexpensive short-order breakfasts, and burgers, sandwiches, and fries for lunch.

Take a break from antiquing for freshly made ice cream and shakes at the **Dairy De-Lite** ice cream shop (695 Main St., Woodbury, 203/263-4450). A great area ice-cream parlor is **Peaches 'N Cream** (U.S. 202, Litchfield, 860/496-7536), popular with local hikers and shoppers.

**Max's Ice Cream** (17 U.S. 202, Litchfield, 860/567-7775) occupies a cute cottage in a colonial-style shopping center, just a short drive west of the Litchfield Green—here you can order homemade gelato, ice cream, espressos, wraps, sandwiches, and other goodies. There are a few picnic tables out front.

## Gourmet Goods and Picnic Supplies

Just north of the traffic circle on Rte. 63, **Nodine's Smokehouse** (65 Fowler Ave., Goshen, 860/491-4009 or 800/222-2059) is behind a white clapboard house. This rickety little shed smokes its own meats and cheeses, for which it's revered throughout the tri-state region; duck sausage, venison, salmon, gruyère, and cheddar are a few possibilities. You can also get a big old bone for your dog to chew on—although some of the bones are bigger than some of the dogs. Although not a restaurant, Nodine's does sell some prepared food, such as sweet Italian sausage and smoked provolone rolls, as well as baked goods, gourmet goodies, and candy. You can dine on the picnic tables out back.

Between Bantam and Litchfield's village green, the **Dutch Epicure Shop** (491 Bantam Rd.,

© ANDREW COLLINS

At Bantam Bread Company, everything—from the bread to the fruit tarts to the pastries—is organic and hearth-baked from scratch.

U.S. 202, 860/567-5586) has an enticing range of prepared foods, desserts, and soups.

A great way to finish off a day of hiking at the White Memorial Foundation is to grab a tomato-garlic focaccia or a loaf of olive-rosemary bread at the **Bantam Bread Company** (U.S. 202, 860/567-2737), where everything is hearth-baked, from scratch, organically. Fruit tarts, pastries, and cakes are also offered, and if you're like many customers, you may have

trouble making it from the door to your car without stopping to devour your purchases while admiring the Bantam River, which runs right beside the shop. For bakery fanatics, this place is a must-visit. **New Morning Natural and Organic Foods** (Main St. S., Middle Quarter Mall, Woodbury, 203/263-4868) is a nice big store with a great daily array of prepared foods that varies according to the season. You can also buy the ingredients to cook up a great healthy meal at home. The organic produce and bulk foods section is particularly commendable.

## INFORMATION AND SERVICES

### Visitor Information

All of the towns in this region are served by the **Litchfield Hills Visitors Bureau** (Box 968, Litchfield, CT 06759, 860/567-4506, www.litchfieldhills.com).

### Getting Around

Two major highways clip the southern and eastern edges of this area: I-84 to the south (which has an exit in Southbury), and Rte. 8 to the east (which cuts through Torrington and Winsted). These are the best ways to get to eastern Litchfield County from other parts of the state, but you should rely on the scenic local roads to get among the area's towns.

# Waterbury and the Naugatuck Valley

The fortunes of Connecticut's fourth-largest city, Waterbury (pop. 107,000), and the largely blue-collar towns strung through the valley north and south of the city, have for two centuries been tied to the success of the Naugatuck River. The Naugatuck, which commences in Torrington, flows for nearly 40 miles to Derby, where it joins with the larger Housatonic River. It is the only major river in the state whose source is in Connecticut, and so it's rather fitting that its history has largely mirrored the Nutmeg State's as a whole.

Like the state's other powerful rivers, the Naugatuck early on provided a source of fish for the first indigenous tribes who lived along it. It later

became a source of food for the first waves of European settlers, who quickly began damming it to maximize the river's power source and start up a number of rudimentary grist, cider, and textile mills. In the early 19th century, towns like Torrington, Waterbury, and Seymour began developing more substantial industrial concerns along the river. And by the close of the 19th century, a busy rail line paralleled the river, and hundreds of enormous factories and municipal sewage systems emptied their waste into the Naugatuck's once pristine waters.

Fishing was a joke at this point, and the Naugatuck was little more than a trail of poisonous,

THE WESTERN HILLS

smelly sludge. It remained this way for most of the 20th century, and as many of the mills and factories closed in the river valley following World War II, towns like Waterbury, Naugatuck, Beacon Falls, Seymour, and Derby were left with a brittle economy, an abundance of empty industrial structures, and a foul gray waterway coursing through their downtowns.

There remains today a stigma associated with the Naugatuck River, one that contrasts with the considerably more positive reputation of the nearby Housatonic River, which the Naugatuck joins in Derby. This reputation is unfortunate, and at this point inaccurate—since the late 1980s, the Department of Environmental Protection has worked with local organizations and city governments to right the course of the Naugatuck.

One problem these groups faced was deciding what to do with the many dams that interrupted the flow of the river, making it difficult for fish to proliferate here, and for recreational boaters to canoe or raft along it. Millions of dollars have been spent by the state DEP and Trout Unlimited to raze or partially remove eight dams, to install fish ladders, and in one case to develop a bypass waterway in Seymour that will allow boaters and fish access around the Tingue Dam. Shad, river herring, eels, sea run trout, and lamprey are expected to return to the Naugatuck, the way they thrived here before the river was ruined—all told about 29 of the river's 39 miles will be reopened to fish. It's now possible to catch trout and striped bass in the Naugatuck, in surprisingly high numbers, all the way along its span.

Of course, the removal of dams means nothing unless the water is clean, and both wildlife and people have incentive for this to happen. Tremendous headway has been made in this regard, with many companies along the river having complied with requests to stop dumping in it—the once horrendous sewage problems have been largely eradicated.

Changing the image of the Naugatuck from a sour trough of waste into a great community asset has taken a good bit of time. Still, to this day the Naugatuck is the butt of many local jokes, and perhaps it will take a new generation of residents to fully appreciate the river's benefits. But even now the about-face of the river has infused Waterbury and the other towns nearby with a spirit of regeneration, and a serious commitment to improve their reputations and economies. Waterways play a vital role in the success and image of communities, and in this case a newly rejuvenated river could lead the way to newly rejuvenated downtowns.

## WATERBURY

Many Connecticutters, even some who live just 5 or 10 miles away, know Waterbury only from having passed over it along I-84, which slices across the city high on an elevated roadbed. From here, you get a nearly perfect view of a tall, electrically lighted crucifix called Holyland, which is perched on a hillside on the west side of downtown. The 52-foot cross, erected in 1968 by one of the area churches, has come to represent the city in the eyes of those uninterested in actually venturing off the highway—for far too many people, Waterbury is "that city with the big cross by the highway."

Once the center of America's brass industry, and now a city striving to create a new and optimistic vision for itself, Waterbury has had a tough go in recent years. Factories and mills largely shut down or were downsized during the 1950s and 1960s. At the same time, massive I-84 was built, piercing the city center, its exits flying off willy-nilly like arms of a serpent, strangling the heart of Waterbury until by the 1970s the city had nearly ceased breathing. The visitor will still find a high number of boarded up or vacant storefronts and buildings, especially in the industrial section south of I-84. A spate of scandals in the 1980s plagued the city's police force and government, and it's a bit early to tell how some of the more recent attempts to reinvigorate downtown will affect Waterbury's future.

The highest-profile civic project was the completion of the Brass Center Mall on the east side of downtown, just off I-84. By all accounts, this sprawling shopping mall and adjoining shopping center, complete with a multiplex movie theater and several restaurants, has tempted a whole new generation of people to exit the highway and

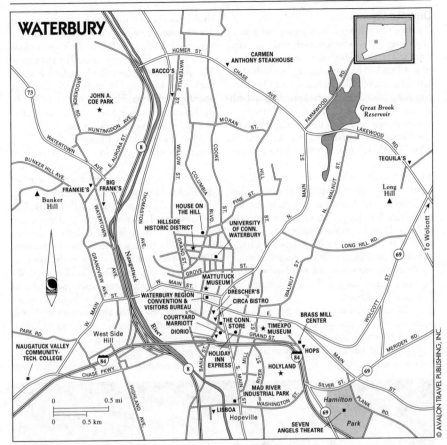

spend a little time (and money) in Waterbury. The flip side, for the time being, is that the mall may have shifted the spotlight—and the retail buzz—away from the existing shops and restaurants downtown, and that visitors to the Brass Center are not actually taking the next step and venturing beyond this highway-side complex.

Indeed, valid arguments have been offered assessing both the positive and negative impacts of the mall. But the fact is, for most residents of the towns in this region, there never was a spotlight shone upon downtown Waterbury, or any part of Waterbury, until the mall opened. And if city planners and commercial developers can continue to infuse the city with new attractions and to beau-

tify some of the neighborhoods in need of a facelift, Waterbury will rise above its downcast image and become a truly desirable place to live and visit.

In addition to the mall, the new Timexpo Museum, opened by the Middlebury-based Timex Company, has helped draw new visitors, and talk now centers on developing perhaps a new sports stadium or arena.

For now, Waterbury easily has enough going for it that any visitor could be entertained here for a full day. And if you're particular interested in industrial history or 19th- and early–20th-century architecture, the city's hilly, densely settled terrain makes for a couple days' poking around and exploring.

## Downtown

The best place to begin looking around is at the city's long green, which is anchored by a small clock tower, several war monuments, and plenty of park benches. It's a nice spot from which to observe the mix of older and newer buildings that run along Main Street, some appealing and others less so. On the north side of the green is one of the state's best (and most underrated) museums, the **Mattatuck Museum** (144 W. Main St., 203/753-0381, http://mattatuckmuseum.org, open Tues.–Sat. year-round, also Sun. fall–spring, $4). It's housed in a beautifully restored building on the west side of Waterbury's town green.

Galleries and exhibits at this multi-use museum trace Waterbury's "brass roots" and show locally made tools, art deco tableware, a rubber desk that belonged to Naugatuck's Charles Goodyear, and 18th- to 20th-century paintings by American impressionists and Hudson River School painters, such as Frederic Church and Maurice Prendergast.

A 300-seat performing arts center hosts a wide variety of presentations and programs, and the museum also offers art classes and lectures regularly. The museum gives an insightful overview of the city's best-known products, including the brass buttons that Yankee peddlers once hawked from town to town and the inexpensive clocks that made it possible for virtually every household to keep time. The chances of Waterbury's downtown finally making a comeback were increased tremendously with the opening of this smartly done museum. Inside, the Exhibition Cafe is an elegant but affordable choice for lunch or afternoon tea.

From the Mattutuck Museum, you can walk along some of the streets just off the green to see some of the many dignified old buildings that bear witness to the prosperity that once touched this region. Leavenworth Street, which runs due south from the green, is particularly notable. Follow Church or Leavenworth to Grand Street, turn right, and proceed by the public library to Meadow Street, where you'll see before you the dramatic 240-foot-tall clock tower, which looms above the city's old rail terminal. The *Waterbury Republican,* which is the city's daily newspaper, makes its home in this building now. The campanile, which is somehow less talked about than the electric cross mentioned earlier, is truly the region's identifying landmark—this fine redbrick tower is modeled after the campanile in Siena, Italy.

On the east edge of downtown, in the corner

Timexpo Museum, Waterbury

© ANDREW COLLINS

of Brass Mill Commons mall's parking lot, the relatively new **Timexpo Museum** (175 Union St., 203/755-TIME or 800/225-7742, www.timexpo.com, open 10 A.M.–5 P.M. Tues.–Sat., noon–5 P.M. Sun., $6) was created by Timex Corporation, which is based in nearby Middlebury, to trace the history of clock making in the Naugatuck River Valley. At this museum, you begin on the top floor, where exhibits detail early Connecticut time pieces, and work your way down to the ground level, where the museum really becomes more of a tribute to Timex itself than to timepiece-manufacturing in general. There's also a rather odd and not entirely cohesive exhibit on the Easter Island adventures of explorer Thor Heyerdahl.

An astounding collection of vintage clocks is exhibited, along with related memorabilia, such as a handwritten note from Mark Twain in which he places an order for one of the Ingersoll Company's impressive $1 pocket watches. Ingersoll was in partnership with Waterbury Clock Company, which was begun in this area as Benedict and Burnham Manufacturing in 1812. Eventually, U.S. Time Corp. bought the entire enterprise in 1944, and that company changed its name to the eminently recognizable Timex in 1969.

Kids enjoy the displays of Disney and Mickey-Mouse watches, which were first developed in 1933. And everybody seems to love watching the monitors showing those old TV commercials where John Cameron Swayze demonstrates that Timex watches can take a licking (or pulverizing or beating or drowning) and keep on ticking. An interesting side note: The original Waterbury Clock Co. plant in Middlebury, which is now the corporate headquarters, was built in 1942 as part of the war effort (the company made the time fuses that went into anti-aircraft missiles). The flat, single-story building was designed so that its roof could be flooded with water, thus fooling potential enemy planes flying overhead into thinking they were looking at a country pond, rather than a clock factory.

> *The campanile . . . is truly the region's identifying landmark—this fine redbrick tower is modeled after the campanile in Siena, Italy.*

The rest of the city is best explored by car, although there are several spots where you can pull over, get out, and walk around. If you don't feel comfortable walking in urban environments, parts of Waterbury may make you nervous. The crime rate here is in keeping with most Northeastern cities, and if you stick to well-traveled and lighted streets, and keep your wits about you, you should encounter no problems.

## Greater Waterbury

One of the less eye-pleasing parts of town is south of I-84, where the city's second highway, Rte. 8, runs, as do rail tracks and the Naugatuck River. The river, as discussed earlier, has been almost entirely cleaned up, but at least in this part of town the neighborhood surrounding it still looks pretty down and out. Still, if old mill buildings and historic factories are your thing, this area bears a look. Note the complex at 815 S. Main St., called Mad River Industrial Park. You may recognize it as the setting of the Jane Fonda and Robert De Niro movie *Stanley and Iris,* which was filmed here in 1989.

Working-class residential neighborhoods, housing Waterbury's considerable populations of German, Irish, Lithuanian, Puerto Rican, Polish, Portuguese, and West Indian immigrants (and their descendants), climb the hillsides east and west of downtown, and also to the north. The neighborhood where many of the brass barons and well-to-do built their mansions, the Hillside Historic District, is immediately north of downtown—just drive up Central Avenue from the city green.

The Hillside Historic District sits about 500 feet above sea level and is dominated by the University of Connecticut Waterbury, although several of its buildings are newer and not particularly charming. There is one lone, elegant painted lady Victorian standing high atop the center of campus, and several more nice houses sit along the street. Where Central Avenue intersects with Hillside Avenue, turn right, and then left onto Prospect Street, and continue up the hill. Turn left onto Buckingham and then right onto Pine, again climbing farther north into the hills. From all of these streets, and the blocks near them, you'll get a look at the many Victorian and Edwardian mansions for which this area is famed.

East of downtown, the 1898 **Hamilton Park** (follow Idylwood Ave. south from Rte. 70) is on the National Register for Historic Places, and has long been a focal point of the city. There's an Arts and Crafts pavilion that houses the Seven Angels Theatre, and also a bridge designed by George Dunkleberger, who is responsible for most of those spanning the historic Merritt Parkway (you'll be able to discern the similarities).

## NORTH AND WEST OF WATERBURY

A good way to get a sense of the Naugatuck Valley, north of Waterbury, is to take a train ride on the Naugatuck Railroad at the **Railroad Museum of New England** (E. Main St. at the rail bridge, exit 38 from Rte. 8, Thomaston, 860/283-RAIL, www.rmne.org, May–Dec., call for schedule, $10), a 17-mile restored historic railroad that runs alongside the Naugatuck River. The "Naugy" pulls a collection of meticulously restored 1920s coaches directly through the middle of a historic factory complex, through vintage rail depots, and beside the stunning banks of the Naugatuck River, at one point actually riding over the Thomaston Dam. There are two runs, one from Thomaston to Waterville (in northern Waterbury) and the other, which takes in more natural scenery, from Thomaston up into Torrington. This rail line opened in 1849 and played a vital role in the industrial success of Waterbury and the towns spread through the Naugatuck Valley during the late-19th and early-20th centuries; it linked with the New Haven railroad in 1887. Following your 20-mile round-trip, you can tour the rail yard, examine the vintage engines and cars, and learn a great deal more about the people and products that were once transported along this rail system.

Whether you journey along the Naugatuck Railroad or not, the best way to explore the valley

north of Waterbury is by heading north alongside the river. From Waterbury, follow Rte. 8 to exit 36 and make a left turn onto Chase River Road. Follow this by the Waterville rail station, where the Naugatuck Railroad rides commence, and up alongside the mills in this area before making a left turn onto Thomaston Avenue. Continue north to enjoy nice views of the river on your left in many spots. Eventually, this road becomes Rte. 262 for a brief spell (stay on it, following signs toward Thomaston and Rte. 8). Route 262 will turn left, but for the prettiest views you should continue north along Waterbury Road, which continues to hug the right bank of the Naugatuck River for a little more than three miles, before crossing over it just south of downtown Thomaston.

### Thomaston

Follow signs north into Thomaston, crossing under Rte. 8 and through the intersection with U.S. 6. Main Street (Rte. 254) leads through the heart of this old clock-making town. Not surprisingly, a huge clock tower crowns the Seth Thomas industrial park, where clocks were manufactured for many years. You'll see the city hall, and the Thomaston Opera House, whose exterior has been gloriously restored (a full restoration of the interior is slated for the future). At the north end of downtown, fork to the right onto Rte. 222 toward Harwinton. This stretch continues along the Naugatuck River through some pretty countryside and leads to the turnoff for **Northfield Brook Lake** (331 Hill Rd., Thomaston, 860/283-5540). Here, you'll find 208 acres of public land set around a massive earth- and rock-fill dam that was completed in 1965, after one too many floods wreaked havoc upon the valley. (The last straw was the great flood of 1955, during which dozens of residents were killed and millions of dollars of damage incurred). The U.S. Corps of Engineers built seven flood control reservoirs in this region, of which this is one. It's about 118 feet tall and 810 feet in length—you can drive across the face of the dam on a paved road that offers hair-raising views down over the valley. This is one of the more amazing feats of engineering in Connecticut. From a parking area, you can climb a 1.7-mile trail up a hill, facing a waterfall; there are several picnic spots and an eight-acre lake stocked with bass. There's also lake swimming (but no lifeguards), and bird-watching is a popular activity.

Return down Rte. 222 into Thomaston, and retrace your steps back down Main Street to U.S. 6, onto which a right turn leads toward Watertown. Soon after, you'll pass the entrance for **Black Rock State Park** (860/424-3200), which is somewhat overlooked by visitors (but not by locals). Evergreens and oaks thrive on the rocky bluffs and fertile slopes of this immense park, which has several marked trails of varying lengths. If you're lucky, you'll stumble upon a flint arrowhead, evidence that this was once the domain of King Philip, the native chieftain who gave Colonial settlers fits when they attempted to settle here.

## Watertown

U.S. 6 continues south into the center of Watertown, where at the junction with Rte. 63 you'll find a hilly town green. Originally part of Waterbury, Watertown was established in 1780 and first included the neighboring towns of Plymouth and Thomaston. Much of the suburban reach of Waterbury has consumed the town, especially its southern and eastern fringes, but the green reminds one of a time in the not-too-distant past when this was a largely agrarian community in the tradition of nearby Litchfield.

Situated on the green is a gazebo, war memorial park, two churches, and some old municipal buildings. Just past the 1839 First Congregational Church at the top of the green is a little redbrick building housing the **Watertown Historical Society Museum** (22 DeForest St., 860/274-4344, limited hours, free). A small, stone Lutheran chapel also sits near the green. Artful landscaping and the angle of the lawns that sweep across the green do their best to hide the fact that it overlooks a busy intersection.

From the green, you can walk or drive along U.S. 6, noting the beautiful neighborhood of Colonial and Victorian homes, almost all of them with white picket or iron fences in front.

Just around the bend, past North Street, is the Taft prep school, whose campus is dominated by a cluster of gabled redbrick buildings with a patchwork of pale-green, gray, and rust-colored slate roofs.

Back at the green, head south along Rte. 63 and coast through Watertown's rather ordinary but not unpleasant downtown. Make a brief detour, a left turn, onto Rte. 73 (Main Street) to reach the Victorian mill community of Oakville, half of which is within the Watertown border, the other half in Waterbury. Among the several old industrial concerns on Main Street is a former tool-making factory that now houses one of the state's most popular microbreweries, **Hammer & Nail Brewers of Connecticut** (Oakville, 860/274-5911, www.hammerbrew.com). Tours and tastings are offered year-round, usually on Saturday, but it's wise to call ahead for the schedule. The name, by the way, is a take on the names of the cofounders of the brewery, Peter Hammer and Kit Nagel (*Nagel* is German for nail). At press time, Hammer & Nail is planning to move into a new facility, and has therefore suspended all tours; it's best to call for the new location and touring schedule.

## Middlebury

Back on Rte. 63, follow the road south into Middlebury, a town that borders Waterbury to the west and yet somehow feels more like a part of Litchfield County, which borders its western flanks. Soon after you pass the town line, you'll come to the entrance to Timex Corporate Headquarters, a massive corporate compound on a site where David Humphreys once operated a successful Spanish-sheep farm and woolen mill, as well as the nation's first spool silk factory (in 1822).

Middlebury, because it is quite hilly and without a major source of waterpower, was never industrialized the way its neighbors along the Naugatuck River were. Settled in 1707, the town's economy depended largely upon dairy farming until well into this century, and only since the 1950s has it developed into one of Waterbury's more desirable suburbs.

Where Rte. 63 intersects with Rte. 64, make

a left turn and head toward Woodbury. After driving along this scenic winding road for a few miles, you'll come to the attraction for which Middlebury has best been known over the years, at least among grade-school kids—the 20-acre **Quassy Amusement Park** (Rte. 64, 203/758-2913 or 800/FOR-PARK, www.quassy.com), which sits over the shores of Lake Quassapaug. This old-fashioned park (it dates from 1908) has 30 rides, with games, swimming, playing fields, food concessions, a small petting zoo, and other fun activities. It's not as extensive or fancy as Lake Compounce, but then the price is right. (Open daily Memorial Day–Labor Day, weekends spring and fall. Admission is free, ride prices vary, all-day and seasonal passes available, parking runs $4).

Head back the way you came on Rte. 64, passing Rte. 188 south (toward Oxford) but turning right onto Rte. 188 north (toward Naugatuck)—it's slightly confusing, because Naugatuck is actually south of Middlebury, but trust in the road signs. Route 188 leads directly into Middlebury's quaint village center, where the imposing Westover Girls' Prep School overlooks the very prettiest town green in the Naugatuck River Valley—a wonderful spot for a picnic or for reading a book.

Westover, founded by a woman named Mary Hillard in 1909, is a long, cream-colored building with a steep pitched roof and rows of dormer windows—it, and the buildings around it, have a formal British air. North Street and South Street, which intersect the west side of the village green, are both lovely streets for a jog or bicycle ride, lined with some of the town's most handsome Colonial homes. Additionally, two churches and the Middlebury Historical Society are within view of this most pastoral spot.

In 2002, the **Golden Age of Trucking Museum** (1101 Southford Rd., Rte. 188, 203/577-2181, www.goldenagetruckmuseum.com, open 10 A.M.–4 P.M. Mon. and Thurs.–Sat., noon–4 P.M. Sun., $8) opened in a massive space on the edge of Middlebury, just off I-84. The collection here include numerous 18-wheelers and about 20 other trucks from all through the history of trucking, including many from the 1950s.

# SOUTH OF WATERBURY

Whereas the towns north and west of Waterbury have a reasonably prosperous and somewhat countrified appearance, the southern part of the region has suffered through considerably harsher economic times since the 1950s, and most of the communities down here have gritty and somewhat depressed downtowns, the lone exception being Oxford, which feels quite a bit like its neighbor Middlebury.

## Naugatuck

From Middlebury, begin this tour by continuing south along Rte. 188 and making a right turn onto Rte. 63, which leads south into Naugatuck. With steep hills hugged by both elaborate and simple homes, towering over a downtown of steeples, redbrick factories, and grand turn-of-the-20th-century buildings, and with a river running through it, Naugatuck looks a lot like a miniature Pittsburgh. You can find great views of the area and its abundance of Victorian architecture by driving up the narrow winding lanes on the west side of downtown, then peering back at the activity below. Naugatuck's charms may not be immediately apparent if you have a disdain for ragged old factory towns, but as far as these go, Naugatuck is one of the finest examples in the state, and the hilliness gives visitors a perspective not gained elsewhere.

As you drive through town, you'll see a number of the buildings that once housed rubber factories—you'll even pass Rubber Avenue. The city's town green is one of several planned industrial villages in the Naugatuck Valley, and although there aren't any museums or especially interesting shopping districts, quite a few beautiful 19th-century civic buildings remain, many of them designed by the prestigious architectural team of McKim, Mead & White. The part of town to the east of the river is called Union City; it's less interesting than Naugatuck proper.

In this book, I generally suggest you get off the limited-access highways and onto the more scenic and atmospheric two-lane local roads. An exception can be made here in the lower Naugatuck Valley, where Rte. 8 cuts a dramatic path

## NAUGATUCK'S INDUSTRIES: RUBBER AND CANDY

Waterbury stakes its claim to industrial fame on shiny brass, and New Britain stakes its on precision-crafted tools. In Naugatuck, the chronically in-debt and generally unsuccessful inventor Charles Goodyear developed a process to vulcanize rubber, making the substance resistant to the corrosive forces of both cold and heat. Goodyear earned very little money from his patent, but the rubber industry did take off as a result, and Naugatuck became a leading producer of rubber-soled shoes, tires, and many other products.

And on Rte. 63, just east of the Rte. 8 highway, you'll see the enormous Peter Paul candy factory. Naugatuck is where York peppermint patties and Almond Joy and Mounds candy bars are manufactured.

gatuck Valley. It does contain one architectural gem, a massive old mill building that has been converted to condos.

Across the street from the mill is a delightfully idiosyncratic turquoise shop called the **Trolley Stop Luncheonette and General Store** (15 N. Main St., 203/720-7597). Go inside and peruse the eclectic offerings: cigars, live bait, grilled cheese sandwiches, candy, comics, milk shakes, maps, and newspapers. On a good day, you'll also see a nice variety of Harley Davidsons parked along the street outside.

### Seymour

At the south end of Main Street (which is Rte. 42 at this point), hop back on Rte. 8 and follow it one more exit to Rte. 67, in Seymour. Another planned factory town, this one has a small but very interesting downtown called **Humphreyville**, which was the very first planned factory community in the nation (named for its founder, David Humphreys). Seymour used to have little going for it, but it's experienced a nice little antiques boom in recent years, and now the streets of Humphreyville have a number of good shops. The leader of this movement is **Seymour Antiques Co.** (26 Bank St., 203/881-2526). Large pieces and period toys and collectibles await inside a 10,000-square-foot showroom, which offers the wares of some 70 dealers. In this same neighborhood, Seymour's little movie theater, the **Strand**, is a great work of art deco.

### Ansonia

At this point, if your patience for depressed downtowns on the river has worn thin, it would be wise to follow Rte. 67 north from Seymour into Oxford. Otherwise, from downtown Seymour, continue south through working-class neighborhoods on the east side of the Naugatuck along Rte. 115. This road takes you into depressed Ansonia, which was incorporated comparatively recently (1889), when it broke from Derby.

It's worth a brief detour east along Elm Street (Rte. 243), toward Woodbridge and New Haven. Just up the hill from Rte. 115 is the restored home of David Humphreys, the Colonial renaissance man who operated a wool mill in

alongside the river, passing south from Naugatuck to where it crosses the Housatonic in Shelton. Through most of the valley, you can also opt to stick with local roads, but it's worth taking Rte. 8 for part of the ride. The most direct way to reach the old industrial village of Beacon Falls is to hop on Rte. 8 in the southern end of Naugatuck, right where Rte. 63 crosses the highway. Note that if you continue a short distance past the highway entrance on Rte. 63, you'll see the enormous Peter Paul candy factory, where Almond Joy and Mounds candy bars are manufactured. (By the way, PEZ candies are made just down the Housatonic, in Shelton).

### Beacon Falls

Once on Rte. 8, head south for about three miles to exit 24, which deposits you at the north end of Beacon Falls. If ever a town failed to live up to its name, Beacon Falls is it—a place that you might imagine to have neat Victorian wooden homes and redbrick shops and banks, Gothic churches, and mills along a roaring river. In fact, there's barely even a town here; it's notable mostly because it illustrates the plight of the lower Nau-

Middlebury, built a factory town in Seymour, and served as an aide to George Washington during the American Revolution and later as a U.S. ambassador. The **General David Humphreys House** (37 Elm St., 203/735-1908, open weekday afternoons, $2) was built in 1698 and contains exhibits detailing Humphreys's fascinating life and the early history of this region.

Continue east along Rte. 243 for about 1.5 miles, then make a left turn onto Benz Street, following it north a little more than a mile until you see a sign for the **Ansonia Nature & Recreational Center** (10 Deerfield Rd., 203/736-1053, open dawn–dusk daily, free). This 104-acre park has more than two miles of easy nature trails, a wildflower garden, fishing pond, playing field and picnic pavilions, and environmental exhibits. It's a great taste of open space and nature, a welcome break from the industrial feel of the Naugatuck River Valley.

## Derby

Back on Rte. 115, drive south; as you enter Derby, a right turn onto Rte. 34 (west, toward Danbury and Newtown) leads you over the Naugatuck River just as it flows into the Housatonic. You'll cut through downtown Derby, yet another downtown that has fallen on hard times, and then Rte. 34 leads along the eastern bank of the lower Housatonic River. The river proved significant in the city's early history as a shipbuilding center.

The towns along the west bank of the lower Housatonic (Newtown, Monroe, and Shelton) make for better exploring than Derby and Seymour on the east. But there are a couple of interesting sites along Rte. 34 before it crosses over the river into Newtown. First, just north of downtown Derby, Rte. 34 passes some intriguing old factory buildings, one housing a quirky shop called **Books by the Falls** (253 Roosevelt Dr., Rte. 34, 860/734-6112), which is packed to the ceiling with vintage books, antiques, and bric-a-brac. As you drive along the river, keep an eye out also for the recently built **Yale Boathouse,** a gorgeous building where the University's crew team is based.

At the north end of Derby, you'll see the entrance off Rte. 34 for **Osbornedale State Park,** 500 Hawthorne Ave., which contains the Kel-

vintage building facades along Main Street in Derby

logg Environmental Center (203/734-2513, open Tues.–Sat., free) and the historic **Osborne Homestead Museum** (203/922-7832, varied hours mid-Apr.–mid-Dec., grounds open daily, donation suggested). These two great facilities can easily keep families entertained for the afternoon. Nature trails and interactive exhibits are found at the grounds of the environmental center, which also hosts informative wildlife educational workshops, and beautiful formal gardens surround the 1850 Osborne mansion, a stately Colonial Revival house furnished with the original occupants' art and antiques.

One of Derby's more unusual claims to fame is **Vintage Motor Cars** (67 Minerva St., 203/734-1302, open weekdays, free), an antique auto restoration company that provides vintage cars for movies shot around the Northeast. Among the nearly 100 classics in this warehouse are a Franklin once owned by Amelia Earhart, and a Lincoln convertible singer Ricky Nelson once tooled around in. You can come to admire not only the cars, but also the restoration experts rehabilitating automobiles. The showroom is downtown, just a couple blocks up from Main Street.

## Oxford

Back on Rte. 34, continue driving north along the Housatonic through the western edge of Seymour, then make a right turn onto Rte. 188, following it up into Oxford. This enchanting drive through rolling farmland and over some steep hills passes through the heart of the town's historic Quaker Farms area, including a number of 18th- and 19th-century homes and farmsteads. At the north end of Rte. 188 is the sign for Schreiber's Farm (see below).

Rte. 188 soon leads by the entrance to **Southford Falls State Park,** where the Eight-Mile Brook rushes through a small wooded gorge. This is technically in the town of Southbury, just beyond the Oxford town line, but it's a pleasant way to end this tour. From here, you're in a perfect position to continue touring up into the eastern Litchfield Hills or to drive west (either by returning to Rte. 34 or taking I-84) into the Housatonic River Valley.

## SHOPPING

As the lower Naugatuck River Valley is not a major spot for tourism, and not terribly well-off, shopping isn't a major pastime here. However, there are good antiques in Seymour, plus a smattering of interesting pick-your-own farms and offbeat shopping opportunities.

The latest big retail draw in the region is the **Brass Mill Center** (495 Union St., exit 23 from I-84 eastbound, exit 22 from I-84 westbound, 203/755-5000, www.brassmillcenter.com), which consists of 130 shops with an 800-seat food court, plus a 12-screen movie theater—it's anchored by Filene's, JCPenney, and Sears, and next door is Brass Mill Commons, which has a Barnes & Noble superstore. A couple of good chain restaurants (Hops microbrewery, Bertucci's), plus the usual slew of fast food, are in the mall itself, while Chili's and TGI Friday's are next door at the Commons.

### Pick-Your-Own Farms

In Oxford, herbalists and gardeners regularly make the trip to **Catnip Acres Herb Nursery** (67 Christian St., Oxford, 203/888-5649), which has gardens, a greenhouse that sells 400 varieties of herbs, scented geraniums, and perennials. In the Quaker Farms section of town,

**Schreiber's Farm** (648 Quaker Farms Rd., Rte. 188, 203/888-0832) offers pumpkin hayrides and has pick-your-own pumpkin harvesting, plus gardens. This farm is also a good spot to watch the farm animals, and mountain biking is popular here.

## Miscellany

For the definitive Nutmegger shopping spree, you need to plan for some time at **The Connecticut Store** (120-140 Bank St., Waterbury, 800/474-6728, www.theconnecticutstore.com). It's the state's oldest department store, in a dramatic cast-iron building downtown, offering random products made or invented instate, including Wiffle balls, PEZ candy dispensers, and all kinds of toys, games, and home furnishings. Set in the 1890s Howland-Hughes department store, the store offers a nice little lesson in local history.

## RECREATION

### Golf

**Crestbrook Park** (Northfield Rd., Watertown, 860/945-5249) is an excellent—though often very crowded—local course, probably the best in this region. There's a nice little nine-holer in Wolcott, the **Farmingbury Hills Golf Course** (141 East St., 203/879-8038), which offers nice views toward the Hanging Hills in Meriden. Down in Naugatuck, **Hop Brook Country Club** (615 N. Church St., 203/729-8013) is another short and fairly simple nine-hole course; the clubhouse has a popular restaurant, Jesse Camille's. Waterbury has a pair of courses, both of which have suffered from uneven upkeep over the years. The most improved is **Western Hills** (Park Rd., Waterbury, 203/756-1211), a par-72, 6,500-yard course.

### Hiking

While this isn't a major hiking area, there are trails at some of the facilities described above, including the **Ansonia Nature & Recreational Center, Northfield Brook Lake, Osbornedale State Park,** and **Southford Falls State Park**—the latter is particularly appealing, as it offers walks by tumultuous cascades, through a covered footbridge, past a handful of long-abandoned mill sites, and up to a soaring lookout tower.

The 38-mile **Mattatuck Trail** extends through a good bit of the area north of Waterbury, beginning in Wolcott, passing through Plymouth, Thomaston, Watertown, and Morris, and ending in Litchfield. Much of it goes through **Black Rock State Park.** Favorite jaunts through this area include a stretch of the trail that passes through the mysterious **Leatherman Cave,** the alleged temporary shelter of an eccentric Frenchman named Jules Bourglay, who wandered the western Connecticut countryside in an apparent stupor sometime around the Civil War. Great legends have surfaced concerning this bizarre figure, who supposedly failed in a leather business in France and arrived in Connecticut destitute, dispirited, somewhat deranged, and clad in a bombastic outfit made almost entirely of leather. This particular cave can be reached by hiking east along the Mattatuck Trail for about a mile from the small parking area on U.S. 6 (about a mile south of Rte. 109). Just before the cave, you'll ascend an impressive little summit, Crane Overlook, from which there are broad views toward the Naugatuck River Valley. Another good stretch of the trail runs along the west side of Black Rock Pond, within the actual park limits in Watertown.

South of Waterbury, your best bet for hiking lies in **Naugatuck State Forest,** which has popular sections in Beacon Falls. To reach the trails from Rte. 8 in the center of town, cross the Naugatuck River via Depot Street, and then make a right onto Cold Spring Road and continue for about a mile to a parking area near some picnic tables. From this area, several well-beaten trails lead up over the eastern wall of the Naugatuck River Valley. More trails extend from the Spruce Brook parking area, which is just a short way north on Cold Spring Road.

## Horseback Riding

**High Lonesome Rose Hurst Stable** (Rte. 188, Middlebury, 203/758-9094) has trail rides year-round, daily by appointment.

## ENTERTAINMENT AND NIGHTLIFE

For such a small area, Waterbury and the Naugatuck Valley have a very nice selection of cultural venues, including the regionally acclaimed **Seven Angels Theatre** (Hamilton Park Pavilion, Plank Rd., Waterbury, 203/757-4676), which stages regional, national, and pre-Broadway shows. The **Waterbury Symphony Orchestra** (203/574-4283, www.waterburysymphony.org) celebrated its 65th anniversary in 2003; performances take place at a variety of venues throughout the area. On the west side of the city, plays and concerts are often held at the **Naugatuck Valley Community-Technical College** (750 Chase Pkwy., Waterbury, 203/575-8036 or 203/575-8037, www.nvctc.commnet.edu) in a multi-use fine arts facility.

Watertown is the home of the **Connecticut Dance Theatre** (523 Main St., 860/274-0004, www.ctdancetheatre.org), and nearby Oakville presents original and published plays staged at the **Clockwork Repertory Theatre** (133 Main St., Oakville, 860/274-5911). Probably the most dramatic venue is the **Thomaston Opera House** (158 Main St., 860/283-6250, www.thomastonoperahouse.org), one of the great restorations in the state, where you can see dance, theater, and concerts year-round. Appropriately, a tall clock tower crowns this 1884 building in the center of one of the great clock-making towns in America. **The Strand** (165 Main St., Seymour, 203/888-0083) presents music and theater throughout the year.

Greater Waterbury has a somewhat limited bar and club scene. Your best bets for catching live music are **Bobby D's** (227 Whitewood Rd., 203/754-0622) and the well-respected **Fat Daddy's Tavern** (675 Main St., Watertown, 860/945-9300), which is known for its great jazz and blues. The **Brass Horse** (26 N. Main St., 203/574-7741) is a convivial spot right on the Waterbury Green, with a great happy hour, close proximity to restaurants and hotels, and live entertainment. There's a fairly popular gay bar in downtown Waterbury, the **Brownstone** (29 Leavenworth St., 203/597-1838).

## FESTIVALS AND EVENTS

### Winter and Spring

From late November through early December, Waterbury celebrates the **Festival of Trees** (Mattatuck Museum, 144 W. Main St., 203/753-0381), which includes holidays parties and events for both adults and children. Throughout December, one of the largest gingerbread houses you'll ever lay eyes on is displayed at Middlebury's **Annual Gingerbread Village and Bazaar** (St. George's Church, Tucker Hill Rd., 203/723-4143); 200 pounds of flour and 600 eggs are used for this immense undertaking.

### Summer and Fall

On the same weekend in mid-September, Thomaston is site of both the **Classic Car Show** (Main St., 860/283-8168), and the **Clocktown Arts & Crafts Fair** (Seth Thomas Park, S. Main St., 860/283-8188). Crafters also delight in the **Holiday Crafts Fair** (Fire Department Building, 65 Tucker Hill Rd., 203/758-9276), and the **Oxford Arts and Crafts Show** (Center School, Rte. 67, Oxford, 203/888-0363), which are both held the first week in November.

## ACCOMMODATIONS

The vast majority of lodging possibilities in this area can be found in the city of Waterbury. The few exceptions include a great B&B in Middlebury and one of the state's best economy motor inns in Wolcott.

### Hotels and Motels

**$50–$100:** The **Courtyard Marriott** (63 Grand St., 203/596-1000 or 800/321-2211) is easily the best hotel in downtown Waterbury, a sparkling-clean property through and through, from the marble and dark woods of the lobby to the clean, light-filled guest rooms. It's within walking distance of Mattatuck and local businesses, and a short drive from the Brass Mill Center mall. Newly opened in downtown Waterbury, the **Holiday Inn Express** (88 Union St., 203/575-1500 or 800/465-4329) was a so-so Quality Inn prior to changing affiliations in winter 2003. This 111-room, eight-floor property has tasteful modern rooms, a fitness center, and an outdoor pool, and rates include a free breakfast.

The neatly kept **Wolcott Inn and Suites** (1273 Wolcott Rd., Rte. 69, Wolcott, 203/879-4618 or 800/424-9466, www.wolcottinnandsuites.com) is one of the finest motels in the area—it's in northern Wolcott, high on a hill and a reasonably short drive from Waterbury. It's also convenient to the Litchfield Hills and towns like Bristol and Southington. Both rooms and suites, with separate sitting areas and kitchens, are available; all have light oak furnishings, pastel color schemes, and clean wall-to-wall carpeting.

### Country Inns and Bed-and-Breakfasts

**$100–150:** There's a magnificent B&B in Waterbury's grand Hillside Historic District, once the realm of wealthy industrialists. The **House on the Hill** (92 Woodlawn Terrace, 203/757-9901, www.houseonthehill.biz), which definitely lives up to its name, is a decadent painted-lady Victorian in six colors surrounded by formal gardens and elaborate fieldstone paths and walls. Inside this 20-room mansion (including five guest rooms) are six fireplaces, pressed-tin ceilings, and fine mahogany and cherry woodworking. Both antiques and tasteful newer pieces fill common and guest areas, and a lavish full breakfast is included. Weekend cooking classes are also offered here.

An easy walk or bike ride from Middlebury's enchanting village green, the **Tucker Hill Inn** (96 Tucker Hill Rd., 203/758-8334, www.tuckerhillinn.com) is a 1923 clapboard Colonial filled with country-style furnishings and operated by outgoing innkeeper Susan Cebelenski. Weddings are one of Cebelenski's specialties—she claims that hundreds have been held here, and hundreds more newlyweds have spent their wedding nights in one of Tucker Hill's four warmly furnished rooms. A gracious library is filled with books, CDs, and video movies, which can all be taken and played in the individual guest rooms. Full breakfast is served.

# FOOD

Most of the towns and cities along the Naugatuck are solid working-class communities, many with a strong ethnic presence. Excellent Italian and Portuguese restaurants are among the region's hallmarks. Beyond that, you'll find a typical mix of traditional American and Continental spots, most of them perfectly nice for a casual meal, but few offering the creative and critically acclaimed cooking found in some of the more tourist-oriented parts of the state.

## Upscale

A sprawling, red, Victorian inn with elaborate white trim and pretty landscaping, the **Milestone** (18 Neumann St., Naugatuck, 203/723-6693, $13–19) is thankfully set back from ugly Rubber Avenue, which looks about as uninspired as a road called Rubber Avenue could expect to look. There's a pub downstairs and more refined dining areas upstairs; in both, you can order from the menu of Italian and Continental favorites, such as boneless breast of capon chicken sautéed and simmered with Madeira wine, served with bits of tomato and wild mushrooms, or roast duckling flamed with Grand Marnier.

*Most of the towns and cities along the Naugatuck are solid working-class communities, many with a strong ethnic presence. Excellent Italian and Portuguese restaurants are among the region's hallmarks.*

**Circa Bistro** (92 Bank St., 203/597-9292, $16–34), a snazzy downtown Waterbury restaurant, has a long and very popular bar up front and a quieter and rather more refined dining room in back. The menu blends contemporary styles with traditional preparations, and portions are huge. Try the lobster-and-crab cannelloni with vodka sauce, or the starter of layered ripe tomatoes, mozzarella, fresh basil, and dark olive oil and aged balsamic. There are often great lobster specials, too. People justly rave about the crab cakes served at **Carmen Anthony Steakhouse** (496 Chase Ave., 203/757-3040, $17–36), a longtime favorite in Waterbury. With an elegant dining room of dark woods and a staff of thoughtful and personable servers, Carmen Anthony has developed into a most elegant steak house. The portions, including those fresh crab cakes, are *big*; think lobsters weighing up to five pounds and Italian-style steaks registering a massive 32 ounces. The preparation and quality of ingredients are always exceptional, and the value—considering a restaurant of this caliber—is extraordinary.

Having pleased Waterbury locals with its fine Italian fare since the 1930s, **Bacco's** (1230 Thomaston Ave., Waterbury, 203/755-0635, $12–24) remains remarkably good in every regard, despite a setting in the uninspiring Waterville section of town. Once inside, however, you'll find a dignified dining room with soft lighting, framed art, and a tasteful clean ambience. Devotees of Italian cooking will no doubt debate back and forth whether Bacco's or Diorio serves the best of this genre—it's worth trying them both. Very good pizzas, house-made onion rings and steak fries, and a long list of pastas and grills are strong bets.

Similarly charming in an old-school sort of way is **Diorio** (231 Bank St., Waterbury, 203/754-5111, $15–25), arguably the best Italian restaurant in the lower Naugatuck Valley (and that's considering some pretty serious competition). Definitely reserve a day or two ahead to be sure of a seat in one of the sumptuous, high-back wooden booths. Other notable decorative elements include fine white napery, pressed-tin ceilings, and a classic mahogany bar with an etched mirror backdrop. The Northern Italian fare is excellent, and many seafood grills are offered as specials; the wine list is also superb.

## Steak, Pizza, Pub Grub, and Seafood

Locals have been coming to **Drescher's** (25 Leavenworth St., Waterbury, 203/573-1743, $9–17) since it opened in 1868—on some days, you'll see folks who look like they may well have attended the grand opening. The National Historic Register building used to stand at another location, but when faced with demolition a few years back, it was saved and relocated just a block south of the village green. The dining rooms ooze with character—in particular the room on the left as you enter, which has a long row of tables facing a large window. The food at Drescher's is hearty and traditional, with an emphasis on German, Italian, and American dishes, such as blackened New York strip, fettuccine carbonara, and Wiener schnitzel à la Holstein (breaded veal cutlet topped with a sunny-side-up egg and anchovies, with red cabbage and German fries).

Oxford doesn't have many dining standouts. Your best bet is the **Oxford House** (441 Oxford Rd., 203/888-6241, $12–18), a somewhat ordinary Colonial-style inn on Rte. 67, just across the street from a handsome white church and a small sliver of a town green. Chicken in Calvados with a cheddar sauce, baked stuffed scallops, baked scrod, and wild mushroom ravioli are among the better options from the no-surprises American and Continental menu.

Located just inside the door of the Brass Mill Center shopping mall, on the east side of Waterbury, **Hops** (495 Union St., 203/757-4677, $7–18) is Connecticut's only branch of the increasingly popular national chain of brewpub restaurants. In addition to sampling several kinds of ale, you can dig into hefty portions of stick-to-your-ribs fare, including burgers, meat loaf, chicken-chili burritos, seared sea scallops, and barbecue baby back ribs. The mood is festive and casual, the portions large enough to satisfy even the hungriest patrons.

A pleasant little restaurant at the Hop Brook Golf Course, with views of Hop Brook and the fairways, **Jesse Camille's** (615 N. Church St., Naugatuck, 203/723-2275, $10–17) has a bright dining room with beamed ceilings, Windsor chairs, floral curtains, and a fireplace. Shrimp cocktail, grilled New York sirloin with a mushroom and port reduction, and barbecued baby back ribs are typical here.

Perhaps the best waterside setting of any restaurant in the Naugatuck River Valley (but of the Housatonic River) is at the **Riverside Restaurant** (337 Roosevelt Dr., Rte. 34, Seymour, 203/736-9969, $6–15), a highly popular family restaurant with good pizza (try the one with barbecued chicken), fried seafood, charcoal-broiled burgers,

and fairly traditional Italian fare. It's in a light-filled many-windowed contemporary wooden building on the banks of the river, and during the day diners are rewarded with outstanding views. Excellent lobster, shrimp, and scallop pizza is served at **Roseland Apizza** (350 Hawthorne Ave., Derby, 203/735-0494, $8–12), which has been a hit since the 1930s, almost as long as some of the grandfathers of American pizza-making have been pleasing palates in nearby New Haven. It's a short distance from Derby's Osborne Homestead and Kellogg Nature Center. Set in a characterful old bank building, **Tartaglia's** (285 Main St., 203/734-2462, $11–16) anchors Derby's downtown, right by the bridge across the Housatonic to Shelton. The menu offers dozens of classic Italian dishes, including a tremendous array of seafood options, such as classic *zuppa di pesce* and veal cacciatore.

## Ethnic Fare

**Tequila's** (733 Lakewood Rd., 203/755-4806, $10–20) is in a strip of mostly chain restaurants in northern Waterbury, yet it's surprisingly good, one of the better Mexican restaurants in the state. In addition to serving what you'd expect (burritos, enchiladas, etc.), Tequila's has a very nice cactus soup (offered sporadically as a special), carnitas asadas (marinated chunks of pork in a blend of lemon and spices), and some delicious seafood paellas. The decor is festive but not overdone.

In a region offering little in the way of Asian eats, the **Golden Palace** (544 Straits Tpke., Rte. 63, Pioneer Plaza shopping center, Watertown, 860/274-6770, $6–14) stands out for its tasty take on Sichuan, Polynesian, and Cantonese cooking. The dining room is done with original art imported from China. An almost ridiculous number of dishes are offered—you'd have to eat here every night for a year to try them all. Specialties include volcano steak (tenderloin of beef spiced and decorated with a ring of fresh broccoli, and served with flaming wine sauce) and the Golden Palace seafood bird's nest (lobster, shrimp, sea scallops, and veggies in a crispy fried "nest").

With Portuguese descendants living all over the state, it's a wonder there aren't more such restaurants in Connecticut. But the Naugatuck

Valley has a pair of great ones. Many say that **Estoril** (152 Church St., Naugatuck, 203/729-7850, $9–15) is the best—dinner here is certainly a bargain. The place consists of a long bar on the left that's a famous haunt for local characters. On the right is a neat little dining room with green leatherette booths and a friendly staff. Some fairly exotic dishes are served, including shish kabob Estoril (skewers of pork, beef, linguica sausage, peppers, onions, tomatoes, and shrimp); a dauntingly big but very tasty shellfish casserole with lobster, shrimp, scallops, mussels, and clams; and baby goat roasted with roast potatoes.

In a rather dreary area, the Portuguese **Lisboa** (19–23 Lafayette St., Waterbury, 203/754-0789, $10–20) is sandwiched between Rte. 8 and rail tracks on one side and the Naugatuck River on the other. Inside, however, is a cheerful, well-run restaurant, with a popular bar and a dining room. The staff is gracious and quite eager to welcome everybody, and the food is delightful. Consider marinated pork chunks with littleneck clams, pickled vegetables, and potatoes, served in a clay pot; Portuguese-style cod boiled with potatoes, chickpeas, and eggs; or shrimp with a spicy sauce.

## Quick Bites

When the weather's good, expect crowds of locals packed into the deck seating and picnic tables at **Al's Hot Dogs** (248 S. Main St., Naugatuck, 203/729-6229, under $8), which has fast-and-filling breakfasts and delicious dogs with all the fixings. There's dining insid, too, but clearly the outdoor tables are the favorites, even if they are in the shadows of a busy highway.

**American Pie** (500 New Haven Rd., Rte. 63, Naugatuck, 203/723-8661, $5–11) is an infectiously fun little pizza and burger joint with 1950s drive-in ambience, photos of vintage Camaros and T-birds, and deco-style chairs and tables. It's a great place for above-average short-order food, three meals a day: blueberry pancakes and breakfast fajitas star at breakfast, while pastas, burgers, French dip sandwiches, and pitchers of beer are the popular choices later in the day.

**Frankie's** (705 Watertown Ave., 203/753-6999, under $10) has been a place to go in Waterbury after little league games and county fairs

since the 1930s, when the Caiazzo brothers opened this wildly popular hot-dog stand. The foot-long wieners are memorable, topped with any number of greasy goodies, including fantastic relish. An absolutely amazing item here is the lobster roll, which is served in a toasted hot-dog bun—no mayo, no filler, no funny stuff: just big pieces of shredded lobster that have been dredged in melted butter. Adjacent to Frankie's is a **Carvel Ice Cream Supermarket**, in case you were hoping for a sweet ending to this meal. It's as much fun to eat here as it is to people-watch; see the lines of loyal customers queuing up at the rows of takeout windows in this long, brick, one-floor building. A neon sign outside proclaims Frankie's honest and catchy motto: "Come in and eat . . . or we'll both starve." Of course, there's no dining room inside, so you actually end up eating in your car, but that's a minor point.

Just down the street from Frankie's is a barbecue spot operated by the same Caiazzo family, called **Big Frank's** (572 Watertown Ave., Waterbury, 203/753-7427), which has been open since 1998 and is a huge success. Carved-wood piggy totem poles greet you as you enter and then proceed to a long counter to order your food: beef ribs, whole barbecued chicken, baby back ribs, pulled pork sandwiches, and great baked beans and corn on the cob, too. The cooking here is oh-so-good, and just the smell of the place is enough to get your heart racing (and arteries clogging).

The most atmospheric ice-cream spot in the area is the **Rich Farm Ice Cream Shop** (691 Oxford Rd., Rte. 67, Oxford, 203/881-1040), an expansive working dairy farm with picnic tables and a friendly staff that happily help you choose a flavor if you're having a tough time with all the great options.

## Gourmet Goods and Picnic Supplies

It's worth the trip to Naugatuck to pick up fresh homemade ravioli and other Italian treats at **Anna Donte** (413 N. Main St., Naugatuck, 203/729-6783) in a homely little storefront in the shadows of Rte. 8. It offers delicious food, and extremely friendly service to boot. Ravioli by the dozen include broccoli, sausage, and fried sweet peppers; wild mushrooms and Swiss chard; and spinach

Florentine with sausage; plus lobster ravioli and the freshly made vodka sauce to go with it.

## INFORMATION AND SERVICES
### Visitor Information

For information on the towns in this region, contact the **Litchfield Hills Visitors Bureau** (Box 968, Litchfield, CT 06759, 860/567-4506, www.litchfieldhills.com).

### Getting Around

Although there's public transportation in Waterbury and several of the towns in the region, the Naugatuck River Valley is best explored by car. The four-lane limited-access highway Rte. 8 runs north–south alongside the Naugatuck River and is the fastest way to get from town to town. I-84 runs east–west through Middlebury and Waterbury, connecting the region with Danbury and Hartford.

# Danbury and the Lower Housatonic Valley

An eclectic chunk of western Connecticut comprising wealthy northern Fairfield County suburbs, rural and heavily wooded communities in the Litchfield foothills, the small multiethnic city of Danbury, and a string of communities along the western bank of the roaring Housatonic River, this region makes for an ideal base to explore all of western Connecticut. It has, if you'll pardon the cliché, a little something for everyone.

Another advantage to basing yourself here is that I-84 cuts through the region, providing extremely easy access to New York City (75 minutes away) and even Boston, which is no more than 2.5 hours away. The character of the terrain varies largely according to population density and the way in which the land has been used historically—although this part of the state is among Connecticut's fastest-growing, farms and state parks still abound. And Connecticut's largest man-made lake, Candlewood, provides plenty of opportunities for boating—to say nothing of the great fly-fishing you'll find along the Housatonic.

## DANBURY

Danbury escaped some of the problems that plagued Connecticut's cities during the latter half of the 20th century, partly because it's surrounded on all sides by fairly prosperous towns, and partly because its economy—like Norwalk's and Stamford's—has relied on a significant mix of both manufacturing- and services-based com-

panies. It could really be called a city within a very hilly suburb, as a large part of Danbury is rather quiet and residential and has the feel of its neighboring towns, while the city center is rapidly righting itself with several ambitious civic projects.

One thing to keep in mind before tackling Danbury is that the city is laid out willy-nilly, with I-84 and a four-lane limited-access span of U.S. 7 crossing through the city at rather strange angles. There is no grid street system, even in the heart of downtown, and as the city is also poorly signed, Danbury can be a little tricky to navigate. With those caveats in mind, a good place to begin your explorations of the area is downtown, which can be reached via I-84 (take exit 5 and head south on Main Street).

### Downtown

As you head down Main Street, make a left turn onto White Street, a quick right again onto Ives Street, and then follow this beside the small, recently created town green to the large—and surprisingly attractive—parking garage. From here, you can walk to several good restaurants and a couple of Danbury's attractions, including the city's new Danbury Ice Arena.

The small aforementioned green is a pleasant spot for a breather on a sunny day—there are a couple of benches here—and although a Firestone Tire center anchors one side of the green, a few restored historic buildings sit along the others.

Walk back to White Street and turn right to reach the **Danbury Railway Museum** (120 White

# GREATER DANBURY

Brookfield

DI GRAZIA
VINEYARD & WINERY ★

TOWER RD.

WHISCONIER RD.

25

202

7

FEDERAL RD.

CANDLEWOOD LAKE RD.

Hawleyville

MOUNT PLEASANT RD.

OLD HAWLEYVILLE RD.

84

6

STONY HILL INN ●
BEST WESTERN

HELGA'S ▼

BEST WESTERN
BERKSHIRE MOTOR INN

PAYNE RD.

SHELLEY RD.

JACKLIN

Dodgingtown

SUNRISE
HERBAL
REMEDIES ■

COONH HILL RD.

WOLFPITS RD.

BLUE JAY
ORCHARDS ●

PLUMTREE RD.

TAYLOR RD.

302

58

GREENWOOD AVE.

Bethel

CHESTNUT ST.

Beaverbrook

SIT DOWN
DINER ▼

SHELTER ROCK RD.

BANGKOK
THAI ▼

NEWTOWN RD.

FEDERAL RD.

202

6

7

84

Candlewood
Lake

STEW
LEONARD'S ■

IVES
CONCERT HALL ★

WHITE ST.

MAIN ST.

DANBURY RAILWAY
MUSEUM ★

TWO STEPS DOWNTOWN GRILLE ▼

DANBURY MUSEUM
& HISTORICAL SOCIETY

MAIN ST.
SOUTH

COALPIT HILL RD.

BETHEL CINEMA/
EMERALD CITY
CAFE ■

GIOVANNI'S ▼

DR. MIKE'S ▼

53

SYCAMORE
DRIVE-IN ★

HOUSATONIC VALLEY
TOURISM DISTRICT

BRUSHY HILL RD.

Margerie
Lake Reservoir

ONDINE ▼

37

PEMBROKE RD.

E. PEMBROKE RD.

THANG LONG ▼

ERNIE'S
ROADHOUSE ▼

DANBURY
CORRECTIONAL
FACILITY ■

BEST INN
& SUITES ●

Danbury

CAIOI CAFE &
WINE BAR ▼

WEST ST.

WEST ST.

LAKE AVE.

TARRYWILE
PARK

SESAME
SEED ▼

WOOSTER HTS.

7

To Ridgefield

PADANARAM RD.

CLAPBOARD RIDGE RD.

39

MILITARY MUSEUM
OF SOUTHERN
NEW ENGLAND

ETHAN
ALLEN
HOTEL ●

DANBURY
FAIR MALL ■

DANBURY
AIRPORT ✈

BACKUS AVE.

MIRY BROOK RD.

Wooster Mountain
State Park

CLASSIC ROCK
BREW PUB ▼

MIDDLE RIVER RD.

West Lake
Reservoir

WESTERN CONNECTICUT
STATE UNIVERSITY

6

203

84

Lake
Kenosia

DANBURY RADISSON
HOTEL & SUITES ●

GEORGE WASHINGTON HWY.

KING ST.

AUNT HACK RD.

RICHTER PARK
GOLF COURSE ▲

CAFE ON
THE GREEN ▼

COMFORT
SUITES ●

HILTON
GARDEN INN ●

MILL PLAIN RD.

DANBURY SHERATON ●

RIDGEBURY RD.

Round
Mountain ▲

1 mi

1 km

0

0

CONNECTICUT
NEW YORK

THE WESTERN HILLS

© AVALON TRAVEL PUBLISHING, INC.

St., 203/778-8337, www.danbury.org/drm, open 10 A.M.–5 P.M. Tues.–Sat., noon–5 P.M. Sun., more limited hours in winter, $5), inside the city's original restored Union Station—you may recognize it as the station from Alfred Hitchcock's thriller *Strangers in a Train*. This is a largely kid-oriented museum, but anybody with an interest in the railroad will get a kick out of the historic exhibits and estimable collection of vintage rail cars assembled in the yard behind the station—an eclectic array of cabooses, coaches, cranes, and engines.

During Danbury's manufacturing heyday, White Street was lined with bawdy old taverns and perhaps a few houses of at least somewhat ill repute. Still anchoring the corner of White Street and Patriot Drive, nearly across from the rail museum, is **Meeker's Hardware,** a hulking old building that's been in business since 1883 and is still great fun to explore. You can even get a cup of Coca-Cola at the counter for five cents, just as you could at the turn of the 20th century.

Continue back along White Street, past Ives Street, and up to Main Street, which has received several face-lifts over the past decade. Running down the Main Street median is a very pretty Elmwood Park, with flower beds, park benches, a fountain, and walkways. It's a nice spot to stroll or to munch on lunch from one of the restaurants in town. Generally, the area along Main north of White Street and closer to I-84 has been the least appealing, although this span has improved of late. A badly laid out housing project was torn down in the early 1990s, and a few interesting stores and some ethnic-food markets have opened along here.

The better walk is had by making a left turn onto Main Street and walking south. Anyone expecting the quaint, tony storefronts of nearby Ridgefield will be disappointed by the spate of workaday and, in some cases, frumpy-looking businesses. But there's no denying the street's rich architectural heritage—there are some lovely old buildings.

Toward the south end of Main is the city's former town green, **Elmwood Park**, a small slice of grass and gardens that marks the spot where 2,000 British troops perpetrated their carnage upon Danbury in 1777, burning virtually every build-

**Elmwood Park in downtown Danbury**

© ANDREW COLLINS

ing in sight. This is the primary reason you'll find very few pre-1800s structures in this town.

Continue a few hundred feet down the street to the small complex of historic buildings that makes up the **Danbury Museum and Historical Society** (43 Main St., 203/743-5200, www.danburyhistorical.org). You can visit three buildings at this site: a genealogical library, the 1785 John & Mary Rider House, and the 1790 John Dodd Hat Shop. A short drive south, at 5 Mountainville Ave., is the 1829 **birthplace of Charles Ives**. The museum is also planning to add the studio of opera singer Marion Anderson, who was born here.

This building is a tribute to one of America's more avant-garde composers. Ives, hardly a household name, even among houses filled with music lovers, was born in 1874 and raised here. His musical talents were not well received in his day, as polytonality and multiple meters were trademarks of his musical philosophy. Ives sold insurance for a living and composed only in his spare time. He first received critical recognition in Europe before gradually getting notice in the Unites States in the 1930s, but this was some two decades after he ceased composing. It wasn't until 1947, seven years before his death, that Ives received a Pulitzer Prize for one of his pieces.

Danbury now goes to great lengths to celebrate the legacy of Ives, having created a tour of city sites that figured in the composer's life. You have to be a serious Ives fan to follow this tour in earnest, taking in what are mostly ordinary though attractively preserved historic buildings, including local churches, houses, and parks. The house is about a half-mile walk from the Danbury Museum and is open by appointment only. Admission to all historical society sites is free, but a donation is suggested. The buildings on the museum's property are open Wednesday–Sunday, but with limited hours (they're mostly open late in the afternoon; it's best to phone ahead).

The **John & Mary Rider House,** which was moved here from another part of town, is decorated with 18th- and 19th-century furnishings that would have been typical of homes at this time.

### Greater Danbury

To explore the rest of Danbury, as well as the lower Housatonic River Valley, you'll want to use a car. From downtown, it's a very short drive to the former estate of hat mogul, Charles Darling Parks, **Tarrywile Park** (Tarrywile Lake Rd., 70 Southern Blvd., 203/744-3130, www.danbury.org/tarry, open dawn–dusk daily, free). To get here, head west on Wooster Street from lower Main Street (near Elmwood Park). Follow Wooster for several blocks, making a left turn onto Jefferson Avenue and then a right onto Southern Boulevard. This neighborhood

## DANBURY'S GLORIOUS REIGN AS OUR "HATTING CAPITAL"

The **Dodd Hat Shop,** at the Danbury Museum and Historical Society, is the most interesting of the structures, as its exhibits illustrate the fascinating story of Danbury's history as the "hatting capital of America."

Danbury's hat industry can be traced officially to a local hatmaker named Zadoc Benedict, records about whom recall that he began a shop in 1780 (in all likelihood there were earlier hatters, but the British burned the town records during their raid of 1777). An abundance of water in what was then a rather marshy wetland attracted beavers, and these two resources were central to creating the hats of the day. The earliest hats were made painstakingly by hand, and an early shop employing 30 workers would have been lucky to produce 15 dozen hats weekly. By the early 19th century, there are a nearly 40 such operations in Danbury.

The glue used to bind the felt lining in hats contained mercury, and any soul who handled this material over a prolonged period of time eventually succumbed to the effects of this highly toxic substance. Mercury turned many a hatter insane, so the legend goes, and this bit of lore largely explains the term "mad as a hatter." Fortunately, a clever entrepreneur named Charles Darling Parks eventually developed a process for making hats without the use of mercury, and so by the end of the 1800s the industry had ceased being so hazardous.

The peak of Danbury's hat production was 1909, when some 36 million hats were made here. By then every fashionable style of hat was coming from here, from cowboy hats to fedoras to top hats. Presidents and Hollywood actors wore Danbury hats, from Harry Truman to John Wayne. But the ascendancy of automobile culture spelled a gradual decline of the hat industry, as car drivers and passengers found it awkward to wear a conventional top hat. Many say that the election of President Kennedy in 1960 hammered the final nail in Danbury's hat-making coffin: Kennedy eschewed hats, which had a profound effect on the styles of the day. Pretty soon, everybody had shelved their hats. By 1966, there was one hat factory left in town—Stetson. It relocated to another state in 1987, and so marked the end of an era.

is an interesting one to explore, as it contains many of Danbury's finest old homes. Tarrywile Park comprises 535 acres, some of it landscaped but most of it quite wild, laced with trails for hiking, biking, cross-country skiing, and horseback riding—none of the trails are more than 1.5 miles long, and all are relatively easy, except for one that leads up a steep hill. There are three scenic ponds (swimming is not permitted) and good spots for bird-watching. Call ahead to find out whether any programs are planned either in the grand old mansion (you might, for example, see crafts demonstrations or lectures there) or out by the old barn, silo, and greenhouse. This is one of western Connecticut's great little secrets, a marvelous place to while away a sunny afternoon.

From Tarrywile, make a left onto Southern Boulevard and continue until you intersect with Wooster Heights, onto which you'll make a left turn. Follow it as it winds over a hill and emerges just east of U.S. 7 and the small municipal Danbury Airport. From this road, you can pull over and get a perfect view of any planes that happen to be landing or taking off—it's a pretty dramatic spot to land a plane, as there are some steep ridges south and east of the airport.

Continue down Wooster and turn right (north) onto U.S. 7, exiting almost immediately after onto Park Avenue and making a right turn (away from the Danbury Fair Mall, which is detailed below). After about three-fourths of a mile, you'll come upon the **Military Museum of Southern New England** (125 Park Ave., 203/790-9277, www.usmilitarymuseum.org, open 10 A.M.–5 P.M. Fri.–Sat., noon–5 P.M. Sun., $4 for adults). A large parking lot outside an otherwise nondescript white building is filled with tanks and other military vehicles, dating from the 1900s. This is a clue as to what lies inside: hundreds of uniforms, photos, medals, and equipment used by the army, navy, air force, coast guard, and marines fill the rooms. This vigorous look at war history is the nation's largest collection of armored battle vehicles used in 20th-century military conflicts, with vehicles and materials dating from World War I through the present.

Head back toward U.S. 7, this time passing under it and continuing toward the immense **Danbury Fair Mall** (7 Backus Ave., exit 3 from I-84, 203/830-4380, www.danburyfairmall.com). The mall sits over what used to be the grounds of a wildly popular agricultural fair, which took place every summer. In 1987, the then-largest mall in the Northeast went up over this 130-acre tract, and it remains the region's leading attraction. Some 225 stores, including such anchors as Macy's, Lord & Taylor, JCPenney, Sears, and Filene's, offer the usual mid- to upscale consumer goodies. There's a double-decker carousel in the center of the rather large food court, a hit with kids. At 7 A.M. daily, a group (open to everybody) called "Mall Walkers" strolls briskly through the several corridors of shops—an exercise regimen particularly appealing to shopaholics.

Just down Backus Avenue from Danbury Fair Mall is a huge outdoor shopping center, some chain eateries (Red Lobster, Olive Garden), and an upscale pool hall, Boston Billiards Club. Several superstores dominate the retail landscape.

Just as few nonresidents know about Tarrywile, a similarly small number know about the appealing little swimming hole and boating lake that's right nearby, within a few hundred yards of busy I-84. From Backus Avenue, make a right turn onto Kenosia Avenue and then, at the cemetery, a left onto W. Kenosia Avenue, to reach **Lake Kenosia,** a rippling body of water with a playing field, a nicely maintained children's playground, and supervised swimming in summer. If you've dragged your kids to the mall, reward them with some fun and games at this pleasant municipal park.

Also on the west side of town, atop a hill just north of I-84, is the sprawling campus of **Western Connecticut State University** (a.k.a. West Conn; off U.S. 6/202, www.wcsu.edu), site of the Charles Ives Performing Arts Center. If you follow the paved road that leads through to its end, you'll come to a small parking lot and trailhead for 33-acre **Westside Nature Preserve**, a dense woodland and wetland that's popular with bird-watchers, hikers, and nature-lovers.

# SOUTH OF DANBURY

## Ridgefield

The easiest and most direct route to explore Ridgefield, immediately south of Danbury, is to follow U.S. 7 south from the I-84, and then turn right onto Rte. 35. But a far more scenic route is to head south from Danbury on Old Ridgebury Road (exit 2 from I-84; it can also be reached from Lake Kenosia, above, by taking Kenosia Avenue north, making a left onto Mill Plain Road (U.S. 6/202), then another left onto Old Ridgebury).

This wooded, winding road (which becomes simply Ridgebury Road once you enter Ridgefield) passes by some of the area's most scenic countryside. You'll see old farms and Colonial houses, as well as quite a few newer (and bigger) suburban homes that reveal the northward march of Fairfield County's affluence. Eventually, you'll come to Rte. 116, where you'll make a left turn to reach Ridgefield's historic and rather quaint downtown (if you take a right turn onto Rte. 116, you'll go for another mile before crossing into North Salem, New York).

Ridgefield is a hybrid of the grand old New England communities of Litchfield County and the wealthy bedroom communities of Fairfield County (of which it is actually a part). Route 116 cuts south right into the center of town; at the blinking yellow light at Rte. 35 (Main Street), turn right (south) and pull into your first parking spot once you've reached the center of this Colonial village.

Towering shade trees line Main Street, and you can still imagine how sleepy this colonial village must have felt when it was too far away to be a commuter town. Judging from the young families that amble about Ridgefield streets today, it remains one of the more pleasant Connecticut towns in which to raise a family.

The infamous traitor Benedict Arnold, before deserting the cause of the Continental Army, directed a small barracks in the center of town, right along Main Street. Following the devastating raid of Danbury by British general William Tryon in spring 1777, the Ridgefield militia attempted to prevent their enemies from retreating

successfully to Long Island Sound. A fierce battle ensued, during which men on both sides were lost. Today, a plaque on Main Street gives a moving tribute to not only the felled American soldiers, but also the redcoats: "In Defense of American Independence at the Battle of Ridgefield, April 27, 1777, died eight patriots—who were laid in this ground companioned by sixteen British soldiers—living, their enemies, dying, their guests." Among those lost was General David Wooster, the first commander of the Connecticut state militia.

A stroll along Main Street reveals a new kind of invasion—one that's familiar in many other Colonial downtowns throughout Fairfield County—upscale chain shopping. But in addition to the Gap and similar such enterprises, downtown Ridgefield possesses a great many boutiques and unusual businesses, plus plenty of places where you can grab a light or substantial meal.

Architecturally and aesthetically, Ridgefield retains many of its ties to the Colonial period. Only in 1998 did Bedient's Hardware Store close down—founded in 1783, it had been the second oldest hardware store in the country (tied with H. C. Lovell Company in Stratford). The store, although it prospered right until the end, closed mostly because the owners felt it was time to move on, but locals continued to favor it over mega-chain stores up until it closed. It is this mindset that typifies Ridgefielders.

Great big Colonial mansions line Main Street south of the downtown commercial district. The public may visit the gambrel-roofed **Keeler Tavern Museum** (132 Main St., Rtes. 33 and 35, 203/438-5485, www.keelertavernmuseum.org, seasonal hours, $5), which sits behind a white picket fence on a fancy stretch of Main Street. The tavern dates from the early 1700s, and it became an inn in 1769, when it served travelers on the inland stage coach route between New York and Boston. It continued to function as an inn until the close of the 19th century. Timothy Keeler opened the inn, and it was his relations who sold it to renowned architect Cass Gilbert (Woolworth Building in New York, the U.S. Supreme Court Building in Washington, D.C.) in 1907. In 1915, Gilbert built the Classic Revival garden house in the back, which is now the site of teas, receptions, and other events these days. The tavern contains dozens of 18th- and 19th-century antiques, but perhaps its most unusual claim to fame is the remains of a British cannonball stuck in one of the building's corner posts—British troops fired at the house during a Revolutionary War battle of April 27, 1777.

Along the same stretch, be sure to visit the **Aldrich Museum of Contemporary Art** (258 Main St., 203/438-4519, www.aldrichart.org, open noon–5 P.M. Tues.–Sun., $5, free on Tues.), which has quarterly changing exhibits and is an outstanding museum with a superb sculpture garden behind it.

## Branchville and Georgetown

Continue south along Main Street (Rte. 33), making a left turn onto Branchville Road (Rte. 102), which winds down to the Branchville section of Ridgefield, where you'll find cute shops, some antiques stores, and a few eateries. The village grew out of the old Branchville rail depot, which still sits just off U.S. 7. Turn right toward Wilton on U.S. 7, and you'll shortly after enter Georgetown, a little hiccup of a village, whose unincorporated borders straddle the "real" town lines of Redding, Wilton, and Ridgefield. Developed in the 19th century as a mill workers' community, it is a lone vestige of industrial history in this tony and historically agrarian section of Fairfield County. Old Gilbert & Bennett Wire Mill presides over the village of Georgetown, which is centered at U.S. 7 and Rte. 107. The 1991 Danny DeVito film *Other People's Money* was filmed at this old mill, as well as the 1984 movie *Reckless*.

## Redding

Turn left onto Rte. 107 to reach one of the most spectacular towns for country driving in Connecticut, Redding. Several scenic routes pass through town, all of which reward drivers (or bikers) with fine views of wooded countryside and Colonial homesteads, and there are three excellent parks in Redding. One option is to make a left turn onto Umpawaug Road, about 1.7 miles from where Rte. 107 branches off from U.S. 7. Follow this road a short ways before making a left onto Topstone Road.

**Topstone State Park** is a remote, dark, wooded park reached via Topstone Road; follow the twisting dirt road and you'll come upon a small dirt parking lot on the right. From this park, return to Umpawaug Road (continuing north), making a left just before the road intersects with Rte. 53, onto Station Road. This leads into West Redding's quaint village center, which is anchored by a train station with a few small shops around it. This is a remarkably rural and quiet community nearly devoid of commercial development, and yet it is in the heart of bustling Fairfield County, an easy commute from Danbury and Norwalk, and even Stamford. Land conservation is a town legacy, and more than 4,000 acres of the town are protected permanently from any kind of development.

*Redding is a truly delightful town for country drives or bicycling jaunts (mind the many hills and twisting, narrow lanes).*

Mark Twain lived out his final two years on a magnificent estate he built called Stormfield—it burned some years later, but most of its 228 acres are among those preserved today (and the town library he founded bears his name and contains an assortment of oddities pertaining to his life). The town center is cute enough to qualify officially as quaint, and the few shops and eateries clustered around West Redding Station look like something out of a 1930s Hollywood period piece on life in the country. It's a truly delightful town for country drives or bicycling jaunts (mind the many hills and twisting, narrow lanes).

At the station, turn right onto Sidecut Road, which will bring you out onto Rte. 53. Make a left turn and drive north to reach Bethel, making a right turn on Rte. 302 to reach downtown.

A longer and more scenic option from Rte. 107 is to follow it until it intersects with Rte. 53. Here, make the very hard right turn onto Rte. 53 and drive south toward Weston—the road winds around swamps and wetlands that feed into the picturesque Saugatuck Reservoir, the northern half of which you'll get a nice view of as you approach from Rte. 53.

Where Rte. 53 breaks right and curves around the reservoir, you should instead make a left turn onto Newtown Turnpike, which winds a bit around the northeastern shore of the reservoir before climbing up a wooded hill past several interesting old homes. Nearly two miles after having turned off of Rte. 53 by the reservoir, you should bear slightly right onto Giles Hill Road and follow the steep ridgeline road until it intersects with the Black Rock Turnpike (Rte. 58). Giles Hill Road is one of the more fetching streets in Fairfield County, with dramatic 18th-century farmhouses, twists over hairpin curves, and sylvan views.

Make a left onto Rte. 58 (heading north) and after about 1.6 miles, just past Hopewell Road on your right, make a right onto Sunset Hill Road and follow this winding route up until you see on your right the sign for the small parking area by **Huntington State Park** (203/938-2285). The southeastern entrance is guarded by enormous bear and wolf statues. You can walk through the park's vast meadows and wooded trails; the park is quite high up with fine views. It's half in Bethel, half in Redding, and just a smidgen in Newtown. Trails wander through meadows downhill into wooded terrain, eventually leading to Huntington Pond. Another popular approach to Huntington is along Dodginton Road, which is not maintained in winter and can be a bit rough if you don't have four-wheel drive. The road passes alongside both a lily pond and Huntington Pond; there appears to be a foundation or former home site at the end.

From Huntington State Park, continue north on Sunset Hill Road; just a couple of hundred yards beyond Old Dodginton Road, make a left onto Williams Road. Work your way down the hill to Rte. 58, where a right turn (north) will lead to **Putnam Memorial State Park** (203/938-2285). The entrance is marked by a 65-ton bronze statue of General Israel Putnam, who led a camp of Revolutionary soldiers through a brutal winter here in 1778–1779. Camps were set up throughout western Connecticut, from here south to the sound, in preparation for a British

invasion. General George Washington established the three brigades to prevent the redcoats from securing control over the Hudson River, thereby keeping New England from being cut off from the rest of the Continental Army. The Americans were successful in keeping them down, and Putnam made an especially impressive stand in Greenwich when he thwarted a group of redcoats led by General Tryon. At the park are many hiking trails, but also a museum (open Memorial Day–Columbus Day, free), reconstructed officers' barracks, the remnants of a munitions magazine, and a cemetery. Putnam is a short drive from Huntington and has the potential to be a much more complete and exciting attraction. Cannons, equestrian statues, and an obelisk mark the entrance to Putnam Ridge.

## Bethel

From here, continue north on Rte. 58 into Bethel, making a right turn on Rte. 302 to reach the little downtown. Bethel, the birthplace of P. T. Barnum, is a modest suburban town with a nice bounty of restaurants. It's a busy little slice of middle-class all-American values. Pretty houses are clustered around the center of town, and there are several good shops and restaurants. The town also has the best arts cinema in the region, and a coffeehouse with poetry readings and such. From downtown, head back to Rte. 53 via Rte. 302 to return to Danbury.

# NORTH OF DANBURY

Like Redding to the south, the towns north of Danbury—New Fairfield and Sherman—have little in the way of formal attractions, but they make for some of western Connecticut's most scenic driving.

## New Fairfield

From downtown Danbury, you can reach New Fairfield via either Rte. 37 (which is the most direct) or Rte. 39 (winding and more scenic). If you go by way of Rte. 37, you have the added bonus of passing the grounds of the Danbury Correctional Facility, a minimum security, so-called "country club" prison where the likes of Leona Helmsley have done time—the complex overlooks the shore of Candlewood Lake.

The center of New Fairfield, at the junction of Rtes. 37 and 39, is a peaceful little suburban town, as is Sherman to the north. Both enjoy a remarkable isolation from the rest of Connecticut, as they are bordered entirely by New York on the west and by Candlewood Lake on the right. For these reasons, the pace of life up here has remained pleasantly slow, despite the rapid expansion of suburbs in Fairfield County—that said, both of these towns are among the state's fastest-growing.

Open primarily on weekends and by appointment (with free admission), the **Northrop House Museum** (10 Rte. 37, Sherman, 860/354-3083) occupies a well-preserved colonial house and features exhibits on the history of chair-making (from Sheraton to Shaker to locally produced Hitchcock chairs). It's operated by the Sherman Historical Society.

You can continue following Rte. 37 north into Sherman, which offers a pretty, often steep and winding ride, or follow Rte. 39, which in several spots hugs the western shore of Candlewood Lake. This 6,000-acre, 15-mile-long body of water is entirely man-made, created in 1925 to supply water for the region. Part of the lake filled in the once heavily wooded Big Basin Valley, and scuba divers still like to check out the bottom of the lake, where they sometimes find stone walls, foundations, and other odd remains of a few farmhouses that once stood here.

One branch of the northwestern part of the lake, **Squantz Pond State Park** (203/797-4165) is an ideal spot for picnicking, swimming, boating, and sunning. There are canoe, rowboat, and outboard-motorboat rentals at the park. Continue along Rte. 39 until you again intersect with Rte. 37 (right by the Sherman Playhouse), and at this point turn right and follow Rte. 37 back down the hill until it joins with U.S. 7. Now you're in New Milford; drive south on U.S. 202 to enter the town of Brookfield, which makes up much of the eastern border of Candlewood Lake and has one very nice drive along the shore.

## Brookfield

About 5.5 miles south of where Rte. 37 joins U.S. 7 (past the many shopping centers and superstores), make a right turn onto Sullivan Road. Continue south about a mile, and then turn right onto Candlewood Lake Road, which will take you along the shore for nearly five miles. At Down The Hatch restaurant, make a left turn onto Elbow Hill Road, which brings you out onto U.S. 202 (called Federal Road at this point). A right turn would bring you down into Danbury, but turn left to continue this tour through Brookfield.

Follow Federal Road north, past where it joins U.S. 7, and make a right turn onto Whisconier Road (Rte. 25). On your right is the **Brookfield Craft Center** (286 Whisconier Rd., Rte. 25, 203/775-4526, www.brookfieldcraftcenter.org), in a former gristmill (ca. 1780), which was fully renovated over the past couple of years. It's one of the nation's leading crafts centers, drawing some 1,200 students of various trades annually. About 200 artisans show their creations here. The center was founded in 1954 and is one of the most prestigious in the state, offering some 300 workshops annually. From mid-November through Christmas, the center hosts the **Annual Craft Exhibition and Sale,** a good time to do some holiday shopping.

Continue south along Rte. 25, and you'll enter Brookfield's small and pleasant town center. A right turn onto Rte. 133 would lead you up into Bridgewater (covered above in the western Litchfield Hills). Continuing south along Rte. 25 leads into Newtown and through towns that flank the western bank of the lower Housatonic River Valley.

For a wine-lovers' detour, head north on Rte. 133 from Brookfield Center for about a half mile, making a right turn onto Tower Road, and follow this south to **DiGrazia Vineyards** (131 Tower Rd., 203/775-1616, www.digrazia.com), one of the longest-running and best-known wineries in the state. Produced here are many French-hybrid varieties, including seyval blancs, vidal blancs, and vignoles, as well as blackberry, black currant, and pear fruit juices. Guided tours and tastings are offered daily May–December, and on weekends the rest of the year. The staff is

THE WESTERN HILLS

extremely knowledgeable and friendly. When you're finished sampling, you can get back to Rte. 25 by continuing south on Tower Road, until it eventually feeds into Obtuse Road before intersecting with Rte. 25 (a left turn leads into Newtown).

## ALONG THE LOWER HOUSATONIC

### Newtown

From Brookfield (or from Danbury via I-84 to exit 9), follow Rte. 25 south into Newtown, one of Connecticut's more rapidly growing towns and—at 60 square miles—an extremely large one geographically.

The heart of Newtown is actually its own borough, and also a designated historic district comprising some 200 early houses and buildings along Main Street (Rte. 25), near where U.S. 6 (Church Hill Road) breaks off from it to the east. Newtown was incorporated in 1711, but a good many structures in this neighborhood are Victorian, since it was during the 19th century that the community prospered. Three major turnpikes intersected in the center of town, where a super-tall flagpole now stands over a slightly confusing traffic circle.

This convergence of commerce and travel translated into formidable revenues for local merchants, as evidenced by the size of some of the houses. All over town, however, you'll notice beautifully preserved old homes—some locals claim there are more Colonial-era structures here than in any other Connecticut town.

Over the years, Newtown has been blessed by the philanthropic spirit of many residents, especially the Hawley family, whose name appears on various roads and buildings, including the local Mary Hawley Inn. Three Connecticut governors have also lived here, as well as the creator of the board game Scrabble, the opera star Grace Moore, and the famed acting team of Garson Kanin and Ruth Gordon (whose historic Newtown home was the setting for the Katharine Hepburn and Spencer Tracy vehicle, *Adam's Rib*).

A good way to familiarize yourself with Newtown's history is to stop inside the **Edmond Town Hall,** which was built in 1929 with funds from, you guessed it, the Hawley family. Benefactress Mary Hawley stipulated that the new town hall have a movie theater, and there's still a wonderful old cinema off the main foyer, presenting second-run movies for just $2. Another distinction is the 60 murals painted throughout the building's

© ANDREW COLLINS

**Housatonic River**

stairwell, which tell the story of Newtown's history. All in all, it's quite a versatile building—in one visit, you can pay off any outstanding traffic fines, catch a movie, apply for a dog license, and take an illustrated historical tour.

As you step outside the town hall onto tree-shaded Main Street, walk a few doors to your right, toward the flagpole, and stop inside the old **Newtown General Store** (203/426-9901), a throwback to the vintage village shops of yore, with old hardwood floors and friendly employees. It's a nice spot for an ice cream cone or milk shake from the soda fountain in back, or a deli sandwich.

While the historic downtown suggests a town stuck in time, Newtown is becoming increasingly suburban in character. As new building lots are increasingly difficult to find in lower Fairfield County, many families are constructing homes here in the northern half of the county. Newtown is still a pretty town with some beautiful old country roads, but it's well past the point of being quaint. Issues about zoning and limiting growth dominate the discussions at town meetings these days.

### Sandy Hook

A second section of Newtown that retains its rustic roots, however, is Sandy Hook, which you reach from the center of town by following Church Hill Road over I-84. Just east of the flagpole, by the way, you'll pass the offices of the local paper, the *Newtown Bee,* which also publishes the regionally famous antiquing newspaper, *Antiques and Arts Weekly.*

The village of Sandy Hook is pierced by the Pootatuck River, a tributary of the Housatonic, and consists of a handful of simple shops and eateries that look the same as they might have in the 1950s. In the center of town, make a left turn from Church Hill onto Glen Road and follow it to Walnut Tree Hill Road, where a left onto this winding scenic lane leads you to Alberts Hill Road. Turn right, and you'll soon come to the signs for **McLaughlin Vineyards** (Alberts Hill Rd., 203/426-1533), a sylvan 160-acre estate with green meadows and split-rail fences. There's a winery here with daily tastings, extensive behind-the-

scenes tours on weekends, and the public is welcome to hike and picnic on the grounds (which fringe the Housatonic River). Other seasonal activities include maple sugaring, food-and-wine pairing seminars, and bald eagle–spotting along the river. The inn also has a small guest house available for overnight stays.

### Stevenson

Retrace your steps back to the village center of Sandy Hook and, rather than heading back on Church Hill Road, follow Washington Avenue southeast under I-84 until it becomes Rte. 34. Remain on this road for about six miles past I-84, and you'll see the right turn onto Rte. 111, which leads south to Monroe. But before you make this turn, continue a short distance farther on Rte. 34 into the Stevenson section of Newtown. You'll soon come to the massive Stevenson Dam and a larger bridge that takes Rte. 34 across the Housatonic River into the towns of Oxford and Seymour (which are described in the Naugatuck River Valley tour). This is a nice spot to admire the roaring river and perhaps stop for a picnic.

### Monroe

Return to Rte. 111 and follow it south several miles into Monroe, a bedroom community with the general wooded and airy disposition of other Fairfield County towns. You'll pass lovely old homes along this hilly road, before coming to Rte. 110, onto which a left turn will lead you toward the town of Shelton (which, if you ask anybody who lives there, is typically referred to as Huntington; see the sidebar "Huntington and Shelton").

### Shelton

Controversies about its identity notwithstanding, Shelton is an ordinary-looking town with relatively few attractions. One of them is right off Rte. 110, on the west bank of the Housatonic River. Here, a signed left turn leads you to **Indian Wells State Park,** which comprises grassy meadows, picnic tables, and playing fields. Across from the more developed side of the park is a trail leading to an interesting old waterfall. This marks the beginning of the **Paugusset Trail,** which eventually wends its way through the western and

# HUNTINGTON AND SHELTON: CONNECTICUT IN MICROCOSM?

A 1999 article in Sunday's Connecticut section of the *New York Times* discussed at length the lively debate over what to call this middle-class suburban town on the Housatonic River—a place that has two distinct personalities, making the issue of nomenclature all the more important. Much of the community is a quiet and residential smattering of Colonial houses and many more Colonial-style ones built in this century. But another side of town, nearest the Housatonic River, is a rather downcast pocket of industry with a faded commercial center, characterized by weathered old Victorian warehouses and storefronts.

The town broke away from northern Stratford and incorporated on its own, in 1789, as Huntington. The name paid homage to Samuel Huntington, a war hero of the American Revolution and subsequent state governor (he was president of the Continental Congress when the Articles of Confederation were ratified, and he signed the Declaration of Independence). For the first century, Huntington was a simple, attractive agrarian town. But as industrialization swept through the state during the 19th century, the town's northern edge, which fringed the powerful Housatonic, was developed into a prosperous manufacturing center.

The great industrial leader of this era was Huntington native Edward Nelson Shelton, who built and financed a number of factories along the river. He himself opened the long-running and highly successful Shelton Tack Company. Of course, the development of the river was not all good—dams ended the once-abundant shad runs, and pollution from the factories killed off whatever fish might have otherwise remained. But by the end of the Civil War, Huntington had become a great place to work and to live, and much of the credit went to Edward Shelton. In 1882, the area nearest the river was designated the borough of Shelton, and shortly after World War I, the citizens of Huntington voted once and for all to change the name of the entire town to Shelton.

Some five decades later, the Great Depression and then the industrial recession that plagued the northeast following World War II left the town in a state of near-ruin. By the 1950s, it was no longer fashionable to hail from Shelton. Residents of the southern end of town, which still had a lovely Colonial village green and several pretty white churches, increasingly identified themselves as living not in Shelton but in the town of Huntington. In 1975, one of Shelton's last important manufactories, the Sponge Rubber Plant, was burned in one of America's most infamous cases of industrial arson—more than 1,000 workers were left without jobs. Shelton's downtown has been in a severe state of decline ever since, while the southern and western edges of town have secured a healthy place in the post-World War II Connecticut economy, luring major corporations and service-oriented businesses to town and constructing gleaming new corporate parks and shopping centers. It's now said that perhaps 9 percent of the town's residents identify themselves as living in Huntington, regardless of what it says on their driver's licenses or their tax forms.

What might sound like an extraordinary, classist debate over a name actually reveals an intriguing tension that underlies a deeper schism within the personality of Connecticut as a whole. Ask many residents of this state where they live, and they'll characterize themselves as inhabiting a land of Colonial houses, sweeping backyards, thriving new office towers, safe and reputable public schools, wooded parks, and upscale shopping centers—an optimistic vision of countrified suburbia. The rest of the Nutmeggers you meet will tell you they live in a place whose downtowns have been struggling economically since the factories closed 40 years ago, about the high dropout rate in the local public school system, and about the redbrick storefronts and vinyl-sided houses sadly in need of rehabilitation. Connecticut, when you get right down to it, is an uneasy patchwork of Sheltons and Huntingtons.

northern reaches of the park, up over Webb Mountain, and into Monroe, where it joins with the Pomperaug Trail. Note that the park is closed to vehicles from October 15–May 24, but you can still park near the entrance and hike the trails.

Back on Rte. 110, continue on as the road becomes Howe Avenue and leads right into downtown, which though raggedy in spots has potential for redevelopment. Talk now centers on a waterfront recapture park and attempting to rectify some of the retail culture that once thrived along Howe Avenue, which is really the town's main street. A smattering of antiques shops lie along here, as well as a quirky little coffeehouse called the **Living Room Cafe.** And a bridge leads across to Derby's similar-looking downtown.

If you head south on Center Street from Howe Avenue, it becomes Bridgeport Avenue, and soon reveals the newer "Huntington" side of town. You'll find a few chain hotels and restaurants and some big new shopping centers. At the end of Bridgeport Avenue, a right turn on Huntington Street will lead you back up into the quaint Colonial center of Huntington Village. Here, just a block northwest of the village green, is the **Shelton History Center** (70 Ripton Rd., 203/925-1803, limited hours, free), a complex of Colonial houses now containing exhibits and memorabilia.

## SHOPPING

The area's most famous excuse for shopping, the **Danbury Fair Mall,** is detailed above, as is the stellar **Brookfield Craft Center.** But many of the towns around Danbury are strong on antiquing or have downtowns filled with odd little one-of-a-kind boutiques. Quite a few shops throughout the area are strong on antiques. Ridgefield has a number of fine shops.

A bit north of Branchville is one of New England's leading distributors of authentic Amish furnishings and crafts, **Amish Outdoor Living** (346 Ethan Allen Hwy., U.S. 7, 203/431-9888). In the downtown area, **Ridgefield Guild of Artists** (34 Halpin Ln., 203/438-8863) has regular exhibits showing a range of media and many works for sale in the gallery. Art courses also are

offered. A bit farther south along Rte. 35, **Books on the Common** (109 Danbury Rd., 203/431-9100) is an interesting little general-interest shop with a thoughtful selection of titles. The **Ridgefield Cafe and General Store** (346 Ethan Allen Hwy., U.S. 7, 203/438-1984) has extremely nice toys, dolls, and high-quality gifts, plus a coffeehouse and tearoom where you might enjoy a light meal.

In Newtown, **Black Swan** (182 S. Main St., 203/426-1230) is an excellent source of country accessories and design elements, from wood stoves to holiday crafts. **Curri Artcraft** (27 Main St., Rte.25, Monroe, 203/268-7919) has been offering an interesting range of home furnishings and handcrafted accessories since it opened in the early 1900s. More country-style furnishings and pieces are found at **Seven Country Ducks** (572 Main St. and 166 Main St., Monroe, 203/452-1903).

Danbury is well known as the home of the **Ethan Allen** furniture company—there's even a hotel filled with examples of its fine Colonial reproduction furnishings. One of the largest showrooms is in Danbury, on Ethan Allen Drive; call 203/743-8500 for details on it or any of the other Ethan Allen showrooms elsewhere in the state—these include branches in Canton, Clinton, Enfield, Groton, Manchester, Milford, Norwalk, Southington, and Stamford.

Although **Stew Leonard's** (99 Federal Rd., just off U.S. 7, 203/790-8030), the theme park–style dairy store that's a hit with both grocers and tourists, began in Norwalk, the newer branch in northern Danbury is actually bigger and more impressive. Kids love it here, where windows into different store departments show how milk and other kinds of food are processed.

### Pick-Your-Own Farms and Nurseries
A favorite spot for picking apples and pumpkins, taking hayrides, and enjoying the yields of a very good farmers market is **Blue Jay Orchards** (125 Plumtree Rd., Bethel, 203/748-0119, www.bluejayorchards.com). **Sunrise Herbal Remedies** (35 Codfish Hill Rd., Bethel, 203/794-0809, www.sunriseherbfarm.com) is a 200-acre nature preserve, petting zoo, and hiking

area that also has a small natural foods café and juice bar. This place specializes in herbal remedies and aromatherapy treatments, and carries many other products related to holistic health. You can also take courses on herbs. The house, a replica of Mt. Vernon, is quite striking. In the lower part of the valley, **Jones Family Farms** (Rte. 110 and Israel Hill Rd., 203/929-8425) has a tremendous array of pick-your-own fruits and berries, plus fall hayrides and pumpkin-gathering. A highly popular cut-your-own Christmas tree program in winter includes a holiday gift shop and visits with "Santa." Monroe is notable for **Twombly Nursery** (163 Barn Hill Rd., 203/261-2133), one of the state's premier such facilities. It sits on 11 acres and contains some 50,000 varieties of flowers, shrubs, and trees. Come wander the 4.5 acres of beautiful gardens.

# RECREATION
## Golf

The star public course of Connecticut, **Richter Park Golf Course** (100 Aunt Hack Rd., 860/792-2550) has a tough, hilly, and beautifully maintained layout, with plenty of water and sand hazards and quite a few tight fairways. You'll want to reserve well ahead for a tee time here, as this place is famous throughout Connecticut and western New York. Overshadowed by Richter's popularity is a second outstanding golf course, **Ridgefield Golf Club** (545 Ridgebury Rd., 203/748-7008), which was designed by noted architect Tom Fazio and offers some very long, tight holes, especially on the back nine.

## Hiking

Many parks detailed elsewhere in this chapter, including **Tarrywile, Huntington State Park, Putnam State Park,** and **Indian Wells State Park,** have great trails of varying lengths and difficulty. For the most part, the terrain in this part of the state is hilly, but without the steep ridges and difficult terrain that characterize Litchfield County. Another excellent resource is **Devil's Den Preserve,** parts of which extend into the southern tip of Redding.

Near northern Redding, the **Wolfpits Pre-**

**serve,** off Wolfpit Road, Bethel—close to both Huntington and Putnam State Parks—is a nice spot for a casual stroll by a feldspar mine and over lightly wooded hills and slopes. In New Fairfield, **Squantz Pond State Park,** near the junction of Rtes. 37 and 39, has an extremely popular trail north along the western slope over the pond, which is an arm of Candlewood Lake. The trail leads from the picnic area at the park, crossing several hillside streams feeding the pond and ending some two miles later at a breezy peninsula.

## Ice-Skating

The state-of-the-art **Danbury Ice Arena** (1 Independence Way, 203/794-1704, www.danburyice.com) anchors the redeveloped part of downtown Danbury and offers year-round skating and instruction.

# ENTERTAINMENT AND NIGHTLIFE

Excellent regional productions are staged at the **Sherman Playhouse** (Rtes. 37 and 39, Sherman, 860/354-3622), a community theater offering both classic and original works. The **Ridgefield Workshop for the Performing Arts** (37 Halpin Ln., 203/431-9850) stages plays throughout the year. The **Charles Ives Center for the Arts,** on the campus of Western Connecticut State University (Westside Campus, off U.S. 6, exit 4 from I-84, 203/837-9226) opened in 1984 and offers outdoor music performances, ranging from symphony recitals to pop, jazz, and folk concerts, with many held at the **Ives Concert Park** (181 White St., Danbury, 203/748-1716). Also at West Conn, the **Berkshire Theatre** (Osborne St., Danbury, 203/837-8732) stages student-directed and -performed plays and musicals.

The **Danbury Music Centre** (256 Main St., 203/748-1716) hosts myriad performances throughout the year, ranging from chamber music to choral presentations. In Newtown, a wide variety of classical works are presented throughout the year at the versatile **Edmond Town Hall** (45 Main St., Rte. 25, 203/426-2475), under the auspices of **Newtown Friends** of Music. Also in Newtown, the **Town Players of Newtown** (Little Theatre, Orchard Hill Rd., 203/270-9144) present a variety of works.

Another very good source of community theater is the **Brookfield Playhouse** (Whisconier Rd., Rte. 25, 203/775-0023), whose Country Players theatrical group presents five shows each season, from dramas to musicals.

There's a huge multiplex cinema in Danbury right off I-84 at exit 7, plus a few other mainstream theaters around the area. The small **Bethel Cinema** (269 Greenwood Ave., 203/778-2100) is one of Connecticut's greatest cinematic treasures, a terrific art house that books the latest and most interesting independent and offbeat movies. A nice selection of baked goods and snacks is sold at the counter, and special deals are sometimes offered in conjunction with a meal at the adjoining Emerald City Cafe.

**Hat City Ale House** (253 Main St., Danbury, 203/790-HATS) has photos commemorating the city's past as hat-making center of America. **Tuxedo Junction** (2 Ives St., 203/748-2561) has live music of all varieties and is a great place to hang out and meet locals—in a great location in downtown Danbury. **Boston Billiards** (20 Backus Ave., 203/798-7665) is the place to go to shoot pool—it's packed on weekends. A big captain's wheel in the window of the **Ancient Mariner** (451 Main St., Ridgefield, 203/438-4771) beckons locals for a somewhat rowdy pub experience; the place has large TV screens with sports, good munchies, and a big singles' scene on weekends. Danbury's **Molly Darcy's Irish Pub and Grill** (39A Mill Plain Rd., 203/794-0449) is a sprawling Irish pub that's a favorite of students from nearby West Conn; there's live music many nights. **Blues Alley Café** (127 Park Ave., 203/744-2394), right by the Military Museum, has live music.

In quiet Newtown, at the rather formal Inn at Newtown, you might be surprised by the hip crowd that frequents **Proud Mary's** (19 Main St., 203/270-1876), a trendy lounge with cushy overstuffed chairs, a fireplace, and a comprehensive list of very fine liqueurs, cognacs, wines, and single-malts.

# FESTIVALS AND EVENTS

## Spring and Summer

In early June, come to the Assumption Greek Orthodox Church in Danbury to partake of the **Greek Experience** (exit 5 from I-84, 203/748-2992), which consists of folk dancing, live music, and traditional Greek fare.

In July, the **Bethel Summer Festival** (downtown Bethel, 203/743-6500) provides visitors with a chance to nosh among food vendors and shop for different odds and ends while listening to live music. In August, similar activities can be found at the **Nutmeg Festival** (St. Stephen's Episcopal Church, 351 Main St., Ridgefield, 203/438-3789). All summer long, **free concerts** are held on Thursday, Friday, and Saturday nights on the green in downtown Danbury.

## Fall and Winter

In early September, there's a lively **Italian Festival** (St. Jude Church, 707 Monroe Tpke., Rte. 111, 203/261-6404) held in Monroe that offers rides, music, and—of course—great food. The following week you can continue satisfying your taste buds by attending the **Annual Taste of Greater Danbury,** on the green (Danbury, 203/792-5095). Also at West Conn, the **Danbury Irish Festival** (203/748-7701) includes food, music, and other entertainment; it's held the third weekend in September. At the end of the month, there's a well-attended **Arts and Crafts Show** (203/938-2004) held in Redding. At the end of November, trolley jollies might bring the family to the **Great Train, Dollhouse, and Toy Show** (Western Connecticut State University, Lake Ave. and University Blvd., Danbury, 203/837-8343), where you'll find amazing train layouts, plus toys, dolls, miniature furniture, and other collectibles and toys.

# ACCOMMODATIONS

Danbury has most of the region's accommodations, but these are largely chain properties that appeal primarily to business travelers. Most of these motels and hotels are on the east side of Danbury or neighboring Bethel, close to a recent spate of development that includes a 10-screen movie theater, several chain restaurants, and a bunch of superstores. Ridgefield has the kinds of grand country inns you might think you have to travel to Litchfield County to find—rooms in the town's three inns are all upscale and modern (though in the Colonial style), which is a negative only if you're seeking a lodging with authentically historic ambience. There are fewer accommodations in the towns that actually fringe the Housatonic, but Brookfield, Newtown, and Shelton all have some pleasant options.

## Hotels and Motels

**$150–250:** The most luxurious of the area's chain properties, the 10-story **Danbury Sheraton** (18 Old Ridgebury Rd., 203/794-0600 or 800/325-3535), is a high-end business-oriented property with first-rate facilities, slick public areas, a personable well-trained staff, and clean upscale rooms—but rather high rates on weekdays owing to the corporate clientele. On weekends, however, rates drop as much as 40 percent—sometimes even more when special weekend packages are offered. The property is just minutes from the New York border in a quiet part of town, and yet also minutes from downtown and the Danbury Fair Mall. Facilities include tennis courts, a restaurant, a large fitness center, a pool, and an extensive business center.

**$100–150:** A somewhat recent entry into the chain hotel sweepstakes, the **Danbury Radisson Hotel & Suites** (42 Lake Ave. Ext., U.S. 6, 203/791-2200 or 800/333-3333, www.radisson.com/danburyct) opened in 1999, just off I-84. It's also quite close to the New York border. About 50 of the 76 units are expansive two-room suites, many with whirlpool tubs. As you might expect, decor and amenities are new and state-of-the-art, making this an excellent all-around option. There are also several long-term suites with full kitchenettes. There's also a restaurant and a fitness center.

Although its location amid gas stations and fast-food restaurants on a busy road is anything but charming, the 199-room **Ethan Allen Hotel and Conference Center** (U.S. 6/202, exit 4 off I-84, Danbury, 203/744-1776 or 800/742-1776)

is all class inside; its spacious rooms filled with the tasteful Colonial reproduction furnishings manufactured by the Ethan Allen furniture company. Behind the hotel is a secluded pool; there's also an exercise room and a racquetball court. Note that the two-room suites are not all that much costlier than the standard rooms—a great value if you're seeking a little extra elbow room.

In tip-top shape, the **Hilton Garden Inn** (119 Mill Plain Rd., 203/205-2000 or 800/HILTONS, www.danbury.gardeninn.com) contains 158 rooms. Amenities include hair dryers, high-speed Internet, dual-line speaker phones, refrigerators, large work desks, and microwaves. There's also a gift shop–grocery and a business center (both open 24 hours), a fitness center, and an indoor pool. Another newcomer to the west side of Danbury is the **Comfort Suites** (89 Mill Plain Rd., 203/205-0800 or 877/424-6423), an attractive property with large rooms that have separate sitting/working areas and many of the same amenities as the Hilton Garden Inn. Both of these are near West Conn's campus.

**AmeriSuites** (695 Bridgeport Ave., Shelton, 203/925-5900 or 800/833-1516) is a modern, business-oriented lodging just off Rte. 8 in front of a leviathan corporate park. With reduced weekend rates, huge rooms with kitchenettes, an impressive breakfast buffet, and a highly professional staff, this is one of the best bases for exploring the lower Housatonic and Naugatuck Valleys.

Similarly appealing, though without rooms as large, is the 155-room **Ramada Plaza Hotel** (780 Bridgeport Ave., Shelton, 203/929-1500 or 800/2-RAMADA), which is also relatively new and just up the road, with clean and well-maintained rooms. It tends to book up fast with business travelers on weekdays, but weekends can be a good deal. There's a Bertucci's pizza restaurant practically next door, and an indoor pool and health club on the premises.

In Shelton is another **Hilton Garden Inn** (25 Old Stratford Rd., 203/447-1000 or 800/HILTONS), which is just off exit 12 of Rte. 8, near the many corporate offices that have sprung up in these parts in recent years. There are 142 rooms here, all with dual phone lines, voicemail, data ports, and other business-oriented amenities, plus a fine fitness center and indoor heated pool.

**$50–100:** One of the better value-oriented properties, the recently refurbished **Best Inn & Suites** (78 Federal Rd., 203/743-6701 or 877/743-6702) has 72 standard-issue rooms, an indoor pool, a business center with high-speed Internet, and an exercise room. It's very close to downtown Danbury. Suites have microwaves and refrigerators.

Easily one of the nicest midprice accommodations in the area is the **Twin Tree Inn** (1030 Federal Rd., U.S. 7/202, Brookfield, 203/775-0220, www.twintreeinn.com), a well-kept motor hotel with a vaguely Colonial style and a cute lobby with old books and numerous brochures on exploring the area. It's close to the New Milford border, making it an ideal choice for anybody exploring the Litchfield County. Rooms are brightly furnished with Colonial-style pieces and floral drapes and bedspreads, and some of the rear units look out onto the wooded lawn behind the place and have private patios accessed through rear sliding doors. The same people operate New Milford's wonderful Heritage Inn.

Bethel has a pair of very nice midpriced motels, both run by the same owner and located close to the Danbury border. The more picturesque of the two is the **Stony Hill Inn Best Western** (46 Stony Hill Rd., U.S. 6, 203/743-5533 or 800/528-1234), a country motel that looks right out of the 1950s—but very well-kept. The rooms, all with private outdoor entrances, overlook a lush meadow with a pond and a gazebo; facilities include a pool, driving range, and a decent restaurant. This is a perfect choice for families, and while the rooms are fairly ordinary, the pleasant setting makes this a romantic getaway that won't break your wallet. Just down the road, a bit closer to I-84 and Danbury, is the sister property, the **Best Western Berkshire Motor Inn** (U.S. 6, 203/744-3200 or 800/528-1234), which is a considerably more modern and businesslike property. Many of its rooms look northwest toward the lower Litchfield Hills (also within view is I-84, but rooms are well-insulated from the traffic noise). Although there's no pool here, guests can use the

facilities at the Stony Hill Inn. Continental breakfast is included at both properties.

## Country Inns and Bed-and-Breakfasts

**$150–$250:** The **Elms Inn** (500 Main St., Ridgefield, 203/438-2541, www.elmsinn.com) consists of two buildings, one dating from 1760 and having served as a hostelry since its inception—there are just a few rooms in this section, however, as the entire ground floor houses the fanatically acclaimed Elms restaurant. Most rooms are in a relatively modern building next door; they're furnished in traditional Colonial style with stenciled walls and, in many cases, four-poster beds. The best of the inn's 20 rooms—all of which have private baths, TVs, and phones—are in the front, overlooking Ridgefield's picturesque Main Street.

Down along a relatively peaceful stretch of normally overdeveloped U.S. 7, **Stonehenge** (U.S. 7, Ridgefield, 203/438-6511) shares certain traits with Ridgefield's other inns. The building, which replaced an 18th-century inn that was lost to a fire in the late 1980s, is a faithful reproduction. Each of the 16 rooms is furnished differently, but with a similar high quality and rather plush Colonial furnishings, including four-poster beds; you'll also find the same modern amenities as at the other inns, plus a highly respected restaurant. Rooms are pricier here than at the competitors, and the inn is a car ride from downtown (not within walking distance of much), but the grounds are quite pretty.

**$100–150:** Slightly less expensive than the Elms, the **West Lane Inn** (22 West Ln., Rte. 35, Ridgefield, 203/438-7323, www.westlaneinn.com) is a 19th-century mansion with a steep pitched roof and a beautiful front porch overlooking the arresting grounds. Rooms are large and handsomely furnished, all with individual climate control, cable TV and VCRs, and phones with voicemail; some have fireplaces. The philosophy has clearly been to provide a country inn setting, but with thoroughly updated accommodations that appeal to the many business travelers who stay here midweek. The inn is an easy walk from downtown attractions and restaurants, and next door to the Inn at Ridgefield restaurant.

A relatively unheralded option is Newtown's **Inn at Newtown** (19 Main St., 203/270-1876, www.theinnatnewtown.com), which is better known for its restaurant. In the late 1990s, new owners took over and did a commendable job updating the three guest rooms with Early American–inspired furnishings and colors, four-poster beds, large TVs and direct-dial phones, and elegant modern bathrooms. Each room has a separate outdoor entrance. The inn anchors Newtown's lovely historic downtown.

Set inside a very distinguished-looking 1911 Tudor mansion in Ridgefield, the relatively new **Stone Ridge Manor B&B** (24 Old Wagon Rd., 203/431-8426) contains a pair of sumptuous guest rooms. One room is anchored by a handsome mahogany-accented sleigh bed, while another is distinguished by its jade-and-gilt-leaf bathrooms fixtures and jade-green antiques bedroom set; this unit also has a sitting room. An elaborate full breakfast is included, and guests are free to use the Olympic-size outdoor pool and cabanas. Ridgefield's charming downtown is a short drive away.

## FOOD

The Housatonic River Valley is blessed with as varied a dining scene as any region in the western half of the state, although there are fewer choices than down along the coast. Danbury is a hot spot for ethnic dining, from Vietnamese to Middle Eastern cooking. Ridgefield has some of the state's finest high-end eateries. And the rest of the towns have at least one or two spots renowned for their creative cooking and refined ambience, plus a smattering of lower-priced family-style eateries. Danbury is the only city in the area, and consequently the only place where you're likely to find a major concentration of chain restaurants and fast-food eateries—both near Danbury Fair Mall and on Newtown Road just off exit 8 of I-84. At the other end of the region you'll find a smaller but still diverse mix of similar restaurants in Shelton south of downtown, along Bridgeport Avenue.

## Upscale

Set romantically in a pink stucco country house on a verdant hillside at the New Fairfield-Danbury border, **Ondine** (Rte. 37, 203/746-4900, Danbury, about $50 prix fixe) is one of Connecticut's greatest culinary treasures (and relative bargains). Within an interior of Oriental rugs and French-influenced country furnishings, you'll be seated at an elegant, linen-draped table and shown a handwritten menu that changes daily each evening and includes an appetizer, soup, entrée, and dessert. The cooking blends contemporary and traditional French styles and ingredients, from filet mignon grilled with marrow and presented with a green peppercorn sauce and an asparagus flan, to a soul-warming roast-duck with apples and calvados.

It's a bit fussier, strictly traditional, and somewhat more expensive, but the **Inn at Ridgefield** (20 West Ln., Ridgefield, 203/438-8282, $22–32) is a classic, fine French restaurant that has been going strong since the 1940s; the restaurant is inside a lovely old house beside the West Lane Inn. The velvety vichyssoise served here is a tradition, as is the filet mignon with a truffle sauce. This is one of the few restaurants in the state where men should wear a jacket and tie. This policy, as well as the Inn's demeanor—which is neither hip nor relaxed—is just fine with its many proponents who welcome a chance to dress up a bit and be treated to impeccable service and urbane French cuisine.

A few years ago, new owners took over the fading Colonial **Inn at Newtown** (19 Main St., Newtown, 203/270-1876, $19–26) and revamped the dull menu by offering an excellent variety of New American and old New England favorites: rosemary-marinated double-cut lamb chops with soft polenta, haricots verts, kalamata olives, and lamb jus; or pan-roasted mahimahi with leeks, tomatoes, and mussels in a citrus-cilantro broth. You can dine in either a formal dining room or a more relaxed tap room, which sometimes has live music and offers some lighter fare. The caliber of cuisine isn't quite up to the big-name restaurants in neighboring Litchfield County, but it's pretty good.

A characterful clapboard country inn with

reasonably priced Continental fare, the historic **Spinning Wheel Inn** (Rte. 58, Redding, 203/938-2511, $16–21) serves food that ranges from just okay to quite sophisticated and adeptly prepared. Yellowfin tuna chargrilled with a cracked peppercorn crust and fresh mango coulis is a somewhat exotic offering, while a steak, mushroom, and ale pie shows off the chefs' love of traditional standards. Service tends to be friendly but somewhat lax.

The venerable restaurant and country inn **Stonehenge** (U.S. 7, Ridgefield, 203/438-6511, $22–36), where in the 1950s Elizabeth Taylor honeymooned with Mike Todd, has endured considerable uncertainty and change in recent years—a major fire requiring a complete reconstruction of the place, and the rather rapid coming and going of some quite well-known chefs. These days, it's tough to find any two people who can agree on the quality and value of the restaurant, which presents an oft-rotating menu of very fine Continental and American cuisine: steaks, Maine lobster whose preparation changes daily, salmon, foie gras, and the like. The gorgeous dining room has dark, clubby, Colonial-style furnishings, with massive windows overlooking the woods and white outbuildings in back.

## Creative but Casual

With a kitchen overseen by New York City culinary star Brendan Walsh, the **Elms Inn** (500 Main St., Ridgefield, 203/438-9206, $8–16 in the tavern, $23–32 in the restaurant) has become one of the hottest restaurants in Fairfield County. You can dine in a main room from a rather serious menu—check out the wood-grilled "dry aged" sirloin steak with baked stuff potato and red wine sauce, or the grilled loin of venison with sweet potato spoonbread—or you can eat in a simpler tavern, where you might sample a grilled chicken sandwich on focaccia with black olive dressing, an excellent burger, or one of the lighter pastas. Both dining areas are inside a 1799 house, which is part of the hotel of the same name, in the heart of downtown Ridgefield.

In the Super Shop & Stop plaza, on a stretch of Bridgeport Avenue that has many of Shelton's corporations and modern office compounds,

**Metro Grille** (882 Bridgeport Ave., 203/929-1000, $7–23) is a quirky spot (mannequins sit along a ledge overlooking the dining—an odd yet somehow appealing touch). It presents an eclectic menu of both traditional and innovative dishes, from Pacific Rim Thai chicken to thin-crust pizzas to porterhouse steaks. This is a popular spot for executives and yuppies, offering one of the nicer dining experiences in the area.

**Gail's Station House Cafe** (378 Main St., Ridgefield, 203/438-9775, $12–19) serves dinner Thursday–Saturday (rosemary-skewered grilled shrimp with white bean and fennel salad; ravioli filled with sweet potato, goat cheese, and caramelized shallots, filet mignon), but breakfast and lunch are the best-known meals. The setting is a sunny storefront on Main Street.

Quiet little Bethel is somewhat overlooked when it comes to culinary achievement, at least beyond several fairly ordinary (though perfectly enjoyable) casual restaurants. A notable exception is the urbane and sophisticated **Emerald City Cafe** (269 Greenwood Ave., 203/778-4100, $10–19). It's a diminutive place, attached to the artsy Bethel Cinema, where you'll find serious food but a lively and engaging staff, and seating at tables or along a counter by the window. An eclectic cooking style has been demonstrated here from the restaurant's very beginning, from burgers and spinach salad with bacon dressing on the lighter side to Indonesian-style coconut-encrusted snapper with a spicy curry and mango chutney. Interestingly, a large rainbow flag (denoting gay-friendliness) hangs outside the front door—a little surprise in this otherwise conservative little suburb.

There's no shortage of good Italian cooking in Ridgefield—many in these parts favor **Biscotti** (3 Big Shop Ln., Ridgefield, 203/431-3637, $14–24), a simple but large restaurant whose dining room is strung with lights and filled with tables and ladderback chairs—there's also a small but charming patio with a fountain and additional seating. The marvelous antipasti (bruschetta, roasted red peppers, grilled calamari, etc.) can be ordered either in small or large portions. Also consider grilled vegetable salad; eggplant sliced and sautéed with plum tomatoes and diced smoked mozzarella over penne; a white puttanesca sauce with angel hair pasta; and filet of catfish broiled with lemon and oil and served over polenta with a roasted pepper sauce and asparagus. Everything on the extensive menu is available to go, including the signature honey-macadamia crème brûlée.

Country French fare is presented with considerable panache at **Cafe Luc's** (1 Big Shop Ln., 203/894-8522, $18–25), an intimate place tucked behind a shopping center near Ridgefield's quaint Main Street—bottles of vinegar, champagne, and wine stand on ledges throughout the dining room. Indeed, Luc's has an excellent wine list. Typical offerings include salmon fillet with mustard sauce and saffron rice, and duck-and-bean cassoulet.

**G. P. Cheffields** (97 S. Main St., 203/270-6717, $16–24) is Newtown's hippest and hottest restaurant, an upscale Mediterranean eatery with a nice range of meat and seafood specialties, all of them presented artfully. A starter of grilled tender calamari with a sauce of minced cherry peppers breathes more fire than some of the spiciest Mexican and Thai food you'll ever eat. Entrées like charred rare tuna with pepper-herb crust, foie gras, spinach, shallots, vinegar, and potato show off the kitchen's tremendous skills. This is a loud and busy spot, and reservations are an excellent idea.

You won't find much in the way of businesses in rural Sherman, but folks from all over the region drive for miles to the town's only (tiny) shopping center, which houses the **American Pie Company** (29 Rte. 37, 860/350-0662, $8–19), a cozy, cheerful eatery that serves a great deal more than just pies—breakfasts are a favorite meal here, but also sandwiches at lunch and hearty American comfort food, often with nouvelle twists, at dinner. But back to the homemade pies—they're terrific.

Owned by the same folks who run Two Steps, across the street, **Ciao! Cafe and Wine Bar** (2B Ives St., Danbury, 203/791-0404, $10–19) showcases a mix of Italian and regional American dishes. Offerings range from stuffed portobello mushrooms with toasted pine nuts, romano cheese, and spinach in a yellow pepper sauce to chicken Monterey stuffed with fresh crabmeat, spinach,

and fontinella cheese in a champagne cream sauce with angel hair pasta. Sandwiches, jerk chicken, and baby back ribs are also offered. The long, narrow eatery with black-and-white checked floors, black booths, and crisp linens has a slick ambience—the staff is accommodating and upbeat.

The latest contemporary regional American restaurant to take Ridgefield by storm has been **Bailey's Backyard** (23 Bailey Ave., 203/431-0796, $17–28), which turns out old favorites with new twists—baked macaroni and Vermont cheddar, crab cakes with chipotle remoulade, classic cioppino, and pecan-crusted trout with a lemon-and-parsley brown sauce. In warm weather, you can dine on the terrace. Golf and fine dining never necessarily go hand in hand, especially at a municipal golf course, but the charming Italian restaurant **Cafe on the Green** (100 Aunt Hack Rd., Danbury, 203/791-0369, $14–23) deserves kudos for both its excellent cooking and romantic setting. Come expecting to find a rose on every table and fine views of Richter Park golf course's fairways. The restaurant is in a contemporary hip-roofed clubhouse, miles away from the din of downtown Danbury. Veal cuoco (veal sautéed with fresh artichokes, mushrooms, and peas with plum tomatoes) and rigatoni in a light mushroom sauce are favorite dishes here.

## Pizza, Pub Grub, and Seafood

A key figure in downtown Danbury's burgeoning dining and entertainment district, **Two Steps Downtown Grille** (5 Ives St., 203/794-0032, $7–16) is a dandy bilevel Southwestern restaurant carved out of the handsome shell of an old redbrick firehouse. The decor inside is fanciful, as piñatas, boots, and colorful paraphernalia dangle from the ceilings, but the building's key architectural elements have been carefully preserved. In summer, green-and-white Rolling Rock umbrellas crowd over an expansive terrace. Excellent dishes include fresh crab, avocado, and brie quesadillas; nachos made with homemade white corn chips; white bean and chicken burritos; and roasted veggies on a bed of greens with a cilantro-lime vinaigrette. Drawing a similarly young crowd to this up-and-coming neighborhood, Two Steps' neighbor **Eleven Ives Street** (11 Ives St., 203/830-3084, $7–18) has a raw bar, patio, and live music, plus many kinds of beer on tap.

For years, locals have flocked to **Roberto's** (505 Main St., Monroe, 203/268-5723, $11–22) for red-sauce Italian fare, from a whole slew of veal and chicken dishes (piccata, marsala, Milanese, and others) to meatball and pepper casserole to linguine with white clam sauce. The place always seems to be packed.

In Shelton, **Roma** (232 Leavenworth Rd., Rte. 110, 203/929-5177, $10–17) is a warmly decorated Italian restaurant in a shopping center up the hill from Indian Neck State Park. Waiters dressed in tuxedo shirts deliver hefty portions of steak Diana, veal bolognese, and other reliable standbys. Good pizzas, too.

**Ernie's Roadhouse** (30 Padanaram Rd., Danbury, 203/790-0671, $10–20) is just what the name conjures up, a fun and slightly kitschy roadhouse with views of a waterfall in back (you might not expect this upon first pulling up, as the Padanaram Brook that runs behind it is not clearly visible). There's a lively bar with stained glass to one side of this 1891 house, which has been a restaurant the whole time. The food—steaks, ribs, and pastas—is decent; come more for the convivial ambience. **Rosy Tomorrow's** (Old Mill Plain Rd., 203/743-5845, $8–$19) is a hugely popular, rambling family restaurant and tavern that's rather close to West Conn.

A cavernous building that stood vacant for what seemed like decades sprouted new life a few years ago as **Belzoni's Red Lion** (619 Danbury Rd., U.S. 7, Ridgefield, 203/438-7454, $11–20). The several rooms are filled with hanging plants, faux columns, and other busy but cheerful design elements. The slightly nouvelle Italian menu offers the likes of gnocchi with Italian tomatoes, shallots, basil, and parmesan cheese; an Italian version of seafood paella; and boneless chicken sautéed with cognac and a touch of cream, braised with piedmontese sauce and wild mushrooms. It's nothing special, but the size of the place and variety of offerings make it a nice choice for families.

With a delightfully odd location (overlooking Danbury's regional airport) and dishes named for 1970s rock anthems (the Freebird salad has grilled chicken, chili-roasted vegetables, mixed grains and greens, and a sweet corn and cumin dressing), the **Classic Rock Brew Pub** (1 Wibling Rd., 203/792-4430, $6–18) is something between a music-theme restaurant and an airport commissary. Of course, rock tunes buzz (not too loudly) in the background, and there's often live entertainment. The cavernous **Colorado Brewing Trading Company** (6 Delay St., 203/791-1450, $7–22) has been packed nightly since it opened, and serves very good designer pizzas, salads, and grills. But it has a few drawbacks, too: a short menu for so large a place, a nonsmoking section with a cement floor and plain walls that give it the feel of an elementary school gym, and extremely uneven service. Still, this looks to become yet another feather in downtown Danbury's increasingly colorful culinary cap.

The food at Brookfield's **Down the Hatch** (292 Candlewood Lake Rd., 203/775-6635, $9–17)—traditional Italian-American favorites like veal Oscar and chicken parmigiana—is less a reason to come here than to enjoy the sparkling views over a small marina and cove on the eastern shore of Candlewood Lake. The deck is so popular that the indoor dining room is closed off in summer. Both yuppies and rowdy drinkers have been known to frequent this place—the staff is exceedingly friendly. Open seasonally; call for hours.

Bargain seekers will want to remember that on Monday and Tuesday, lobster dinners cost under $15 at the rollicking **Georgetown Saloon** (8 Main St., 203/544-8003, $8–19), a lively little spot in the industrial neighborhood near the Ridgefield and Wilton borders. The Western-style facade more evokes Dodge City than Colonial Connecticut, and live music keeps the younger set coming back. Typical offerings include BLTs, pork chops with applesauce, and smoked chicken. A raw bar and dining rooms wallpapered in vintage newsprint are among the draws of **Redding Roadhouse** (406 Redding Rd., 203/938-3388, $8–16), a convivial spot with live music and hearty comfort food in the center of Redding. Linguine with clam sauce, beef kabobs, and burgers are popular offerings.

THE WESTERN HILLS

Head to the **Villa Restaurant** (4 Riverside Rd., Sandy Hook, 203/426-4740, $9–20, large pizzas $14–17) for traditional Italian food prepared with admirable attention to detail and considerable flair. A starter of wild mushroom risotto with truffle oil and grated parmesan is memorable; you might move on to rigatoni with hot Italian sausage, baby peas, and a light tomato cream sauce, or caramelized sea scallops with basil pesto. A wide selection of grinders and pizzas are served—try the Villa Special, with feta, fresh tomatoes, mozzarella, spinach, and garlic. The setting is an attractive stone villa-like building with a formal dining area up front and a small bar in the back.

## Ethnic Fare

Credited with introducing Thai food to Connecticut, **Bangkok Thai** (72 Newtown Rd., Danbury, 203/791-0640, $7–16) remains one of the top Asian eateries in the region, with food that compares favorably with the better Thai restaurants in Boston and New York City. The dining room is filled with Thai artifacts and crafts, and the kitchen specializes in whole fresh fish deep-fried and smothered with onions, peppers, tomatoes, and pineapples, plus the usual variety of yellow, green, and red curry sauces. This place is packed on weekends, which is when the staff sometimes appears overwhelmed.

**Thang Long** (56 Padanaram Rd., Danbury, 203/743-6049, $5–15) has a less appealing setting than Bangkok Thai, but also serves commendable Thai food. The specialty here, however, is Vietnamese fare: sautéed vermicelli noodles with seafood, vegetable pancakes, pan-fried salmon, and sautéed pork with ginger. Every dish is available in small or large portions.

In a rambling, old, pale-blue shingle house west of downtown, **Sesame Seed** (68 W. Wooster St., 203/743-9850, $6–13) is testimony to Danbury's visible Middle Eastern community. This place serves excellent cuisine from around the Mediterranean, including *foul mudammas* (fava beans in tahini and lemon), falafel, tabouli, hummus, kebabs, and kibbeh. The dining room, with its vintage board games, mismatched plates and saucers, and old black-and-white photos, imparts

a comfy feel. Service can be brusque, but chances are you won't have to wait long for your meal.

A homey little German-American restaurant with dwarf figurines and a festive, flower-filled beer garden, **Helga's** (55 Stony Hill Rd., Bethel, 203/797-1860, $14–18) is a great spot for Wiener schnitzel, sole amandine, and other rich old-world dishes. In Monroe, **Señor Pancho's** (262 Main St., Rte. 25, 203/261-1399, $7–14), a branch of the popular Southbury Mexican restaurant, serves a nice selection of Tex-Mex dishes, plus very good margaritas.

Danbury has a fast-growing Brazilian community, and you'll find a few groceries and cafeteria-style fast-food **Brazilian** eateries along the east end of Main Street, mostly around the intersection with Wooster Street. In these stores, you can pick up not only a wide range of imported foods and groceries, but also affordable and quite authentic cooking at low prices.

## Quick Bites

The **Marcus Dairy** (5 Sugar Hollow Rd., 203/748-5611, $3–7) is a local institution that dates from the days when the famous Danbury Fair was held on the adjacent grounds (now the Danbury Fair Mall); the dairy still supplies milk and related products to groceries all around the region. Additionally, this is a full-service diner (not an especially attractive one, but that's not the point) serving the usual grub, plus very good ice cream.

The **Sandy Hook Diner** (98 Church Hill Rd., 203/270-5509, under $8) is a peculiar little spot with a somewhat nontraditional clapboard exterior and a quiet setting on this little village's main thoroughfare; the pumpkin pancakes are legendary. However, the **Blue Colony Diner** (just off I-84 on U.S. 6, Newtown, 203/426-0745, under $10), while it lacks its competitor's ambience, has great food, too, and is open 24 hours (the Sandy Hook Diner closes at 2 P.M.).

**Chez Lenard** (Main St., 203/431-6324, $2–4) may be just a hot-dog car on a sidewalk in downtown Ridgefield, but this place has a loyal following. Le Hot Dog Garniture Suisse has imported fondue cheese with white wine and kirsch. Pelligrino, juices, and sodas are served, too. It's great fun to nosh here on a warm afternoon at one of the benches along Main Street. **Le Patisserie des Anglaises** (408 Main St., Ridgefield, 203/894-8482), a dainty café and sandwich shop, serves tempting pastries and gourmet coffees.

An excellent 1950s-style diner with an unusually good menu is **Sit Down Diner** (69 Newtown Rd., U.S. 6, 203/778-0887, $4–10), which was taken over by new and ambitious owners rather recently.

The **Sycamore Drive-In** (282 Greenwood Ave., Bethel, 203/748-2716, under $7) is a shimmering, stainless-steel beauty oozing character and dishing out hefty ice-cream sundaes and blue-plate specials. Vintage cars are invited to pull in on Saturday nights, giving the place the air of an authentic 1950s-style drive-in. For the best breakfast in the area, head to **Rickyl's Brookfield Luncheonette** (800 Federal Rd., 203/775-6042, $3–8), a casual luncheonette that's been a local favorite for years. At lunch, folks crowd in for the tasty sandwiches.

With two locations, **Dr. Mike's** (158 Greenwood Ave., Bethel, 203/792-4388, and 444 Main St., Monroe, 203/452-0499) is something of a household name in the lower Housatonic Valley, having specialized in top-of-the-line homemade ice cream for more than 25 years. Another area favorite with a pair of locations is **Sprinkles** (28 Rte. 39, New Fairfield, 203/746-1484), which also has a branch in New Milford at 60 Railroad St., 860/355-1664. There are about 150 flavors (more than a quarter of them appearing daily), plus hefty sundaes. In Georgetown, **Inside Scoop** (951 Danbury Rd., U.S. 7, Georgetown, 203/544-9677) is a cute, little, brick ice-cream stand where little league players, high school kids, and more than a fair share of adults munch on chili cheese fries, burgers, hot dogs, and delectable frozen desserts. There's no dining room, but you will find several chairs and tables (with umbrellas) outside.

## Java Joints

Set in a historic building in Danbury's revitalized arts-and-entertainment district, **Downtime**

**Online Cafe** (1 Ives St., 203/205-0620), next to Two Steps Grille, is a nice stop for coffee or to browse the Web.

## Gourmet Goods and Picnic Supplies

**Giovanni's** (211 Greenwood Ave., Bethel, 203/744-7368, $4–11) may be inside an ordinary-looking Connecticut shopping center, but it could easily pass for something on Court Street in Brooklyn's Carroll Gardens (New York's best-known Little Italy). This first-rate Italian market and brick-oven pizza parlor specializes in gourmet sandwiches (consider the capriccio with fresh mozzarella, prosciutto, roasted red peppers, oil, and balsamic vinegar), fresh-made calzones and strombolis, delicious salads, and feather-light butter cookies.

You can't officially eat at Ridgefield's **Hay Day Market** (21 Governor St., 203/438-3211), but you can have the premade soups, salads, and casseroles heated up in the adjacent coffee bar and enjoy them there. This fancy and pricey market—often compared with gourmet luminaries like Balducci's and Dean & DeLuca in Manhattan—has fresh and exotic produce, cheese, fish, and meats flown in daily from all over the country, plus delicious baked goods. A full wine shop and florist are attached.

Berry-picking and berry wines are available at tranquil **White Silo Farm** (32 Rte. 37, Sherman, 860/355-0271), where an old dairy barn has been converted into a winery producing dry fruit wines (which you can taste here and also buy in bottles). Rhubarb, raspberries, and blackberries are used. In September and October, you can drop in to pick your own berries.

# INFORMATION AND SERVICES

## Visitor Information

Most of the towns in this region are served by the **Litchfield Hills Visitors Bureau** (Box 968, Litchfield, CT 06759, 860/567-4506, www .litchfieldhills.com). Monroe and Shelton are handled by the **Coastal Fairfield County Convention & Visitor Bureau** (20 Marshall St., Suite 102, Norwalk, CT 06854, 203/840-0770 or 800/866-7925, www.coastalct.com).

## Getting Around

The area is easily accessible via East–West I-84, which links Danbury and environs to Westchester and Putnam County in New York state, and Waterbury and Hartford to the east. North–south U.S. 7, which is a limited-access highway part of the way through, is the main route down to coastal Fairfield County and up into the Litchfield Hills. The state road Rte. 25 runs north–south through the lower Housatonic River Valley, from Brookfield down to Bridgeport along the coast.

# The Eastern Hills

As in the Litchfield Hills, the relatively high and rugged terrain of the region east of the Connecticut River Valley kept settlers from developing the land until many parts of the state had already been established. Woodstock, which at the time of its founding was part of the Massachusetts Bay Colony, was the region's first community, having been settled in the late 1680s. There's comparatively little hard evidence of the Native American cultures that lived in these woodlands, as so few Europeans traveled through these parts and interacted with them. By the time of Woodstock's settlement, the repression of southern New England's Indians following King Philip's War had resulted in the dispersion of what tribes may once have thrived here.

Woodstock was one of the few towns in these parts founded by a cohesive unit of Puritan settlers. Most of the other towns were developed by land speculators, and so right from the start, there were skirmishes among the residents of various towns over borders and land rights.

Northeastern Connecticut developed less organically than much

Roseland Cottage, Woodstock

© ANDREW COLLINS

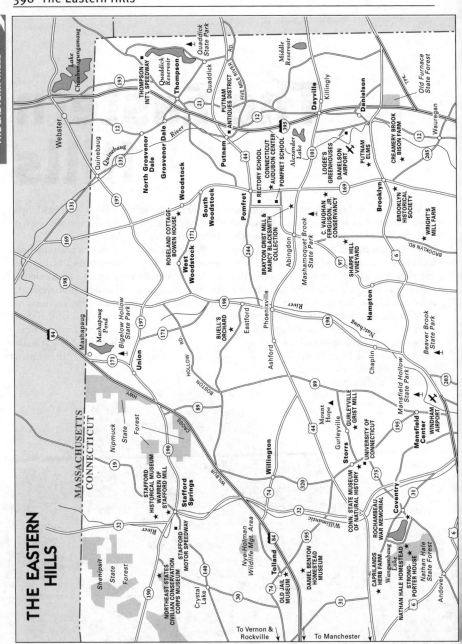

# THE EASTERN HILLS

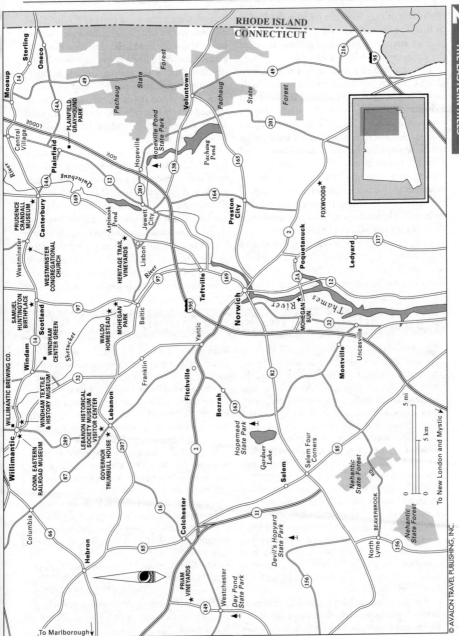

RHODE ISLAND
CONNECTICUT

© AVALON TRAVEL PUBLISHING, INC.

of the rest of the state, and perhaps that's why, to this day, nobody has been able to come up with an effective term that characterizes either the entire region or its people.

The eastern and northernmost towns, from about Coventry and Lebanon east to the Rhode Island border, and from about Plainfield and Lebanon north to the Massachusetts border, are often collectively dubbed Connecticut's "Quiet Corner." Most of these towns are administered by the Northeast Connecticut Visitors District, and share a common history of dairy farming, textile milling, and otherwise limited commercial development. This is the least heralded portion of the state—many Connecticutters from other areas would be hard-pressed to name more than three or four towns in the Quiet Corner.

Except for Lebanon, which is on the edge of this district, none of the towns in the Quiet Corner have played a particularly vital role in the state's history. Economically, the area is a bit less

well-off than some other parts of Connecticut. Tourists might imagine that because the area lacks a major city like Hartford or New Haven, or a major attraction like Mystic Seaport or Beardsley Zoo, there's little reason to come here. But in addition to this area's peaceful and unhurried pace, the land and the early architecture have remained largely unspoiled by the kind of sprawl found along the coast and in the Connecticut River Valley.

The Quiet Corner is closest in character to the Litchfield Hills, but without nearly as developed and sophisticated a network of inns, restaurants, and antiques shops. This doesn't mean there aren't inviting historic inns, acclaimed eateries, and both quirky and highly respected shops in northeastern Connecticut, but there are far fewer of them than in the northwestern corner. There are also fewer celebrities and weekending New Yorkers—meals and accommodations cost comparatively less here, and roads are

## SAMPLING CONNECTICUT'S AGRICULTURAL SIDE

Eastern Connecticut's agricultural legacy is somewhat less talked about than its history as a textile producer, but touring this part of the state provides a wealth of opportunities to visit working farms. In fact, the tourist boards produce a useful brochure on Eastern Connecticut, *Farms Family Fun*, which you can obtain by contacting the **Southeastern Connecticut Tourism District** (470 Bank St., Box 89, New London, Ct 06320, 860/444-2206 or 800/TO-ENJOY, www.mysticmore.com).

The brochure details attractions that possess an agricultural angle, including many establishments detailed elsewhere in this book. There are B&Bs, such as Applewood Farms Inn and Fitch Claremont House, and several museums that touch on the manner in which tilling the land has shaped the eastern half of the state. These include the Brayton Grist Mill, Nathan Hale Homestead, and Waldo Homestead.

You can visit and observe animals at **Creamery Brook Bison Farm, McCulloch Farm** (famous for its Morgan horses), and UConn's **Kellogg Dairy**

**Barn** (3636 Horsebarn Rd. Ext., Storrs, 860/486-2023). At the latter, visitors will especially want to come by in the springtime when the farm animals give birth to newborns. Dozens of farms in this region are open to the public for purchases of every imaginable kind of produce, including apples, peaches, blueberries, raspberries, tomatoes, pod peas, honey, dairy products, and maple syrup.

Early March, in fact, is the time for syrup lovers to gather for the annual **Hebron Maple Festival** (www.hebronmaplefest.com), when several area maple-sugaring houses offer self-guided tours and perform maple-sugaring demonstrations. Other events staged in the village center this time of year include a pancake breakfast, roast beef supper, dog-sled exhibition, folk dancing, and games for children.

**The Connecticut Department of Agriculture** (Marketing Division, State Office Building, 765 Asylum Ave., Hartford, CT 06105, 860/713-2503, www.state.ct.us/doag/pubs/sugarhs.htm) also produces a brochure listing the state's many sugarhouses.

generally uncluttered, even during peak summer and fall weekends.

The Quiet Corner is less gentrified than the Litchfield Hills, and also without quite the dramatic scenery, such as the formidable Berkshire foothills and roaring Housatonic and Naugatuck Rivers. The hills and rivers are gentler in eastern Connecticut, the sweeping vistas fewer. But the dense woodland, sparkling lakes and ponds, and Colonial villages that define Litchfield County are similarly prevalent here. And when you're seeking a quieter and less expensive alternative to northwestern Connecticut, the Quiet Corner deserves serious consideration.

The towns of the Quiet Corner have traditionally been more oriented toward Providence and Rhode Island than toward Hartford and the rest of Connecticut, and this focus partially explains why this area remains less known among many Nutmeggers. Providence is just 25 miles from the easternmost towns, while Hartford is roughly 40 miles away. The first major east–west roads in this area were constructed into Providence, rather than into the Connecticut River Valley.

The kinship also helps explain why at least 10 percent of the mills in New England are concentrated in this very small region. Most of these hulking facilities, many of which stand empty and others that have been retrofitted for new uses, were textile producers. The textile industry in the New World developed in earnest around Providence, where a man named Samuel Slater successfully brought technologies he'd learned as an apprentice in England to Rhode Island. Throughout the 1790s and early 1800s, mill development flourished throughout Rhode Island and spread rapidly into central and southern Massachusetts and northeastern Connecticut, as new sources of waterpower and more land were constantly needed.

The Quiet Corner's rivers provided just the power necessary for milling, and when British exports were embargoed during the War of 1812, a young America's milling and manufacturing capabilities increased exponentially. It was the rapid emergence of textile production in eastern Connecticut, and the development of interchangeable parts in the Connecticut River Valley that partly precipitated this nation's industrial revolution.

And so throughout the 19th century, as larger and more prolific mills opened in communities like Attawaugan, Dayville, North Grosvenordale, Putnam, Wauregan, and Willimantic, waves of immigrants settled into the Quiet Corner. All the while, those areas considered by textile barons to be unsuitable for mill works remained agrarian. Although the eastern uplands have always had better farming terrain than the Litchfield Hills, it's still not an enviable place for planting crops on a wide scale. Dairy farming, on the other hand, was a perfect fit, and so the industries of textile and dairy production fueled the economy until well into the 20th century.

Today, most of the mills have left the area, just as the manufactories that once proliferated throughout the Connecticut River Valley and along parts of the coastline have long since shut down or moved to areas with cheaper labor. Relatively few dairy farms still exist, with more closing each year. Those that remain supplement their income by offering B&B accommodations, pick-your-own crops, ice-cream stands, and similar diversions that can be great fun for visitors.

The inner edges of Connecticut's eastern uplands, the swath of towns cushioning the Quiet Corner from the coast to the south and the Connecticut River Valley to the west, maintain their own distinct identities. This latter group of towns—Manchester and Vernon chief among them—falls along the Bolton Range, a long ridge that forms the eastern wall of the Connecticut River Valley. Historically, these communities developed much in the same way their counterparts in the Quiet Corner did, as agricultural and textile mill communities. But in recent decades, the suburban sprawl of Hartford has crept gradually into this region, and once-sleepy towns like Bolton and Marlborough are mushrooming.

The upland towns that buffer the Quiet Corner from the densely settled coastline form the Mohegan Range, with the small city of Norwich anchoring them. Like the Bolton Range communities, this string of towns has rapidly been suburbanized by its proximity to urban life, namely Groton and New London. Further spurring the growth of this region has been the advent in the 1990s of big-time casino gambling in Ledyard and Norwich.

Many residents of towns lying along the Bolton and Mohegan Ranges would identify themselves more as living along Connecticut's coastline or in the state's central river valley, but geographically and historically speaking, these regions combine with the Quiet Corner to make up Connecticut's eastern uplands.

## A FEW PRACTICALITIES
### Media
*The Chronicle* (860/423-8466, www.thechron-icle.com), published daily in Willimantic, serves an eight-town region that includes Coventry, Storrs, and Lebanon. Manchester's daily *Journal Inquirer* (860/646-0500, www.journalin-quirer.com) serves 17 towns in the North-Central part of the state, including Tolland, Vernon, and Bolton. And the *Norwich Bulletin* (860/887-9211) is the daily news source for Norwich, Ledyard, and surrounding towns.

### Getting There
East–West I-84 and North–South I-395 are the region's major limited-access highways. State roads also connect the region with other parts of the state, as well as with eastern Rhode Island and south-central Massachusetts.

An extensive network of interstate train, bus, and ferry providers serves the eastern hills. The region also is served by Bradley International Airport near Hartford and T. F. Green Airport in Providence, Rhode Island.

### Tours
Departing from the marina in downtown Norwich, **Norwich Harbor Cruises** (American Wharf, Main St., Rte. 82/32, 877/248-6964) offers three types of excursions along the Thames River. The 50-minute narrated Harbor Cruise takes in the river, the historic Norwich harbor, and the waters nearby; the 90-minute Evening Cruise runs all the way down the river; and the 2.5-hour Nautilus Cruise runs all the way to U.S. submarine base in New London Harbor.

# The Quiet Corner

The Quiet Corner is pierced by Rte. 169, which runs north–south. A 32-mile span of this was designated one of America's 14 Scenic Byways in 1996 by the Federal Highway Administration. It also encompasses part of the vast Quinebaug and Shetucket Rivers Valley Corridor, which begins to the north in Massachusetts and has been described by the National Park Service as "the Last Green Valley in the sprawling metropolitan Boston-to-Washington corridor." It's the biking and country-driving highlight of the region, and it's been serving travelers since the earliest days of the colony (it was incorporated as the Norwich and Woodstock Turnpike in 1801). While federal recognition is an important honor, it's worth mentioning that several of the shorter routes crossing Rte. 169 east–west are equally deserving of praise—in general, this sparsely settled, well-preserved chunk of Connecticut is

enchanting. Along Rte. 169, there are nearly 200 homes dating from the mid-1900s or even earlier, and many more neatly preserved homesteads line the east–west routes.

## WOODSTOCK TO POMFRET
### Union
A great place to begin a tour of this region is in one of its largest towns, Woodstock, where a Colonial aesthetic pervades to this day. To get there from most parts of the state, take I-84 and exit at Rte. 190 to the sparsely populated town of Union. Follow Rte. 190 north, turning right after a couple miles onto Rte. 197, which leads east into Woodstock.

On your way along this pretty road, note the entrance on your left to **Bigelow Hollow State Park** (Rte. 197, Union, 860/346-2372). This largely pristine reserve adjoins Nipmuck

State Forest and abuts two scenic ponds, Bigelow Pond down near the south end of the park and Breakneck Pond, which is long and narrow. The road into the park leads to the largest body of water, which is quite popular for both swimming and boating: Mashpaug Pond (it and Bigelow Pond have boat launches). Be aware that the eastern border of Mashpaug Pond is private property; be sure to study the maps posted near the parking areas, so as not to venture onto private land. From several turnouts from the road, signs direct hikers onto trails. The Mashapaug Pond View Trail skirts the southern edge of lovely Mashapaug Pond, the Bigelow Loop Pond offers a shorter jaunt around that rippling pond, and the Breakneck Pond View Trail requires a longer but still easy trek through dense woodland. Only the East Ridge Trail, which runs over a north–south ridge through the forest before linking with other trails, is considered rather challenging—but none of these journeys requires an investment of more than two or three hours. Note that Bigelow Park is actually a small section within Nipmuck State Forest, which exists in several independent parcels throughout Union, both adjacent to the park and west of it on the other side of I-84.

## Stafford Springs

Detour from Union into the town of Stafford Springs to visit the **Northeast States Civilian Conservation Corps Museum** (166 Chestnut Hill Rd., off Rte. 190, Stafford Springs, 860/684-3430, noon–4 P.M. daily late May–Labor Day and by appointment, free), which consists of a blacksmith's forge, forest fire-fighting equipment, and memorabilia from the Depression. The **Stafford Historical Museum** (207 Orcuttville Rd., Stafford Springs, 860/684-5115, limited hours, free) shows of many of the wares created by local mills, including pearl buttons. And once a month, you can tour the historic **Warren of Stafford Mill** (29 Furnace Ave., Stafford Springs, 860/684-2766, open year-round, reservations required), which includes a walking tour.

## Woodstock

From Bigelow, Rte. 197 runs east into Woodstock, a large, heavily wooded town containing scores of Colonial homesteads. When you reach Rte. 169, make a right turn toward the heart of the town. You'll soon pass the majestic Inn at Woodstock Hill and then the **Roseland Cottage—Bowen House** (Rte. 169, 860/928-4074, www.spnea.org, open 11 A.M.–4 P.M. Wed.–Sun., June–mid-Oct., $5), one of the most remarkable house-museums in the state. This distinctive estate is as well known for its salmon-pink Gothic Revival exterior—the house has worn some 13 shades of pink throughout its life—as for such exotic accoutrements as a carriage house with a one-lane bowling alley; it's said to be the oldest surviving private alley in the nation.

The original owner, Henry Chandler Bowen, built the house in 1846 with monies he'd accrued as a merchant in Manhattan. A prominent abolitionist and founder of the politically charged newspaper the *New York Independent,* Bowen attracted some powerful names into his coterie of friends and confidantes. His annual Fourth of July parties were the stuff of legend, drawing visits from four different U.S. presidents (Grant, Harrison, Hayes, and McKinley) and a glittering roll call of other notable individuals. Today, you can tour the house and outbuildings, admiring their often exotic and lavish contents, and in warm weather enjoy a walk through the boxwood parterre garden, which blooms with roses in summer. The garden is thought to be the oldest formal one in New England that still contains original plants; it was laid out in 1850 with plants ordered by Bowen from Dyer's Nursery, down the road in Brooklyn. These included 600 yards of dwarf box hedging (the hedging dwarfed passersby for many years, growing as high as eight feet, until the garden was restored in the late 1970s). A series of twilight concerts and afternoon teas are held June–September; call for exact dates.

In South Woodstock, make a left turn (east) onto Rte. 171 and follow it until it joins with U.S. 44 about 3.5 miles later. Continue east just a short way into Putnam, before making a left turn north onto Rte. 12, which leads into the northeasternmost town in the state, Thompson.

For a sense of geographical perspective, consider that Thompson is just over an hour from Boston, and about three hours from Manhattan, whereas Greenwich—at the opposite southwestern corner of the state—is 45 minutes from Manhattan and just over three hours from Boston.

## Thompson

The Colonial heart of Thompson lies at the junction of Rtes. 193 and 200, both of which fork to the right off of Rte. 12. It's worth parking the car by the White Horse Inn and walking around the green to admire the fine old Congregational church, the many white mansions, and the legions of mature oak and maple trees. The White Horse is a good place for a bite to eat; it's been in continuous operation as a tavern since 1830, 12 years after it was constructed.

Beyond this quaint village, Thompson reveals a variety of landscapes—it's a pretty town for driving or bicycling. One idea is to continue north along Rte. 193 for a bit more than five miles to the Massachusetts border town of Webster—you might even venture just a short ways into Webster to observe the shores of Lake Chaubunagungamaug (try saying that 10 times fast).

Back in Thompson, turn left onto Sand Dam Road, just south of the state border, and continue for roughly two miles before bearing right onto E. Thompson Road—the views are of both old homesteads and newer suburban housing, mostly surrounded by woodland. After passing the entrance to the **Thompson International Speedway,** make a left onto Spicer Road and then a right at the stop sign onto Quaddick Town Farm Road. This lane winds a couple of miles through Quaddick State Forest, eventually to **Quaddick State Park** (860/424-3200). An entry road leads to a grove of picnic tables and a boat launch for Quaddick Reservoir, a few very short trails through the lightly wooded forest, and a larger parking area with more picnic tables, snack concessions (in summer), changing facilities, and a nice beach for swimming. Several spots around the reservoir are ideal for fishing. From the park entrance, it's about a mile farther to Quaddick Road, onto which a right turn leads about three miles back into the center of town, where you started.

## North Grosvenor Dale

Following Rte. 200 west from the village for a very different view of the area, cross under I-395 and into the Victorian industrial communities of Grosvenor Dale and North Grosvenor Dale. The Grosvenor Dale section to the right, at the junction of Rtes. 200 and 12, is a fascinating frozen-in-time mill village with hulking old redbrick buildings and a few rows of run-down workers' houses. The scene offers a window into a rather sad and now passed industrial period. Follow Rte. 12 north up into North Grosvenor Dale; another enormous old mill looms over the Thompson Library and Community Center. This one leases space to several companies, including Crabtree and Evelyn's toiletries division. Knights of Columbus and American Legion halls retain great social significance in this solid working-class community, still peopled largely with the children and grandchildren of the Southern and Eastern European immigrants who first came here to work the textile mills.

## Quinebaug

A left onto Rte. 131 leads into one final, sleepy (but in this case prosperous-looking) village, Quinebaug, which hugs the Massachusetts border at the junction with Rte. 197. There are a few shops and eateries in these parts.

From Quinebaug, you can either follow Rte. 197 south into Woodstock and continue on to Putnam via Rte. 171, as described earlier, or simply retrace your path back down Rtes. 131 and 12. The heart of Putnam lies at the junction of U.S. 44 and Rte. 12.

## Putnam

As recently as 1990, Putnam was emblematic of the problem facing outmoded industrial settlements throughout New England. Having weathered a flood that destroyed more than 200 homes during the 1950s, and witnessing simultaneously the exodus of its many textile mills to other parts of the country, the city grew quite dreary. It's still not as charming and quaint as the Colonial villages in Woodstock and Thompson, and it probably never will be—but there's a positive buzz about Putnam these days. It's now one of Connecticut's leading centers for antiques shopping.

The turnaround began when an antiques dealer named Jerry Cohen bought the grand (but vacant) 1880 Bugbee department store building, restored it, and began leasing it to some 250 antiques dealers. Each was given a stall. Soon, other stores opened in the town center, many with antiques concerns. A few good restaurants followed, the old vaudeville Bradley Playhouse was restored, a Holiday Inn Express opened in nearby Dayville, and most recently, the 1.3-mile **Putnam River Trail** was created alongside the Quinebaug River, which runs through the center of downtown. A new state-of-the-art bandstand is planned—this will be a spot for festivals and concerts. This is now an engaging community, enjoyable among all manner of antiques shoppers (everything, from rare high-end pieces to highly affordable bric-a-brac and collectibles, is sold here) but also for anybody who appreciates historic urban architecture.

An attractive driving or biking loop can be made by following U.S. 44 east out of downtown. About 4.5 miles later, where the road crosses Five Mile River, there's a nice little waterside grove of picnic tables and benches—at this point you're just 25 miles from Providence, Rhode Island. East Putnam, like East Thompson, is rural and quite pleasant to drive through. Continue east a short distance and turn right onto East Putnam Road, and then a half mile later right onto Five Mile River Road. This meandering and highly scenic Colonial road eventually wends back in a westerly direction, crossing Rte. 21 and taking you back into downtown Putnam.

Turn left (south) down Rte. 21 if you'd like to continue this ride through bucolic eastern Connecticut. Less than a mile later, make a left turn onto Aspinock Road, which you should follow until it becomes Putnam Road. At this point, you will actually have crossed the border into the rural Pineville section of Dayville. You'll soon come to an ancient old bridge that is no longer in use for cars. The bridge, which is okay for bikes and pedestrians, crosses Five Mile River and a

small picturesque waterfall—it's a wonderful little spot made all the more interesting by an easily overlooked historical marker that reads: Stone Round Historical Trail. A description notes that this is the site of one of the earliest textile mills in America (ca. 1715), and, indeed, if you look down into the woods you'll see the old stone foundation of this early Dayville mill. Note that Keep Out signs on either side of the bridge make it clear that the old mill sits on private property, but you can easily walk across the bridge and view the river, falls, and stone remnants.

## Pomfret

From Putnam, it's a short drive west to reach one of the most scenic towns in the region, Pomfret, which during the latter half of the 1800s was a summer getaway for wealthy New Yorkers and Bostonians—the railroad came through the area in 1872, and Pomfret attained a cachet in New England second only to Newport. Quite a few enormous and spectacular summer "cottages" still stand in these parts, many of them right along U.S. 44 and Rte. 169. But a less-traveled and arguably more scenic route through town is along Rte. 97, which winds through the Pomfret Historic District. Along here are several fine Queen Anne and shingle-style Victorians, plus several Georgian Revival and Colonial Revival school buildings belonging to the prestigious **Pomfret School** prep academy, which was established in 1894. Note the medieval-inspired Clark Memorial Chapel (1907)—one of its windows comes from 13th-century France. A Victorian inn stood across from the school for many years (it was torn down in the 1960s); the school continues to use several of its buildings, however. Not far from here is the **Rectory School,** a 1920s facility that educates children in grades four–nine. Pomfret, along Rte. 169, also has three 19th-century churches, all of them quite elaborate and well-preserved.

Follow Rte. 97 southwest from the intersection of U.S. 44 and Rte. 169 to pass by the aforementioned buildings; when this road again crosses U.S. 44—in the Abington section of town—make a left turn and head east to Mashamoquet Brook State Park, home of the **Brayton Grist**

**Mill and Marcy Blacksmith Collection** (U.S. 44 at entrance to park, Pomfret, 860/424-3200, open weekend afternoons late May–mid-Sept., free). A collection of tools that were used in an area mill and a blacksmith shop around the turn of the 20th century illustrates the technology employed by artisan-businessmen of this era.

You might break up your trip with a stop at **Sharpe Hill Vineyard** (108 Wade Rd., 860/974-3549, www.sharphill.com). There are tastings held in the vineyard's vintage Colonial barn Friday–Sunday, and you can order a light meal from a spa-style menu and, in the warmer months, munch away at a table in the lovely gardens. There are about 20 acres of vineyards here, and the winery continues to expand its acreage. To reach the vineyard, return to Rte. 97 via U.S. 44, turn left, head south for a little more than two miles, make a left turn onto Carter Road, a right onto Brooklyn Road, and then another left shortly after onto Wade.

## Ashford

If you occasionally hear stories about actors Paul Newman and Joanne Woodward wandering around these parts, stopping by local eateries and shops, it's because Paul Newman established the **Hole in the Wall Gang Camp** (860/429-3444, www.holeinthewallgang.org) in 1995 on a 300-acre spread in neighboring Ashford. The camp serves the needs of children with cancer and serious blood diseases—about 900 enrollees per summer—and has received awards for its innovative architectural design. The name of the camp comes, of course, from *Butch Cassidy and the Sundance Kid,* in which Paul Newman starred with fellow Fairfield County resident Robert Redford. The camp is not open to the public, except by invitation.

# BROOKLYN TO SCOTLAND

## Brooklyn

From Pomfret, a particularly scenic stretch of Rte. 169 leads south into rural Brooklyn, which is anchored by one of the Quiet Corner's most alluring greens. It's best to park at the small library, which was constructed in 1822 as the town

bank (it was transformed into its current literary function in 1913), where you can set out to explore the village on foot.

At the south end of the green, on Rte. 169, is a **statue of Israel Putnam,** the great general (1718–1790) of both the French and Indian Wars and the Revolutionary War. It was Putnam who, while commanding troops at the Battle of Bunker Hill, exclaimed, "Do not fire until you see the whites of their eyes!" Putnam was soon made second-in-command of the Continental Army, subordinate only to George Washington. He later operated a tavern on the Brooklyn town green, and the bronze equestrian statue that commemorates his life was erected in 1888, nearly a century after his death.

Across the green is the **Daniel Putnam Tyler Law Office** (Rte. 169, Brooklyn, 860/774-7728, limited hours, free), a small 1820 building in which Tyler practiced law for some 50 years and enjoyed an illustrious career in state politics and newspaper publishing. The office is run by the **Brooklyn Historical Society Museum** (25 Canterbury Rd., 860/774-7728, open 1–5 P.M. Wed. and Sun. Memorial Day–Labor Day, free), which is right behind the Putnam statue and contains documents, artifacts, and exhibits on the town's past.

Another notable building is the **Unitarian Universalist Church** (860/779-2623), which was established here in 1882, thus becoming the first such congregation in the state. The building actually dates from 1771, when it was consecrated as the Congregational Meeting House. The green's other church, **Trinity Episcopal Church,** contains four stained-glass windows created by Louis Comfort Tiffany, whose ancestors operated a mill in the eastern side of town. This comparatively decadent structure wears a Gothic Revival facade that marks an intriguing contrast to the Unitarian church. In the nearby town hall (ca. 1820), which served as the county courthouse in the 1800s, Canterbury's Prudence Crandall was tried for establishing her then-controversial school for young black women; she even spent one night here in the town lockup.

Just south of the green are the town fairgrounds, the site of America's oldest extant agricultural fair, which has been going (and moo-ing, and baaa-ing, and oink-ing) strong since 1852—it's held the weekend before Labor Day.

A bit south of the green, make a left turn onto Rte. 205, and soon after take a left onto Creamery Brook Road. You may never have expected to find buffalo roaming in Brooklyn, Connecticut, but here in this pastoral section of town is the **Creamery Brook Bison Farm** (19 Purvis Rd., just off Creamery Brook Rd., 860/779-0837, www.creamerybrookbison.com). The remarkable thing about this working dairy farm is that you can tour it on a 40-minute wagon ride, (tours offered at 1:30 P.M. on weekends, July–Sept., rides are $6 for adults, $4.50 for kids). The owners began their dream of raising buffalo with the purchase of five animals in 1990; there are now more than 60. There's also a farm store (open 2–6 P.M. weekdays, 10 A.M.–2 P.M. weekends, year-round) where farm-raised buffalo meat is sold.

Head back toward Rte. 205, but just before the intersection, make a right turn onto Gorman Road and follow it 1.5 miles before making a right onto Prince Hill Road. Shortly after, you'll come to U.S. 6, at which point you should go through the intersection and continue up Church Street to see the **Old Trinity Church.** This structure is unusual for being one of the earliest Anglican houses of worship in the state, having been erected with funds from Godfrey Malbone, a wealthy Tory from Newport, Rhode Island. It's something of a wonder that the Old Trinity wasn't burned to the ground by offended patriots during the American Revolution. When the Episcopal Church was formed officially in Woodbury, Connecticut, in 1783, Old Trinity became the local Episcopal church. It's no longer a full-time house of worship, as the Episcopalians built a new church on Brooklyn's village green in 1866, but annual services are now held here on Father's Day and All Saints' Day, and you can also visit by appointment.

A short distance farther up Church Street is **Putnam Elms** (191 Church St., 860/774-3059, www.putnamelms.org, seasonal hours, typically Wed. and Sun. afternoons, free), the former mansion of Godfrey Malbone. When Malbone passed on in the early 1780s, a son of General Israel Put-nam, Daniel, purchased the house and lived there with his bride, Catherine Hutchinson (Malbone's niece). The tension resulting from the son of a famous patriot general wedding the niece of a noted loyalist no doubt caused a scandal in little Brooklyn—imagine if a member of the Kennedy clan had married one of Barry Goldwater's nieces in the early 1960s, and you'll get the idea. This house-museum contains various artifacts and documents from the 18th and 19th centuries.

Back at U.S. 6, you can either drive west a short distance back to the Brooklyn green and continue your journey south along Rte. 169, or make a left turn onto U.S. 6 and head east for a detour into some of the area's more industrial communities, Danielson and Dayville. These communities are actually sections of the larger town of Killingly. If time is short, it's more worthwhile to stick with Rte. 169 and follow it south to Canterbury.

## Danielson and Dayville

U.S. 6 intersects with Rte. 12 in the heart of Danielson, a rough-and-tumble compact city that has seen better days. North up Rte. 12 is a smaller and similarly downcast community called Dayville—you will pass some of the region's hulking old mills in both of these towns. Follow U.S. 6 east out of Danielson to reach one of the area's less-heralded but quite inviting parks, **Old Furnace State Forest,** just off U.S. 6 east of the I-395 overpass. From the parking area, blue-blazed trails lead down to a river, where an old forge once stood—when there's sufficient flow, water tumbles over the falls. Near the waterfall is a small meadow with picnic tables.

## Plainfield

From Danielson, Rte. 12 runs south—parallel to I-395—into the suburban town of Plainfield and, to the east, Sterling. Plainfield's main attraction is the **Plainfield Greyhound Park** (137 Lathrop Rd., 860/564-3391 or 800/RACES-ON, www.trackinfo.com/pl). There are restaurants at the track (not worth checking out solely on the merit of the food, but okay if you're already here). Call for times.

From Plainfield, follow Rte. 14A nearly to the Rhode Island border to reach one of the more engaging attractions in the area, especially for kids—the **River Bend Mining & Gemstone Panning and Wildlife Exhibit** (41 Pond St., just south of Rte. 14A, 860/564-3440, www.river-bendcamp.com, open daily mid-Apr.–mid-Oct., $10 to enter the mine and pan in the sluice, exhibits and grounds free). Adjacent to the River Bend Campground, you can enter a re-created above-ground gem mine and look for your own minerals, fossils, shells, and such—the management "stocks" the mine with more than 125 varieties from around the world. Additionally, you can pan for gemstones in a small sluice. There are also nature and wildlife exhibits, and another with fluorescent rocks on display.

Turn back toward Plainfield on Rte. 14A and notice the left turn for Rte. 49. This rural road passes through some of eastern Connecticut's prettiest countryside, and is ideal for biking or country driving clear from this point down

through Voluntown and into North Stonington. A 19.5-mile stretch of Rte. 14A (between downtown Plainfield and the junction with Rte. 49) and Rte. 49 south were designated a state scenic highway in 1995; indeed, the stone-walled cattle farms and stately farmhouses, which this route passes, make for a charming excursion.

## Canterbury

To reach Canterbury from Plainfield, follow Rte. 14A west until you join with Rte. 14, and continue on to intersect with Rte. 169, the road you would have taken straight down from Brooklyn if you skipped the detour through Killingly. This junction defines Canterbury Center, which was recently named a National Historic District—many fine Georgian and Federal Colonial homes fringe this village and its shaded green, which dates from the town's settling in 1697. Also note the **Cleaveland Cemetery,** just north of the green on Rte.

## PRUDENCE CRANDALL, COURAGEOUS PIONEER OF RACIAL EQUALITY

Canterbury is the home of the **Prudence Crandall Museum** (860/546-9916, open 10 A.M.–4:30 P.M. Wed.–Sun. Apr.–mid-Dec., $3), which occupies a large late-Georgian house on the village green. In this building, on April 1, 1833, the courageous, progressive Prudence Crandall established New England's first academy of education for girls of color. Crandall was forced to close the school less than two years later, marking an ugly but fairly typical-for-the-times chapter in the state's history. She was initially hired by local residents in 1832 to open an academy on the Canterbury green for area schoolchildren. Controversy arose, however, when Crandall welcomed a young black woman to her classroom—the town immediately turned on her.

A woman of her convictions, Crandall convened with William Lloyd Garrison—a noted abolitionist of the day—and with his encouragement opened a boarding academy to serve the needs of young girls of color. These students were drawn from throughout southern New England. Locals responded to this seeming outrage by vandalizing the building, scorning Crandall, and

harassing the students (an interesting precursor to events that occurred during desegregation in the South more than 100 years later). Then the unsympathetic state assembly passed the "Black Law," a short-lived edict that forbade the establishment of any school or academy for instruction of "colored persons who are not inhabitants of this state." Finally, after thwarting arson attempts and an attack by a local mob of citizens, Crandall shut down the school, fearing for her own and her students' safety.

Today, the museum is a lesson in racial discrimination; rooms contain exhibits on this bleak episode and also on African American history through the ages. A small research library is open to the public with advance reservation. Visitors often come away surprised that such hostility toward blacks was perpetrated—was in fact sanctioned by the state government—in Connecticut, which has often been credited with an antislavery bent and a record of racial tolerance long before either was popular. In fact, Connecticut's racial problems were on par with those in many other states, albeit a few decades before the Civil War.

169—entombed here is Moses Cleaveland, the land speculator who founded the Ohio city that bears his name (albeit minus one letter).

A good old Yankee town through and through, Canterbury also developed a strong following among Finnish immigrants in the early part of the century. Testimony to possessing the largest such community in the state is the **Finnish Hall** (76 N. Canterbury Rd., Rt. 14A, near the Plainfield town line, 860/546-6671), which was constructed in 1924. Occasionally events, dances, and festivals held at the hall are open to the public, such as the **Finnish Pancake Breakfast** in late April; call ahead if you're curious.

## Scotland

Follow Rte. 14 through the historic Westminster section of town. Note the **Westminster Congregational Church** (395 Westminster Rd., Rte. 14) near where Rochambeau's troops encamped during their march back from Yorktown. Route 14 soon passes into Scotland. At the center of this village, where Rte. 14 intersects with Rte. 97, is the **Samuel Huntington Birthplace** (36 Huntington Rd., 860/456-8381, http://huntingtonhomestead.org, extremely limited hours, or by appointment, open May–Oct., free), where the great Connecticut statesman was born in 1731. This small farmhouse is currently under restoration. It is the only home of a signer of the Declaration of Independence that is open to the public. At Rte. 97, make a short detour south (about three miles each way) to reach the historic **Waldo Homestead** (96 Waldo Rd., 860/456-0708, open by appointment, free). This is a beautifully preserved 1714 Colonial farmstead containing the moving and thought-provoking letters home from Joseph and John Waldo, while they served in the Revolutionary War. Antiques from the Colonial period also fill the house.

## WILLIMANTIC AND LEBANON

### Windham

From Scotland, continue west on Rte. 14, the route taken by Rochambeau and his 6,000 troops when they marched from Newport, Rhode Island, to Yorktown, New York, in 1781.

About two miles after crossing the border of Windham, a marker on the north side of the road, just east of Ballamahack Road, marks the field the soldiers camped in when returning to Newport following the battle.

Windham is overshadowed by the attention given to its urban western half of town, which encompasses the small city of Willimantic. But here, where Rte. 14 enters the town from the east, you'll find a quaint Colonial hamlet focused around the **Windham Center Green** (junction of Rtes. 203 and 14). This picturesque expanse was the site of fervent patriotism during the American Revolution. In 1765, 500 citizens gathered here to protest the British Stamp Act, burning an effigy of the state stamp master, Jared Ingersoll, on the green (Ingersoll would resign from his post as a result of this uprising). Windham supplied more than 1,000 troops to the Continental Army, plus large supplies of food, livestock, and arms. Overlooking the green is the 1832 **Windham Free Library.** If you get a chance to poke inside, be sure to check out the crude wooden statue of Bacchus, the Greek god of wine. This was carved by three British war prisoners who were held in Windham in 1776; they later escaped, leaving behind the statue.

### Lebanon

Rather than continuing along Rte. 14 into Willimantic, consider a highly rewarding detour south to Lebanon, via Rte. 203, and then make a left turn (south) onto Rte. 32. When you reach the village of North Franklin, make a right onto Rte. 207, which leads you directly to the town center.

The Lebanon town green extends for a full mile and is one of the best in the state to stroll along; you can park at the **Lebanon Historical Society Museum and Visitor Center** (856 Trumbull Hwy., Rte. 87, 860/642-6579, www.lebanonct.org/visitor_services.html, open afternoons Wed. and Sat. year-round and by appointment, $3). This recently opened museum and visitor center is a good place to orient yourself and learn a bit more about the other house-museums nearby before you visit them; it contains a history library, genealogical research center, and numerous exhibits on the town's Colonial legacy.

Next, move along the green to the **Governor Trumbull House** (169 W. Town St., 860/642-7558, open afternoons Tues.–Sat. mid-May–mid-Oct., $2). In this 1740 house, Trumbull and his wife Faith raised six children, four of whom served in the Revolution (and one of whom perished during it). Family possessions, furnishings, and other curious artifacts fill this house in which the likes of Washington, Rochambeau, Henry Knox, and Lafayette convened on various occasions. Beside the house is the Palladian high-style stable that once stood on Main Street, in Hartford, on the Wadsworth homestead (now the site of the Wadsworth Atheneum). The stable actually stood beside what is now the Travelers Insurance Tower, before it was moved here in 1954 with funds raised by the Daughters of the American Revolution (DAR). It now contains a fine collection of early oxcarts, wagons, and iron tools and implements.

Trumbull had a fairly short commute to work; his **War Office** (149 W. Town St., no phone

number, seasonal hours, generally weekends Memorial Day–Sept.; nominal donation suggested) stands nearly beside his home, having been constructed in 1720 and used originally as the base for his shipping business. Governor Trumbull oversaw the provisioning of the Continental Army and the operations of the Connecticut militia from this very chamber, which today contains artifacts relevant to the period.

Also on this same street is the **Dr. William Beaumont House** (W. Town St., 860/642-7247, seasonal hours, generally afternoons Sat. mid-May–mid-Oct., $1). Because of his pioneering research and studies on human digestion, Dr. Beaumont has earned the distinguished, if obscure, title "The Father of Gastric Physiology." Inside the doctor's birthplace, which is administered by the Lebanon Historical Society, visitors can observe some of the rather primitive-looking instruments of medicine from the early 19th century, and see a re-created doctor's examining room.

Across the green on the north side of Rte. 87 is the house of Trumbull's son, the **Jonathan Trumbull, Jr., House** (780 Rte. 87, 860/642-6100,

## AMERICA'S REVOLUTIONARY WAR SUPPLY CHEST

The Revolutionary War was victorious in part because of the Continental Army's vast supply chest, which was based in Lebanon—a rather unsung player in America's independence. Some historians have argued that only Boston and Philadelphia played a more vital role in the American Revolution than this now almost-forgotten community. The town's significance stems largely from the fact that Lebanon was the home of Connecticut governor Jonathan Trumbull, the only Colonial governor to side (fervently, at that) against the Crown during the war.

Prior to the war, Trumbull had run a successful mercantile operation in Lebanon, which during the War of Independence was transformed into the War Office—the headquarters from which Trumbull and his officers oversaw the day-to-day operations of the state militia and navy. Connecticut, because of its strategic position bridging the New England and Mid-Atlantic colonies, and because of the mercantile skills of Trumbull, became

known as the "Provisions State" during the Revolutionary War. It supplied the Continental Army, and later Rochambeau's French troops (who landed at Newport), with munitions, tents, clothing, food, hardware, and other goods—all of this complicated routing was undertaken by Trumbull's office. During the winter of 1780–1781, about 250 of Rochambeau's French soldiers, under the command of Duc de Lauzan, encamped in fields just west of the town green, near where the Lebanon town library now stands.

Quite a few of the sights in the northeastern corner of the state that played a prominent part in the war are open to the public and described within the tours in this chapter. If you're interested in exploring this region with this angle in mind, consider beginning in Lebanon, a still-rural town with one of the state's best-preserved village greens and several of the buildings that figured in the lives of Jonathan Trumbull and his dedicated family.

seasonal hours, generally afternoons Sat. mid-May–mid-Oct., \$2). This 1764 house is noted for its remarkable interior and exterior design elements, such as the carved fireplace with a cherrywood balustrade in the main living room area.

The younger Trumbull shared his father's military and political acumen, having served as the first comptroller of the U.S. Treasury and as a military secretary to General George Washington. He later served as a U.S. senator and then as the state governor, one of the last Federalist governors to serve before Oliver Wolcott, Jr., would become the first non-Federalist to govern the state. Interestingly, both Wolcott and Trumbull came from respected and famous families of Congregational Federalists. This party of George Washington was closely tied to the blue-blooded WASPy image that is today associated with old-time New England Yankees. These men advocated a strong cohesive union and bitterly opposed the radical republican ideals of America's third president, Thomas Jefferson. They also practiced a fairly obvious brand of nepotism and exclusion: they ran the banks, the government, and the churches, and they tended to prevent dissenting voices, races, and classes the opportunity to break through their tight network.

Federalists like Trumbull and his father, and of course George Washington and John Adams, were noble men who helped secure the nation's independence and thwart the tyranny of English rule. As you visit the historic sites of Lebanon and consider the reverence with which men like the Trumbulls have been regarded, it's fascinating to think that the tenets embraced by these men would be found acutely unjust and tyrannical by today's political barometer.

The home of another Trumbull son, David, is at the south end of the green, at 589 Rte. 207. This 1778 house, **Redwood,** stands on the site of the first Trumbull homestead and is not open to the public. During the winter of 1780–81, when a band of French soldiers encamped in Lebanon, David allowed the leader of the troops, Duc de Lauzan, to use his home as a headquarters. The soldiers encamped just west of the green, but held their military training and marching directly on the green. In vehemently anti-Catholic

Connecticut, it was significant that these French Catholic troops conducted themselves with the utmost discipline and decorum—their visit marked one of the first instances in Connecticut where the Puritan-rooted distrust of outsiders and non-Congregationalists was softened. The residents of Lebanon came to admire and befriend the soldiers, and were said to enjoy watching Duc de Lauzan drill his horse-mounted troops, who dressed in riotously colorful uniforms. The **French Ovens Plaque,** just north of the town library, on the green and facing Rte. 87, marks the spot where ovens once stood that supplied the French men with baked bread.

Just southeast of the green is the now private **William Williams House,** 876 Rte. 87, in which noted merchant William Williams resided during the American Revolution. Williams served as a delegate to the first Continental Congress and is one of four Connecticut residents whose signatures appear on the Declaration of Independence (Oliver Wolcott, Samuel Huntington, and Roger Sherman being the others).

A final spot worth visiting is the **Lebanon Meetinghouse** 588 Rte. 207, a striking white building that dates from the late 1930s but is built to the exact design of Jonathan Trumbull Sr.'s, fourth son, John (not to be confused with his aforementioned second son, Jonathan Jr.). The nearly identical original of this building went up according to Trumbull's design in 1804, but was toppled by the great hurricane of 1938. John, who was barely 20 at the beginning of the Revolution, served for a few years in the war effort, then sailed to Europe in 1780 to follow his passion to become an artist. His family name and ties to Washington (he served as a second aide-de-camp under the general briefly back at home) led to his arrest in London on charges of espionage—he served for eight months in a British jail. But his dream to become a renowned painter was eventually realized, and his famed historical and religious works now hang in museums and civic buildings all over the country. His mural *The Declaration of Independence* is in the rotunda of the U.S. Capitol, and he founded America's first college art museum, the Trumbull Gallery at Yale, which today contains many of his works.

## Willimantic

From Lebanon, drive north on Rte. 289 for about seven miles to reach Willimantic, a former textile-milling center known during its heyday in the late 1800s as "Thread City." The enormous American Thread Company complex on Main Street in Willimantic, now called **Windham Mills**, dates from 1854 and accounts for the city's nickname. At more than one million square feet set over 40 acres, it was the largest such mill in the world, producing some 90,000 miles of thread—every day. In its heyday, it employed some 3,200 workers, making it the state's largest employer and a harbinger of the industrial revolution. One building, which is about 700 yards long, was designed by Thomas Edison and erected in the 1880s—it was the first factory in America illuminated by electricity. While most textile mills moved south following the Depression and World War II, Windham Mills kept chugging away at a strong pace well into the 1970s, when it still employed more than 1,000 workers. In the late 1980s, the company finally caved into the economic realities of the times and moved to North Carolina. The city was left with an enormous, albeit unwieldy, industrial dinosaur—one whose condition deteriorated rapidly.

Willimantic, its leaders realizing it would cost a small fortune and an irreplaceable degree of civic pride to tear the complex down, absorbed the property by public domain. It tore down those buildings that could not be rehabilitated but kept the massive ones fashioned out of blocks of gneiss, which had been quarried locally. The primary building No. 2 is now the Windham Mills Technology Center; it's about five stories tall and crowned with an immense tower. Mainly small businesses, many of them high-tech, now occupy this building. There's a movement afoot to create a surge of biotech industries in eastern Connecticut—to bring in companies from the coastal cities of Groton and New London clear up to the University of Connecticut—and it's hoped this movement will spawn a new use for some of the many still-vacant mill compounds that dot this region.

In the meantime, Willimantic takes on the look and ambience rather typical of other small New England cities—you'll notice an abundance of towering Victorian and early–20th-century church spires crowning the skyline and a downtown in the throes of revitalization. The transformation of the mills has been a major coup, but economic and social problems remain to some degree; you may see a few down-and-out characters lurking around. And while many of the community's gorgeous old buildings have been or will soon be restored, several leftover architectural disasters from the 1960s catch one's eye: note the hideous YMCA on Main Street, with a garish concrete ornamental facade that looks a bit like a radiator grate.

Just down the way, across from the Downtown Cafe, the distinctive 1906 Willimantic footbridge spans 635 feet across the Shetucket River, railroad tracks, and a parking lot, connecting downtown with a residential neighborhood to the south. Be sure to take a quick walk across this wooden-plank bridge, which consists of five steel segments.

One part of the old Windham Mills complex has been retrofitted into the **Windham Textile and History Museum** (Main and Union Sts., 860/456-2178, www.millmuseum.org). Exhibits offer a fascinating look at the conditions of factory workers of this period, and include a reproduced mill floor, millworkers' tenement, a few rooms from the mill managers' mansion, and a mill library (open 1 P.M.– 4:30 P.M. Wed.–Sun. in summer, 1–4 P.M. Fri.–Sun. in winter, and by appointment, $4).

The city also contains the **Connecticut Eastern Railroad Museum** (off Bridge St., 860/456-9999, www.cteastrrmuseum.org, open 10 A.M.–4 P.M. weekends in summer, free), with artifacts concerning the region's rail history. This museum operates on a fairly small scale and is staffed by volunteers (it's run by the Connecticut Eastern Chapter of the National Railroad Historical Society), but it continues to grow. It's set in downtown Willimantic in old Columbia Junction Freight Yard and encompasses a collection of vintage trains, some railroad buildings, and the six-stall roundhouse. A more substantial visitor center, plus further restorations of historic railroad buildings, is planned for the future.

A great place to satisfy your interest in the

brewing process is the **Willimantic Brewing Company** (967 Main St., 860/423-6777, www.willibrew.com), where you can watch the brewmaster at work. There's also a restaurant and brewery inside this restored 1909 building (see Food, below).

If you approach Willimantic via Rte. 32, be sure to note the so-called **Frog Bridge,** a popular nickname for the Thread City Crossing bridge, which carries traffic over the Willimantic River into town. Completed in fall 2000, and replacing an 1850s bridge that is being converted to pedestrian use, this dramatic structure has become a favorite with locals. The bridge supports are crowned with concrete "thread spools," as a tribute to the city's industrial heritage. And atop each of these four spools is a massive bronze frog statue.

These peculiar works of art were inspired by the so-called "Battle of the Frogs," which took place on Willimantic in 1754. No human lives were lost in this debacle, but the local townspeople were reportedly quite scared. As the legend goes, locals awakened one hot summer night to the most horrible screeches and shrieks—they feared everything from Armageddon to an attack by wild animals. In fact, a drought had plagued Willimantic that spring, and the area's considerable population of frogs, having run out of sources for water, apparently went berserk as they struggled to survive. The morning following the eerie noises, townspeople found several hundred dead or dying bullfrogs around the community's nearly dry millpond.

## COVENTRY, STORRS, AND MANSFIELD

### Coventry

From Willimantic, continue north on Rte. 32 as it crosses U.S. 6 and leads into Coventry (pronounced "CAH-ven-tree" in these parts), the family home of one of America's great martyrs, Captain Nathan Hale, and the site of a few renowned pick-your-own farms and wineries. At the quiet village of Perkins Corner, bear left onto Rte. 31, driving through Coventry's unassuming downtown (there are a few antiques shops, but little else to see here), and make a left

turn onto Lake Street when you reach the town center. In this quiet village, you'll see the **Rochambeau War Memorial,** which was erected in 1998 to pay tribute to the contributions of the French army in the American Revolution, and to remember the sacrifice of seven French soldiers who died in Coventry during the march to Yorktown. Overlooking Coventry Lake is the **Nathan Hale Monument and South Cemetery,** where a 45-foot-tall granite obelisk commemorates the life and sacrifice of Nathan Hale.

Continue south a short distance on Lake Street, bear right onto Cross Street, and then make a right turn onto South Street, which leads to the **Nathan Hale Homestead** (2299 South St., 860/742-6917, open 1–4 P.M. Wed.–Sun. mid-May–mid-Oct., $5). Nathan Hale, as in "I only regret that I have but one life to lose for my country," never lived in this red Colonial mansion—it was constructed the year that he was captured as a spy and hanged by the British (1776).

Members of the Hale family continued to live in this massive (by period standards) red house for the next several decades. The Antiquarian & Landmarks Society bought the house in 1945, and has since operated it as a museum, continuing to acquire furnishings and artifacts of the Colonial period, including more than a few belongings that were once Hale's or his family's. A kitchen ell jutting off the back of the house, which historians believe actually predates the

© ANDREW COLLINS

**Coventry's Nathan Hale Homestead was built in 1776, the year the famous patriot was captured and hanged.**

main structure by some 40 years, has been fully re-created with the design and kitchen implements you'd expect to find in an authentic Colonial home. To see the house, you must take one of the highly informative and engaging tours, which are given every 30 minutes and included in the price of admission. Upon arrival, you register in an old barn behind the house, watch a short video about Hale's life, and at your leisure browse the several books and various crafts and gifts in the barn's museum shop.

Beside the Hale Homestead is the **Asher Wright Monument.** Wright was the loyal and affectionate boyhood friend and military assistant of Nathan Hale. He served dutifully in the Continental Army, but never recovered emotionally from his companion's death; he died at the age of 90 in 1844, sad and lonely, never having married.

A few doors down is another Coventry house-museum, the **Strong-Porter House** (2382 South St., 860/742-7847, open weekend afternoons in summer and by appointment, $1), part of which dates from 1730 and the rest from 1748. It contains antiques, a carpenter's shop, carriage sleds, and changing exhibits.

## Mansfield

Retrace your steps to downtown Coventry and head east toward Mansfield via Rte. 275. After about 4.5 miles, make a right turn (south) toward Mansfield Center. Shortly after this turn you'll come to the **Mansfield Historical Society Museum** (954 Storrs Rd., 860/429-6575, open afternoons Thurs.–Sun. June–Sept., $1), part of which occupies the former town hall (ca. 1843). Inside the town hall and the society's adjoining building are exhibits tracing Mansfield's rural roots, its impressive milling history, and the eventual opening of the Storrs Agricultural School (1881), which has evolved into what we now know as the University of Connecticut. Because of its proximity to the university, this historical society draws more interest and is better curated than many in the state.

Continue the drive south, and you'll pass the **First Church of Christ Congregational** (549 Storrs Rd.), which is where the town of Mansfield passed a "Declaration of Freedom" in 1774, a

full two years before the new nation made its famous Declaration of Independence. A bit farther south you'll enter the little village of Mansfield Center, which was settled in 1692, originally as a part of Windham. Here are a considerable number of Colonial houses—very charming.

A left turn onto Mansfield Hollow Road takes you into **Mansfield Hollow State Park,** one of the state's most popular spots for hiking, boating, fishing, and other outdoors activities. You'll often see moon-eyed romantics, many of them students from nearby UConn, lying under the evergreens on a bluff high above a lake.

## Storrs

Head back up Rte. 195 toward the Storrs section of town to reach the main campus of the University of Connecticut (UConn). A slight detour from Rte. 195 just south of Storrs involves a right turn onto East Street, which winds down a narrow hill. Follow it to the left, and pause after passing a small pond with a waterfall. A historic marker notes the significance of Hanks Hill—on this pond Rodney Hanks built America's first silk mill in 1810. It's private property now, and only the pond and foundation are left. The original mill was moved to the Henry Ford Museum in Dearborn, Michigan, in 1930. From here, travel 1.2 miles and turn right onto Stonemill, which becomes a dirt road.

After crossing a narrow bridge, the pavement resumes and you'll see on your left the little center-chimney **Gurleyville Grist Mill** (Stone Mill Rd., Mansfield, 860/429-9023, open Sunday afternoons May–Oct., nominal donation requested), which dates from 1835 and is the only stone grist-mill in the state, one of only a handful in all of New England. On hand is the original milling machinery and tools of the mid-19th century, thus allowing visitors a firsthand look at how grist-mills functioned. The mill was owned by Samuel Cross, father of former governor Wilbur (who was born in the nearby cottage across the street). This entire detour offers an authentic drive back through time, and yet it's minutes from UConn. Retrace your steps back to Hanks Hill Road, but this time turn right and follow the road back to Rte. 195, just south of UConn campus.

The heart of the **University of Connecticut** campus is along Rte. 195, between U.S. 44 and Rte. 275 (860/486-3530, www.uconn.edu). Founded in 1881, as the Storrs Agricultural School, UConn now has a student body of about 12,000 undergraduates and another several thousand graduate students. The campus itself lacks the stately aplomb of many New England academic institutions—this collection of stiff brick, steel, and concrete monoliths, with functional but institutional-looking blue signs and gangly smokestacks, evokes the utilitarian aesthetic of a World War II internment camp. Nowhere on UConn's campus are there the sorts of visual cues found at many universities that might invite the passerby to pull the car over, get out, and wander around. Storrs isn't an overly commercial town, but there are a few shops and cheap collegiate restaurants around campus (mostly along Rte. 195, south of the main entrance), plus some museums on campus.

One of the more unusual museums on UConn's campus is the **Ballard Institute and Museum of Puppetry** (Willimantic Cottage, Weaver Rd., UConn Depot Campus, off U.S. 44, 860/486-4605, www.sp.uconn.edu/~wwwsfa/bimp.html), where a collection of some 2,000 puppets and a considerable cache of related material serve to educate the public on puppetry as an art form (open noon–5 P.M. Fri.–Sun. Apr.–mid-Nov., $2).

The **William Benton Museum of Art** (University of Connecticut, 245 Glenbrook Rd., 860/486-4520, www.benton.uconn.edu) is open Tuesday–Sunday year-round and is free to the public. This is primarily an exhibition museum whose collections change, but the quality of the shows is very high. Recent exhibits have included "Past & Present: Santos from Puerto Rico" and "After the Photo-Secession: American Pictorial Photography, 1910–1955." There's also a very good museum shop attached. Quite a few lectures and programs are held, and it's always a good idea to call periodically to see what's coming. There is also a small permanent collection. The school's art building also contains the **Atrium Gallery** (860/486-3930, open weekdays Sept.–mid-May, free), which exhibits the works of undergraduate and graduate students.

Here also is the **Connecticut State Museum of Natural History** (2019 Hillside Rd., next to Gampel Pavilion, University of Connecticut, Storrs, 860/486-4460, www.mnh.uconn.edu, open 9 A.M.–4 P.M. weekdays and 1–4 P.M. Sun., $1 donation requested), which moved to a larger space in 2000, part of which is still under construction. Once completed, this large facility's exhibits will show mounted wildlife, greenhouses containing an extensive collection of plant life, and displays pertaining to Native American life.

The university is perhaps best known, from a national perspective, for its excellent football and basketball programs. Both the men's and women's teams are among the top few in the nation, and several Huskies of recent years have gone on to the NBA, including Donyell Marshall, Ray Allen, and Travis Knight. America truly opened its eyes to the success of these programs when the men's Huskies edged Duke for the NCAA championship in 1999, and when the women's Huskies won the NCAA championship in 1995, 2000, and 2002. As you might expect, scoring tickets to UConn basketball games these days can prove a major challenge.

## SHOPPING

The Quiet Corner isn't a major retail hub; there are no shopping malls or boutique-lined streets to speak of. Antiquers, however, know this to be one of the best parts of the state for treasure-hunting, especially downtown Putnam. There are also dozens of farms and nurseries open to the public, and a few other distinctive opportunities for browsing. Many of these stores are open seasonally, and often only on weekends, so always call ahead before making a special trip.

### Coventry

Among horticulturists, Coventry is nearly synonymous with **Caprilands Herb Farm** (534 Silver St., 860/742-7244, www.caprilands.com), a system of some 30 herb gardens set around a restored 18th-century farmhouse. There are 300 varieties of herbs sold here, plus books and gifts that any gardener shall appreciate. High tea is served at 2 P.M. on Sundays and lecture luncheons are held many

Fridays and Saturdays (May–Dec.)—reservations are required for both.

Along U.S. 44, **Edmondson's Farm** (2627 Boston Tpke., 860/742-6124) has a large greenhouse with about 200 kinds of herbs, plus a country gift and floral shop and pick-your-own fruits during various times of the year. In the fall, call and find out about the farm's weekend hayrides.

## Putnam

In Putnam, anybody with even a mild interest in antiquing could easily spend a full day browsing—maybe even two or three days. Several of the antiques centers are marketplaces with dozens of stalls showing all types of antiques, and these have all been carved out of what were once ordinary-goods shops, from an old Montgomery Ward department store to a characterful old bank. Included in the mix of shops are custom and estate jewelers, estate liquidation, architec-

tural elements, frame shops, art galleries, decorative arts, Persian and Oriental rugs, and such. All told there are 20 shops with stalls representing some 400 dealers.

Most famous here is the **Antiques Marketplace** (109 Main St., 860/968-0442), a consortium of some 300 merchants dealing in just about every conceivable style and ware. Within walking distance are several other multi-dealer and independent shops. One of the best sources of unusual imported furnishings, many of them quite ornate, is the **Little Museum Co.** (86 Main St., 860/928-2534), which also carries very fine Oriental rugs. **Antique Corner** (112 Main St., 860/963-2445) sells Fiestaware, mod 1950s lamps, shag carpets, and lots of cool retro furniture. It's perfect if you're going for that Lucy-and-Ricky look.

Putnam is also home to **Wonderland Books** (120 Main St., 860/963-2600), a general-interest shop that also has gifts, cards, and music. Foodies

## THE MARTYR-SPY OF THE AMERICAN REVOLUTION

It often comes as a surprise in this era, when James Bond movies are major blockbusters, that espionage was looked upon with disdain during Colonial times, even when undertaken for the right cause. In the case of Nathan Hale (1755–1776), now celebrated as one of America's great national heroes, it's theorized that Hale's own family felt slightly shamed, or at least a bit awkward, about the fact that their son lost his life not on the front line, but in an act of subterfuge. To Hale's credit, he volunteered to spy on the British solely out of duty—it had become necessary for a patriot soldier to sail to Long Island and attempt to glean a sense of where the British troops were organizing and in what numbers. He saw an opportunity to help the patriot cause, and he jumped at it.

Hale posed as a schoolteacher of modest means, but in keeping with his (and his culture's) disapproval of deceit and presenting oneself falsely, he refused when confronted by the British to carry on his charade. Rather, he identified himself simply as Nathan Hale, soldier of the Continental Army. This act of honesty would result in his hanging, at the hands of British general William Howe, on

the following day, September 22, 1776.

Hale was one of many children and the son of a successful farmer. He attended Yale and, at the age of 18, graduated near the top of his class; soon after he took a position as a schoolteacher at a boys' school in New London. A progressive thinker for his day, Hale believed firmly that young girls deserved to have the same opportunities in education that boys of that period enjoyed. To this end, he instructed a separate class of young women for two hours very early each morning on his own time, before his paid teaching job commenced.

Upon the spread of news that war had broken out between the Massachusetts colony and the British, Hale enlisted immediately, and soon served as a first lieutenant in the Seventh Connecticut regiment, participating in several maneuvers in Boston. It was in the early fall of 1776 that General Washington implored one of his subordinate commanders to find a soldier willing to sneak into New York to collect information on the activities of the British. Only Hale volunteered, and the rest is history.

and Anglophiles love to browse the goodies at **Mrs. Bridge's Tea Shop and Pantry** (136 Main St., 860/963-7040), which is chock full of tea and related accessories, British recipe books, British and American gourmet packaged foods, and many other gifts, from needlepoint materials to soaps and bath oils.

## Woodstock and Pomfret

Woodstock is an excellent source of various arts and crafts shops. Best known is **Scranton's Shops** (300 Rte. 169, South Woodstock, 860/928-3738), a small complex set around a Colonial blacksmith, where the works and antiques of some 90 local artisans are featured. Adjoining these businesses is **Fox's Fancy Sweet Shoppe** (860/928-2558), where you can find ice cream, truffles, and other cures for a sweet tooth. Other potential stops include the **Christmas Barn** (835 Rte. 169, 860/928-7652), which—despite the name—is open from summer through the end of the year and displays both holiday-oriented and general country furnishings and crafts; and the **Chocolate Saltbox Stenciler** (1250 Rte. 171, 860/974-1437), where hand-stenciled table linens and accessories are sold, plus some 10,000 stencil designs.

Fans of multi-dealer antiques stores should look beyond Putnam at the 90-stall **Pomfret Antique World** (Rte. 101, near junction with U.S. 44, 860/928-5006). Fans of gardening and cooking should be certain to drop by **Martha's Herbary** (junction of U.S. 44 and Rtes. 169 and 97, Pomfret, 860/928-0009), a memorable shop where you can also tour magnificent gardens and a touching pet cemetery that dates to 1889. Classes on cooking and herbs are offered throughout the year.

## Elsewhere

Roughly at the Brooklyn town line, Canterbury's **Wright's Mill Farm** (63 Creasey Rd., 860/774-1455, www.wrightsmillfarm.com) is a 250-acre spread of pumpkins in the fall, and Christmas trees in November and December (plus a Christmas shop inside a silo). Year-round this makes for an interesting excursion

to see the five antique water-powered mill sites on the property, or to explore the farm's hiking trails. Seasonally, horse-drawn carriage and wagon rides are also offered—call ahead for details.

Overlooking the quaint village green in Brooklyn, **Heirloom Antiques** (8 Wolf Den Rd., 860/774-7017) sells both original and reproduction antiques, most with a country American feel—lamps, tin chandeliers, kitchen chairs, and the like. If you're interested in high-quality finely crafted reproductions of Windsor chairs and Early American tables and cabinets, pay a visit to Ashford's **Classics in Wood** (271 Ashford Center Rd., U.S. 44, 860/429-6020).

Fans of holiday festivity should be sure to drop by **G & L Christmas Barn** (Rte. 14, Windham, 860/456-1154 or 888/737-5600), where you'll find a huge selection of Christmas crafts, decorations, figurines, ornaments, and such.

Near the intersection of U.S. 44 and Rte. 89 in Ashford, **Crooke Orchards** (317 Bebbington Rd., 860/429-5336) has apples, peaches, pears, and various vegetables, sold in the farm store or seasonally you can pick your own. You can visit New England's lone automated candy-apple factory in Eastford: the hundred-acre **Buell's Orchard** (108 Crystal Pond Rd., off Rte. 198, 860/974-1150) also has pick-your-own apples, blueberries, peaches, and pears, and is the site of an annual Fall Festival. Right at the Brooklyn town border on Rte. 169, Pomfret's **Lapsley Orchard** (403 Rte. 169, 860/928-9186) is another great pick-your-own farm with a roadside farm stand: expect to find apples, peaches, pears, pumpkins, jams, honey, and juices depending on the season. **Anderson Organics** (369 Pomfret Rd., Rte. 169, Brooklyn, 860/774-8856, www.andersonorganics.com) grows more than 80 varieties of medicinal and culinary herbs and also is a great source of heirloom vegetables, flowers, shrubs, and trees. A tradition for more than a century, **Logee's Greenhouses** (141 North St., Danielson, 860/774-8038) comprises some seven greenhouses rife with every imaginable kind of plant.

# RECREATION

## Auto Racing

The **Stafford Motor Speedway** (55 West St., 860/684-2783, staffordmotorspeedway.com) hosts NASCAR events April–Labor Day on its half-mile track.

## Bicycling

Northeastern Connecticut is arguably the best biking territory in the state, as rural and scenic as the Litchfield Hills but slightly—and only slightly—less hilly. The Northeast Connecticut Visitors District distributes a remarkably thorough and detailed brochure, *Northeast Connecticut's Bike Guide*, with maps and point-by-point directions of 10 loops in the region, plus routes connecting these loops. These self-guided cycling tours are 5–25 miles and pass by historic homesteads and museums, B&Bs, and even a handful of restaurants.

Throughout the spring and summer months, organized rides are sponsored by different bike shops in the area. It's best to call these places individually for details, and if you want information on rentals. These include the **Ordinary Bike Shop** (21 Furnace St., Danielson, 860/774-1660), **Scott's Cyclery** (1171 Main St., Willimantic, 860/423-8889), and **Silver Bike Shop** (6 Livery St., Putnam, 860/928-7370).

## Hiking

The 78-acre **C. Vaughan Ferguson, Jr. Conservancy,** off Rte. 169 near the Brooklyn–Pomfret border, has several easy red-blazed trails through rolling woodland and low-lying marshes, both of which provide ample opportunities to observe area wildlife. You'll find about 5 miles worth of well-maintained and exceptionally pristine trails in the Connecticut Audubon Society's **Bafflin Sanctuary** (Day Road, off Rte. 169, Pomfret, 860/928-4041), a 700-acre preserve. The new **Connecticut Audubon Center at Pomfret** (189 Pomfret St., Rte. 169, 860/928-4948) is an attractive nature center with exhibits, an excellent book and gift shop, kids programs, seasonal lectures and workshops. Naturalists here also lead walks through Bafflin Sanctuary.

A span of an old railroad bed, the **Air Line Walking Trail** (860/928-6121) extends from Putnam through Pomfret for 26 scenic miles into the town of Windham. This trek is less for rugged hiking than for jogging or walking, whether you want to keep fit or simply to appreciate the scenery. There are several access points, including James L. Goodwin Forest in Hampton, the aforementioned Bafflin Sanctuary in Pomfret, and behind the Willi Bowl in North Windham.

**Mansfield Hollow State Park** (off Bassetts Bridge Rd., Mansfield, 860/455-9057), which sits on 26,000 rolling acres, is laced with color-coded hiking trails, some passing over footbridges on the Fenton River and one that leads up to a cliff offering great views back over the countryside.

# ENTERTAINMENT AND NIGHTLIFE

The Theatre of Northeastern Connecticut performs at Putnam's late–19th-century **Bradley Playhouse** (30 Front St., Putnam, 860/928-7887, www.tnect.org), which has gradually been renovated by the group throughout the 1990s. This regional theater group presents popular Broadway-style shows and revivals, from Shakespeare to Tennessee Williams to Agatha Christie to popular musicals. It's not expensive (not much more than the price of a movie, in fact). A children's show is presented throughout August, and the season runs year-round with about six productions. The theater is in the heart of the downtown antiques district, within walking distance of several restaurants.

Drive-in movies are all but a memory in much of the world, but you can still enjoy this form of entertainment at the **Mansfield Drive-In Theatre** (junction of Rtes. 31 and 32, 860/423-4441, www.mansfielddrivein.com), the state's only three-screen drive-in. There's a full playground here, plus a snack bar. This is a great place to bring the kids, but (who are we kidding?) couples seem to find plenty of reasons to keep this drive-in popular. Films are shown daily June–August and on Friday and Saturday evenings in April, May, and September.

Most of the area's other opportunities for nightlife and the arts revolve around the campus of UConn, in the Storrs section of Mansfield. About 40 plays, musical performances, lectures, plays, operas, and other arts presentations are held at UConn's **Jorgensen Center for the Performing Arts** (2132 Hillside Rd., 860/486-4226, www.jorgensen.ct-arts.com, Sept.–May). Some of these shows are produced by the **Connecticut Repertory Theatre.**

For nightlife, stop by **Huskies** (28 King Hill Rd., 860/429-2333), a rowdy hangout and sports bar popular with UConn students—you'll find pool tables, video screens, video games, and plenty of drink specials.

## FESTIVALS AND EVENTS
### Spring and Summer
About 25 nurseries and garden shops in the Quiet Corner offer demonstrations and events during **Getaway Gardens Weekend** (various locations, 860/928-1228, in late April). A day-long **Fourth of July Jamboree** (Woodstock Common, 860/928-7449) on July 4 includes a petting zoo, crafts, relay races, and local foods. The second weekend in August, the **Lebanon Country Fair** (Mack Rd., 860/423-4886) features arts, crafts, livestock competitions, entertainment, food, and carnival rides. The **Brooklyn Fair** (town fairgrounds, Rte. 169, 860/779-0012, www.brooklynfair.org, in late August) is America's oldest continuously running agricultural fair, having first been held in 1851.

### Fall and Winter
Observe stage and livestock shows, visit a petting zoo, browse arts and crafts, and watch go-cart races at the **Woodstock Fair** (Rtes. 169 and 171, 860/928-3246), the second-oldest fair in the state, dating from 1861. That same early September weekend, **Prudence Crandall Day** (Prudence Crandall Museum, Rtes. 14 and 169, 860/546-9916) celebrates the birthday of the courageous headmistress, with children's games, entertainment, crafts sales and demonstrations, and museum tours. Late in the month, the **Lebanon Outdoor Antiques Show** (Lebanon green, Rtes. 87 and 207, 860/642-7247) is one of the longest-running such events in the state.

The Waldo Homestead in Scotland plays host each October to the **Annual Highland Festival** (96 Waldo Rd., 860/423-9634); come watch traditional Highland dance competitions, bagpipes, amateur sports, folk music, Highland cattle, and clan tents. Each October you can attend the **Walking Weekend** (866/363-7226, www.thelastgreenvalley.org), which is organized by the Quinebaug-Shetucket National Heritage Corridor. Over three days, a series of guided walks are held on town greens, through woodlands, across farmsteads, and along other interesting properties all through this corridor that extends from South-Central Massachusetts into the Quiet Corner. This is one of the best outdoors events in the state, and attendance keeps growing each year. Later in the month, the **Festival at Roseland Cottage** (860/928-4074) draws as many as 10,000 onlookers; this event includes 175 juried arts and crafts exhibitors.

Late in November, gather the kids to watch the **Grand Arrival of Santa** (Wright's Mill Farm, 63 Creasey Rd., Canterbury, 860/774-1455); Santa and the elves arrive by wagon, and children are welcome to have their picture taken with Santa, take a wagon ride, and visit with the barnyard animals. There's also a Christmas shop.

## ACCOMMODATIONS
The Quiet Corner has a great many B&Bs and a smattering of motels, but on the whole there are far fewer lodging options than elsewhere in the state. If you're seeking a midrange business-oriented chain property that's still convenient to this region, go with one of the several in Vernon, Manchester, or Norwich (although a new Holiday Inn Express did open in Putnam in 1999, remedying the area's need for such a property). On the other hand, for so remote and sparsely populated a region, there are dozens of B&Bs, many of which are reviewed below, and many more can be booked through area reservations services.

## Hotels and Motels

**$100–150:** The **Best Western Regent Inn** in Mansfield (123 Storrs Rd., Rt. 195, just north of U.S. 6, 860/423-8451 or 800/528-1234) is one of the few large properties in northeastern Connecticut; it's an 88-room hotel just 10–15 minutes south of UConn, and so its availability depends almost entirely on when university-related events are taking place (homecoming weekend, reunions, parents' weekends, etc.). This well-kept Colonial-style building has an exercise room and an outdoor pool, and there are plenty of restaurants nearby. UConn recently got an on-campus hotel with the opening of the 100-room **Nathan Hale Inn & Conference Center** (855 Bolton Rd., Storrs, 860/427-7888, www.nathanhaleinn.com). Spacious, colonial-style rooms have large windows, desks, and two-line phones with voicemail; some units have high-speed Internet, microwaves, and mini-refrigerators. Facilities include a state-of-the-art fitness center, indoor pool, lounge, and a very good full-service restaurant, the Blue Oak Cafe, which serves creative contemporary New England fare. The hotel is in the middle of campus, an easy walk to UConn's museums.

**$50–100:** The relatively new, 77-room **Holiday Inn Express Hotel and Suites** (16 Tracy Rd., Dayville, 860/779-3200 or 800/HOLIDAY, www.hiexpress.com) is just a short drive south of the antiquing mecca, Putnam—it's one of northeastern corner's only full-service hotels (without a restaurant, but with a very nice complimentary breakfast buffet). This attractive property has an indoor pool, exercise room, and a guest laundry.

Another to consider in this price range is the **Sleep Inn** (327 Ruby Rd., Rt. 320, Willington, 860/684-1400 or 800/753-3746), which is also fairly new and is smack in the midst of a truck stop off I-84 (meaning Burger King, Dunkin' Donuts, and Country Pride are steps from the lobby). Despite what may sound like a charmless location, it's rather quiet and peaceful here, and the hotel faces a wooded area and has a small outdoor pool; it's also quite handy to all Quiet Corner attractions, and a mere 20–30-minute drive from Hartford.

For basic accommodations, consider the

**Plainfield Yankee Motor Inn** (55 Lathrop Rd., Plainfield, 860/564-4021, a 49-room two-story property with among the nicest and cheeriest rooms of the four.

## Country Inns and Bed-and-Breakfasts

**$150–250:** There's only one large-scale grand country hotel in the Quiet Corner, but the **Inn at Woodstock Hill** (94 Plaine Hill Rd., South Woodstock, 860/928-0528) has been a fixture in the region since it opened in 1987. There are 22 rooms, furnished uniformly with Colonial-style pieces; some are inside the main 1816 farmhouse and its adjoining barn, while others are in a century-old smaller building nearby. The house was built originally for William Bowen, a relative of Roseland Cottage owner Henry C. Bowen. There's a full-service restaurant on the premises. The regal **Lord Thompson Manor** (Thompson Hill Rd., Rte. 200, Thompson, 860/923-3886) is set down a long, horribly pocked driveway—the poor condition somehow adds to the charmingly remote location on 42 wooded acres, yet this inn is minutes from I-395. The house is often the site for weddings, parties, and various functions, but you can also book a stay in one of the six guest rooms. Each has the sort of majestic furnishings you might expect to find in a British manor house; three have large bathrooms with antique tiling and fireplaces, and the rest share a bathroom. Full breakfast included.

**$100–150:** Another excellent option in Woodstock is the **Elias Child House B&B** (50 Perrin Rd., 860/974-9836 or 877/974-9836, www.elias childhouse.com), which is on 40 acres of woodland and can be reached via an extremely quiet country road—a perfect place to spend a peaceful weekend. The house dates from the early 1700s and contains nine fireplaces, two remarkable walk-in hearths (cooking demonstrations are often given), a beehive oven, a chamber for smoking meats, and an attached outhouse (which indicates that the Colonial occupants were quite well-off). Original architectural details like 12-over-12 double-hung windows, wide-plank floors, and original wavy-glass windows further reveal the house's intriguing history. All three rooms have fireplaces and private baths, and guests have the use of an in-ground pool and a massage session (by prior arrangement). Full breakfast is included.

In Brooklyn, the **Friendship Valley B&B** (60 Pomfret Rd., Rte. 169, 860/779-9696, www.friendshipvalleyinn.com) offers among the most inviting accommodations in the area, and also a glimpse into the region's Civil Rights history: A stop on the Underground Railroad, the home was owned in the 1830s by an abolitionist-minded Quaker named George Benson who took an unpopular stand by supporting and hosting Prudence Crandall. A 1795 Georgian Colonial on 12 acres and surrounded by a white-picket fence, the house contains five antiques-filled bedrooms, all with private baths, furnished with an eclectic and memorable collection of antiques. There's a pool out back, and full breakfast is included.

Sometimes when you stay at a B&B you're afforded the pleasure of playing with the innkeepers' cat or dog; at the **B&B at Taylor's Corner** (880 Rte. 171, Woodstock, 860/974-0490 or 888/503-9057, www.bnbattaylorscorner.com) you'll meet the resident Scotch Highland cow, Jessie-Brown, and her calf, Earlene (well, they don't actually live inside the house, but you get the idea). This extremely charming and low-keyed hostelry is in a large 18th-century house with eight fireplaces, including one large fireplace where the owners sometimes give hearth-cooking demonstrations. There are three guest rooms, each with private bath and air-conditioning. Full breakfast is included.

The **Chickadee Cottage** (70 Averill Rd., Pomfret, 860/963-0587, www.chickadeecottage.com) evokes the spirit of the adjacent 500-acre Audubon Nature Sanctuary, rather than the playful words of W. C. Fields. Here, at this early–1900s, Cape-style cottage situated on 10 pastoral acres, guests can choose from two country-style rooms filled with antiques, four-poster beds, and art. Some of the art is from Pennsylvania's sylvan Chester County (which is where the owners hail from)—the walls of one room are painted with a garden mural. The cottage has fully modernized rooms and a wonderful gourmet kitchen, where you can take breakfast; a screened porch overlooking beautiful gardens is another option for dining or lounging.

A tavern in the early 1800s, **Bird-in-Hand** (2011 Main St., Coventry, 860/742-0032, www.thebirdinhand.com) was built in 1731—and an exact replica of the original tavern sign greets visitors. The inn sits on two wooded acres, with glorious herb and flower gardens, and contains three guest rooms, each with period Colonial antiques and Oriental rugs. One room has a double-whirlpool tub, while two others have fireplaces. In the Mary Rose Room, you'll find a discreetly situated closet that is said to have hidden slaves traveling north via the Underground Railroad. There's also a small cottage that's nice for extended stays; it has a VCR/TV, private phone, fireplace, and full kitchen. Breakfast is served in a charming formal dining room.

**Celebrations Inn** (330 Pomfret St., Pomfret, 860/928-5492 or 877/928-5492, www.celebrationsinn.com) is a warm and richly decorated 1885 Queen Anne Victorian property in the heart of Pomfret. The five rooms here are filled with cushy, lavish furnishings—one contains a gas fireplace and a sumptuous iron canopy bed; the two-room master suite also has a gas fireplace, as well as a daybed, rocking chair, and antique white-iron bed. The common areas of this 19-room mansion are similarly romantic. Set on a serene 80-acre farmstead, the 1730s **Daniel Trowbridge House** (193 Hampton Rd., Rte. 97, Pomfret, 860/974-3622, www.danieltrowbridgehouse.com) has just a pair of guest rooms, but is adding two more in the near future. The owners bought this property, which was in rather dire condition, several years ago and have been working hard to restore it ever since. Rooms contain a number of pieces built by one of the hosts, Tom Campbell, who uses wood salvaged from old barns and other vintage structures to create fine beds, tables, cabinets, and other furnishings. This is one of the most relaxing and secluded properties in the Quiet Corner, a lovely old home surrounded by acres of fields and lush gardens.

**$50–100:** It has just three rooms, but the **Fitch House** (563 Storrs Rd., Rte. 195, Mansfield Center, 860/456-0922, www.fitchhouse.com) exists on a grand scale. Its spacious accommodations are decorated with a meticulous eye for how they might have looked during the 1830s and 1840s, when the original owners resided in this stunning white Greek Revival mansion. One room has a working wood-burning fireplace, all three have four-poster beds, TVs, private baths, and an elegant yet restrained assortment of period antiques. A full country breakfast is served in a sunny dining area whose tall windows afford inviting pastoral views, and UConn and Mansfield Hollow State Park are just a short drive away.

Less than two miles from the campus of UConn (and across from the Mansfield Historical Museum), the **Altnaveigh Inn** (957 Storrs Rd., Rte. 195, 860/429-4490, www.altnaveigh-inn.com) is popular for its reasonably priced rooms (two of five have private baths) and dependable restaurant. The attractive inn dates from 1734, and rooms are simple but romantic (without phones or TVs), with inviting fluffy beds with quilts and plush pillows. Continental breakfast is included.

Despite its name, the **Old Eagleville Inn** (670 Stonehouse Rd., Rte. 275, Coventry, 860/742-1872 or 800/721-8058, www.oldeaglevilleinn.com) is not old at all—the attractive house was built in 1997. However, it's a perfect replica of an 18th-century saltbox Colonial. It's a great choice if you love the style of old, but prefer a newer accommodation with modern comforts (efficient air-conditioning, phone jacks for your laptop computer, music that can be piped into guest rooms as desired, and attractive bathrooms). Rooms are tasteful and cozy, brightened with country quilts and four-poster beds. The largest unit has a grand double-whirlpool. The inn occupies a secluded, wooded property.

## Campgrounds

The Quiet Corner contains many very nice camping facilities, from full-scale RV resorts to peaceful groves of tents in secluded state parks. One of the best-known large-scale sites is **Brialee RV & Tent Park** (174 Laurel Ln., Ashford, 860/429-8359 or 800/303-CAMP, www.brialee.net), a 195-site compound with RV rental

units also available. This is a popular spot with families, owing to the Olympic-size pool, stocked trout pond with 200-foot sandy beach, grocery store and coffee shop, hiking trails, and numerous organized activities and entertainment. Another one big with families is **Water's Edge Family Campground** (271 Leonard Bridge Rd., Lebanon, 860/642-7470 or 800/828-6478, www.watersedgecampground.com). This is a 150-site facility with both wooded and lakefront sites and a slew of outdoors activities—boating, fishing, volleyball, swimming, horseshoes—and entertainment possibilities; here, too, is a grocery store and a small restaurant.

Woodstock has been home to Connecticut's only nudist campground since 1934: the **Solair Recreation League** (65 Ide Perrin Rd., 860/928-9174) has 150 sites and welcomes families. A bit smaller and more adult-oriented is Chaplin's **Nickerson Campground** (1036 Phoenixville Rd., (Rte. 198, 860/455-0007), which fringes Natchaug Forest (great for hiking) and the Natchaug River (great for fishing and swimming). **Mashamoquet Brook/Wolf Den Campgrounds** (Wolf Den Dr., Pomfret, 860/928-6121), a small state park-managed operation, is a peaceful place for tent camping (there are no RV sites here). **Roaring Brook Cooperative Campground** (8 South Rd., Rte. 190, Stafford Spring, 860/684-7086, roaringbrookcampground.com) has extensive grounds with a few hundred sites, ball fields, volleyball, ponds for swimming and trout or bass fishing, a pool, a store and small short-order restaurant, and various social activities.

## FOOD

Given the low population density of the area, few Quiet Corner towns have more than a half dozen restaurants, and that's including basic diners, luncheonettes, and pizzerias (a few of the more intriguing are described below). There are very few chain and fast-food establishments—what few you'll find are near UConn (both off I-84 and along Rte. 195) and in Putnam. Recently, several higher-profile upscale restaurants have opened in the area, finally meeting the culinary demands of the increasingly sophisticated crowd of antiquers and other visitors who have begun to discover the joys of northeastern Connecticut.

## Upscale

It's taken a little time, but the Quiet Corner is rapidly catching up to the rest of the state in culinary panache. The **Laurel House** (8 Tracy Rd., next to the Holiday Inn Express, Dayville, 860/779-2900, $15–25) is an upscale space with a gorgeous mahogany bar and paneling, and a menu that focuses on chiefly Continental fare. Specialties include shellfish Savannah—lobster, mussels, clams, shrimp, and scallops over angel hair pasta with a light tomato sauce and a piquant rouille—and fresh rotisserie duck with ginger-black cherry sauce.

While Brooklyn's **Golden Lamb Buttery** (Brush Hill Road, 860/774-4423) is indisputably fine dining, a meal in this barn overlooking Jimmie and Bob Booth's 1,000-acre Hillendale Farm can hardly be called traditional. Dining is by reservation only (booking at least a month ahead is advised), offered only on Friday and Saturday evenings (it's a $65 prix fixe that typically features a choice of lamb, chateaubriand, duck, or salmon, plus heaps of tasty vegetable sides and desserts—most of the ingredients fresh from the farm). There's one seating, and no rush to finish up and be on your way—the Booths have worked hard to create an experience that may be savored for hours. Before sitting down to your meal, you're invited (but by no means required) to embark on a brief hayride through the Buttery's adjoining fields. Dining is in four breathtakingly charming rooms, decked with antiques that include a vintage automobile, and you'll be serenaded by singing staff members (should you request it) during dinner. It's open mid-May–December.

A favorite of parents visiting their kids at nearby UConn, **Altnaveigh Inn** (957 Storrs Rd., Rt. 195, Storrs, 860/429-4490, $17–26) is well-regarded for its fine traditional dining room, where Continental fare is presented. Specialties include tenderloin of beef Wellington, lobster Newburg, and coquilles St. Jacques Mornay.

The chef at **Harvest** (37 Putnam Rd., U.S. 44, Pomfret, 860/928-0008, www.harvestrestaurant.com, $15–26) has long been known around

these parts, having based his establishment in a few different buildings over the years. In 1996, he moved his operation to an 18th-century farmstead, shaded by mature tulip, maple, and pine trees, plus herb and perennial gardens. In this rustic building, you'll discover exemplary Continental and American cuisine, from sage-roasted chicken served with its natural juices to a more daring cedarplank-roasted salmon with lemon, ginger butter, and white wine. Steaks and chops are also specialties.

The **Inn at Woodstock Hill** (94 Plaine Hill Rd., South Woodstock, 860/928-0528, $16–26) is hidden off a back road in peaceful seclusion among forested hills, rolling meadows, and historic homes—the old-world dining room is the perfect setting for crab cakes with chipotle aioli or escargot with garlic, tarragon, scallions, mushrooms, and butter; another specialty is pork tenderloin with a cranberry-peach chutney.

## Creative but Casual

The **Depot Restaurant** (57 Middle Tpke., U.S. 44, Mansfield Depot, 860/429-3663, www.thedepotrestaurant.com, $12–22) couldn't quite be called nouvelle, but the American and Italian menu does manage a reasonable degree of complexity, from pan-seared trout with an almond crust and Dijon-caper aioli to porcini-mushroom ravioli with a wild-mushroom cream sauce, fresh herbs, and frizzled leeks; thin-crust stone-baked pizzas are another option. The setting is noteworthy (if tried and true): a converted rail station, complete with an old red caboose permanently docked beside it. It has dark-wood tables, wood paneling, and dim lighting that imparts both a romantic and a festive mood, making this an ideal choice for both couples and groups of friends.

Set among the potpourri of antiques shops in Putnam is the **Vine Bistro** (85 Main St., 860/928-1660, $13–23), a snug storefront eatery with twinkly lights strung vertically in the windows and neatly framed art on the walls. Vodka rigatoni with gulf shrimp, eggplant layered with ricotta and mozzarella, and fine Caesar salads are among the tasty specialties—with many dishes, you'll be offered a choice between creamy or low-fat versions; unless you're seriously dieting, opt for the creamy one. And, if you're feeling especially relaxed about your figure, take a shot at the pumpkin and cognac cheesecake for dessert. The owners are adding a trendy martini bar next door.

## Pizza, Pub Grub, and Seafood

Worth a visit if you happen to be in the area, the 1820s **Bidwell Tavern** (1260 Main St., Coventry, 860/742-6978, $7–17) serves the expected roster of pub favorites: steaks, chops, wings, onion rings, burgers, and a few seafood entrées like scallops baked with asiago cheese. The space is dark and homey, with old brick archways, dark-wood overhanging beams, and tables set around a central bar.

The most recent addition to Putnam's antiques district is the **Courthouse Bar and Grille** (121 Main St., 860/963-0074, $8–16), set in a small handsome building that was in fact a courthouse from the late 1880s to the 1940s. Pub fare—such as burgers, steaks, and similar casual American favorites—set the culinary tone at this cozy hangout that's popular for both lunch and dinner. Grilled swordfish and Montréal-style steak are favorites. Owned by the same folks as the popular Brannigan's Ribs in Southington, **Uncle D's Log Cabin** (383 Rte. 87, Lebanon, 860/456-7663, $8–13) serves up reasonably priced Italian and American fare.

**Chuck's and Margaritas** (1498 Stafford Rd., Rte. 32, Mansfield, 860/429-1900, $10–20) serves a menu of Mexican food from both the Chuck's steakhouse chain and the Margaritas Tex-Mex chain (there are other Chuck's and Margaritas throughout New England). The food is fairly basic, although the jerk chicken fajitas are a standout. And, as you might guess, drinking margaritas and fruity daiquiris accounts for much of the fun. Although part of a regional chain with just okay food (the steaks at Chuck's are better than the Tex-Mex from the Margaritas side of the menu), this popular hangout is set in a dramatic retrofitted barn with a towering adjacent silo and a giant fireplace inside, It has a pleasing ambience (especially, it seems, among young singles).

Foodwise, the new branch of Middletown's renowned **Coyote Blue Tex Mex Cafe** (50 Higgins Hwy., Rte. 31, Mansfield, 860/423-4414, $7–14) earns considerably higher marks. The spacious, airy restaurant, decked in tasteful southwestern art, presents a happy mix of dishes inspired by Mexican, Texan, and New Mexican food.

Giving new meaning to the term "going postal," the ambitious developers of the **Willimantic Brewing Company** (967 Main St., Willimantic, 860/423-6777, www.willibrew.com, $6–17) took a long-vacant neoclassical 1909 post office in the center of town and reinvented it as a lively, artful, and vibrant brewpub. Amid the old tellers' windows, the terrazzo and marble floors, and the soaring vaulted ceilings, a WPA-style mural evoking a 1930s street scene watches over the din of happy eaters chomping on tempting American vittles. The menu is big, and most dishes are named for area towns to which mail once flowed from this very space: note the Lebanon Greens salad, the Voluntown veggie primavera, Plainfield parmesan-crusted tuna steak, and the Canterbury chili. Fresh-baked pizzas are another specialty.

**Willington Pizza House** (25 River Rd., Rte. 32, 860/429-7433, large pies are $15–18, grinders and dinner are $4–10) is famous—for miles around—for its red potato pizza (with sour cream, sliced red potatoes, sharp cheddar, chives, and your choice of bacon, broccoli, or both), but some of the others are nearly as enticing. The California pie has garlic, mozzarella, artichoke hearts, black olives, and sundried tomatoes; the Cheeseburg Pizza is a white pie with ketchup, mustard, hamburger, pickles, diced onions, sharp cheddar cheese, and bacon. Grinders and Italian platters are also offered. Willington Pizza seats 200; it's not only a pizza parlor, but a local institution and a town meetinghouse, set in a long gray sprawling building with walls lined with photos, banners, and beer signs. A tavernesque ambience prevails. And the food lives up to the impressive billing. It's near the Mansfield line, so it's a hit with UConn students.

In Putnam, **Pyzzz** (8 Harris St., 860/928-7424, pies are $9–13, no credit cards accepted) is set rather oddly inside an old converted storage building whose exposed stone-and-mortar construction gives the place a warm and distinguished ambience. All of the pizzas are hand-spun and slid right into a fiery brick oven. Locals rave about the hot-boneless-chicken-wing-and-blue-cheese pie. Great salads, grinders, and quesadillas are available as well, plus a nice selection of beer and wine that you might also sample while sitting at the cozy deco bar.

## Asian

There simply aren't many ethnic restaurants in this part of the state, but Willimantic does have what many consider a first-rate Chinese restaurant, **Peking House** (1601 W. Main St., 860/456-7271), with extremely cheap food ($4–12, most entrées under $8). Of the some 160 dishes offered here, there aren't too many surprises—the usual chow meins, shrimp with lobster sauce, orange chicken, and such. Several dishes can be prepared with no-fat, low-cholesterol, and all-natural ingredients. It's in an unattractive shopping center on the west end of town, and the staff could not be friendlier, although the dining room is ordinary.

## Quick Bites

In Plainfield, stop by **Hank's Dairy Bar** (1006 Norwich Rd., 860/564-2298) for burgers, dogs, fish and chips, lobster rolls, and soft-serve ice cream, among other tasty, if not especially good-for-you, treats. **Jason's** 274 Riverside Dr., Rte. 12, Thompson, 860/923-2908, $3–8) is a cute and cheap family-oriented place adjacent to a miniature-golf center; expect to find fried seafood, burgers, ice cream, and the like. **Sweet Evalina's** (688 Rte. 169, North Woodstock, 860/928-4029, under $7) is a nice spot for a light lunch or breakfast.

The **Bar-B-Q-Hut** (1 Mechanics St., Putnam, 860/928-6499, $5–$14) is a simple, almost dowdy, little roadside stand in Putnam with simply delicious barbecue. You order at the counter and will find just a few tables to enjoy your meal. Full dinners come with baked beans, coleslaw, and corn bread. Dinner platters include the honey-lemon chicken, St. Louis–style ribs, spicy wings, and baby back ribs. Several sandwiches are also offered. Peanut-butter pie makes a nice dessert.

At the north end of UConn's campus, **Kathy-John's** (U.S. 44 and Rte. 195, 860/439-0362, $4–7) is an old-fashioned family restaurant, ice-cream parlor, and gift shop (stocked with kids' books, penny candy, toys, and strange little novelties). Sandwiches—like grilled cheese with roasted pepper, or hot corned beef with Swiss cheese, or fried clam strips, or spinach salad—are typical, but the real draw here is ice cream: chocolate-chip cookie ice-cream sandwiches, chocolate raspberry sundaes, malted vanilla shakes, and a particularly evil banana split with five scoops of ice cream and gobs of whipped cream. Loud and rollicking most nights, it's a great place to bring the kids.

Within steps of the antiques shops around Putnam, **Nikki's Dog Place** (35 Main St., 860/928-0252, under $6) is an endearingly simple gray house beside the old train station, with brightly painted picnic tables outside and vinyl booths within. Coney Island–style hot dogs are the favored bill of fare, but don't overlook the greasy but great bacon-mushroom burgers or any of the other hefty sandwiches. **Stoggy Hollow General Store and Restaurant** (860/974-3814, Woodstock) has fine grilled crab cakes with herb-tomato mayo.

In little Willington, the vintage rail station is now a quirky jewelry shop, a historic green-clapboard station right beside the cozy **Track Nine Diner** (12 Tolland Tpke., U.S. 44 near Rte. 32, 860/487-1619, $3–6), a homey family-oriented restaurant with good food, open only for breakfast and lunch. **Traveler's** (1257 Buckley Hwy., Rte. 171, Union, 860/684-4920, $3–10) is a strange little family-style restaurant just off I-84 at the Massachusetts border, serving basic American fare with one interesting perk: every party receives a free used book with the meal.

Not a ramshackle roadside stand oozing with nostalgic charm, the **UConn Dairy Bar** (3636 Horsebarn Rd. ext., 860/486-2634, under $5) is in a rather squat, institutional-looking, redbrick building appended to the rear of the University Animal Sciences center, which you find by turning onto the unnamed road off Rte. 195, marked by a blue "Dairy Products Sales Room" sign. In Pomfret, the **Vanilla Bean Cafe** (450 Deerfield

Rd., 860/928-1562, $8–11) has for years been the favorite place in the Quiet Corner to stop for lunch—there's dining both inside and out, and on warm days, the patio provides a nice setting for a meal. At dinner, popular entrées include smoked mozzarella and basil ravioli, and the bean burritos. **Thread City Cafe** (931 Main St., Willimantic, 860/456-3344, funder $5) is a cute diner, with framed prints of vintage Willimantic on its brick walls, and some counter seating. On weekends it's breakfast only (until 1 P.M.), Tuesday–Friday breakfast and then lunch are served. Chili dogs, blueberry pancakes, omelets, and cheese steaks are among the tasty offerings in this cheerful storefront space in the heart of downtown. Dayville's classic stainless-steel **Zip's Dining Car** (Rtes. 12 and 101, 860/774-6335, $3–9) packs in a never-know-who-you'll-see crowd of locals for home-style diner cooking.

The creative, filling breakfast fare at **Bill's Bread & Breakfast** (5149 Providence St., Putnam, 860/928-9777), a down-home diner-style eatery that's open for three meals, earns raves from locals. In Putnam's antiquing district, **Pickled Pepper Cafe** (172 Main St., 860/963-0401, $4–9) is a quaint little luncheonette, open only for breakfast and lunch. An oft-changing roster of house-made soups and sandwiches makes this a nice break from window-shopping. Head to **Chelle's 1950s-style Car Hop Diner** (107 W. Stafford Rd., Rte. 190, Stafford Springs, 860/684-6622, $3–10) when you're craving great short-order cooking and a touch of retro nostalgia. There's live entertainment some nights.

## Java Joints

**Calabash Coffee Co.** (Rte. 169 and U.S. 6, 860/774-8263) is Brooklyn's favorite little java joint; it occupies what was many years ago the Brooklyn Academy boys' school. There's also an art gallery and gift shop attached. It's a good source for tasty sandwiches, like the one with sliced apples, cheddar cheese, and golden onions, grilled on cinnamon bread, or the smoked turkey with honey mustard and cheddar on honey-whole wheat bread. Mochaccino and chai are among the warm elixirs. A beautiful, relatively new coffeehouse in scenic Woodstock, **Java Jive**

Zip's stainless-steel diner, Dayville

© ANDREW COLLINS

(283 Rte. 169, 860/963-7477), serves up tasty drinks, pastries, and desserts, and also sells exotic gourmet goods, from Russian caviar to fine imported ground coffee. A homey spot with sofas and lounge seating, **Cafe Downtown** (713 Main St., Willimantic, 860/423-7682, under $6) presents an assortment of fresh-made coffees, pastries, crème brûlée, spinach pies, sandwiches, and ice cream.

## Gourmet Goods and Picnic Supplies

In Plainfield, **Rising Moon Natural Foods** (708 Norwich Rd., Rte. 12, 860/564-4811) is a great source of organic foods and other products.

# INFORMATION AND SERVICES
## Visitor Information

For information on the towns in this region, contact the **Southeastern Connecticut Tourism District** (470 Bank St., Box 89, New London, CT 06320, 860/444-2206 or 800/TO-ENJOY, www.mysticmore.com).

## Getting Around

Where major highways are concerned, you can take I-84 from Hartford, exiting in Willington or Union to reach the northeasternmost towns in the region. From the coast, I-395 runs north directly through the region, passing eventually into Worcester, Massachusetts. Other major north–south routes include Rtes. 169 and 97; popular east–west routes include U.S. 6 and 44.

The latter, from the Rhode Island border to I-384 by the Manchester town line, is a pleasing, largely undeveloped drive (except for the stretch through busy Putnam) through pastoral countryside; hardly a traffic light to spoil the ride and nice views along the way.

# Vernon, Manchester, and Environs

Towns like Vernon and Manchester cultivate a fast-growing suburban population, and formerly quiet farming towns like Marlborough and Tolland now contain tract after tract of mostly upper-middle-class residential housing. As far as attractions go, the area has relatively few cultural and historic sites, but there are some nice state parks and a few good recreational opportunities.

## Vernon

Vernon, within whose town limits exists the small industrial city of Rockville, offers a reasonable representation of what you'll find throughout this area: Victorian mills rub elbows with bedroom communities, and shopping-center sprawl competes for space with the town's few remaining farms. There's little to interest the tourist in Vernon proper, but from the center of town (or I-84, if you view it via it), follow Rte. 83 north a couple miles and make a right turn east onto Rte. 74. This takes you east into Rockville—a.k.a. "Loom City," owing to its past as a textiles manufacturing hub.

## Rockville

The Vernon Historical Society distributes an engaging walking tour of the city center. Rockville was incorporated in 1889 as a city within the somewhat pastoral town of Vernon, and it existed expressly in the name of textile production, its mills fueled by the waterpower of the Hockanum River. The first textile factory went up along the banks of the river in 1821; it and the first few that followed made satinet, a "coarse fabric having a cotton wrap and a wool filler," according to a description in the brochure.

In 1841, a loom was introduced to production, thus sparking the creation of fine cassimere and the wools for which the city was best known. In 1864, Florence Mill went up, the first-known example of a Second-Empire–inspired mansard

roof on an industrial building; it's on the National Register. Silk production began in the late 1860s, and from the late 1890s to the turn of the 20th century, production of very fine fabrics peaked—Rockville mills produced the cloth used in the inaugural suits of Presidents William McKinley and Teddy Roosevelt. The five mills here were consolidated into Hockanum Mills in 1906, and closed down for good in 1952. About 13 mill buildings, dating from 1834–1906, still line the river, which drops nearly 300 feet over the course of 1.5 miles. Rockville is quiet today, and many of these mills stand vacant.

As you wander through the center of this once-thriving community, you'll see the imposing George Maxwell Memorial Library, an enormous, impressive structure befitting what was once a substantially larger town. You'll also see massive stone and redbrick churches that seem to touch the sky, a reflection of the prosperity these mills brought to Rockville—no doubt evidence that local citizens realized their houses of worship should not be dwarfed by their places of business, the hulking mills.

## Tolland

Continue east for several miles along Rte. 74 to reach one of eastern central Connecticut's best-preserved Colonial villages, Tolland. Close as it is to Hartford, this former county seat of Tolland County retains an air of tranquillity, especially around its classic long and narrow town green—the anchor of a historic district comprising about 50 structures. Beyond the green lie wooded hills that have been developed residentially quite a bit since the 1980s, but which remain for the most part rural in character. The town is bereft of shopping plazas and commercial development.

Absent of the statuary and formal landscaping that mark many Connecticut town greens, Tolland's is rather a purist's common. Although the planners laid out the town in 1715, most of the historic buildings of note date from the late 18th through the late 19th centuries, when the county seat moved to neighboring Rockville. Lining the green are the former Tolland County Courthouse (1822) and town jail (1785), the former Tolland County Bank (ca. 1830), a country store where you can buy penny candy and Colonial-inspired bric-a-brac, and many fine examples of Victorian, Federal, and Georgian architecture.

The former courthouse now contains the Tolland Genealogical Library and the French Canadian Genealogical Society.

The **Old Jail Museum** (52 Tolland Green, 860/870-9599, open mostly on Wed. and Sun. in summer, and by appointment) functioned as the county jail 1856–1969—note that thick iron bars still guard the windows. You can tour the cells these days, getting an intriguing sense of what it would have been like to be incarcerated here. Other displays show early farming and household implements, Indian artifacts, and historic photos.

A few doors down, the **Hicks-Stearns Museum** (42 Tolland Green, 860/875-7552, open afternoons Sun. and Wed. mid-May–mid-Oct.) combines several architectural styles. It opened as an inn in the 1700s, but a variety of Victorian elements were added to the house throughout the 19th century, including Tudor details and a three-story tower. The house now contains family possessions of the occupants of the home.

The **Daniel Benton Homestead Museum** (Metcalf Rd., 860/872-8673, open afternoons Sun. mid-May–mid-Oct.) is a couple miles south of the Tolland Green. This ancient homestead contains great examples of Early American furnishings, plus five fireplaces and timber walls joined by original wooden pegs. The grounds are laced with stone walls, peaceful footpaths, and old apple trees.

## Manchester

From Tolland, retrace your steps to Rockville and turn south on Rte. 31, making a right turn onto U.S. 44, which leads to Manchester. Along the way, you'll pass through the still largely rural town of Bolton, south of which are the similarly agrarian communities of Hebron (reached via Rte. 85 to Rte. 94) and Andover (reached via U.S. 6). These three towns have no formal museums or attractions per se, but each has a handful of farms open to the public—complete with farm shops and pick-your-own crops, plus excellent and quite scenic terrain for country driving and bicycling.

There's also great hiking and other outdoors fun to be had at historic **Gay City Park** (Rte. 85, 860/424-3200), the entrance of which is at the Bolton-Hebron town line (parts of the park also extend into Glastonbury to the west). This is a hilly park, set along the ridge defining the eastern slope of the Connecticut River Valley; several trails (ranging 1.5–5 miles) span the park, many of them crossing the Blackledge River. Some run by an old mill and dam site, and by a small beach with swimming.

Back at U.S. 44, continue west from Bolton until you enter the cultural heart of this area, Manchester. This city of about 56,000 has an impressive-looking downtown that's part of the Manchester Main Street Historic District, a collection of mostly brick buildings dating from the early part of this century, and including some rather dramatic facades, many with classical design influences. This stretch of Main lies mostly below U.S. 44, and includes a few businesses that have been serving the town since the early 20th century, including Manchester Hardware and Bray Jeweler. Downtown Manchester has a pleasant, all-American feel to it; it's not overly cutesy, but it's also fairly free from the chain shops and overdevelopment that typify the section of town out by I-84.

The name Cheney dominates Manchester's history, as it was noted clockmaker Timothy Cheney who established a homestead in the town's south end in 1784. It was his five grandsons who began the Cheney Brothers Silk Manufacturing Company in this part of town in the 1840s. The Cheneys built many grand redbrick textile mills

> *In 1841, a loom was introduced to production, thus sparking the creation of fine cassimere and the wools for which Rockville was best known.*

and were responsible for the prosperity of Manchester for many decades and for creating much of its private and municipal infrastructure. They also constructed a compound of mansions set around Park Street. You can visit the **Cheney Homestead** (106 Hartford Rd., 860/643-5588, www.manchesterhistory.org/cheneyhomestead.htm), which contains engravings, portraits, and quilts made from Cheney silk. A restored 18th-century schoolhouse is on the premises (open 10 A.M.–3 P.M. Fri.–Sun., $2). The museum is one part of the impressive **Manchester Historical Society** (126 Cedar St., 860/647-9983), whose headquarters incorporate the Old Manchester Museum (open 9 A.M.–noon Mon. and 1–4 P.M. Sun., $2). The museum is filled with artifacts and changing exhibits, as well as a number of historic buildings around town, including the 18th-century Keeney Schoolhouse (same hours as Cheney Homestead, admission included with Cheney Homestead). The society also gives tours of the historic Cheneyville section of town, which includes several of these buildings.

A couple of the attractions in downtown Manchester work well if you've got kids with you. The **Fire Museum** (230 Pine St., 860/649-9436, www.thefiremuseum.org) is in the 1901 Manchester Fire House. Exhibits include early leather fire buckets from Colonial times, hand-pulled engines, and old prints and lithographs of fires. The museum is a couple of miles west of Main St., off Hartford Rd. (open 10 A.M.–5 P.M. Fri.–Sat., noon–5 P.M. Sun., mid-Apr.–mid-Nov., $4). Also consider the **Lutz Children's Museum** (247 S. Main St., 860/643-0949, www.lutzmuseum.org, open 9 A.M.–5 p.m. Tues.–Fri., noon–5 P.M. weekends, $4); highlights include a hall of live animals, a picnic area, and interactive learning exhibits.

In the northwestern end of town, near the East Hartford border, both kids and adults appreciate the many activities available at **Wickham Park** (1329 W. Middle Tpke., U.S. 44/6, 860/528-0856), the estate of Clarence W. Wickham, an early Manchester industrialist. The park consists of 215 acres of gardens, woodland, meadows, and ponds. Shaded picnic groves, flower gardens, tennis courts, softball diamonds, fitness

trails, and other free sporting facilities are available. You can while away a pretty afternoon strolling the 10 acres of ornamental gardens, statuary, and bridges, or visit the aviary that's home to some 50 native and exotic birds. There's also a cedar log cabin sitting on the park's highest point, whose front lawn boasts views of Hartford and five other area towns.

The eastern half of Manchester ascends the eastern wall of the Connecticut River Valley; this is especially obvious if you have the chance to climb I-384 en route to Bolton. There are some remarkable natural features on this eastern upland side of town. Birch Mountain is one of the more dramatic spots and encompasses **Case Mountain Park.** Bikers and hikers can follow a trail to the top of the mountain, crossing Birch Mountain Brook and a rather striking dam (it's across the street from an old redbrick mill and close to some grand old estates. Parking for the trail is off Spring Street, just opposite the turn to Glen Road. There's also a back way to the mountain, with the trailhead just off of Birch Mountain Road (on the right-hand side, a short way after turning onto the road from Camp Meeting Road, just beyond the I-384 underpass).

## SHOPPING

Off I-84 is the massive **Buckland Hills Mall** (exit 62 from I-84 or the Tolland Tpke. exit from I-291, Manchester, 860/644-6369, www.bucklandhills.com), which serves the eastern side of greater Hartford and virtually the entire eastern and northern quadrant of the state. A bit less glamorous than Westfarms Mall in West Hartford, Buckland is fairly run-of-the-mall and includes such anchors as Lord & Taylor, Filene's, JCPenney, Dick's Clothing and Sporting Goods, and Sears. This retail citadel sits high on a bluff with views of the Hartford skyline. Downtown Manchester also has a lot of great old stores and restaurants. This is one of those dry-goods stores famous for its tremendously varied selection—if it exists, they appear to have it here.

If the stagnant air and artificial lighting of indoor mega-malls get you down, drop by the **Marlborough Country Barn** (N. Main St., Rte.

66, 860/295-8231 or 800/852-8893), a quaint (in the legitimate sense of the word) retail village of Colonial buildings housing about a dozen home-furnishing and decorative shops, plus a restaurant. Braided rugs, four-poster beds, Windsor chairs, and holiday wreaths galore.

**Fish Family Farm** (20 Dimlock Lane, Rte. 85, just off exit 85 of I-384, Bolton, 860/646-9745) is one of state's most popular publicly accessible farms—one of the few dairy farms that milks its own cows and pasteurizes and bottles its own milk. A long winding drive leads past a gracious manor house to a handsome hip-gambrel–roofed white dairy barn. Inside, a small shop sells delicious homemade ice cream (by the quart, or cones on weekends); there are also fresh herbs, some produce, and a few other gourmet items. Kids enjoy the food and the self-guided tour of the facility, where you can watch the cows being milked. Also in Bolton, the **Liberty Candle Company** (263 Boston Pike, U.S. 44, 860/649-3822) produces fragrant, scented candles of all shapes, colors, and sizes—there are about 70 fragrances in all. Styles include votives; apothecary candles in small, charming jars; and floaters, designed to sit in water. The scents are wide-ranging: butterscotch, eucalyptus, gardenia, maple sugar, and watermelon are a few top sellers.

Three generations have operated the **Hurst Farm and Country Store** (746 East St., Andover, 860/646-6536), which differs a bit from many farms around the state. The 36 acres are maintained with old-fashioned, antique equipment. The shop here, open year-round, sells fresh-fruit preserves, horticultural goods, home-canned foods, herbs, maple syrup, and fresh honey. In late winter, folks come to watch the maple syrup being made. The Hursts also added formal gardens in spring 2000, so you can tour them while visiting the farm.

In Andover, make the trip to **Black Iron Ventures** (214 Bear Swamp Rd., 860/742-9080), a fascinating place that crafts horse-drawn carriages and wagons, but is also a favorite site of weddings and events. The farm offers hayrides and sleigh rides seasonally, horse-drawn tours of nearby Nutmeg Vineyards in Coventry. Elegant black Percheron, draft horses lead the tours. So, whether or not you're actually in the market for a new carriage, this farm set in lovely woodland makes for a fun visit.

## ENTERTAINMENT AND NIGHTLIFE

Most of the folks in this area hit the bars, clubs, theaters, and performing arts halls of Hartford when seeking an after-dark scene. However, don't overlook the **Little Theatre of Manchester** (Cheney Hall, 177 Hartford Rd., 860/647-9824, www.cheneyhall.org), an 1860s structure created by the fortunes of the great Cheney silk-producing family. Folk, jazz, classical, and other musical programs are presented here throughout the year, and tours of this oldest operating theater in the state are given by appointment.

## FESTIVALS AND EVENTS

Hebron hosts a popular **Harvest Fair** (Lion's Park, Rte. 85, 860/228-9403) with games, entertainment, rides, and the usual aggie fair festivities; it's in early September. Later that month, artists and craftspeople display their wares at the **Creative Arts Festival** (Blish Memorial Park at Lake Terramuggus, 860/295-9162), where you'll also see live music, dance, and theatrical performances. Late in October, there's a **Crafts Fair** (Manchester Community-Technical College, 60 Bidwell St., 860/647-6137) in Manchester. Get a head start on your holiday shopping in late November at the **Annual Christmas Fair** (St. Maurice Church, 32 Hebron Rd., Bolton, 860/643-4466).

## ACCOMMODATIONS

Quite a few chain motels and inviting B&Bs dot this region, making it a nice strategic base from which to explore both the hills and the river valley—even downtown Hartford is only a 10-minute drive from properties in Manchester and Vernon.

### Hotels

**$100–$150:** The **Clarion Suites Inn** (191 Spencer St., just off I-384, Manchester, 860/643-

5811 or 877/424-6423) offers clean, bright condo-style units with plenty of space, making it a perfect spot for families. The deluxe suites have fireplaces and pull-out sofas, so they sleep four (and cost only $10 per person extra, beyond the standard double-occupancy rate). The decorating is not especially memorable—mirrors and pastels are used to increase the sense of space—but neither is the look unpleasant. There's an exercise room and outdoor pool, and a daily breakfast buffet is included in the rates, as is dinner Monday–Thursday. This is really an ideal base, whether you're visiting the eastern hills or nearby Hartford.

A great alternative is the **Courtyard Marriott Manchester** (225 Slater St., 860/533-8484 or 800/321-2211), which is near Buckland Hills Mall. It has 90 rooms, a restaurant, and a slew of business amenities. Ideal for longer stays, the relatively new **Residence Inn Hartford/Manchester** (201 Hale Rd., 860/432-4242 or 800/331-3131) has 96 spacious suites with separate living and sleeping areas, fully equipped kitchens, plus an outdoor pool, hot tub, and exercise room. Buckland Hills Mall and its many good restaurants are very close by.

**$50–100:** A very nice **Holiday Inn Express** (346 Kelly Rd., Vernon, 860/648-2000 or 800/HOLIDAY), off Rte. 83, has 63 clean, quite contemporary rooms, and a setting just off I-84 that's not especially pleasant, but is close to area attractions and a short drive from Hartford. A plus is that it's on the edge of the shopping center sprawl around the intersection of Rtes. 30 and 83 (as opposed to being directly in the center of it). As with all Holiday Inn Express hotels, the rates include a free Continental buffet breakfast, morning paper, local phone calls, and other handy amenities. The 69-room **Comfort Inn** (425 Hartford Tpke., Rte. 30, Vernon, 860/871-2432 or 800/235-INNS, www.comfortinnvernon.com), despite having rather garish bedspreads, is a safe and comfortable bet with reasonable rates—and it's steps from Lotus and Rein's Deli restaurants.

The **Quality Inn** (51 Hartford Tpke., Rte. 30/83, Vernon, 860/646-5700 or 800/235-INNS) is a dependable, midrange accommodation with a popular steak and seafood restaurant, George's,

and a courteous staff. Rooms are nicer than at some of the chain properties in nearby East Hartford, and cheaper (but smaller) than those in Manchester. There's an outdoor pool, and the hotel is set back off a busy road, so it's not too noisy.

**Under $50:** One of the best budget options in the state, the **Best Value Inn** (400 Tolland Tpke., just off I-84, Manchester, 860/643-1555) has nice new TVs with cable, touch-tone phones, and all the other amenities you might expect, along with tasteful furnishings, soft colors, and new carpeting. There's a Roy Rogers restaurant on the premises, and the staff works hard to keep everything clean and discourage unwanted guests (in other words, it's a family-friendly setting). The only drawback is noise from I-84, but for the price, this one is hard to top.

## Country Inns and Bed-and-Breakfasts

**$100–$150:** The Federal-style **Tolland Inn** (63 Tolland Green, Rte. 195, 860/872-0800, www.tollandinn.com) is the largest of the town's accommodations, with two suites and five double rooms, plus extensive common areas—everywhere there are antiques, walls with hand-stenciling or vintage wallpapering, and homey decorative touches. A honeymoon suite, the Pacific room, contains a spectacular four-poster bed, a two-sided gas fireplace that faces both the bed and the sitting area, and a two-person hot tub. In warm weather you can loll on the rocking chair on the wraparound porch. Breakfast is a big to-do here: it might consist of orange-walnut French toast or oat scones with maple butter. All rooms have private baths and cable TV.

The **Mansion Inn** (139 Hartford Rd., Manchester, 860/646-0453, www.themansioninn-nct.com) occupies the grand 17-room home once owned by Manchester's illustrious Cheney family—it was one of more than a dozen such mansions owned by Cheneys during the heyday. The white 1910 house with Greek Revival details sits on a neatly groomed, tree-shaded property, and contains five guest rooms, each with private bath, working fireplace, phone, cable TV/VCR, electric blanket, and clock radio. Each room is named for the floral pattern of wallpapers that adorns it: Iris, Rose, Ivy, Tulip, and Lilac. The Lilac has an elegant queen sleigh bed and a separate study, while the lavish Rose Suite has both a sitting area and its own porch. The location is ideal as a base for Hartford or heading into the hills east of the Connecticut River Valley.

**50–$100:** The **Jewell Inn** (5 Bolton Rd., Vernon, 860/872-7822, www.jewellinn.com) is one of the region's newer accommodations, although the house itself is a lovely yellow Federal Colonial that dates from 1835. The four rooms are named for gems and are warmly furnished in period style—in the Diamond Room, you'll find handsome maple furniture, a writing desk, lace curtains, and a large bathroom with a pedestal sink. Deep-blue fabrics with rose accents give the Sapphire Room a cool, sophisticated look. All rooms have phones. Breakfast includes sweet-potato pancakes with locally produced maple syrup.

# FOOD

As with lodging, Vernon and Manchester have the bulk of the area's restaurants, including some excellent takes on both Italian and Asian fare. Otherwise, you'll find a lot of fairly basic family restaurants, pizza joints, and whatnot. Bear in mind that Glastonbury, a hub of trendy New American restaurants, fringes this area and is covered in the Food section of the Connecticut River Valley chapter.

## Upscale

**Cavey's** (45 E. Center St., Manchester, 860/643-2751), which was founded in the 1930s but has in no sense lost its sophistication, is actually two restaurants in one. On the lower level is a somewhat formal and traditional French restaurant ($27–36) that presents a fine menu of Gallic specialties, including roast pousson with a fricassee of crayfish, asparagus, and black trumpet mushrooms. Marinated salmon with ginger, Beluga caviar, and a cucumber coulis makes a fine appetizer. A few critics have called it overrated, but most regulars can't get enough of this place. Upstairs is Cavey's Northern Italian component ($16–25), a brighter, lighter, and more casual

space where you might sample chicken piccata with potato gnocchi or grilled Atlantic salmon with spring vegetables, preserved lemon, and horseradish juice. In both spaces, service is friendly and inviting.

An ancient, white, gambrel-roofed house in the center of a quiet (but fast-growing) community, the **Marlborough Tavern** (3–5 E. Hampton Rd., Rte. 66, 860/295-8229, $15–23 in dining room, $7–13 in tavern) also offers two separate dining experiences. In a slightly more formal dining room, dark-wood tables with vases of flowers and deep fireplaces convey an Early American ambience, while a second, still-rustic feeling space presents a lighter menu. On both, you'll find somewhat standard American and Continental fare, such as prime rib, sole Oscar, and veal marsala. Come more for the ambience than to be dazzled by the cuisine.

## Creative but Casual

**Monet's Table** (Rte. 74, Tolland, 860/875-7244, $10–20) is one of relatively few restaurants in this region that actually merits a trip from afar, partly because of its rustic but refined location inside a 1750s brown-clapboard Colonial house, complete with local artwork, fresh flowers, and wide-plank wooden floors, and partly because of the skillfully prepared New American fare. Just over the Tolland line, a few minutes from Rockville, the restaurant makes for a nice lunching venue, when dishes like tequila-grilled shrimp salad and balsamic marinated and grilled portobello mushroom sandwiches with goat cheese and fresh tomatoes keep patrons happy. Typical at dinner is the apricot-glazed duck breast with plums, mushrooms, and roasted garlic, or the peanut noodles with tofu and ginger vegetables.

A bit higher in quaint factor than Marlborough Tavern, **Sadler's Ordinary** (61 N. Main St., Marlborough, 860/295-0006, $7–17) occupies a creaky, red, center-chimney Colonial that's part of the antiques barn complex, with wide-plank floors, Windsor chairs, and a big fireplace. This place is a favorite any time of day, with excellent breakfast burritos and blueberry pancakes, and rest-of-the-day favorites ranging from hearty chicken potpie or salmon cakes, to a more inventive seafood croissant with shrimp, crab, fish, and melted jack cheese and honey-mustard barbecued tuna steak with basmati rice.

## Pizza, Pub Grub, and Seafood

In the spirit of family-style, red-sauce Italian restaurants where the portions are absurdly enormous, **Angellino's** (346 Kelly Rd., Vernon, 860/644-7702, $9–17) serves heaps of tasty kettle-fried sea scallops, calamari marinara, veal saltimbocca, eggplant parmigiana, and pasta with of several kinds of sauce (it's a mix-and-match deal). Whatever you order, you'll probably end up taking some of it home with you. The restaurant is right beside the Holiday Inn Express, decorated with sponged ochre walls and booth seating. **Pagani's Brick Oven Restaurant** (55 E. Center St., Manchester, 860/645-7777, $8–14, $10–15 for large pizzas) serves soul-satisfying large pizzas; the much-loved South-End pie has crushed tomatoes and basil, mozzarella and fontina cheeses, andouille sausage, and jalapeño peppers. Other options include artichoke shrimp scampi, veal scallopine marsala, and mix-and-match pastas. This cheap, simple family-popular restaurant is right by Cavey's, and more than a few folks consider the food here tastier.

**Cheney's** (623 Main St., Manchester, 860/646-5356, www.cheneys.com, $11–20) is a dark and classy Irish pub with brick walls and simple wooden tables with Windsor chairs. The food here is quite good—consider roasted Cornish game hen, butter bean and leek pie, Guinness and oysters, and rosemary pork loin. If you just have the munchies, try one of the tasty starters, such as brie-and-cranberry purses or steamed mussels. The beer list includes Harp, Boddingtons, Ten Penny Ale, and many other imported favorites.

A beautiful restored mill on the Hockanum River, a few minutes' south of Buckland Hills, **Adam's Mill** (165 Adams St., Manchester, 860/646-4039, $12–19) is a popular setting for weddings and parties; it's a huge space, with exposed brick, tall windows, hanging plants, and artifacts from the building's original incarnation (tools and whatnot) hanging on the walls. The menu is as long as the building is big, and both lo-

cals and tourists love this place, more for its ambience than the food, which is fine but geared toward pleasing big crowds. Chicken teriyaki, pork Normandy (grilled and stuffed with apple dressing and served with a light mushroom sauce), and house combinations where you can request two of six potential grill items (sort of a broad variation on surf and turf) are among the featured dishes.

## Asian

**Lotus** (409 Hartford Tpke., Rte. 30, Vernon, 860/871-8962, $10–17) is an anomaly among area Asian restaurants: there's no takeout, the menu describes and names each dish rather than assigning it a number, and the dining room is elegantly decked in pink napery. Prices are also a bit higher than what you might be used to, but Lotus serves some of the most sophisticated Vietnamese fare in Connecticut, including five-spiced Cornish hen, catfish baked in a clay pot, peppered shrimp, and ribs barbecued with honey and lemongrass. **Bombay Raj Mahal** (836–840 Main St., Manchester, 860/646-5330, $7–14) is a pleasant, economical Indian restaurant in downtown Manchester—a cozy and atmospheric space occupying a pair of neighboring storefronts. You might start with the coconut soup or onion fritters, before moving on to shrimp Bengal cooked in a pineapple curry sauce or lamb with a fiery madras tomato curry. An unusual dessert is the *rasmalai*, a ball of farmers cheese in sweetened milk with pistachio nuts.

## Mexican

**Pancho Loco** (218 Talcottville Rd., Rte. 83, Vernon, 860/871-1819, $9–14) presents fairly interesting Mexican food, notably crab (not the imitation kind) and shrimp quesadillas, chicken mole, and a few home-style American dishes like honey-mustard barbecue chicken, Texas-style chili, ribeye steaks, and burgers—the menu goes on and on. It's a modest space near the center of Vernon, arguably the best Mexican in this part of the state. Still, if you want your food spicy, you need to ask. There's live music on Fridays.

## Quick Bites

Many folks driving from Massachusetts down through Connecticut on I-84 make it a point to stop at the regionally famous Jewish deli **Rein's** (435 Hartford Tpke., Vernon, 860/875-1344, www.reinsdeli.com, $3–10). It's a lot like the famous delis of Manhattan's Lower East Side—places like Katz's Delicatessen and 2nd Avenue Deli—except that at Rein's, the staff won't bark at you or give you dirty looks for taking your time ordering. And, there's a bright spacious dining room with table service, and a full bar behind that. Otherwise, expect beautiful sandwiches, like the Boston Harbor, with whitefish salad, nova lox, lettuce, tomato, and Spanish onion, or a turkey-pastrami Reuben whose meat is so fresh and tender it will bring tears to your eyes. Sides like chopped herring salad, borscht, cheese blintzes, bagels with sturgeon and cream cheese, cheddar fries, and thick dill pickles round out the selection. For dessert, note the cheesecakes from the famed S&S bakery in Manhattan, or pick up a box of cinnamon-nut rugalach. Breakfast dishes are also served any time. Rein's is a destination in and of itself.

People trek to **Shady Glen** (840 E. Middle Tpke., Manchester, 860/649-4245, under $6), a perky redbrick building on the east side of town, from all over the land. It looks like a prototype for Friendly's, but serves much, much better food: burgers and fresh-made ice cream (try the tasty pumpkin in fall). The waiters wear old-fashioned white uniforms with endearingly (and embarrassingly) old-fashioned soda-jerk hats.

**Cafe On Main** (985 Main St., 860/647-7444, $3–8) is a cute spot for breakfast or lunch; this simple and affordable spot is on Manchester's bustling Main Street. It's also popular as a coffeehouse. **Natural Rhythms** (764 Main St., Manchester, 860/645-9898, $4–7) open only for lunch, is a bright and cheerful storefront dining room that serves creative vegetarian fare. The eggplant pocket has roasted eggplant, roasted peppers, organic mozzarella, and lettuce), and a delicious cucumber gyro in spinach-feta flatbread overflows with chopped cukes, tomatoes, scallions, and a dill dressing on spinach feta flatbread. The soups are great, too.

## Gourmet Goods and Picnic Supplies

For great biscotti and fresh breads, visit **Iuliano's Bakery** (207 Spruce St., 860/643-7956), which has been a fixture in downtown Manchester since the 1920s. Almost an antidote to the several farm stands and fruit markets lining U.S. 6 in Bolton, **Munson Chocolates** (U.S. 6, Bolton, 860/649-7209 or 800/321-7008, www.munsonschocolates.com) is a showroom of sweets, from fresh peanut-butter-cup fudge to every variety of truffle imaginable. It's very difficult to poke your nose into this spacious shop and leave without less than a pound of chocolates. This is the original of a growing chain that has been around since 1946; it also does a brisk Internet (www.munsonchocolates.com) and mail-order business. Anyone who thinks that Connecticut's only serious Polish food is found in Hartford or New Britain needs to check out Vernon's **Unicorn Polish Bakery** (378 Kelly Rd., 860/645-7322). It's a great source of both sweet and savory breads, cakes and pastries, butter cookies, and imported Polish groceries and sundries—candies, jams, sauces, newspapers, magazines. Homemade Polish sausages are also sold here.

## INFORMATION AND SERVICES
### Visitor Information
The towns in this region are served by the **Greater Hartford Tourism District** (31 Pratt St., 4th Fl., Hartford, CT 06103, 860/244-8181 or 800/793-4480, www.enjoyhartford.com).

### Getting Around
From Hartford, I-84 cuts through this region, and I-384 branches off into Manchester before intersecting with U.S. 44 in Bolton. Limited-access Rte. 2 also cuts across the southwestern corner of this area.

# Norwich and Casino Country

There's little question that the high-profile casinos of Foxwoods and Mohegan Sun have put Norwich and the surrounding area on the map. Before these places opened, most people associated these towns with greater New London and Mystic, which are a short drive to the south. The casinos, however, don't especially shed light on the area's history and what it looks and feels like today.

Norwich is a tough little port city that has worked extremely hard in recent years to turn itself around—a familiar story, of course, throughout Connecticut. But you can really sense the potential in Norwich when you consider the truly remarkable cache of both residential and commercial architecture, dating from Colonial times until the city began to slip following World War II. The solid middle-class towns surrounding Norwich have historically based their economics on farming and milling, just as other towns in the eastern hills have. In Salem and Colchester, you're likely to see horse farms, while gritty blue-collar communities like Occum and Taftville contain the remnants of riverside redbrick factories.

## Norwich

In 1659, settlers from Old Saybrook established Norwich at the head of the Thames River, near the confluence of the Yantic and Shetucket Rivers—inland about 15 miles from Long Island Sound. Before a bridge was built in the early–20th century, connecting Groton with New London, all coastal transport had to jog inland through Norwich to get around the Thames, which is quite wide from Norwich south to the sound. Taking advantage of this strategic position and a deep waterway capable of accommodating sizable ships, residents built a wharf in the 1680s in what is now Chelsea, the port section of the city. Prosperity followed almost immediately, and by the American Revolution this was the state's second-largest and wealthiest port (after New Haven).

Evidence of Norwich's prosperity lies in the many mansions north of downtown, in the Norwich-town section, where wealthy merchants

settled in significant numbers. The town developed further prominence with the advent of steamship travel in 1817, and then the construction in 1835 of the Norwich & Worcester Railroad. Steamships transported passengers from Norwich to New York City during the 19th and early 20th centuries, further securing the city's prominence. Three large hotels opened downtown near the wharf and the railway, and neighboring towns like Preston City and Taftville grew to become important textile manufacturing centers, their goods sent by ship or by rail through Norwich. In the mid-19th century, only New Haven and Hartford exceeded Norwich in population in Connecticut.

By the turn of the 20th century, industry had begun to die a bit in Norwich, particularly with the construction of the bridge from Groton to New London, which allowed trains and automobiles to bypass the city. Downtown remained somewhat prosperous for a few more decades, but the Depression set in deeply here, and Norwich has struggled since that time.

During the 1990s, residents hoped the area casinos would give the city a boost, either directly or indirectly. But up to this point there has been more tension than cooperation between residents and the two tribes that control the Mohegan Sun and Foxwoods casinos. It's also unclear to what degree the presence of the casinos has drawn visitors into Norwich itself—it appears they've had little positive effect, at least to this point. Fortunately, the city planners have worked hard in recent years to promote existing assets, especially the abundance of fine architecture, and to develop new attractions.

In addition to those described below, at press time there were a few other attractions planned for Norwich. A new Civil War museum will be set inside the restored home of Connecticut's governor during the Civil War, William A. Buckingham. And the old Central Fire Station is slated to become the Norwich Fire Equipment Museum, which will house one of the most comprehensive collections of antique fire equipment and memorabilia in existence. A final development will be the Heritage Center at Chelsea, where interactive high-tech exhibits will let visitors explore the role the area's rivers played in Norwich's industrial boom. It will also be the main information center, where visitors can find out about exhibits and collections at other museums in the area.

Today's Norwich, with a population of 36,500, is a mix of classes, races, and ethnicities. Hilly downtown is filled with wonderful old buildings, although many of them have difficulty attracting suitable tenants. Although it's somewhat

undervisited, Norwich has plenty going for it, especially in the way of museums, which are free of some of the crowds you might encounter down on the coast, in Mystic.

You can get a good sense of the city by beginning in Chelsea nearby the harbor, at **Howard T. Brown Memorial Park** (860/886-6363), a picturesque lawn with a gazebo near one of the deepest points in the Thames. Right next to the park is a marina, and several local festivals and events are held here each year. The Norwich Office of Tourism is right nearby, and up the hill along Broadway you'll come to the rather deca-

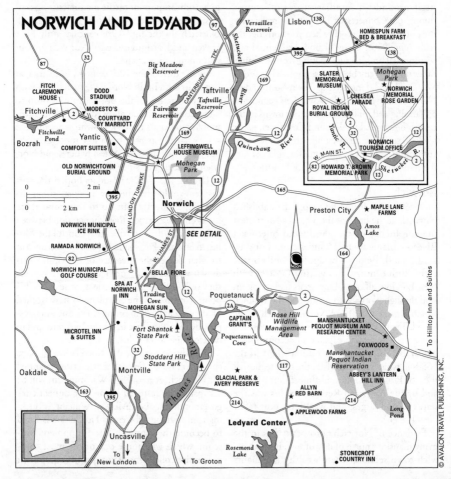

NORWICH AND LEDYARD

dent **Norwich City Hall,** which went up in 1873, back when the city had no shortage of funds—the Second Empire building cost $250,000, and that's without the four-sided clock tower that was added in 1909. Much of the interior contains original furnishings and architectural details from the Victorian era.

Norwich Tourism Council produces a handful of excellent brochures detailing the town's sites and describing the architecture and points of interest in several historic neighborhoods. The "Broadway & Union Street" tour is 1.5 miles past the mostly late-Victorian homes of mill owners and successful merchants. It extends in a loop from the south side of Chelsea Parade down Broadway and then along parallel Union Street into downtown and beside the harbor, and then works you back up along Broadway to around the Norwich Free Academy. The tour discusses the major Norwich industries during the city's boom years, firearms (especially during the Civil War) and textiles. While you can't enter most of the nearly 30 homes and buildings along this tour, the brochure gives an exceptionally well-researched commentary on the history and architecture of each one.

The "Washington & Broad Streets" tour is 1.25 miles and takes you through the neighborhood immediately west of that covered in the "Broadway & Union Street" tour. You begin on Washington Street (up where Broadway intersects it), walk south several blocks, make a right on Broad and follow it to Broadway, and then retrace your steps, finishing at the Chelsea Parade. As with the neighboring tour, many of the buildings along this walk are mansions built during the city's 19th-century industrial heyday, but quite a few notable examples of both late-18th-century and 20th-century architecture are also identified. Washington Street was particularly fashionable among the owners of mills along the Yantic River, which is just a couple blocks west. Along this loop tour you'll also pass beside the historic marker that notes the site of Benedict Arnold's birthplace, the infamous Revolutionary War turncoat who hailed from Norwich.

The triangular **Chelsea Parade,** which figures prominently in each of the aforementioned

tours, was established in 1797 as a public green, and from its earliest days it has served as a venue for military functions (hence the name "parade"). It's a nice spot to sit and enjoy the grand homes lining the streets bordering it, and contemplate the extensive collection of war memorials—11 in all, ranging from the *USS Maine* monument to the POW-MIA memorial that was placed here in 1992.

Overlooking Chelsea Parade is the **Slater Memorial Museum** (108 Crescent St., Norwich, 860/887-2506, www.norwichfreeacademy.com/slater_museum, open 9 A.M.–4 P.M. Tues.–Fri., 1–4 P.M. weekends, $3), a Romanesque-Revival, 1886, mansion that contains a fascinating array of artifacts and art bequeathed by various estates over the years—the prosperous legacy of Norwich is well-preserved here. Apollo, Julius Caesar, Nike, Venus de Milo, and Hermes are among the 150 plaster-cast replicas of famous classical statuary. You'll also find impressive collections of African, Egyptian, and Asian art; a gun collection; and a textiles exhibit—plus Early American furnishings, American paintings, and Native American, African, Oriental, and European art. There are also changing exhibitions in the adjoining Converse Art Gallery, which was built in 1906. The museum is on the campus of the **Norwich Free Academy,** a privately endowed but public high school—the second largest high school in the state. It's also the only public high school in America with an art museum on its grounds. The school has offered free education since it opened in 1856.

There are fine houses on each side of the academy's campus, and the **Royal Indian Burial Ground** (Sachem St., Rte. 32) is just off the parade's southwest corner, across Washington Street. Follow Sachem Street west from the green, and make a left onto Sherman Street to reach Yantic Falls and the Heritage Walkway. Here you have access to a 1.8-mile walkway from the Upper Falls of the Yantic River down to where it flows into the Thames River, right at Brown Park and Norwich Harbor. The waterfalls and old Power House—now a small museum at the northern terminus of the trail—mark the origins of the city's industrial history, as a gristmill was first developed at this fast-moving point in the river in the late 1600s.

A few hundred yards south of Slater Museum, turn east onto Mohegan Park Road to reach 385-acre **Mohegan Park** (860/823-3759), one of Connecticut's great urban sanctuaries. Most of the park is wooded hilly terrain, well suited for a brisk walk along one of the many trails. But you will also find a small petting zoo, playing fields, picnic areas with grills, and the beloved **Norwich Memorial Rose Garden,** a two-acre plot with some 120 varieties of roses (about 2,500 bushes). Norwich has been called the rose of New England, as it's situated on five hills, which have been compared to the five petals of a wild rose, and so this garden is really a symbol of the city's local pride. The most exciting thing about Mohegan, however, will soon be the Chelsea Botanical Gardens, a 50-acre haven of plant life patterned after the famous Butchart Gardens in Victoria, British Columbia.

Somewhat longer is the "Norwichtown" tour, which is 2.5 miles and takes about 90 minutes to walk. Norwichtown is the neighborhood north of the Chelsea Parade, where the town of Norwich was first settled in the mid-1600s, when James Fitch and John Mason purchased an 81-square-mile tract of land from the indigenous Mohegan Indians. Here at the heart of the settlement, three houses from 1660 still stand, and many others built over the next 150 years have been neatly preserved. Many of the buildings sit around the old Norwichtown Green, including the First Congregational Church, where the tour begins, before looping around this neighborhood. The church is the fifth in a succession of meetinghouses that have stood on this spot since 1660 (the current one dates from 1801).

Here, the **Leffingwell House Museum** (348 Washington St., Norwich, 860/889-9440, open Fri.–Sun. mid-May–Oct. and by appointment, $5) preserves the legacy of one of Connecticut's great early industrialists and merchants, Christopher Leffingwell, who operated a paper mill along the Yantic River. From an architectural standpoint, this is one of America's most interesting early homes. The core of the house was built in 1675 by Stephen Backus, but in 1701, owner Thomas Leffingwell added to the house to make it suitable for innkeeping. Thomas's descendant, Christopher Leffingwell, owned the inn by the time of the American Revolution, during which he played a vital role helping to supply the troops of the Continental Army with various goods. Inside the house today are numerous examples of Early American furnishings, including clocks and works of silver. As you walk among the rooms, note how those that were part of the original differ from the still extremely old addition. The Tavern Room, part of the original, still contains original wood paneling, along with furnishings that date mostly from the early 1700s.

Walk a short way north to reach the **Samuel Huntington House** (34 E. Town St.), which was built by the noted Colonial statesman in 1783 (although it's been remodeled extensively over the years). Huntington was a member of the first Continental Congress of 1776—he was later elected president of this body, and some historians argue therefore that he was truly America's first president. He signed the Declaration of Independence, and served as governor of Connecticut for 10 years prior to his death in 1796. The house is now private. Nearby, The **Old Norwichtown Burial Ground,** off Lee Street, contains the headstones of many prominent early Norwich residents.

Head northeast from downtown via Rte. 169 to reach the Taftville section of town, which is known for the old Ponemah Mills that once thrived here—during its existence this was believed to be the largest cotton mill in the world.

## Mohegan Sun

Just south of Norwich in Uncasville, **Mohegan Sun** (Rte. 2A, exit 79A from I-395, 860/204-7163 or 888/226-7711, www.mohegansun.com) is the newest casino complex in the state, which—thanks to an knock-your-socks-off expansion completed in 2002—competes favorably with Foxwoods, and has helped turn this region into a mini Las Vegas. Here at this 24-hour facility, which has two huge gaming areas, you'll find nearly 300,000 square feet of gaming (part of it non-smoking). The casino has 6,000 slot machines, 120 blackjack tables, a

1,400-seat bingo hall, and a 20,000-square-foot race book with hundreds of TV monitors showing various races and games around the country (including jai alai in Milford). There's also a 10,000-square-foot children's area called Kids Quest, where young'uns can frolic and play under the watchful eyes of child-care professionals.

The squat-looking building occupies a prime piece of land on the west bank of the Thames River. There are several restaurants (including a large food court beneath a massive atrium) and bars, an Indian-themed promenade of shops, and live entertainment—call for info on upcoming acts; past performers have included Anita Baker, Duran Duran, Tony Bennett, and Luther Vandross, plus several world-class boxing spectacles.

The 2002 expansion added a 34-story, 1,200-room hotel whose upper floors have views clear to Long Island Sound; a 175,000-square-foot shopping mall; a 10,000-seat arena; and, of course, more gaming space. This move will surely inspire Foxwoods to add to *its* already enormous casino compound, and it has given Mohegan Sun its first hotel. Up to this point, Foxwoods had the state's only casino-hotel rooms. In the opinion of many, Foxwoods and Mohegan Sun have—for better or for worse—helped southeastern Connecticut to eclipse Atlantic City as the East Coast's premier gaming destination.

## Foxwoods

From Mohegan Sun, continue east on Rte. 2A a few miles to reach **Foxwoods** (Rte. 2, Ledyard, 860/885-3000 or 800/FOXWOODS, www.foxwoods.com), whose hotel towers rise up out of the otherwise sleepy southeastern Connecticut countryside. This property was the first of the state's two casinos to grow to a size and prestige on par with the largest casino resorts in America—it's a gaming, dining, entertainment, and hotel complex on par with anything in Las Vegas. It's amazing that the whole place remains fairly tasteful, given its size and the opportunities that exist to make it tacky. An enormous amount of money has gone into this mega-casino, and the investment continues to pay huge dividends, even though the glitzy expansion at Mohegan Sun has stolen some of Foxwoods's thunder.

Between the two casinos, at the Mashantucket Pequot Reservation—off Rte. 2, about 1.5 miles west of Foxwoods—the **Mashantucket Pequot Museum and Research Center** (110 Pequot Trail, 860/396-6838 or 800/411-9671, www.pequotmuseum.org, open 9 A.M.–5 P.M. daily with last admission at 4 P.M., $15) opened to considerable acclaim a few years ago. The entrance of this magnificent facility sits beneath a 185-foot observation tower on a ridge in Ledyard. State-of-the-art exhibits that, frankly, blow away many of those found in the majority of New England's staid and traditional history museums, open the doors to the 10,000-year history of indigenous life in this part of the world. As you enter the museum, an escalator carries you deep into a re-created 18,000-year-old glacial crevasse, to a life-size mastodon exhibit, and through a 16th-century Pequot village with dozens of life-size characters. Computer exhibits throughout the museum have touch-screen graphics and videos, and an epic film interprets the great Pequot War of the 1630s. There's also a 150,000-volume research library that provides information on native peoples throughout North America, as well as on conservation and archaeology—the library also contains artifacts and art from throughout the ages. A children's library has about 10,000 titles, and other services include a storytelling and activity room, a full-service restaurant, and a 6,000-square-foot museum shop. Of course, a drawback is that this facility has the highest admission cost of any museum in the state, and possibly in New England.

## Preston City

From the casino, drive east a short distance, making a left (north) turn onto Rte. 164, which leads into Preston City, a pretty little rural village near Ledyard with a pair of historic districts. Poquetanuck Village served as a small manufacturing center as early as the late 17th century, and a handful of buildings here date to this period. A later development is the Hallville Historic District, which reveals evidence of the town's industrial history throughout the later part of the 19th century, when a massive woolen mill thrived here. The mill, which has undergone several additions over the years, still stands, as do many of the original mill workers' houses.

## Voluntown

Continue from Preston City east about seven miles into Voluntown, which was established by "volunteer" soldiers who defended the Connecticut Colony in King Philip's War. It is notable primarily for the 24,000-acre **Pachaug State Forest,** the largest such tract in the entire state. It also encompasses **Green Falls Recreation Area,** where you'll find 35 miles of hiking and bridle trails, extensive picnic and camping sites, a lake with a boat launch, fishing, and great swimming. The official entrance to the forest is off Rte. 49, and admission is $5 per car for residents, $8 for nonresidents.

## Lisbon

From Voluntown, drive west along Rte. 138 for about 10 miles until you come to the southern end of the 32-mile stretch of Rte. 169 that was made a National Scenic Byway in 1996. The village of Libson broke from Norwich in 1718. Then called Newent, it was incorporated and renamed Lisbon in 1786, allegedly as a tribute to the Portuguese port city with which area traders executed considerable business in the Colonial days. A worthwhile stop is the **John Bishop House Museum** (Rtes. 169 and 138, 860/376-6866, seasonal hours, free), which is administered by the local historical society. The 1810 farmhouse incorporates characteristics of both

## THE LORE OF CONNECTICUT TOWN NAMES

The name of Voluntown has a rather odd origin; one that you could probably guess if you thought about it for a second or two. Yes, Voluntown was established by volunteers. Local military figures Thomas Leffingwell and John Frink served their colony, voluntarily, in the various Indian battles of the 1660s and 1670s, which culminated in King Philip's War. In 1696, the two men petitioned Hartford for compensation—namely, some land. The original Volunteers Town, as the six-square-mile plantation was first known, was incorporated as Voluntown in 1721. As you might expect, Voluntown today has a loyal and dedicated volunteer fire department.

The neighboring community of Sterling broke off from Voluntown and incorporated separately in 1794, taking its name from a prominent resident, Dr. John Sterling. So loved was he by the townspeople that they named the community after him—though he sweetened the deal by promising that if the town were named for him, he'd build it a big, beautiful library. In the event, Sterling failed to hold up his end; the library was finally completed with funds accrued after months of soliciting private donors.

It's fitting that the first president of the United States should have dozens of towns and villages named for him, and indeed there's a Washington, Connecticut, right in the heart of Litchfield County. It was the first community to honor Washington in such a way—in fact, so impressed were its citizens with the acclaimed statesman and general that they named their town for him while he was still alive. But wait: Samuel Huntington, of Norwich, the elected president of the Continental Congress when the Articles of Confederation went into effect in 1781, was according to many interpreters of U.S. history the new nation's first true president. How many towns are named after him? Alas, none are, at least officially. The town of Huntington was named for him when it was incorporated, but many years later the citizens voted to change the name to Shelton, after a local industrialist. The town did this not because Shelton had promised to build the town a library, but because he had already succeeded in developing a series of mills that had turned Huntington into an industrial powerhouse.

Meanwhile, the name of Huntington's neighboring community, Trumbull, remains in effect as a tribute to Jonathan Trumbull, Sr., of Lebanon. Trumbull was Connecticut's governor during the Revolutionary War, and the only governor in the New World to side with the patriots.

Speaking of Lebanon, you could color in a good bit of the world map by shading all the countries and cities that share their names with communities in Connecticut. Of course, dozens of towns took the Federal and Georgian periods, and is notable for its indoor well and attic smoke chamber.

This part of the state is gradually becoming a hub of winemaking (see the Connecticut Coast chapter for additional vineyards in Stonington and Clinton), and one of the more popular such facilities is Lisbon's **Heritage Trail Vineyards** (291 N. Burnham Hwy., 860/376-0659, www.heritagetrail.com), which offers free tastings and tours Friday–Sunday. The six-acre property consists of an 18th-century farmhouse, and the tasting room is decorated with period antiques and warmed by a fireplace. During the warmer months you can sip wines on the sundeck overlooking the tranquil grounds. A café is planned for near future.

## Colchester and Salem

To see the largely agrarian towns to the west, drive west along Rte. 2 from Norwich into Colchester, which is notable for its downtown historic district, situated around a large town green. If you stop by the town hall, you can pick up a self-guided tour of historic homes in this district. Drive a short ways southwest of town on Rte. 16 and look for signs that mark the turnoff for **Comstock Bridge,** which was built in 1873 and is one of five remaining covered bridges in the state. Route 85 and the limited-access highway Rte. 11 lead south from Colchester in Salem, which is known for its horse farms.

their names from cities in England—Bristol, Canterbury, Coventry, Cornwall, Kent, Litchfield, New London, Norfolk, Oxford, Stamford, Stratford, Wilton, Woodstock, and many others. But also note such communities as Berlin, Lisbon, and Scotland. Or good old Brooklyn, where you're unlikely to meet anybody with the sort of Brooklyn accent much of the world is accustomed to hearing. And then, of course, there's the city of Cleveland. Ohio, that is. It's named for Moses Cleaveland (the "a" was somehow dropped), who was born in Canterbury but established Cleveland in 1796 (it was not formally incorporated and named for Cleaveland until many years after his death, in 1836).

Bethlehem, Canaan, Goshen, and Sharon are among the many Connecticut town names with biblical associations. But before you guess that these names shed light on the pious nature of the town founders, consider that many were named by land speculators hoping to lure residents. They figured, correctly in many cases, that if you gave a town a name of great biblical prominence, you'd have a much easier time convincing folks to travel to it for the promise of arable land and a balmy climate. In fact, most are in the far northern reaches of Litchfield County, a harsh terrain of rocky ledges and fierce winters. So much for truth in advertising.

Have a sense of déjà vu when you cross into the Litchfield County town of Warren? Maybe it's because you've traveled too much already throughout New England. Warren is the only incorporated town name that appears in all six New England states.

Some things take their names from Connecticut towns, for better or for worse. Take Lyme disease, for instance, which was first identified in the town of Lyme.

Connecticut has both a Hampton and an East Hampton. Not too strange really, except that Hampton is about 25 miles northeast of East Hampton. Shouldn't that be the other way around?

A few of Connecticut's best-known towns are not towns at all, but sections of larger incorporated towns. Keep that in mind that next time you drop by Winsted (which is really part of Winchester), Willimantic (part of Windham), Mystic (part of Groton and Stonington), Rockville (part of Vernon), and Dayville and Danielson (both within the Killingly town limits).

Native American names are common across Connecticut for rivers, lakes, mountains, forests, and many other geographical features, but only two of the state's 169 incorporated towns bear Native American names. Can you come up with them? A hint: They both start with "N". (See the Introduction if you're stumped.)

Colchester is the site of one of the state's younger wineries, **Priam Vineyards** (11 Shailor Hill Rd., 860/267-8520, www.priamvineyards.com), a 27-acre property set on a hill with commanding 35-mile views of the countryside. The emphasis here is on Northern France- and Germany-style wines, such as cabernet francs, gewurtztraminers, and reislings, but several American hybrids are also produced, including Seyval and St. Croix.

## RECREATION
### Amusement Parks
If you're looking for a place to take the kids, consider **Putts Up Dock** (1 Chelsea Harbor Dr., 860/886-PUTT or 888/48-WHARF), an impressive course fronting Norwich Harbor with an exploding volcano, a misty cave, and other elaborate layout elements. There's also bumper boating. **Gardner Lake Park** (38 Lakeview Ave., Rts. 82 and 354, Salem, 860/859-3340, open Memorial Day–Labor Day, $3) has swimming, rafting, paddleboats, food concessions, kiddie rides, and an arcade.

### Baseball
This double-A affiliate of major league baseball's San Francisco Giants (it was a New York Yankees affiliate until 2002) is based right in Norwich, where you can see the stars of tomorrow, today: The **Norwich Navigators** (860/887-7962, www.gators.com) play at **Dodd Stadium** (New Park Ave. from Rte. 32, Apr.–Sept.).

### Bicycling
The historic sections of Norwich and the rural, relatively undeveloped areas east of the city, around Preston, Ledyard, and Voluntown, are prime areas for scenic cycling—just bear in mind that the roads are somewhat narrow, and traffic, especially near the casinos, can be heavy. Another nice spot for a ride is from Colchester down Rte. 85 into Salem. Area shops with bike rentals are **Rose City Cycle** (427 W. Main St., Norwich, 860/887-7442) and **Sunshine Cycle & Sport** (467 S. Main St., Colchester, 860/537-2788).

### Golf
**Norwich Municipal Golf Course** (685 New London Tpke., Norwich, 860/889-6973), is the best public facility in the region. Another good bet is **River Ridge Golf Course** (Rte. 164 Griswold, 860/376-3268, www.riverridgegolf.com), a scenic 18-hole layout.

### Hiking
There are a number of great spots for hiking in the area; one of the most popular is Voluntown's **Pachaug State Forest.** Other possibilities include **Fort Shantok State Park** (Rte. 32, 860/424-3200) in the Uncasville section of Montville, where trails fringe the west bank of the Thames River. In Griswold, **Hopeville Pond State Park** (193 Roode Rd., 860/424-3200) has trails, freshwater swimming, a food concession, and overnight camping. In Bozrah, hikers and freshwater-fishing enthusiasts should try **Hopemead State Park** (Rte. 163, 860/424-3200); **Day Pond State Park** (Rte. 149, 860/424-3200) is a popular option in Colchester. Wildlife-seekers and bird-watchers should take to the trails in Ledyard's **Glacial Park and Avery Preserve** (Avery Hill Rd., 860/464-8740).

### Hot-Air Ballooning
**Eastern Connecticut Balloon Sevices** (Jewett City, 860/376-5807, www.easternctballoon.com) offers sunrise and pre-sunset balloon flights over the Norwich region April–December.

### Ice-Skating
The indoor **Norwich Municipal Ice Rink** (641 New London Tpke., Norwich, 860/892-2555, www.norwichrink.com) has skate rentals and is open year-round for public skating for two hours daily (at different times depending on the days). A day pass is $5.

## SHOPPING

Fans of pick-your-own produce can visit **Allyn Red Barn** (610 Colonel Ledyard Hwy., Ledyard, 860/464-9316) for apples (including cider and pies) September–December. In Preston, **Maple Lane Farms** (57 N.W. Corner Rd., 860/889-3766 or, for 24-hour information, 860/887-8855, www.maplelane.com) has a variety of pick-your-own crops; depending on the season you'll discover strawberries, raspberries, blueberries, pumpkins, and Christmas trees. Ledyard's **Holmberg Orchards** (12 Orchard Dr., off Rte. 12, in the Gales Ferry section of town, 860/464-7107) has pumpkins, apples, and raspberries seasonally, plus a variety of pies, gift baskets, and other gourmet items.

Mohegan recently added about 175,000 square feet of retail space. Highlights include Chico's, Joseph Abboud, Brookstone, Yankee Candle, the Nostalgia Store, and many others—you'll find music, electronics, fashion, gifts, and just about anything else you'd find in a typical shopping mall. Also at Mohegan are shops selling Native American art, crafts, and clothing; casino logo stuff (like hats and t-shirts); jewelry; and tobacco products (remember: they're tax-free). Foxwoods Casino has an extensive range of shops, about 12,000 square feet worth of retail, but most of it is no different than what you'd find elsewhere in the region (and often at better prices). There are clothiers and jewelry shops, basic souvenir shops, and several places that specialize in tobacco (which is not taxed on the Native American lands). Some of the more unusual shops sell Indian arts and accessories, from pottery to baskets.

There are a few good spots for antiquing in and around Norwich. The historic district around the village green in Colchester has a half dozen good stores, including **N. Liverant & Son** (168 S. Main St., 860/537-2409) and **Wild Geese** (191 Broadway, 860/537-4010). In Norwich, you'll find a small stretch of antiques stores along Main Street, down near the harbor: these include **Antoinette's** (860/887-1879); **Antiques Etc.** (860/887-0699); and **Lawson's** 860/887-5562). Given the many old estates that have been liquidated in Norwich over the years, it's no surprise that these places carry some wonderful treasures.

## ENTERTAINMENT AND NIGHTLIFE

Attached to Bella Fiore restaurant (see below) is a cigar-friendly nightclub called **Bella Notte** (543 W. Thames St., Norwich, 860/887-

9030), with daily theme nights (comedy, singles, live jazz, Top 40, Latin dance). In Norwich, the **Lincoln Inn Cafe** (W. Main St., 860/889-4977) has great drink specials and features live music regularly, making it a hit with locals. One of the most prominent live music venues in the region is the **Hill Side Cafe** (241 High St., Baltic, 860/822-6282). Try the **Chelsea Landing Pub & Gallery** (86 Water St., Norwich, 860/889-9932) for live rock music many nights.

At Foxwoods Casino, **Club B. B. King** (Rte. 2, Ledyard, 860/885-3000 or 800/FOX-WOODS, www.foxwoods.com) hosts rocking blues, jazz, and rockabilly bands. The Casino's **Fox Theatre** books well-known comedians and musicians, from Michael Bolton to Jackie Mason. **Mohegan Sun Casino** (Rte. 2A, exit 79A from I-395, 860/204-7163 or 888/226-7711, www.mohegansun.com) also has a full arena that hosts major performers and sporting events, a cabaret, and the smaller Wolf Den concert hall. In Norwich, the **Spirit of Broadway Theater,** at the Historic Chestnut Street Fire House (860/886-2378, www.spiritofbroadway.org), presents high-caliber off-Broadway plays, cabarets, and other performing-arts fare throughout the year.

## FESTIVALS AND EVENTS
### Spring and Summer

Preston hosts a popular **Bluegrass Festival** (Strawberry Park RV Resort, Pierce Rd., 860/886-1944) in late May and a **Cajun-Zydeco Music Festival** in early June. **Home and Garden Tours** of some of the imposing mansions of Norwich are held in mid-June; call 860/887-3288 or 860/887-3303. Fourth of July weekend is the time for **Independence Day at Howard Brown Park,** in Norwich, (860/886-6363); expect games, concerts, fireworks, and picnics. Later in the month, the Norwich Regional Vocational Technical School is the site of the **Eastern Connecticut Antique and Custom Auto Show** (860/887-1647).

### Fall and Winter

Mid-September is busy: the **Annual Ledyard Fair** (Ledyard Fairgrounds, Rte. 117, 860/886-0329) comes to town then, bringing livestock shows, agricultural exhibits, rides, and a midway; Howard Brown Park in Norwich hosts a **Taste of Italy** (860/889-0864), an all-day fair with live music, arts and craft, and—of course—great Italian fare; and the **Lisbon Fall Festival** (John Bishop House, 860/376-0869) is an annual celebration of history, music, food, crafts, and other fun events. There's a **Grecian Food Festival** (Holy Trinity Greek Orthodox Church, 247 Washington St., 860/887-1458) in Norwich, in late September. Caroling, music, horse-drawn wagon rides, and an appearance from Santa highlight Norwich's **Light Up City Hall party** (City Hall, Union Square, 860/889-0754), the last weekend in November. More than 20 floats—plus magicians, clowns, and bands—take part in the **Norwich Winterfest** (860/892-1813), the following weekend, in December.

## ACCOMMODATIONS

If you're looking for a comfy—and action-packed—base from which to explore the area, definitely consider the three big hotels at Foxwoods Casino and the massive new hotel tower at Mohegan Sun, which offer not only clean new rooms and oodles of amenities, but also a location equidistant to Mystic and greater Norwich. Another strength of this area is the very high number of B&Bs, a few of them quite luxurious, but the majority offering cozy but informal antiques-filled guest rooms and serene rural settings. Beyond these options, you'll find a smattering of chain motels in and around Norwich, but if this is the sort of accommodation you're seeking, you'll find a bigger and better selection down along the coast in both Mystic and New London—just a 15- to 20-minute drive away.

### Hotels and Motels

**$150–250: Foxwoods Casino** (Rte. 2, Ledyard, 860/885-3000 or 800/FOXWOODS, www.foxwoods.com) has three large, contemporary resort hotels with rates that fit several budgets. It's worth remembering that a love of casino gambling is but one reason to stay at these properties; Foxwoods has a stake in attracting guests so that they'll

be close to the gaming areas and thus able, ultimately, to increase the casino's revenues. This means rates are actually a bit lower than you might expect to pay for comparable accommodations in many other parts of Connecticut. It can be a great deal, but even with nearly 1,500 rooms among the three properties, Foxwoods is still sometimes booked solid. At the high end of the spectrum is the massive 825-room **Grand Pequot Tower,** which has a full health club and spa, several restaurants, 24-hour room service, a business center, and its own high-stakes gaming area. It's ideal if you want to be in the thick of the action. Just slightly less expensive, and also right at the casino compound, the 312-room **Great Cedar Hotel** has an indoor pool, exercise room, and 24-hour room service.

Perhaps the most exciting, and controversial, hotel development in Connecticut has been the construction of a 34-story, 1,200-room hotel tower at **Mohegan Sun Casino** (Rte. 2A, exit 79A from I-395, 860/204-7163 or 888/226-7711, www.mohegansun.com), which is also home to the state-of-the-art, 20,000-square-foot Elemis Spa. This mammoth deluxe hotel has large rooms (a minimum of 450 square feet) with high-speed Internet access, dual-line speaker phones, irons and ironing boards, in-room safes, and marble baths. Room decor is sleek and urbane, with beige, white, and either black or blue color schemes and high quality contemporary furniture. As there are no other tall buildings near it, and Mohegan is situated on a river bluff, you'll generally get a pretty nice view, even from rooms on lower floors. Of course, requesting a room on an upper floor will ensure the farthest-reaching views, which can take in the entire Thames River valley. This is an upscale property, but rates do vary greatly according to occupancy. There's a business center, concierge, indoor pool, and complimentary valet parking. The gaming areas and Mohegan's extremely impression array of restaurants are just an elevator ride from your room.

The **Spa at Norwich Inn** (607 W. Thames St., Rte. 32, Norwich, 860/886-2401 or 800/ASK-4SPA, www.thespaatnorwichinn.com), which is also owned by Foxwoods Casino, offers perhaps the most luxurious and sybaritic full-service lodging experience in greater Norwich. The large, brick, Colonial-style spread on a hill high above the Thames River has two good restaurants and 103 sumptuous rooms, but is perhaps best known for its spa, where every imaginable kind of body and mind treatment is available, from a native Norwich flower wrap to an anti-aging facial. You can also take classes on massage; call for details. Among accommodations, the fanciest are the private villas, with private balconies, galley kitchens, and total seclusion. The Norwich public golf course is next door to the inn.

Although it's in North Stonington, which is covered chiefly in the Coastal Connecticut chapter, the **Hilltop Inn & Suites** (373 Rte. 2, 860/535-0500 or 877/965-0500, www.hilltopinnrt2.com) is one of the closest properties to Foxwoods, just three miles down the road. This is an upscale, contemporary motel hotel with 120 rooms. It's also a gated facility, not that this is a particularly crime-ridden part of the state. Complimentary breakfast is included. The main draw, and the reason the rates are relatively high, is proximity to the casinos—if you're not planning to visit Foxwoods or Mohegan Sun, it might make sense to spend less and stay elsewhere.

**$100–150:** The **Ramada Norwich** (10 Laura Blvd., 860/889-5201 or 888/298-2054) is a somewhat dated property, but it's just off I-395 (convenient to casinos), and the management has done an excellent job keeping the rooms clean and attractive—all of the 127 large rooms have data ports, irons and ironing boards, and coffeemakers, and some have mini-refrigerators and microwaves. There's a nice indoor pool off the lobby.

The 280-room **Two Trees** ($100–150) has the more low-key Colonial ambience of the three—it's a gray clapboard building with very pretty grounds, and if you're looking to get away from all the action while still being close enough to get there in a snap (there's a 24-hour shuttle), this is your best bet.

**$50–100:** Guests interested in longer stays—or those traveling with friends or a family—might do well to consider **Comfort Suites** (275 Otrobando Ave., Norwich, 860/892-9292 or 800/847-SUITE), whose rooms all have ample

space and attractive, modern furnishings, and pull-out sleeper sofas that enable each room to accommodate four to six guests. The eight two-room suites have Jacuzzi tubs, microwaves, and refrigerators. There's also an exercise room, indoor pool, and game room. Built in 1997, it's a well-kept property and an excellent value. Another relatively recent addition is the **Courtyard by Marriott** (181 W. Town St., Norwich, 860/886-2600), a cheerfully decorated and efficiently run chain property with an indoor pool and exercise room. There are 120 rooms set over five floors; all have speaker phones, work desks, in-room movies, coffeemakers, and irons and ironing boards. The **Microtel Inn & Suites** (1954 Norwich–New London Tpke., Uncasville, 860/367-0880 or 888/771-7171) is the closest budget property (rooms often go for as low as $50–60 nightly) to Mohegan Sun Casino. Long-term guests love this property in part because nearly half the 120 rooms are suites with microwaves, refrigerators, second phone lines, and plenty of space to spread out. This is a nicely kept property, and if you can do without a pool, restaurants, or exercise room, it's an exceptional value.

## Country Inns and Bed-and-Breakfasts

**$150–250:** The **Stonecroft Country Inn** (515 Pumpkin Hill Rd., Ledyard, 860/572-0771 or 800/772-0774, www.stonecroft.com) consists of a magnificent yellow Georgian-style farmhouse that dates from 1807, along with a pretty, restored carriage house in back that contains additional guest rooms and an outstanding restaurant (see the Food section, below). The house sits back off the road on 6.5 wooded acres, preserving a sense of history and rusticity in a neighborhood that has unfortunately become increasingly modern and suburban in character. There are stone walls everywhere, plus herb gardens, broad lawns, and an exercise track—you might also see the owners' cute shelties sprinting about the grounds. There are 10 antiques-filled guest rooms, all with fireplaces and several with private terraces. Breakfast is a four-course candlelight affair.

**$100–150:** One of the most sophisticated small inns you'll find in greater Norwich, the **Fitch Claremont House** (83 Fitchville Rd, Bozrah, 860/889-0260, www.fitchclaremonthouse.com) is on the grounds of a historic (and still operating) 300-acre vineyard. There are four simply but smartly decorated rooms in this brown, 1790s, gambrel-roofed house, all with antiques and soft quilts, but also a full slate of plush amenities: fireplaces, TVs, phones, and private baths. Also on property is a secluded cottage with its own kitchen and laundry and room to sleep up to four guests. A highly acclaimed full breakfast is included.

A lovely old 1750s house on a hill with unusual double front door, **Captain Grant's** (109 Rte. 2A, Poquetanuck, 860/887-7589 or 800/982-1772, www.captaingrants.com) sits in a small village about midway between the two casinos. The house looks out on a large field and is filled with wonderful old wooden floors and beams, and quite a few antiques. The friendly, down-to-earth innkeepers cook up an impressive five-course full breakfast—specialties include apple crisp and carrot cake. The house has an intriguing history: It served as a garrison during the Revolutionary War. Next door is the 1790 Avery Home, which contains three more rooms.

Slightly northeast of Norwich, but also very convenient to the Quiet Corner, the **Homespun Farm Bed & Breakfast** (306 Preston Rd., Rte. 164, Griswold, 860/376-5178, www.homespunfarm.com) is one of the region's oldest extant farmsteads; the main house (and its rough-hewn beams) dates from 1740. An orchard of pear, apple, peach, and cherry trees adjoins the home, as do spectacular gardens and a koi pond. There are two rooms here, one of which is an impressive two-room suite with a handmade white oak bed, hand-stenciled walls, dark-wood floors, pitched ceilings, cable TV, and a private bath with a claw-foot tub. The sitting room has a twin bed and sofa, making it perfect if you've got children with you. The second room is equally gracious, but without the sitting area. Freshly made muffins, breads, and jams, plus fresh fruit, are presented in the morning. There's an excellent golf course just across the street, and a wonderful little crafts shop is at-

tached to this most distinctive inn, where you'll find hand-poured scented votive candles, dried flowers, and casual clothing.

On a rural 33-acre spread, the early-19th-century **Applewood Farms Inn** (528 Colonel Ledyard, Ledyard, 860/536-2022 or 800/717-4262, www.visitmystic.com/applewoodfarmsinn) has six spacious guest rooms (one of them a mini-suite) with soft antique featherbeds (ideal on a nippy evening), crooked and creaky wide-plank floors, private baths, and in some rooms working fireplaces. Behind the house is an old red barn and fields laced with white wooden fences; one field has been transformed into a golf fairway and putting green. There's also a secluded jacuzzi tub hidden in another small barn out back. The hosts, who are laid-back and friendly, have a pair of even friendlier basset hounds and a cute cat; your own small pets are welcome, but call ahead to confirm the arrangements.

**Abbey's Lantern Hill Inn** (780 Lantern Hill Rd., Ledyard, 860/572-0483, www.abbeyslanternhill.com) presents an intriguing alternative to the big hotels at Foxwoods—it's an attractive collection of contemporary shingled cottages just down the hill a quarter mile from Foxwoods, within a short drive or even a walk. Rooms are individually themed: the Down East has nautical artifacts, for example, and the Southwest has colors and fabrics suggesting that region. There are eight different rooms; many have private decks, private entrances, and jacuzzis, and two have fireplaces. A full country breakfast is included on weekends. Kids are welcome. Great hiking and climbing are within walking distance of the inn.

## Campgrounds

Camping is a hugely popular activity in eastern Connecticut, and more than a dozen large, well-equipped commercial facilities are in greater Norwich. These include **Acorn Acres** (135 Lake Rd., Bozrah, 860/859-1020 or 800/772-4691), with 200 sites; **Odetah Campground** (38 Bozrah St., Bozrah, 860/889-4144 or 800/448-1193, www.odetah.com), with 280 sites; **Campers World of Connecticut** (28 Nowakowski Rd., Jewett City, 860/376-2340, www.campersworldcampground.com), with about 100 sites; **Ross Hill Park** (170 Ross Hill Rd., Lisbon, 860/376-9606 or 800/308-1089, www.rosshillpark.com), with 250 sites; **Laurel Lock Family Campground** (15 Cottage Rd., Oakdale, 860/859-1424), with 130 sites; **Hidden Acres Family Campground** (47 River Rd., Preston, 860/887-9633), with 180 sites; **Strawberry Park Resort Campground** (42 Pierce Rd., Preston, 860/886-1944 or 888/794-7944, www.strawberrypark.net), with 440 sites; **Indianfield Campgrounds** (Gardner Lake, 308 Old Colchester Rd., Rte. 354, Salem, 860/859-1320), with 228 sites; **Salem Farms Campground** (39 Alexander Rd., Salem, 860/859-2320 or 800/479-9238, www.salemfarmscampground.com), with 182 sites; **Witch Meadow Lake Campground** (139 Witch Meadow Rd., Salem, 860/859-1542, www.campconn.com/witch_meadow), with 280 sites; **Salt Rock Campground** (199 Scotland Rd., Baltic, 860/822-8728), with 128 sites; **Circle C Campground** (21 Bailey Pond Rd., Voluntown, 860/564-4534 or 800/424-4534, www.campcirclec.com), with 80 sites; and **Nature's Campsites** (96 Ekonk Hill Rd., Rte. 49, Voluntown, 860/376-4203), with 150 sites. Also, **Hopeville Pond State Park** (193 Roode Rd., Rte. 201, Griswold, 860/376-0313 or 860/376-2920), on the site of several former mills, has about 80 tent sites.

## FOOD

The presence of Foxwoods and Mohegan Sun casinos have greatly transformed the dining scene in this part of the state, with both facilities offering excellent culinary options. Beyond these, you'll find a handful of very good restaurants, but mostly inexpensive family-oriented pizza parlors, pubs, and fast-food restaurants, particularly in Norwich, which might be the largest city in the state lacking a bona fide culinary star.

### Upscale

A handsome Italian restaurant with a teal-and-pink color scheme, just down the road from the Norwich Inn and Spa, **Bella Fiore** (543 W. Thames St., 860/887-9030, $12–25) has excel-

lent food, an extensive wine list, and effusive service. Favorite dishes include Gamberi shrimp (sautéed in garlic, capers, and olive oil and served with white wine sauce over linguine) and an appetizer of scallops in bacon cream sauce. With so many venerable old country inns with noted restaurants in southeastern Connecticut (Copper Beech, Bee and Thistle, Randall's Ordinary, etc.), the **Stonecroft Country Inn** (515 Pumpkin Hill Rd., Ledyard, 860/572-0771, $20–34) has taken a little time to catch everybody's attention. But this sophisticated, understated eatery, in a revamped barn behind the inn's main house, serves finely tuned, Asian-influenced, regional American fare, including a starter of sake-and-miso-broiled salmon over a seaweed salad with a cellophane noodle salad and a soy reduction, pickled ginger, and wasabi oil. A top entrée is the five-spice seared duck breast with black lentil–and–ginger confit pudding, asparagus–and–wild mushroom hash, and a tangerine-soy glaze. For a special occasion, the Stonecroft is a more refined and romantic option than any even the best eateries at Foxwoods and Mohegan Sun, and it's a relatively short drive from either casino.

### Creative but Casual

It's kind of unexciting-looking, but **Modesto's** (10 Rte. 32, North Franklin, 860/887-7755, $13–26) serves imaginative, first-rate Mexican, American, Continental, and Italian fare—that's right, four great culinary traditions that, strangely, all work well together. The number of available dishes is huge—menus this long are usually only found at Chinese restaurants and all-night diners. There are great chiles rellenos, Norwegian salmon in a shallot-dill sauce, steamed or broiled Maine lobster, blackened New Zealand lamb loin with Cajun spices, and much more.

**NuNu's Bistro** (45 Hayward Avenue, 860/537-6299, $9–18) has a weird, yet strangely appealing location tucked down a driveway on the green in quiet Colchester. The restaurant occupies a handsome old Victorian carriage house. Inside, you'll be treated to consistently good American and Italian fare, most of it not really true to the restaurant's "bistro" name, but it's great tasting nonetheless. There's an outstanding antipasto

# CASINO DINING

Whether or not you're keen on dice and slots, Connecticut's casinos offer some of the region's finest noshing opportunities. If a meal is your sole reason for visiting, Mohegan Sun is probably a better bet than Foxwoods—the restaurants serve consistently better food, and access to Mohegan's eateries (valet parking up front or a large self-parking garage behind the casino) is easier than at Foxwoods, which is bigger and often a long walk or short shuttle ride from parking. A plus at Foxwoods is that many restaurants are inside the casino's resort hotels, or at least sufficiently far from the gaming areas to keep the noise of clattering slot machines from souring your appetite.

It's hard to say whether casino dining offers a better value than other dining in the area. There are inexpensive food courts and buffet options at both places, but why trek all the way to a casino for cheap fare when eastern Connecticut abounds with diners and seafood shacks? These simpler casino dining venues make sense mostly if you're already on-site for some gambling. However, both casinos have a few restaurants that merit a visit solely on their cooking laurels, and prices here are generally 15–30 percent lower than at comparable non-gaming restaurants.

## Foxwoods

Dining options at Foxwoods Casino (Rte. 2, Ledyard, 860/885-3000, www.foxwoods.com) include a decent New York–style deli, a big ol' pigging-out buffet, and a four-outlet food court—plus some lounges and bars with light late-night dining. **Han Garden,** off the casino's massive concourse, specializes in upscale Chinese fare ($14–62). A popular starter is Malaysian satay. Consider the filet mignon with black pepper sauce, and if you're

in a big-spending mood, sample the braised abalone (a hefty $60). Better and less pricey is the **Golden Dragon,** which offers an eclectic pan-Asian menu ($8–18) of dishes like marinated Korean beef short ribs, smoked salmon sushi rolls, dim sum, roast suckling pig, and a house rice congee special of beef, squid, and vegetables. This restaurant is in the Grand Pequot hotel tower.

Also in the Grand Pequot Tower, **Fox Harbour** serves commendable seafood ($18–28), with the usual raw bar favorites, sushi rolls, great chowders and bisques, smoked fish, and a nice chilled lobster salad.

The restaurant most associated with fine dining, **Al Dente,** presents snazzy Italian cuisine ($13–30), such as traditional *pasta e fagioli* soup, show-stopping swordfish puttanesca and flawless veal osso bucco. Other nice picks include **Cedars Steak House** ($18–60), with a typical repertoire of hefty meats and seafoods. Arguably Foxwoods's most acclaimed eatery, **Paragon** ($25–42) is on the 24th floor of the Grand Pequot Tower. French-Asian delicacies are served, including Chilean sea bass and herb-crusted rack of lamb for two. A meal doesn't come cheaply here—a side of humble mustard greens with garlic sets you back about $10.

## Mohegan Sun

If fine dining is one of your top reasons for visiting a casino, make a beeline for Mohegan Sun (I-395 and Rte. 2, 888/777-7922, www.mohegansun.com). Foxwoods led in this department until 2001, when Mohegan Sun underwent a vast expansion that added numerous trendy restaurants, some of them helmed by celebrity chefs.

Mohegan Sun has two main gaming areas, connected by a large shopping mall with restaurants.

In the original casino, you'll find a handful of pretty good eateries, most of them set together near the back of the immense gaming area. Unfortunately, noise from slots can be a nuisance, but the higher-end places have recessed dining alcoves set back from the action. Mohegan has a good food court with pizzas, sandwiches, burgers, Asian food, etc. Still inexpensive, but with table service, are **Chief's Deli** ($4–13), where you'll find bigger-than-average sandwiches and platters, and **Mohegan Territory** ($6–16), a pub-cum-diner where you can get lobster rolls, steak and eggs, and buffalo burgers.

The cream of the culinary crop in this part of the casino are three adjoining restaurants. **The Longhouse** ($16–70) serves elaborate steaks, seafood, and other high-ticket American dishes, including gilled venison chops with herb polenta, root vegetables, baby fennel, and lingonberries. This dining room is farthest from the crowds and decorated tastefully—a legitimate venue for a romantic date. **Bamboo Forest** ($12–65), with bamboo walls, Asian-inspired colors and design motifs, and servers in elegant costumes, presents creative Pacific Rim (especially Thai, Malaysian, and Vietnamese) fare. A specialty is the three-course Beijing duck in hoisin sauce; also note the appetizer of chilled jellyfish with abalone over pickled veggies.

Between the other two restaurants, **Pompeii & Caesar** ($14–48) offers credible takes on northern Italian cuisine, such as smoked-duck salad with frisee and tomatoes; and lobster fra diavolo over linguini.

The real showstoppers, however, are in the newer casino area, beginning with **Todd English's Tuscany** ($15–50), which is set beneath a massive cascading waterfall—this might be the best and most distinctive eatery in either casino. English, who is famous for restaurants in Boston and Las Vegas, among other cities, designed a menu of creative Mediterranean favorites, such as wood-fired littleneck clams and chorizo in a saffron-tomato broth; and sturgeon baked in parchment with Yukon potatoes, fennel, and lemon confit. Another noted chef opened **Jasper White's Summer Shack** ($7–25), an homage to seafood eateries made to look like a New England shanty—favorites include lobster, raw oysters, fried-clam rolls, and the signature shack bouillabaisse.

Look no farther than **Michael Jordan's Steak House** ($27–52) if you have a craving for red meat. This is not sports-themed, despite Jordan's interest in it, but is a high-rollers spot for delicious but expensive food. The space is dark and urbane, and some say the service here is the best of any of the casino eateries. A final temple of haute cuisine is **Rain** ($25–65), where you could try a first course of rabbit with lentils, applewood-smoked bacon, and chanterelles; followed by tenderloin of buffalo with new potatoes, carrot purée and fava beans.

Highlights among the casual eateries are lively **Big Bubba's BBQ** ($7–13), decked out with vintage signs and 1950s roadhouse memorabilia. Wood-smoked po'boys, pulled-pork sandwiches, brisket, and fried oysters are offered. **Lucky's Lounge** ($7–12) is done up retro 1950s, with red banquette seating and cheesy decor. Italian grinders, pizzas, and salads are served.

Among Mohegan Sun's fun lounges and bars, the most distinctive is **Leffingwell's,** a martini bar with a fake–night sky ceiling and bizarre lighted sculptures. This one is hard to believe until you see it.

platter of cured meats, fresh cheeses, and such. Entrées include risotto with porcini mushrooms and a fresh sausage as well as seafood over a red-sauced linguine.

A new spot in Groton, but right on the Ledyard border close to the casinos, is the **Wobbly Dog** (Rte. 184, 860/572-9564, $8–16), operated by Drew Egy, who is the chef at the acclaimed Stonecroft Inn. This more casual spot draws raves for the baby back ribs, pulled-pork sandwiches, roast chicken dinners, burgers, and other barbecue. There's also a long list of beers on tap.

## Quick Bites

Near the junction of Rtes. 2, 11, and 85, **Herman's Diner** (Rte. 85, Colchester, 860/537-2591, under $7) is a cute little roadside diner with a wooden clapboard facade. It's a reliable spot for affordable home-style fare.

**Salem Valley Farms Ice Cream** (20 Darling Rd., Salem, 860/859-2980) makes exceptionally rich and delicious ice cream, and has an astounding array of flavors—especially when you consider that this little red building looks like a miniature dairy barn in the middle of nowhere. You order at the window and eat in your car. Many flavors rotate seasonally, such as Indian pudding, mint julep swirl, and raspberry fudge ripple.

A favorite spot with families and visitors, near Hopeville State Park, is **Stu's House** (801 Hopeville Rd., Rte. 201, Griswold, 860/376-5068, $3–7). The restaurant serves huge plates of spaghetti, fried seafood, burgers, homemade fries

and onion rings, and clam chowder. The shakes, sundaes, and floats are a great way to top things off.

In the center of little Voluntown, you'll find decent breakfasts, American fare, grinders, and pizzas at the **Town Pizza Restaurant & Olde Town Tavern** (junction of Rtes. 138, 49, and 165, 860/376-3378, $4–12).

# INFORMATION AND SERVICES

## Visitor Information

The region is served by the **Southeastern Connecticut Tourism District** (470 Bank St., P.O. Box 89, New London, CT 06320, 860/444-2206 or 800/TO-ENJOY, www.mysticmore.com). Another good source of information, specifically on Norwich, is the **Norwich Tourism Office** (69 Main St., 860/886-4683 or 888/4-NORWICH, www.norwichct.org). On the Web, www.visit-connecticut.com/mystic.html is a useful site with links to numerous attractions, B&Bs, and other useful sites.

## Getting Around

Norwich is at a fairly major junction of both limited-access and surface highways: I-395 runs north–south through the city, connecting the region with the southeastern Connecticut coastline (and I-95), and with the Quiet Corner towns. Route 2 is a limited-access highway that runs west from Norwich, and then northwest up toward Hartford. Routes 12 and 32 are additional north–south state roads that cut through the region, while Rtes. 82 and 165 are useful east–west routes.

# Resources

# Suggested Reading

Connecticut hasn't exactly been written about to death, but there are a number of useful and colorful books out there on the Nutmeg State. Most of those listed below focus exclusively on Connecticut, or at the very least on Southern New England, but bear in mind that a number of additional titles, general guidebooks, B&B guides, and historical reviews discuss the state as a component of its greater identity, New England.

For further information on other states in the Northeast, including Connecticut's neighbors, check out the following cousins of *Moon Handbooks Connecticut: Moon Handbooks Rhode Island,* also by yours truly; *Moon Handbooks Maine,* by Kathy Brandes; *Moon Handbooks Massachusetts,* by Jeff Perk; *Moon Handbooks New Hampshire,* by Steve Lantos; and *Moon Handbooks New York,* by Christiane Bird.

You may recognize the "Images of America" series, by Arcadia Publishing (888/313-BOOK, www.arcadiapublishing.com), from the trademark sepia covers of its hundreds of small, softcover historic photo essays on more than 1,000 communities across the country. These fascinating books are produced by a small firm in Charleston, South Carolina, and each title typically contains 200–250 early black-and-white photos of a particular region, along with running commentary that is usually authored by a local historian, librarian, or archivist from that area. The books cost $15–25, and presently there are 70 titles on Connecticut. These cover dozens of cities and towns in the state, and then a variety of special topics, including *University of Connecticut, Route 15: The Road to Hartford,* and *Connecticut Whistle Stops: Greenwich to New Haven.*

## Description and Travel

Boyle, Doe. *Fun With the Family in Connecticut.* Globe Pequot Press, 2002. Where to look for advice on how to enjoy the coast with kids.

Boyle, Doe. *Guide to the Connecticut Shore.* Globe Pequot Press, 2003. A guidebook focusing on Connecticut's shoreline towns.

Hubbell, William (photographer), and Roger Eddy. *Connecticut.* Graphic Arts Center Publishing Co., 1989. This is the quintessential coffee-table book—the one local teenagers schlep abroad to their host families when embarking on foreign exchange programs. The photography is, indeed, quite stunning in many places.

Laschever, Barnett D., and Andi Marie Fusco. *Connecticut: An Explorer's Guide.* Countryman Press, 2002. A general-interest guidebook on the state.

Kelley, Brooks Mather. *Yale, A History.* Yale University Press, 1999. This book sheds considerable new light on that world-renowned New Haven educational institution.

Mills Brown, Elizabeth. *New Haven: A Guide to Architecture and Urban Design: Fifteen Illustrated Tours.* Yale University Press, 1976. For a detailed look at the buildings that have contributed to the look of one of Connecticut's most famous cities, pick up a copy of this book.

Ritchie, David, and Deborah Ritchie. *Connecticut: Off The Beaten Path.* Globe Pequot Press, 2002. The Connecticut version of the popular series, which emphasizes lesser-known and out-of-the-way attractions.

Rocheleau, Paul, Henry Wiencek, and Donald Young. *Southern New England.* Stewart Tabori & Chang, 1998 (part of the Smithsonian Guides to Historic America series). Beautiful book with excellent writing and vibrant photography; this edition covers Rhode Island, Connecticut, and Massachusetts.

Workers of the Federal Writers' Project of the Works Progress Administration for the state of Connecticut. *Connecticut—A Guide to its Roads, Lore, and People.* Houghton Mifflin, 1938 (out of print). Arguably the best treatment of the state ever written is this dense and fascinating work compiled by the Works Progress Administration (WPA) Workers of the Federal Writers' Project. Part of the amazingly well-executed and thoroughly researched American Guide Series, the book is long since out of print (many titles within this series have been picked up in recent years and reprinted by current publishing houses, but not yet Connecticut, alas). Your best hope of finding a copy of this wonderful tome is by scouring the racks of used bookstores or websites such as eBay. Depending on its condition and age (and whether it has its original cover and map), this guide should sell for anywhere from $15–75.

## Maps and Orientation

There are a number of decent folding maps on Connecticut, and if you call the state tourism office, 800/CT-BOUND, you'll be sent the free annual *Connecticut Vacation Guide,* which contains a very good general state map.

Unquestionably, the most precise maps on the state are published by Rand McNally. The easy-to-read and well-labeled Rand McNally StreetFinder series breaks the state down into six distinct regional atlases: Fairfield County, Northwestern Connecticut, New Haven and Middlesex Counties, Hartford County, Northeastern Connecticut, and Southeastern Connecticut. You need to buy all six to cover the state in its entirety, although they each overlap considerably into neighboring turf. Each contains an exhaustive street index. Hagstrom also publishes several regional Connecticut atlases.

DeLorme. *Connecticut/Rhode Island Atlas and Gazetteer.* DeLorme Publishing, 2002. DeLorme publishes a state atlas that includes both Connecticut and neighboring Rhode Is-

land as part of its Gazetteer series. While this series shows much greater detail than your run-of-the-mill atlas, it's not very trustworthy as a serious navigational aid. A disturbing number of errors appear on these pages—in particular, the DeLorme atlas has a tendency to show dirt roads and even trails as primary paved thoroughfares, creating the potential for all sorts of frustrating wild goose chases.

Microsoft. *Microsoft Streets and Trips.* Microsoft, 2003. A very useful digital tool, Microsoft Expedia Streets covers the entire United States (and Canada). With this CD-ROM, you can type in virtually any street address in Connecticut (or any other state for that matter) and instantly have it pinpointed on a full color, detailed map on your computer screen.

Rand McNally. Series includes *Rand McNally StreetFinder: Fairfield, Litchfield, and New Haven Counties; New London, Tolland, and Windham Counties; Hartford;* Rand McNally & Co., 2000–2002. Very precise maps on different regions of the state, with great detail, including city coverage—these may be the best overall print maps you'll find.

## History

Bushman, Richard L. *From Puritan to Yankee: Character and the Social Order in Connecticut, 1690–1765.* Harvard University Press, 1980. This detailed history sets out to illustrate the colony's earliest years.

Crowder, John F. *Jeopardy.* Escapade Games Inc., 1997. If you're the kind of person who can't get enough of TV's *Jeopardy,* and also a loyal Nutmegger, then you'll probably get a kick out of this little-known-fact–filled book.

Phillips, David E. *Legendary Connecticut/Traditional Tales from the Nutmeg State.* Curbstone Press, 1992. Phillips proves to be an able and highly entertaining raconteur with this lively and chatty collection of oftentimes bizarre happenings and controversies that have played out over the centuries—from sightings of the "wild man of Winsted" to the mysterious noises of Moodus.

Radde, Bruce. *The Merritt Parkway.* Yale University Press, 1996. Provides a provocative and colorful account of this historic road, one of the nation's first limited-access highways, and one that is today a National Historic Landmark. The book contains numerous historical photographs, too, which give a nice sense of Fairfield County on the eve of its transformation into a bustling suburb.

Staubach, Suzanne. *Connecticut—Driving Through History.* Douglas Charles Ltd., 1998. Despite its name, this book is not written as a driving tour, but rather as individual listings of every incorporated town in the state, by county. Each entry lists the major roads through town, the date of incorporation, the name of the Native Americans who first settled there, a number of general historical facts, a list of notable buildings, and a list of recognized historic districts.

## Hiking and Recreation

Join the Connecticut Forest and Park Association, and you'll receive a copy of the *Connecticut Walk Book,* which offers explicit directions through and maps of every single blue-blazed hiking trail in the state. If you're a serious hiker, you don't want to be without this book.

Alden, Peter, and the National Audubon Society. *National Audubon Society Field Guide to New England.* Knopf, 1998. A great field guide on New England.

Borland, Hal. *This Hill, This Valley.* Johns Hopkins University Press, 1990. Armchair naturalists will want to seek out all books by the late renowned writer from Falls Village, Hal Borland, but this is arguably the best.

Hardy, David, with Gerry Hardy and Sue Hardy. *50 Hikes in Connecticut: From the Berkshires to the Coast.* Countryman Press, 2002. One of the most extensive and descriptive outdoors books you'll find—Hardy uncovers the pleasures of trails both famous and obscure.

Milne, George McLean. *Connecticut Woodlands: A Century's Story of the Connecticut Forest and Park Association.* Connecticut Forest and Park Assn, 1995. A great read on the state's conservation history.

Mullin, Edwin, and Jane Griffith. *Short Bike Rides in Connecticut.* Globe Pequot Press, 1998. Indispensable resource for avid cyclists.

Passante, Jeff. *Housatonic River: Fly Fishing Guide.* Frank Amato Publishers, 1998. Anglers should also be certain to read the this short but helpful guide.

Tuckerman, Steve. *AMC River Guide: Massachusetts–Connecticut–Rhode Island.* Appalachian Mountain Club, 1991. The Appalachian Mountain Club publishes a favorite book of kayakers, rafters, canoeists, and fishing enthusiasts.

Wilson, Alex. *Quiet Water Canoe Guide: Massachusetts, Connecticut, Rhode Island.* Appalachian Mountain Club, 1993. If it's advice on freshwater boating that interests you, check out this well-written volume.

## Environment, Ecology, and Geology

Baptist, Thomas R., George A. Clarke, Jr., and Joseph D. Zeranski. *Connecticut Birds.* University Press of New England, 2002. This detailed guide gives the a sense of which birds visit Connecticut and where.

Bell, Michael. *The Face of Connecticut: People, Geology, and the Land.* Department of Environmental Protection Maps and Publications

Sales, 1995. This easy-to-follow book offers an absolutely mesmerizing glimpse into the geology and landscapes that shape the state in so many ways. Somehow one imagines this book has been used more as a college textbook than for armchair reading, but keep in mind that Bell writes vividly and lucidly, and somehow turns themes that many laypersons find intimidating into a great read. The geographical organization of *Moon Handbooks Connecticut*—with its major divisions being the Connecticut River Valley, the Western Hills, the Eastern Hills, and the Connecticut Coastline—is based largely on Bell's model for explaining the state's human and geological history. (Bell would no doubt point out the Western and Eastern "hills" should truly be labeled "uplands." Sorry, "hills" just has a nicer ring to it.)

Henshaw, Carol, and Grace H. McEntee. *Natural Wonders of Connecticut and Rhode Island; A Guide to Parks, Preserves, and Wild Places*. McGraw Hill/Contemporary Books, 2000. Gives vivid and detailed descriptions of several good hiking and outdoors areas in the state.

Kricher, John C., and Gordon Morrison (illustrator). *A Field Guide to Eastern Forests North America* (Peterson Field Guide Series). Houghton Mifflin Co., 1998. The best all-around guide on New England's geology, flora, and fauna.

Patton, Peter Charles, with James M. Kent. *A Moveable Shore: The Fate of the Connecticut Coast (Living with the Shore)*. Another excellent and highly engaging book—it focuses on the state's ever-shifting and always-vulnerable waterfront.

Wetherell, W. D. (editor). *This American River: Five Centuries of Writing About the Connecticut*. University of New England Press, 2002. A collection of essays and tales about the Connecticut River.

# Biography, Memoir, Fiction, and Literature

Dozens of famous authors live in Connecticut—now there is a handful of work that actually focuses on the state itself. Perhaps the definitive work of fiction with a local theme is Mark Twain's satirical concoction, *A Connecticut Yankee in King Arthur's Court*, which, though published in 1889, is still widely in print and available in most bookstores. The story centers on Hank Morgan, an everyday Joe at one of one of Connecticut's many munitions factories, who's bonked on the head and awakens many centuries earlier in Camelot. On a related note, the audio-cassette *A Visit to Mark Twain's House: The Complete Live Radio Broadcast from Hartford*, by Garrison Keillor, makes for an engaging and amusing listen.

Black, Stephen A. *Eugene O'Neill: Beyond Mourning and Tragedy*. Yale University Press, 2002. Fans of the dramatist have lauded this new and gripping critical biography, which offers insights into the man and the tragedies and sufferings that fueled his creative drive.

Clark, Mary Higgins. *We'll Meet Again*. Pocket Books, 2000. The noted mystery writer weaves one of her typically suspenseful yarns at a hoity-toity prep school in Greenwich, Connecticut.

Ellis, Erika. *Good Fences: A Novel*. Random House Inc., 1998. Traces the life of an African American family in Connecticut and its relentless attempt to assimilate within progressively WASPier and wealthier neighborhoods—a semi-comical journey that leads, as one could easily guess, right into the town of Greenwich.

Hoffman, Andrew. *Inventing Mark Twain: The Lives of Samuel Langhorne Clemens*. William Morrow & Co., 1998. You can understand more about the life of Connecticut's most famous author by thumbing this well-researched biography.

Hosley, William. *Colt: The Making of an American Legend*. University of Massachusetts Press, 2000. One of the better biographies of a Connecticut luminary, this book documents not only the life of this dynamic manufacturing but also the history of gun-making in America.

Levin, Ira. *The Stepford Wives*. Perennial, 2002. Levin's creepy and campy story shines a bright light of suspicion upon the happily posh and rarified bedroom communities of Fairfield County; much of the movie on which the book was based was filmed in Westport, Weston, and Easton.

MacNeill, Mary. *The Widow Down by the Brook: A Memoir of a Time Gone*. Scribner, 1999. One of the more moving Connecticut-related works of recent years is Mary MacNeill's personal recounting of her move in the 1950s, along with her cancer-stricken husband, into a small and quiet community of Canton Corner, where they rehabilitate a country barn in which they'll live. MacNeill's memoir recounts his passing and her coping with the loss and her new life in rural Connecticut. The book is cobbled together from notes and letters the author kept hidden away for nearly 50 years before unearthing them to write this book, at the ripe old age of 93.

Moody, Rick. *The Ice Storm*. Back Bay Books, 2002. One of several Connecticut-based novels to be interpreted successfully on the big screen, this chilly tale paints a disturbing—and at times very funny—picture of shallow, embittered, circa-1973 Connecticut suburbanites and their bleak travails.

Saxon, A. H. *P. T. Barnum: The Legend and the Man*. Columbia University Press, 1989. Reveals the "Greatest Showman on Earth."

Steel, Danielle. *Bittersweet*. Dell Publishing Co., 2000. Steel set this novel in tony Westport.

Her lead character lives an unhappy life of suburban monotony, but eventually breaks free and rejects the cushy trappings of the Gold Coast (for Rawanda, no less).

Updike, John. *Marry Me: A Romance*. Ballantine Books, 1979. John Updike offered one of the earlier studies of life—and marital infidelity—in Fairfield County with this engaging novel set in the early 1960s.

Yates, Richard. *Revolutionary Road*. Vintage Books, 2000. This recently re-released 1961 novel chronicles the lives of a young, well-to-do, and seemingly happy family in Connecticut and the troubles that lie deep within. The commentary on bleak 1950s suburbia is still gripping today.

## People, Politics, and Current Events

The famous woman and Westport resident behind a television show and an entire magazine about home living, Martha Stewart has penned countless coffee-table books on entertaining, gardening, wedding planning, cooking, decorating, and crafting—in general, on leading the sort of life that quite a few authors have both satirized and celebrated in the several works of fiction described above.

Benedict, Jeff. *Without Reservation: How a Controversial Indian Tribe Rose to Power and Built the World's Largest Casino*. Perennial, 2001. This none-too-flattering account of how the Mashantucket Pequot tribe rose to operate Foxwoods has rankled many; it's an intriguing work that casts doubt as to the very legitimacy of the present-day tribe.

Byron, Christopher M. *Martha Inc.: The Incredible Story of Martha Stewart Living Omnimedia*. John Wiley & Sons, 2002. A salacious and reasonably balanced tell-all about controversial Martha Stewart, as told by her Westport neighbor.

Dunne, Dominick, and Mark Fuhrman. *Murder in Greenwich: Who Killed Martha Moxley?* Harper-Collins, 1999. One of the great Connecticut scandals of recent years, the unsolved murder of teenager Martha Moxley in 1975 and her death's connection to the Kennedy clan (yes, *that* Kennedy clan), has made for great tabloid journalism in recent years. Connecticut resident and frequent *Vanity Fair* contributor Dominick Dunne, and infamous O.J. Simpson trial witness Mark Fuhrman, wrote this book that argued that the killer was Michael Skakel—indeed, a jury found him guilty of the murder in 2002, three years after this book came out.

Febbroriello, Courtney. *Wife of the Chef.* Clarkson Potter, 2003. The wife of chef Christopher Prosperi and, with him, co-owner of their Simsbury restaurant Metro Bis (which is reviewed in the Farmington Valley section of this book) wrote this funny memoir and commentary on the good and the bad of being married to the guy in the kitchen.

Smith, Diane. *Absolutely Positively Connecticut.* Globe Pequot Press, 2000. New Haven–based TV news anchor Diane Smith has become well-known locally for a segment she does about inspiring local stories called "Positively Connecticut." Her book of the exact same name, published in 1998, recounted many of these tales, and this equally popular sequel offers more of the same. These are large-trim books with about 200 photos, making them ideal as gifts.

Weller, Sheila. *Saint of Circumstance: The Untold Story Behind the Alex Kelly Rape Case: Growing Up Rich and Out of Control.* Pocket Star, 1997. This highly sensational and rather moralistic book chronicles the infamous Connecticut court case of a young, good-looking Darien High School student who, after being charged with the rape of a former female friend in 1986, fled to Europe for about a decade of eluding the law, hanging around posh ski resorts, and living the good life. Since the 1997 publication of this book, Alex Kelly has, by the way, been convicted on one count of rape (he was actually accused of at least one other).

# Internet Resources

Connecticut has only a handful of regional websites, but there are several detailed statewide ones. Furthermore, a number of national sites covering everything from transportation to the outdoors have specific pages on just Connecticut.

## Tourism and General Information

### The Hartford Courant
**www.ctnow.com**

This website produced the state's most widely read paper, and may be the most comprehensive and informative online resource in Connecticut. This site also contains stories, reviews, and information from about 15 other newspapers and TV stations. On this site, you'll find the same in-depth news coverage you will in the daily *Courant* newspaper, and you can search for older stories. There are extensive sections on dining (with many restaurant reviews culled from several sources), travel, arts and theater, attractions, and events.

### CitySearch
**www.hartford.citysearch.com;**
**www.newhaven.citysearch.com**

This internationally known site is better for bigger cities than those in Connecticut, but it does contain listings and limited editorial information on new restaurants, museum exhibitions, which movies are playing where, and where to find hotels. While the coverage is chiefly about Hartford and New Haven, you'll also find listings for the other towns and cities throughout the state. Unfortunately, outdated information appears routinely on this site.

### Digital City
**www.digitalcity.com/hartford**

The competing web company of Citysearch, Digital City has better coverage not only of Hartford and New Haven, but of other parts of the state. Both sites also include ratings by site users, which can be very useful and extremely entertaining.

### The Official State of Connecticut Home Page
**www.state.ct.us**

The official state website comes in handy when you're looking for detailed information on state and local politics, regional demographics, the state library, and local laws.

### The Official State of Connecticut Tourism Home Page
**www.tourism.state.ct.us**

The mother of all Connecticut travel and tourism websites, with links to the state's five regional tourism sites: **Litchfield Hills** (www.litchfieldhills.com), **Greater Hartford** (www.enjoyhartford.com), **Coastal Fairfield County** (www.coastalct.com), **Greater New Haven** (www.newhavencvb.org), and **Mystic and Southeastern Connecticut** (www.mysticmore.com). Within each site, you'll find a trove of links to regional attractions, dining, lodging, events, transportation, and other valuable information.

## Transportation

Several sites are very useful for exploring the different transportation options in Connecticut, from flying to training to catching the ferry.

### Bradley International Airport
**www.bradleyairport.com**

Find out about parking, airlines, check-in information, and arrivals and departures the state's main airport.

### Amtrak
**www.amtrak.com**

Homepage for the national rail service with several stops in Connecticut.

### Metro-North Railroad
**www.mta.nyc.ny.us**
Metro-North offers frequent commuter service from New York City to southwestern Connecticut.

### Bonanza Bus Lines
**www.bonanzabus.com**
Has details on interstate bus service to and from Connecticut.

### Greyhound
**www.greyhound.com**
The nation's leading bus line makes a number of stops in Connecticut.

### New London to Orient Point ferry
**www.longislandferry.com**
Find out about rates and scheduling for this ferry connecting southeastern Connecticut to eastern Long Island.

### Bridgeport to Port Jefferson ferry
**www.bpjferry.com**
Find out about rates and scheduling for this ferry connecting southwestern Connecticut to central Long Island.

### Connecticut Department of Transportation
**www.dot.state.ct.us**
Provides extensive information on numerous publications, traveler resources and road conditions, licenses and permits, upcoming roadwork and projects, legal notices, and construction bid notices.

## Sporting and the Outdoors

### Connecticut Department of Environmental Protection (DEP)
**http://dep.state.ct.us**
Among Connecticut's top Internet resources for outdoors enthusiasts, the DEP home page provides information and policies pertaining to boating, hiking, hunting, fishing, beachgoing, and many other activities.

### Connecticut State Parks and Forests
**http://dep.state.ct.us/stateparks/index.htm**
This site provides links to every property in the state park system. Also has information on primitive camping at state parks.

### Connecticut Chapter of the Nature Conservancy
**www.tnc.org/states/connecticut**
Hikers might want to visit this site, which contains information about the Conservancy's many Ocean State refuges and preserves.

### Connecticut Audubon Society
**http://ctaudubon.org**
Great site for birding, with specifics on the society's Connecticut chapter.

### Connecticut Forest and Park Association (CPFA)
**www.ctwoodlands.org**
An invaluable resource for fans of hiking, conservation, and woodland strolls.

### Connecticut Campground Owners Association, Inc.
**www.campconn.com**
Great ideas about where to find a desirable commercial campground.

### Connecticut State Golf Association
**www.csgalinks.org**
Here golfers can learn all about the state's many public courses.

### Connecticut Golfer
**www.ctgolfer.com**
Another great website for Nutmeg State golfing enthusiasts.

### Connecticut Ski Conditions
**www.goski.com/resorts/rusact/conn.htm**
Gives information on the state's five ski resorts.

# Index

## A

Abbey of Regina Laudis: 342
abolitionist movement/abolitionists: Connecticut Freedom Trail 20; Prudence Crandall 408; John Norton 265; Harriet Beecher Stowe 333; Torrington groups 329
accommodations: 44–48; *see also specific place*
Action Wildlife Foundation: 338
Adriaen's Landing: 204–205
agricultural tourism: 39–40
airports: 57–58
American Revolution: general discussion 18; battlefields 170; Litchfield's participation in 330, 331; supplies for 410
*Amistad* case: 20
amphibians: 10
Amtrak: 55
amusement parks: Lake Compounce 266; Ocean Beach Park 165; Putts Up Dock 442; Quassy Amusement Park 364
ancestry, cultural: 31
anesthesia, developer of: 215
Ansonia: 365–366
antiques: general discussion 51–52; Putnam 405; Stamford 80; *see also specific place*
aquariums: Maritime Aquarium at Norwalk 83; Mystic Aquarium 173
Archer-Gilligan, Amy: 249
architecture: Alliance for Architecture 128; Armsmear 210; art deco 328, 329, 350; Belle Haven 75; Connecticut State Capitol 201–202; driving tour of homes 91; Glass House 82; Goodspeed Opera House 286–287; Greek Revival 270; Leffingwell House 438; Lockwood-Mathews Mansion 85; New London 167; overhanging second-story 228; *see also specific place*
area codes: 65–66
Armsmear: 209, 210
Arts Council, Greater Hartford: 203
Ashford: 406
ATMs: 63–64
Audubon Society: Connecticut Audubon Birdcraft Museum 91; Connecticut Audubon Coastal Center 131; Fairfield Center 91; Glastonbury Center 273; Sharon Center 310
auto racing: 418
auto restoration: 366
aviation: first attempt at human 120; National Helicopter Museum 121; New England Air Museum 247
Avon: 230–232

## B

Bacon, Henry: 270
bald eagles: 9
banks: 63–64
Bantam: 335
Barkhamsted: 232
Barnum, Phineas Taylor: 118–119

## Art Museums and Galleries

Aldrich Museum: 379
Austin Arts Center: 212
Bruce Museum: 75
Canton Artists Guild: 230
Connecticut River Artisans Cooperative: 289
Fairfield: 91
Farmington Valley Arts Center: 230
Hill-Stead Museum: 228
Huntington Museum: 249
Lyman Allyn Art Museum: 168
Lyme Academy of Fine Arts: 164
Lyme Art Association: 164

Mattatuck Museum: 360
New Britain: 263
Silo: 304
Slater Memorial Museum: 437
Wadsworth Atheneum: 205–206
Washington: 305
Washington Art Association: 306
Webb-Deane-Stevens Museum: 261
William Benton Museum of Art: 415
Yale Center for British Art: 130
Yale University Art Gallery: 130
*see also specific place*

Barnum Museum: 119–120
beaches: 150–151
Beacon Falls: 365
Bear Mountain: 4, 315
bed-and-breakfasts: 46–47; *see also specific place*
Benedict, Zadoc: 376
Benedictine abbey (Hotchkissville): 342
Berkshire Balloons: 39, 191
Berlin: 264
Bethany: 133
Bethel: 380
Bethlehem: 338–339
bicycle manufacture: 196
Bigelow Hollow State Park: 402–403
biking: general discussion 40; Case Mountain Park 429; Norwich area 442; Putnam 405; Quiet Corner 418; Rte. 169 402; Soapstone Mountain 253; Steep Rock Reservation 306; Tarrywile Park 376–377; Topstone State Park 379; White Memorial Foundation 334; Wilton 88; *see also specific place*
bird-watching: general discussion 40–41; Essex 290; Hammonasset State Park 150; Holbrook Bird Observatory 334–335; Northfield Brook Lake 362; Tomasso Nature Park 266; Westside Nature Preserve 377; *see also* Audubon Society; *specific place*
"Black Laws": 408
Black Rock: 120
Black Rock State Park: 363, 368
Block, Adriaen: 13
Bloomfield: 245
Blue Laws: 129
Bluff Point State Park: 151
boating: Housatonic River 313; Lake McDonough 232; Mt. Tom State Park 335; museums 171; Squantz Pond State Park 381; *see also specific place*
books: 131
bookstores: 136
Borden, Gail: 329
boroughs: 24
Bowen, Henry Chandler: 403
Branchville: 379
Branford: 148–149
breweries: 363
Bridgeport: general discussion 114–122; accommodations 123–124; dining 124–126; history 115–118; industry 117; recreation and entertainment 122–123

Bridgewater: 304–305
Bristol: 266
broadleaf trees: 7–8
Brookfield: 381–382
Brooklyn: 406–407
Brown, John: 329
Burlington: 229
Burr, Aaron: 330–331
Bushnell, Reverend Horace: 201
Bushnell Park: 200–201
business hours: 68
bus travel: 56
butterflies: 9
Buttolph-Williams House: 261

**C**
Campbell Falls: 326
camping: general discussion 41; *see also specific place*
Canaan: 312
Candlewood Lake: 381
candy industry: 365
Cannon Museum: 311
canoeing: general discussion 43; Farmington River 235; Housatonic River 313; *see also specific place*
Canterbury: 408–409
Canton: 229–230
Carousel Museum: 266
car rentals: 58
cartoons, museum of: 267–268
car travel: 53
casinos: dining in 448–449; Foxwoods 439; Mohegan Sun 438–439
celebrities: 28–29, 86, 299
cellular phones: 66
Central Shoreline: general discussion 148–162; accommodations 155–157; beaches 150–151; Branford 148–149; dining 157–162; entertainment 154; festivals 154–155; Guilford 149–152; shopping 153–154
Charter Oak: 206; incident 16, 195
Chatfield Hollow State Park: 292
Cheney family: 428–429
Cheshire: 267–269
Chester: 289, 290–291
children, traveling with: 62–63; *see also* Children's Activities
Christ Church Cathedral: 200
Civic Center, Hartford: 203

## Children's Activities

Amy's Udder Joy Exotic Animal Farm: 271
Bruce Museum: 75
Bushnell Park Carousel: 202
Children's Museum: 429
Children's Museum of Southeastern Connecticut: 165
Discovery Museum: 118
Flamig Farm: 232
Kidcity: 271
Lake Compounce: 266
The Last Post: 311
New Britain Youth Museum: 263
Ocean Beach Park: 165
pony rides: 348
Putts Up Dock: 442
Quassy Amusement Park: 364
Science Center of Connecticut: 227
Smiles Amusement Center: 136
Stamford Museum and Nature Center: 78
Stepping Stones Museum for Children: 85
Wethersfield Nature Center: 261

climate: 7
Clinton: 153
clock museums: 361
Clock Tower, Keney Memorial: 200
Clock and Watch Museum, American: 266
coast guard academy: 169
Colchester: 441
Colebrook: 325, 326–327
Colebrook church controversy: 325
colleges. *see* Schools and Universities
Collins, Samuel: 229
Collinsville: 229
Colonial legacy: Phelps Tavern Museum 232; preserving 2; Salmon Brook Settlement 246; *see also specific place*
colonists, European: general discussion 13–17; Dutch explorers 194; governing doctrine for 13–17
Colt, Samuel: 23, 196, 210
Colt firearms: 202
Colt Village and Park: 209–211
Columbia Bicycle: 196
comics, museum of: 267–268
communications: 65–67

Compo Beach: 87–88
Comstock, Ferre & Co.: 261
conifers: 7
Connecticut Colony: 16
Connecticut River: 190, 191
Connecticut River Valley: general discussion 187–297; Farmington River Valley 226–244; Hartford 192–225; heart of Connecticut 260–285; lower 2, 285–297; maps 188–189; Tobacco Country 244–259; tours 190–192
copperheads: 10
Cornwall: 309–310
Cornwall Bridge: 309
Cos Cob: 77
Coventry: 413–414
crafts: 35
Crandall, Prudence: 407–408
credit cards: 64
crime: 59
Cromwell: 271
cross-country skiing: Hurd State Park 275; linear park 276; Northwest Park 249; Peoples State Forest 232–233; Tarrywile Park 376–377; Tobacco Country 254–255; Topsmead State Forest 337; White Memorial Foundation 334; Winding Trails Cross Country Ski Center 234
cruises: 190–191, 402
cultural ancestry: 31
currency exchange: 64
Curtis House: 341

### D
Danbury: 373–377
Danielson: 407
Darien: 82, 102
Davenport, Reverend John: 129
Dayville: 407
Deep River: 289
deer ticks: 61
deforestation: 11–12
Derby: 366
development, urban: coastal 2–3; and industrialization 22; riverfront 204–205
Devil's Den Preserve: 95
Devil's Hopyard State Park: 292
dining: 48–51; *see also specific place*
Dinosaur State Park: 271–272
dinosaur tracks: 272
disabilities, travelers with: 63
distances, driving: 54

Dodd Hat Shop: 376
downhill skiing. *see* skiing
DuBois Beach: 151
Durham: 286
Dutch explorers: 194

**E**

eagle-watching trips: 9
Eastern Hills: general discussion 397–450; casinos 438–439; Manchester 428–429; maps 398–399; Norwich 435–438; Quiet Corner 402–427
eastern Litchfield Hills: general discussion 324–357; accommodations 351–353; Colebrook 326–327; dining 353–357; entertainment 348–350; Hotchkissville 341–342; Litchfield 330–338; Norfolk 324–326; shopping 343–347; Torrington 328–329; Woodbury 339–341
East Haddam: 286–287
East Hartford: 273
East Haven: 135
Easton: 89–90
East Windsor: 250
economy: general discussion 25–27; Hartford 196–197; *see also* industry; manufacture
electricity, standards for: 68
Elizabeth Park: 214–215
Ellington: 253
Ellsworth, Oliver: 248
emergencies: 10
endangered animals: 10
Enfield: 250–252
environmental groups: 38
environmental issues: 11–12
Environmental Protection Agency (EPA): 43
Episcopal Church, America's: 340
Essex: 289–290, 291
ethnic cuisine: 50
expenses, traveling: 64

**F**

Fairfield: general discussion 90–94; dining 112–113; history 90–91; population 31
Falls Village: 311–312
Farmington: 228–229
Farmington Canal: 22
Farmington Canal Linear Park: 276
Farmington River: 226
Farmington River Valley: general discussion 226–244; accommodations 237–238; Avon 230–232; Canton 229–230; dining 238–244; Farmington 228–229; recreation and entertainment 234–236
farms and nurseries: Amy's Udder Joy Exotic Animal Farm 271; Anderson Organics 417; Caprilands Herb Farm 415; Collins Powder Hill Farm 253; Creamery Brook Bison Farm 407; Fish Family Farm 430; Flamig Farm 232; Holmberg Orchards 443; Kassandra—Herbs Unlimited 253; Loon Meadow Farm 302; McCulloch Farm 164; Noden-Reed House and Barn 248; Pleasant View Farm 253; Wagon Shed Nursery 254; Wood Acres Farm 302; Wright's Mill Farm 417; *see also* Pick-Your-Own Farms
ferries: general discussion 56–57; oldest operational 272
festivals: Connecticut River Eagle Festival 9; dogwood 91; Music Mountain 311; by season 36–37; *see also* Food Festivals; *specific place*
firearms, Colt: 209
firearms, manufacture of: 23
Fire Museum: 250, 429
fishing: general discussion 41–42; Housatonic River 314, 343; Mansfield Hollow State Park 414; Quaddick Reservoir 404; Saugatuck Reservoir 89; *see also specific place*
Fitzgerald, F. Scott: 86

## Food Festivals

Annual Apple Harvest Festival: 277
Annual Taste of Greater Danbury: 387
Apple Festival: 98
Goshen Agricultural Fair: 350
Greek Experience: 387
Harvest Fair: 430
Hungarian Bazaar: 123
Italian Festival: 387
Lobsterfest: 176
Norwalk Oyster Festival: 97–98
Old Saybrook Apple Festival: 155
Pumpkin Festival: 236
Sharpe Rib Burn-off: 218
Taste of Hartford: 218
Taste of Litchfield Hills: 350
Wapping Fair: 255

Flanders Nature Center: 344–345
flora: 7–8
food: 48–51
Fort Trumbull State Park: 167
fossils, dinosaur: 272
Foxwoods casino: 439, 444, 448
Freedom Trail, Connecticut: 20
Frisbee, invention of: 117
Frisbee, William R.: 117
Frog Hollow: 212
frogs: 10
Fuller Brush Company: 23, 196

**G**

gardens: Bartlett Arboretum 81; Beardsley Gardens 310; butterfly 273; Colonial 286; Connecticut College Arboretum 168; Gertrude Jekyll Garden 340; Norwich Memorial Rose Garden 438; Pardee Rose Garden 135; Phelps-Hatheway House 246; rose 218; Roseland Cottage—Bowen House 403; Sundial Gardens 285; Wickham Park 429

gay and lesbian travelers: 62
gear: 69
genealogical libraries: 248
*Genius of Connecticut:* 202
geography: 2–7
geology: 3–7
Georgetown: 379
Gillette, William: 288
Gillette Castle State Park: 288
Gillette Corner (Massachusetts): 247
glacial activity: 5–6
Glass House: 82
Glastonbury: 272–273
Glebe House: 340
Gold Coast: general discussion 73–113; accommodations 98–101; dining 101–113; entertainment 96–97; Fairfield 90–94; festivals 97–98; Greenwich 75–77; maps 72, 76; North Stamford 78–81; Norwalk 83–85; recreation 95–96; services 113; shopping 94–95; Stamford 78
Golden Hill Indians: 116

## Hiking

general discussion: 42–43
Ansonia: 366
Appalachian Trail: 314
Bigelow Hollow State Park: 402–403
Black Rock State Park: 363, 368
Burr Pond State Park: 329
Case Mountain Park: 429
Chatfield Hollow State Park: 292
Cockaponset State Forest: 291–292
Denison Pequotsepos Nature Center: 173
Devil's Den: 95
Devil's Hopyard State Park: 292
Earthplace: 87
eastern Litchfield Hills: 348
Fairfield County: 96
Farmington Canal Linear Park: 276
Farmington River Valley: 235–236
Gay City Park: 428
heart of Connecticut: 274–276
Heublein Tower: 231
Huntington State Park: 380
Indian Wells State Park: 383–385
lower Housatonic Valley: 386

Mohegan Park: 438
Mt. Tom: 335
Mt. Tom State Park: 348
Naugatuck Valley: 367–368
New Canaan Nature Center: 81
Northwest Park: 249
Norwich area: 442
Peoples State Forest: 232–233
Quiet Corner: 418
Riverbound Farm Sanctuary: 268–269
Roaring Brook Nature Center: 230
Sharon Audubon Center: 310
Sleeping Giant State Park: 134
Stanley Quarter Pond: 264
Steep Rock Reservation: 306
Tarrywile Park: 376–377
Tobacco Country: 254–255
Tomasso Nature Park: 266
Walnut Hill Park: 264
Western Litchfield County: 314–315
Westside Nature Preserve: 377
White Memorial Foundation: 334

# Historic Districts

Burlington—Harmony Hill Roads Historic District: 330
Canterbury Center: 408
Colchester: 441
Enfield Shakers Historic District: 252
Hallville Historic District: 439
Hamilton Park: 362
Hillside Historic District: 361
Lakeville Historic District: 310
Litchfield—South Roads Historic District: 330
Madison Green Historic District: 152
Manchester Main Street Historic District: 428
Marion Historic District: 267
Millington Green Historic District: 288
Mystic Seaport: 171–172
New Britain Downtown District: 262
New Canaan Historical Society: 81

Newtown: 382
Norwich: 437
Old Lyme Historic District: 164
Pine Grove Historic District: 230
Poquetanuck Village: 439
Round Hill Historic District: 76
Salisbury Historic District: 311
Salmon Brook Settlement: 246
Simsbury Center Historic District: 232
Stratford Historical Society: 121
Thomsonville: 252
Tolland: 427
West Hill Historic District: 228
Westport: 87
Worthington Ridge Historic District: 264
*see also specific place*

golfing: 42, 95–96, 275; *see also specific place*
Goodspeed Opera House: 286–287, 292
Goshen: 337–338
Goshen Agricultural Fair: 350
government: general discussion 24–25; colonial 16
Granby: 245–246
granite formation: 6–7
gratuities: 64–65
graveyard, Hartford's oldest: 204
graveyard tours: 191
Greater Hartford Open: 275
Greens Farms: 87–88
Greenwich: 75–77, 94, 102
Griswold, Florence: 163
Groton: 166, 169–170
Groton Long Point: 170
Guilford: 149–152

## H

Haddam: 286
Haddam Meadows State Park: 286
Hale, Nathan: 413–414, 416
Hamburg: 288
Hamden: 134
Hammonasset State Park: 150, 152
"Hardware City": 263
Harness Memorial State Park: 151
Harral-Wheeler House: 117

Hartford: general discussion 192–225; accommodations 219–220; dining 220–225; economy 192, 196–197; entertainment 216–218; history 194–197; maps 193, 198–199; and the Patriots 187; riverfront development 207–208; services 225; shopping 215–216; sights 197–215
Hartford Wolf Pack: 216
Hartland: 233
Harwinton: 329–330
"hatting capital of America": 376
Hawley family: 382
Haystack Mountain: 326
health care: 59
heart of Connecticut: general discussion 260–285; accommodations 277–279; Bristol 266; Cheshire 267–269; dining 280–284; entertainment 276–277; Middletown 269–271; New Britain 261–264; Plainville 265–266; recreation 274–276; shopping 273–274
Helmsley, Leona: 92
Henri Bendel estate: 80
Heublein Tower: 231, 254
Higganum: 285
history: general discussion 12–24; Charter Oak incident 16, 195; colonial 13; *see also specific place*
Hitchcock Chair Factory: 233
Hooker, Thomas: 14, 15, 195

horseback riding: High Lonesome Rose Hurst Stable 368; Roraback Wildlife Management Area 330; Western Litchfield County 315; White Memorial Foundation 334, 348; *see also specific place*
hospitals: 59
hot-air ballooning: general discussion 39; Connecticut River Valley 191; Norwich area 442; Western Hills 302
Hotchkissville: 341–342
hotels: 47
Housatonic Railroad: 116
"House that Sherlock Holmes Built": 288
hunting: 41–42
Huntington: 384
Huntington State Park: 380
Hurd State Park: 275

**I**
ice-skating: International Skating Center of Connecticut 236; Mt. Tom State Park 335; Norwich Municipal Ice Rink 442
income, per capita: 25–26
Indians. *see* Native Americans
indigenous peoples. *see* Native Americans
industrialization: 19, 22, 262
industry: collapse 384; financial 19; and manufacture 23–24; maritime 19; and mass-production 22, 23; milling 401; rubber 365; shipbuilding 18; tobacco 244–245; wartime 117; *see also specific place*
inns: 46–47; *see also specific place*
insects: 9, 60
insurance, travel: 60
insurance industry: 196
Internet services: 66–67
inventors: 117, 134
invertebrates: 8–9
ironworks: 3
Italian neighborhoods, Hartford's: 222–223
Ives, Charles: 375–376
Ivoryton: 290
Iwo Jima Memorial: 264

**JKL**
jazz: 201
Johnson, Philip: 82
Katharine Ordway Preserve: 95
kayaking: 43, 235
Kemp, G. Leroy: 93

Kensington: 264
Kent: 308–309
Kent Furnace: 308
Kettletown State Park: 343
Killingworth: 285–286
King Philip's War: 16
Lake Compounce: 266
Lakeville: 310–311
Lake Waramaug: 307
landscape: 2–7
leaf-viewing, fall: 305
Leatherman Cave: 368
Lebanon: general discussion 409–411; geography 400; and the American Revolution 410
Ledyard: 436
lesbian and gay travelers: 62
lighthouses: Sheffield Island Lighthouse 83; Stonington 174
Lime Rock: 310
Lisbon: 440–441
Litchfield: general discussion 330–338; Congregational church 336; history 330–332; maps 331; shopping 343; White Memorial Foundation 334
Litchfield County: 30
*Litchfield County Times*: 299
Litchfield Hills: 2
Little Italy: 222–223
Lock 12 Historical Park: 268
Long Island wineries: 349
Lord's Hill: 212–213
lower Connecticut River Valley: accommodations 293–295; Chester 289; dining 295–297; East Haddam 286–287; Essex 289–290; general discussion 285–297; Killingworth 285–286; recreation 291–292
lower Housatonic Valley: accommodations 387–390; Danbury 373–377; dining 390–395; recreation 385–386; Redding 379–380
Lyme: 288
Lyme disease: 61

**M**
Madison: 150, 152–153
Malbone, Godfrey: 407
mammals: 10–11
Manchester: 428–429
Mansfield: 414
manufacture: candy 365; Hartford as center of

196; technology and 22; *see also* industry
maple sugaring: 344–345, 400
maps: resources for finding 38; *see also specific place*
marching band museum: 290
marine animals: 8
Marion: 267
maritime festivals: 292
maritime galleries: 172
mass-production: 23
mass transit: 54–57
Mattatuck Trail: 368
McLean Game Refuge: 245–246, 254
media: 65
Meridian: 269
Merritt Parkway: 74
Merwinsville: 307
Metacomet Ridge: 274
Metacomet Trail: 254
metalworks: 22
Middlebury: 363–364
Middletown: 269–271
Milford: 131–133
Milldale: 267
mills: Gurleyville Grist Mill 414; historic 3; in the Quiet Corner 401; thread 412
Milton: 335–336
mines, copper: 246
mining tools: 308
Mirror Lake: 269
Mohegan Sun casino: 438–439, 444, 448–449
Mohegan tribe: 12–13
money: 63–65
Monroe: 383
Moodus: 288–289
Morris: 338
Morris Academy: 338
motels: 47
motion sickness: 60
mountain biking: 253
Moxley, Martha: 92
Mt. Higby: 274
Museum of Political American Life: 227
music: Battell-Stoeckel House 325; Hot Steamed Jazz Festival 292; Music Mountain 311; New Haven 135; Performance Pavilion 201; Yale Collection of Musical Instruments 130–131; *see also specific place*
Music Mountain: 311
Mystic: 2, 166, 171–173
Mystic Seaport: 171–172

**N**
Native Americans: history of 12–13; Institute for American Indian Studies 306; land rights 116; modern-day 16; resist European colonization 16; tools 252–253; *see also specific tribe*
Naugatuck: 364–365
Naugatuck River: 357–358
Naugatuck Valley: general discussion 357–373; accommodations 369; dining 370–373; Middlebury 363–364; recreation 367–368; Waterbury 357–362
New Britain: 261–264, 281
New Canaan: 81–82
New Fairfield: 380–381
New-Gate Copper Mine: 246
New Hartford: 232
New Haven: general discussion 2, 126–148; accommodations 139–141; dining 141–147; entertainment 137–138; maps 127, 132; Milford 131–133; recreation 136–137; shopping 135; surrounding towns 131–135; Yale University 129
New Haven Colony: 15
Newington: 261
New London: 165–169
New Milford: 303–304
New Preston: 307
Newtown: 382–383
nightlife: 37; *see also specific place*
Nipmuck tribe: 12
Noah Webster House and Museum: 227
Noank: 170–171
Nook Farm: 213–214
Norfolk: 324–326, 346
North, Simeon: 22
Northfield: 337
North Grosvenor Dale: 404
North Stamford: 78–81
Norton, John: 265
Norwalk: 83–85, 94, 107–109
Norwalk Oyster Festival: 97–98
Norwich: general discussion 435–438; accommodations 444–446; dining 447; history 435; maps 436
"Notch, the": 247
nuclear plants: 286

**O**
Ocean Beach Park: 165
off-season travel: 70

Old Greenwich: 77–78
Old Lyme: 163–164
Old Saybrook: 153
Old State House (Hartford): 197
Oliver Ellsworth Homestead: 248
O'Neill, Eugene: 169
Opera House, Goodspeed: 286–287
Orders, the: 15
Overbrook Nature Center: 80
Oxford: 366–367

**P**
packing: 69
Parsons, Martha A.: 251–252
patents, New Britain: 262
Patriots, New England: 187
Paugusset tribe: 116
Peak Mountain: 254
peddling: 21
Penwood State Park: 254
people: 27–32
Peoples State Forest: 236
Pequabuck River: 265
Pequot tribe: of Bridgeport 116; general discussion 12–13; Pequot War of 1637 14–15; resists Puritan colonization 14
Pequot War of 1637: 14–15
performing arts: 35; *see also specific place*
pharmacies: 60
Philip, King: 16
Plainfield: 407–408
Plainville: 265–266
planetariums: Copernican Observatory and Planetarium 264; North Stamford 80
plant life: 7–8
Police Museum: 263
Polish cuisine: 281
politics: general discussion 24–25; colonial 16
polo: 255
Pomfret: 405–406, 417
Pope Manufacturing Company: 196
population: general discussion 27–32; African-American 116; and environmental issues 11; growth 31–32; indigenous 12; statistics 27
Pratt & Whitney: 196
preservation, environmental: general discussion 11–12; Eightmile River Watershed Project 288
Preston City: 439
Provisions State: 18
puppetry, museum of: 415

## Pick-Your-Own Farms

general discussion: 39
Allyn Reed: 442
Berry Farm: 343
Bishop Farms: 273
Blue Jay Orchards: 385
Brown's Harvest: 253
Buell's Orchard: 417
Catnip Acres Herb Nursery: 367
Crooke Orchards: 417
Easy Pickin's Orchard: 253
Flamig Farm: 232
4-H Farm Resource Center: 253
Hickory Hill Orchard: 273
Johnny Appleseed's Farm: 253
Jones Family Farms: 386
Lapsley Orchard: 417
Loon Meadow Farm: 302
Lyman Orchards: 273
Maple Lane Farms: 442–443
Pickin' Patch: 233
resources, agricultural: 400
Rose's Berry Farm: 273
Schreiber's Farm: 367

Puritans: colonization by 13; religious intolerance of 18; settlement in Windsor 248–249
Putnam: 404–405, 416–417
Putnam, Israel: 406
Putnam Memorial State Park: 380

**QR**
Quaddick State Park: 404
Quiet Corner: general discussion 402–427; accommodations 419–422; Brooklyn 406–407; dining 422–426; industry 401; Lebanon 409–411; population 30; Putnam 404–405; shopping 415–417; Williamantic 412–413; Woodstock 403–404
Quinebaug: 404
Quinnipiac River: 265
rabies: 10, 60
rafting: 43; Housatonic River 313; *see also specific place*
Railroad Museum of New England: 362
railroads: 22
railways: 55–56

rattlesnakes: 10
Ray, Margaret: 93
recycling plants: 211
Redding: 379–380
religion: colonial 18; and politics 19, 21; and Puritan colonists 13–14; Shaker 252
reptiles: 10
resources, online: 458–459
resources, outdoor: 38
Ridgefield: 378–379
Ringling Brothers Barnum & Bailey Circus: 119
riverboat rides: 43, 290
Riverfront Recapture: 207
Riverton: 233
Roaring Brook Park: 268
Robeson, Paul: 251
Rockville: 427
Rocky Hill: 271–272
Rocky Neck State Park: 150, 164
Roraback Wildlife Management Area: 330
Roseland Cottage—Bowen House: 403
Rose Weekend: 218
Rowayton: 83
Roxbury: 30, 305
rubber industry: 365

**S**
safety, urban: 59
salamanders: 10
salaries, average: 25–26
Salem: 441
Salisbury: 311
Sandy Hook: 383
Saugatuck: 85–86
scandals, Fairfield County: 92–93
scenic drives: 53
Scotland: 409
seafood: 50
seals: 11
Seaside Park: 120
seasons, and travel plans: 68–69
seed suppliers: 261
senior citizens: 62
Sequin tribe: 13, 194
Seymour: 365
Shaker community: 252
Sharon: 310
shellfish: 8
Shelton: 383
Shelton, Edward Nelson: 384

## Schools and Universities

**M** Index

Central Connecticut State University: 264
Connecticut College: 168
Fairfield University: 91
Gunnery Prep School: 306
Housatonic Community-Technical College: 120
Little Boston School: 165
Loomis-Chaffee School: 249
Morris Academy: 338
Pomfret School: 405
Quinnipiac College: 133
Rectory School: 405
Skip Barber Racing and Driving School: 310
Tapping Reeve's Law School: 333–334
Trinity College: 211–212
United States Coast Guard Academy: 169
University of Connecticut: 415
University of Connecticut School of Law: 214
Wesleyan University: 270–271
Western Connecticut State University: 377
Yale University: 129

Shenipset State Forest: 253
Shenipset Trail: 276
Sherwood Island State Park: 151
shipbuilding: 18, 172
shopping: 51–52
shrubs: 7–8
Simsbury: 232
skiing: general discussion 43; Mohawk Ski Area 314; Mount Southington 276; Ski Sundown 235; Woodbury Ski Area 347; see also cross-country skiing
Skip Barber Racing and Driving School: 310
slavery: Freedom Trail 20; see also abolitionist movement/abolitionists
sledding: 276
Sleeping Giant State Park: 133–134
snakes: 10
Soapstone Mountain: 4, 253
Somers: 252–253
Southbury: 342–343
Southeast Coastline: general discussion 163; accommodations 177–181; dining 181–186; East Lyme and Niantic 164–165; Groton 169–170; Mystic 171–173; New London

165–169; Noank 170–171; Old Lyme 163–164; recreation and entertainment 175–176; shopping 174–175; Stonington 173–174; Waterford 165

Southington: 267

South Windsor: 250

spas: 95

speed limits: 54

Squantz Pond State Park: 386

Stafford Springs: 403

Stamford: general discussion 78; growth of 73; maps 79; shopping 94

steamboats: 21

Steep Rock Reservation: 306

Sterling, Dr. John: 440

Stevenson: 383

Stewart, Martha: 93

Stonington: 173–174

Stony Creek: 149

Storrs: 414–415

Stowe, Harriet Beecher: 213

Stratford: 121–122

students: 62

submarines: manufacturing 23; museums 169, 271; Subfest 177

Suffield: 246–247

Sunny Valley Preserve: 314

"Swedish Nightingale": 119

syrup, maple: 344–345

**TUV**

Talcott Mountain State Park: 235

telephones: 65–66

temperature: 7

textiles: 22, 427

Thimble Islands: 149

Thomaston: 362–363

Thompson: 404

Thomsonville: 252

Thumb, Tom: 118–119

Timexpo Museum: 361

time zone: 68

tipping: 64–65

tobacco: 244–245, 249

Tobacco Country: general discussion 244–259; accommodations 255–257; dining 257–259; Enfield 250–252; Granby 245–246; McLean Game Refuge 245–246; recreation 254–255;

shopping 253–254; Windsor 248–250; Windsor Locks 247–248

Tolland: 427–428

Tomasso Nature Park: 266

Topsmead State Forest: 337

Topstone State Park: 379

Torrington: 328–329

tourist information centers: 67

tours, water: Connecticut River Valley 190–192; Farmington River 235; Long Island Sound 43

town names: 440–441

transportation: 53–58; *see also specific place*

Travelers Tower: 5, 205

travel insurance: 60

trees: 7–8

Trinity College: 211–212

Trolley Museum: 250

trucking museum

Trumbull, Jonathan: 410

tubing: river 235; snow 276

turtles: 10

Twain, Mark: 213, 214, 379

Underground Railroad: 20

Union: 402–403

Unionville: 229

universities. *see* Schools and Universities

Vernon: 427

Vintage Motor Cars: 366

visitor information centers: 67

Voluntown: 440

## Vineyards and Wineries

Chamard Vineyards: 153

DiGrazia Vineyards: 381–382

Haight Vineyard: 336–337

Heritage Trail Vineyards: 441

Hopkins Vineyard: 307

Jonathan Edwards Winery: 174

Land of Nod Winery: 312

McLaughlin Vineyards: 383

Nutmeg Vineyards: 430

Priam Vineyards: 442

Sharpe Hill Vineyard: 406

Stonington Vineyards: 174

wine trail: 349

**WXYZ**
Wadsworth Atheneum: 34, 205–206
Wadsworth Falls State Park: 274
Wallingford: 134
Wampanoag tribe: 16
Wappinger: 13
Warner Theatre: 350
War of 1812: 19
Warren: 307
Washington: 305–306
Washington Depot: 306
Waterbury: general discussion 357–362; accommodations 369; dining 370–372; map 359
water conditions: 43
waterfalls: Campbell Falls 326; Kent Falls State Park 308; Roaring Brook Park 268; Wadsworth Falls 274
Waterford: 165
water safety: 60
water tours: Connecticut River Valley 190–192; Farmington River 235; Long Island Sound 43
Watertown: 363
wealth: 25–26
Webster, Noah: 227
Weindenmann, Jacob: 201
Weir, J. Alden: 89
Wells, Horace: 215
Westbrook: 153
West Cornwall: 309
Western Hills: general discussion 299–396; eastern Litchfield Hills 324–357; Kent 308–309; lower Housatonic Valley 373–396; maps 300–301; media 299–302; tours 302; Washington 305–306; Waterbury 357–362; Western Litchfield County 302–324
Western Litchfield County: general discussion 302–324; accommodations 316–319; Cornwall 309–310; dining 319–323; entertainment 315; Lakeville 310–311; New Milford 303–304; recreation 313–315; shopping 312–313
West Hartford: 226–228
West Haven: 133
Weston: 89
Westport: general discussion 86–87; dining 109–112; maps 84
Wethersfield: 260–261

## Wildlife Preserves

Action Wildlife Foundation: 338
Denison Pequotsepos Nature Center: 173
Devil's Den: 89
Flanders Nature Center: 342
Katharine Ordway Preserve: 95
Lake Zoar Wildlife Area: 343
McLean Game Refuge: 245–246
Ragged Mountain Memorial Preserve: 275
Riverbound Farm Sanctuary: 268–269
Roraback Wildlife Management Area: 330
Seaside Park: 120
Sunny Valley Preserve: 314
Sunrise Herbal Remedies: 385
Tomasso Nature Park: 266
Westside Nature Preserve: 377

whale-watching: 11
whaling industry: 19, 172
Whitehead, Gustave: 120
White Memorial Foundation: 334
Whitney, Eli: 22, 134
wildlife: 60
Willimantic: 412–413
Wilton: 88–89
Winchester Center: 326
Windham: 409
Windham Mills: 412
Windsor: 248–250
Windsor Lock Canal: 255
Windsor Locks: 247–248
wineries. see Vineyards and Wineries
Winsted: 327–328
Winthrop, Jr., John: 16
Wolcott, Governor: 21
Woodbridge: 133
Woodbury: 339–341, 346–347
woodland: 3
Woodstock: 397, 403–404, 417
World War II memorials: 264
Yale, Elihu: 129
Yale University: 129, 325
zoos: 118–119

# Acknowledgments

First and foremost, I could not have written this book without the support and inspiration of two individuals aged 65 years apart: Yoav Broum, born in 1976, accompanied me on road trips across every corner of the state, kept me from losing my mind as the deadline of this manuscript approached rapidly and furiously, and—in general—put up with more aggravation while standing by me than anybody should have to. I will forever stand by him. Anne Collins, born in 1911, is, strictly speaking, my grandmother. More significantly, she is one of my closest friends and has been, especially during the years I've spent cobbling together this guidebook, an indispensable fellow researcher—accompanying me to museums and nature preserves, dining out with me at numerous restaurants, and putting a roof over my head during my many visits.

Various dedicated employees of the travel and tourism industry have provided me with constant updates on statewide goings-on, and have given me access to many parts of Connecticut I'd have never unearthed on my own. To the following individuals, I'm ever grateful: Remo Pizzichemi in Enfield, Mary Woods in Norwalk, Molly McGrath Curry in Danbury, Renny Loisel in New Haven, Diane Moore in Middletown, Janet Serra in Litchfield, Eileen Jacobs Sweeney in New Britain, Eliza Baron in New London, Rosanne Poynton in Waterbury, Sherry Smardon in Hartford, and Michelle Mineo in Putnam.

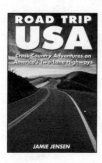

# U.S.~Metric Conversion

|  | | |
|---:|:--:|:---|
| 1 inch | = | 2.54 centimeters (cm) |
| 1 foot | = | .304 meters (m) |
| 1 yard | = | 0.914 meters |
| 1 mile | = | 1.6093 kilometers (km) |
| 1 km | = | .6214 miles |
| 1 fathom | = | 1.8288 m |
| 1 chain | = | 20.1168 m |
| 1 furlong | = | 201.168 m |
| 1 acre | = | .4047 hectares |
| 1 sq km | = | 100 hectares |
| 1 sq mile | = | 2.59 square km |
| 1 ounce | = | 28.35 grams |
| 1 pound | = | .4536 kilograms |
| 1 short ton | = | .90718 metric ton |
| 1 short ton | = | 2000 pounds |
| 1 long ton | = | 1.016 metric tons |
| 1 long ton | = | 2240 pounds |
| 1 metric ton | = | 1000 kilograms |
| 1 quart | = | .94635 liters |
| 1 US gallon | = | 3.7854 liters |
| 1 Imperial gallon | = | 4.5459 liters |
| 1 nautical mile | = | 1.852 km |

To compute Celsius temperatures, subtract 32 from Fahrenheit and divide by 1.8. To go the other way, multiply Celsius by 1.8 and add 32.

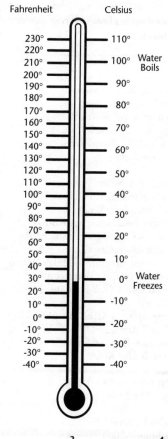

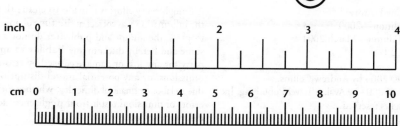

# Keeping Current

Although we strive to produce the most up-to-date guidebook humanly possible, change is unavoidable. Between the time this book goes to print and the moment you read it, a handful of the businesses noted in these pages will undoubtedly change prices, move, or even close their doors forever. Other worthy attractions will open for the first time. If you have a favorite gem you'd like to see included in the next edition, or see anything that needs updating, clarification, or correction, please drop us a line. Send your comments via email to atpfeedback@avalonpub.com, or use the address below.

*Moon Handbooks Connecticut*
Avalon Travel Publishing
1400 65th Street, Suite 250
Emeryville, CA 94608, USA
atpfeedback@avalonpub.com
www.moon.com

Editor: Mia Lipman
Series Manager: Kevin McLain
Copy Editor: Kate Willis
Graphics Coordinator: Susan Snyder
Production Coordinator: Justin Marler
Cover Designer: Kari Gim
Interior Designers: Amber Pirker, Alvaro
    Villanueva, Kelly Pendragon
Map Editors: Olivia Solís and Naomi Adler
    Dancis
Cartographers: Mike Morgenfeld,
    Kat Kalamaras, Olivia Solís
Proofreader: Damion Searls
Indexer: Rachel Kuhn

ISBN: 1-56691-543-0
ISSN: 1545-2190

Printing History
1st Edition—2000
2nd Edition—March 2004
5 4 3 2 1

Text © 2004 by Andrew Collins.
Maps © 2004 by Avalon Travel Publishing, Inc.
All rights reserved.

Avalon Travel Publishing is a division of Avalon Publishing Group, Inc.

Some photos and illustrations are used by permission and are the property of the original copyright owners.

Front cover photo: © Paul Rezendes
Table of Contents photos: © Andrew Collins

Printed in China through Colorcraft Ltd. Hong Kong.

Moon Handbooks and the Moon logo are the property of Avalon Travel Publishing, a division of Avalon Publishing Group, Inc. All other marks and logos depicted are the property of the original owners.